Hong Kong
and Macau

THE ROUGH GUIDE

There are more than one hundred and fifty Rough Guide titles
covering destinations from Amsterdam to Zimbabwe

Forthcoming titles include
Argentina • Croatia • Ecuador • Switzerland

Rough Guide Reference Series
Classical Music • Drum'n'Bass • English Football • European Football
House • The Internet • Jazz • Music USA • Opera • Reggae
Rock Music • Techno • World Music

Rough Guide Phrasebooks
Czech • Dutch • Egyptian Arabic • European Languages • French
German • Greek • Hindi & Urdu • Hungarian • Indonesian
Italian • Japanese • Mandarin Chinese • Mexican Spanish • Polish
Portuguese • Russian • Spanish • Swahili • Thai • Turkish • Vietnamese

Rough Guides on the Internet
www.roughguides.com

Rough Guide Credits

Text Editor:	Gavin Thomas
Series Editor:	Mark Ellingham
Editorial:	Martin Dunford, Jonathan Buckley, Jo Mead, Kate Berens, Amanda Tomlin, Ann-Marie Shaw, Paul Gray, Chris Schüler, Helena Smith, Judith Bamber, Kieran Falconer, Orla Duane, Olivia Eccleshall, Ruth Blackmore, Sophie Martin, Geoff Howard, Claire Saunders, Anna Sutton, Andrew Tomicic, Lisa Nellis, Joe Staines, Alexander Mark Rogers, Polly Thomas (UK); Andrew Rosenberg, Mary Beth Maioli (US)
Online Editors:	Alan Spicer, Kate Hands (UK); Kelly Cross (US)
Production:	Susanne Hillen, Andy Hilliard, Link Hall, Helen Ostick, Julia Bovis, Michelle Draycott, Anna Wray, Katie Pringle
Cartography:	Melissa Baker, Maxine Burke, Nichola Goodliffe, Ed Wright, Catherine Robertson
Picture Research:	Eleanor Hill, Louise Boulton
Finance:	John Fisher, Katy Miesiaczek, Gary Singh, Ed Downey
Marketing & Publicity:	Richard Trillo, Simon Carloss, Niki Smith, David Wearn (UK), Jean-Marie Kelly, Myra Campolo (US)
Administration:	Tania Hummel, Charlotte Marriott, Demelza Dallow

Acknowledgements

From **Jules Brown**: thanks to Sophy for all her efforts with this edition, which are much appreciated. Thanks also to Gavin for patient editing; love to Katie for helping; and commiserations to Capt. I. Little following his bold, but ultimately futile, attempt to paddle across the South China Sea in a bath-tub.

From **Sophy Fisher**: thanks to Michael Sheridan, Shelagh Lester-Smith, Michael Timperley, Yuen Chi Kei, Judith Clarke, Tim Jepson, Corky Addis, Vicky Findlay, Fionnuala McHugh, Chantal Hooper, Kirsty Norman, Paul Boulding, HK Magazine, the HKTA staff in Jardine House, Thea Baird at the Macau Information Bureau, and to Tony and Wendy Fisher, without whom I would never have come to Hong Kong.

Thanks also to Nick Thomson for research in the US, Cameron Wilson for Australian research and indexing, Cathy McElhinney for typesetting, Laurence Larroche for proof-reading, and cartographers Nichola Goodliffe and Sam Kirby for tackling a big job with unfailing patience and skill.

This edition published July 1999 by Rough Guides Ltd, 62–70 Shorts Gardens, London WC2H 9AB. Reprinted June 2000.

Distributed by the Penguin Group:

Penguin Books Ltd, 27 Wrights Lane, London W8 5TZ.

Penguin Books USA Inc, 375 Hudson Street, New York 10014, USA.

Penguin Books Australia Ltd, 487 Maroondah Highway, PO Box 257, Ringwood, Victoria 3134, Australia.

Penguin Books Canada Ltd, 10 Alcorn Avenue, Toronto, Ontario, Canada M4V 1E4.

Penguin Books (NZ) Ltd, 182–190 Wairau Road, Auckland 10, New Zealand.

Printed in England by Clays Ltd, St Ives PLC.

Typography and **original design** by Jonathan Dear and The Crowd Roars.

Illustrations throughout by Edward Briant.

ISBN 1-85828-435-X

Hong Kong
and Macau

THE ROUGH GUIDE

Written and researched by
Jules Brown

This edition researched and updated by
Sophy Fisher

THE ROUGH GUIDES

Help us update

We've gone to a lot of trouble to ensure that this fourth edition of the *Rough Guide to Hong Kong and Macau* is accurate and up-to-date. However, things inevitably change, and if you feel we've got it wrong or left something out, we'd like to know: any suggestions, comments or corrections would be much appreciated. We'll credit all contributions and send a copy of the next edition – or any other *Rough Guide* if you prefer – for the best correspondence.

Please mark letters "Rough Guide to Hong Kong and Macau" and send to:
Rough Guides, 62–70 Shorts Gardens, London WC2H 9AB or
Rough Guides, 375 Hudson St, 9th floor, New York, NY 10014.

Email should be sent to:
mail@roughguides.co.uk

Online updates about Rough Guide titles can be found on our website at www.roughguides.com

The author

Jules Brown first visited Hong Kong and Macau in 1989. Apart from this book he has also written and researched Rough Guides to Scandinavia, Barcelona, Washington DC, and England, and contributed to guides on Portugal, Spain, the Pyrenees, Italy, and Malaysia and Singapore. He is a regular contributor to the *Daily Mail* travel pages and to various Fodor's publications.

Readers' letters

Daniel Annoot, Carole Brewer, Barbara Carson, K.K. Chan, Judy Cheung, Dan Colwell, Adam Coulter, Keith Davies, C. Griffin, Annalisa Henderson, Gerard Hosek, Javier Jimenez, R.A.Lee, P.J. Mahaffey, Jan A. Mann, I.S. Nicholson, Nathan Roberts, Samantha Robinson, Bruce Seymour, Jane Seymour, Steve Taylor, Owen Walker, Robin Womersley, Liz Wright.

Rough Guides

Travel Guides • Phrasebooks • Music and Reference Guides

We set out to do something different when the first Rough Guide was published in 1982. Mark Ellingham, just out of university, was travelling in Greece. He brought along the popular guides of the day, but found they were all lacking in some way. They were either strong on ruins and museums but went on for pages without mentioning a beach or taverna. Or they were so conscious of the need to save money that they lost sight of Greece's cultural and historical significance. Also, none of the books told him anything aboutGreece's contemporary life – its politics, its culture, its people, and how they lived.

So, with no job in prospect, Mark decided to write his own guidebook, one which aimed to provide practical information that was second to none, detailing the best beaches and the hottest clubs and restaurants, while also giving hard-hitting accounts of every sight, both famous and obscure, and providing up-to-the-minute information on contemporary culture. It was a guide that encouraged independent travellers to find the best of Greece, and was a great success, getting shortlisted for the Thomas Cook travel guide award, and encouraging Mark, along with three friends, to expand the series.

The Rough Guide list grew rapidly and the letters flooded in, indicating a much broader readership than had been anticipated, but one which uniformly appreciated the Rough Guides' mix of practical detail and humour, irreverence and enthusiasm. Things haven't changed. The same four friends who began the series are still the caretakers of the Rough Guide mission today: to provide the most reliable, up-to-date and entertaining information to independent-minded travellers of all ages, on all budgets.

We now publish more than 100 titles and have offices in London and New York. The travel guides are written and researched by a dedicated team of more than 100 authors, based in Britain, Europe, the USA and Australia. We have also created a unique series of phrasebooks to accompany the travel series, along with the acclaimed series of music guides, and a best-selling pocket guide to the Internet and World Wide Web. We also publish comprehensive travel information on our Web site: www.roughguides.com

Contents

List of maps

MAP SYMBOLS

══════	Major road	🛕	Monastery	☾	Mosque
═════	Minor road	♠	Temple	■━■	Cable car
≡ ≡ ≡	Tunnel	♀	Museum	⭕	Stadium
- - - -	Path	⟊	Gardens	▬	Building
━━━	Railway	⌂	Caves	✛	Church
— —	Ferry route	لرزل	Rocks		Beach
··········	River	◉	Hotel		Built up area
▬▬ ▪ ▪	District boundary	▣	Restaurant	┼┼┼	Cemetery
— — —	Chapter division boundary	★	Bus/taxi stop		Marshland
▲	Mountain peak	ⓘ	Tourist information		Park
◆	Point of interest	✉	Post office	╱╱	Reclaimed land
✈	Airport	✡	Synagogue		

Introduction

Hong Kong is a beguiling place to visit: a land whose aggressive capitalist instinct is tempered by an oriental concern with order and harmony. Indeed, whatever you've heard about it, the most important thing to remember is that, despite 150 years of British colonial rule and the modern city's cosmopolitan veneer, Hong Kong is, and always has been, Chinese. The glittering skyline imitates others throughout the world; the largest department stores are Japanese-owned; you can take English high tea to the accompaniment of a string quartet; there's cricket and horse-racing, pubs and cocktail lounges. But for most of the Chinese locals – 98 percent of a population of almost seven million – life still follows a pattern that many mainland Chinese would recognize as their own: hard work and cramped housing; food bought from teeming markets and street stalls; and a polytheistic religion celebrated in the home, in smoky temples, and during exuberant festivals.

Recent years, however, have been far from easy for Hong Kong. The enormous political upheaval that accompanied the **handing back of the territory** to China in 1997 was followed almost immediately by the **Asian economic crisis**, during which the stock market and property values collapsed and unemployment reached its highest levels for 25 years. And though fears that the Chinese government would interfere in the running of Hong Kong after the British left have proved to be generally unfounded, they have been replaced by concerns that the territory's own leadership lacks the experience necessary to run such a sophisticated and fast-changing society, with local officials trying to second-guess the wishes of Beijing.

Even so, visitors to Hong Kong will find that little has changed – superficially at least – since the handover. Many practical matters, such as entry requirements, have remained unaffected, and the city has lost none of its interest: the **architecture** is an engaging mix of styles, from the stunning towers of Central to ramshackle town housing and centuries-old Chinese temples; the **markets and**

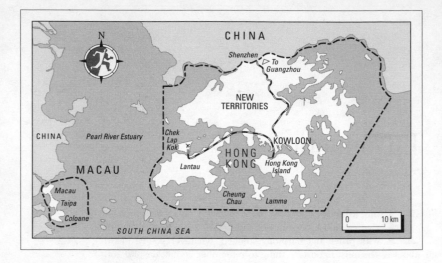

streetlife are compelling; while the **shopping** – if no longer the bargain it once was – is eclectic, from open-air stalls to hi-tech malls. Hong Kong is also one of the best places in the world to eat **Chinese food** (and a good many other cuisines besides), while the territory's Western influence has left it a plentiful selection of **bars and nightspots**. If there's a downside, it's that commercialism and consumption tend to dominate life. **Cultural** matters have been less well catered for, though a superb Cultural Centre, several new or improved museums, and an increasing awareness of the arts – both Chinese and Western – are beginning to change that.

Sixty kilometres west across the Pearl River estuary, **Macau** (due to be returned to China in December 1999) makes Hong Kong look like the gaudy *arriviste* colony it is. In 1557, almost three hundred years before the British arrived in southern China, the Portuguese set up base here, and although Hong Kong and its harbour later surpassed the older enclave in terms of trading importance, Macau absorbed its Portuguese associations and culture in a way that Hong Kong never did with Britain.

Smaller and more immediately attractive than its neighbour, Macau remains a pleasant contrast to the madness across the water in Hong Kong. It's one of Asia's most enjoyable spots for a short visit, its Chinese life tempered by an almost Mediterranean influence, manifest in the ageing Catholic churches, hilltop fortresses and a grand seafront promenade. Of course, like Hong Kong, Macau is Chinese – 95 percent of its population speak Cantonese. All the temples and festivals of southern China are reproduced here, but few come to Macau to pursue them, believing – perhaps rightly –

Average temperatures and humidity

Note that the figures below are *averages*. In summer, the temperature is regularly above 30°C, and the humidity over 90%. The winter is comparatively chilly, but the temperature rarely drops below 15°C.

	Average Temperature °C (°F)	Average Humidity	Monthly Rainfall (mm)
Spring (March to May)	18 (70)	84%	137
Summer (June to mid-Sept)	28 (82)	83%	394
Autumn (mid-Sept to mid-Dec)	23 (73)	73%	43
Winter (mid-Dec to Feb)	16 (60)	75%	33

Storm Signals

Once a typhoon is in full swing (after the no. 8 signal has been announced), planes will start to be diverted, local transport like buses and cross-harbour ferries will eventually stop running, and you would be wise to stay indoors and away from exposed windows. Heavy rainstorms – which are not accompanied by the winds which characterize typhoons – can also be extremely disruptive, and businesses and transport links may close. Weather signals for both typhoons and rainstorms are displayed as an icon on top of the pictures of local TV channels.

Red Rainstorm Warning is an indication that very heavy rain is either falling or expected within the next two hours. Roads may be inundated, flash floods and landslides can occur.

Black Rainstorm Warning is issued when 100mm or more of rain is predicted or recorded within two hours. It will not necessarily be accompanied by exceptional winds. Many public facilities are closed, roads are flooded and landslides are a serious danger.

Typhoon Signal 1 means a tropical cyclone (and thus the wind, or typhoon, associated with it) is within 800km of Hong Kong.

Typhoon Signal 3 indicates that winds are expected across Hong Kong of up to 60 knots/hr. This generally means a typhoon is on its way: you're supposed to tie things down on balconies and rooftops, and check transport availability. Some public facilities, such as kindergartens and swimming pools, will close.

Typhoon Signal 8 means be prepared for storm-force winds of between 63 and 117km/hr and gusts up to 180km/hr.

Typhoon Signal 9 indicates storm-force winds are set to increase significantly.

Typhoon Signal 10, known melodramatically as a "direct hit", means there will be a hurricane of 118km/hr and upwards, with gusts up to and above 220km/hr. The effects are extremely destructive and dangerous.

that such things are done bigger and better in Hong Kong. Instead, Macau offers alternative attractions. **Eating** here is one of the highlights of any trip to the region – even on a short visit to Hong Kong it's worth taking the jetfoil over for a meal: Macanese food is an exciting combination of Portuguese colonial cooking, with dishes and ingredients taken from Portugal itself, Goa, Brazil, Africa and China, washed down with cheap, imported Portuguese wine, port and brandy. And with gambling illegal in Hong Kong, except for betting on horse-races, the Hong Kong Chinese look to Macau's various **casinos** to satisfy their almost obsessive desire to dice with fortune.

When to go

Hong Kong and Macau's **subtropical climates** are broadly similar. Apart from a couple of months a year during which the weather is reliably good, for most of the time it's generally unpredictable, and often downright stormy. The heat is always made more oppressive by the **humidity**: in very humid weather you'll find your strength sapped if you try to do too much walking, and dehydration can be a serious problem. You'll need air-conditioning in your hotel room or – at the very least – a fan. Macau does have the bonus of the cool breeze off the sea in summer, which makes nursing a beer on the waterfront the pleasant experience it rarely is in Hong Kong.

The best time is undoubtedly **autumn**, when the humidity is at its lowest and days are bright and warm. In **winter**, things get noticeably cooler (you'll need a jacket), and though the skies often stay clear, there will be periods of wind and low cloud – don't expect reliable, clear views from the Peak at this time. Temperatures and humidity rise during **spring**, and while there can be beautiful warm blue days towards April, earlier in the season the skies usually stay grey and there are frequent showers and heavier rain. The **summer** is dramatically different: it's terribly hot and humid, and best avoided, if possible. If you do visit, you'll need an umbrella to keep off both the rain or the sun; raincoats are hot and aren't much use in heavy downpours.

The summer also sees the **typhoon season**, which lasts roughly from July to September. Getting stuck in a typhoon can be quite an experience. The word comes from the Chinese *dai foo*, or "big wind", an Asian hurricane, and over the years typhoons whistling through Hong Kong have had a devastating effect – scores of people dead and millions of dollars' worth of damage. Listen to the radio or TV weather broadcasts to find out what's happening and check the box on p.xi for Storm Signal details.

The Basics

Getting there from Britain

The simplest way to reach either Hong Kong or Macau from Britain is to fly. All the main routings are to Hong Kong in the first instance, from where it's around an hour by boat to Macau; for details of travel on to Macau from Hong Kong, see pp.323–325. Macau also has an international airport, with services from Singapore, Kuala Lumpur, Bangkok, Manila and a number of cities in China. For more details on approaching the region from elsewhere in Southeast Asia see p.4. There's also the possibility of following one of the world's classic overland trips, by train from London, through Russia and Mongolia to China, and from there to the end of the line in Hong Kong. Travelling this way takes at least twelve to fourteen days and requires making the necessary travel and visa arrangements well in advance, but as a route it has few equals. See p.6 for more details.

Flights from Britain

The least demanding way to reach Hong Kong is to **fly non-stop** with one of the three major airlines – just under a thirteen-hour flight **from London** Heathrow. British Airways and Cathay Pacific fly non-stop twice daily; Virgin has a once-daily non-stop service. Prices have fallen considerably in recent years, though the cheapest fares carry various restrictions – usually a minimum stay of seven days and a maximum of one, two or three months, plus a penalty payment for

changing your flights. Low-season fares (generally Oct–Feb) cost from around £410-470 return, shoulder season around £570, while in high season (mid-June to Sept, the fortnight before Christmas, the fortnight before Chinese New Year, and Easter), you'll pay between £650 and £900 depending on the type of ticket.

Of the big three only Cathay Pacific flies direct **from Manchester** (once daily via Amsterdam or Paris) – fares are pegged to those from Heathrow. However, British Airways can provide add-on connections from Manchester and other regional airports to Heathrow, starting at around £75.

Several **other airlines** fly to Hong Kong (from London and Manchester) but touch down two or three times on the way, sometimes giving the opportunity of a stopover: the Middle East and Southeast Asia are standard stops, while Air China (China's national airline) – one of the cheapest options – flies via Beijing. These flights are usually better value than non-stop services but can take sixteen to twenty hours. Depending on the time of year, they cost from around £400-700 return, though seats at Christmas, Chinese New Year and Easter are hard to come by: book well in advance.

Shopping for tickets

You can try the airlines direct (see p.4) for their current prices and special offers: some don't sell tickets directly to the public and will point you in the direction of their appointed agent. Generally you're best off booking through an established **discount agent** which can usually undercut airline prices by a significant amount. See the box on p.5 for a list of recommended agents or check the ads in the national Sunday newspapers, in the weekly London listings magazine *Time Out* or London's *Evening Standard*, and in Manchester's weekly listings magazine *City Life*. If you are a **student or under 26**, you may be able to get further discounts on flight prices, especially through agents such as Usit Campus, Council Travel and STA Travel.

Most of the specialist agents will also be able to sell you a **Round-the-World** or **Round-Asia** ticket, routed out of London, which includes Hong Kong in the itinerary. These are, of course, more expensive – between £700 and £1000 depending on your chosen route – but, as they're usually valid for six to twelve months, they're just the thing if your Hong Kong visit is part of a longer trip.

Package tours

The other option is to travel to Hong Kong on an inclusive **package tour**, something that can be very good value out of season. For a week (2 nights on a plane and 5 nights in Hong Kong), including flights and three-star hotel accommodation, expect to pay from around £650 per person. Obviously, the price goes up during high season (mid-June to Sept and Christmas, Chinese New Year and Easter) and according to which class of hotel you choose to stay in – at peak times, the same holiday will be closer to £1000. However, all the hotels used are more than adequate and you can sometimes get extremely good deals for a stay in the very best hotels; in low season some operators can get you a return

flight and five nights in a five-star hotel for around £750. If you want to stay longer, all operators offer a daily add-on charge for around £20–40, depending on the hotel.

Packages to Hong Kong are fairly standardized and the **tour operators** listed in the box opposite all offer holidays based on three- and five-star hotels on Hong Kong Island and in Kowloon, with various add-on local tours. If you have a particular hotel in mind, mention it when making enquiries. For longer holidays incorporating travel into China, China Travel Service, British Airways Holidays and Magic of the Orient are good first calls. For details of China Travel Service's Trans-Siberian Express package to Moscow, Beijing and Hong Kong, see "Overland by train", p.6.

Travelling via Southeast Asia and China

With more time on your hands, you could see Hong Kong and Macau as part of a longer, Southeastern Asian trip or use the territories as the start or end points of a trip further into China. Moreover, since certain Southeast Asian countries (Thailand in particular) have opened up as long-

---

Airlines

Air China
☎0171/630 0919
Good deals on flights to Beijing, where you can change for Hong Kong.

Air India
☎0171/495 7951
Stopovers in Bombay.

Biman Bangladesh
☎0171/629 0252
Flies via Dacca; no direct sales to the public.

British Airways
☎0345/222111
Non-stop from London Heathrow.

Cathay Pacific
☎0171/747 8888
Non-stop from London Heathrow; from Manchester via Amsterdam or Paris.

Emirates Airlines
☎0171/808 0808
Flies via Dubai; possible stopovers in Bangkok.

Gulf Air
☎0171/408 1717

Usually among the cheapest flights; stopovers in Bahrain, Muscat and Bangkok.

Lufthansa
☎0345/737747
Flies via Frankfurt.

Qantas
☎0345/747767
Flies via Singapore.

Royal Brunei
☎0171/584 6660
Flies via Brunei. No direct sales to the public.

Singapore Airlines
☎0181/747 0007
Flies via Singapore.

Thai International
☎0171/499 9113
Flies via Bangkok.

Virgin Atlantic
☎01293/747747
Non-stop from London Heathrow.

Agents and Operators

DISCOUNT FLIGHT AGENTS

Council Travel
London ☎0171/437 7767
Specialist in student discounts.

Far East Travel Centre
London ☎0171/414 8844
*Flight and package tour agent, with lots of
options to Hong Kong.*

Globepost Ltd
London ☎0171/587 0303
Flight agent specializing in Hong Kong.

STA Travel
London ☎0171/361 6262
Bristol ☎0117/929 4399
Cambridge ☎01223/366966
Glasgow ☎0141/338 6000
Leeds ☎0113/244 9212
Manchester ☎0161/834 0668
Newcastle ☎0191/233 2111
Oxford ☎01865/792800
*Worldwide specialists in low-cost flights and
tours particularly for students and under-26s.
Branches on university campuses nationwide.*

Trailfinders
London ☎0171/938 3939
Birmingham ☎0121/236 1234
Bristol ☎0117/929 9000
Glasgow ☎0141/353 2224
Manchester ☎0161/839 6969
*One of the best-informed and most efficient
agents.*

Travel Bag
London ☎0171/287 5558
*Discount flights to the Far East; official
Qantas agent.*

Travel Bug
London ☎0171/835 2000
Manchester ☎0161/721 4000
Large range of discounted tickets.

Usit Campus
London ☎0171/730 8111
Birmingham ☎0121/414 1848
Brighton ☎01273/570226
Bristol ☎0117/929 2494
Cambridge ☎01223/324283
Edinburgh ☎0131/668 3303
Manchester ☎0161/833 2046
Oxford ☎01865/242067
*Student youth-travel specialists with branch-
es on university campuses all over Britain
and also in YHA shops.*

TOUR OPERATORS

British Airways Holidays
☎0870/242 4245

China Travel Service (CTS)
☎0171/836 9911

Jade Travel
☎0171/494 2461

Kuoni Worldwide
☎01306/740500

Magic Of The Orient
☎01293/537700

Premier Holidays
☎01223/516677

Regent Holidays
☎0117/921 1711

Somak Holidays
☎0181/423 3000

Thomas Cook Holidays
☎0990/666222

haul package destinations from Europe and North America, flight prices to some cities are cheaper than those to Hong Kong.

Flights via Southeast Asia and China

At most times of the year you should be able to find a flight from London to Bangkok, Singapore or Kuala Lumpur for around £360–460 return.

Once there, **discounted air tickets to Hong Kong** are no problem, available from most local travel agencies and tour operators. For a return ticket, you can expect to pay in the region of £150–220/US$250–350 from Bangkok, £180–240/US$300–400 from Kuala Lumpur and £220–240/US$350–400 from Singapore. There are also now regular non-stop services to **Macau**

SOUTHEAST ASIA

Beijing
NORTH KOREA   JAPAN
Seoul
SOUTH
KOREA   Tokyo

CHINA

BANGLADESH

Shanghai

INDIA   EAST CHINA SEA

N

Guangzhou   Taipei
MYANMAR   Macau   TAIWAN
(BURMA)   Hanoi
LAOS   Hong Kong

SOUTH
CHINA
SEA
THAILAND
Bangkok   THE PHILIPPINES   PACIFIC
OCEAN
VIETNAM   Manila
CAMBODIA

Ho Chi Minh City

0   1000 km

MALAYSIA
Kuala Lumpur   BRUNEI   Sabah

SINGAPORE   Sarawak

PAPUA
NEW
GUINEA

Jakarta

INDONESIA

from Kuala Lumpur (with Malaysia Airlines) and Singapore (Singapore Airlines), as well as flights from Bangkok, Manila and a dozen Chinese cities, including Beijing. Official prices, booked through the airlines, are high, but agents should be able to undercut them substantially. In the end though, since the two territories are only an hour apart by hydrofoil, you'd probably do best to take the cheapest available Hong Kong flight.

Another alternative is to fly first to **China**, specifically to Beijing, and travel on to Hong Kong from there, either overland (24hr by express train) or by air. The best deals are with Air China (booked through the China Travel Service) whose return fares from London to Beijing start at around £350 in low season, rising to £600 in summer. British Airways often have similarly priced deals to Beijing at certain times of the year. The train journey from

Beijing to Hong Kong (via Guangzhou) costs from around £50.

Overland by train

The **overland train route from London** passes through Eastern Europe, Russia and Mongolia to China and Beijing, from where trains run south to the end of the line in Hong Kong. It's a supremely satisfying – though exacting – journey, but it doesn't save you any money. Prices start at around £470 one-way for the Moscow–Beijing/Hong Kong journey, with fares at their highest (£550) between May and October. Prepare for a very long haul: from London to Moscow is two days, Moscow to Beijing five or six days depending on the route, and it's another 24 hours from there to Hong Kong. Note that the cheapest tickets are for four-berth hard-sleeper accommodation, but this is intolerably uncomfortable over a six-night journey; the two-berth so-called "1st-class deluxe" is no such thing, but for an extra £100 or so it's not a lot to pay for the possibility of sleep during the week's travel.

If this doesn't put you off, you'll have to decide upon the route and train you want to take – services are operated by both the Russians and Chinese, either passing through, or bypassing, Mongolia (for which you need a separate visa). To sort it all out, talk to an experienced agent like Regent Holidays or China Travel Service, who can organize all tickets, visas and stopovers and can arrange a cheap flight back to London – you'll need to plan at least six weeks ahead. CTS also offers a 22-day organized trip from London, which starts at about £1600 per person (more if you're travelling on your own) – this includes the flight to Moscow, the train to Beijing, accommodation in Beijing (3 nights), Xi'an (3), Guilin (2) and Hong Kong (2), and a flight back to London.

Insurance

Most travel agents and tour operators will offer you insurance when you book your flight or holiday, and some will insist you take it. These policies are usually reasonable value, though as ever, you should check the small print. If you feel the cover is inadequate, or you want to compare prices, any travel agent, insurance broker or bank should be able to help. If you have a good "all risks" home-insurance policy it may well cover your possessions against loss or theft even when overseas, and many private medical schemes also cover you when abroad – make sure you know the procedure and the helpline number.

Travel insurance schemes are sold by various specialist companies. A couple of weeks' inclusive cover for Hong Kong and Macau starts at around £38; a month at around £55. Good-value policies are issued by Usit Campus or STA Travel (see "Discount Flight Agents" for addresses), Columbus Travel Insurance (☎ 0171/375 0011) and Endsleigh Insurance (☎ 0171/436 4451).

Getting there from Ireland

The smoothest route from Ireland to Hong Kong is to fly with British Airways **from Belfast** via Heathrow (a once-daily service), giving an optimum flight time of around fifteen hours – though this stretches depending on how long you have to wait in London for the connection. Official fares start at around IR£800 in low season (generally Oct–Feb), rising to around IR£1100 in high season (mid-June to Sept, the fortnight before Christmas, the fortnight before Chinese New Year, and Easter), though it's worth keeping an eye out for special offers which can undercut these prices considerably. Tickets are valid for a minimum of seven days and a maximum of one, two or three months. A specialist agent like USIT (see box on p.8 for telephone numbers) can often find students and under-26s better deals – though you're still looking at return fares of around IR£650 from Belfast (and not much scope for changing departure times or dates).

From Dublin, the problem is that many international flights are routed in the first instance to Gatwick, meaning you have to switch airports to make the Hong Kong leg of the journey.

Airlines and Agents

AIRLINES

Aer Lingus
Belfast — ☎ 0645/737747
Dublin — ☎ 01/705 3333 or 844 4777

British Airways
Belfast — ☎ 0345/222111
Dublin — ☎ 1800/626747

British Midland
Belfast — ☎ 0345/554554
Dublin — ☎ 01/283 8833

Malaysia Airlines
Dublin — ☎ 01/676 2131

Ryanair
Dublin — ☎ 01/609 7800

Singapore Airlines
Dublin — ☎ 01/671 0722

Virgin Atlantic
Dublin — ☎ 01/873 3388

DISCOUNTED FLIGHT AGENCIES

Apex Travel
Dublin — ☎ 01/671 5933

Joe Walsh Tours
Cork — ☎ 021/277959
Dublin — ☎ 01/676 3053

Student & Group Travel
Dublin — ☎ 01/677 7834

Trailfinders
Dublin — ☎ 01/677 7888

Twohigs
Dublin — ☎ 01/677 2666 or 670 9750

USIT
Belfast — ☎ 01232/324073
Cork — ☎ 021/270900
Derry — ☎ 01504/371888
Dublin — ☎ 01/602 1700
Galway — ☎ 091/565177
Limerick — ☎ 061/415064
Waterford — ☎ 051/872601

Williames
Belfast — ☎ 01232/230714

World Travel Centre
Dublin — ☎ 01/671 7155

TOUR OPERATORS

Liffey Travel
Dublin — ☎ 01/878 8322
Package tour specialists.

Silk Road Travel
Dublin — ☎ 01/677 1029 or 677 1147
Far Eastern specialist.

Thomas Cook
Belfast — ☎ 01232/554455
Dublin — ☎ 01/677 0469
Package holiday and flight agent.

Through-flight prices from Dublin are prohibitively expensive, and even though Virgin Atlantic and Cathay Pacific in London can both arrange an add-on Dublin–London fare with another airline in conjunction with their regular London–Hong Kong flights, these are usually much higher than the budget fares that you can book yourself with a variety of airlines, Ryanair, Aer Lingus and British Midland among them – the cheapest cost from around IR£50–70 return. You may want to consider taking advantage of these discounted air fares between Ireland and Britain and picking up an onward flight from London with another airline (see "Getting There from Britain", on p.3), though you'll need to plan connections carefully.

If you intend to see Hong Kong as part of a wider **Southeast Asian trip**, you may well find that you can turn up cheaper flights to destinations like Kuala Lumpur, Singapore and Bangkok, all of which will be routed through London in the first instance. Talk to a specialist travel agent for the best deals; and see p.4 for more details on travel from the region to Hong Kong.

Alternatively, check on details of package holidays, on which the Ireland–Britain section of your trip will be included in the overall price. A one-week holiday (2 nights on a plane, 5 nights in Hong Kong), staying in a three-star hotel, costs around IR£1100 in peak summer season, with add-on nights possible for another IR£20–40 or so. In the low season (Oct–Feb, excluding Christmas and New Year), you'll find you can get much better deals than this, either shaving ten to fifteen percent off the price or substituting a five-star hotel for around the same price.

Travel **insurance** is best obtained through a travel specialist such as USIT (see box opposite). Their policies start at around IR£36 for 6–10 days' worldwide cover (around IR£55 for one month). Discounts are offered to students of any age and anyone under 35.

Getting there from the US and Canada

There are any number of possible routes to Hong Kong from North America, with wide variations in fares. Although the recent influx of Hong Kong Chinese into Canadian cities and the subsequent surge in competition and discounted fares from Canada has now abated, there are still good deals to be found. Check the ads in newspaper travel sections, and shop around, being aware that discount travel agents and consolidators can almost always quote you a fare substantially lower than the airlines' discounted rates.

Shopping for tickets

Barring special offers, the cheapest of the airlines' published fares are usually **Apex** tickets, although these carry certain restrictions: you have to book – and pay – at least 21 days before departure, spend at least seven days abroad (maximum stay three months), and you will also be penalized if you change your schedule. Some airlines also issue Special Apex tickets to **under 24s**,

often extending the maximum stay to a year, while others offer youth or student fares to **under 26s**, though these tickets are subject to availability and may carry eccentric booking conditions. It's worth remembering that most cheap return fares involve spending at least one Saturday night away and that many will only give a percentage refund if you need to cancel or alter your journey, so make sure you check the restrictions carefully before buying a ticket.

You can normally cut costs further by going through a **specialist flight agent** – either a **consolidator**, who buys up blocks of tickets from the airlines and sells them at a discount, or a **discount agent** who, in addition to dealing with discounted flights, may also offer special student and youth fares and a range of other travel-related services such as travel insurance, rail passes, car rentals, tours and the like. Bear in mind, though, that penalties for changing your plans can be stiff. Remember too that these companies make their money by dealing in bulk – don't expect them to answer lots of questions. Some agents specialize in **charter flights**, which may be cheaper than anything available on a scheduled flight, but again departure dates are fixed and withdrawal penalties are high (check the refund policy). If you travel a lot, **discount travel clubs** are another option – the annual membership fee may be worth it for benefits such as cut-price air tickets and car rental.

Don't automatically assume that tickets purchased through a travel specialist will be cheapest – once you get a quote, check with the airlines and you may turn up an even better deal. Be advised also that the pool of travel companies is swimming with sharks – exercise caution and *never* deal with a company that

Airlines

Air Canada
USA ☎ 1-800/776 3000
Canada ☎ 1-888/247 2262
Non-stop flights from Vancouver four times a week plus connections from most other major Canadian cities.

Asiana Airlines
☎ 1-800/227 4262
From Seattle and Los Angeles via Seoul; from New York and Vancouver via Seattle and Seoul.

Canadian Airlines
USA ☎ 1-800/426 7000
Canada ☎ 1-800/665 1177
Daily non-stop from Vancouver and direct from Montréal and Toronto with connections from most other major Canadian cities.

Cathay Pacific
USA ☎ 1-800/233 2742
Daily non-stop flights from Vancouver, Los Angeles and San Francisco; direct flights from New York via Vancouver and Toronto via Anchorage.

China Airlines
☎ 1-800/227 5118
Daily from Los Angeles, San Francisco, Honolulu and Anchorage via Taipei.

EVA Airlines
☎ 1-800/695 1188
Daily flights from New York via Seattle and Taipei and from Seattle, San Francisco and Los Angeles via Taipei.

Japan Airlines
☎ 1-800/525 3663
Daily flights from Los Angeles, San Francisco, Dallas, New York and five days a week from Vancouver to Hong Kong via Tokyo.

Korean Air
☎ 1-800/438 5000
To Hong Kong via Seoul daily from New York, San Francisco and Los Angeles and on certain days from Atlanta, Chicago, Washington DC, Dallas/Fort Worth, Toronto and Vancouver.

Northwest/KLM Airlines
☎ 1-800/447 4747
Daily direct flights from Seattle, New York, Los Angeles, San Francisco, Detroit and, with a change of plane, from Minneapolis. All via Tokyo.

Singapore Airlines
☎ 1-800/742 3333
Non-stop daily from San Francisco, and from New York via Singapore.

Thai Airways International
USA ☎ 1-800/426 5204
Canada ☎ 1-800/668 8103
Los Angeles to Hong Kong daily via Bangkok.

United Airlines
☎ 1-800/538 2929
Daily non-stop from Los Angeles, San Francisco and Chicago. Daily direct service from New York via Tokyo. Connections from major US and Canadian cities.

---

demands cash up front or refuses to accept payment by credit card.

Regardless of where you buy your ticket, the fare will depend on the **season**. Fares are highest in December and June–September, lowest from January to March, and midway between during the "shoulder" seasons which make up the remainder of the year. Bear in mind though that seasonal boundaries may differ from airline to airline, so always double-check to make sure you're getting the best deal. Flying at weekends can add $50–$60 to the cost of a round-trip ticket: prices quoted in the sections below assume midweek travel and exclude taxes (approximately $50 in the US; CDN$10 in Canada).

Flights from the US

Singapore Airlines, Cathay Pacific and United Airlines are the only airlines with **non-stop services to Hong Kong** from the **West Coast**, with a flying time of approximately fourteen hours. United also fly non-stop from Chicago. Other carriers, such as China Airlines, Japan Airlines, Korean Air and Thai Airways International make connections from Los Angeles or San Francisco via Taipei, Tokyo, Seoul and Bangkok. The cheapest low-season fare is with Singapore Airlines (around $730); during high season, Northwest/KLM's direct service via Tokyo at roughly $1060 is best. Asiana's flight from Seattle via Seoul costs roughly $620 (low season) or

$890 (high), but takes around four hours longer. From the **East Coast**, the major carriers offer the most convenient service, with Cathay Pacific, United, Northwest/KLM and Singapore all flying direct daily via Vancouver, Tokyo or Singapore. The cheapest published fares are on Northwest/KLM, with return fares from New York at around $920 (low season)/$1110 (high); their flights, including a two-hour stop in Tokyo, take around 22 hours. Discount agents such as STA may have better deals, probably on a smaller carrier like Korean Air, with fares from the West Coast for as little as $610 (low season)/$770 (high) and from the East Coast for $600 (low)/$900 (high).

Many airlines offer a stopover in Hong Kong on a **round-trip fare** to another city in Asia. This is ideal if Hong Kong is not your only destination. With Singapore Airlines, for instance, a stopover in Hong Kong en route to Singapore, costs $100.

Flights from Canada

The cheapest published fares from Canada to Hong Kong are with Canadian Airlines, who have daily non-stop flights from Vancouver (13hr) and direct flights from Toronto and Montréal (21hr). From the **West Coast** the fare is around CDN$1410 (low season)/CDN$1780 (high); from the **East Coast** approximately CDN$1990 (low)/CDN$2195 (high). Other carriers include Cathay Pacific and Air Canada. Bargain round-trip fares are available on Korean Air through discount travel agents such as Travel Cuts – from Toronto CDN$1075 (low season)/CDN$1560 (high); from Vancouver CDN$1025 (low)/CDN$1410 (high). Prices can drop even lower towards the end of the month, when carriers are struggling to fill empty seats.

Round-the-World tickets

If Hong Kong is only one stop on a longer journey, you might want to consider buying a **Round-the-World** (RTW) or **Circle-Pacific** ticket. Some travel agents can sell you an "off-the-shelf" RTW ticket with stops in half a dozen cities (Hong Kong is on several itineraries); others will assemble one for you, which can be tailored to your needs but is apt to be more expensive. Circle-Pacific airfares, with four or so stops, can work out a bit cheaper. A good way to familarize yourself with routes and fares is to check High Adventure's Web site (*www.highadv.com*), which

lists hundreds of possible combinations and sample fares.

Also worth considering is Cathay Pacific's **All Asia Pass** which allows you, in theory at least, to touch down in as many as fifteen Asian cities. The pass, which must be booked through a travel agent, with all itineraries planned in advance, is valid for a minimum seven days/maximum 21 days on departures from San Francisco, Los Angeles or New York at a flat rate of $999 (low season) or $1199 (high). The pass is also available in Canada, flying out of Vancouver or Toronto, for a roughly equivalent price. You can increase the time limit of the pass to 31 days for an extra $100; to 45 days for $150; to 60 days for $200; and to 90 days for $300.

Packages and organized tours

Air/hotel **packages and tours** are available either for Hong Kong alone or as part of a trip to China and other regions of Asia. The major airlines offer a range of **city holidays** which can be good value – United Vacations, for example, offer six nights in Hong Kong including air fare, airport transfers and a half-day sightseeing tour from around $1185 (West Coast departures) and $1205 (East Coast). TBI Tours offer a range of exclusive Hong Kong packages plus more extensive Asia tours incorporating Hong Kong stopovers of at least three nights, whilst Asian Pacific Adventures are worth checking, particularly for those interested in customizing their own package.

A trip on the **Trans-Siberian Express** from Moscow to Beijing, then on to Hong Kong is a great way to arrive in the city (see p.6 for more details). Train tickets can be purchased from agents in the US and package tours including overnight stays in Beijing and Moscow are available. Mir Corp in Seattle offer a wide range of packages – a fourteen-night trip from Moscow to Hong Kong, for example, costs around $1600.

Insurance

Before buying an **insurance policy**, check you're not already covered. Canadian provincial health plans typically provide some overseas medical coverage, although they're unlikely to pick up the full tab in the event of a mishap. Holders of official student/teacher/youth cards are entitled to coverage – and the annual membership is far less than the cost of comparable insurance. Students may also

Agents and Operators

DISCOUNT AGENTS

Air Brokers International
☎ 1-800/883 3273; 415/397 1383
Consolidator and specialist in RTW and Circle-Pacific tickets.

Council Travel
☎ 1-800/226 8624; 888/COUNCIL; 212/822 2700
Nationwide specialists in student travel.

Educational Travel Center
☎ 1-800/747 5551; 608/256 5551
Student/youth and consolidator fares.

High Adventure Travel
☎ 1-800/350 0612; 415/912 5600
Round-the-World and Circle-Pacific tickets. Web site features interactive database that lets you build and price your own RTW itinerary.

Moment's Notice
☎ 718/234 6295
Discount travel club.

Overseas Tours
☎ 1-800/323 8777
Discount air tickets and hotel packages.

STA Travel
☎ 1-800/777 0112
Student/youth fares, student IDs, travel insurance and car rental.

Travel Cuts
☎ 1-800/667 2887
Canadian discount travel organization.

TOUR OPERATORS

Asian Pacific Adventures
☎ 1-800/825 1680
Customized tours and China-wide packages.

International Gay and Lesbian Travel Association
☎ 1-800/448 8550
Trade group with lists of gay-owned or gay-friendly travel agents and accommodation.

Mir Corps
☎ 1-800/424 7289
Trans-Siberian Express trips and Asia packages with Hong Kong stopovers, plus customized tours.

Saga Holidays
☎ 1-800/343-0273
Specialists in group travel for seniors.

TBI Tours
☎ 1-800/223 0266
General Asian tours plus exclusive Hong Kong packages.

TEI Tours
☎ 1-800/435 4334
Trans-Siberian Express packages and customized tours.

United Vacations
☎ 1-800/328 6877
City breaks.

find that their student health coverage extends during the vacations and for one term beyond the date of last enrollment. Bank and credit cards (particularly American Express) often provide certain levels of medical or other insurance, as do some homeowners' or renters' policies.

After exhausting the possibilities above, you might want to contact a **specialist travel insurance** company. The best premiums are usually to be had through student/youth travel agencies – the current rates for STA (see listing under "Discount Agents", above), for example, are $35 (7 days); $55 (8–15 days); $115 (1 month); $180 (2 months); then $55 for each extra month. Other insurers include Access America (☎1-800/284 8300), Carefree Travel Insurance (☎1-800/323 3149), Travel Guard (☎1-800/826 1300) and Travel Insurance Services (☎1-800/937 1387).

Getting there from Australia and New Zealand

The most convenient way to travel between Australasia and Hong Kong is to **fly non-stop** with Qantas, Cathay Pacific, Ansett or Air New Zealand. Practically all the Southeast Asian airlines fly to Hong Kong via their home airports, though these fares are usually – but not always – more expensive. Prices for flights and flight/accommodation packages vary according to season and demand. High season is mid-May to late August and December to mid-January; shoulder season from March to mid-May and September; low season the rest of the year. You should always check out what the specialist **independent travel agents** have on offer (see box on p.14). Look, too, in the travel sections of the weekend newspapers, which carry adverts for special offers on flights.

From Australia

From Australia, Qantas fly **non-stop to Hong Kong** daily from Sydney and Melbourne (9hr) and Perth (8hr), with less frequent flights from Brisbane, Adelaide and Cairns, for around A$1300 return (high season)/A$920 (low); it's a couple of hundred dollars cheaper from Perth. Youth/student fares offer a slight saving on these prices. Ansett fly daily (except Tues & Thurs) from Sydney, and Cathay Pacific daily from Sydney and Melbourne, with less frequent services from other main cities. Fares are comparable with Qantas.

There's a wide choice if you want to fly **via an Asian stopover city**, although fares with Thai Airways, Singapore Airlines and Malaysia Airlines via their home ports are more expensive than those on the non-stop services.

If Hong Kong is your only destination, an **all-inclusive package** is almost certainly the cheapest option. You should be able to find a package including return airfare, transfers, five nights' accommodation and a half-day sightseeing tour from around A$1000 (per person, twin share) in low season. Qantas, Cathay Pacific and Ansett all have package deals, but these can only be booked through travel agents.

Airlines

Air New Zealand

Sydney	☎ 13/2476
Auckland	☎ 09/357 3000

Five times weekly from Auckland.

Ansett

Sydney	☎ 13/1414
Auckland	☎ 09/379 6409

Five times weekly from Sydney.

Cathay Pacific

Sydney	☎ 13/1747
Auckland	☎ 09/379 0861

Daily from Sydney, Melbourne and Auckland.

Malaysia Airlines

Sydney	☎ 13/2627
Auckland	☎ 09/373 2741

Flies via Kuala Lumpur.

Qantas

Sydney	☎ 13/1211
Auckland	☎ 09/357 8900;
	toll-free ☎ 0800/808767

Daily from Sydney, Melbourne and Perth, plus services from Brisbane, Adelaide and Cairns.

Singapore Airlines

Sydney	☎ 13/1011
Auckland	☎ 09/379 3209;
	toll-free ☎ 0800/808909

Flies via Singapore.

Thai Airways

Sydney	☎ 1300/651960
Auckland	☎ 09/377 3886

Flies via Bangkok.

Discount Flight Agents

Accent on Travel
Brisbane ☎ 07/3832 1777

Anywhere Travel
Sydney ☎ 02/9663 0411

Asian Travel Centre
Melbourne ☎ 03/9654 8277

Budget Travel
Auckland ☎ 09/366 0061;
toll-free ☎ 0800/808040
for nearest branch

Destinations Unlimited
Auckland ☎ 09/373 4033

Flight Centres
Sydney ☎ 02/9235 3522
Melbourne ☎ 03/9650 2899,
plus other branches nationwide
(☎ 13/1600 *for nearest branch*)
Auckland ☎ 09/309 6171,
plus branches nationwide
(☎ 0800/FLIGHTS *for nearest branch*)

Harvey World Travel
Sydney ☎ 02/9261 2800
plus branches nationwide
(☎ 13/2757 *for nearest branch*)

Northern Gateway Travel
Darwin ☎ 08/8941 1394

STA Travel
Sydney ☎ 02/9212
Melbourne ☎ 03/9654 7266;
plus branches nationwide
(☎ 13/1776 *for nearest branch*).
Auckland ☎ 09/309 4058
Christchurch ☎ 03/379 9098
Wellington ☎ 04/385 0561

Topdeck Travel
Adelaide ☎ 08/8232 7222

Tymtro Travel
Sydney ☎ 1300/652 969

UTAG Travel
Sydney ☎ 02/9956 8399

If Hong Kong is part of a longer world trip, it's worth looking at **one-way fares** and **Round-the-World** (RTW) tickets. RTW tickets are based on mileage: you are allowed a number of stop-offs (usually six) within a maximum number of miles. For example you should be able to put together a Sydney–Hong Kong–London–New York–Los Angeles–Honolulu–Sydney ticket with Qantas/British Airways for around A$2700 (high season)/A$2200 (low season), but it's worth shopping around.

From New Zealand

From New Zealand, Air New Zealand flies **non-stop** from Auckland to Hong Kong five times a week (11hr), while Cathay Pacific goes daily. Fares start around NZ$1300 in low season, rising to NZ$1900 in high season. Qantas via Australia, Singapore Airlines via Singapore and Malaysia Airlines via Kuala Lumpur are generally more expensive than the direct services, although Malaysia Airlines currently offer a low-season special of NZ$1345, while a four-night holiday package flying Qantas costs NZ$1410 per person, twin-share.

Round-the-World fares from New Zealand are not particularly cheap. Figure on around NZ$3300 (high season) for Christchurch–Australia–Hong Kong–London–New York–Los Angeles–Christchurch in high season (NZ$2800 low).

Insurance

Travel insurance is put together by the airlines and travel agent groups in conjunction with insurance companies. For Hong Kong (and the rest of Southeast Asia), a month's comprehensive insurance policy will typically cost about A$150/NZ$190. Australian insurers include Cover-More (☎ 02/9202 8000; toll-free ☎ 1800/251881), Ready Plan (☎ 1300/555017), or UTAG (☎ 02/9956 8399; toll-free ☎ 1800/809462). In New Zealand, contact STA Travel (see box above).

Visas and red tape

Most people need only a valid passport to enter Hong Kong or Macau. Depending on your nationality, you'll be allowed to stay for various periods, from seven days to six months, without a visa. However, it's recommended that you check first with the relevant authorities in your own country before travelling. To enter the **Chinese mainland** from Hong Kong you need a separate visa, readily obtainable in Hong Kong from travel agencies, major hotels, branches of the China Travel Service or the visa office of the Ministry of Foreign Affairs of the PRC – see "Onward travel: into mainland China" on p.56 for details.

Hong Kong

Citizens of the **United Kingdom, Eire, USA, Canada, Australia, New Zealand**, all other Commonwealth passport holders and citizens of most European countries do not require a visa and can stay for up to three months. Everyone else should consult the relevant Chinese Embassy, Consulate or High Commission in their country of origin for visa requirements. If in any doubt, contact the **Immigration Department**, Immigration Tower, 7 Gloucester Rd, Wan Chai, Hong Kong ☎(00-852) 2824 6111.

There shouldn't be any trouble with the **immigration officers** on arrival, all of whom speak English. You may be asked how long you intend to stay and, if it's a fairly lengthy period, for referees in Hong Kong and proof that you can support yourself without working, unless you have an employment visa (see p.32).

Given the length of time most people are allowed to stay in Hong Kong, you shouldn't need to **extend your stay** if you're just a tourist. If you do, the simplest solution is to go to Macau or China for the weekend and come back, and nine times out of ten you'll just get another period stamped in your passport. If you want to ensure a longer stay, though, you'll need to apply for a visa in advance of your visit from the Immigration Department (see above); as you will if you're intending to work in the territory, for details of which see "Staying On", p.32. Allow at least six weeks for most visa applications.

If you're in trouble or lose your passport, or you want details of the visas necessary for travel on to neighbouring countries, consult the relevant **foreign consulate in Hong Kong** – there's a list on p.312.

Customs

You're allowed to bring the following duty-free goods into Hong Kong: 200 cigarettes (or 50 cigars or 250g of tobacco), 1 litre of wine or spirits, 60ml of perfume and 250ml of toilet water. Apart from alcohol, which is taxed, you can take most other things into Hong Kong with little difficulty. Prohibited items include all firearms and fireworks, and if you're caught carrying any kind of illegal drugs you can expect very tough treatment. Indeed, if you're arriving from anywhere that has a high drugs profile, and are young and scruffy, or have long hair, your baggage might come in for some extra attention.

Macau

Macau's **handover to the Chinese** on 20 December, 1999 isn't expected to change entry requirements for citizens of most countries, though it's worth double-checking with your nearest Chinese embassy, consulate or high commission. Currently, citizens of the **UK, Eire, Australia, New Zealand, Canada, USA** and most European countries need only a valid passport to enter Macau, and can stay up to twenty days;

Chinese Embassies and Consulates Abroad

AUSTRALIA

Embassy: 15 Coronation Drive,
Yarralumla, ACT 2600 ☎02/6273 4783
Consular Offices: 539 Elizabeth St,
Surry Hills, Sydney ☎02/9698 7929
plus offices in Melbourne ☎03/9822 0607
and Perth ☎08/9321 8193

CANADA

515 St Patrick's St,
Ottawa, ON K1N 5H3 ☎613/789 3434
240 St George St,
Toronto, ON M5R 2P4 ☎416/964 7260
3380 Granville St,
Vancouver, BC V6H 3K3 ☎604/736 3910
1011 6th Ave SW,
#100 Calgary, Alberta T2P 0W1 ☎403/264 3322

IRELAND

40 Ailesbury Rd,
Dublin 4 ☎01/269 1707

NEW ZEALAND

Consulate-General: 588 Great South Rd,
Greenland, Auckland ☎09/525 1588

UK

Cleveland Court, 1–3 Leinster House,
London W2; Visa Section is at
31 Portland Place, London W1 ☎0171/631 1430
visa-line ☎0891/880808

USA

2300 Connecticut Ave NW, ☎202/328 2517;
Washington DC 20008 202/265 9809
520 12th Ave,
New York, NY 10036 ☎212/330 7410
100 W Erie St,
Chicago, IL 60610 ☎312/803 0095
3417 Montrose Blvd,
Houston, TX 77006 ☎713/524 4311
443 Shatto Place,
Los Angeles, CA 90020 ☎213/807 8018

Hong Kong residents can stay for ninety days. Most other nationals can buy an individual visa on arrival, valid for twenty days.

If you need to **extend your stay**, the simplest thing is to return to Hong Kong and re-enter Macau at a later date.

You'll barely notice the **customs officials** as you arrive in Macau, though there might be the odd spot check, with the same severe penalties as Hong Kong for any drugs or firearms offences. Otherwise, the only thing to watch for is when returning to Hong Kong: there's no export duty on goods taken out of Macau, but the Hong Kong authorities will only allow you to bring in one litre of wine (or spirits) sold in Macau, and 200 cigarettes or fifty cigars.

Health matters

You don't need to have any inoculations to enter Hong Kong or Macau. The only stipulation is that if you've been in an area infected with cholera or typhoid during the fourteen days before your arrival, you'll need certificates of vaccination against the two diseases. These requirements might change, so ask your doctor if you're unsure about what constitutes an infected area. If you're travelling elsewhere in Asia or China, before or after Hong Kong and Macau, it's a good idea to make sure that all your inoculations (against typhoid, cholera, tetanus, polio and hepatitis) are up to date.

Health problems

You shouldn't encounter too many problems during your stay. The **water** is fit for drinking everywhere (except from old wells on some of Hong Kong's outlying islands), though bottled water always tastes nicer. Be aware in Hong Kong, however, that despite the Western veneer, **hygiene standards**, particularly to do with food preparation and bathrooms, are not generally high. Many traditional small eating places still just rinse their bowls and chopsticks with lukewarm water, or sometimes tea. Fruit and vegetables from the market should be washed very carefully – many are grown in mainland China where pesticide and fertiliser use is rampant and uncontrolled. Meat and fish are often sold alive, which guarantees it's fresh, but check any shellfish which may have been dredged out of the sometimes less-than-clean bays and waters around the islands.

The summer **heat** can be a problem if you aren't prepared for it or don't take it seriously. Both Hong Kong and Macau can be terribly humid and hot, and skin rashes are not uncommon, something you can combat by showering often and using talcum powder, renting a room with air-conditioning and wearing light cotton clothing. It's also very easy to get dehydrated, particularly if you are drinking alcohol or hiking (or both). If you come down with stomach trouble, the best advice is not to eat anything for 24 hours, drink lots of water or weak tea, and take it easy until you feel better. Once on the mend, start on foods like soup or noodles, though if you don't improve quickly, get medical advice.

Turn to the appropriate pages for details and addresses for the following **medical services**.

Hong Kong

Contraception	p.312
Dentists	p.313
Doctors	p.313
Hospitals	p.314
Pharmacies	p.315

Macau

Doctors	p.377
Hospitals	p.377
Pharmacies	p.377
Vaccination Centres	p.378

While **AIDS** is not as prevalent as in some other Southeast Asian cities, there's a growing awareness of the threat caused by the virus, and TV advertising campaigns and educational programmes have been set in motion.

Pharmacies, doctors and hospitals

Pharmacies can advise on minor ailments and will prescribe basic medicines: they're all registered, and (in the centre of Hong Kong, less so in

A Travellers' First-aid Kit

First aid items are readily available in Hong Kong. If you're planning to travel on into China, or elsewhere in Southeast Asia, a useful kit might include:

Antiseptic cream
Plasters/band aids
Lints and sealed bandages
Knee supports
A course of flagyl antibiotics
Imodium (Lomotil) for emergency diarrhoea treatment
Paracetamol/aspirin
Multi-vitamin and mineral tablets
Rehydration sachets
Water sterilization tablets
Hypodermic needles and sterilized skin wipes

Medical Resources for Travellers

AUSTRALIA
Travellers' Medical and Vaccination Centre, Level 7, 428 George St, Sydney ☎02/9221 7133; Level 2, 393 Little Bourke St, Melbourne ☎03/9602 5788; Level 6, 29 Gilbert Place, Adelaide ☎08/8212 7522; Level 6, 247 Adelaide St, Brisbane ☎07/3221 9066; 5 Mill St, Perth ☎08/9321 1977; general info/health line ☎1902/261560.

BRITAIN
Most general practitioners in the UK have a travel surgery from which you can obtain advice and certain vaccines on prescription, though they may not administer some of the less common immunizations. For up-to-the-minute information, contact one of the following organizations:

British Airways Travel Clinic, 156 Regent St, London W1 (Mon–Fri 9am–5.15pm, Sat 10am–4pm ☎0171/439 9584). *This can be visited without an appointment; there are also appointment-only branches at 101 Cheapside, London EC2 ☎0171/606 2977 and at the BA terminal in London's Victoria Station ☎0171/233 6661. BA also operates regional clinics throughout the country (call ☎01276/685040 for your nearest one). All these clinics sell travel accessories, including mosquito nets and first-aid kits.*

Hospital for Tropical Diseases, St Pancras Hospital, 4 St Pancras Way, London NW1 (Mon–Fri 9am–5pm ☎0171/388 9600). *This also operates a recorded message service on ☎0839/337733 which gives hints on hygiene and illness prevention as well as listing appropriate immunizations.*

MASTA (Medical Advisory Service for Travellers Abroad), London School of Hygiene and Tropical Medicine ☎0891/224100. *Operates a travellers' health line 24 hours a day, 7 days a week, giving written information tailored to your journey by return of post.*

IRELAND
All these places offer medical advice before a trip and medical help afterwards in the event of a tropical disease.

Travel Medicine Services, P.O. Box 254, 16 College St, Belfast 1 ☎01232/315220.

Tropical Medical Bureau, Grafton St Medical Centre, 34 Grafton St, Dublin 2 ☎01/671 9200.

Tropical Medical Bureau, Dun Laoghaire Medical Centre, 5 Northumberland Ave, Dun Laoghaire, Co. Dublin ☎01/280 4996.

NEW ZEALAND
Travellers' Medical and Vaccination Centre, 1/170 Queen St, Auckland ☎09/373 3531; 6 Washington Way, Christchurch ☎03/379 4000.

NORTH AMERICA
International Association for Medical Assistance to Travellers (IAMAT), 417 Center St, Lewiston, NY 14092 ☎716/754 4883; 40 Regal Rd, Guelph, ON N1K 1B5 ☎519/836 0102. *Provides lists of English-speaking doctors, climate charts and leaflets on various diseases and inoculations.*

International SOS Assistance, PO Box 11568, Philadelphia, PA 19116 ☎1-800/523 8930. *Overseas emergency services.*

Medic Alert, 2323 Colorado Ave, Turlock, CA 95381 ☎1-800/432 5378; in Canada, ☎1-800/668 1507. *Sells bracelets engraved with the traveller's medical requirements in case of emergency.*

Travel Medicine, 351 Pleasant St, Suite 312, Northampton, MA 01060 ☎1-800/872 8633. *Sells first-aid kits, mosquito netting, water filters and other health-related travel products.*

Travelers Medical Center, 31 Washington Square West, New York, NY 10011 ☎212/982 1600. *Immunization service.*

Macau) usually employ English speakers. They are generally open daily 9am–6pm.

At some stage, even if it's just to look, go into one of the **Chinese herbal medicine shops**, found throughout Hong Kong and Macau, which are stacked from floor to ceiling with lotions, potions and dried herbs. The people in these shops are less likely to speak English, but if you can describe your ailment they'll prescribe and mix for you a herbal remedy that might or might not cure it. Opinions – Western opinions certainly – divide on whether or not the herbal cures really work. On balance, though, there's a strong case to be made for the holistic approach of Chinese medicine, particularly for some chronic problems. Nevertheless, remember that Chinese herbalists are not required to have formal training to set up shop – although many do.

For a **doctor**, look in the local phone directories' Yellow Pages (under "Physicians and Surgeons" in Hong Kong; "*Medicos*" in Macau), or contact the reception desk in the larger hotels. Many doctors have been trained overseas, but you should ask for one who speaks English. You'll have to pay for a consultation and any medicines they prescribe; ask for a receipt for your insurance.

Hospital treatment is infinitely more expensive, which makes it essential to have some form of medical insurance. Casualty visits are free, however, and hospitals in both territories have 24-hour casualty departments. Finally, both doctors and **dentists** are known as "doctor" in Hong Kong, so be sure you're not wasting your time at the wrong place. Having dental work done costs a lot, so if you possibly can, wait until you get home for treatment.

Travellers with disabilities

There are **organized tours and holidays** specifically for people with disabilities – the contacts in the box will be able to put you in touch with specialists for trips to Hong Kong. If you want to be more independent, it's important to become an authority on where you must be self-reliant and where you may expect help, especially regarding transport and accommodation. It is also vital to be honest – with travel agencies, insurance companies and travel companions. Read your travel **insurance** small print carefully to make sure that people with a pre-existing medical condition are not excluded. And use your travel agent to make your journey simpler: airline or bus companies can cope better if they are expecting you, with a wheelchair provided at airports and staff primed to help. A **medical certificate** of your fitness to travel, provided by your doctor, is also extremely useful; some airlines or insurance companies may insist on it. Make sure that you have extra supplies of drugs – carried with you if you fly – and a prescription including the generic name in case of emergency. Carry spares of any clothing or equipment that might be hard to find; if there's an association representing people with your disability, contact them early in the planning process.

Hong Kong

Physically disabled travellers, especially those reliant upon wheelchairs, will find **Hong Kong** easier to manage than they might have imagined. There are special access and toilet facilities at the airport, as well as on the main Kowloon–Canton Railway (KCR) and LRT system, and at some MRT stations, though other forms of public transport – particularly buses and trams – are virtually out of bounds. However, wheelchairs are able to gain access to the lower deck of cross-harbour and outlying island ferries, taxis are usually obliging, and there's a special bus service, Rehabus, which operates on a dial-a-ride system – see p.313 for details. There are fewer facilities for visually disabled visitors, though assistance is offered by braille signage in KCR elevators and clicking poles at the top and bottom of escalators.

All other facilities for the disabled in public buildings, hotels, restaurants and recreational buildings are listed in a very useful and comprehensive free booklet, *A Guide for Physically Handicapped Visitors to Hong Kong*, distributed by the Hong Kong Tourist Association.

On the whole you'll find people willing to help as you go. If you can, use the telephone numbers given in the text to phone ahead if you think there's likely to be a problem with access at any hotel, restaurant or public building. There's a list of **useful numbers** given on p.313 if you require more information when in Hong Kong.

Contacts for Travellers with Disabilities

AUSTRALIA
ACROD (Australian Council for Rehabilitation of the Disabled)
Curtin, ACT ☎ 02/6282 4333
Cabarita ☎ 02/9743 2699
General travel information.

Barrier Free Travel
North Bellingen, NSW ☎ 02/6655 1733
Hotel, transport and other information.

BRITAIN
Holiday Care Service
Horley, Surrey ☎ 01293/774535
Information on all aspects of travel.

RADAR
London ☎ 0171/250 3222
minicom ☎ 0171/250 4119
Good advice on holidays and travel abroad.

CANADA
Jewish Rehabilitation Hospital
Chomedy Laval, PQ ☎ 514/688 9550, ext 226
Guidebooks and travel information.

Kéroul
Montréal ☎ 514/252 3104
www.craph.org/keroul
Organization promoting and facilitating travel for mobility-impaired people.

Twin Peaks Press
Vancouver ☎ 206/694 2462 or 1-800/637 2256
Publisher of the Directory of Travel Agencies for the Disabled, listing more than 370 agencies worldwide; Travel for the Disabled; the Directory

of Accessible Van Rentals *and* Wheelchair Vagabond, *loaded with personal tips.*

IRELAND
Disability Action Group
Belfast ☎ 01232/491011
Information about access for disabled travellers abroad.

Irish Wheelchair Association
Dublin ☎ 01/833 8241
A national voluntary organization working with people with disabilities with related services for holidaymakers.

NEW ZEALAND
Disabled Persons Assembly
Wellington ☎ 04/801 9100
Advice and general travel information.

USA
Mobility International USA
Eugene, OR ☎ 541/343 1284
Information and referral services, access guides, tours and exchange programs. Annual membership $35.

Society for the Advancement of Travel for the Handicapped (SATH)
New York ☎ 212/447 7284
www.sittravel.com
Non-profit travel-industry referral service.

Travel Information Service
☎ 215/456 9600
Telephone information and referral service.

Macau

Macau is far less easy to negotiate for most physically disabled travellers. The streets are older, narrower, rougher and steeper, and there isn't the same hi-tech edge – overhead ramp-ways, wide, modern elevators, etc – that makes Hong Kong relatively approachable. Visitors in wheelchairs will first have to contact the STDM office in Hong Kong (in the Shun Tak Centre; see p.81), which can assist with travel arrangements on the jetfoils. Some of the larger hotels are also geared towards disabled visitors; contact the MGTO for more information.

Information and maps

Both Hong Kong and Macau maintain **tourist offices** in several cities abroad, where you can pick up information, maps, brochures and leaflets before you go. Don't go mad, though: once you're there, you'll get better, more detailed information from local tourist offices. For addresses and opening hours, see Hong Kong, p.45, Macau, p.326.

The **Internet** is a useful source of information and advice, although many web sites are geared to the business traveller. The Hong Kong Tourist Association (*www.hkta.org*) provides one of the most detailed and up-to-date sites, featuring festivals, weekly events, shopping, food and entertainment listings, plus full visa and visitor information. The official web site of the Macau Government Tourist Office (*www.macautourism.gov.mo*) is similarly useful;

and check out the Macau Municipal Council site (*www.cityguide.gov.mo*) for stats, data, tourism, sport and cultural information.

Maps

The **street plans** given away by the tourist offices are fairly good, but if you want more detailed **regional maps** of Hong Kong and Macau or Southeast Asia, visit one of the map outlets listed in the box on p.22. If you're in Hong Kong for any length of time, you'll need a detailed street **gazetteer**, which names all the streets and buildings in English as well as Chinese: the *Hong Kong Guide* (Lands Department) is a reliable one. Good travel bookshops and map stores should stock them, and they're also widely available in Hong Kong; see p.291.

Tourist Offices Abroad

HONG KONG TOURIST ASSOCIATION (HKTA)

Australia
Level 4, 80 Druitt St,
Sydney, NSW 2000 ☎02/9283 3083

Canada
3rd Floor, 9 Temperance Street,
Toronto, ON M5H 1Y6 ☎416/366 2389

USA
401 N Michigan Ave, #1640,
Chicago, IL 60611 ☎312/329 1828;
10940 Wilshire Blvd, Suite 1220,
Los Angeles, CA 90024 ☎310/208 4582

UK and Ireland
6 Grafton St,
London W1X 3LB ☎0171/533 7100,
brochure line ☎0891/661188

MACAU GOVERNMENT TOURIST OFFICE (MGTO)

If your country has no representation, contact the relevant Portuguese National Tourist Office for information.

Australia
Level 17, 456 Kent St,
Sydney, NSW 2000 ☎02/9285 6856;
local call-rate ☎1300/300236

Canada
Suite 157, 10551 Shellbridge Way,
Richmond, BC V6X 2W9 ☎604/231 9040;
13 Mountalan Ave, Toronto,
Ontario M4J IH3 ☎416/466 6552

New Zealand
c/o 101 Great South Rd,
Remuera, Auckland ☎09/309 8094

UK and Ireland
1 Battersea Church Rd,
London SW11 3LY ☎0171/771 7006

USA
5757 W. Century Blvd, #660,
Los Angeles, CA 90045 ☎1-877 MACAU 00
(toll free); 310/568 0009

Map Outlets

AUSTRALIA
Adelaide
The Map Shop, 16a Peel St,
Adelaide, SA 5000 ☎ 08/8231 2033
Brisbane
Worldwide Maps and Guides, 187 George St,
Brisbane, QLD 4000 ☎ 07/3221 4330
Melbourne
Mapland, 372 Little Bourke St,
Melbourne, VIC 3000 ☎ 03/9670 4383
Perth
Perth Map Centre, 884 Hay St,
Perth, WA 6000 ☎ 08/9322 5733
Sydney
Travel Bookshop, Shop 3, 175 Liverpool St,
Sydney, NSW 2000 ☎ 02/9261 8200

BRITAIN
London
Daunt Books,
83 Marylebone High St, W1 ☎ 0171/224 2295
National Map Centre,
22–24 Caxton St, SW1 ☎ 0171/222 2466
Stanfords,
12–14 Long Acre, WC2 ☎ 0171/836 1321;
52 Grosvenor Gardens, SW1 ☎ 0171/730 1314;
56 Regent St, W1 ☎ 0171/434 4744
The Travel Bookshop,
13–15 Blenheim Crescent, W11 ☎ 0171/229 5260
Cambridge
Heffers Map Shop, 3rd Floor,
Heffers Stationery Department,
19 Sidney St, CB2 3HL ☎ 01223/568467
Glasgow
John Smith and Sons,
57–61 St Vincent St, G2 ☎ 0141/221 7472
Manchester
Waterstone's,
91 Deansgate, M3 2BW ☎ 0161/832 1992
Newcastle
Newcastle Map Centre,
55 Grey St, NE1 6EF ☎ 0191/261 5622
Oxford
Blackwell's Map and Travel Shop,
53 Broad St, OX1 3BQ ☎ 01865/792792

Maps by **mail or phone order** are available
from Stanfords ☎ 0171/836 1321

CANADA
Montréal
Ulysses Travel Bookshop, 4176 St Denis,
Montreal H2W 2M5 ☎ 514/843 9447
Toronto
Open Air Books and Maps, 25 Toronto St,
Toronto, ON M5C 2R1 ☎ 416/363 0719
Vancouver
International Travel Maps & Books, 552
Seymour St, Vancouver, V6B 3J5 ☎ 604/687 3320

IRELAND
Belfast
Waterstone's, Queens Bldg, 8 Royal Ave,
Belfast BT1 ☎ 01232/247355
Dublin
Easons Bookshop, 40 O'Connell St,
Dublin 1 ☎ 01/873 3811
Fred Hanna's Bookshop, 27–29 Nassau St,
Dublin 2 ☎ 01/677 1255
Hodges Figgis Bookshop, 56–58 Dawson St,
Dublin 2 ☎ 01/677 4754
Waterstones, 7 Dawson St,
Dublin 2 ☎ 01/679 1415

NEW ZEALAND
Auckland
Auckland Specialty Maps,
58 Albert St ☎ 09/307 2217

USA
Chicago
Rand McNally ☎ 1-800/234 0679
for the nearest store or for direct mail maps
New York
The Complete Traveller Bookstore,
199 Madison Ave, New York,
NY 10016 ☎ 212/685 9007
San Francisco
The Complete Traveler Bookstore,
3207 Fillmore St, San Francisco,
CA 94123 ☎ 415/923 1511
Seattle
Elliot Bay Book Company, 101 S Main St,
Seattle, WA 98104 ☎ 1-800/962 5311
Washington
The Map Store Inc., 1636 I St NW, Washington,
DC 20006 ☎ 1-800/544 2659

Costs and money

It's difficult to pinpoint an average daily cost for staying in Hong Kong and Macau, though it's true to say that both places come more expensive than most other Southeast Asian destinations in terms of food and accommodation. If you've just come from China or Thailand, for instance, you're in for a substantial increase in your daily budget. The details below should help you plan exactly how much to allow for.

The easiest and safest way to carry your money is as **travellers' cheques**, available for a small commission (usually 1–2 percent of the amount ordered) from any bank, whether or not you have an account, and from branches of American Express and Thomas Cook. Make sure to keep the purchase agreement and a record of cheque serial numbers safe and separate from the cheques themselves. In the event that cheques are lost or stolen, the issuing company will expect you to report the loss forthwith to their office; most companies claim to replace lost or stolen cheques within 24 hours.

You can use all major **credit cards** in Hong Kong in return for goods and services. However, watch out for the three to five percent commission that lots of travel agencies and shops try to add to the price. It's illegal, but there's not much you can do about it except shop around: always ask first if there's an extra commission charge with a credit card. And inform your credit card company when you get home.

In addition, American Express, Mastercard and Visa cardholders can use the **automatic teller machines** (ATMs) at various points in both territories to withdraw local currency; details from the companies direct. Make sure you have a personal identification number (PIN) that's designed to work overseas. Remember that all cash advances are treated as loans, with interest accruing daily from the date of withdrawal; there may be a transaction fee on top of this.

If you need to **transfer money from overseas**, go to one of the major international banks (preferably one which is linked with your bank back home) and get them to have your bank telex the money to a specific branch in Hong Kong. This will probably take a day or so, and you'll be charged a small handling fee. Or you can use **Western Union Money Transfer**, which typically charges eight to ten percent of the sum transferred to effect a money transfer to Hong Kong. For addresses and contact numbers in Hong Kong see "Directory", p.311 and p.317.

Hong Kong

The vast consumer choice in Hong Kong leads to a few contradictions in terms of how much things cost. There is no limit to the amount of money you could spend; certain hotels, restaurants and shops are among the priciest in the world. But the overwhelming majority of the population doesn't command the same income as the super-rich, and consequently it's possible to survive as they do: eating cheaply, travelling for very little and staying in low-cost accommodation.

At the bottom end of the scale, staying in hostels and dormitories costs as little as £7/US$10.50 a night, and cheap Chinese meals at street stalls and in cafés go for another £2–3/US$3–4.50 a time. **Living frugally** this way, for a fairly short time, you could survive on around £13/US$20 a day.

Eat out more, or go to better restaurants, take a taxi or two, have a drink in a bar, and an average day easily costs £25–30/US$38–45 or more. Upgrade your accommodation to a room with en-suite facilities, eat three meals a day and

> For **banking information** and opening hours in both territories, see Hong Kong, p.311, Macau, p.376.

don't stint on the extras and this figure at least doubles: a reasonable estimate for a good time in the territory, without going over the top, is anything from £40–60/US$60–90 a day. Obviously, if you're planning to stay in one of the very expensive hotels, this figure won't even cover your room – but then you'll either be on a package tour or, if not, you probably won't be bothered about sticking to any kind of budget.

The bonus of Hong Kong is that once you've accounted for your room and a decent meal every day, most of the extras are very cheap: snacking as you go from the street, or lunching on *dim sum*, is excellent value; public transport costs are among the lowest in the world; the museums and galleries are mostly free; and the active, colourful street life doesn't cost a cent either.

Currency

The unit of currency is the Hong Kong dollar, often written as HK$, or just $, and divided into 100 cents (written as c). Bank notes are issued by the Hongkong and Shanghai Banking Corporation, the Standard Chartered Bank and the Bank of China, and are of slightly different design and size, but they're all interchangeable. **Notes** come in denominations of $10, $20, $50, $100, $500 and $1000; there's a nickel-and bronze $10 coin; **silver coins** come as $1, $2 and $5; and **bronze coins** as 10c, 20c and 50c. It's a good idea to buy at least a few Hong Kong dollars from a bank before you go; that way you don't have to use the airport exchange desk (which has poor rates) when you arrive.

The current **rate of exchange** fluctuates around $12–13 to the pound sterling, $5 to the Australian dollar, $4 to the New Zealand dollar; it is pegged at $7.78 to the US dollar. There's no black market and money, in any amount, can be freely taken in and out of the territory.

Macau

You'll find **living costs** in Macau similar to those in Hong Kong, though there are significant differences. You'll pay slightly more for the very cheapest beds, but will get much better value in the larger hotels – which drop their prices even further in midweek; it's always worth shopping around. Meals, too, are particularly good value: wine and port is imported from Portugal and untaxed, and an excellent three-course Portuguese meal with wine and coffee can be had for as little as £10/US$15. Transport costs are minimal, since you can walk to most places, though buses and taxis are in any case extremely cheap. All in all, you can live much better than in Hong Kong on the same money, or expect to be around ten to twenty percent better off if you watch your budget.

Currency

The unit of **currency** is the *pataca*, made up of 100 *avos*. You'll see prices written in several ways, usually as M$100, MOP$100 or 100ptcs (as in this book), all of which mean the same thing. **Coins** come as 10, 20 and 50 *avos*, and 1 and 5ptcs, **notes** in denominations of 10, 50, 100, 500 and 1000ptcs.

The *pataca* is pegged to the Hong Kong dollar (see above), though officially worth roughly three percent less. In practice, **you can use Hong Kong dollars (notes and coins) throughout Macau to pay for anything**, on a one-for-one basis, though you can't use *patacas* in Hong Kong – in fact, you'll find them almost impossible to get rid of there, so spend all your *patacas* before you leave Macau.

Opening hours, holidays and festivals

Hong Kong has a fairly complicated set of different opening hours for different shops and services. Generally, **offices** are open Monday–Friday 9am–5pm, and some open Saturday 9am–1pm; **banks**, Monday–Friday 9am–4.30pm, Saturday 9am–12.30am; **shops**, daily 10am–7/8pm, though later in tourist areas (see p.286 for more details); and **post offices**, Monday–Friday 8am–6pm, Saturday 8am–2pm. **Museums** usually close one day a week; check the text for exact details. **Temples** often have no set hours, though they are usually open from early morning to early evening; again, the text has full details.

In **Macau**, opening hours are more limited, with government and official offices open Monday–Friday 8.30/9am–1pm and 3–5/5.30pm, Saturday 8.30/9am–1pm. Shops and businesses are usually open throughout the day and have slightly longer hours.

On **public holidays** and some religious festivals (see below) most shops and all government offices in both territories will be closed. Annual public holidays in Hong Kong and Macau are listed below; Macau has several more than Hong Kong, due to its Portuguese (and consequently Catholic) colonial heritage.

Festivals

You're in luck if you can time a visit to coincide with one of the many **festivals** that bring whole streets or areas in both Hong Kong and Macau to a complete standstill. At the most exuberant festival of all – Chinese New Year – the entire population takes time out to celebrate. With roots going back hundreds (even thousands) of years, many of the festivals are highly symbolic and are often a mixture of secular and religious displays and devotions. Each has its own peculiarities and attractions: not all are as vibrant and lively as New Year, but each offers a unique slice of Hong Kong and Macau and, by extension, China.

Confusingly, not all the festivals are also public holidays, when most things will be closed. But all mean a substantial increase in the number of people travelling on public transport, higher prices for certain services and large crowds in the festival centres. Also, as the Chinese use the **lunar calendar** and not the Gregorian calendar, many of the festivals fall on different days, even different months, from year to year. The likely months are listed below, but for exact details contact the HKTA or MGTO. For a description of the major festivals, turn to p.282 (Hong Kong) and p.328 (Macau).

Chinese Festivals

January/February: Chinese New Year; Yuen Siu (Lantern Festival).

April: Ching Ming Festival.

April/May: Tin Hau Festival.

May: Birthday of the Lord Buddha; Tai Chiu Festival.

June: Tuen Ng (Dragon Boat Festival).

July: Birthday of Lu Pan.

August: Maiden's Festival; Yue Lan Festival.

September: Mid-Autumn (Moon Cake) Festival; Birthday of Confucius.

October: Cheung Yeung Festival.

Public Holidays

HONG KONG

Hong Kong's public holidays are changing as China jettisons the old colonial holidays in favour of its own celebrations. For now, the following public holidays are observed.

January 1: New Year.

January/February: three days' holiday for Chinese New Year.

March/April: Easter (holidays on Good Friday, Easter Saturday and Easter Monday).

April: The day after the Ching Ming Festival.

May: Labour Day, Buddha's Birthday.

June: Dragon Boat Festival.

July 1: HKSAR Establishment Day.

September: Mid-Autumn Festival.

October 1:Chinese National Day, Cheung Yeung Festival.

December 25 and 26: Christmas.

MACAU

Macau's public holidays are likely to change following the reversion of sovereignty to China.

January 1: New Year.

January/February: three days' holiday for Chinese New Year.

March/April: Easter (holidays on Good Friday and Easter Monday).

April: Ching Ming Festival.

April 25: anniversary of the 1974 Portuguese revolution.

May 1: Labour Day.

June 10: Camões Day and Portuguese Communities Day, commemorating Portugal's national poet.

June: Dragon Boat Festival; also Feast of St John the Baptist.

September: Mid-Autumn Festival.

October 5: Portuguese Republic Day, to mark the establishment of the Portuguese Republic in 1910.

October: Cheung Yeung Festival.

November 2: All Souls' Day.

December 1: Portuguese Independence Day.

8: Feast of Immaculate Conception.

22: Winter Solstice.

25 and 26: Christmas.

Communications

As befits one of the world's greatest business centres, Hong Kong's **communications** are fast and efficient. The phones all work and the postal system is good, sending mail home is quick and relatively cheap, and the poste restante system is well organized. Macau is slightly more laid back, but you should have few problems getting in touch.

Hong Kong

Post offices throughout the territory are open Monday–Friday 8am–6pm, Saturday 8am–2pm. The post offices by the Star Ferry on Hong Kong Island and at 10 Middle Road in Tsim Sha Tsui are also open on Sundays 8am–2pm. Letters sent poste restante will go to the GPO building in Central (see p.315 for addresses) – take your passport along when you go to collect them. Letters and cards sent airmail take three days to a week to reach Britain or North America. Surface mail is slower, taking weeks rather than days; rates are listed in a leaflet available from most post offices.

If you're sending parcels home, they'll have to conform with the post office's packaging regulations. Either take your unwrapped parcel along to a main post office – together with your own brown paper and tape – and follow their instructions, or buy one of their cardboard boxes.. It's a good idea to insure your parcels, too: the post office will have the relevant forms, as well as the customs declaration that must be filled in for all goods sent abroad by post. Your parcel will go by surface mail unless you specify otherwise – the price obviously increases the bigger the parcel and the further it has to go.

The Hong Kong telephone system works well, perhaps inspired by the fact that everybody, roadmenders to millionaires, seems to have their own portable phone. Making a local call – which means throughout the territory of Hong Kong – from a private phone is free. Public coinphones cost HK$1 for five minutes, while there are also creditcard phones and cardphones. You'll find phones at MTR stations, ferry terminals, in shop-

Telephone Numbers

The Hong Kong Chinese consider certain phone numbers to be unlucky, principally because the words for some of the numbers sound like more ominous words – 4 (*sei*), for example, which sounds like the Cantonese word for "death". Lots of people won't accept the private numbers they're allocated by the telephone company for this reason, and there's a continuous struggle to change numbers. Conversely, other numbers are considered lucky because they sound fortuitous – particularly 3 (longevity), 8 (prosperity) and 9 (eternity) – and people will wheedle, pay or bribe to have these included in their telephone number. The same applies, incidentally, to car number plates: each year there's a government auction of the best ones, some of which fetch thousands of dollars.

ping centres and hotel lobbies, while most shops and restaurants will let you use the phone for free. You can buy phone cards from HK Telecom Service Centres (see p.28) and from tourist offices and convenience stores such as 7-Eleven; they come in units of $50, $100, $200 and $300.

Making a call is easy: on every pay and card phone there are instructions in English – the ring-

---

To phone Hong Kong from abroad

Dial the international access code (given opposite) + ☎852 (country code) + number
International access codes

Australia ☎0011	Canada ☎011
Ireland ☎010	New Zealand ☎00
UK ☎00	USA ☎011

To phone abroad from Hong Kong

Dial ☎001 + IDD country code (see below) + area code minus first 0 + subscriber number

IDD country codes

Australia ☎61	Macau ☎853
Canada ☎1	New Zealand ☎64
China ☎86	UK ☎44
Ireland ☎353	USA ☎1

Home Direct codes

Australia ☎96/0061
Canada ☎800 1100

Ireland ☎800 0353
Macau ☎800 0853
New Zealand ☎96/0064
UK (BT numbers only) ☎800 0044
USA   (AT&T) ☎800 1111
       (MCI) ☎800 1121
       (Sprint) ☎800 1877
       (TRT/FTC) ☎800 1115

ing, engaged and number-unobtainable tones are similar to those used in Britain and America. All telephone numbers contain eight digits and there are no area codes. For **international calls**, use the International Direct Dialling (IDD) phones found around the territory, or go to one of the several **Hong Kong Telecom Service Centres** throughout the territory; there's a list of the central ones on p.316. Here you can make overseas calls, including **reverse-charge** ("collect") calls and faxes. Another method of making cashless international calls is to use Hong Kong's **Home Direct** service (see box on p.27), which gives you access to an operator in the country you're calling, who can either charge calls collect or to an **overseas telephone card**. These include the **BT Chargecard** and the card issued by **AT&T Direct Service**. Both cards are free and they work in the same way – just ring the company's international operator, who will connect you free of charge and add the cost of the connected call to your domestic bill. For a list of **useful telephone numbers** in Hong Kong, see p.316.

Internet and **email access** is available at branches of the *Pacific Coffee Company* and other cyber cafés (see p.235) or in the business centres of major hotels.

Macau

The main **post office** in Macau (see p.377 for address) is open Monday to Friday 9am–1pm and 3–5.30pm, Saturday 9am–12.30pm. Otherwise, little booths all over Macau sell **stamps**, as do the larger hotels, and there are post offices on Taipa and Coloane. Letters and cards sent from Macau to Europe and North America take around the same time as from Hong Kong – between five days and a week.

The Macanese **telephone system** is operated by Companhia de Telecomunicações de Macau (CTM). **Local phone calls** from a pay phone cost 1ptc though, as in Hong Kong, local calls are free from a private phone or from the courtesy phones in shops and restaurants. There are no area codes; just dial the five- or six-figure number given. Instructions on most phones are in English as well as Portuguese. You can make **international calls** from the telephone office at the back of the main post office; some of the staff there speak English. As in Hong Kong, there's a **Home Direct** service (*Pais Directo*), which gives you access to an operator in the country you're calling, who can either charge calls collect or to your overseas phone card (see "Hong Kong" above). For a round-up of **useful and emergency telephone numbers** in Macau, see p.377.

To phone Macau from abroad

Dial the international access code (see p.27) + ☎853 (country code) + number

---

To phone abroad from Macau

Dial ☎00 + IDD country code (see p.27) + area code minus first 0 + subscriber number

To Hong Kong – classed as an international call – dial ☎01 + number.

Home Direct Codes

Australia ☎0800-610	**UK** (BT numbers only) ☎0800-440
Canada ☎0800-100	**USA** 0800-11
Hong Kong ☎0800-852	(AT&T) ☎0800-111
New Zealand ☎0800-640	(MCI) ☎0800-131
	(Sprint) ☎0800-121

Police and trouble

Hong Kong and Macau are both very safe places for tourists, certainly compared to other Asian cities. The only real concern is the prevalence of **pickpockets**: the crowded streets, trains and buses are the ideal cover for them. To guard against being robbed in this way, keep money and wallets in inside pockets, sling bags around your neck (not just over your shoulder) and pay attention when getting on and off packed public transport.

Apart from this, **avoiding trouble** is a matter of common sense. Most of the streets are perfectly safe, as is Hong Kong's MTR underground system, which is clean, well lit and well used at night. Taxis, too, are reliable, though it's still wise to use registered taxis from proper taxi ranks only.

In both territories, it's rare that you'll be wandering around areas of the city at night that are a bit dodgy and, if you are, there's nothing you can do to avoid standing out. The best advice if you're lost, or somewhere vaguely threatening, is to look purposeful, don't dawdle, and stick to the main roads. If you are **held up and robbed** – an extremely unlikely event – hand over your money and *never* fight back: local villains have large knives which they have few compunctions about using.

More common problems are those associated with **drunkenness** in Hong Kong. If it's your scene, be careful in bars where the emphasis is on buying hugely expensive drinks for the "girls":

if you get drunk and can't/won't pay, the bar gorilla will help you find your wallet. And unless you like shouting and fighting, try to avoid the bars when the sailors of various fleets hit the city.

Police and offences

Probably the only contact you'll have with the olive- or blue-uniformed **Hong Kong Police** (who are armed) is if you have something stolen, when you'll need to get a report for your insurance company. On the street, police officers who speak English wear a red flash under their shoulder number. Otherwise, contact one of the police stations, whose addresses are given on p.315. In **Macau**, police wear a dark blue uniform in winter, and sky-blue shirts and navy blue trousers in summer. The main police station, where you should go in the event of any trouble, is listed on p.377.

There are a few **offences** you might commit unwittingly. In Hong Kong, you're required to carry some form of **identification** at all times: if you don't want to carry your passport around, anything with your photograph will do, or your driving licence. Residents (and those thinking of staying and working in Hong Kong) need a special ID card – see p.34 for details. As a Westerner it's unlikely you'll be stopped in the street and asked for ID, though you might be involved in the occasional police raid on discos and clubs, when they're usually looking for known Triad members, illegal immigrants and drugs. They'll prevent anyone from leaving until they've taken down everyone's details from their ID.

Buying, selling or otherwise being involved with **drugs** is extremely unwise. If you're caught in possession, no one is going to be sympathetic, least of all your consulate.

Other than these things, you'll be left pretty much alone, though don't think of **bathing topless** on any of Hong Kong or Macau's beaches:

Emergencies

In both Hong Kong and Macau, dial ☎ 999 for any **emergency service** (police, ambulance or fire).

---

you'll draw a lot of attention to yourself, offend some people and in any case it's illegal.

Sexual harassment

Harassment is not common, and **women travelling in Hong Kong and Macau** are more likely to be harassed by sexist foreign expats than by Chinese men, which at least has the advantage of being more familiar and so easier to deal with. You're not likely to mistake unwelcome advances from a Westerner as cultural inquisitiveness, and the same tactics as at home are the ones to use to get rid of creeps. To minimize what physical risks there are, try to avoid travelling alone late at night on Hong Kong's MTR; don't be tempted by any work offers as "hostesses" (see "Staying On", p.33); and generally use your common sense. For local womens' organizations in Hong Kong, see p.317.

Organized crime: the Triads

Much of the lurid crime you read about every day in Hong Kong's English-language newspapers is related to the **Triads**. The historical reasons for the existence of these organized crime societies (similar to the Mafia) is discussed in "History" (p.389), but at street level they're directly and indirectly responsible for most of the drug dealing, prostitution, corruption and major crime in the territory. Needless to say, the average visitor won't come into contact with any of this, though drug addicts support their habit by pickpocketing and mugging, and the shop you bought your camera from or the restaurant you eat in may pay protection money to one Triad society or another, or may buy their supplies through a Triad-related company.

In recent years Macau has experienced a wave of small but violent incidents. Cars and motorcycles have been blown up, grenades and small bombs have been thrown and a number of people have been shot or attacked with meat cleavers in gangland style hits. The attacks, which usually take place in the small hours, are generally either targeted at local officials or related to turf wars between different Triad groups. It's extremely unlikely that, as a visitor, you'll notice anything untoward, and even more unlikely that you will become personally involved.

Religion

Most major **religions** are represented in Hong Kong and Macau, though it's the three main Chinese ones – **Taoism**, **Confucianism** and **Buddhism** – that are of most interest to visitors. Everywhere, you'll come across temples and shrines, while many of the public holidays are connected with a particular religious occasion. The whole picture is further confused by the contemporary importance attached to **superstition** and **ancestor worship**.

The religions

The main local religion, **Taoism**, dates from the sixth century BC. A philosophical movement, it advocates that people follow a central path or truth, known as *Tao* or "The Way", and cultivate an understanding of the nature of things. This search for truth has often expressed itself in Taoism by way of superstition on the part of its devotees, who engage in fortune telling and the like. The Taoist gods are mainly legendary figures, with specific powers – protective or otherwise – which you can generally determine from their form: warriors, statesmen, scholars, and so on. Taoist temples are generally very colourful, hosting the rowdiest of the annual festivals.

Confucianism also began as a philosophy, based on piety, loyalty, education, humanitarianism and familial devotion. In the 2500 years since Confucius died, these ideas have permeated every aspect of Chinese social life, and the philosophy has acquired the characteristics of a religion. However, it's the least common of the Eastern religions in Hong Kong, with few temples and fewer regular observances. Rather it's a set

Gods and Goddesses

For the most part, the Chinese gods and goddesses honoured in Macau are the same as in Hong Kong, with occasional variations in spelling and importance – the deity A-Ma, for instance, is the same as Hong Kong's Tin Hau. You'll find further information about the following deities throughout the text, usually under the entry for the main temple at which they're worshipped.

Kuan Ti (or Kuan Yue): god of war; a warrior.

Kuan Yin (or Kwun Yum): Buddhist goddess of mercy.

Pak Tai: god of order and protection; also known as Emperor of the North.

Pao Kung: god of justice.

Shing Wong: a city god, responsible for those living in certain areas.

Sui Tsing Paak: a god who cures illness; also known as the "Pacifying General".

Tai Sui: a series of sixty different gods, each related to a year in the Chinese calendar.

Tin Hau: goddess of the sea, and one of the most popular deities, unsurprising in a land where fishing has always been important; known as A-Ma in Macau.

Wong Tai Sin: a god who cures illness and brings good fortune.

of principles, adhered to in spirit if not in practice.

Also represented in Hong Kong and, to a lesser extent, Macau is **Buddhism**, which was originally brought from India to China in the first century AD. It recognizes that there is suffering in the world, which can be relieved only by attaining a state of personal enlightenment, *nirvana*, or extinction, at which point you will find true bliss. The method of finding this enlightenment is by meditation. Various Buddhist sects follow different practices, and in Hong Kong the situation is made more complicated by the way in which deities from various religions are worshipped in each other's temples – it's common for Buddhist deities to be worshipped in Taoist temples, for example. Buddhist temples are relaxed places, less common and less bright than Taoist, but often built in beautiful, out-of-the-way places and with resident monks and nuns.

Inside a temple: the deities

The majority of the temples described in the text are Taoist, and what goes on inside is fairly similar everywhere. Most temples are **open** from early morning to early evening and people go in when they like, to make offerings or to pray; there are no set prayer and service times.

The **roofs** of Taoist temples are usually decorated with colourful porcelain figures from Chinese legend, while inside you'll find stalls selling joss sticks, and slow-burning **incense** spirals which hang from the ceiling. In most temples there's a stall or special room for **fortune telling**, most commonly achieved by shaking sticks in a cylinder until one falls out: the number on the stick corresponds to a piece of fortune paper, which has to be paid for and interpreted by a fortune teller at a stall. Go with someone who can speak Chinese if you want to try this, or visit Hong Kong's massive Wong Tai Sin temple in Kowloon (see p.140), where fortune telling takes place on a much more elaborate scale: here you'll find lots of long-established fortune tellers, as well as palmists and phrenologists, who are used to foreign tourists, and lots of explanatory notes.

Obviously, coinciding with one of the main religious **festivals** (see "Opening Hours, Holidays and Festivals", on p.26) is an invigorating experience, and this is when you'll see the various temples at their best: lavishly decorated and full of people. There'll be dances, Chinese opera displays, plenty of noise and a series of **offerings** left in the temples – food, and paper goods which are burned as offerings to the dead.

Staying on: working and living in Hong Kong

Hong Kong has always been full of foreigners working and living in the territory, although as ties with the UK weaken, fewer of them are British. These days the biggest immigrant group in Hong Kong is from the Philippines – mostly women who come here to work as servants and house maids (*amahs*). What European expatriate workers (expats) there are tend more and more to have been posted to the territory by their company, or have applied for jobs with Hong Kong firms from abroad. That said, the dream still persists with many travellers that they can turn up, find work and make their fortune. You *can* find work and accommodation in Hong Kong, but you'll probably need to lower your sights and be aware that since the Asian economic crisis the situation has become much tougher.

Hong Kong isn't an easy place to live, job or no job. It's crowded, hot and humid, with few prospects of getting away from it and all the frustrations of living in a country where you probably don't speak the native language. You'll find the basic rules below, together with ideas about how to get a job and somewhere to live. However, there are no short cuts to making the kind of money Hong Kong is famous for – though you can be happy with the thought that it's several times easier to become a Hong Kong dollar millionaire than a sterling or US dollar millionaire.

Finding work

Everyone – including British citizens – needs an **employment visa**, which you have to apply for before you arrive, at a Chinese embassy or consulate. Any general enquiries should be addressed to the **Immigration Department**, Immigration Tower, 7 Gloucester Rd, Wan Chai, Hong Kong ☎ 2824 6111. If you're staying and working longer than six months, you'll also need an ID card (see p.34).

The economic downturn and the resulting rise in local unemployment means there are fewer jobs than ever before for foreigners. In addition the government now imposes stringent tests on employers, who have to show that the job cannot be done by a local person. What is most likely to be on offer is **skilled and highly specialized work**, or work which requires fluency in English or other languages. Flick through the jobs pages of the *South China Morning Post* – it's on sale in foreign Chinatowns – or look at the paper's Web site (*www.scmp.com*) and you might be able to apply before you leave. Note, though, that if you find a job while you're a visitor in Hong Kong, you'll have to leave the territory and apply for a visa before being allowed to take up the position – and that takes weeks, if not months.

If you don't want to apply for anything specific, you can always try **writing and ringing** around once you're in Hong Kong. Ideally, you'll need a base (your own or someone else's flat and phone), plenty of experience in the field you're trying to bust into, and lots of time. Bring copies of all relevant qualifications. You can get a free list of many different Hong Kong companies from the **Employment Services Division**, Labour Department, 17th Floor, Harbour Building, 38 Pier Rd, Central ☎ 2852 4158.

Failing that, the other option is to look for **semi- and unskilled work**, which is more widely available, but has the disadvantage of being fairly badly paid. Some ideas are listed below and though you'll make enough to live on with most of the jobs, you're in competition with young Chinese people, who are mostly well-educated, bilingual and prepared to accept lower wages than you'd expect for the same job.

Employment agencies

Employment agencies are listed in the Yellow Pages. Most will ask to see your CV/résumé before registering you. The longer you plan to work, the more chance you have of getting a job – you might need to be economical with the truth about the length of time you intend to spend in Hong Kong. The following agencies will register people looking for as little as six weeks' clerical work:

Drake International, 9 Queen's Road, Central ☎ 2848 9288.

Swift Recruitment Ltd, California Tower, Lan Kwai Fong, Central ☎ 2845 3280.

Career opportunities

• **Bar and restaurant work**. Poorly paid – around HK$35 an hour plus tips – but there are still vacancies in English and Australian pubs and often in non-Chinese restaurants. Ask around the bars, look in windows for notices of "help wanted", check the noticeboard in the *Travellers' Hostel*, Chungking Mansions, or look in the classified advertisements of *HK Magazine*.

• **Film extras**. Hong Kong is a big film-making centre, although the industry is in the doldrums at the moment. There are sometimes jobs going as extras for films and commercials, paying around HK$250 a day. Watch noticeboards and newspapers.

• **Hostess/modelling/escort work**. You might see adverts seeking any of these three categories of people, though in general they're worth avoiding. At best, hostessing/escort work consists of drinking lots of fake champagne with fat old businessmen; at worst it consists of sleeping with them as well.

• **Hotel work**. Fairly hard to come by for foreigners, but watch out for advertising by the big hotels for cleaning, kitchen and desk staff. Some of the hostels in Chungking Mansions also occasionally take on helpers; ask at the ones used to Western travellers, like the *Travellers' Hostel*.

• **Office work**. The Hong Kong papers are full of office jobs – clerking, dogsbodies, gofers and sales people – but you'll often need to speak Cantonese, and many firms may be unwilling to employ you without the right papers. Law companies are among the few businesses which employ only English-speaking people; phoning them direct can be very effective – but you will need some experience or qualifications. Reckon on earning from HK$6000 a month and upwards, not a fortune by any means, though many jobs also offer commission.

• **Smuggling**. The noticeboards at the *Travellers' Hostel* and elsewhere sometimes advertise for people to take items – electronic gear and the like – to other countries, where it can be sold at a premium. You'll get the air ticket for your trouble, and maybe paid too, but if customs stamp the gear in your passport you'll be expected to have it when you leave the country you've brought it into – and if you don't know exactly what it is you're taking, or haven't checked the goods, it could well be drugs. Not at all recommended.

• **Teaching**. Eminently possible, though again not brilliantly paid (around HK$70–100 an hour). However, you don't always need experience or a TEFL qualification. Look in the *South China Morning Post* for jobs in private and government schools, or for people wanting private tuition; or advertise yourself. The language schools listed in the Yellow Pages are worth checking.

Finding an apartment

If you're staying in Hong Kong for any length of time, you'll need to get out of your hostel or hotel and into an apartment. Space is at a premium in the territory, and don't expect to get the same space or facilities for your money as at home. But as long as you don't want to live on Hong Kong Island itself, you should be able to find somewhere that's reasonably priced, especially if you can share accommodation.

If you've been sent to Hong Kong by your company, or have come for a job that's been offered to you by a large company, then you shouldn't have to pay all or indeed any of your rent. Your initial hotel bills should be paid, too, while you look for apartments on **Hong Kong Island** – perhaps in the quieter, greener areas on the south side by the beaches, or in Mid-Levels above Central. If you *are* paying your own rent, however, these places are likely to be out of your price range. A flick through the papers at the property pages will show you that you're talking a lot of money, but then living on The Peak itself has always been reserved for the phenomenally wealthy. Mere mortals will have to look else-where for accommodation. Generally, the further out you get the cheaper it becomes – so Kowloon is a good place to start, or perhaps Kennedy Town or Chai Wan on the Island. The **New Territories** towns are good places to look: Sha Tin may be the most central place you'll be able to afford, only a quick train ride from Kowloon Tong; Tsuen Wan and Tuen Mun are further out and plagued by rush-hour congestion, but connected with Central by hoverferry. If you don't mind the travelling time, and being isolated as one of the few foreigners around, towns fur-ther up the KCR rail line are substantially cheap-er: like Tai Po and developments in and around Fanling and Sheung Shui. Living on one of the **outlying islands** (Lamma, Cheung Chau or Lantau particularly) is popular with many foreigners – it's certainly quieter and often cheaper too, although commuting in every day can be a real pain, and in typhoon season the ferry services are often suspended altogether.

You can start to look for **apartments** in the classified sections of the *South China Morning Post*, the *Hong Kong Standard* or in freesheets like *HK Magazine*, distributed in many bars and restaurants. Places are mostly rented unfurnished and are advertised by the square foot; you'll soon work out what's big and what isn't, although a lot of places count crazy things in the square footage like the lift lobby, the pipe ducts, or even the windowsills – so don't be surprised if it looks smaller than it sounds. The price in dollars will be the monthly **rent** – around HK\$7000 and upwards for anything halfway decent – and you'll probably have to pay around two months' rent as

a deposit as well. It's also worth contacting let-tings agencies; look for names in the papers or Yellow Pages. Or wander around the shopping centres in the New Territories towns, like Sha Tin, and go into the agents you see to ask about apartments: they're the shops with coloured cards in the windows, generally in Chinese, but with explicable square footage and price signs.

Once you're in your apartment, you'll be responsible for furnishing it and all the bills. Lots of the new buildings have security guards and video-protection services, but otherwise give some thought to **securing your apartment**: change the locks or get a steel door like every-one else. Crime is still rare in Hong Kong, but bur-glary is on the increase.

ID cards

Every resident of Hong Kong has to carry an **identity card**. You may be asked to produce it – or a passport if you are not a taxpaying resident – by the police doing spot-checks for illegal immigrants. So if you are staying on you should think about getting hold of one as soon as pos-sible – technically, you're supposed to apply for one within thirty days of arrival if you're going to stay in Hong Kong.

ID cards are **issued** free of charge at the terri-tory's Immigration Department at Immigration Tower, 7 Gloucester Rd, Wan Chai ☎ 2824 6111. Take your passport and a few dollars in change which you'll need for making photocopies and having a couple of photos taken. They'll take your name and address and you'll have to return about a month later to pick the card up. Lose it and a replacement will cost around HK\$170.

Hong Kong

Chapter 1

Introducing Hong Kong

A mainland peninsula and more than 260 islands of assorted shape and size on the southeastern tip of China make up the territory of **Hong Kong**, which has a total land area of just under 1100 square kilometres. Almost seven million people live here, but despite the congestion on the roads and in the urban areas, it's fairly easy to get around. You could travel the 40km from the Chinese border in the north to the south coast of Hong Kong Island in a couple of hours or so. Indeed, it's compact enough to make seeing the whole territory in just a few days eminently possible – though the geographical and cultural diversity packed in between could take weeks of careful exploration if you have the time.

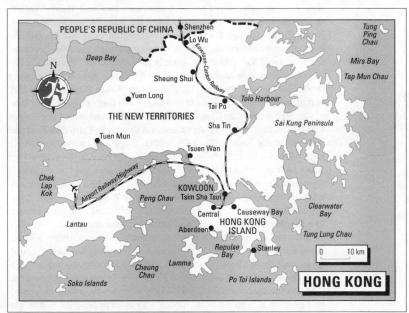

Hong Kong Island, which later gave its name to the entire territory, was the original British settlement. If you're on the island, you're "Hong Kong-side". The southern tip of the Kowloon peninsula (just 12 square kilometres) was added to the colony in 1860, giving the British control of the deep-water harbour between the two: here, you're "Kowloon-side". North of Kowloon lie the New Territories – acquired in 1898 along with most of the outlying islands – these extend to the former border with China, which now serves as the dividing line between the Special Administrative Region of Hong Kong and the rest of the People's Republic of China.

If your time is at all limited in Hong Kong, you'll do nearly all your sleeping, eating and sightseeing on the island or in Kowloon, crossing between the two on the cross-harbour ferries or on the MTR underground system. However, if you stay on the island and in Kowloon, you're only seeing a fraction of Hong Kong, and – arguably – little of the real Chinese part of the territory.

Orientation

Most visitors start with **Hong Kong Island** (Chapter 2), whose main business centre is called **Central**. To the west, it shades into the old **Western** district, around the area called Sheung Wan, while further west still, at the edge of the island, is **Kennedy Town**. Moving east from Central, the built-up areas change little in outer appearance as they run through **Wan Chai** to **Causeway Bay** and **Happy Valley**, though beyond here – certainly beyond the island's northernmost tip, **North Point** – things become more residential. South of Central the land becomes immediately steeper, rising through the **Mid-Levels** to the heights of **Victoria Peak**, usually just known as "The Peak". The island's **south side** is characterized by its bays and beaches, running from **Aberdeen** in the west, through **Deep Water Bay**, **Repulse Bay** and **Stanley**, around to **Shek O** and **Big Wave Bay** on the eastern side.

Cross to **Kowloon** (Chapter 3) and you leave the island geography firmly behind. The tip of the peninsula is known as **Tsim Sha Tsui** and it's here, along **Nathan Road** especially, that every consumer durable under the sun is sold, stolen or traded. To the east is **Tsim Sha Tsui East**, an area of flash hotels and shopping centres built on reclaimed land, and **Hung Hom** train station. North of Tsim Sha Tsui, the crowded grids of streets become less recognizably Western and more Asian the further you go: through noisy residential and shopping centres like **Yau Ma Tei** and **Mongkok**, 3km from Tsim Sha Tsui.

You should try to make at least one trip to the **outlying islands** (Chapter 5), the southwestern group – **Lamma, Lantau, Cheung Chau** and **Peng Chau** – especially, as they're only around an hour away from Central by ferry. But it's the **New Territories** (Chapter 4) that give an insight into the real Hong Kong: they help feed the colony and provide it with housing, labour and enterprise. New towns like

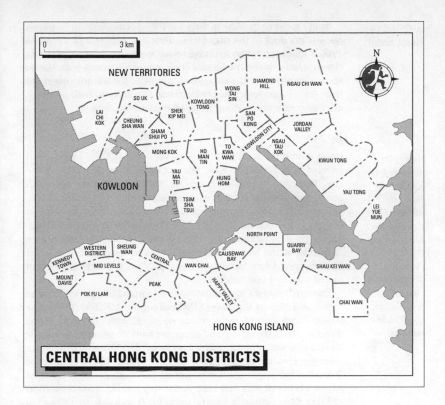

CENTRAL HONG KONG DISTRICTS

Sha Tin, Tsuen Wan, Tuen Mun and Yuen Long are all easily reached by public transport; or you can take the New Territories train line (the KCR) from Hung Hom to **Sheung Shui** and **Lo Wu** – the end of the line on the Hong Kong side of the border – for a fifty-minute tour through the region. To the east, the **Sai Kung peninsula** is a glorious region of country parks, islands, bays and beaches. In the west, traditional Chinese fishing villages like **Lau Fau Shan** are also easily reached on a good day out from central Hong Kong.

Arriving in Hong Kong

Most travellers now arrive at **Hong Kong International Airport** on **Chek Lap Kok**, just off the north coast of Lantau. The terminal, designed by British architect Sir Norman Foster, was built on land formed by literally flattening the small rocky islet of Chek Lap Kok and connecting it to the neightbouring island of Lantau. The entire project, including transport links, was one of the world's biggest construction projects, and cost in the region of US$20 billion.

Arriving in Hong Kong

Sadly, arriving by **ship** is only for the spectacularly rich, whose cruiseliners dock at the ritzy Ocean Terminal at the tip of Tsim Sha Tsui. It's easy, however, to arrive on more modest boats from points closer to hand, given the regular ferry connections with both Macau and mainland China. It's also possible to enter the territory **overland** from the Chinese cities of Shenzen and Guangzhou, both of which are well connected to Hong Kong by rail and bus.

By air

Helicopter arrivals from Macau with East Asia Airlines touch down on the helipad above the Macau Ferry Terminal (see "By sea" on p.44), where you'll clear customs.

Hong Kong International Airport (☎2181 0000), more often referred to as **Chek Lap Kok**, is about 34km from the centre of the city. There are foreign-exchange facilities land- and air-side (with poor rates, and the air-side exchanges may only take cash), a left-luggage office, and an office of the Hong Kong Hotel Association (see p.213), which can help you find a room with its member hotels. For arriving passengers the Hong Kong Tourist Association (see "Information and Maps", p.21) has a desk in the transit area, open from 6am–midnight, where you can pick up a plastic bag full of tourist literature and brochures.

The most efficient way to get from the airport to the city is by the high-speed **Airport Express (AER) rail service** (☎2881 8888). The station forms part of the terminal building, with platforms joined directly to both the arrival and departure halls. Trains to Central take 23 minutes, with stops at Tsing Yi (12min) and Kowloon (19min) in carriages boasting air conditioning, back-of-seat TVs, a reasonable amount of luggage space, but no toilets. Services operate every eight minutes between 6am and 1am. A one-way journey from the airport to Hong Kong Station in Central costs $150, to Kowloon $90 and to Tsing Yi $60. Tickets can be bought with cash or credit cards from machines or customer service desks. There are taxi ranks, bus stops and hotel shuttle bus stops at the AER stations, and a left-luggage service at Hong Kong and Kowloon stations (6am–1am; ☎2868 3190). Hong Kong Station is also linked to the MTR station at Central – it's a five-minute walk between the two.

A much cheaper but time-consuming alternative to the AER is to take bus #S51 or #S61 to Tung Chung on Lantau (about $4). From here, the **Tung Chung MTR Line** runs alongside the AER line all the way into Kowloon and Central ($23 one way) It's a slower, commuter line, with stops at five stations in addition to the AER stations. Services run every eight minutes; the journey to Central takes about forty minutes

The cheapest way into the city (and to most hotels) is by bus. For the **Airbus**, follow the signs out of the terminal. There are six routes,

When **flying out**, it's possible to check in at Hong Kong Station in Central up to ninety minutes before the train departs, but you need to buy an AER ticket first. Airport departure tax is HK$50, although this is expected to rise.

Airbus Routes

Enquiry Hotline: for #A11 #A12 #A21 #A22, ☎2873 0818. For #A31 #A41, ☎2786 6036.

· **#A11** to Causeway Bay (Moreton Terrace) via Sheung Wan, Central, Admiralty and Wan Chai (daily 6am–midnight, every 12min; $40). Travels via *Mandarin Oriental Hotel, Furama, Island Shangri-La/Conrad/Marriott, Wesley Hotel, Warney Hotel, Empire, New Harbour, Luk Kwok, Century Hong Kong, The Charterhouse, South Pacific, The Excelsior, The Park Lane, New Cathay, Regal Hong Kong.*

· **#A12** to Sai Wan Ho Ferry Pier via Sheung Wan, Central, Admiralty, Wan Chai, Causeway Bay, Tin Hau, Fortress Hill, North Point Quarry Bay, Tai Koo (daily 6am–midnight, every 15min; $45). Travels via *Mandarin Oriental, Ritz Carlton, Grand Hyatt, Renaissance Harbour View, Harbour View International House, Park Lane, Newton Hong Kong, City Garden, South China, Grand Plaza.*

· **#A21** to Kowloon KCR Station via Tsim Sha Tsui, Jordan, Yau Ma Tei, Tai Kok Tsui (daily 6am–midnight, every 10min; $33). Travels via *Island Hotel, Concourse, Grand Tower, Stanford, YMCA International House, Booth Lodge, Caritas Bianchi Lodge, Eaton, New San Diego, Nathan, Bruton Prudential, BP International House, Miramar, Kimberley, Windsor, Holiday Inn Golden Mile, New Astor, Sheraton, The Peninsula, Hyatt Regency, Chungking Mansions, the Regent, New World Renaissance, Kowloon Shangri-La, Royal Garden, Regal Kowloon, Park, International, Ramada, Stanford Hillview.*

· **#A22** to Lam Tin MTR Station via Kwun Tong, Ngau Tau Kok, Kowloon Bay, Kowloon City, To Kwa Wan, Hung Hom, Jordan (daily 6am–midnight, every 15min; $39). Travels via *Jordan Hotel, Eaton, New San Diego, Nathan, Regal Kai Tak.*

· **#A31** to the New Territories and Tsuen Wan (Discovery Park) via Tsuen Wan MTR Station, Kwai Chung Road, Kwai Fong, Tsing Yi Road (daily 6am–midnight, every 15min; $17). Travels via *Panda Hotel.*

· **# A41** to the New Territories and Sha Tin via City One Sha Tin, Sha Tin Central (daily 6am–midnight, every 20min; $20).Travels via *Regal Riverside Hotel, Royal Park.*

For the location of Airbus stops, see the accommodation maps on pp.218–219 (Hong Kong Island) and p.221 (Tsim Sha Tsui). English-language announcements on board the buses tell you where to get off for your hotel.

detailed above, all of which have very regular departures between 6am and midnight, and there's plenty of room for luggage. The airport customer service counters sell tickets and give change; on the buses themselves you'll need to have the exact fare. The average journey time is about an hour. There are also 21 cheaper **city bus** routes, used mainly by local residents. Some offer 24-hour services.

Taxis into the city are metered and reliable (see "Getting Around", p.55, for more details). You might want to get the tourist office in the Buffer Hall to write down the name of your destination in Chinese characters for the driver, though they should know the names of the big hotels in English. It costs roughly $300 to get to Tsim Sha Tsui, about HK$350 to Hong Kong Island. There may be extra charges for luggage and for tunnel tolls – on some tunnel trips the passenger pays the return charge too. **Rush-hour traffic** can slow down journey times considerably, particularly if you're using one of the cross-harbour tunnels to Hong Kong Island.

The new airport is open 24 hours a day, although onward transport from **early or late flights** can be a problem. Between midnight and 6am the rail connections are closed. There are four night-bus services, but otherwise you'll have to take a taxi.

By sea

Almost all the various jetfoil and ferry services **from Macau** arrive at the **Macau Ferry Terminal**, in the Shun Tak Centre, 200 Connaught Road, Sheung Wan, Hong Kong Island. The MTR (from Sheung Wan station, accessed directly from the Shun Tak Centre) links with most places from there; the bus terminus is next door. Some services from Macau (hoverferries and Jetcats) dock instead at the **China Ferry Terminal** at 33 Canton Road, in Tsim Sha Tsui, behind Kowloon Park, from where most of the area's accommodation is within walking distance, though taxis are available too.

All sea arrivals **from China** also dock at the China Ferry Terminal. Services include the ferry and Jetcat from **Guangzhou**, the hoverferry from **Shekou** (close to Shenzhen) and **Whampoa**, the Turbocat from **Fu Yong** Ferry Terminal (for Shenzhen airport), the catamaran service from **Zhuhai** (west of Macau), and the ferry from **Shanghai**. For departure details, see the box on p.58.

By train and bus

For details of travel into mainland China from Hong Kong by train or bus, see the box on pp.56–57.

Express trains from Guangzhou arrive at **Hung Hom Railway Station** (train enquiries ☎2602 7799), east of Tsim Sha Tsui, also known as the **Kowloon–Canton Railway Station** (or KCR). Signposted walkways lead from here to an adjacent bus terminal, taxi rank and – ten minutes around the harbour – the Hung Hom Ferry Pier: for Tsim Sha Tsui, take bus #5C to the Star Ferry. For Hong Kong Island, take the cross-harbour ferry to Wan Chai or Central.

Local trains from Guangzhou drop you at the Chinese border city of Shenzhen, from where you walk across the border to Lo Wu on the Hong Kong side and pick up the regular KCR trains to Kowloon: it's a fifty-minute ride, the trains following the same length of track to Hung Hom Station.

You might conceivably arrive **by bus** from a couple of Chinese cities, though the services are mostly used by the local Chinese. It's an easier and quicker route than it once was, since the opening of the Guangzhou–Shenzhen highway, and will, in time, become an increasingly popular method of reaching Hong Kong. The main bus service, the CTS bus **from Guangzhou**, makes stops in Sheung Shui, Sha Tin and at Kowloon Tong MTR Station, before terminating at Hung Hom train station (though some services also run on to the CTS branch offices in Mongkok or Wan Chai). There's also an increasing number of minor routes and services. From Shenzhen, for instance, the Citybus stops at the corner of Middle Road and Kowloon Park Drive, Tsim Sha Tsui (behind the YMCA); whilst its service from Dongguan stops at Admiralty and China Hong Kong City.

Information, maps and addresses

At the **airport** HKTA assistants will sidle up to you and hand over a bag full of brochures. If you miss out, visit the HKTA **information office** in the Buffer Hall and transit area (daily 8am–midnight, accessible to arriving passengers only).

There are two more information centres in the city at Shop 8, Basement, Jardine House, 1 Connaught Place, Central (Mon–Fri 9am–6pm, Sat 9am–1pm) and at the Star Ferry Concourse, Tsim Sha Tsui (Mon–Fri 8am–6pm, Sat & Sun 9am–5pm). Both are staffed by English-speakers and have a wealth of free handouts, including transport timetables, accommodation brochures and sightseeing guides. The most useful are the magazine *Hongkong Now!*, which has listings of events in the territory; the guides to Sightseeing and Culture, Shopping, and Dining and Entertainment; the factsheets on individual temples, sights and areas; and the monthly *Official Hong Kong Guide*, which has restaurant recommendations (updated each month) and coverage of current festivals and events.

There's a general, multilingual HKTA **Telephone Information Service** on ☎2508 1234 (Mon–Fri 8am–6pm, Sat & Sun 9am–5pm). They also have a Web site at *www.hkta.org.hk*.

Maps

Our maps of Hong Kong should be sufficient for most purposes. For anything more detailed you'll need one of the **commercial maps and gazetteers** – vital if you're intending to do any serious travelling around the territory. Best is the paperback-format *Hong Kong Guide*, a couple of hundred pages of indispensable maps, street and building indexes, transport timetables and other listings, available for around $70 from the large bookshops selling English-language books (see p.291).

You might also want to visit the **Government Publications Centre**, in the Queensway Government Offices, Low Block, Ground Floor, 66 Queensway, Admiralty (Mon–Fri 9am–6pm, Sat 9am–1pm;

See the colour section at the end of the book for comprehensive street maps of Hong Kong

☎2537 1910). As well as government publications, this sells the *Countryside Series* of maps, which come in very useful if you plan to go **hiking** on the outlying islands or in the New Territories.

Finding an address

Finding your way around Hong Kong isn't particularly difficult, though there are certain local peculiarities to be aware of. **Addresses** make great use of building names – often designated "Mansions" or "Plazas" – as well as street names and numbers, and usually specify whether the address is in Hong Kong (ie, on Hong Kong Island) or Kowloon. Abbreviations to note are HK (Hong Kong Island), Kow (Kowloon) and NT (New Territories).

The shop or office **numbering system** generally follows this format: no. 803 means no. 3 on the 8th floor; 815 is no. 15 on the 8th floor; 2212 is no. 12 on the 22nd floor, and so on. Floors are numbered in the British fashion: ie, the bottom floor is the ground floor. Most abbreviations are straightforward: G/F is the ground floor; B the basement (sometimes subdivided B1, B2, and B3 – of which B3 is usually the lowest); M (mezzanine) and L (lobby) are also used. Because many buildings are built on slopes, floors marked "G/F" are not always at ground level – the exit to street level may be either above or below G/F, or even on different floors on opposite sides of the same building.

We've listed hotels and many restaurants and bars by area, under subheadings which correspond to districts covered in the guide, such as Tsim Sha Tsui, Central, Wan Chai and Causeway Bay. These different areas are most easily reached by the **MTR underground stations** (see opposite) of the same name. Occasionally, a district has more than one MTR station – Tsim Sha Tsui is served by both Tsim Sha Tsui MTR and Jordan MTR; Causeway Bay by Causeway Bay MTR and Tin Hau MTR – so it's always worth checking which is nearest. MTR exits and entrances are marked on the maps.

Getting around

Hong Kong has one of the world's most efficient integrated **public transport** systems. Underground and overground trains, trams, buses and ferries connect almost every part of the territory, and services are extremely cheap and simple to use, which encourages you to roam far and wide. Two problems, however, are universal on all types of transport. First, travelling in the rush hour anywhere in the urban area is a slow and crowded business, worth avoiding. Secondly, don't expect too many people to speak English – sorting out your route back in advance is a good idea; getting someone to write down your destination in Chinese characters is also helpful.

The Mass Transit Railway (MTR)

Getting around

Hong Kong's transport pride and joy, the underground **Mass Transit Railway** – always shortened to MTR – has four lines: the **Island Line**, which runs along the north side of Hong Kong Island; the **Tsuen Wan Line**, which crosses under the harbour from Admiralty on the island and heads out to Tsuen Wan in the western New Territories; the **Tung Chung Line**, which follows the same route as the Airport Express, linking Central and Tung Chung; and the **Kwun Tong Line**, which links Yau Ma Tei in Kowloon with Kwun Tong to the east, then runs back under the harbour to Quarry Bay on Hong Kong Island. **Interchange stations** between lines are clearly marked on maps and boards at the stations and there's a handy interchange at Kowloon Tong (Kwun Tong Line) with the Kowloon–Canton East Railway (see p.48). The MTR station at Central also provides a link to the airport railway and the Tung Chung line – it's a five-minute walk between the two stations.

See the colour plates at the back of the book for a map of the MTR and KCR.

The MTR is the fastest public transport in the territory, and the most expensive – the harbour crossing from Central or Admiralty to Tsim Sha Tsui costs around $9, considerably more than the Star Ferry. However, it's also air-conditioned, fully automated, sparkling clean and very easy to use. **Hours of operation** are daily from 6am to 1am, with trains running every few minutes; the first and last train times are posted on boards at the stations. Avoid travelling during the morning and evening **rush hours** (8–9.30am & 5.30–7pm); in the morning especially, the crowds piling onto the escalators and trains are horrendous, and the MTR authorities have taken to hiring people to "help" passengers onto trains and get the doors closed. Don't even think about taking heavy luggage onto the train during the morning rush hour.

There's a **no smoking** policy on all trains; you're not supposed to eat anything either. There are also **no toilets** on any of the MTR platforms. However, everything is marked and signposted in **English**, as well as in Chinese characters, so you shouldn't get lost. See the colour MTR map at the back of the book for full details; for the **MTR Passenger Information Hotline**, call ☎2881 8888.

Tickets

Tickets cost from $4 to around $26 for a one-way journey. There are no returns and tickets are only valid for ninety minutes, so don't buy one for your return journey at the same time. Feed your money into the machines on the station concourse and you'll get your ticket, which looks like a thin plastic credit card. Some machines don't give change and some take only coins, but there are small change machines in the stations, and you can change notes or buy tickets at the information desks. **Children** under 12 need a special Child Ticket ($3–5), also available from the machines.

To **use the system**, you feed your ticket into the turnstile, walk through and pick it up on the other side. At the end of your journey, the turnstile will retain your ticket as you exit.

For more than one journey, there's a souvenir MTR **Tourist Ticket**. It costs $25, but gives only $20 worth of travel (it's valid on the KCR as far as Sheung Shui too). Feed it into the turnstile and at the end of each journey the cost is deducted, the turnstile indicator showing how much money is left on the ticket. For your last ride it doesn't matter if there isn't enough credit left to cover the full cost of your last trip, the ticket will still work and you'll get it back to keep at the end of your final journey. The ticket is available from MTR and KCR East Rail offices, except Lo Wu.

Locals use an **Octopus Card** (☎2993 8880 for information), a rechargeable stored-value ticket valid for travel on the MTR, KCR, LRT, the Airport Express and some ferries and buses. You pay a deposit of $50 to get the plastic card, then add credit to it by feeding it and your money into machines in the MTR. An added benefit is that you don't have to feed it into the turnstile but can simply leave it in your wallet or handbag and pass the entire thing over the sensor pad on the top of the turnstile. They're worth buying if you're going to do a lot of travelling and you get your deposit back when you return the card.

As everything is completely automated on the MTR, it seems simple enough to leap the turnstiles and **travel without a ticket** – which, indeed, is what you'll see some people doing. The stations, however, are patrolled by inspectors and swept by TV cameras – there's a fine of $5000 if you're caught.

New Territories' trains

There are two main **train networks** in the New Territories – the KCR East Rail (see below) and the LRT – plus the Airport Express (AER), which as well as serving the airport also has stops at two places en route (see p.42). You're likely to use the AER if you arrive or depart by air, though you probably won't have occasion to use the KCR and the LRT unless you intend to do a bit of out-of-the-way sightseeing. Like the MTR, all stations, signs and trains are marked in English.

The Kowloon–Canton East Railway (KCR)

*More details
on using the
KCR to leave
Hong Kong are
given in
"Onward
Travel: Into
Mainland
China", p.57.*

The **Kowloon–Canton East Railway** – (KCR) (information on ☎2602 7799) – runs from Hung Hom station in Kowloon to the border with China at Lo Wu, a fifty-minute journey. Regular, electric trains travel the line, calling at various New Territory towns on the way, while some non-stop express trains run right the way through to Guangzhou (Canton). Even if you're only staying in Hong Kong, a ride on the KCR is thoroughly recommended, giving you a first-hand view of life in the New Territories.

The ticketing and turnstile system is the same as that on the MTR. One-way **tickets** cost from around $3.50 (the Kowloon Tong–Mongkok section) to $9 (for the journey from Kowloon to Sheung Shui). **Children** under 3 travel for free, those under 12 pay half-fare. There's a **first-class** compartment, staffed by a guard, for double the standard fare. You'll pay a $100 **fine** if caught travelling without a ticket, or travelling first-class with an ordinary ticket. The Tourist Ticket and Octopus Card (see opposite) are both valid on the KCR, and are used in exactly the same way as on the MTR.

Kowloon Tong is the interchange station for the KCR and MTR; just follow the signs between the two. More importantly, **Sheung Shui is the last Hong Kong stop** that you can get off at on the KCR. Although most trains run through to **Lo Wu**, which is still in Hong Kong, it's a restricted area and you'll need to have travel documents valid for entering China to alight here (and a special Lo Wu ticket, which costs around $33 one-way from Kowloon).

The air-conditioned trains **operate** from around 5.30am to 1am, running every three to ten minutes or so. They're generally less crowded than MTR trains (except during rush hour at the Kowloon stations – Kowloon Tong and Mongkok), but be aware that **pickpockets** tend to ply their trade on this route. Again, there's **no smoking** and no eating on board, but there are **toilets** on all the station concourses.

The Light Rail Transit (LRT)

A second train system, the **Light Rail Transit** – LRT (information on ☎2468 7788) – links two towns in the western New Territories, Tuen Mun and Yuen Long. There are plans to extend the system further into the New Territories, creating a West Rail system that will link the LRT to the KCR, but that won't be completed until 2003. At the moment it's the Hong Kong rail system you're least likely to use.

For a map of the LRT, see the colour plates at the back of the book.

The trains are electric, running alongside – and down the middle of – the New Territories' roads, and the system is zoned. Automatic ticket machines on the platforms tell you which zone your destination is in and how much it'll cost. Fares are comparable to the KCR, around $4–6 per journey; feed your money in and wait for your ticket. One branch of the line starts at **Tuen Mun Ferry Pier**, which you can reach direct by hoverferry from Central; the northernmost LRT station, **Yuen Long**, is connected by bus #77K to the Fanling KCR station.

Buses

Double-decker **buses** are operated by three companies: New World First Bus (☎2136 8888) run the orange and green buses, Citybus (☎2873 0818) the yellow ones, while the Kowloon Motor Bus Company (☎2745 4466) operate the cream and red ones in Kowloon. **Fares** are low – from $1.20 to around $35 a trip – the amount you have to pay is posted at most bus stops and on the buses as you get on. Put the exact fare into the box by the driver (who is unlikely to speak much English); there's no change given, so keep a

**Getting
around**

supply of coins with you. The buses run on fixed **routes** from various
terminals throughout the city, from around 6am to midnight: some of
the main **bus terminals**, and the buses which depart from them, are
detailed below; for more information check the text. Not all buses are
air-conditioned (those that are cost more), and they can get very
crowded during rush hour. However, on longer journeys, to the
south of Hong Kong Island and out in the New Territories, they're an
excellent way to see the countryside.

Minibuses are cream-coloured vans with red markings, seating
14–16 people. They run regularly throughout the territory on routes
which are not always fixed and will stop (within reason) wherever
you flag them down or ask to get off. Their destination is shown on a
card on the front, but as they're used almost exclusively by locals,

---

Useful Bus Routes: Numbers and Terminals

Each double-decker bus is marked with the destination in English and a
number. "K" after the number means that the bus links with a stop on the
KCR line; "M"-suffixed buses stop at an MTR station; buses with an "R"
only run on Sundays and public holidays; and "X" buses are express buses
with limited stops. Note that some buses still have destinations marked as
the "Jordan Road Ferry Pier". This is no longer a ferry stop, because of the
land reclamation, but it's still a bus terminus.

Hong Kong Island
Central Bus Terminal (Exchange Square) to: Aberdeen #70; Ap Lei
Chau (Aberdeen) #90; Deep Water Bay #6A, #64, #260; Mid-Levels
#15; Ocean Park #90; The Peak #15; Repulse Bay #6, #6A, #61, #64,
#260; Stanley #6, #6A, #260; Taikoo Shing #21, #721.

Outlying Islands Ferry Piers Bus Terminal to: Aberdeen #7; Admiralty
#11, #681; Causeway Bay #11, #681; Central #11; Mid-Levels #12;
Pokfulam/Western #7; Wan Chai #681. Also maxicabs to Central/Shun
Tak Centre #54, #55.

City Hall (Edinburgh Place): maxicabs to The Peak #1. Also express bus
to Ocean Park; and free shuttle bus to Lower Peak Tram terminus.

Happy Valley (tram terminus) to: Admiralty/Central #5, #5A; Kennedy
Town via Queen's Rd East, Des Voeux Rd, Connaught Rd & Des Voeux
Rd West #5A; Mongkok/Sham Shui Po #117.

Macau Ferry Terminal to: Causeway Bay #2; Shau Kei Wan #2; Wan
Chai #2.

Rumsey St to: Cotton Tree Drive (Hong Kong Park) #3B; Happy Valley
#1; Lower Peak Tram Terminus #3B; Wan Chai #1.

Kowloon
KCR (Hung Hom) Station to: Airport #A21; Hankow Rd #8, minibus
#6; Mongkok #87D; Star Ferry #5C, #8A, #87D; Tsim Sha Tsui East
#87D; Whampoa Garden #8A.

Star Ferry to: Jade Market #6, #6A, #7, #9; Jordan Rd Ferry #8;
Kowloon KCR station (Hung Hom) #87D, #5C; Kowloon Park #1, #1A,

---

this is usually in Chinese characters, with a tiny English version. Either make sure you know the number you want (given in the text where useful) or flag them all down until you find the right one. They're quicker than the double-deckers, and fares – posted inside the vehicle – are similar ($2–20; pay when you get off, and try to have the right change). They can be really useful for jumping short distances (up Nathan Rd, say) when you're in a hurry, although the driving can be a bit hair-raising. When they want **to get off**, the Chinese shout *yau lok*; in practice, you can say almost anything as long as you make it clear you want to alight. On Sundays, public holidays, race days and when it's raining, fares shoot up to around twice the normal rate. Hours of operation are from around 6am until well after midnight on some routes.

#2, #6, #6A, #7; Lai Chi Kok #6A; Mongkok (via Nathan Rd) #1; Science Museum #5, #5C, #8; Temple Street Night Market #1, #1A, #2, #6, #6A, #7, #9; Waterloo Road (for YMCA) #7; Whampoa Garden #8A. Also maxicabs to Tsim Sha Tsui East #1, #1M.

Cross-Harbour services
There are around a dozen **cross-harbour bus services**: ones you might use include the #170 (Ocean Park/Hennessy Rd/Causeway Bay/Waterloo Rd/Sha Tin KCR), #111 (Chatham Rd North/Wan Chai/Admiralty/Central/Macau Ferry Terminal) and #103 (Waterloo Rd/Wan Chai/Admiralty/Cotton Tree Drive). Otherwise, the two that use the cross-harbour tunnel all night are the #N121 (Macau Ferry Terminal–Choi Hung) and #122 (North Point Ferry Pier–So Uk).

New Territories
Choi Hung to: Clearwater Bay #91; Pak Tam Chung/Wong Shek Pier #96R; Sai Kung #92.

Fanling to: Hok Tau Wai #52K; Luen Wo Market and Sha Tau Kok #78K; Luk Keng #56K.

Pak Tam Chung to: Wong Shek #95R (weekends and public holidays only).

Sai Kung to: Nai Chung #99; Pak Tam Chung #94; Sha Tin #299; Wong Shek #94.

Sha Tin to: Sai Kung (via Nai Chung) #89R, #299.

Sheung Shui to: Fanling #78K; Jordan Road Ferry Pier/Kowloon AER station #70; Lok Ma Chau 76K; Luen Wo Market #70; Shau Tau Kok #78K; Yuen Long #76K and #77K.

Tai Po Market to: Kam Tin #64K; Tai Mei Tuk (for Plover Cove) #75K; Yuen Long #64K.

Tsuen Wan to: Kam Tin #51; Sham Tseng #34B or minibus #96M; Yuen Long (via Tuen Mun, for Ching Chung Koon Temple and Mui Fat Monastery) #68M.

Yuen Long to: Jordan Road Ferry Pier/Kowloon AER #68, #68X; Kam Tin #54; Lau Fau Shan #655; Sheung Shui (via Lok Ma Chau) #76K; Sheung Shui (via Kam Tin) #77K; Tai Po Market KCR #64K; Tuen Mun #68M.

The green and yellow minibuses, called **maxicabs**, seat the same number of people but run on fixed routes with marked stops – some of the most useful are given in the box on pp.50–51. Again, fares are fixed, ranging from around $1.50 to $18 depending on distance, paid in exact coins into a moneybox as you get on. Operating hours are around 6am to midnight.

The HKTA puts out some very useful free **timetables** listing bus routes, frequencies, fares and the Chinese characters for all the major destinations in Kowloon, Hong Kong Island and the New Territories. Timetables are also posted at most bus stops.

Trams

Double-decker **trams** rattle along the north shore of Hong Kong Island, from Kennedy Town in the west to Shau Kei Wan in the east, via Western, Central, Admiralty, Wan Chai and Causeway Bay; some detour around Happy Valley and the racecourse. Not all trams run the full distance, so check the destination (marked in English) on the front and sides before you get on. From Central, east to Causeway Bay takes around forty minutes, to Shau Kei Wan around fifty minutes, and west to Kennedy Town around half an hour.

Climb aboard at the back. If you're staying on for a long journey, head upstairs for the views. Otherwise, start working your way through to the front and, when you get off, drop the **flat fare** ($2 for adults, $1 for senior citizens and children) in the box by the driver: there's no change given. Trams operate from 6am to 1am, though services on some parts of the line finish earlier; avoid rush hours if you actually want to see anything as you go – seats are in short supply. For **information**, call Hong Kong Tramways ☎2559 8918.

The most famous tram of all is the **Peak Tram**, not really a tram at all but a funicular railway, which climbs swiftly from the Lower Peak Tram Terminal on Garden Road to the Peak Tower on Victoria Peak (with a couple of local commuter request stops on the way). The journey takes about eight minutes; services run from 7am to midnight every ten minutes. Tickets cost $18 one-way, $28 return (children under 12, $5 and $8 respectively); see p.90 for more details. Information from Peak Tramways ☎2522 0922.

Ferries and hoverferries

An enduring image of Hong Kong is of countless ferries and boats zipping across the harbour. The views are rightly lauded, and on a clear day the ferries provide an unforgettable first sight of Hong Kong Island. All services are very cheap and reliable: the only days to watch out for are in **typhoon** season, when crossings sometimes become very choppy, though at really blustery times, they're suspended altogether.

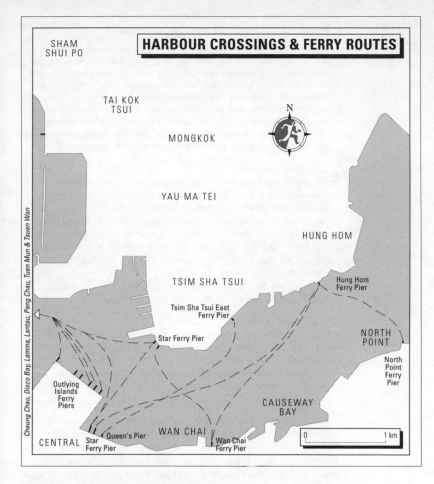

SHAM
SHUI PO

HARBOUR CROSSINGS & FERRY ROUTES

TAI KOK
TSUI

MONGKOK

N

YAU MA TEI

HUNG HOM

TSIM SHA TSUI

Hung Hom
Ferry Pier

Tsim Sha Tsui East
Ferry Pier

Star Ferry Pier

NORTH
POINT

North
Point
Ferry
Pier

Outlying
Islands
Ferry
Piers

CAUSEWAY
BAY

CENTRAL   Star
Ferry Pier

Queen's Pier   WAN CHAI

Wan Chai
Ferry Pier

0   1 km

Cheung Chau, Disco Bay, Lamma, Lantau, Peng Chau, Tuen Mun & Tsuen Wan

Of all the **cross-harbour ferry services**, the quickest and most
famous is the **Star Ferry** (information on ☎2366 2576), an eight-
minute crossing between Tsim Sha Tsui and Central on one of the
ten double-decker, green and white passenger ferries. The service
runs every four minutes at peak hours and operates from 6.30am
to 11.30pm; it costs just $2.20 to travel on the upper deck, $1.70
on the lower deck. Check you're in the right channel at the ferry
pier, feed your coins into the relevant turnstile and join the waiting hordes at the gate, which swings open when the ferry docks. It
all looks chaotic, but the numbers allowed on board are controlled, and if there are too many people you'll have to wait for the
next ferry – though this will never be more than a few minutes
behind.

Getting around

Main Cross-Harbour and New Town Services

The location of ferry piers is in a state of flux while land reclamation work continues in Central and Kowloon. One result has been the disappearance of the Jordan Road Ferry Pier in West Kowloon (although the place name is still used in bus routes). Some services have already relocated to the new Outlying Islands Ferry Piers just west of the Star Ferry Pier in Central; others may follow or move elsewhere since even the famous Star Ferry Pier in Central may be redeveloped. Current departures are listed below; for up-to-date information, contact the HKTA. Services are daily unless otherwise stated.

Hong Kong Island

Outlying Islands Ferry Piers: ferry (Mon–Fri 3 daily) and hoverferry (6.45am–8.20pm, every 8–20min) to Tuen Mun; ferry (Mon–Fri 4 daily) and hoverferry (7am–7pm, every 15–30min) to Tsuen Wan.

Central Star Ferry Pier: ferry to Tsim Sha Tsui (6.30am–11.30pm, every 4–10min); ferry to Hung Hom (7am–7.20pm, every 12–20min); hoverferry to Discovery Bay, Lantau (24hr service, every 20min at peak times).

Queen's Pier (Edinburgh Place): hoverferry to Tsim Sha Tsui East (8am–8pm, every 20min).

Wan Chai: ferry to Hung Hom (Mon–Sat 7am–8pm, every 15–20min); ferry to Tsim Sha Tsui (7.30am–11pm, every 7–20min).

Kowloon

Hung Hom Ferry Pier: ferry to Central (7am–7.20pm, every 12–20min); ferry to Wan Chai (Mon–Sat 7am–8pm; every 15–20min); ferry to North Point (7am–7pm, every 20–30min).

Tsim Sha Tsui Star Ferry Pier: ferry to Central (6.30am–11.30pm, every 4–10min); ferry to Wan Chai (7.30am–11pm, every 7–20min).

There are several other cross-harbour ferry services, too, operated either by Star Ferry or the Hong Kong and Yaumatei Ferry Company, with regular services throughout the day. These include the fifteen-minute **Central–Hung Hom** crossing (for the KCR station); the **Tsim Sha Tsui–Wan Chai** and **Wan Chai–Hung Hom** runs; there are also links from **North Point** to Hung Hom and Kowloon City. While you may have no real cause to use any of these services, they're worth thinking about simply as trips in their own right: splendid, cheap sightseeing.

Quicker harbour crossings are provided by a fleet of **hoverferries**, most usefully the one that links Central (Queen's Pier, in front of City Hall) with Tsim Sha Tsui East, stopping at the pier in front of the *Shangri-La Hotel* (8am–8pm, every 20min; $5.70). Hoverferries also run from Central to the **new towns** of Tsuen Wan and Tuen Mun in the New Territories and to Discovery Bay on Lantau – details are given in the text. In addition, another series of ferries and hoverferries serve the **outlying islands** from Central and elsewhere; for full details see pp.184–185.

Taxis

Hong Kong's **taxis** are relatively cheap – many people treat them as a branch of public transport. You can flag them down in the street or pick one up at the **ranks** you'll find at major MTR and KCR stations and at both Star Ferry terminals. Taxis can't drop or pick up on yellow lines. Look for a red "For Hire" flag in the windscreen; at night the "Taxi" sign on the roof is lit. Make sure the driver turns the meter on when you get in (though rip-offs are rare). On **Hong Kong Island** and **Kowloon**, taxis are red: minimum charge is $15 (for the first 2km) and then it's $1.30 for every 200m. In the **New Territories**, taxis are green and slightly cheaper. The island of **Lantau** has its own taxi service, though there's no taxi service on any other island.

Taxis can be extremely hard to come by when it rains, during typhoons, on race days, after midnight, and at driver changeover time (around 9.30am and again at 4pm). Many drivers don't speak English, although they'll know the names of major hotels – and they should have a card somewhere in the cab with major destinations listed in Cantonese and English. Otherwise you'll need to have someone write down where you're going on a piece of paper to show to the driver. If you get really stuck, gesture to the driver to call his control centre on the two-way radio, and state your destination into the microphone. Someone there will translate.

Although the red taxis are supposed to work on Hong Kong Island and in Kowloon, drivers will often only pick up fares on one side or the other. In practice, this means that if you want to use the **cross-harbour tunnel**, the driver is allowed to charge you double the toll on top of the fare, since they assume they won't get a fare back. More annoying is the practice of drivers heading back to base and putting a sign in their window saying either "Hong Kong" or "Kowloon", depending on where they are; they'll only take you if you're headed their way, but more often than not will still charge you double the actual toll. If you're not happy with this – and that might depend on how difficult it is to get a taxi at the time – check before you set off, and be prepared to kick up a fuss and get out. You'll also have to pay tolls ($5–15) on top of your fare at the other tunnels in the territory, such as the Aberdeen tunnel and the Lion Rock tunnel to Sha Tin – there should be a yellow sign inside each taxi telling you how much the tolls are. You'll also have to pay an extra $5 for each piece of **luggage**.

There's a 24-hour **Taxi Complaints Hotline** (☎2527 7177): take a note of the taxi licence number displayed inside the vehicle if you want to pursue a complaint.

Renting cars and bikes

There are comparatively few private cars in Hong Kong: only nineteen percent of the territory's vehicles are privately owned and run; the rest are public transport, goods and work vehicles. And you soon

Onward Travel: Into Mainland China

It's becoming ever easier to visit mainland China from Hong Kong, with the nearest major Chinese city of note, Guangzhou (Canton), as little as two hours away by train. There are even organized bus tours starting at around HK$600 for a day-trip to Shenzhen, the nearest city, rising to around $1100 for a day-trip to Guangzhou itself; details from any Hong Kong travel agent (see p.316). You won't, however, see much of anything in such a short visit, and it's far better to allow at least one night in Guangzhou. Just make sure you avoid travelling at Chinese New Year or at any other major festival time, when local transport in and out of China is packed solid.

Entry requirements, visas and money

To enter China you need a valid passport and a **visa** which can be easily obtained in Hong Kong and is generally valid for three months from the date of issue (*not* the date of entry); one-month extensions are available in China. As well as the two official organizations listed below, just about any travel agency in Hong Kong can arrange a visa for you, and can also sort out your transport to China and accommodation once there if you wish. It currently takes one to three working days to get a single-entry visa, for which you'll pay around $180–300, depending on how quickly you need it and what kind of passport you hold. Same-day visas cost over $300. For a dual-entry visa, count on another $150. You'll also need two passport photographs.

At the border you may be asked to declare all your valuables at **Chinese customs** (including things like personal stereos and cameras) and how much money and travellers' cheques you're carrying. This is entered onto a declaration form, which you keep until you leave China; don't lose it, as it's designed to prevent you selling such items in China. As always, don't carry anything through customs for anyone else, however innocent it may seem.

The unit of **currency** is the yuan (¥), which is divided into ten jiao (further divided into ten fen). You can now buy yuan in Hong Kong banks before your trip, and there are exchange offices at Shenzhen and Guangzhou train stations, but you'll find that Hong Kong dollars are freely accepted in Shenzhen (where it's legal currency) and for various services in Guangzhou.

Ministry of Foreign Affairs of the PRC

Visa Office, 5th Floor, Lower Block, 26 Harbour Rd, China Resources Building, Wan Chai ☎2827 1881; Mon–Fri 9am–12.20pm & 2–5pm, Sat 9am–12.20pm.

China Travel Service (CTS)

4th Floor, CTS House, 78 Connaught Rd, Central ☎2853 3888; 2nd Floor, China Travel Building, 77 Queen's Rd, Central ☎2525 0450; Southorn Centre, Johnston Rd, Wan Chai ☎2832 3888; 1st Floor, Alpha House, 27–33 Nathan Rd, Tsim Sha Tsui ☎2315 7188; 10–12, 1st Floor, China Hong Kong City, 33 Canton Rd, Tsim Sha Tsui ☎2736 1863; all open Mon–Fri 9am–5.30pm, Sat 9am–5pm, Sun 9am–1pm & 2–5pm.

By local train

The cheapest route to Guangzhou, though a little time-consuming, is to take any of the local KCR trains from the Kowloon–Canton Railway Station at Hung Hom to the border station of Lo Wu; the one-way, fifty-minute trip costs $33. Lo Wu is on the Hong Kong side of the border but is a restricted area: you must be going on into China to come here. From here, follow the signs and walk across the border, through passport control and customs, into Shenzhen, the Chinese frontier city. From the new train station here, there are hourly trains to Guangzhou, which cost around $100. You can pay for your Guangzhou ticket in Hong Kong dollars, and the journey takes another two to three hours, depending on the train and the time of day. Note that the last border-crossing train to Lo Wu from Hung Hom is at around 10pm; the border closes before 11pm. This local route to Guangzhou is to be avoided at all costs on public and religious holidays, at Easter and at Chinese New Year, when most Hong Kong families visit relations over the border.

By express train

It's much easier to travel directly to Guangzhou by express train, with four daily services from the Kowloon–Canton Railway Station. Although the departure times occasionally change, there is usually one in the early morning, two around lunchtime and one later in the afternoon; the standard trains take two hours forty minutes, while one service a day is designated "high speed" and takes just two hours. Tickets cost $190 one-way on the standard train; $230 on the high-speed. Children pay half-fare on all services. You can buy tickets in advance from CTS offices in Hong Kong (see opposite for addresses), and at the office in the Kowloon–Canton Railway Station. Outside holiday times, it's generally not necessary to buy in advance.

By bus

There are plenty of local buses into China's Guangdong province (which encompasses both Shenzhen and Guangzhou). Services to Guangzhou take two to three hours and are straightforward enough: Citybus (☎2873 0818) operate five services every day, between 7.30am and 2.30pm, departing from China Hong Kong City, next to the China Ferry Terminal on Canton Road in Tsim Sha Tsui. They also pick up at Sha Tin City One Station in Sha Tin and at Admiralty on Hong Kong Island. They drop you at the *Garden Hotel* in Guangzhou. Fares are $150 one way. Tickets can be bought from CTS offices or MTR Travel Service Centres at Central, Admiralty, Tai Koo and Mongkok. The other operator on the route is the Motor Transport Company of Guangdong, with eleven services daily departing from Hung Hom Railway Station. Some also pick up in Sha Tin, on Centre Street. The fare is $100. Tickets are available from CTS or from the company itself, at 501 Canton Rd, Tsim Sha Tsui. Citybus also run services to Shenzhen, departing either from Admiralty Station, Sha Tin City One, or China Hong Kong City (six to nine daily; $85 one-way) and Shenzhen Airport, departing from the same pick-up points (six or seven daily; $85). Tickets are available from CTS or the MTR Travel Service Centres.

continued overleaf

Onward Travel: Into Mainland China (continued)

By air

Flights from Hong Kong to China are competitively priced. To Guangzhou, it'll cost you about $500 one-way for the 35-minute trip; there are also direct services to Beijing and Shanghai, with connections to most other Chinese cities. Various airlines (Dragonair among them) serve each destination several times daily. You can get more information from any of the travel agents listed on p.316 or at any CTS office – it's worth shopping around since prices can vary sharply and even on the major airlines special seasonal deals and discounts are often attractively priced.

By boat

You now have quite a choice if you want to go to Guangzhou by sea. Most services leave from the China Ferry Terminal (Canton Rd, Tsim Sha Tsui); tickets can be bought from CTS offices, most travel agents, or directly at the ferry terminal. There are six daily catamaran services to Shenzhen ($196), four hoverferries daily to Shekou, the port closest to Shenzhen ($155), and six daily Turbocat services to Fu Yong Ferry Terminal (for Shenzhen airport; $196).

Other useful services from the China Ferry Terminal include boats to Zhuhai, Zhaoqing, Zhongshan and Xiamen. Longer-term China travellers might also consider the two-and-a-half-day ferry voyage to Shanghai (departures every week) or the ten-hour hovercraft link between Hong Kong and Wuzhou which means if you're ultimately heading for the Guilin area, you can cut out the long ferry ride from Guangzhou to Wuzhou. For current ticket prices and departure times, contact CTS or the ferry terminal.

For bus and ferry services to China from Macau, see p.376.

get an idea of who does drive when you look at the other figures: there are more Rolls Royces in Hong Kong per head of population than anywhere else in the world, and more in number than everywhere except Britain and the US.

Renting your own car in Hong Kong isn't a sensible idea. The public transport system is so good that it's rarely quicker to drive, and in any case one dose of rush-hour traffic would put you off for ever. If you really need a car, out in the New Territories, say, or on Lantau, it's always cheaper just to take a taxi. There's also the problem of parking: finding a space in the centre is nigh impossible, and the multi-storey car parks are generally expensive and located where you least want them. If you're determined, turn to p.312 for the addresses of **car rental** agencies and central **car parks**.

Bike rental is a more likely possibility, though again, not in crowded central Hong Kong or Kowloon. There are several places in the New Territories where it's fun: there are cycle lanes around Sha Tin and stretching all the way along Tolo Harbour to Tai Po. To use these, go to Tai Wai KCR station and rent a bike from the open space next to the amusement park there; the cheapest are only a few dollars an hour (for more details, see p.147). You can also rent bikes at the Plover Cove Country Park, near Tai Po (see p.155). The best places, though, for bikes are the less congested outlying islands: there are some for rent at Mui Wo on Lantau and on Cheung Chau.

Getting around

Walking

The best way of getting around much of the territory is **walking**. It's unavoidable on nearly all the outlying islands, good fun in the country parks of the New Territories and essential on the view-laden circuit of the Peak. The old street markets of Kowloon are fascinating to stroll around, whilst in Central there's a hi-tech edge to being a pedestrian: step off the Star Ferry and head up the nearest set of steps and you needn't touch the ground again for hundreds of metres as you walk above the traffic on footbridges, escalators and moving walkways – in fact, you can keep above ground right the way from the Star Ferry to the Macau Ferry Terminal in the west and Admiralty in the east, or head up to Mid-Levels via the Hillside Escalator Link (p.92).

For details of Hong Kong's country parks and long-distance hiking trails, see p.302.

Rickshaws and helicopters

Every time you step off the Star Ferry on Hong Kong Island you'll pass a handful of idle red **rickshaws** in the concourse, the last survivors from the time when these were the only way to travel around Hong Kong, for the monied classes at least. The old men squatting next to their vehicles are touting for custom, though what this generally means is a photo opportunity: bargain before you snap away and expect to pay a hefty $50 or so for a picture. You can even ask them to take you around the block, something that with bargaining will cost around $100. Try to get them to take you any further and you could end up on manslaughter charges, as most of them don't look fit enough to blow their own noses.

If you're really intent on wasting your cash on frivolous transport, you could always charter a **helicopter** (for five people or less) for a jaunt over Hong Kong Island, Lantau or the New Territories. Prices start at $5440 for a thirty-minute spin with Heliservices ☎2802 0200.

Organized tours

There are more **organized tours** of Hong Kong than you can shake a stick at, and if you're only staying a couple of days some may be worth considering – the more exotic tram- and boat-related extravaganzas especially. Some of the better ideas are detailed below. Also, if you really can't bear to make your own arrangements, a whole range of companies will organize your trip to Macau or China, though this is extremely easy to do yourself. For more help, turn to the list of **travel agencies** on p.316.

China Travel Service Local tours and China trips with the official Chinese government organization. See box on p.56 for a list of offices.

Gray Line Tours, 5th Floor, Cheong Hing Building, 72 Nathan Rd, Tsim Sha Tsui ☎2368 7111, fax 2721 9651. An international organization whose Hong Kong arm runs predictable coach tours ($220 upwards) plus longer trips to Macau and China.

Hong Kong Archaeological Society, Block 58, Kowloon Park, Tsim Sha Tsui ☎2723 5765 (ask for the honorary secretary). Field trips, lectures and excavations.

HKTA Any of the HKTA offices can book you onto one of their tours, which include everything from escorted visits to various attractions to harbour cruises and full-day New Territories tours. Some of the more offbeat itineraries include a trip on an antique tram; an evening cruise with unlimited free drinks; a Family Insight Tour which includes a visit to a public housing estate; a day at the races; and a day's sport at the Clearwater Bay Golf and Country Club. From around $280–450 a head; more expensive China daytrips, too.

Watertours, B17, Star House, 3 Salisbury Rd, Tsim Sha Tsui ☎2724 2856 or ☎2739 3302, fax 2735 1035. From around $200 for a two-hour harbour cruise. Most of their tours include at least a few drinks; the $650 ones come with dinner and unlimited booze.

Museums and galleries

Full details are given for each museum and gallery reviewed in this guide – address, public transport links, opening hours and adult admission (where applicable). For up-to-date admission information call the numbers listed below, or see the relevant page. Note that on **public holidays** (there's a list on p.26), museums adopt Sunday opening hours, while most are closed for a few days over Christmas and Chinese New Year.

A special **Visitors' Pass** ($50) gives one month's unlimited admission to the Museum of Art, Museum of History, Science Museum (excluding special exhibitions) and Space Museum (excluding Space Theatre). Buy it at any of the museums or from the HKTA.

Chinese University Art Musuem, Chinese University, Sha Tin, New Territories ☎2609 7416. See p.152.

Hong Kong University Museum and Art Gallery, University of Hong Kong, ☎2975 5600. See p.86.

Lei Cheng Uk Han Tomb Museum, 41 Tonkin St, Sham Shui Po ☎2386 2863. See p.141.

Museum of Art, Cultural Centre Complex, 10 Salisbury Rd, Tsim Sha Tsui ☎2734 2167. See p.126.

Museum of History, 100 Chatham Rd South, Tsim Sha Tsui ☎2724 9042. See p.131.

Museum of Tea Ware, Flagstaff House, Hong Kong Park, 10 Cotton Tree Drive, Central ☎2869 0690. See p.78.

Police Museum, 27 Coombe Rd, Wan Chai Gap ☎2849 7019. See p.95.

Railway Museum, 13 Shung Tak St, Tai Po Market, New Territories ☎2653 3455. See p.153.

Sam Tung Uk Museum, Kwu Uk Lane, Tsuen Wan, New Territories ☎2411 2001. See p.162.

Science Museum, 2 Science Museum Rd, Tsim Sha East ☎2732 3232. See p.131.

Sheung Yiu Folk Museum, Pak Tam Chung, Sai Kung Country Park, New Territories ☎2792 6365. See p.177.

Space Museum, Cultural Centre Complex, 10 Salisbury Rd, Tsim Sha Tsui ☎2734 2722. See p.127.

T.T. Tsui Museum of Art, 4th Floor, Henley Building, 5 Queen's Rd, Central ☎2868 2688. See p.74.

Chapter 2

Hong Kong Island

To many people – visitors and residents alike – **Hong Kong Island** *is* Hong Kong. Seized by the British in 1841, the colony took its name from the island (Heung Gong in Cantonese, or "Fragrant Harbour") and created its initial wealth here, despite Lord Palmerston's famous disappointment that all Britain had grabbed was a "barren rock" in the South China Sea. The rich, industrious and influential carried on their business around the enormous harbour, building warehouses, offices and housing, in support of which communications, roads and transport developed as best they could. The island still doesn't look planned, though it has taken a kind of mad, organizational genius to fit buildings into the space allowed by the terrain. First impressions are of an organic mass of concrete and glass, stretching back from the water to the encroaching green hills behind. This is **Central**, the economic hub of the island and territory. Like Manhattan, which it superficially resembles, film and TV familiarity does nothing to prepare you for the reality of a walk through Central's streets, which hold as tightly constructed a grouping of buildings as can be imagined: there's little available space to drive, walk or even breathe at ground level, and the only way left to build is up.

The wealth generated in this urban concentration is part of the reason that Hong Kong exists at all, and brash, commercial Central

---

HONG KONG ISLAND: TOP TEN ATTRACTIONS

Racing at Happy Valley (p.106)
Hong Kong Park, Botanical and Zoological Gardens (pp.76–78)
The Hongkong and Shanghai Bank (p.71)
Man Mo Temple (p.83)
Ocean Park amusement park (p.110)
The tram ride up The Peak (p.90)
A walk around Sheung Wan (p.80)
Shopping in Central and Admiralty
Stanley village and market (p.112)
T.T. Tsui Museum (p.74)

---

is interesting for just that – though the island also encompasses the more traditional districts of **Western** and **Wan Chai**, and the tourist and shopping zone of **Causeway Bay**. There are rural pockets and walks, too, that make Hong Kong Island an attractive target for a few days' gentle sightseeing. Half an hour's bus ride from the city leaves you on the island's **south side** or **east coast** with a diverse series of attractions: beaches, small villages and seafood restaurants, an amusement park, markets and walks. Closer to Central, you can escape the city by getting on top of it, either by a walk through the residential areas of **Mid-Levels** or **Wan Chai Gap**, or by going one better and scaling **Victoria Peak** itself, the highest point on the island, reached by the famous Peak Tram, a perilously steep funicular railway.

Central

HONG KONG ISLAND

The financial, business and administrative heart of the territory, **CENTRAL** is packed into a narrow strip of land, much of it reclaimed, on the northern side of Hong Kong Island. It forms the southern edge of Victoria Harbour and is just a few minutes from the mainland by ferry. Still technically the "capital" of Hong Kong, the district was originally named Victoria, following the planting of the Union Jack and the claiming of the island for Britain just to the west of here in 1841. The name still survives in the harbour, but the district's no-nonsense, latter-day tag reflects what this part of Hong Kong has become in the last fifty years: the most expensive piece of real estate in the world, supporting some of the planet's priciest (and most exciting) buildings and a skyline for the twenty-first century.

Central is emphatically a place to **walk** around. Much of the area can be seen from the elevated walkways and escalators that lead along the harbourfront and through the shopping malls and lower floors of the skyscrapers that stack back from the water, passing above the snarling streets and construction jackhammers. Nearly all the sights are contemporary – of buildings, shops and conspicuous consumption – but there are also markets and street traders among the monolithic

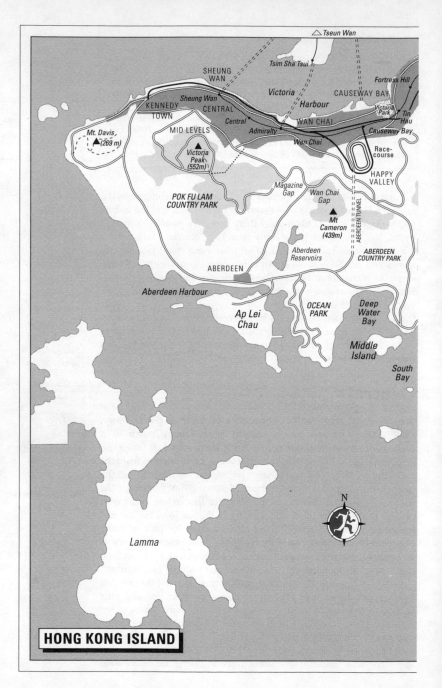

HONG KONG ISLAND

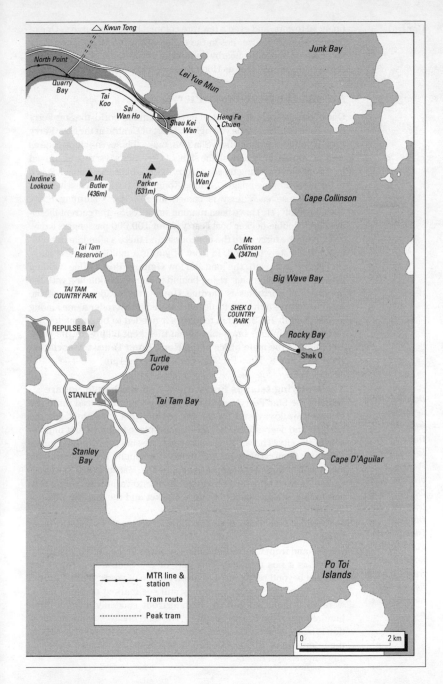

financial towers, and even a few rare colonial buildings survive. One of these, Flagstaff House, lies in the highly attractive **Hong Kong Park** and it's here and in the nearby **Zoological and Botanical Gardens** that the district gets as close as Hong Kong ever does to winding down.

Around the Star Ferry Pier

One of the cheapest and greatest ferry rides in the world, the Star Ferry from Tsim Sha Tsui lands you right in heart of Central at the **Star Ferry Pier**. If you're staying in Tsim Sha Tsui, make this seven-minute ride as soon as you can after arrival: the sight of Central's skyscrapers, framed by the hills and looming up as the ferry skips across the channel, is one of the most thrilling images of Hong Kong. The ferries themselves (so-called because each ferry is named after a star: "Morning Star", "Evening Star", etc) have been running since 1898 – the current diesel-operated, double-decker boats carry about 100,000 passengers a day.

Step off the ferry onto the concourse and there's a huddle of buildings immediately to hand. In front of you is a multi-storey car park. City Hall is to the left; the long and low **General Post Office** building is to the right of the pier; rising behind it, the white building with the hundreds of portholes is **Jardine House**, the headquarters of the Jardine group – although its design has inspired a ruder name among locals. Built in 1972, within ten years it needed to be completely re-faced in aluminium, since its original tiles kept falling off. Its basement houses the main office of the **Hong Kong Tourist Association** (HKTA) (Shop 8; Mon–Fri 9am–6pm, Sat 9am–1pm).

The Outlying Islands Ferry Piers and Exchange Square

Details of ferry departures from the Outlying Islands Ferry Piers are given on p.54; for bus routes from the Outlying Islands Ferry Piers bus terminal and from Exchange Square bus terminal, see p.50.

Leaving the Star Ferry concourse, steps on the right lead up to the **elevated walkway and footbridge** system that runs alongside the harbour and deeper into Central – a good place to gain a first impression of the city. The walkway leads west, passing the Airport Express terminal, then turning to run above Connaught Road Central for about half a kilometre before reaching the Macau Ferry Terminal. Offshoots head off over Connaught Road into various shopping centres, one of which leads to Central Market and the starting point of the Mid-Levels escalator (see p.92).

Heading west from the Star Ferry also leads to the **Outlying Islands Ferry Piers,** the terminal for most ferry and hoverferry services to and from Central (including services to the outlying islands), as well as a bus terminal. This part of the Central waterfront has changed beyond recognition in just a couple of years: Blake Pier and the old ferry piers, which you may still see marked on some maps, were all demolished and the harbourfront suddenly jumped three hundred metres out into the water. The land created by the reclamation is being used for the Hong Kong Airport Express railway station, the International Finance Centre on top of the station and – eventually – more skyscrapers.

Victoria Harbour

Central is the best place from which to ponder the magnificent **Victoria Harbour**, one of the major reasons that the British took possession of Hong Kong Island in the first place. This was once the best and busiest deep-water harbour in the world, though the waterfront warehouses – or "godowns" – are long gone, and the money-making has shifted into the office buildings of Central, many of which are built upon land reclaimed from the sea. In 1840 the harbour was 2km wide; now it is half that original width. What's more, further reclamation – between Central and Wan Chai – is already on the drawing board. As well as affecting the view, this narrowing of the harbour has drastically reduced its natural ability to flush itself clean. This could prove catastrophic since the water is already dangerously polluted, as a peer over the side of any Star Ferry will prove: 1.5 million cubic litres of untreated sewage are discharged here daily, and new sewage treatment facilities are still some years from completion.

It's still difficult, even so, to beat the thrill of crossing the harbour by boat. Apart from the Star Ferry, there are many other **ferry** routes and **harbour cruises** worth taking, all of them with fine views of the port and its vessels. Alternatively, simply park yourself near the Outlying Islands Ferry Piers for a view of the maritime activity that originally made Hong Kong great – junks, ferries, motorboats, container ships, cruiseliners, hoverferries and sailing boats. Twenty thousand ocean-going ships pass through the harbour every year, with scores of thousands of smaller boats heading from here on their way to the Pearl River Estuary and China.

Just behind the reclamation site, accessible by raised walkway, are the pastel-pink, marble and glass buildings which house Hong Kong's **Stock Exchange**, the second largest in Asia after Tokyo. The territory's four exchanges were merged in April 1986 and rehoused in Swiss architect Remo Riva's **Exchange Square**, whose three towers, open piazza (with sculptures by Henry Moore and Elizabeth Frink) and fountains add a rare touch of grace to the area. There are sometimes free lunchtime concerts, making it a good place for an al fresco sandwich, and you can even watch the latest prices on video screens inside the building. Everything inside the exchange itself is computer-operated: the buildings' environment is electronically controlled and the brokers whisk between floors in state-of-the-art talking elevators. There's exhibition space, too, inside **The Forum**, the restaurant and meeting area in the middle of the complex.

Underneath Exchange Square (reached by escalators) is Hong Kong's **Central Bus Terminal**, also referred to as Exchange Square Bus Terminal. Buses leave from here for Aberdeen, Stanley, Repulse Bay and The Peak among other places; see p.50 for details.

City Hall to HMS Tamar

East of the Star Ferry Pier, the two blocks of the **City Hall** are a mean exercise in 1960s civic architecture, all the worse given that the previous City Hall – a grand mid-nineteenth-century French classical

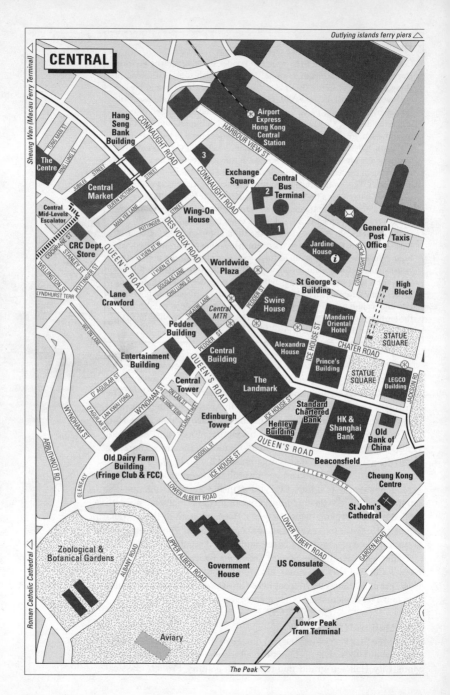

CENTRAL

Outlying islands ferry piers △

Sheung Wan (Macau Ferry Terminal) △

Hang Seng Bank Building

CONNAUGHT ROAD

HARBOUR VIEW ST

Airport Express Hong Kong Central Station

The Centre

TUNG MAN ST

HING LUNG ST

JUBILEE STREET

3

CONNAUGHT ROAD

Exchange Square

Central Bus Terminal

2

1

Central Market

STREET

QUEEN VICTORIA

Wing-On House

Jardine House

General Post Office

Taxis

Central Mid-Levels Escalator

MAN YEE LANE

POTTINGER

DES VOEUX ROAD

CONNAUGHT PLACE

CRC Dept. Store

COCHRANE ST

STANLEY ST

POTTINGER ST

LI YUEN ST W

LI YUEN ST E

QUEEN'S ROAD

DOUGLAS LANE

Worldwide Plaza

St George's Building

High Block

WELLINGTON ST

LYNDHURST TERR

CHIU LUNG ST

PEDDER STREET

Swire House

Mandarin Oriental Hotel

STATUE SQUARE

Lane Crawford

THEATRE LANE

Central MTR

ICE HOUSE ST

CHATER ROAD

WO ON LANE

Pedder Building

PEDDER ST

Central Building

Alexandra House

Prince's Building

STATUE SQUARE

JACKSON RD

Entertainment Building

Central Tower

The Landmark

LEGCO Building

D'AGUILAR ST

WYNDHAM ST

ON LAN ST

ON HING TERR

Edinburgh Tower

Standard Chartered Bank

HK & Shanghai Bank

Old Bank of China

D'AGUILAR ST

LAN KWAI FONG

QUEEN'S ROAD

Henley Building

WELLINGTON STREET

DUDDELL ST

QUEEN'S ROAD

Old Dairy Farm Building (Fringe Club & FCC)

ICE HOUSE ST

Beaconsfield

BATTERY PATH

Cheung Kong Centre

ARBUTHNOT RD

GLENEALY

LOWER ALBERT ROAD

St John's Cathedral

LOWER ALBERT ROAD

GARDEN ROAD

Roman Catholic Cathedral △

Zoological & Botanical Gardens

ALBANY ROAD

UPPER ALBERT ROAD

Government House

US Consulate

Aviary

Lower Peak Tram Terminal

The Peak ▽

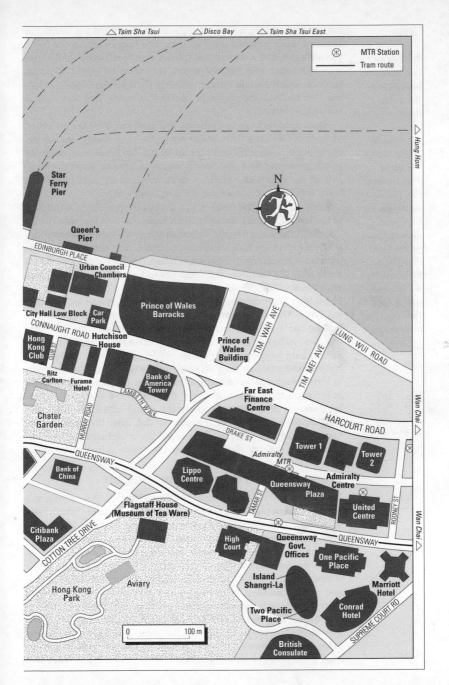

Central

The City Hall Low Block houses clean, free public toilets.

A free double-decker shuttle bus leaves from between City Hall and the adjacent Edinburgh Place car park for the Lower Peak Tram Terminal; the #1 minibus goes to The Peak from the same place.

structure – was with Hong Kong's usual disregard for aesthetics knocked down to make way for them. The Low Block, to the front, has a theatre and a concert hall (plus a café, a gift shop, and a *dim sum* restaurant with harbour views), as well as an enclosed garden through which parade regular wedding parties. The High Block to the rear holds a succession of libraries, a recital hall and various committee rooms.

Hoverferry services to Tsim Sha Tsui East run from Queen's Pier, in front of City Hall. This is also where the corporate junks belonging to local businesses and bigwigs tie up. On Friday and Saturday evenings around 6pm and Sunday mornings around 11am the quayside is jammed with expensive craft, manned by uniformed boat boys, waiting to pick up some of Hong Kong's elite.

The area just to the east – which until 1997 was the headquarters of the British military forces in Hong Kong – is now the base for the People's Liberation Army of China, although it's rare to see any PLA soldiers except for those manning the gates, who stand as immobile as statues. Contrary to local expectation the base kept its colonial name after the handover and continues to be known as **HMS Tamar** after the naval supply ship that docked here in 1878 and became the Royal Navy's administrative HQ in 1897. The ship was scuttled during World War II to prevent the Japanese getting their hands on it, but the name survived and is now used as shorthand for the entire complex, including the weird **Prince of Wales Building**, which looks as if its base has been partly cut away by a giant axman. In 1993 the Navy moved to a new base on Stonecutters Island and the dockyard at HMS Tamar was reclaimed and turned into a parade ground. It was here, on the night of the handover, that the British staged their sunset lowering of the Union Jack, to the sound of a lone piper, with HMS *Britannia* floodlit on the quay behind. After the handover the space was supposed to be redeveloped for government offices, but cost-cutting put that plan on hold, and its future is now uncertain.

From the Star Ferry to Statue Square

The pedestrian underpass from the Star Ferry concourse emerges near the **Cenotaph** war memorial in Statue Square, which pro-democracy demonstrators decked in flowers, banners, letters and poems after the massacre at Tiananmen Square in June 1989. The **Hong Kong Club**, a bastion of colonial privilege since Victorian times, still faces the Cenotaph, though it's no longer housed in the stately building that went up at the end of the nineteenth century – and was demolished in the 1970s – but instead occupies several floors of a modern, bow-fronted tower. In the northeastern corner is the **Mandarin Oriental Hotel**. Built in 1963 it was the first of the new wave of luxury hotels in Hong Kong and is still rated "best hotel in the world" almost every year – though it hides its riches well inside a fairly dull box-like structure. Taking tea or a drink inside is one way for riff-raff to get a glimpse, or you can march in and use the toilet facilities, which as well as being almost the last word in urinary comfort offer telephones, grooming facilities and chaise longues.

Cross Chater Road and you're in the southern half of **Statue Square**, the statue in question – typically – being that of a banker, Sir Thomas Jackson, a nineteenth-century manager of the Hongkong and Shanghai Bank. The square once gave Hong Kong its colonial focus, open down to the water, surrounded by fine buildings and topped with a statue of Queen Victoria, but it's lost all its character – and even the cricket pitch that once adorned it – to visionless late twentieth-century development. Plans are occasionally mooted to try to improve the current mish-mash of concrete, ponds and sculpture, but for now it does at least come to life on Sunday when it and the surrounding areas are packed with the territory's 100,000 Filipina *amah*s, or maids, who gather here on their day off. People from the Philippines have been coming to Hong Kong for a century and now form the territory's largest immigrant grouping. Most are women who come to work here as maids, sending money back home to support their families. At weekends and public holidays they descend upon Statue Square, where they picnic, shop, read, sing and have their hair cut. Coming from the Star Ferry you will hear them before you see them – Jan Morris once memorably likened the noise of their talk to an "assembly of starlings".

The LEGCO Building

One of the most important of Central's surviving colonial buildings sits on the eastern side of Statue Square. Built in the first decade of this century, the former **Supreme Court** (now the **LEGCO Building** – home of Hong Kong's Legislative Council), a granite structure with dome and colonnade, is the only colonial structure left in the square. It's as safe from future development as anything can be in Hong Kong, though unfortunately you can't go into what is the territory's nearest equivalent to a parliamentary building.

The Hongkong and Shanghai Bank and around

Crossing Statue Square and busy Des Voeux Road puts you right underneath one of Hong Kong's most extraordinary buildings, Sir Norman Foster's headquarters for the **Hongkong and Shanghai Banking Corporation**, first opened in 1986. It cost around a billion US dollars to complete, although the structure itself is far more impressive than any statistics. Wearing its innards on the outside, the battleship-grey, ladder-like construction hangs from towers like suspension bridges stacked one on top of the other. The whole building is supported on eight groups of four pillars. Walk under the glass canopy and you look up through the glass underbelly into a sixty-metre-high atrium, the floors linked by long escalators that ride through each storey, open offices ranged around the central atrium.

Hong Kong's Government

Under Hong Kong's British colonial system the head of government, the Governor, was appointed by the Queen and served in office without limit. Traditionally, the Governor was appointed from the ranks of senior British civil servants or diplomats. The last incumbent, Chris Patten, appointed in 1992, after the Conservative Party's general election victory – but following his own personal defeat in his British parliamentary seat – was unique in that he was the first career politician to hold the post.

The Governor was head of both the Executive Council (known as EXCO), which wielded effective administrative power and advised the Governor on his day-to-day decisions, and of the Legislative Council (LEGCO), which formulated the territory's laws and controlled its expenditure. The only matters the Governor had no responsibility for were defence and foreign relations, which until the handover to China remained in the hands of the British government. The other governmental body, the Urban Council, held responsibility for raising local taxes to finance municipal services like markets, sports and cultural facilities.

In the past, both EXCO and LEGCO were staffed solely by appointed and ex-officio members, approved by the Governor. Representative rule had never had any place in Hong Kong and there were no legal political parties until 1990. However, following direct elections in September 1991 – the territory's first – roughly a third of Legislative Council members were elected, most of them belonging to Hong Kong's main pro-democracy political party, the United Democrats (now the Democratic Party). After the arrival of Chris Patten the future of LEGCO's democratically elected members soon became a point of conflict between the Governor (and, by extension, Britain) and China, with Chris Patten making it clear that he regarded an extension of the franchise in Hong Kong as of paramount importance. China, for its part, remained adamant that it wanted the democratic content of Hong Kong's "parliament" to be as limited as possible when it took control of the territory. Despite this, the Governor

The public banking facilities are on the first two floors of this, so no one minds you riding the first couple of escalators from street level to have a look. The bronze lions at the front were saved from the previous building (torn down to make way for this one) – one still shows damage from World War Two shrapnel.

The Standard Chartered Bank and the Bank of China
Next door to the Hongkong and Shanghai Bank is the headquarters of the **Standard Chartered Bank**, a thin and fairly anonymous tower squeezed between opposing blocks that – by design – just overtopped the Hongkong and Shanghai's building.

The only serious conceptual rival to Foster's creation, however, is the Chinese-American architect I.M. Pei's **Bank of China Tower**, slightly along to the east, across Garden Road. Built between 1985 and 1990, Pei's blue and grey spear-like building – seventy storeys and just over 300m high – was the territory's tallest until Central pressed ahead with his proposals to increase the number of directly and indirectly elected LEGCO members and widen the franchise from around 200,000 voters to around 2.6 million – more than 1 in three of the population. These actions prompted some virulent and memorable invective from Beijing during which the Governor was described, among other things, as a "prostitute for a thousand years" and the "triple violator".

Further elections in September 1995 – the first time that each of LEGCO's sixty seats was contested – brought more democracy and more pro-democracy gains. Not all seats were decided by direct election, and only around forty percent of those eligible to vote actually voted, but that was almost twice as many as had ever voted previously in Hong Kong. After the results were declared, the Democratic Party could count on the support of around 28 of LEGCO's members. Their main opposition in LEGCO, and outside, was the considerably less well-represented Democratic Alliance for the Betterment of Hong Kong, the biggest pro-China political grouping.

At midnight on 30 June 1997, when Hong Kong became a Special Administrative Region of the People's Republic of China, the Governor was replaced by a Chief Executive, the first incumbent being Tung Chee-hwa, a shipping billionaire. China also carried out its promise to dissolve the elected LEGCO, replacing it with its own body, Provisional LEGCO, which had been elected by a complex committee system. Provisional LEGCO sat until May 1998 when new elections were held, with a far more limited franchise and redrawn constituency boundaries. The highly complex voting system allocated 20 seats through voting lists in geographical constituencies, 30 through so-called functional constituencies – such as lawyers, bankers, or property developers – and ten through a committee, elections for which had been held earlier. To general amazement – and despite torrential monsoon rains – there was a record turnout of 53 percent and a resounding success for the Democratic Party who took 13 seats, almost all in directly elected geographical constituencies, making them the largest party in the new LEGCO.

Plaza went up in Wan Chai (local lore has it that the Bank of China and the Hongkong and Shanghai Bank continually tried to outdo each other in the height of their buildings, so that the *taipan* of one could sit in his top floor office and spit on the head of his rival). It's an engineering triumph since it has no internal columns and is supported by the remarkable strength of its glistening shaft walls. The interior, however, is disappointingly ordinary.

The **Old Bank of China**, which the new Bank of China Tower superseded, still stands next to the Hongkong and Shanghai Bank. A solid stone structure dating from 1950, it's not open to the public since it's now occupied by another bank and, at the top, the ritzy members-only China Club.

Along Queen's Road and Des Voeux Road

Queen's Road is Central's main street, as it has been since the 1840s when it was on the waterfront and described by contemporaries as a

Hong Kong Geomancy

For all their modernity, even the most hi-tech of Hong Kong's buildings is expected to conform to the dictates of **feng shui** (literally "wind and water"), a complex discipline reflecting Taoist beliefs in the interconnectedness of all parts of the universe. *Feng shui* seeks to preserve a harmonious relationship between natural forces – wind, water, mountains, hills – and peoples' living environments; getting it wrong is believed to result in insomnia, business failure, romantic disappointment or even death. Consequently, *feng shui* masters, or geomancers, are frequently called in to advise on new building projects, offering guidance on anything from the way a desk or chair is placed in a room to the positioning of an entire skyscraper – even the angle of the escalators in the Hongkong and Shanghai Bank was fixed according to their instructions. It's not difficult to spot smaller manifestations of *feng shui* around buildings, such as mirrors hung above doors or woks placed outside windows to deflect bad influences and negative currents. Fishtanks and other water features – such as the waterfalls outside the Bank of China – create positive *feng shui* (it is believed that wealth is borne along by the water), meaning that buildings with a clear view of the harbour are extremely popular. By contrast, the old Government House was always said to have very bad *feng shui*: it's cut off from the sea, is overlooked by high buildings, and some of the surrounding skyscrapers are placed so that their corners point towards it – the *feng shui* equivalent of being stabbed. The run of bad luck Hong Kong has had since Government House was left unoccupied, however, has led to some to question the accuracy of this diagnosis.

"grand boulevard" (or *dai ma lo* in Cantonese, a name by which it's still known by the Chinese). Running west from **Chater Garden**, after the Hong Kong and Shanghai Bank building you'll reach the Henley Building, on the fourth floor of which you'll find one of the best private art collections in Hong Kong. The **T.T. Tsui Museum of Art** (Mon–Fri 10am–6pm, Sat 10am–2pm; $30) is small but its exhibits are of superb quality. There are three thousand pieces of Chinese art on rotating display, including ceramics, bronzes, furniture and paintings. The museum has also recreated rooms from stylistically important periods of Chinese history, which give a fascinating picture of how scholars and nobles lived.

A little further on is the junction with **Ice House Street**, named for a building that once stored blocks of ice for use in the colony's early hospitals, imported from the United States since there were no commercial ice-making facilities in Hong Kong. A wander up Ice House Street to the junction with Lower Albert Road gives you a view of a later storage building, the early twentieth-century **Old Dairy Farm Building**, in brown and cream brick, which today houses the Fringe Club (see "The Arts and Media", p.277) and the Foreign Correspondents' Club, a members-only retreat for journalists, diplomats and lawyers.

To the west, beyond Ice House Street, Queen's Road and parallel **Des Voeux Road** take in some of the most exclusive of the territory's shops and malls, including **The Landmark** shopping complex, on the corner of Pedder Street and Des Voeux Road, opened in 1980 and boasting an impressive fountain in the huge atrium. You'll doubtless pass through at some point since the Landmark is a key hub in the **pedestrian walkway** system that links all the major buildings of Central to the Airport Express Station, Star Ferry and harbour.

It's worth leaving the indoor walkways at some stage to reach **Pedder Street** itself, where the turn-of-the-century **Pedder Building**, now filled with discount clothes outlets and businesses, is a solid old structure that's somehow escaped demolition over the years. Back across the street, between The Landmark and the Central Building, you should be able to make out a red oval plaque which marks the approximate position of the 1841 waterfront – a remarkable testament to the quantity of land reclaimed since then.

West to Central Market

It doesn't matter which of the two main streets – Queen's Road or Des Voeux Road – you follow west from Pedder Street, though it's useful to know that **trams** run straight down the latter, either to Western or east into Wan Chai. Stay on foot, though, until you've walked the few hundred metres west to Central Market (see below), and you'll pass the parallel cross alleys of **Li Yuen Street East** and **Li Yuen Street West**, which run between the two main roads. Both are packed close with stalls touting clothes and accessories: the contents of the two alleys are much the same – women's clothes, silkwear, children's clothes, fabrics, imitation handbags and accessories. Emerge from Li Yuen Street East onto Queen's Road and you're opposite the more upmarket shopping experience of **Lane Crawford**, one of the city's top – and most staid – department stores, with a smart café at the top and aisles full of heavily made-up charge-card queens.

Just beyond Lane Crawford, on the same side of the street, the steps of Pottinger Street are lined with small stalls selling ribbons, flowers, locks and other small items – it still looks remarkably similar to how it did in photographs taken in the 1940s and 50s. Pottinger Street leads up to Hollywood Road and SoHo, in Mid-Levels, which has so far managed to resist the worst effects of redevelopment.

A little further on, the district's western end is marked by **Central Market** (daily 6am–8pm), which – like all markets in Hong Kong – is about the most fun you can have outside a hospital operating room. Fish and poultry get butchered on the ground floor, meat on the first, with the relative calm of the fruit and veg selling taking place one floor higher. It's virtually all over by midday (although the smell remains) so aim to get here early and (if you've the stomach for it) take a break at one of the food stalls inside. There's a shopping arcade on the upper floor, from where the **Central–Mid-Levels escalator link** takes off, snaking up the hill above street level (see p.92 for details).

Just west of Central Market at 99 Queen's Road Central is **The Centre**, by night one of the most eye-catching features of the island's skyline. It was designed by the same architect, Denis Lau, who was responsible for Central Plaza in Wan Chai. Here he went even further, installing horizontal bars of light which change colour every few minutes and put on a dancing light show nightly at 9pm.

South of Queen's Road: Lan Kwai Fong

In addition to the Luk Yu Teahouse *(p.238), another famous Cantonese restaurant in the area, the* Yung Kee, *32–40 Wellington Street (p.238), is a great spot for lunch.*

The network of streets south of Queen's Road – Stanley Street, Wellington Street, D'Aguilar Street and Wyndham Street – contains a fancy array of shops, galleries, restaurants and bars in which the emphasis is firmly Western. You may well find yourself eating and drinking in this area, particularly off D'Aguilar Street on a sloping L-shaped lane known as **Lan Kwai Fong**. This once housed a major flower market, and a couple of florists still survive, but Lan Kwai Fong is known now exclusively for its burgeoning array of trendy pubs, bars, restaurants and clubs. They've now spread out of the 'Fong itself, into Wing Wah Lane, D'Aguilar Street and others, so the name is now used to refer to the entire area (for full details see chapters 7 and 8). They're all late-opening – you can eat and drink here until 5am – and mostly frequented by expats and well-to-do Chinese yuppies (called, predictably enough, "chuppies"). Every August, the area takes part in the **Hong Kong Food Festival**, with outdoor events, food promotions and general good times. It hasn't always been so pleasant. During street celebrations in Lan Kwai Fong for New Year's Eve in 1992, the steep streets became slippery with spilled drinks, a few revellers lost their footing and panic set in among the twenty thousand or so people crowded into the area. Twenty people died in the ensuing crush, a sobering thought as you trawl around the various bars, and an event which has left the local police somewhat paranoid about crowds.

There is one small, traditional enclave amid this contemporary barrage of bars and restaurants. **Wo On Lane**, off the western side of D'Aguilar Street, retains an Earth God shrine, a couple of basic cafés, a calligrapher and a working street-barber – a rare sight these days. Alternatively, try to grab a table in the **Luk Yu Teahouse** at 24–26 Stanley Street, a traditional Chinese tea house (also renowned for its traditionally rude staff) which relocated here in 1975, using the lovely wooden furniture and decorations from its original building, which had stood on Wing Kut Street since the 1930s.

From the Zoological Gardens to St John's Cathedral

Perching on the slopes overlooking Central are the **Zoological and Botanical Gardens**, opened in 1864 (entrances on Glenealy and on Albany Road; daily 6am–7pm; free). The views of the harbour disappeared years ago, replaced by spectacular close-ups of the upper storeys of the Bank of China Tower and the Hongkong and Shanghai Bank. Early in the morning it's a favourite venue for people practising *tai chi*, a balletic discipline in which protagonists appear to be walking through treacle. The Botanical Gardens' aviary is the most pleasant retreat, home to a collection of pink flamingos, cranes, toucans and all kinds of ducks. The zoological section to the west (cross Albany Road using the underpass) is less worthwhile, its unhappy captives – including stir-crazy simians – sitting bored in cramped cages.

Follow the path near the orangutan cage that slopes downwards from the northwest corner of the gardens towards Arbuthnot Road, followed by a left up a driveway, and you'll reach the city's **Roman Catholic Cathedral**, finished in 1888 and financed largely by Portuguese Catholics from Macau. If it's open take a look at the stained-glass west windows, made in Toulouse.

Central

Bus #23A runs directly to the gardens from stops along Connaught Rd; get off at the Caritas Centre.

Government House and the Cathedral

Beneath the gardens, on Upper Albert Road, **Government House** was the official residence of Hong Kong's colonial governors from 1855 to 1997. It's a strange conglomeration of styles, with several additions having been made over the years, the most unusual being those of a young Japanese architect who redesigned the building during the Japanese occupation of Hong Kong in World War II. He's responsible for the turret. The house is now used only for receptions and official functions and is normally closed to the public, although charity events such as concerts are occasionally held here – watch the local press for details. However the gardens, which are famous for their rhododendrons and azaleas, are opened to the public for a few days every year in early spring. The current Chief Executive, Tung Chee-hwa, works from the Government Offices in Lower Albert Road and prefers to live in his apartment in Magazine Gap Road. It's rumoured that he and his wife were put off by the notoriously bad *feng shui* of Government House, although it may just have been the Colonial ambience which disturbed him. His successors may think differently.

Down Garden Road, past the **Lower Peak Tram Terminal** (see p.90), is the other dominant symbol of British colonial rule, the Anglican **St John's Cathedral**, founded in 1847 but damaged during World War II when the Japanese army used it as a club. It's the only building in Hong Kong which is freehold, as opposed to standing on land leased from the Government – presumably the Colonial administrators felt God would accept nothing less than perpetuity. Supposedly the oldest Anglican church in the Far East, it's been restored since and despite being dwarfed by almost everything around, its pleasant aspect gives you an idea of the more graceful proportions of colonial Hong Kong. The main doors, incidentally, were made from the wood of the supply ship HMS *Tamar*, which was docked down at the harbour for nearly fifty years until 1941 (see p.70), and which lent its name to the British Naval HQ. There's also an interesting bookstore in the grounds selling souvenirs and cards.

You can regain Central's lower reaches by continuing down Garden Road, past the contorted towers of **Citibank Plaza** towards the **Cheung Kong Centre** and the Bank of China. But it's rather more appealing to stroll across the leafy cathedral grounds to the early nineteenth-century redbrick building at the edge of the hill known as **Beaconsfield**, after Disraeli, the Earl of Beaconsfield. It has had several uses: once the French Mission Building; subsequently the Victoria District Court. Now it's where the Court of Final Appeal sits – the body set up to take the role of the UK's House of Lords following the handover. From Beaconsfield, a path drops down to Queen's Road near the Hongkong and Shanghai Bank building.

Hong Kong Park

Heading straight for the park, bus #12 from Connaught Rd stops near the entrance; get off at the first stop on Cotton Tree Drive. From Admiralty MTR take bus #12A or head into Pacific Place and look for the signs to Hong Kong Park.

The other route from the Zoological Gardens is to head down **Cotton Tree Drive**, which sounds charmingly rural but is in fact choked with traffic. However, beyond the Lower Peak Tram Terminal, on the eastern side of the drive, is the remarkably attractive **Hong Kong Park** (daily 6.30am–11pm; free), which contains the elegantly colonial Flagstaff House and its Museum of Teaware (see below).

Opened in 1991, and beautifully landscaped in tiers up the hillside, the award-winning park contains an interesting **conservatory** with dry and humid habitats for its plants and trees, as well as the superb **Edward Youde Aviary** (daily 9am–5pm; free), named after a former Governor. This is designed as an enormous mesh tent inside which is a piece of semi-tropical forest and its resident bird species. Wooden walkways lead you through and above the trees, bringing you face-to-face with exotically coloured hooting birds; signs point out which ones are currently rearing chicks. As you exit the aviary at the lower end are some pools of water for aquatic birds – you can see the pelicans being fed at 10am and 3pm. Elsewhere in the park and throughout Mid-Levels you may see flocks of wild cockatoos. These are not native to Hong Kong but are escaped pets which have bred successfully. They are very pretty – white with yellow or orange crests – but unfortunately they are killing many local trees by ripping off branches and bark.

The rest of Hong Kong Park features ornamental lakes, a visual arts display centre, a children's playground, a bar-restaurant, and a sadly under-used open-air theatre. It's also a popular wedding spot (there's a registry office inside the park), so bridal parties framed by Central's surrounding skyscrapers are a common sight.

Flagstaff House: the Museum of Tea Ware

At the northern corner of the park, in the lee of the massive Bank of China building, is **Flagstaff House**. Built in 1844, this impressive piece of colonial architecture was the residence of the Commander of the British Forces in the territory for well over a century – a cool, white, shuttered building; its simple pillars and surrounding garden an elegant contrast to the skyscrapers all around. That it still stands is down to the donation by one Dr K.S. Lo of his fine teaware collection to the Urban Council, which promptly restored the house and opened the **Museum of Teaware** inside (daily except Wed 10am–5pm; free). The house alone – with its high-ceilinged rooms and polished wooden floors – is worth seeing, but the displays of teaware and related items from China throughout the ages are engaging too, and there are some explanatory English notes.

Admiralty

Latterly, Central has expanded east, with a batch of striking new buildings down **Queensway**, beyond Hong Kong Park, into the area known as **ADMIRALTY**. All the buildings are connected by overhead walkways which you can join from the bottom of Cotton Tree Drive, and use to go west into Central or east to Pacific Place. Most of the land here was originally part of the old colonial Victoria Barracks, which were decommissioned at the turn of the 1980s; Hong Kong Park, too, sits on former military turf.

Admiralty MTR has several entrances in the neighbourhood, one at the Lippo Centre itself, another at Queensway Plaza, which brings you out near buses and taxis.

The **Lippo Centre**, at the junction of Cotton Tree Drive and Queensway, is the most eye-catching structure, designed by American architect Paul Rudolph and formerly owned by the Australian entrepreneur Alan Bond (after whom it used to be named). Supported on huge grey pillars, interlocking steel and glass spurs trace their way up the centre's twin towers, while in the central lobby a ten-metre-high stone relief of a dragon and junk dominates.

Walkways connect the Lippo Centre to other office and retail buildings, including Queensway Plaza, the gold block of the NEC building (the one that looks like a giant cigarette lighter) and Hutchison House, from where you can get back to the walkways that lead around Central's office blocks and across Queensway to the Government Offices and the modern **High Court** building – a disappointingly squat, grey block – and, along from it, to the vast development of **Pacific Place**, with yet more shops, offices, cinemas, restaurants and three luxury **hotels** – the *Island Shangri-La*, the *Conrad* and the *Marriott*.

Western District: Sheung Wan To Kennedy Town

HONG KONG ISLAND

The oldest settled parts of Hong Kong Island are all in **WESTERN DISTRICT**, which starts only a few hundred metres from the skyscrapers and office blocks of Central. Not long after the seizure of the island, the British moved out of Western, leaving what was a malarial area to the Chinese, who have been living and trading here ever since. Full of traditional businesses, small temples and crowded residential streets, it could claim to be the most characterful part of the island, but it's by no means a homogeneous mass, and encompasses several quite distinct areas.

Sheung Wan, at the western end of the MTR Island Line, is the part of the district closest to Central. This area is what's generally thought of as "Western", a web of street markets and traditional shops that unfolds back from the **Macau Ferry Terminal**, which you can reach by the walkway from the Star Ferry in Central. South of Sheung Wan, climbing up the island's hillside, **Hollywood Road** is one of the more important of the district's thoroughfares, where you'll find the famous **Man Mo Temple**; nearby, the **Tai Ping Shan** district conceals a set of lesser-known temples. Further west, you can skip the less appealing bits of Western by taking the bus to the **University of Hong Kong**, where there's a fine collection of Chinese art in the **University Museum and Art Gallery**. Or take the tram direct to **Kennedy Town** – the island's westernmost point of interest – which retains much of its mid-nineteenth-century character in a series of streets and warehouses alive with the trade based around its harbour.

Sheung Wan

SHEUNG WAN begins immediately west of Central Market, its streets a mixture of traditional Chinese shops and merchants, tucked into the narrow lanes that run between the main roads. Some of the more fascinating trades have been lost as redevelopment rips out old alleys to replace them with new office and retail buildings. This is especially true of the nooks and crannies immediately west of Central Market, between Bonham Strand and Queen's Road Central to the south, and Des Voeux Road to the north, where skyscraper developments such as The Centre (with its high-tech light display at night) are pushing out the older buildings. However, you should still find enough to occupy a morning's stroll. You can follow the routes outlined below, or simply wander as you fancy: it's difficult to get lost since the main roads are always close by, and once you start climbing you know you're heading away from the harbour.

From Central Market to Man Wa Lane

Heading west down Des Voeux Road, a couple of blocks up on the left is **Wing On Street**, formerly known as "Cloth Alley" because of the fabric stalls that used to cluster here. They've now been relocated to Western Market (see p.82), although you'll still find some other cloth shops on Queen's Road, at the junction with Wellington Street. Neighbouring alleys are still devoted to traditional trades, though, with the amount of redevelopment in this area, how much longer they will be there is anyone's guess: **Wing Kut Street** features stalls selling clothes, accessories, socks and scarves; in **Wing Wo Street**

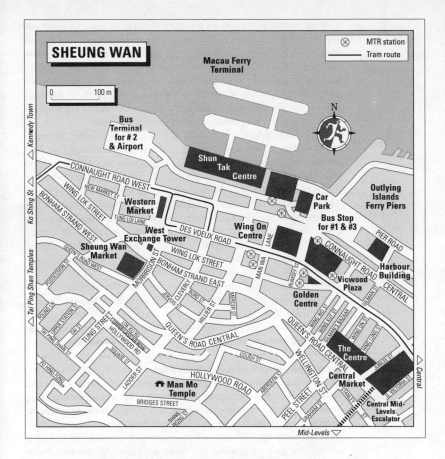

SHEUNG WAN

the shops specialize in imitation jewellery. Walk west up Wing Lok Street to the stalls of **Man Wa Lane**, where another old Chinese trade is practised: carving seals, or "chops", as the carved name stamps they make here are called. They're used to tourists, and lots of the stalls display signs and prices in English. The craftsmen will translate your name or message into Chinese characters, which are then carved onto the seal you've picked, usually made of wood, soapstone or porcelain. The process takes around an hour, making it possible to wander round the rest of Sheung Wan while you're waiting.

Around the Macau Ferry Terminal
Down at the waterfront, catamarans and jetfoils to Macau leave from the **Macau Ferry Terminal**, part of the massive, twin-towered **Shun Tak Centre**, a shopping mall and apartment complex built in 1986. The complex replaced "temporary" Macau ferry piers that had stood

for over twenty years and its futuristic design, for once, doesn't yet appear dated. In a nice touch, the red trimming at base, middle and apex of both towers is echoed in the design colours of the Jetfoils that whip off to Macau from the parallel piers. If you want to circle back to Central from here, head inside up to the main shopping level, where there are a few shops and some travel agents – from the eastern section an **elevated walkway** runs right the way along the harbour to the Star Ferry terminal, a fifteen-minute walk.

Across Connaught Road from the Shun Tak Centre, **Western Market** (daily 10am–7pm), built in 1906, retains its Edwardian shell but has undergone a marked interior transformation. A Chinese food market for over eighty years, much like Central Market to the east, it was renovated and in 1991 reopened as an arts and crafts centre – which means it has retained its fine original brick- and ironwork but that the noisy market has been replaced with a two-floor shopping mall. Ground-floor stalls sell arts and crafts, while the first floor houses the cloth shops moved here from Wing On Street; the second floor is a galleried restaurant, *Treasure Inn Seafood* (open until 11pm) – a good place for a *dim sum* lunch.

For a traditional Chinese market, head up Morrison Street: the large white complex on the right is the **Sheung Wan Market**, packed full of meat, fish, fruit and vegetable stalls. The second floor is a cooked food centre (open 6am–2am), with *dai pai dongs* in operation almost around the clock.

Wing Lok Street and Bonham Strand

There's more sustained interest in the long streets to the south and west, which provide glimpses of the trades and industries that have survived in this area since the island was settled. **Wing Lok Street**, in its lower reaches at least, and **Bonham Strand** retain some of their older, balconied buildings and a succession of varied shops and businesses that merit a browse, and there are plenty of *dai pai dongs* along **Hillier Street**.

This area of Sheung Wan is also known as **Nam Pak Hong** – "North–South Trading Houses" – and many of the businesses are herbal and medicinal wholesalers, with snake recipes among their many products. Glass cases fronting Bonham Strand contain a whole host of Chinese medicinal ingredients, of which **ginseng** is the most famous – and one of the most expensive. The root of a plant found in Southeast Asia and North America, there are over thirty different varieties of ginseng, including the pricey red from North Korea, white from the United States and wild from mountainous northeast China. It's prescribed for a whole host of problems, from saving those faced with imminent death by illness (which wild ginseng is purported to delay for three days) to curing hangovers (white ginseng in boiled water). Some of the larger ginseng trading companies have their offices along **Bonham Strand West**, the most venerable ones boasting impressive interiors of teak and glass. Here you'll see people sorting through newly arrived boxes of ginseng root, chopping it up and preparing it for sale.

Ko Shing Street, at the western end of Bonham Strand West, is devoted to the wholesale medicinal trade. Great sacks and wicker baskets are taken off a line of trucks by men carrying a wicked hook in one hand: they spear the sacks and hoist them onto their shoulders, dumping them onto the pavements where others unload and sort their contents. The shops here, open to the street, display ginseng alongside antlers, crushed pearls, dried sea horses, birds' nests and all the assorted paraphernalia of Chinese **herbalists**. In keeping with the traditional nature of the trade, some of the names are straight from the nineteenth century – one company here has a sign proclaiming it to be the "Prosperity Steamship Company".

Ko Shing Street bends back round towards Connaught Road West (along which the tram runs). The stretch from here to as far west as Centre Street is devoted to stores selling dried mushrooms, salted and preserved fish, dried squid, oysters, sea slugs, seahorses, sharks' fins, scallops and seaweed. They make for colourful displays and, even if the priciest goods are out of your range, you could always pick up a string of Chinese sausages or a bottle of oyster sauce.

Along and around Hollywood Road

Hollywood Road, running west from the end of Wyndham Street in Central, and the steep streets off it, form one of Western's most interesting areas: a run of antique shops, curio and furniture stores. There's some wonderful Asian applied art here – furniture, old and new ceramics, burial pottery, painted screens, prints, jewellery and embroidery – and a group of more upmarket antique shops at the eastern end of Hollywood Road. As you move further west towards Cat Street the selection becomes more mixed (and prices get lower), with any number of smaller places selling bric-a-brac and junk, as well as "genuine" antiques. The western end of Hollywood Road is also known for its coffin sellers, and there are a few surviving shops as well as some that sell funeral clothes for the dead, made from silk.

Man Mo Temple

Follow Hollywood Road west and just before the junction with Ladder Street is the **Man Mo Temple** (daily 8am–6pm), one of Hong Kong's oldest, built in the 1840s and equipped with impressive interior decorations from mainland China. It's recently been restored so it is not as dark and smoky as some other Chinese temples, but there is still plenty of atmosphere with the hanging, pyramidal incense coils belching out scented fumes. It's not intimidating, however, and no one will mind you poking about the interior. It's generally busy, too, as plenty of people pop in to pay their respects to the two gods honoured here, while others have their fortunes told by shaking inscribed sticks out of bamboo cylinders (there are half-hearted attempts to charge tourists $100 for this, and $20 for entrance, but this is unlikely to be enforced). The name of the temple means "civil" (Man) and "martial" (Mo) and it's dedicated to these two characteristics which are represented by separate gods. The "civil" aspect belongs to the God of Literature, Man Cheong, who protects civil servants (he's the red-robed statue wielding a writing brush); the "martial" is that of the God of War, Kuan Ti (represented by another statue, in green, holding a sword). Kuan Ti, particularly, is an interesting deity, worshipped by both Buddhists and Taoists, and a protector of – among other things – pawn shops, policemen, secret societies and the military. On the left by the main door as you enter, the carved nineteenth-century chairs (which look like shrines) in the glass cases were once used to carry the statues through the streets at festivals. The other altars in the temple are to Pao Kung, the God of Justice, and to Shing Wong, a God of the City, who protects the local neighbourhood.

Just west of the temple, at the junction of Hollywood Road and Sing Wong Street, a sign indicates the start of **Sun Yat-sen Historical Trail**, an easy-to-follow walk around thirteen sites related to the Chinese revolutionary's life, all in and around Hollywood Road, where he lived briefly during the 1890s.

Ladder Street to Possession Street

Back outside the temple, Hollywood Road is crossed by **Ladder Street**, not so much a street as a steep flight of steps linking Caine Road with Queen's Road. Built to ease the passage of sedan-chair bearers as they carried their human loads up to the residential areas along Caine Road in the nineteenth century, it's the only surviving street of this kind, one of several that used to link Central and Western with Mid-Levels. The lower part retains some of its older, shuttered houses, their balconies jutting over the steps.

Turn right, down the steps, and immediately on the left, **Upper Lascar Row** is what's left of the area known to the late nineteenth-century citizens of Hong Kong as "Cat Street". The names have various interpretations: *lascar* is an Urdu word, meaning an East Indian seaman, and the area is probably where these seamen lived – the "Cat Street" tag probably derives from its consequent role as a red-light area. The other theory is that Cat Street was a "thieves' market", all the goods at which were provided by cat burglars. These days Upper Lascar Row is a mixture: an increasing number of upmarket antique outlets occupy the shops, while the flea-market vendors have moved to the pavement outside, with old banknotes, coins, jade, watches and jewellery spread out on the ground alongside broken TVs and other junk. The flea market really only comes alive at weekends, while the antique shops are open every day, although some close on Sunday. There is also one gallery of shops, the **Cat Street Galleries**

(Mon–Fri 11am–6pm, Sat 10am–6pm), selling a mixture of modern china, contemporary paintings and antiques in showrooms ranged over several floors.

Hollywood Road continues west past **Possession Street**, where in 1841 the British landed, claiming the island by planting the Union Jack – though the street's name is the only reminder of this symbolic act. The only interesting thing about Possession Street, in fact, is how far inland it is today, land reclamation having pushed the shoreline hundreds of metres north over the years.

A little further on, Hollywood Road meets **Queen's Road West**, which carries another mix of age-old shops and trades. You can follow Queen's Road right back into Central, a long walk past wedding shops full of embroidered clothes and goods; shops selling paper offerings to be burnt at religious festivals; art-supply shops with calligraphy sets, paper and ink; tea stores; and all manner of other traditional trades, conducted from a variety of gleaming windows and dusty shop fronts.

Tai Ping Shan

Up Ladder Street from the Man Mo Temple and off to the right lies the district of **TAI PING SHAN** or "Peaceful Mountain". One of the earliest areas of Chinese settlement after the colony was founded, it was anything but peaceful, notorious for its overcrowded housing and outbreaks of plague, and known as a haunt of the early Hong Kong Triad societies. An exiled Chinese scholar, Wang Tao, took a walk through the district in the late-nineteenth century and was disappointed by the quality of the "singsong girls" available in the brothels, most of who had large feet instead of the "tiny bowed feet" he considered attractive.

Tai Ping Shan is a far less dramatic place these days, but it's worth a stroll down **Tai Ping Shan Street** itself, beyond Bridges Street, to see the neighbourhood's surviving temples, which cluster together at the junction with Pound Lane. Raised above the street, the temples are easily missed, seeming more a part of someone's house than a place of worship, an impression that persists until you see the incense sticks and are hassled for money by the old women sitting outside. First is the **Kuan Yin Temple**, dedicated to the Buddhist Goddess of Mercy and reached by climbing the steps on the left of the junction. The altar in the main hall of the green-tiled **Sui Tsing Paak Temple** next door holds a statue of the god Sui Tsing Paak, known as the "Pacifying General" and revered for his ability to cure illnesses – the statue was brought here in 1894 during a particularly virulent outbreak of plague. One of the rooms off the main hall is used by fortune tellers, and you should also look for the rows of *Tai Sui* in the temple – a series of statues of sixty different gods, each one related to a specific year in the sixty-year cycle of the Chinese calendar. In times of strife, or to avert trouble, people come to pray and make offerings to the god associated with their year of birth. Further along the street, towards the junction with Upper Station Street, you'll find more shrines, as well as stalls selling incense, oranges and other offerings.

The most interesting temple is further down the street, past the little red Earth God shrine at the junction with Pound Lane which protects the local community. The **Paak Sing** ("hundred names") ancestral hall was originally established in the mid-nineteenth century (and rebuilt in 1895 after the buildings in the area were razed because of plague) to store the bodies of those awaiting burial back in China, and to hold the ancestral tablets of those who had died in Hong Kong, far from their own villages. Usually such halls are for the sole use of one family or clan, but this one is used by anyone who wishes to have an ancestral tablet made for their relatives – there are around three thousand people commemorated here. Several small rooms hold the ancestral tablets – little wooden boards with the name and date of birth of the dead person written on them, and sometimes a photograph, too. Behind the altar there's a courtyard, whose incinerator is for burning the usual paper offerings to the dead, on the far side of which is a room lined with more tablets, some of them completely blackened by years of incense and smoke.

West to Kennedy Town

If you've followed the route through Western district this far, you won't want to **walk** on to Kennedy Town as it's a long haul from Central. Either head straight there on the **tram** down Des Voeux Road, or follow the route outlined below, which takes you most of the way there by **bus**, and allows you to stop off at a couple of points of interest along the way.

The University Museum and Art Gallery

You can also reach the museum direct from Causeway Bay on bus #103 to Pokfulam; it's much quicker than taking the tram.

Bus #3 from the stop in front of Jardine House, on Connaught Road Central, takes around ten minutes to run along Caine Road and Bonham Road. Get off opposite St Paul's College at the university; the entrance to the **University Museum and Art Gallery** (UMAG) is at 94 Bonham Road (Mon–Thurs & Sat 9.30am–6pm, Sun 1.30–5.30pm; free), opposite an old, yellow-plastered house of the type that once lined this residential road.

An impressive museum of Chinese art, the collection is in two adjacent buildings, the **T.T. Tsui Building** and the **Fung Ping Shan Building**, through which you enter (the two are linked on the second floor). Inside, the quiet and uncrowded exhibition is rich in interest, and the quality of the ceramics and bronzes especially makes it worth a detour on the way to Kennedy Town. There's also some interesting furniture and woodcarving, some scroll paintings, and a collection of contemporary Chinese art.

The collection is displayed on a rota basis, so not all the items are on display at any one time. The buildings are also often used for interesting visiting exhibits (see press for details). However, among the items that are worth looking out for are a unique group of **Nestorian bronze crosses**, relics of the Yuan Dynasty (1271–1368 AD) from the Ordos region of northern China. There are 966 crosses in all, each just a few centimetres across and every one different from every other, though only a fraction of the collection is displayed here. The bronzes were decorations for a heretic Christian group, which had survived in central and east Asia since the fifth century AD; most are cruciform in shape, though a few are bird-shaped (also a Christian symbol), star-shaped or circular, or use a swastika pattern. Each has a flat back and a fixed loop, designed to be attached to a leather thong and probably worn as a pendant.

The **ceramics** collection ranges from Neolithic pottery through to the later ruling dynasties. There are many fine pieces here. There is a good selection of items from the Tang Dynasty (618AD – 907AD) including some remarkably realistic glazed camels and horses from tombs, and a selection of three-coloured pottery – dishes, jars, and even an arm- and head-rest. There is white ceramic ware from the Sui to the Song Dynasties, including two Song Dynasty ceramic pillows, one round and one rectangular, both decorated with black and white line-drawings. More colourful are the Ming (1368–1644) and Qing (1645–1911) Dynasty bowls and dishes, displaying rich blues, greens and reds. In other rooms you can find a selection of woodcarvings and some Ming and Qing dynasty furniture, laid out as a room, and a large, impressive Six Dynasties' bronze drum. There are also swords, vessels, bird figures and decorative items, and the contemporary Chinese paintings are also worth a look. On the ground floor of the T.T. Tsui Building there is a good book and gift shop, selling some reasonably priced books on Chinese art.

From the University to Lu Pan Temple

From the museum, you can walk up into the car park and through the grounds of the **University of Hong Kong**, whose buildings have stood here since its foundation in 1912, when it had less than a hundred students (today it has eight thousand). Architecturally, it's less than gripping, though you might as well walk around to Loke Yew Hall on your left, inside which some quiet cloisters planted with high palm trees make for a bit of a break from the traffic outside.

Follow the road through the grounds, cross Pokfulam Road by the footbridge and then walk up the right-hand side of Pokfulam Road (you'll have to dodge under a subway initially). A few hundred metres up, after no. 93 and just before the garages, a white tiled flight of steps leads down on the right to a terrace overlooking the elaborate, multicoloured roof carvings of figures and dragons on top of the **Lu Pan Temple**. It's the only temple in Hong Kong dedicated to Lu Pan, the "Master Builder", blessed with miraculous powers with which (according to legend) he repaired the Pillars of Heaven and made carved birds which could float in the air. He's commemorated every year on the thirteenth day of the sixth moon (see "Festivals", p.284), when building and construction workers hold a feast and make offerings to him in the temple here. At most other times of the year it's dark and empty inside, but take a look at the interesting carvings on either side of the door and above the two internal doors.

From the temple's terrace, steps continue down and turn into a wide, stepped path, Li Po Lung Path, which descends to Belcher's Street, at which point you're in Kennedy Town.

Kennedy Town

Most people come out to **KENNEDY TOWN** for the ride on the tram, and then catch the first one back again to Central. This offers good views of the moored junks and warehouses, but doesn't begin to give you the real flavour of the place – a sort of down-at-heel Sheung Wan, supporting a fascinating mixture of maritime and trade businesses. Much of the district (named after Sir Arthur Kennedy, Governor from 1872 to 77) is built on reclaimed land, piled high with decrepit tenements, the streets busy with traders and jammed traffic. Since the mid-nineteenth century, it's seen its goods arrive and leave by sea, at a harbour that still retains its working flavour, though like so many areas of the island's north coast it's already being changed by land reclamation.

If you've walked down from the university, make for the **tram terminus**, to your left at the end of Catchick Street, passing the large covered market of Smithfield on the way. The **Kennedy Town Abattoir Market** is where the trams turn round before heading back to Central. The waterfront strip a couple of blocks down is known as the **Praya**, a Portuguese word meaning "waterfront" (used more commonly in Macau) that's evidence of the once-strong Portuguese influence in the whole of the South China Sea. The Praya is lined with cranes unloading into the waterfront **godowns** (warehouses). The tram runs back along part of the Praya, but before you go take a walk through the small streets back from the shore. One of them, **North Street**, has a lively food market, and there are basic restaurants and cafés everywhere where you can get a cheap bowl of noodles or a plate of roast meat with rice.

Victoria Peak

HONG KONG ISLAND

As one of Hong Kong's main attractions, you have to visit **VICTORIA PEAK** (or simply "The Peak") sooner or later, and since you're going up primarily for the views, try to do so on a clear day. It's a fine ride up, by bus or tram, and the little network of paths and gardens at the top provides one of the world's most spectacular cityscapes – little wonder that this is *the* place to live in the territory, as it has been since the mid-nineteenth century.

Yet even on the murkiest days The Peak is worth the journey. It's cooler up here, the humidity is more bearable, there's foliage and birdlife, and a series of paths gives you a choice of quiet, shady **walks**. Bring a picnic and enjoy the respite from the crowds below.

The Peak

The 550-metre heights of Victoria Peak give you the only perspective that matters in Hong Kong – down to the outlying islands, the towers of Mid-Levels and Central and the magnificent harbour that frames

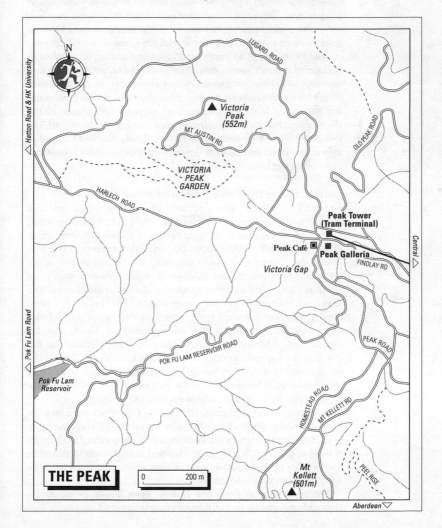

the island. It didn't take long for the new British arrivals to flee the malarial lower regions of Hong Kong Island and set up cool summer homes here. The first path up to The Peak, as everyone soon learned to call it, was made in 1859, and within twenty years it was a popular retreat from the summer diseases and heat below. Access was difficult at first, by sedan chair only, ensuring it remained the preserve of the colony's wealthy elite. Things changed in 1888 with the opening of the Peak Tram, and the first road connection was made in 1924, since which time the territory's power brokers and administrators have settled it properly with permanent houses – and, latterly, apartment buildings – that rival each other in terms of position, views and phenomenal rental value. Along the racist lines of other colonial haunts elsewhere in the world, the Chinese weren't allowed on The Peak except to carry up Europeans and supplies on their backs, and it didn't see its first Chinese-owned house until well into modern times. Now, of course, money is the only qualification necessary for residence here. Among the super-rich currently maintaining houses up here are Martin Lee, barrister and leader of the Democratic Party; the chairman and deputy chairman of the Hongkong bank; members of the Hotung family, the first Chinese to live on The Peak; and various Consul-Generals, business people and assorted celebrities.

Getting there: the Peak Tram and other routes

Since 1888, the **Peak Tram** – actually a funicular railway – has been transporting passengers from a terminal close to St John's Cathedral to the end of the line at Victoria Gap, a 1.4-kilometre ride which climbs up to around 400m above sea level. It's an extraordinary sensation, the 27-degree gradient providing an odd perspective of the tall buildings of Central and Mid-Levels, which appear to lean in on the tram as it makes its speedy journey. The terminals at either end have been renovated over the years, and in 1989 there was a complete overhaul of the tram system itself, during which the old cars made way for computer-controlled replacements. Fundamentally, though, there's been little change. The route's the same as that followed in the late nineteenth century and it's still reputed to be the safest form of transport in the world: there's never been an accident yet, and the track brakes fitted to the wheels can stop the tram on the steepest part of the system within six metres.

Most tourists take the tram right to the top, which disguises the fact that for the whole of its life it's been primarily a commuter system. There are four intermediate stops at which you can flag the tram down – at Kennedy, Macdonnell, May and Barker roads – but unless you've been up before and have time to explore on the way, stick with the journey right to the top.

The tram departs from the **Lower Peak Tram Terminal** (in Garden Road, just up from Citibank Plaza in Central) daily from 7am to midnight, every 10–15 minutes; **tickets** cost $28 return, $18 one-way. If you've just come from the Star Ferry, rather than walk you can head over to the City Hall car park and catch the **free shuttle bus** from there to the Lower Terminal; it runs daily, every twenty minutes from around 9am to 7pm. Be warned that on Sundays and public holidays the queues at the terminal can be interminable: get there early.

You can also reach Victoria Gap by **bus**, a route worth considering in its own right, whatever the queues are like for the tram. Bus #15 runs from the Central Bus Terminal, underneath Exchange Square (every 13–20min; 6.15am–11.30pm), a splendid ride up the switchback road to The Peak offering arguably even more spectacular views than those from the tram; it costs less too – $8.80 – though count on the journey taking at least half an hour. The other service is the #1 minibus from the City Hall car park (Edinburgh Place), a slightly quicker bus ride, though a bit pricier. You can do the trip by **taxi** as well, though this costs around $70 from the Star Ferry.

Walks around The Peak

The trams pull up at the terminal in the **Peak Tower** (sometimes referred to derogatorily as the Flying Wok) which has indoor and outdoor viewing terraces, restaurants and various other facilities. There are further splendid views across the road from the upper terrace of the **Peak Galleria**, a fancy complex with a computerized fountain outside and high-class stores and restaurants with views inside. **Buses and taxis** stop at ranks underneath the Galleria.

The first thing to know is that you're not yet at the top of The Peak itself. Four roads pan out from the tower, one of which, **Mount Austin Road**, leads up to the landscaped **Victoria Peak Garden** – all that remains of the old governor's residence here which was destroyed by the Japanese during their occupation of the territory in World War II. It's a stiff climb, but you're rewarded by more of those views that leave your stomach somewhere in Central.

Nearly everyone makes the circuit of The Peak, a circular walk that takes around an hour depending on how many times you stop for photo calls. A noticeboard beside the Peak Tower details the various walks – follow the green arrows for Victoria Peak Garden, the blue arrows to descend Old Peak Road to May Road tram station, and the yellow arrows for the Harlech and Lugard roads walk.

Start at **Harlech Road** and you'll get the very best views at the end. It's a shaded path for most of the route, barely a road at all, and you'll be accompanied by birdsong and cricket noises as you go: other wildlife is less conspicuous, certainly the mythical monkeys that are said to frequent the trees, but you might catch sight of the odd alarmed snake. First views are of Aberdeen and Lamma; as you turn later into **Lugard Road**, Stonecutter's Island, Kowloon and Central eventually come into sight – with magnificent views of the latter especially, just before you regain the Peak Tower. It's a panorama

Victoria Peak

The Café Deco Bar and Grill in Peak Galleria and the Peak Café, opposite Peak Tower, are two good places for coffee or lunch; see p.255.

If short of time do the walk to Victoria Peak Garden rather than circular

that is difficult to tire of – if you can manage it, come up again at
night when the lights of Hong Kong transform the city into a glittering box of tricks, the lit roads snaking through the buildings, with
Kowloon glinting like gold in the distance.

Walks from The Peak

More adventurous types can make one of several **walks from The
Peak** that scramble steeply downhill to either side of the island. None
takes more than a couple of hours, but you'll need to carry some
water if you're going to tackle them during the heat of the day, as
there are no facilities en route.

Head down Harlech Road from the Peak Tower and after about
five minutes a signposted path runs down to **Pok Fu Lam Reservoir**,
a couple of kilometres away to the south and a decent target for pic-
nics and barbecues. You can reach the same place by way of Pok Fu
Lam Reservoir Road, which starts close to the car park. Either way,
once you're there, the path runs past the reservoir to join the main
Pok Fu Lam Road, from where you can catch any of several buses
back to Central.

You could also do this walk and then catch a bus in the other direction, on **to Aberdeen**, but if you're feeling energetic it's more fun to
walk there direct from The Peak. To do this, follow Peel Rise (down,
and then off, Peak Road) for around an hour, a lovely shaded and
signposted walk down the valley, passing an immense cemetery on
the way into Aberdeen. Huge swathes of graves are strung across the
terraces, which are cut into the hillside above the town, from where
there are great views of the town's harbour.

Finally, if you follow Harlech Road to just past the junction with
Lugard Road, **Hatton Road** makes a steep descent down to the
streets above the **University of Hong Kong**, one possible approach
to Kennedy Town (see p.88) or Mid-Levels (see below).

Mid-Levels

The area halfway up The Peak, back from the flat strip around the
harbour, is known – reasonably enough – as **MID-LEVELS**. A notch
or two down the social scale from The Peak, it retains a reputation as
a swanky, if rather dull, residential area – although the forest of
apartment buildings may strike you as having a rather depressing
concrete-jungle quality.

Easiest access to the area is by the **Central–Mid-Levels Escalator
Link**, an eight-hundred-metre-long series of elevated walkways, esca-
lators and travelators which cuts up the hillside from Central Market
(at the footbridge across Queen's Road by the corner of Jubilee
Street) to Cochrane Street, Hollywood Road and Robinson Road to
Conduit Road. It is capable of carrying thirty thousand people a day

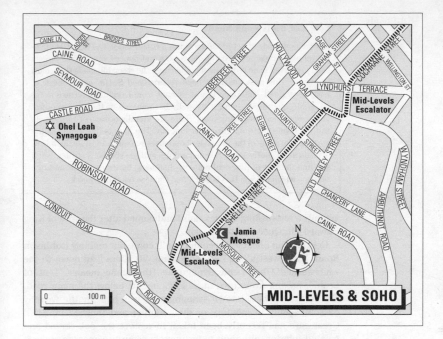

on a one-way system, which changes direction during the day depending on the flow of passengers: uphill from 10.20am to midnight, downhill from 6am to 10am. All told, it's a twenty-minute ride from bottom to top.

Caine Road to Robinson Road

Mid-Levels proper begins just above **Caine Road**, which leads past the Roman Catholic Cathedral (p.77) to Shelley Street, a left turn up which – at no. 30 – is the **Jamia Mosque**, or Shelley Street Mosque, an important place of worship for the territory's fifty thousand Muslims. A mosque has stood on this site since the 1850s, though the present building dates from 1915, a pale-green structure set in its own quiet, raised courtyard above the surrounding terraces. The cool interior isn't always open, but the courtyard behind should be accessible, flanked by three-storeyed houses with wooden, railed balconies hung about with drying washing. The mosque and Islamic Society accounts are pinned to the doors, enabling the faithful to see how much has been spent on sending the Imam on overseas trips.

This part of Mid-Levels is very peaceful, with plenty of incidental interest in the peeling residential terraces around. One of the terraces off the other side of Shelley Street is **Rednaxela Terrace**, an unlikely name even for Hong Kong until you reverse the letters – it's actually a misspelling of Alexandra and named after the wife of King Edward VII, Queen Victoria's son.

Continue up Shelley Street and you'll come out on busy **Robinson Road**. Head west along here and at no. 70 stairs lead down to the whitewashed **Ohel Leah Synagogue** (the name means "Tent of Leah"), lurking in its own quiet leafy hollow below the main road. The territory's best known synagogue, it was built by the wealthy Sassoon family in memory of their mother and finished in 1902. Great care has recently been taken to restore the oak-carved and painted interior, although unfortunately security concerns make it difficult simply to drop in for a look round – bring ID and ask at the entrance if you want to go in.

Wan Chai Gap

HONG KONG ISLAND

The other hillside section of town, east of The Peak, is a better bet than Mid-Levels for an extended stroll: the tree-planted paths leading to **WAN CHAI GAP** offer some fine views and a couple of rather peculiar points of interest. As the approach to the walk is by the #15 bus, it's a tour you can make on your way back from The Peak if you wish.

Along Bowen Road

Get off the #15 bus on Stubbs Road at the stop closest to the Highcliff Apartments and Monte Rosa, two apartment buildings whose signs you can't miss if you're watching out for them. Steps opposite the apartments lead down to **Bowen Road**, which runs west above the city, right the way back to the Peak Tram line.

A short way along Bowen Road, a red-railed path runs up to the right to an **Earth god shrine**, a painted red image on the rock fronted by a neat altar at which there are usually incense sticks burning and small food offerings lying about. Protectors of the local community, earth gods have been worshipped for centuries on the mainland; in Hong Kong you still find them tucked into street corners and against buildings, but this is easily the most spectacularly sited, with views over the Happy Valley racecourse below and the gleaming teeming tower blocks beyond.

Continue along shaded Bowen Road – a marvellous walk at rooftop level – passing further shrines. After about fifteen minutes you'll reach the so-called **Lover's Stone Garden** or Lover's Rock. This steep landscaped area is dotted with more shrines and incense burners, through which steps lead up past a motley succession of red-painted images, tinfoil windmills (representing a change in luck), burning incense sticks and porcelain religious figures. At the top is the **Yan Yuen Sek**, "Lover's Rock", a nine-metre-high rock pointing into the sky from the top of the bluff. It's one of several focuses of the Maiden's Festival, held in mid-August, and since the nineteenth century unmarried women, wives and widows have been climbing up here to pray for husbands and sons. There are also superb views from here.

Beyond the garden, passing various other small shrines along the way, it's about another ten minutes to the junction with **Wan Chai Gap Road**, where a sharp right leads down into Wan Chai itself, past the Pak Tai Temple (p.100). The left turn heads back up to Stubbs Road to Wan Chai Gap proper, and the Police Museum.

The Police Museum

Returning back up to Stubbs Road, a signpost at the junction with Wan Chai Gap Road points to the **Police Museum** (Tues 2–5pm, Wed–Sun 9am–5pm; free), housed in the old Wan Chai Gap Police Station, 100m up Coombe Road at no. 27, on the hill to the right behind the children's playground. Inside, displays chart the history of the Royal Hong Kong Police Force (officially formed in 1844, though there was a volunteer force as early as the initial 1841 landing under the command of Captain William Caine, who was in charge of 32 ex-soldiers) and there are displays of old photos, uniforms and guns, as well as police statements, seized counterfeit cash and a tiger's head (a huge beast shot in Sheung Shui in 1915). Another room displays every kind of drug you've ever heard of and shows you exactly how to smuggle them – hollowed-out bibles and bras stuffed with heroin are just some of the more obvious methods. There's also a mock-up of a heroin factory, and a Triad room, complete with ceremonial uniforms and some very offensive weapons retrieved by the police.

The #15 bus from Central Bus Terminal stops close to the Police Museum, at the junction of Stubbs Road and Peak Road.

Back on Peak Road, you can wait for the #15 bus up to The Peak or follow Wan Chai Gap Road down into Wan Chai. Coombe Road itself climbs on to **Magazine Gap**, another of the hillside passes, from where – if you've got a decent map and lots of stamina – you can eventually strike The Peak from yet another direction.

HONG KONG ISLAND

Wan Chai

East of Central, long, parallel roads run all the way to Causeway Bay, cutting straight through **WAN CHAI**, a district noted for its bars, restaurants and nightlife. Wan Chai first came to prominence as a red-light district in the 1940s, though its real heyday was twenty years later when American soldiers and sailors ran amok in its bars and clubs while on R&R ("rest and recreation") from the wars in Korea and Vietnam. Richard Mason immortalized the area in his novel, *The World of Suzie Wong*, later made into a fairly bad film, whose eponymous heroine was a Wan Chai prostitute. (Oddly, when the film was made in 1960, Wan Chai itself wasn't deemed to be photogenically sleazy enough, filming taking place around Hollywood Road instead.)

The tram from Central to Causeway Bay, via Wan Chai, follows this route: Des Voeux Rd, Queensway, Johnston Rd, Hennessy Rd, then Yee Wo St or Percival St.

Set against those times, present-day Wan Chai is fairly tame, though its eastern stretch is still a decent venue for a night out – packed with places to eat and drink, from *dai pai dongs* on the street corners to restaurants and bars; full of local colour during the day and vibrant at night. However, the westernmost part of Wan Chai, beyond Queensway, belies its traditional, rather seedy good-time image. As the rents have increased in Central, businesses have moved into the area. This development acquired extra momentum with the opening of the enormous **Convention and Exhibition Centre** (CEC) in 1988, and its extension which was finished just in time for the 1997 handover ceremonies to be held there. **Walking** through Wan Chai you can follow one of three parallel main roads – Lockhart Road, Jaffe Road or Hennessy Road – all of which reach down to Causeway Bay. If you're going by **tram**, note that it detours down Johnston Road instead, which is fine for the Pak Tai Temple and Queen's Road East, but not so handy if you're aiming for the Arts Centre, Convention and Exhibition Centre or the waterfront – for these, take the #18 **bus** (not Sun) from Connaught Road Central, the MTR to Wan Chai or the **Star Ferry** from Tsim Sha Tsui to Wan Chai Ferry Pier.

The Arts Centre and Academy for Performing Arts

For events and box office details for the Arts Centre and Academy for Performing Arts, see pp.276–277

Since 1976 much of Hong Kong's arts and drama has been centred on the fifteen-storey **Hong Kong Arts Centre** at 2 Harbour Road. Despite the competition posed by the Cultural Centre in Tsim Sha Tsui (see p.126), it's still a leading venue for drama, film screenings and various cultural events. It also houses the Goethe Institute and, on the fifth-floor, the Pao Sui Loong Galleries (daily 10am–8pm; free), which maintain temporary exhibition space for contemporary art: local and international painting, photography and sculpture. It's worth dropping in to see what's on, especially as you can take advantage of the Arts Centre's good-value café (8.30am–10pm) and restaurant, *The Open Kitchen* (8am–11pm). Both enjoy good views over the harbour.

Close by, on Gloucester Road, the building with the triangular windows houses the **Academy for Performing Arts** (APA). Here many of the productions are performed by the students themselves – local works to Shakespeare – though in addition you'll regularly come across visiting shows, as well as modern and classical music and Chinese and western dance. Other than during performances, the facilities are only open to the students.

Wan Chai

The Convention and Exhibition Centre and around

Massive development over recent years has changed – and will probably continue to change – the Wan Chai harbour front enormously. Huge buildings loom over the water, the grandest of which is the gigantic **Convention and Exhibition Centre**, the largest of its kind in Asia. The curved roofed **CEC Extension**, built on an island of reclaimed land and joined by a bridge to the original centre, was the location for the handover ceremonies in June 1997 – the building was finished only days before the event, although rumour has it that the roof wasn't totally watertight and that some VIPs got dripped on by the typhoon that hit town that night. The CEC is joined to two luxury hotels, the ultra-flash *Grand Hyatt* and the slightly cheaper *New World Harbour View*. Both are aimed at the expense-account business people who come here to wheel and deal at the CEC's various trade exhibitions, but some of the better package tours also put up here.

The Wan Chai Ferry Pier, for services to Tsim Sha Tsui (7.30am–11pm), is across from the Convention and Exhibition Centre.

Further east over Harbour Road, joined to the CEC by raised walkways, is the **China Resources Building**, which contains an interesting Chinese arts and crafts store in its Low Block. A small enclosed, slightly grubby, Chinese garden sits in the middle of the block, while the adjacent building, the Causeway Centre, houses the so-called **Museum of Chinese Historical Relics** (Mon–Sat 10am–6pm, Sun 1–6pm; free), which isn't really a museum but a commercial gallery with the emphasis on the hard sell.

The Sun Hung Kai Centre – the building to the east of the Causeway Centre and linked to it by walkways – contains some good restaurants. See Chapter 7, "Eating", for details.

Central Plaza

With the completion of the 78-storey **Central Plaza** in October 1992, Hong Kong Island acquired another high-tech, high-profile addition to its already cluttered skyline. Sited opposite the Convention and Exhibition Centre, at 18 Harbour Road, it pipped the Bank of China Tower by eight storeys, becoming for a while Asia's tallest building. It's built of reinforced concrete (which, almost interestingly, makes it the world's tallest reinforced concrete building), though more impressive is its height – 374m to the top of its mast – and its extraordinary design and exterior cladding. Triangular in shape, it's topped by a glass pyramid from which a 64-metre mast protrudes: the locals, always quick to debunk a new building, promptly dubbed it "The Big Syringe". As if this wasn't distinctive enough, the American design

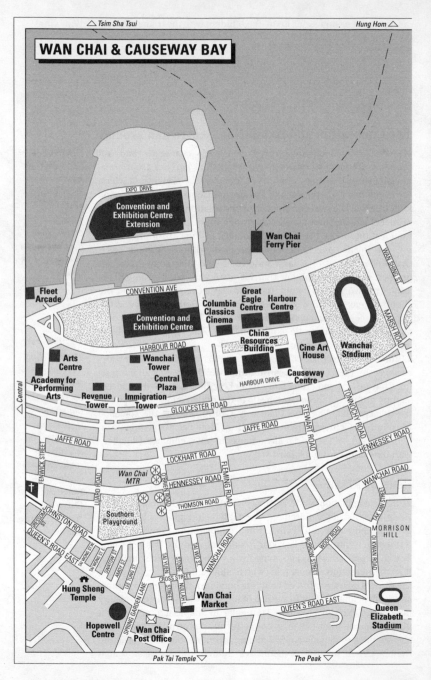

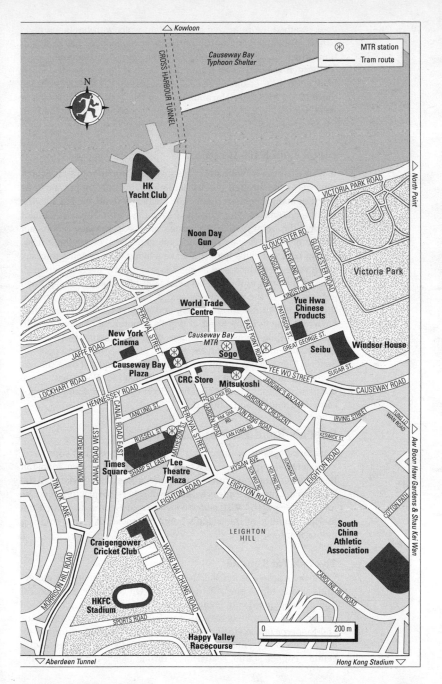

team swathed the reflective glass curtain walls with luminous neon panels, while the spire on top of the pyramid changes has four sections which change colour every 15 minutes to show the time.

Elevated walkways run from inside Central Plaza's soaring lobby back to the CEC or into Wan Chai. To return to Central by bus, take the #18 or #88 from Harbour Road or the #20, #M21, #104 or #260 from Gloucester Road. Alternatively, walk back to the the Wan Chai Ferry Pier for ferry services to Tsim Sha Tsui.

Along Lockhart Road

If Wan Chai has a main street it's probably **Lockhart Road**, which runs west–east through the district before finishing up in Causeway Bay. For many, Lockhart Road – and Hennessy Road one block to the south – epitomizes Wan Chai. Its heady days as a thriving red-light district, throbbing with US marines on leave, are now gone, but that's not to say the area has become gentrified, or anything near. Lots of bars and clubs here still make a living from fleecing tourists, and a walk down the street at night is still a fairly lively experience. Most of the **pubs and clubs** between Luard Road and Fleming Road are rowdy until the small hours, and it's easier to get a late meal in the hundreds of restaurants along and around Lockhart Road than anywhere else in Hong Kong. If there's a merchant or naval fleet in town, Wan Chai occasionally echoes with the sounds of yesteryear, though the most pleasant experience is to stroll down here on Sunday. This is a day off for the Filipina housemaids all over the territory and, after meeting in Central, many head for Wan Chai, where the bars and clubs around Lockhart Road open their doors early for some wild singing and dancing.

Queen's Road East and around

If the brashness of Lockhart and Hennessy roads isn't to your taste, head south towards the more traditional streets between Johnston Road – where the tram runs – and **Queen's Road East**, where all the traditional Chinese trades, from pawnbrokers to printers, can be found. Buses #15, #61 and #64 run from Central to **Wan Chai Market**, another of the island's municipal meat, fish, fruit and veg indoor markets.

The Pak Tai Temple

From the market, Stone Nullah Lane (*nullah* is a ravine or gutter) leads uphill; off to the left, down Lung On Street, is the **Pak Tai Temple**, decorated with colourful, handmade roof pottery and wood carvings. The temple is dedicated to Pak Tai, the Military Protector and Emperor of the North, whose task it is to maintain harmony on earth. He's represented inside the main hall by a tall, seventeenth-century copper statue, seated on a throne facing the door. Up the steps behind, four figures of warriors and scholars guard a second image of the ebony-faced and bearded god, resplendent in an embroidered jacket with a writhing dragon motif. In a room off to the left craftsmen practise the age-old Chinese art of making **burial offerings** from paper and bamboo – delicate works of art that are burned in order to equip the deceased for the afterlife. Around the walls hang half-finished and finished items: a car, an apartment building, houses, money, furniture and aeroplanes, all painted and coloured.

From Wan Chai Post Office to Johnston Road

Queen's Road East leads back towards Central, a route that traces the nineteenth-century shoreline. It's a good street for browsing, with many shops selling **rattanware** products, a tropical cane or palm used extensively here for making furniture. It's all fairly cheap, and often very elaborate. You'll soon pass an old, whitewashed building, the former **Wan Chai Post Office**, opened in 1915 and positively ancient by Hong Kong standards, before reaching the circular **Hopewell Centre**, once Hong Kong's tallest building, though it's now rather dingy and dwarfed by more recent constructions. You can still take the lift to the sixtieth floor, where there's a revolving *dim sum* restaurant.

A hundred metres or so further along, the **Hung Sheng Temple** at no. 131 is built right into the rocks that bear down upon Queen's Road East at this point. A long, narrow temple, it started life in the mid-nineteenth century as a shrine by the sea to the scholar Hung Sheng, a patron saint of fishermen because of his reputed skill in forecasting the weather.

Opposite the temple, over the main road, **Tai Wong Street West** runs through to Johnston Road, the bottom half of the alley filled with birdcages, the air thick with the calls of songbirds, budgies and their dinner – crickets tied up in little bags. A couple of streets further up

Wan Chai

From the temple, you can climb the steps at the back up to Kennedy Road, turn right to Wan Chai Gap Road and follow this road left up to Bowen Road to join the walk described under "Wan Chai Gap", on p.94.

Hundred-Year-Old Eggs

Every Hong Kong market sells a variety of fresh eggs – from ducks, quails, pigeons and geese, as well as chickens – which are inspected under a light by traders for their freshness. Most also contain a massive range of preserved eggs, including the so-called "hundred-year-old eggs". These are made using duck eggs, which are covered with a thick mixture of lime, ash and tea leaves, soaked for a month and then wrapped in ash and rice husks for around six months, when they are peeled and eaten with pickled ginger. They're an acquired taste: green and black inside, with a strong odour, they have a jelly-like consistency and a rich yolk. Salted eggs, too, are produced, covered with a black paste made from salt and burnt rice – in street markets you'll see men plunging the eggs into murky vats of the paste and stirring slowly. These eggs are Cantonese delicacies, which you can try in plenty of restaurants as an appetizer. Failing that, buy a moon cake during the Mid-Autumn Festival (see "Festivals", p.285), which uses the preserved yolk as a filling.

---

is **Gresson Street**, which has a produce market where you can buy freshly peeled bamboo shoots and **preserved eggs** (see the box on p.101) among the more usual items. Johnston Road itself is a handy place to finish up, because you can catch the **tram** from here, either back to Central or on to Causeway Bay.

HONG KONG ISLAND

Causeway Bay

Completing the list of Hong Kong Island's major tourist destinations is **CAUSEWAY BAY**, one of the original areas of settlement in the mid-nineteenth century. There are a few low-key attractions here, and the rattling tram ride from Central is pleasant, but the main reason to visit is for the **shops**. Having said that, there's nothing here you can't find elsewhere in the territory – you'll do as well in Central if you want to go upmarket, or in Tsim Sha Tsui if you want to go down – but Causeway Bay, with its sheer concentration of people and purchasing, does retain a certain atmosphere.

The Bay and the Noon Day Gun

Before land reclamation, Causeway Bay was just that – a large, natural bay, known as Tung Lo Wan in Chinese, that stretched back into what's now Victoria Park and the surrounding streets. The British settled here in the 1840s, erecting warehouses along the waterfront and trading from an area they called East Point. Filled in since the 1950s, all that's left of the bay is the **typhoon shelter**, with its massed ranks of junks and yachts, and **Kellet Island**, now a thumb of land connected to the mainland and harbouring the Hong Kong Yacht Club. Development around here really got under way with the opening of the two-kilometre-long **Eastern Cross-Harbour Tunnel** in the early 1970s, which runs under Kellet Island to Kowloon. With the improved access that this brought (though massive congestion at peak hours threatens its benefit these days), hotels, shops and department stores moved in, effectively making Causeway Bay a self-perpetuating tourist ghetto. White high-rises now girdle the typhoon shelter, but if it's not the prettiest of the territory's harbour scenes, there's something stirring about the hundreds of masts and bobbing boats that carpet the water.

Tram Routes from Causeway Bay

From Causeway Bay to Central: Yee Wo St, Hennessy Rd, Johnston Rd Queensway, Des Voeux Rd.

From Causeway Bay to Happy Valley: Percival St, Wong Nai Chung Rd, Morrison Hill Rd, Ting Lok Lane, Hennessy Rd.

From Causeway Bay to Shau Kei Wan: Causeway Rd, King's Rd, Shau Kei Wan Rd.

In front of one of the modern hotels, the **Excelsior** on Gloucester Road, stands one of Hong Kong's best-known monuments, the **Noon Day Gun**, made famous by one of Noel Coward's better lyrics:

In Hong Kong
They strike a gong
And fire off a noonday gun
To reprimand each inmate
Who's in late
(from *Mad Dogs and Englishmen*)

Apart from a few local street names, this is the only relic of the influence that the nineteenth-century trading establishments wielded in Causeway Bay, in particular Jardine, Matheson & Co, which had its headquarters here. The story is suitably vague, but it's said that the small ship's gun was fired by a Jardine employee to salute one of the company's ships, an action which so outraged the Governor – whose traditional prerogative it was to fire off salutes – that he ordered it to be fired every day at noon for evermore. Some of the short harbour cruises (see "Organized Tours", p.59) take in the daily noon firing of the gun, and there's a more elaborate ceremony every New Year's Eve, when the gun is fired at midnight. The whole story is recorded on a plaque by the gun, which you reach by crossing Gloucester Road: the easiest way is to go through the underground *Wilson* car park on Gloucester Road, next to the *Excelsior*; a tunnel runs under the road and emerges right next to the gun. After all the fuss in print, though, it's simply a rather tiresome gun in a railed-off garden.

Proposed land reclamation means that the Causeway Bay typhoon shelter is slated for redevelopment, although no date has been given for work to start.

From the gun, you can walk further up the tatty promenade towards Victoria Park, where you can negotiate the hire of a **sampan** with the women from the typhoon shelter. Settle on a price and you'll be paddled into the shelter, whereupon other sampans will appear to sell you fresh seafood and produce, which is cooked in front of you and washed down with beer bought from other boats. It's not the bohemian night out it once was, and you'll need to bargain every step of the way.

Victoria Park

The eastern edge of Causeway Bay is marked by the large, green expanse of **Victoria Park**, one of the few decent open-air spaces in this congested city. Built on reclaimed land, it's busy all day, from the crack-of-dawn *tai chi* practitioners to the old men spending an hour or so strolling with their songbirds in little cages along the paths. There's a swimming pool and sports facilities here, too, and if you wander through you might catch a soccer match or something similar. A couple of times a year the park hosts some lively festivals, including a flower market at Chinese New Year, a lantern display for the Mid-Autumn Festival, and the annual candle-lit vigil for the victims of Tiananmen Square on June 4.

At the park's southeastern corner, up Tin Hau Temple Road (by the Tin Hau MTR station), lies Causeway Bay's **Tin Hau Temple**, a couple of centuries old, sited on top of a little hill which once fronted the water. These days it's surrounded by tall apartment buildings, but the temple is one more indication of the area's strong, traditional links with the sea.

Shopping in Causeway Bay

For lunch, try the Sogo supermarket, which has cheap takeaway sushi, sit-down Japanese snack bars and a coffee shop. Or there's good dim sum at Maxim's Chinese Restaurant; see p.239 for a review.

Doing your shopping in Causeway Bay means splitting your time between two main sections. The grid of streets to the north, closest to Victoria Park, contains the modern shops and businesses, many of them owned by the Japanese who moved here in the 1960s. There are large **Japanese department stores** on and around the main Yee Wo Street – Mitsukoshi on Yee Wo Street and Sogo on Hennessy Road – stuffed with hi-tech, high-fashion articles, open late and normally packed with people. The other main store here is the CRC Department Store on Yee Wo Street, one of the biggest of the stores specialising in products from mainland China, such as silk and porcelain. **Vogue Alley**, a covered Art-Nouveau-ish mall running between Kingston Street and Gloucester Road, has clothes as well as restaurants and bars. Benches and a fountain make it a pleasant place to rest your feet.

The area **south** of Yee Wo Street is immediately different. It's the original Causeway Bay settlement and home to an interesting series of interconnected markets and shopping streets. **Jardine's Bazaar** and **Jardine's Crescent**, two narrow, parallel lanes off Yee Wo Street, have contained a street market since the earliest days of the colony (their names echoing the trading connection) and they remain great places to poke around. Cheap clothes abound, while deeper in you'll find *dai pai dongs*, a noisy little market and all manner of traditional shops and stalls selling herbs and provisions. There are similar sights the further back into these streets you go: **Pennington Street**, **Irving Street**, **Fuk Hing Lane** and others all reward making a slow circle through them, perhaps stopping for some tea or to buy some herbal medicine.

Times Square and Lee Theatre Plaza

The most startling fixture in the Causeway Bay shopping scene is the beige blockbuster of a building that is **Times Square**, at Matheson and Russell streets. It's a towering conceit, a vertical shopping mall supported by great marble trunks and featuring a cathedral window and giant video advertising screen. From the massive open-plan lobby, silver bullet elevators whiz up to the various themed shopping floors – levels nine to thirteen, *Food Forum*, are devoted to restaurants and bars, the best of them reviewed in Chapters 7 and 8; at ground level there's a cinema and access to Causeway Bay MTR station.

Times Square is paradigmatic of late twentieth-century Hong Kong architecture, where space can only be gained by building upwards and distinction attained by unexpected design. There's another fine example nearby, at the end of Percival Street, where the architect of the **Lee Theatre Plaza** – faced with an awkward corner on which to build – obviously took New York's Flatiron Building as a starting point. Up soars the steel, glass and marble tower of shops, offices and restaurants, presenting its sharp rib to the front – which is then chopped out above atrium level, leaving the building resembling a face without a nose.

Aw Boon Haw Gardens

The last stop in Causeway Bay is at the gross **Aw Boon Haw Gardens** (daily 9.30am–4pm; free), a landscaped nightmare also known as the "Tiger Balm Gardens" and another of Hong Kong's accredited "sights". It's not strictly in Causeway Bay, though you could easily walk here, up Tai Hang Road. Direct from Central Bus Terminal, the #11 bus takes about twenty minutes, stopping right outside the gardens by a row of souvenir stalls.

The person responsible for the gardens was Mr Aw Boon Haw, a millionaire who made his money by manufacturing Tiger Balm ointment (hence the gardens' other name), which you'll see on sale everywhere in Hong Kong and is used for soothing aches and pains. Aw Boon Haw began building in 1935, and opened this landscaped concoction of coloured statues from religious tales, pagodas, garish staircases and animals to the public in 1950. It's said that the demons and grottoes were a reflection of his subconscious. A fortune teller apparently told the millionaire that he would loose his wealth and die if he stopped building. There's a good view from the top of the Tiger Pagoda (which alone cost a cool million dollars in the 1930s), but otherwise what charm the place had is entirely lost under the daily deluge of visitors. The only vaguely interesting part, the Haw Par Mansion at the gates, is closed to the public. Aw Boon Haw's daughter, the newspaper publisher Sally Aw Sian, has now sold the park to one of Hong Kong's biggest developers, Li Ka-shing, so it is likely to be demolished to make way for more shops, offices and apartments.

Happy Valley

Travel south on the branch tram line from Causeway Bay and you're soon in **HAPPY VALLEY** (or Pau Ma Tei in Cantonese). After Western district, which was soon discovered to be rife with malaria, Happy Valley was one of the earliest parts of the island to be settled, in the hope that it would be healthier and more sheltered. Plenty of houses were built before the "yellow mud stream" that gave Happy

HONG KONG ISLAND was one of the

Valley its original Chinese name (Wong Nai Chung) appeared with a vengeance – the settlers had unknowingly built on a fever-ridden swamp. Everyone moved out, the land was drained and the flattest part turned into a racecourse in 1846, which survives and thrives famously today.

There's not a great deal to see in Happy Valley apart from the racecourse, though a walk up the main **Sing Woo Road** reveals a small market and plenty of good restaurants. The area is a popular expat haunt, many of whom live locally – witness the **Craigengower Cricket Club** at the junction with Leighton Road. Ride on the top deck of the tram past here, however, and you'll discover that there is in fact no cricket pitch inside the walls, crown-green bowling being the preferred sport.

Happy Valley Racecourse

*The Happy
Valley tram
terminus (for
trams to
Causeway Bay
or back
towards Wan
Chai/Central)
is at the back
(southern end)
of the race-
course, on
Wong Nai
Chung Road,
where the
spectator
entrance is.*

The only legal gambling allowed in Hong Kong is on horseracing, and the **Happy Valley Racecourse** is the traditional centre of this multimillion-dollar business (though there's a second racecourse at Sha Tin in the New Territories). It's controlled by the (formerly Royal) Hong Kong Jockey Club, one of the colony's power bastions since its foundation in 1884, with a board of stewards made up of the leading lights of Hong Kong big business. A percentage of the profits go to social and charitable causes – you'll see Jockey Club schools and clinics all over the territory – and such is the passion for betting on horses in Hong Kong (or indeed betting on anything) that the money involved defies comprehension: the racing season pulls in over $91 billion. Jan Morris recounts how even the stabled horses have air-conditioned quarters and swimming pools: "Happy Valley on race day . . ." she maintains "is a bitter, brilliant, grasping place."

The season runs from September to May and there are usually meetings every Wednesday night. Weekend racing is at Sha Tin, but although that course is more modern it doesn't have the intense atmosphere of Happy Valley, which with its tight track and high stands is rather like a Roman amphitheatre. Entrance to the public enclosure is $10, and bilingual staff at the various information desks can help make some sense of the fairly intricate accumulator bets that Hong Kong specializes in. Or give the HKTA's **racing tour** a whirl. They'll take you there, feed you before the races, get you into the members' enclosure and hand out some racing tips: you need to be over 18 and have been in Hong Kong for less than three weeks – and take your passport to any of the HKTA offices at least a day before the race.

*You can book
the racing tour
at any of the
HKTA offices;
see p.45 for
addresses. It
costs around
$500 per
person.*

The cemeteries

It's tempting to think that the series of **cemeteries** staggered up the valley on the west side of the racecourse is full of failed punters. In fact, they provide an interesting snapshot of the territory's ethnic and religious mix: starting from Queen's Road East and climbing up, the five mid-nineteenth-century cemeteries are officially Muslim, Catholic, Protestant Colonial (the largest, with a berth for Lord Napier, the first Chief Superintendent of Trade with China), Parsee and Jewish. For a quick look the #15 bus (to The Peak from the Central Bus Terminal) runs past them, up Stubbs Road, though the best views are the virtually airborne ones from Bowen Road, the path that runs to Wan Chai Gap (see "Wan Chai Gap", p.94). The #6 (to Stanley) also goes by. If you want to explore them at closer quarters (most are open 8am–6pm), take the Happy Valley tram around Wong Nai Chung Road; there's a stop close to the Catholic and Colonial cemeteries, from where you can walk around to further entrances on Stubbs Road.

The South Side

HONG KONG ISLAND

Apart from The Peak, the other great escape from the built-up north side of Hong Kong Island is to the **south side**, a long, fragmented coastline from Aberdeen to Stanley punctured by bays and inlets. Unfortunately, a large proportion of the Hong Kong population escapes there, too, particularly at the weekend. It's worth braving the crowded buses and roads, however, for some of the territory's best **beaches** and a series of little villages which pre-date the arrival of the British in the mid-nineteenth century – though none of them are exactly traditional or isolated these days. Most have somewhere to eat and you needn't worry about getting stuck as the **buses** are all very regular, and run until late in the evening.

The quickest and most obvious trips are to **Aberdeen** and **Repulse Bay** in the west, and most will find time to move on to **Stanley**, too, which is probably the most interesting place to aim for if you've only got the time for one excursion. If you have children in tow, then **Ocean Park** – Hong Kong's biggest theme and adventure park – is a great outing.

Aberdeen

ABERDEEN was one of the few places on the island already settled when the British arrived in the 1840s – the bay here was used as a shelter for the indigenous local people, the Hoklos and Tankas, who fished in the surrounding archipelago. It's still really the only other large town on the island, with more than sixty thousand people, several hundred of them living as they've done for centuries, on sampans and junks tied up in the harbour (though they're gradually being moved into new housing estates). The British named the town that grew up here after their Colonial Secretary, the Earl of Aberdeen, but the Chinese name – Heung Gong Tsai – gives the better hint as to its

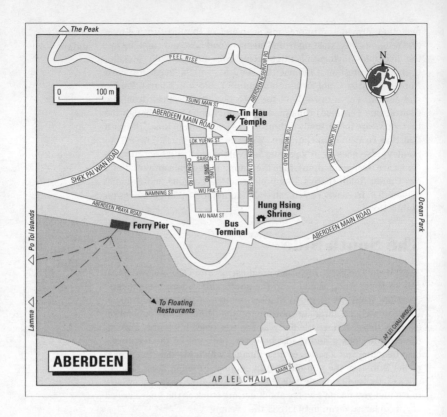

water-based character: "Little Hong Kong", reflecting the attractions
of its fine harbour.

The harbour and town

Arriving by bus, you'll either be dropped at the Bus Terminal or on
Aberdeen Main Road, but it makes no difference since the central
grid of streets is fairly small. It's best to make your way down to the
harbour first, if you want to understand the importance of water to
the town. Cross the main road by the pedestrian footbridge to the
long waterfront and you'll soon be accosted by women touting **sampan rides** through the typhoon shelter, a good way to take a closer
look at the floating homes that still clog the water. A bit of bargaining should get you a twenty- or thirty-minute ride for around $50 a
head. More sampans and ferries at the harbour take you to other
nearby destinations: to Lamma Island (p.183) and the Po Toi group
of islands (see p.110).

Sampans also run across to the large island just offshore, **Ap Lei
Chau** (Duck's Tongue Island); there's also a connecting bridge, with

bus services. This is one of the territory's main boat- and junk-building centres. Wandering around the yards is fascinating, particularly if you can find someone to tell you what's going on. The workshops here are mostly family-owned, the skills handed down through generations, with only minimal reliance on proper plans and drawings. Ap Lei Chau is also becoming a centre for warehouse outlets selling everything from antique furniture to discount fashion. Bus #90 runs here directly from Central's Exchange Square.

Back in town, the small centre is worth a look around, over-touristed these days but with some interesting shops that can enliven a spare hour or so. At the junction of Aberdeen Old Main Street and Aberdeen Main Road, the **Hung Hsing Shrine** is dedicated to a local god who protects fishermen and oversees the weather. Towards the top of town, at the junction of Aberdeen Main Road and Aberdeen Reservoir Road, a hollow in the ground contains the more important **Tin Hau Temple**, built in 1851, with circular-cut doorways inside leading to the furnace rooms. From here, the energetic can continue up the main Aberdeen Reservoir Road, looking for a left turn, **Peel Rise**, which climbs up over the town to the stepped terraces of an immense **cemetery**, offering fine views of the harbour and Ap Lei Chau. The path continues ever upwards from the cemetery, eventually reaching The Peak, though this is really only a climb for those with their own oxygen tents.

Practicalities

It's around half an hour by **bus** to Aberdeen from Central: take the #7 from the Outlying Islands Ferry Piers (via Pokfulam Road, getting off on Aberdeen Main Rd) or the #70 (via Aberdeen Tunnel, getting off at the end of the line) from Central Bus Terminal; or bus #72 from Moreton Terrace in Causeway Bay. Aberdeen's **Bus Terminal** is off Wu Nam Street at its eastern end, close to the water.

There's plenty of choice if you want **something to eat** in Aberdeen. The traditional thing to do is to take the free shuttle ferry from the harbourfront to the two **floating restaurants**, the *Jumbo* and the *Tai Pak*, which are moored in the yacht bays over to the east of the harbour (see p.246 for details), although these are now little more than tourist traps and the food is very poor. Alternatively, take the *kaido* across to **Lamma** and its seafood restaurants (p.185); the regular service stops in the early evening, but it's easy to find a sampan to take you across and pick you up again after a couple of hours – it shouldn't cost more than $120. There are, of course, restaurants in Aberdeen town, too, though they're nothing special. For something more traditional, look out for the *Tse Kee*, a well-known fishball and noodle shop, where you can get a tasty and inexpensive bowl of food. It has two entrances, at 80 & 82 Old Main Street (just up from the bus terminal) and opens from 10.30am to 6pm.

The Po Toi Islands

Aberdeen harbour is the jumping-off point for a visit to the southerly **Po Toi Islands**, an hour's ferry ride away. Like all the minor outlying islands, their population is dwindling, but the main island, with
its prehistoric rock carvings, is good for an isolated stroll and some
secluded swimming. There's a small Tin Hau **temple** near the ferry
pier at Tai Wan, and a couple of simple seafood restaurants that only
really see any business on a Sunday (when you should book). Fans of
John Le Carré will know this island as the setting where the denoue-
ment to his *The Honourable Schoolboy*, a thriller largely set in Hong
Kong, takes place.

Ferries leave Aberdeen on Tuesday, Thursday and Saturday at
9am, but unfortunately they come straight back again and there's
nowhere to stay on the island. Come instead on Sunday, when there
are several departures, including return services to St Stephen's
Beach near Stanley; phone ☎2554 4059 for more details.

Deep Water Bay and Ocean Park

East of Aberdeen, the road cuts across a small peninsula to **Deep
Water Bay**, one of Hong Kong Island's better beaches, offering
views of the cable cars strung across the Ocean Park headland; you
can get there on bus #73 from Stanley and Aberdeen or the #6A or
#260 from Exchange Square in Central.

Ocean Park

The adjacent peninsula is wholly taken up by **Ocean Park** (Mon–Sat
10am–6pm; $140, under-11s $70); a thoroughly enjoyable open-air
theme park, funfair and oceanarium which is adding new rides and
attractions every year. The latest are a pair of Giant Pandas, An-An
and Jia-Jia, for whom a special $80 million complex has been creat-
ed, complete with fake slopes and misting machines to mimic mountain mists.

The **ticket** price seems steep but includes all the rides, shows and
displays on offer – enough in fact to take up most of a day. A couple
of **warnings**, though: there's food on sale inside, but it's plastic and
pricey (hot dogs, burgers and the like), so you might want to take
your own picnic; and try to go early if you're determined to get your
money's worth. It'll take a good four hours to see all parts of the
park, wait in line for a couple of rides and see the marine shows –
with kids, and in the busy summer season, expect it to take longer,
and expect to have to wait for all the popular rides. If you possibly
can, avoid going on Sundays and public holidays.

The first section, the **Lowland** area, is a landscaped garden with
greenhouses, a butterfly house, various parks, a theatre and a kiddies'
adventure playground. There's also a 3D film simulator, and a popular
dinosaur discovery trail, with realistic full-size moving models. This is
also the departure point for the **cable-car**, which hoists you a

kilometre-and-a-half up the mountainside, high above Deep Water Bay, to the **Headland** section. Here, there's a mix of rides (including the truly frightening Dragon roller-coaster built on the headland so that it seems ready to throw you into the sea at 80km per hour) and marine displays – a massive aquarium, a seal, sea lion and penguin sanctuary, and ocean theatre, where performing sharks and whales are put through their paces a couple of times a day. Looming over the lot is the **Ocean Park Tower**, 200m above sea level, giving superb views from its viewing platform and panoramic elevator. After this, you can head down the other side to the **Tai Shue Wan** area, by way of the world's longest outdoor escalator. There are more fine views on the way down, more rides at the bottom, and access to **Middle Kingdom**, a Chinese theme park with pagodas, traditional crafts and all the associated entertainment, including Chinese opera performances.

Back at the main entrance to the Lowland site, you'll find a separate entrance for the adjacent **Water World** (daily 9am–9pm; $65, children $33). This is a water-based fun park – slides and chutes – which gets incredibly packed in the summer, but is just the place to cool down after tramping around Ocean Park.

Bus Routes to Ocean Park

The easiest way to get to Ocean Park is to take the Citybus Tour, which includes round-trip transportation – from Admiralty MTR or Exchange Square Bus Terminal in Central – and entrance to the park. A number of ordinary bus services also pass the park. Unless otherwise shown, buses run every ten to fifteen minutes right up until around midnight, though check the Ocean Park opening times above.

From Aberdeen
#48, #70 and #72 from Aberdeen Main Rd. Get off at the stop before the tunnel.

From Admiralty MTR
Citybus to Ocean Park every 30min (8.40am–3.40pm). You can also buy an all-in-one bus and entrance ticket for around $160 (children half-price) on this route.

From Causeway Bay
#72 from Yee Wo St; get off just after emerging from Aberdeen Tunnel and follow the signs along Ocean Park Rd; on Sun the bus stops right outside Ocean Park. The bus goes on to Aberdeen. Also the #72A, #92, #96 and #592.

From Central Bus Terminal
#70, #75, #90, #97, #260, #262 and #590: get off just after emerging from Aberdeen Tunnel and follow the signs along Ocean Park Rd.

From Hong Kong-side Star Ferry/Edinburgh Place
#6 minibus (daily except Sun and public holidays).

From North Point
#38, #42 and #99.

From Repulse Bay/Stanley
Bus #73 runs past the park en route to Aberdeen.

Repulse Bay

*For Repulse
Bay, take bus
#6, #6A, #61,
#64, #66 (not
Sun) or #260
from the
Central Bus
Terminal; or
the #73 from
Aberdeen.
Buses #6, #6A
or #260, and
the #73, con-
tinue through
Repulse Bay to
Stanley, a fine
ride.*

The next bay along, **REPULSE BAY**, has lost whatever colonial attraction it once had, when the grand *Repulse Bay Hotel* stood at its centre, hosting graceful tea dances and cocktail parties. The hotel was torn down without ceremony in the 1980s (the only surviving portion is the ludicrously expensive *Verandah* restaurant, at 109 Repulse Bay Rd) and the hill behind the bay is now lined with flash apartments contained within a high-rise curvilinear wall washed in pink, yellow and blue. The **beach** itself is clean and wide, though the water quality isn't all it could be, and it's backed by a concrete promenade containing some unmemorable cafés and a garish two-in-one McDonalds and KFC. On summer afternoons tens of thousands of people can descend on the sands – the record is 70,000. Even without such crowds it's all fairly downmarket, though connoisseurs of kitsch may want to amble down to the little Chinese garden at the end of the prom, where a brightly painted group of goddesses, Buddha statues, stone lions and dragons offer some tempting photo opportunities. All in all, it doesn't take great imagination to work out the derogatory, locally inspired tag the bay has acquired over the years – Repulsive Bay.

The people packing the beach are mostly oblivious to Repulse Bay's fairly grim history during World War II. The old hotel was used as a base by British troops, but in 1941, after three days of fierce fighting, the Japanese took the hotel, capturing and executing many of the defenders. Others were taken off to prison camps. The bay here had always been an attractive target for new arrivals: the name itself comes from the ship HMS *Repulse*, from which the nineteenth-century British mopped up the local pirates operating out of the area. If the beach is too crowded for comfort you can try the nearby beaches at **Middle Bay** and **South Bay**, fifteen minutes' and thirty minutes' walk around the bay respectively.

Stanley

The major attraction on the south coast is the village of **STANLEY**, sited on its own little peninsula and with much more appeal than all the other villages along the coast of the island. If you have the time, you could fill a day here, certainly if you're planning to do any shopping in the market.

Stanley has been one of the main areas of settlement throughout the island's history. In 1841 there were two thousand people living here, earning a decent living from fishing; today, it's a small residential place, popular with Westerners as it's only 15km from Central, and fairly lively at most times of the year. The name, incidentally, is down to another nineteenth-century Colonial Secretary, Lord Stanley, but as with Aberdeen the original Chinese name is much more evocative – Chek Chue or "robber's lair", after the pirates who once used the village as a base.

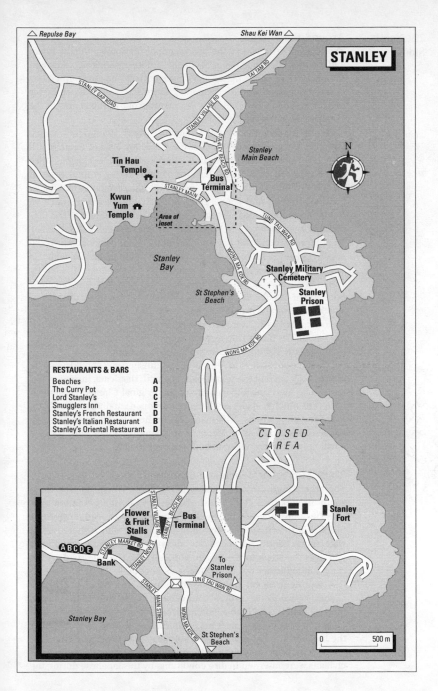

STANLEY

STANLEY GAP ROAD
TAI TAM RD
STANLEY VILLAGE RD
STANLEY BEACH RD

N

Stanley
Main Beach

Tin Hau
Temple

Bus
Terminal

STANLEY MAIN ST.

Kwun
Yum
Temple

Area of
inset

TUNG TAU WAN RD

Stanley
Bay

WONG MA KOK RD

Stanley Military
Cemetery

St Stephen's
Beach

Stanley
Prison

WONG MA KOK RD

RESTAURANTS & BARS

Beaches	A
The Curry Pot	C
Lord Stanley's	C
Smugglers Inn	E
Stanley's French Restaurant	D
Stanley's Italian Restaurant	B
Stanley's Oriental Restaurant	D

CLOSED
AREA

Stanley
Fort

Flower
& Fruit
Stalls

STANLEY VILLAGE RD
STANLEY BEACH RD

Bus
Terminal

A B C D E   STANLEY MARKET RD

Bank

STANLEY NEW ST

To
Stanley
Prison

TUNG TAU WAN RD

STANLEY MAIN STREET

Stanley Bay

WONG MA KOK RD

St Stephen's
Beach

0	500 m

Around the village

The bus will drop you at the **bus terminal** on Stanley Village Road,
and the **main beach** is just a couple of minutes' walk away, down on
the eastern side of the peninsula. This is narrow and stony, ringed by
new development, and for swimming there's actually a much better
one, St Stephen's Beach, about ten minutes out of the centre in the
opposite direction (see below).

Stanley's main attraction is its **market** (daily 10am–7pm), which
straddles the streets and alleys around Stanley Market Road, just a
step over from the bus terminal. It's best known for its cheap clothes
(though they're not actually that cheap), and rooting around turns up
all sorts of fake designer gear, silk, T-shirts, cashmere, handbags,
good sportswear and jeans. The more usual market items such as
food, household goods, crockery are also available, as are the predictable tourist souvenirs. When you've done, you can follow Stanley
Main Street around the bay and across the small roundabout to the
small **Tin Hau Temple** on the western side of the peninsula, which is
now isolated in the centre of a residential development. It's old by
Hong Kong standards, built in 1767, and survived the Japanese
bombing of Stanley in the last war, though a large tiger, the skin of
which hangs on the wall inside, was less fortunate: killed by an Indian
policeman in 1942. There are also lanterns and model ships, remind-
ing you of Tin Hau's role as protector of fishermen, though there's
precious little fishing done from Stanley any more.

When the construction work here has finished you should again be
able to walk beyond the temple, along a path that leads through what
used to be Ma Hang Village, site of the original Chinese settlement
here (but which has already been redeveloped) and up to the **Kwun
Yum Temple** gardens. The main feature here is the six-metre-high
statue of the Goddess of Mercy, Kwun Yum (or Kuan Yin), set in a
pavilion from where you can look out over the bay.

To St Stephen's Beach and Stanley Fort

The other route through Stanley is to follow Wong Ma Kok Road
south through the village, down the peninsula. After about ten minutes (just after the playing field), signposted steps lead down to **St
Stephen's Beach**, a nice stretch of clean sand with a short pier, a
watersports centre, barbecue pits, showers and decent swimming. If
you miss the steps to the beach, you can take the side road on the
right a little further on, by St Stephen's School.

A few minutes on down the main road, the **Stanley Military
Cemetery** has some graves dating back to the mid-1840s, but is
mostly full of those killed defending Hong Kong from the Japanese in
1941 and later in the war. It's a poignant spot to stop and remember
the brave stand that many of the soldiers took, especially since the
other significant landmark, **Stanley Prison** – where hundreds of
civilians were interned in dire conditions by the Japanese during the

*Very
built up
but look
around*

war – is just over the way. Nowadays, it's a maximum-security prison, housing among others forty convicted murderers who were on Hong Kong's death row until 1993, when capital punishment was finally removed from the statute books. The death sentence hadn't been carried out since 1966 – it was always commuted to terms of imprisonment – but the worry was that China might have carried out the penalty after 1997 if it had remained in law. The prison gallows are destined for one of the territory's museums.

The road continues past the cemetery, climbing up to **Stanley Fort**, formerly a British military base. The area is closed to the public (signs here say "Caution – Troops Marching"), though there's nothing to stop you going as far as you're allowed for the views over Stanley Bay.

Practicalities

Stanley isn't far beyond Repulse Bay, reached on **buses #6, #6A** or **#260** (an express) from the Central Bus Terminal, the **#73** from Aberdeen/Repulse Bay, or – coming around the other side of the island – **#63** from North Point and Causeway Bay or bus **#14** from Sai Wan Ho and Shau Kei Wan (which is on the MTR and tram route; see below). The journey takes about forty minutes from Central and is a terrific ride, the road sometimes swooping high above the bays.

You can get something cheap to eat at the *dai pai dongs* on both sides of Stanley Market Road – noodles and the like, and there's fresh fruit on sale, too. More formally (and expensively), there are several good **restaurants**, reviewed in Chapter 7. Stanley being the *gweilo* hangout it is, there are also a couple of **pubs** on Stanley Main Street; the rather unpleasant *Smuggler's Inn* and, more attractively, with seats by the pavement, *Lord Stanley's Bar* – both serve pub food too. You'll also find a **post office** in Stanley (2 Wong Ma Kok Rd), a couple of **banks** and a **supermarket**.

The South Side

Stanley's restaurants are reviewed on the following pages:
Curry Pot *(p.254)*
Pepperonis *(p.256)*
Stanley's Oriental Restaurant *(p.255)*
Tables 88 *(p.255)*

[handwritten note: Get a 6 or 6A drive up spectacular]

The East Coast

There's little incentive to travel much further **east** than Causeway Bay, although the tram ride is fairly entertaining – along King's Road, through **North Point**, the northernmost point of Hong Kong Island, and the residential areas of **Quarry Bay** and **Tai Koo Shing** before reaching **Shau Kei Wan** at the end of the line. Once, this whole stretch was lined with beaches, but the views these days are of high-rise apartments. Improvements in transport infrastructure are making the area more popular: the **Eastern Island Corridor**, a highway built above and along the shoreline, provides some impressive views if you're speeding along it in a car, while the tunnelled **MTR** link across the harbour from Quarry Bay gives much quicker access to Kowloon. It's probably best to go out on the tram – around half an hour from Causeway Bay to the end of the line – and return by MTR; each place along the tram route also has its own MTR station.

HONG KONG ISLAND

Beyond Shau Kei Wan, heading south, you soon escape into more
rural surroundings. Some of the island's best beaches are on its east
coast, the ones around **Shek O** particularly, while you've a better
chance of avoiding the crowds if you take one of the high hill walks
from **Tai Tam Reservoir** which run over the centre of the island.

North Point

If you're going to jump off the tram anywhere before Shau Kei Wan,
NORTH POINT is as good a place as any. Home to many of
Shanghainese descent, it doesn't get many tourists, which isn't surprising since the apartment buildings and busy main road don't hide
any real attractions, but there is a good **market** on Marble Street, a
couple of blocks up from North Point Ferry Pier. It sells cheap T-
shirts and light summer clothes, and has the usual produce section.
Down at the ferry pier, there's a fresh fish market, too, while the **ferries** run across to Hung Hom in Kowloon (7am–9pm). Buses #10
through Central to Kennedy Town and #65 (Sun only) to Stanley also
leave from the ferry pier.

Quarry Bay, Tai Koo Shing and Sai Wan Ho

Further east, the tram runs through **QUARRY BAY**, where the second cross-harbour tunnel terminates. There's an MTR interchange
here, from where you can take the Kwun Tong Line across to
Kowloon.

If you're on the tram, the only other stop you might want to make
is at **TAI KOO SHING**, a massive new development just beyond
Quarry Bay. If you don't have time to see one of the New Territories'
instant cities that have sprung up over recent years, then Tai Koo
Shing will do just as well – a large-scale residential city with its own
monster shopping and entertainment complex, **Cityplaza**, featuring
shops, skating rinks (ice and roller), restaurants, free children's
shows and lots more indoor entertainment – not a bad place for a wet
day. Taikoo Shing has its own MTR station, from which you can walk
straight into Cityplaza.

A few minutes' further on, at **Sai Wan Ho**, you can catch a ferry
across the Lei Yue Mun channel to Sam Ka Tsuen ferry pier, near the
seafood restaurants of Lei Yue Mun (see p.141).

Shau Kei Wan

The tram finishes its run in **SHAU KEI WAN**, which is an important
transport terminus as well as somewhere you could profitably spend
an hour before heading back. Close to the tram terminus you'll find a
Taoist **Shing Wong Temple**, dedicated to the local City God. Further
up, by the water and on the other side of the Eastern Corridor
expressway there's the **Tam Kung Temple**, dedicated to a lesser-
known fishermen's god. The temple was built at the turn of this

century and is the venue of a lively festival, usually at the beginning of May, when it's decorated and there are processions around the whole area. You could take a look around Shau Kei Wan's market stalls, too, before either catching the tram or the MTR back. The **bus terminal** is outside the MTR station; the #2 runs into Central from here.

Shek O and around

The easternmost limb of land on the island holds the enjoyable beach and village of **SHEK O**, reached by bus #9 from the Shau Kei Wan bus terminal, a glorious half-hour ride down a winding road, with splendid views of Tai Tam reservoir, as well as Stanley and the south coast.

The bus drops you at the small bus station in Shek O village. Walk down the road to the roundabout and the **beach** is ahead of you, behind the car park. It's one of Hong Kong's best: wide, with white sand and fringed by shady trees, though it can get very full at the weekend. There's a mini-golf course next to the beach to help while away the afternoon; bikes for rent from the back of the car park; and a few **restaurants** in the village, including a decent one right on the roundabout and a recommended Thai place (see p.260). There's a pub here, too, and on Sunday extra shops and stalls open up, serving food and snacks to the crowds who come down to swim.

The bucket-and-spade shops and basic restaurants in the village don't give the game away, but Shek O is actually one of the swanki-est addresses in Hong Kong, and there are some rich houses in the area. You can get a flavour of things by walking through the village and following the path up to **Shek O Headland**, where you'll be faced with yet more sweeping panoramas. To the right is **Cape D'Aguilar**; to the left, **Rocky Bay**, a nice beach, though with heavily polluted water – which means the sand is generally empty.

Heading back to Shau Kei Wan from Shek O, you don't have to return to the bus station but can instead take a **minibus** from the car park: they're more frequent and a little quicker.

Big Wave Bay

If you want more space and fewer people, head further north to **Big Wave Bay**, where there's another good beach (and one that, unlike Rocky Bay, you can swim from), barbecue pits and a refreshment kiosk. You'll have to walk from Shek O, which takes about half an hour: if you're heading straight here, get off the bus on the way into Shek O at the fork in the road just before the village.

Turtle Cove and Tai Tam Reservoir

The second of the bus routes down the east side of the island, the #14 (also from Shau Kei Wan), runs down the other side of Tai Tam Harbour to Stanley, calling at **Turtle Cove**, a popular beach with all the usual facilities.

The East Coast

On the way back you could call at **Tai Tam Reservoir**, the first in Hong Kong and starting-point for several excellent **hill walks** (maps available from the Government Publications Office; see p.45). The easiest is northwest to Wong Nai Chung Gap, a two-hour walk along Tai Tam Reservoir Road to the Gap, just beyond which is Happy Valley (walk on to Stubbs Road and you can pick up the #15 bus into Central). A longer walk (around 4hr) goes due north along Mount Parker Road, between Mount Butler and Mount Parker, to Quarry Bay, from where you can pick up the MTR or tram back into Central.

Chapter 3

Kowloon

The peninsula on the Chinese mainland, which became part of Hong Kong in 1860 – almost twenty years after the British nabbed the island over the water – is called **Kowloon**, an English transliteration of the Cantonese words, *gau lung*, "nine dragons". The dutiful historical explanation of the name is that the fleeing boy-emperor of the Song Dynasty, who ran to the Hong Kong area to escape the Mongols in the thirteenth century, counted eight hills here, purported to hide eight dragons – a figure which was rounded up to nine by sycophantic servants who pointed out that an emperor is himself a dragon. Since that flurry of imperial attention, Kowloon's twelve square kilometres have changed from a rolling green peninsula to one of the most built-up areas in the world.

There was an unruly Chinese village here, at the tip of the peninsula, since the very earliest days of the fledgling island colony across the harbour, alongside fortified walls and battlements protecting a Chinese garrison. But after the peninsula was ceded to the British, development gathered pace, and colonial buildings and roads were laid out as the growing population spread across from Hong Kong Island. Today, that gradual development – from village to colonial town – has been subsumed into the packed, frenetic region of Kowloon that is **Tsim Sha Tsui**, which takes up the tip of

---

KOWLOON: TOP TEN ATTRACTIONS

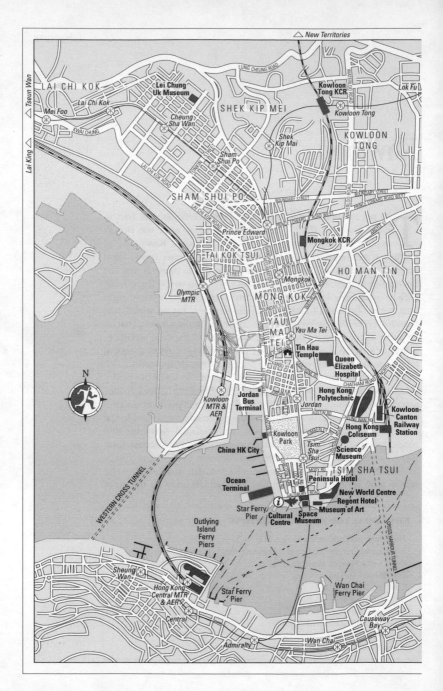

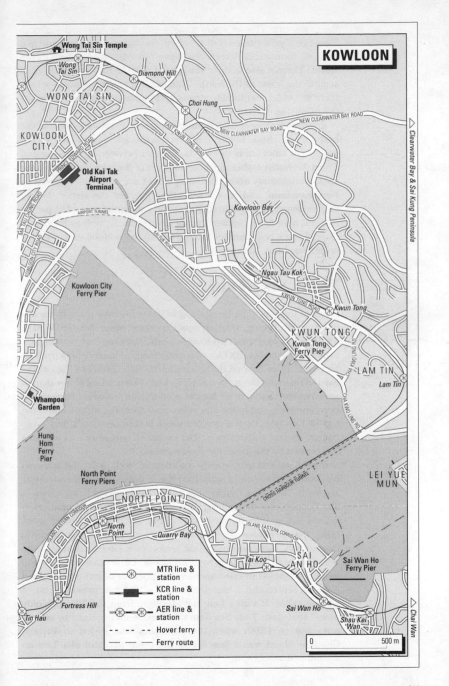

KOWLOON

the peninsula. This is where many visitors stay, eat and – almost Tsim Sha Tsui's *raison d'être* – shop, finding endless diversion in a pack of commercial streets that have few equals anywhere in the world. There's also a more traditional side to Kowloon, however, seen in the areas to the north – **Yau Ma Tei** and **Mongkok** – where there are older, explorable streets and buildings that have retained their Chinese character.

Kowloon proper ends at **Boundary Street**, about 4km north of the harbour. In 1860, before the New Territories were added to the colony (in 1898), this formed the frontier between Hong Kong and China. Nowadays, although officially part of the New Territories, the areas immediately above Boundary Street are sometimes known as **New Kowloon**, and have a few attractions for the visitor. Mostly they're densely populated shopping and residential areas, but people ride out here for a couple of minor diversions, as well as for one of Hong Kong's best temples and the trip to the seafood-eating village of **Lei Yue Mun**, to the east.

Tsim Sha Tsui

If lots of tourists think Hong Kong Island is the only place in the territory worth seeing, then an equal number swear that **TSIM SHA TSUI** is the only place to shop – both mistakes, but both understandable given the HKTA's encouragement of such beliefs in all its literature. Even beyond the brochures, though, Tsim Sha Tsui works hard to maintain the myth that all tourists like nothing better than to spend money: most of its notable monuments are swish commercial developments, and in the kilometre or so from the waterfront to the top of Kowloon Park a devoted window-shopper could find every bauble, gadget and designer label known to humanity – as well as a few pirated by the locals for good measure.

If it all sounds gruesomely commercial, well, it is. But it would be churlish to knock it, since the type of enterprise and endeavour shown in Tsim Sha Tsui are the main reason Hong Kong exists at all. Despite the dampening effect of the Asian economic crisis there's still an infectious vibrancy in the "get rich, get ahead" mentality that pervades the streets, and it rubs off in the markets, restaurants, bars and pubs that make Tsim Sha Tsui one of the best places in Hong Kong for a night out. Look close enough, and amid the morass of consumerism are pockets of culture – a good cultural centre and a museum or two – that can provide a bit of serious relief. It's all a long way, though, from the "sharp, sandy point" that gave Tsim Sha Tsui its Chinese name. Hard to believe now, but in 1860, when the peninsula was ceded to Britain, Chatham Road was a beach and the point of Tsim Sha Tsui an abandoned sandy spit.

The Tsim Sha Tsui Skyline

Major land reclamation and redevelopment projects are changing the face of the neighbourhoods immediately to the north (see "Yau Ma Tei" and "Mongkok", p.132 and p.136), a process which Tsim Sha Tsui has still largely escaped. What is set to change, however, is the skyline. Until now, views of Tsim Sha Tsui have, understandably, been compared unfavourably to the megalopolis of Central over the water, a legacy of the height restrictions imposed during the days when the old Kai Tak airport was in use. Dodging mountains was difficult enough for the pilots; having to circumnavigate skyscrapers as well would have been too much. However, now the airport has moved to Chek Lap Kok, Kowloon building restrictions are set to be relaxed – within a few years there's expected to be a forest of towers, spires and needles to match those of Central. There are even ambitious plans to build what would be the world's tallest building here, on top of the Kowloon Airport Express railway station. The proposed 97-storey Kowloon Landmark Tower would be 574m high, easily dwarfing the 374m of Central Plaza – currently Hong Kong's tallest – as well as the 452-metre Petronas Towers in Kuala Lumpur, which currently hold the world record. The silvery glass structure would contain space equal to 31 football pitches, housing a six-hundred-room luxury hotel, offices, restaurants and an observation deck.

Around the Star Ferry

Walk down the gangway from the **Star Ferry** into its Kowloon-side terminal and you're at the best possible starting place for a tour of Tsim Sha Tsui. The concourse is full of newspaper sellers and hawkers; there's an HKTA office (Mon–Fri 8am–6pm, Sat & Sun 9am–5pm), a decent bookshop and, just opposite, a major bus terminal and taxi rank.

*For bus routes
from the Star
Ferry, see
p.50.*

On the waterfront, on the left as you leave the Star Ferry terminal, tour boats are tied up. Beyond them steps and escalators lead up into an immense, gleaming, air-conditioned shopping centre, reputedly the biggest in Asia (although that's not a unique claim in Hong Kong) – all marble, swish shops and bright lights. It's actually several interconnected centres which run along the western side of Tsim Sha Tsui's waterfront, with luxury apartments studding the upper levels and commanding priceless views over the harbour. The first section, **Ocean Terminal**, which juts out into the water, is where cruise liners and visiting warships dock. There's a passport control here for the international passengers, who usually spend a night or two in Hong Kong before sailing on. Exclusive boutiques line the endless and confusing galleries that link Ocean Terminal with the adjacent **Ocean Centre**, and, the next block up, **Harbour City** – more shops, a couple of swanky hotels, and clothes and shoes the price of a small country's defence budget.

If you want to get back down to street level, signs everywhere will direct you out on to **Canton Road**, which runs parallel to the water. Continue up it, north, past Harbour City, and you'll pass the **China**

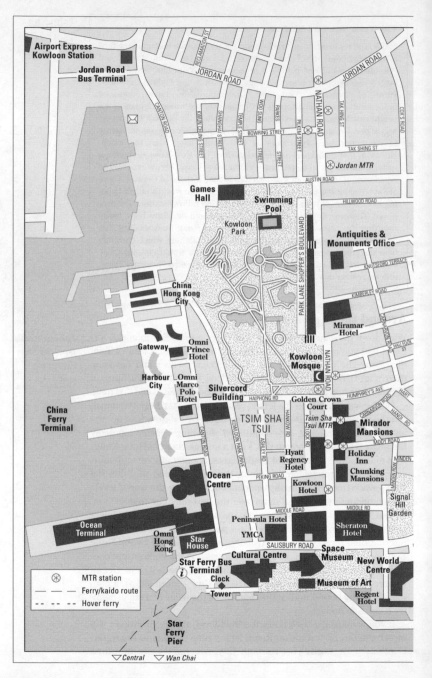

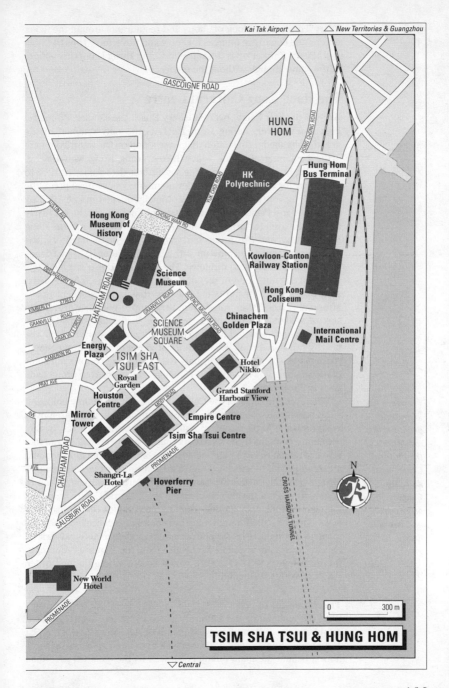

GASCOIGNE ROAD

HUNG HOM

HK Polytechnic

Hung Hom Bus Terminal

Hong Kong Museum of History

CHONG WAN RD

Science Museum

Kowloon-Canton Railway Station

Hong Kong Coliseum

GRANVILLE ROAD

SCIENCE MUSEUM SQUARE

Chinachem Golden Plaza

International Mail Centre

Energy Plaza

TSIM SHA TSUI EAST

Hotel Nikko

KIMBERLEY STREET

GRANVILLE ROAD

GRAN VIEW ROAD

CAMERON RD

Royal Garden

Grand Stanford Harbour View

PRAT AVE

Houston Centre

Mirror Tower

Empire Centre

Tsim Sha Tsui Centre

CHATHAM ROAD

Shangri-La Hotel

Hoverferry Pier

CROSS HARBOUR TUNNEL

SALISBURY ROAD

N

PROMENADE

New World Hotel

PROMENADE

0   300 m

TSIM SHA TSUI & HUNG HOM

Ferry Terminal, a block of shops and restaurants around the ticket offices and departure lounges for ferry and hoverferry trips to China and Macau. Further up is the adjacent China Hong Kong City – more of the same, though without the ferries.

The Hong Kong Cultural Centre

Back at the Star Ferry, over Salisbury Road, the slender, 45-metre-high clock tower, dating from 1921, is the only remnant of the grand, columned train station that once stood on the waterfront here – the beginning of a line which linked Hong Kong with Beijing, Mongolia, Russia and Europe. The station was demolished in 1978 to make way for a new waterfront development, whose focal point, the Hong Kong Cultural Centre, was officially opened in late 1989 by the Prince and Princess of Wales. Its construction put the cat firmly among the architectural pigeons. Given six hundred million Hong Kong dollars and *the* prime harbourside site in the territory, the architect managed to come up with a building that has few friends and – astonishingly – no windows. The plain exterior is shaped like a vast winged chute; one of the more generous interpretations sees it as a bird's wings enshrouding the egg that is the adjacent Space Museum. A brick skirt runs around the entire complex, forming a sort of wedge-shaped cloister, while out in the landscaped plaza, lines of palm trees sit either side of a man-made water channel. The nearby two-tiered walkway offers great views of Hong Kong Island, particularly at night, and is usually full of courting couples, amateur photographers and fishermen. From here, the waterfront promenade goes to Hung Hom.

There are free foyer programmes and exhibitions at the Cultural Centre most days; see Chapter 10 for other events and box office details.

Whatever you think of the Cultural Centre, it's certainly bold, and – the contentious design aside – represents an optimistic attempt to position Hong Kong as one of Asia's major cultural centres. Inside, the centre contains three separate venues – a concert hall, grand theatre and studio theatre – as well as a pleasant book and gift shop and a café. Adjacent blocks harbour an art museum, a space museum, a library, cinema, restaurants and a small formal garden. If you're unable to catch a performance inside the Cultural Centre, consider taking one of the daily guided tours of the complex (in English daily at 12.30pm; $10), although tours are sometimes cancelled when the theatres are being used for performances or rehearsals – call first to check. Tickets are available in advance from the enquiries counter in the main foyer (☎2734 2009), which is also where the box office (☎2734 9009) is situated.

The Museum of Art

With the opening of the Cultural Centre came the eagerly awaited establishment of Hong Kong's Museum of Art (Mon–Wed, Fri & Sat 10am–6pm, Sun 1–6pm; $20), six well-appointed galleries on three floors, behind the main building. As well as the galleries described below, there's space for touring exhibitions of both Western and Chinese artefacts; audio guides are available for $10. A **museum shop** by the entrance stocks books, gifts and some original and reproduction Chinese paintings – unfortunately the staff aren't very helpful, so don't expect much advice if you want to buy.

The museum's permanent exhibitions begin on the second floor with the **Xubaizhai Gallery of Chinese Painting and Calligraphy**, primarily featuring a series of hanging scrolls of ink on silk, some up to 4m high. Many depict rural Chinese scenes, though there are simpler representations, too – Jin Nong's podgy and overweight *Lone Horse* (1761) is an appealing example. Next door, the **Contemporary Art Gallery** features changing exhibitions of mostly post-1950s work, including silkscreen painting, calligraphy, ceramics, and paintings by Hong Kong artists in both Western and Chinese styles.

These galleries are captivating enough, but the museum's real highlights are up on the third floor. The gallery devoted to **Chinese Antiquities** alone contains more than five hundred exhibits, from daily artefacts and decorative items to burial goods. The Han Dynasty (206 BC–220 AD) ceramics are particularly interesting – look out for a green-glazed watchtower, just over a metre high. Pot-bellied tomb figures from the Tang Dynasty (618–907 AD) and an entire side gallery of carved bamboo brush pots and ornamental figures complete the collection. The ceramics section shades into the **Chinese Decorative Arts Gallery**, laden with carved jade, ivory and glassware, as well as a collection of costumes, embroidery and textiles. Also on the third floor, you'll find the **Historical Pictures Gallery**, which displays a selection (from a larger permanent collection) of about sixty oils, watercolours, drawings and prints that trace the eighteenth- and nineteenth-century development of Hong Kong, Macau and Guangzhou as trading centres, as seen by both western and local artists. The collection includes the earliest known painting of Hong Kong; executed by William Havell in 1816, it depicts a waterfall near Aberdeen. Other works, by army draughtsmen, traders and local professional painters (known as "China trade painters"), are of great historical interest: an 1854 oil painting of Victoria, as Central was then called, shows just a few score buildings ranged along the empty waterfront, while contemporary paintings of Guangzhou show it as a thriving centre of warehouses and junks, its buildings sporting the flags of various trading nations. The museum ends on the fourth floor with the **Chinese Fine Art Gallery**, which shows exhibits from a collection of three thousand works, including modern Chinese art and animal and bird paintings.

The Space Museum

Opened in 1980 as the first stage of the Cultural Centre, the **Space Museum** (Mon & Wed–Fri 1–9pm, Sat & Sun 10am–9pm; $10) is devoted to a hands-on display of space- and astronomy-related objects and themes. The Hall of Space Science is well laid out, with push-button exhibits, video presentations, telescopes and picture boards which take you through astronomical and space history, with a perhaps understandable Chinese bias – you learn that the Chinese were the first to spot Halley's Comet, the first to plot star movements and the first to use gunpowder. Upstairs, the Hall of Astronomy is duller, a brief introduction to all things solar, with explanations of eclipses, sun spots and the like. Most people (certainly most children) will want to catch one of the regular daily showings at the Space Theatre ($32; 6- to 15-year-olds, students and senior citizens $16; under 6s free), which has a choice of films shown on the massive Omnimax screen, providing a thrilling sensurround experience – worth going to if you've never seen one before. Call ☎2734 2722 for show times.

Along Salisbury Road

Over the road from the Space Museum stands an equally recognizable monument, and one of Tsim Sha Tsui's few throwbacks to colonial times: the **Peninsula Hotel**. Built in the 1920s, its elegant wings reaching around a fountain, the hotel used to lord it over the water before land reclamation robbed it of its harbourside position – a high, central tower, boasting top-floor picture windows and the splendid *Felix* restaurant (see p.255), has rescued its erstwhile views. It was the *Peninsula* that put up the travellers who had disembarked from the Kowloon–Canton railway; for decades the glitterati frequented it as they frequented other grand Asian colonial hotels like the *Taj Mahal* in Bombay and *Raffles* in Singapore. It's still one of the most expensive places to stay in Hong Kong and one of those with the most social clout, and even if your budget won't stretch to a room here, you can drop into the opulent lobby for afternoon tea – serenaded by a string quartet – and a bit of window shopping in the glitzy arcades. It's worth knowing that if you're dressed "inappropriately" (no shorts or sandals) you'll be gently steered to the door whatever the size of your bank balance.

If you book far enough in advance, you can get a room at the **YMCA** (see p.226), next door to the *Peninsula* but only a fraction of the price. Further along Salisbury Road, past the *Sheraton* at the bottom of Nathan Road, the *New World* and the *Regent* form part of the waterfront **New World Centre** – a hotel and shopping complex built on reclaimed land. The lobby of the *Regent* has twelve-metre-high windows looking out over the harbour, which make a humble drink a spectacular affair; if you work your way outside to the **waterfront promenade**, you can walk all the way up to Hung Hom or back to the Star Ferry.

Nathan Road

Between the *Peninsula* and the *Sheraton* hotels, **Nathan Road** is Tsim Sha Tsui's – and Kowloon's – main thoroughfare, running north from the waterfront all the way to Boundary Street. This is the commercial artery for the whole area, buildings crowding to a point in the distance, festooned with bright neon signs. It's always packed and noisy, split by fast-moving traffic which stops occasionally at the periodic lights to allow an ocean of people to cross from side to side.

Turn-of-the-century photographs show Nathan Road as a tree-lined avenue, with grass verges and no traffic. Built originally in 1865 (and called Robinson Road), there was little prospect of its development until Sir Matthew Nathan, a professional engineer, took up the Governorship of Hong Kong in 1904. Under his orders the road was widened and extended as far north as Yau Ma Tei, but even with the gradual enlargement of Tsim Sha Tsui, the road remained so underused it gained the sobriquet "Nathan's Folly". In 1950 there was only one building more than ten storeys high and not until the 1960s was there real development, when large hotels began to appear in Tsim Sha Tsui and the shopping arcades sprouted.

Shopping on Nathan Road

Today, other than eating and drinking in the surrounding streets, most pedestrians on Nathan Road are intent on trawling the **shops** that have provided the road with its modern tag, the "Golden Mile". It's not just the neon along here that glitters, but the windows too – full of gold and silver, precious stones, hi-fi and cameras, watches and calculators, clothes, shoes and fine art. Window-shopping can be more of a struggle than usual since, apart from the crowds, you also have to contend with hustlers and the pavement hawkers selling goods at knock-down (and knock-off) prices – you'll soon tire of the insistent offers of a "copy watch".

*For full details
of shopping in
Tsim Sha Tsui
and elsewhere,
see Chapter 12.*

As well as the mainstream jewellery and hi-fi shops, Nathan Road has its own **shopping centres**, some of which – in the hotel galleries, like that of the *Hyatt Regency* – are as impressive as those anywhere else. It also has a selection of fairly grim mansion blocks, whose crumbling corridors contain numerous shops and stalls – fun to browse through even if you don't find a real bargain. The best known is **Chungking Mansions**, at nos. 36–44, on the east side before the *Holiday Inn*, which is notorious for its plethora of guest houses and Indian restaurants, although there are some great places to buy cheap silk, T-shirts and other clothes at the shops on the ground and first floors. **Mirador Mansions**, further up on the same side of the road (nos. 56–58), is more of the same.

Buses that head up and down **Nathan Road** include the #1, #1A, #2, #6, #6A, and #9. The **MTR** is less useful for short hops; the five stops on Nathan Rd are Tsim Sha Tsui (for Chungking Mansions and Kowloon Park), Jordan (for Jordan Rd), Yau Ma Tei (Waterloo Rd), Mongkok (Argyle St) and Prince Edward (Prince Edward Rd) – with around 3km between the first and last.

The side streets off both sides of Nathan Road are alive with similar possibilities – just saunter around and take your pick. On the east side, **Granville Road** in particular is famous for its bargain clothes shops, though you'll also find clothes, accessories and jewellery stores all the way along **Carnarvon, Cameron** and **Kimberley** roads. On the west side of Nathan Road, department stores and shopping centres reign: there's a large Yue Hwa Chinese Products store at the corner of Peking Road and Kowloon Park Drive, with HMV's megastore nearby.

Kowloon Park

There's breathing space close by in **Kowloon Park** (daily 6am–midnight), which stretches along Nathan Road between Haiphong Road and Austin Road. Typically, for such a built-up territory, it's not actually at ground level, but suspended above a "Shoppers' Boulevard"; steps lead up into the park from Nathan Road. Parts of it have been landscaped and styled as a Chinese garden with fountains, rest areas, children's playground and an aviary (daily: March–Oct 6.30am–6.45pm; Nov–Feb 6.30am–5.45pm; free), and there's also an outdoor and indoor swimming complex (daily 6.30am–9.30pm; $19), an indoor games hall and a sculpture walk (illuminated at night) featuring work by local artists.

In the southeastern corner of the park at 105 Nathan Road is the large **Kowloon Mosque**, built in the mid-1980s for nearly $30 million to serve the territory's fifty thousand Muslims (of whom about half are Chinese). It replaced a mosque originally built in 1894 for the British Army's Muslim troops from India, and retains its classic design, with a central white marble dome and minarets – surprisingly, it doesn't look out of place, standing above the street. Sadly, however, unless you obtain permission in advance (☎2724 0095), you're not allowed in for a further investigation of the mosque and Islamic Centre it contains.

Leave the park at the southern end and you can drop down to Haiphong Road and its covered **market** at the Canton Road end (daily 6am–8pm).

Tsim Sha Tsui East

After the rambling streets and businesses of Tsim Sha Tsui, **TSIM SHA TSUI EAST** couldn't be more different. Starting at the New World Centre, all the land east of Chatham Road is reclaimed, and the whole of the district has sprung up from nothing over twenty years. It is almost exclusively a wedge of large hotels, connected shopping centres and expensive restaurants and clubs, which you can bypass by sticking to the **waterfront promenade** that follows the harbour around from the Cultural Centre. From here there are superb views across the harbour to the island, and the chance to be horribly fascinated by whether or not the people fishing off the promenade are actually going to eat what they haul out of the vile water. Halfway up, outside the *Shangri-La* hotel, there's a small pier from where you can catch a **hoverferry** over to Queen's Pier on Hong Kong Island.

Hong Kong Science Museum

The **Hong Kong Science Museum**, at 2 Science Museum Road (Tues–Fri 1–9pm, Sat & Sun 10am–9pm; $25), is an enterprising venture worth setting aside a few hours for, certainly if you have children to amuse. Its three floors of hands-on exhibits are designed to take the mystery out of all things scientific – since this includes everything from the workings of kitchen and bathroom appliances to the finer points of robotics, computers, cellular phones and hi-fi equipment, even the most Luddite of visitors should be tempted to push buttons and operate robot arms with abandon. Avoid Sundays if you can, and try to go early or late in the day, since the attraction palls if you have to wait in line for a turn at the best of the machines and exhibits.

Hong Kong Museum of History

The **Hong Kong Museum of History**, next to the Science Museum (Mon–Thurs & Sat 10am–6pm, Sun 1–8pm; $20), shows a cross-section of the museum's enormous archeological and ethnographic collection, covering the history of Hong Kong from Neolithic times to the present day. Old photographs, prehistoric finds and other cultural relics add up to an hour or so well spent here. The Special Exhibition Gallery hosts visiting shows from overseas. Check to find out what's on (☎2724 9042).

Tsim Sha Tsui East

Minibus #1M runs from the Star Ferry to Tsim Sha Tsui East (Granville Square). For the Science Museum, take bus #5, #5C or #8 from the Star Ferry.

Hung Hom

Keep to the Tsim Sha Tsui East promenade, past the line of hotels, and eventually (beyond the International Mail Centre) steps take you up into the labyrinthine corridors and overhead walkways which feed into one of several destinations in **HUNG HOM**, the next neighbourhood to the north. All told, it's a twenty- to thirty-minute walk from the beginning of the promenade.

The most noticeable building is the **Hong Kong Coliseum**, completed in 1983, an inverted pyramid which contains a 12,500-seater stadium, used for sports events and concerts. Remarkably, it's built over the concourse and platforms of the **Kowloon–Canton Railway (KCR) Station**, relocated here in 1975 once it had been decided to demolish the old station down by the Star Ferry. This is where you'll have to come if you want to take the train to China, a route which has

Hung Hom

Heading directly for the Kowloon KCR Station, take bus #5C or #8A from the Star Ferry.

The UCC Coffee Shop, in the Whampoa Garden ship, serves a superb array of different types of coffee, as well as iced tea and snacks.

been in existence since 1912 and which provides a link with London via the trans-Siberian railway. There are also KCR trains to the New Territories from here.

Land reclamation has been continuing in earnest in this area for several years now, filling in a kink in the shoreline. A signposted walkway leads you to the **Hung Hom Ferry Pier**, another ten minutes' walk north from the station, from where services go to Central, Wan Chai and North Point.

If you're coming down this way, it's worth taking the time to look at **Whampoa Garden**, near the ferry pier, a housing and commercial development built around an old dry dock; bus #8A runs here directly from the Star Ferry via Hung Hom KCR Station. The Kowloon Dockyard operated on this site from 1870 to 1984, but with the land filled in around it, the dock now supports an impressive hundred-metre-long concrete "ship", open to the public and stacked with shops, restaurants and recreational facilities. Climb up to the top deck for a surreal view of the surrounding buildings – across to tenth-floor apartments from a ship that looks like it could sail at any minute. North of here is the main Hung Hom shopping area, which has a few **factory outlets** selling clothes and jewellery in the block of streets between Man Yue Street and Hok Yuen Street and in the Kaiser Estates building. You can reach these directly on bus #5C from the Star Ferry/KCR Station.

Yau Ma Tei is a 20-minute walk up Nathan Rd; or take the bus (#1, #1A, #2, #6, #6A, #7 or #9 from Star Ferry), the MTR to Jordan or Yau Ma Tei. The Jordan to Central ferry service no longer runs.

Yau Ma Tei

North up Nathan Road, beyond Jordan MTR, you enter an older part of Kowloon, **YAU MA TEI**, one of the first areas to be built upon after the English acquired Kowloon in 1860 and now, with a pleasing symmetry, at the heart of Hong Kong's most wide-ranging development programme. The **West Kowloon Reclamation Project** has reclaimed an entire district from the water on the west side of the peninsula here, with the new land earmarked for residential, office and retail buildings centred on the **West Kowloon rail terminal**, from which the Airport Express and Tung Chung MTR lines head out west to the airport.

The name of the district recalls the sesame seed farming that the first inhabitants made their living from (*ma* is sesame). The most interesting streets are the long straight ones north of Jordan Road, on the west side of Nathan Road, which – like Western district on Hong Kong Island – conceal a wealth of traditional shops, businesses, markets, *dai pai dongs*, and even a temple of some repute: in particular, Yau Ma Tei is the site of the **Jade Market** and the **Temple Street Night Market**, neither of which should be missed.

The streets

Starting from Jordan Road, it barely matters which street you follow north. Most are a pot-luck mix of endless fascination, though certain blocks and areas are devoted to specific trades. One block south of Jordan Road, **Bowring Street** has an outdoor market selling clothes and other household items, plus a number of Chinese medicine shops; you can exit Jordan MTR directly onto the street. Most of the other major streets run parallel and to the west of Nathan Rd, though some are broken into two parts, with a gap between Kansu and Public Square streets, which can be confusing. One of these, **Shanghai Street,** contains an eclectic and attractive mix of shops and stalls selling items as diverse as bright red Chinese wedding gowns, embroidered pillow cases, lacquered shrines, statuettes, chopping blocks, incense and kitchenware. It is also famous for its red and yellow Chinese signs, offering a range of exotic and specialist sexual services.

Running parallel and to the west is **Reclamation Street.** Here, between **Nanking** and **Kansu** streets, you'll find one of the most intense street markets in the area, concrete proof that the Chinese prefer to buy their food while it's still hopping about. You'll see fish, frogs and turtles cut up on slabs while still alive, calf's heads on the pavements, trays of chicken hearts and livers, and butchers wielding bloodied cleavers. It does little for the appetite, but there are *won ton* makers scattered here and there and *dai pai dongs* between Ningpo and Saigon streets. Just to the east, down **Saigon Street**, there's a small enclave of pawnshops and *mahjong* schools. At the end of the open-air market, at Kansu Street, the **Yau Ma Tei Covered Market** is a more sober affair. Just west of here on the opposite side of the road is the Jade Market (see p.134) while a block to the north, at 627 Public Square Street, is the old colonial **police station**, still in service. Heading east from here will bring you to the Tin Hau Temple (see p.134).

Reclamation Street recommences a block east of the police station and continues to run north. There's a large wholesale **fruit market** at the junction with Waterloo Road, with wicker baskets and tiered boxes of oranges stacked under shelters, the interior alleys echoing to the clack of *mahjong* tiles, although this is destined to move some time soon because of work on the nearby West Kowloon Reclamation Project. Immediately north of here, the street is clogged with traders and workers handling steel rods, metal drums, and heavy-duty kitchen equipment, and there's also the odd shop specializing in Buddhist utensils and decorations – shrines, joss sticks, urns and pictures by the windowful.

The next street to the west, **Canton Road**, is another old thoroughfare that is now split into two. At the southern end, near the junction with Public Square Street, are jade and ivory shops (*mahjong* sets a speciality), while the middle section from Waterloo Road as far as Dundas Street is a varied produce market, less stomach-turning than the one in Reclamation Street. The wholesale market trade is encamped around the Pitt Street junction, whilst the section around Dundas Street has twitching fish and shrimps in shallow plastic buckets. The northern section, from Dundas St to Soy St, is devoted to mechanical and electrical shops – hardware, engines and engineering works piled high at the side of the road. Look out for the medicinal tea shops with their wonderful copper and brass urns decorated with dragons.

Tin Hau Temple

That Yau Ma Tei was once a working harbour is clear from the presence of the **Tin Hau Temple** (daily 8am–6pm), just off Nathan Road on Public Square Street, even if following successive bouts of land reclamation it's now way inland. The small area fronting the complex is usually teeming with men sitting around or gambling at backgammon and *mahjong*, and people may ask for alms from you as you go in. The main temple, around a century old, is dedicated to Tin Hau, but there are three other temples here, too: the one to the left is dedicated to Shea Tan, protector of the local community; to the right are ones to Shing Wong, the City God, and Fook Tak, an Earth God.

Jade Market

You'll find the **Jade Market** (daily 10am–4pm) underneath the Gascoigne Road flyover on Kansu Street (Jordan or Yau Ma Tei MTR). Several hundred stalls display an enormous selection of coloured jade, from earrings and jewellery to statues, and though there's some serious buying and bargaining going on here between dealers, it's a lot of fun just to poke around the stalls to see what you can turn up for a few dollars. In part, jade owes its value to the fact that, as an extremely hard stone, it's very difficult to carve; it's also said by the Chinese to bestow "magical", or at least medicinal, qualities on the wearer. Certain shapes represent wealth (deer), good luck (tiger) or power (dragon). All the best stuff goes before lunch, and if you're serious about buying real jade, you should get hold of the HKTA's factsheet about the market, which tells you what colour and quality to look out for. Basically, there are two kinds: nephrite (which can be varying shades of green) and the rarer jadeite, much of which comes from Burma and which can be all sorts of colours. A rough guide to quality is that the jade should be cold to the touch and with a pure colour which remains constant all the way through; coloured tinges or blemishes can reduce the value. However, since the scope for being misled is considerable, if you don't know what you're doing you're best advised to stick to small trinkets – rings, pendants, paperweights, earrings – if all you want is a souvenir. You'll also see a dying phenomenon in the market: scribes with typewriters writing letters for people who are illiterate or who need business letters typed. True literacy in Chinese can require the memorization of ten thousand characters, so even those educated enough to read simple newspapers can require help with letters.

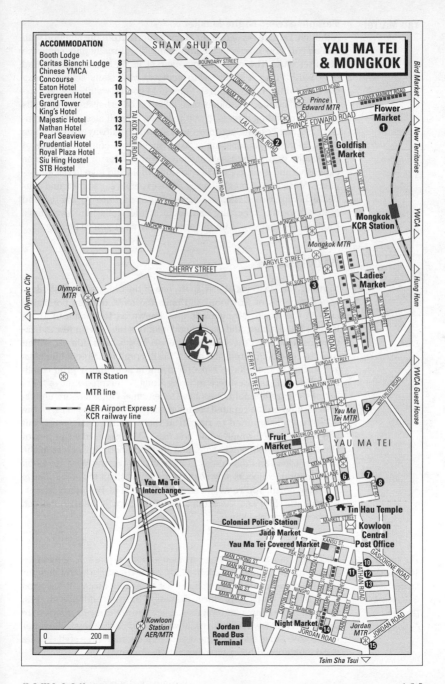

Yau Ma Tei

Temple Street Night Market

Although **Temple Street Night Market** (north from the junction with Jordan Rd) now opens in the afternoon, it still really only comes to life after dark. The most famous market in the area, from around 6pm until 11pm it's alive with activity, with stalls selling cheap clothes (for men particularly), household goods, watches, CDs, cassettes and jewellery, while fortune tellers and herbalists set up stalls in the surrounding streets. If you're lucky, there'll also be impromptu performances of Cantonese opera. About halfway up you'll see stalls laden with an amazing array of shellfish: a couple of plates of sea snails, prawns, mussels or clams, with a beer or two, won't be expensive and it's a great place to stop awhile and take in the atmosphere. More formal meals, hardly more expensive, can be found a little further up, where there's a covered *dai pai dong*. Again, fish and seafood are the speciality and some of the stalls here even have English menus if you want to know exactly what you're getting.

Mongkok

North of Yau Ma Tei is **MONGKOK**, one of the oldest and most dilapidated sections of Kowloon, and once the most densely populated area in the world. Mongkok is also known as the home of Hong Kong's Triad gangs, and the living conditions here give a few indications as to why secret societies flourish in this area. Almost within touching distance across the roads, the decrepit apartment buildings are stuffed to the gills with people living in some fairly grim conditions, though, as elsewhere in Hong Kong, attempts to move them out of their traditional homes have taken time. Outsiders are unlikely to pick up on the reputed community spirit that keeps many of the inhabitants determined to remain in their peeling apartments, but you might walk through while you can – Mongkok, like the rest of Hong Kong, is extremely safe, and there's a certain interest in the street markets and day-to-day goings on, though the West Kowloon Reclamation Project is slowly changing this district too.

To the north, you're within striking distance of **Boundary Street**, which until 1898 and the acquisition of the New Territories marked the boundary with China.

Ladies' Market

The nearest MTR for the Ladies' Market is Mongkok (eastern Nelson St exit).

At Tung Choi Street, a huge women's clothes market, sometimes known as the **Ladies' Market** (daily noon–10.30pm) stretches for four blocks north from Dundas Street to Argyle Street. It's a good place to pick up bargain skirts, dresses, T-shirts, children's clothes, small electrical items and watches, and there are *dai pai dongs* here too. You'll find few fixed prices, however, and bargaining is the order of the day. Since the same gear turns up on stall after stall, have a good look around before making a move for anything.

The goldfish market to the flower market

Still on Tung Choi Street, directly north of the Ladies' Market, is the **goldfish market**, its shops festooned with plastic bags containing all kinds of ornamental and tropical fish. Goldfish are a variety of carp, a popular symbol of good fortune. You'll often see drawings of carp – particularly in pairs – or carp-shaped lanterns in temples or on display during Chinese festivals. Consequently, great care is taken with their breeding, and some can cost thousands of dollars.

One block east of Tung Choi Street is **Fa Yuen Street**, where there's another mixed street market during the day. The next street east, **Sai Yee Street**, has a number of wedding shops and photo studios, with pictures of idealized Chinese brides in their windows. At the junction with **Bute Street** a pedestrian walkway links these streets directly to the **Mongkok KCR** station.

A block north of the top end of Tung Choi Road, just to the east of Prince Edward MTR, is **Flower Market Street**. There are dozens of flower and plant shops here (daily 10am–6pm) and at the weekend many more vendors bring in trucks full of orchids, orange trees and other exotica. It's particularly good around Chinese New Year, when many people buy narcissi, orange trees and plum blossom to decorate their apartments.

The bird market

Mongkok's **bird market** is housed in a purpose-built Chinese-style garden (daily 7am–8pm) in **Yuen Po Street**, at the point where Flower Market Street meets the KCR flyover. There are two or three dozen stalls crammed with caged songbirds, live crickets tied up in little plastic bags (they're fed to the birds with chopsticks), birdseed barrels and men varnishing newly made bamboo cages – minus bird they start at $60 or so, though the more elaborate ones run into the hundreds. Little porcelain bird bowls and other paraphernalia cost from around $10. It's also interesting just to watch the local men who bring their own caged birds here for an airing and to listen to them sing. Taking your songbird out for a walk is a popular pastime among older Chinese men, one you'll see often in the more traditional areas of town.

New Kowloon

The area north of Boundary Street, so-called **NEW KOWLOON**, has much less going for it than the streets of Tsim Sha Tsui and Yau Ma Tei, but if you've got the time there are one or two districts that show a different side of Hong Kong, and a couple of places close enough to tack onto the beginning or end of a day's sightseeing (although the Sung Dynasty Village, formerly a major attraction in this part of town, is now closed). All are still firmly in built-up parts of the city – access is easiest by MTR.

Kowloon City

Boundary Street, Prince Edward Street and Argyle Street all run east from Mongkok, converging on **KOWLOON CITY**, the area immediately surrounding the old **Kai Tak airport** site. An airport first opened here in the 1930s, though it wasn't until 1956 that the impressive runway – almost 4km long – was built right into the middle of Kowloon Bay. The area now feels rather strange, as if the 350,000 people who used to have planes whistling past their windows are still getting used to the relative peace and quiet. The Government has ambitious plans to redevelop the area and reclaim large parts of the harbour on both sides of the old runway: the four-phase **Southeast Kowloon Development Plan** is intended to create parks, shopping centres, industrial areas and housing for a quarter

---

Kowloon Walled City

For years, one of the more notorious districts of Hong Kong lay close to the airport, down Carpenter Road. **Kowloon Walled City** was a slum of gigantic proportions, which had occupied an anomalous position in Hong Kong since the acquisition of the New Territories by the British in 1898, when the Chinese managed to retain judicial control over it by a legal sleight of hand. Originally the site of a Chinese garrison, and walled in (hence the name), it developed into a planned village, rife with disease but thriving from the trade that a nearby wharf brought. There was constant friction between the British authorities and the residents, who felt able to call on the Chinese government whenever they were threatened with resettlement, and the Walled City became a bizarre enclave, virtually free from colonial rule. During the Japanese occupation of Hong Kong, the walls were dismantled and used to extend the airport, and many of the buildings were destroyed. But any hopes the British had of taking over the district were dashed after the end of the war, when thousands of refugees from the Chinese mainland moved into the Walled City and made it their own. Compromise plans came to nothing and for years the Walled City remained a no-go area for the police, becoming a haunt of Triad gangs and fugitive criminals, leading some to call it the "cancer of Kowloon".

Sweat-shops and unlicensed factories employed the refugees, who never left the Walled City in case they were arrested; wells were sunk to provide water and electricity was tapped from the mains; every inch of its tattered surface was covered with wire cages tacked on by the inhabitants to create extra space; there was even a temple and basic restaurants. But life in the city took place amid the most primitive surroundings imaginable: in gloomy, wet corridors, lined with festering rubbish, and with little semblance of order, let alone law. Things improved slightly in the 1970s and 1980s, when residents' associations got together and began to clean up the brothels, abortion clinics, unlicensed medical and dental shops, drinking, drugs and gambling dens that infested the six-hectare site. Finally, in 1987 a planned evacuation programme was agreed with the thirty thousand residents, and by 1991 all of them had been rehoused elsewhere and compensated. The site was levelled and turned into a park, ending one of the more unsavoury of the territory's historical quirks.

---

of a million people on the Kai Tak site; there's also been talk of a cruise ship terminal. Unusually for Hong Kong, however, the plan has met stiff opposition. Environmentalists say damage to the harbour (what's left of it) would be excessive and local residents feel the plans – tower blocks and a park surrounded by motorways – are a badly thought-out and unimaginative use of a wonderful site. Eventually the old airport buildings will be knocked down, but while it waits for plans to be finalized the Government is trying to find uses for the buildings and the runway – charity runs, concerts and car races have already been staged on the tarmac.

New Kowloon

In the meantime the old *Regal Airport Hotel* is still in business, with its *China Coast Pub*, bars and restaurants, and there are some excellent and well-priced **Thai restaurants** in the streets behind.

For details of Kowloon City's Thai restaurants, see pp.258–260.

Lok Fu

Just to the northwest of the old airport, the district of **LOK FU** is a large-scale residential area with huge apartment buildings towering close to the Lok Fu MTR station. It sees few tourists, though an off-beat attraction might tempt you here. Leave the MTR station by exit A and aim for **Wang Lok House** (above the bus terminal), where – on level 1 – the Government Housing Department has constructed a series of model, single-room apartments open to the public (Mon–Fri 9am–4.30pm; free). It's a rare opportunity to delve behind the tourist facade of Hong Kong and see the dreadfully cramped conditions in which much of the population lives, although these examples are cleaner and less crowded than in real life. If you take the lift to the sixteenth floor and walk through the corridors you'll probably be able to see into one or two ordinary flats, as people tend to leave their doors open to create a breeze. It's not so much the size of each apartment that's frightening as the number of people living in each one. It's not unusual for five or six adults (plus perhaps some children) to live in a flat no more than seven metres square. From this height you also get a good view over Kowloon and the **Chinese Christian Cemetery**, spread across a pyramid-shaped hill.

Kowloon Tong

West of the airport, **KOWLOON TONG** is a wealthy, residential area, packed with English and American kindergartens and expensive schools like St George's, while nearby **Broadcast Drive** is home to most of the radio and TV stations in the territory. You are hardly likely to find yourself strolling around here, though Kowloon Tong is the site of the **interchange** between the MTR and KCR train systems. Kowloon Tong is also noted for its nest of euphemistically tagged "short-time hotels". These aren't as seedy as they might sound: many cater to ordinary couples wanting to get away from tiny apartments and the rest of the family. Drive along Waterloo Road and down the adjacent side streets and you can't miss them: all sumptuously decorated and equipped, sitting behind security cameras and grilles.

Wong Tai Sin Temple

There are more strange goings-on a couple of MTR stops east of Kowloon Tong at the massive and colourful **Wong Tai Sin Temple** (daily 7am–5.30pm; small donation expected), next to Wong Tai Sin MTR station. Built in 1973, it's one of the territory's major Taoist temples, dedicated to Wong Tai Sin, whose image was brought to Hong Kong in 1915 from the mainland and moved here from a temple in Wan Chai six years later. Over three million people come to pay their respects here every year. The god, a mythical shepherd boy with the power of healing, has an almost fanatical following, primarily because he's famous for bringing good luck to gamblers, and there are always crowds at the temple, which shows no restraint in its decoration and lavish grounds. As you enter, you'll find hawkers and stalls selling paper money, incense, oranges (very auspicious because of their colour) and Chinese decorations.

You're not always allowed into the main temple building, but from the courtyard you'll still be able to see the altar, which supports the portrait of Wong Tai Sin brought from China. On the left is a small hut where you can borrow a pot of bamboo prediction sticks (free). People stand in front of the shrine shaking the pot until one of the (numbered) bamboo sticks drops out – this stick is then exchanged for a piece of paper bearing the same number, which has a prediction written on it.

Behind the main building is the pleasant Good Wish Garden (Tues–Sun 9am–4pm; $2), with Chinese pavilions, carp ponds and waterfalls. Inside this is the smaller Nine Dragon Wall Garden, which houses a copy of the famous mural in the Imperial Palace in Beijing. The whole complex is good for an hour or so; just watching people making offerings and praying for good luck is diverting enough. There's also a clinic here, the upper floor of which offers **Chinese herbal medicine.**

Just inside the main entrance, on the left, is a covered street of booths. Some sell paraphernalia for worshippers or Chinese medicine, but most are **fortune tellers,** who read palms, bumps, feet and faces. It's a thriving industry in Hong Kong and many of these fortune tellers have testimonials of authenticity and success pinned to the booths, with prices and explanations displayed for the sceptical. There are about 160 practitioners to choose from. Some speak English (there's a map at the end of the building which indicates the English speakers with a red dot) so if you want to find out whether or not you're going to win at the races, this is the place to ask. Busiest days at the temple are around Chinese New Year, when luck is particularly sought, and at Wong Tai Sin's festival, on the twenty-third day of the eighth lunar month (usually in September).

The Lei Cheng Uk Han Tomb Museum

In 1955, between what are now the MTR stations of Sham Shui Po and Cheung Sha Wan, a couple of kilometres northwest of Mongkok, workmen flattening a hillside in order to build a new housing estate unearthed Hong Kong's most ancient historic monument – a Han Dynasty tomb almost two thousand years old. It's been preserved *in situ* and now forms the major part of the **Lei Cheng Uk Han Tomb Museum**, 41 Tonkin Street (Mon–Wed, Fri & Sat 10am–1pm & 2–6pm, Sun 1–6pm; free), an offshoot of the Museum of History in Tsim Sha Tsui.

In truth the small museum is not really worth a special journey, but is interesting if you're in the area. There's a brief explanation of how the tomb was found, with photographs and a few funerary exhibits; the glass-fronted tomb itself is out in the garden, encased in concrete to preserve it. It's simple enough to make out the central chamber, which is crossed by four barrel-vaulted brick niches, but the best idea of what it looked like can be gleaned from the diagrams back inside.

To reach the museum, either take **bus #2, #6 or #6A** from the Star Ferry to Tonkin Street, or the **MTR** to Cheung Sha Wan and walk north for five minutes up Tonkin Street, past grim factories and some fairly dense housing.

Lei Yue Mun

LEI YUE MUN, as befits its name ("carp fish gate"), sits at the narrowest entrance to the harbour. It's probably the biggest and most commercialized of the places to come and eat seafood in Hong Kong, with around 25 restaurants and as many fresh fish shops, the slabs and tanks twitching with creatures shortly to be cooked. The recognized procedure is to choose your fish and shellfish from a shop, where it will be weighed and priced, and then take it (or you'll be taken) to a restaurant, where it's cooked to your instructions: you generally pay the bill at the end; one to the fishmonger and one to the restaurant for cooking the fish and for any rice and other dishes you may have had. The strongest possible warnings about **rip-offs** are applicable here. You *must* ask the price of the fish you choose before it's bashed on the head and carted off to a restaurant or you're just inviting someone to choose what will allegedly be the most expensive creature in the tank for you. A good way to proceed is to name a price to the fishmonger that you want to spend. Alternatively, if there's a group of you, get the tourist office or a Chinese friend to ring one of the restaurants before you go and sort out a fixed-price set menu, which can work out fairly inexpensively. Evenings are the best time to come, when you can sit at the restaurant windows and look out over the typhoon shelter.

New Kowloon

Getting there

The easiest way – particularly if you are in a group – is to take the MTR to **Lam Tin** and then get a taxi. If possible get someone to write the destination in Chinese. If you want to be more adventurous you can get off the MTR one stop away at **Kwun Tong**, a massive residential and industrial area. Follow the signs (exit D1) outside to Kwun Tong Road and pick up **bus #14C** at the terminus in Yue Man Square. The bus runs down to **Sam Ka Tsuen** typhoon shelter, which is where the ferry from Sai Wan Ho arrives. You can walk round to the restaurants or, from behind the ferry terminal, you can take a sampan across to the village of Lei Yue Mun, passing through moored and inhabited fishing boats.

Chapter 4

The New Territories

T oo many visitors miss out on the best that Hong Kong has to offer – namely the 740 square kilometres of mainland, beyond Kowloon, leased to Britain in 1898 and known as the **New Territories**. Around half of the colony's population lives here, both in large new cities and small, traditional villages, and the area is the source of much of Hong Kong's food and water. It's in the New Territories, too, that you'll find the most resonant echoes of the People's Republic. Massive housing estates built around gleaming New Towns don't completely obscure the rural nature of much of the land, and although it's not as easy as it once was to spot water buffalo in the New Territories, some country roads still feature teeming duck farms and isolated houses, while a few decrepit walled villages survive, surrounded by their ancestral lands and with their traditional temples and meeting halls intact. What's more, large parts of the New Territories have been designated country parks, some of them offering excellent hiking opportunities. The **Sai Kung peninsula**, to the east, is the best example, though the adventurous could see the whole of the New Territories from a hiker's viewpoint by following the cross-territory **MacLehose Trail** (see pp.178–179) from Sai Kung to the far west.

Don't expect it to be all peace and quiet. Parts are as busy and boisterous as anywhere in Kowloon, though there is at least always the impression of more space. Some of the **New Towns** are sights in

---

NEW TERRITORIES: TOP TEN ATTRACTIONS

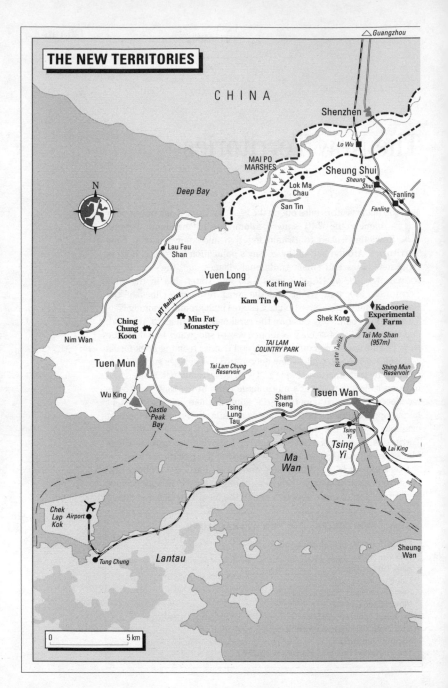

THE NEW TERRITORIES

△ Guangzhou

CHINA

Shenzhen

Lo Wu

MAI PO
MARSHES

Deep Bay

Sheung Shui

Sheung
Shui

Fanling

Lok Ma
Chau

Fanling

San Tin

N

Lau Fau
Shan

Yuen Long

Kat Hing Wai

Kam Tin

Kadoorie
Experimental
Farm

LRT Railway

Miu Fat
Monastery

Shek Kong

Ching
Chung
Koon

Tai Mo Shan
(957m)

Nim Wan

TAI LAM
COUNTRY PARK

Route Twisk

Shing Mun
Reservoir

Tuen Mun

Tai Lam Chung
Reservoir

Wu King

Sham
Tseng

Tsuen Wan

Castle
Peak
Bay

Tsing
Lung
Tau

Tsing
Yi

Lai King

Ma
Wan

Tsing
Yi

Chek
Lap
Kok

Airport

Sheung
Wan

Lantau

Tung Chung

0   5 km

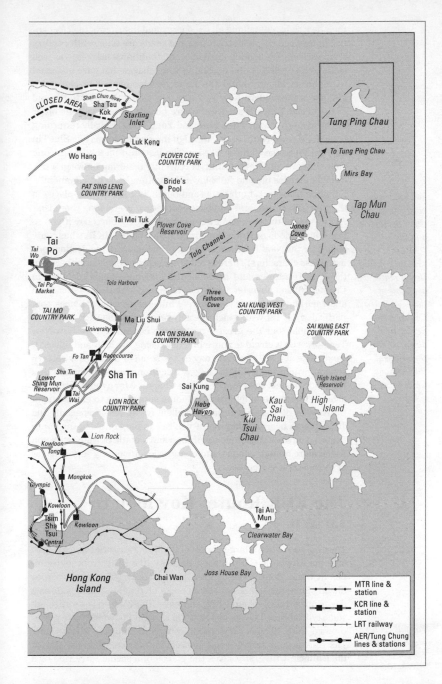

their own right, containing all the energy and industry of the city centre. In between the new structures and roads are nineteenth-century temples, some fascinating museums and traditional markets – as well as the walled villages and coastal fishing villages that have managed to retain an identity amid the rapid development. You can get a glimpse of the modern New Territories by riding the MTR to the end of the line at **Tsuen Wan**, from where buses connect with the other major western towns, **Tuen Mun** and **Yuen Long**. Equally rewarding is the **KCR train route** north, through interesting towns like **Sha Tin** and **Tai Po** to the Chinese border. The last stop on the Hong Kong side, the town of **Sheung Shui**, is currently teetering between a traditional Chinese life and full-blown Hong Kong-style development.

For full transport details, check the text and see "Getting Around", p.46. Useful maps are those of the Countryside Series, available from the Government Publications Centre (see p.45).

Public transport, both trains and buses, is good to most places in the New Territories, and minibuses can prove useful too. There isn't any one place that you can't get to and back from in a day if you're based in Kowloon or Hong Kong Island; pick up the HKTA's bus route leaflet for the New Territories, which prints many of the destinations in Chinese characters. There are also some ferry connections between the New Territories and a few of the outlying islands (detailed in Chapter 5), and hoverferry services between Central and Tsuen Wan and Tuen Mun. Note that you can rent **bikes** at a couple of places, too, particularly at Tai Wai, which is easily reached on the KCR.

You could tour the greater part of the central and western New Territories on a **circular route** in a day, using the KCR and buses; it would take at least one more day to see some of the smaller eastern section, where the going is slower. **Accommodation** is limited to a few youth hostels and campsites (see Chapter 6 for a full listing). You shouldn't have too much trouble finding somewhere **to eat**. Some of the New Territories' towns have excellent restaurants (especially Sha Tin), though bear in mind that if you're camping or using the youth hostels, you should take plenty of food and a bottle of water with you as the more remote villages and countryside are poorly served as far as eating out is concerned.

The KCR Route: Kowloon to Lo Wu

For full details about the KCR, see p.48.

The best way to see a large chunk of the New Territories quickly is to take the **Kowloon–Canton East Railway** (the KCR) from its terminus in Hung Hom north to the Chinese border. The whole trip to Sheung Shui, the last stop you can make on the Hong Kong side as a day-tripper, takes around fifty minutes. The route passes through some typical New Towns, like **Sha Tin** and **Tai Po**, which have mushroomed from villages (or sometimes from nothing) in a few years. There are several temples and markets in between, while the stop at the **Chinese University** gives the choice of a scenic ferry ride or a visit to one of the territory's better art galleries. **Sheung Shui** itself is probably the most interesting place to break the journey, while from Tai Po and **Fanling** it's only a short bus ride into some quite beautiful countryside to the east, at **Plover Cove** and **Starling Inlet**.

If you're going on into China later, you'll pass through the border crossing at **Lo Wu**, at the end of the Hong Kong part of the KCR line, an otherwise restricted area. Visitors can also peer over the border at a couple of points, particularly **Lok Ma Chau**, where there's been a lookout post for years.

Tai Wai

The first stop after the MTR/KCR interchange at Kowloon Tong is TAI WAI, nowadays less a town in its own right (though there's been a village here since the fourteenth century) than an extension of Sha Tin. Its most obvious attraction is easy to spot from the train: **Amah Rock** (in Cantonese, Mong Fu Shek) – to the right across the valley after emerging from the tunnel – though it's debatable to what extent it resembles the human figure it's supposed to be. In legend, a woman climbed the hill to wait for her husband to return from fishing; when he failed to appear the gods turned her to stone. Young women make the pilgrimage up here during the annual Maiden's Festival (see p.284); if you want to clamber up yourself there's a path from the end of Hung Mui Kuk Road, which runs east of the train station.

The other immediately noticeable thing in Tai Wai is the ageing **Happy Dragon Recreation Park** right by the station, which should be open daily but doesn't always bother midweek or during bad weather. There are the usual rides here, and a water world with chutes.

The open space over the way is always busy at the weekend with people renting **bicycles**. Cycle paths start next to the park and run up through Sha Tin, along the river, before skirting Tolo Harbour all the way to Tai Po – a popular route and a good way to get to grips with the New Territories. Bikes cost around $10 an hour, $40 a day, though there's room for bargaining.

Che Kung Temple

A five-minute walk from Tai Wai station, the **Che Kung Temple** is a Taoist temple dedicated to the Chinese general Che Kung, who is supposed to have beaten off the plague which once stalked this valley. From the KCR station, follow the signs for "Che Kung Miu" to the main road, turn left and then cross the road using the subway; the temple is a modern black-roofed building by the road (the prettier green-roofed building behind is private property). The entrance is guarded by old women, who press lucky red paper symbols into your hand in return for dollars, and there are also some fortune tellers. Inside, beyond the courtyard, is a huge, aggressive-looking statue of the general with a drawn sword and a collection of metal fans, which people turn when making their devotions. Che Kung's festival is held on the third day of Chinese New Year, when the temple is packed with people coming here to pray for good luck.

Come out of the temple and keep on up the main road – Che Kung Miu Road – towards Sha Tin and, after another hundred metres or so on the right, you'll find a little garden containing a **Four-Faced Buddha Shrine**. This is a symbol more commonly found in Thailand: you're supposed to pray to each face, moving around the shrine in an anti-clockwise direction.

Tsang Tai Uk

From the shrine it's only a few minutes up the main road to one of the New Territories' lesser-known walled villages, **TSANG TAI UK**, curiously dwarfed by the modern apartment buildings on nearby Sha Tin's riverfront. To get there, follow the main road (which becomes Tai Chung Kiu Rd as it approaches Sha Tin) and look for Sha Kok Street on the right: walk down here and the village is behind the recreation ground to the right, under a green bank of hills.

The name Tsang Tai Uk means "Tsang's Big House", though in effect it's a rectangular, walled village of grey stone, built in the mid-nineteenth century to shelter members of the Tsang family clan. It's survived well and bears comparison with the more frequently visited villages in the Kam Tin area near Yuen Long (see p.169). The thick

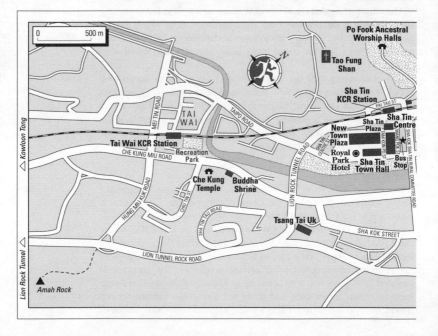

walls incorporate separate rooms with grilled windows, and at each corner there's a tall, square watchtower, adorned with faded stone decoration. High doorways lead into the village, which is based around a central courtyard, with wide alleys running its length split by a network of high-ceilinged rooms and storerooms. Most of the Tsang family have moved out, attracted abroad or by jobs in central Hong Kong, but even so there's a powerful atmosphere here – kids scuttling along the corridors, and washing and cooking going on in corners, much as it has always done.

Sha Tin

Built on both sides of the Shing Mun river in the southern New Territories, **SHA TIN** is one of the most interesting stops on the KCR line. The name means "sandy field", a relic of the days when the area consisted of arable land made fertile by sediment washed down by the river. This productive land supported farming villages, like Tai Wai, for centuries, though it's only since the 1970s that Sha Tin has taken on its ultra-modern appearance. Much of the New Town building here has occurred on land reclaimed from the mud and sand, which you can still see and smell in the murky channelled river.

The town – already home to more than half a million people, and still growing – splits into several distinct areas served by separate

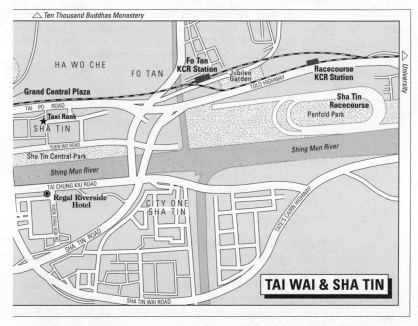

Sha Tin is one
of the few
places outside
central Hong
Kong where
you might
want to stay;
the Regal
Riverside and
Royal Park
hotels are
reviewed on
p.229.

Eating in Sha Tin

You could do worse than plan a day in the New Territories to include lunch or dinner in Sha Tin, since there's a fine selection of local restaurants. Try one of the following:

Laisan Korean BBQ, New Town Plaza, 6th Floor. Korean restaurant with good barbecue.

Lung Wah Hotel and Restaurant, 22 Ha Wo Che. Renowned Cantonese pigeon specialist (see p.247 for more details).

Maxim's Chinese Restaurant, 669–674 New Town Plaza, 6th Floor. Packed and boisterous *dim sum* restaurant.

Regal Riverside, Tai Chung Kiu Rd. Asian buffet lunch and dinner in the hotel restaurant.

KCR stations: Tai Wai is covered above; to the north is Fo Tan, a residential area overlooking the racecourse; while Sha Tin town itself is reached from the central KCR station, also called Sha Tin. From here, signs point you to the **New Town Plaza**, a huge shopping and recreation centre, which offers an accurate view of contemporary local life and manners: solidly Chinese, with crowded shops and good-value restaurants full of local families. If you're here at the right time, you can join the crowds of kids who gather to watch the central musical fountain with its coloured lights and thirty-foot sprays (displays at 12.45pm, 9.30pm, plus 10.00am and 5.30pm at weekends).

Walk through the plaza and there are walkway connections to other nearby shopping centres, as well as the pleasant riverside park (open 7am–11pm) and Sha Tin Town Hall, at weekends a popular place for weddings. The fashion is mostly for meringue-like dresses, but you might also see some Chinese brides dressed in traditional red and gold.

The town is best known for the **Sha Tin Racecourse**. It's probably the most modern in the world and, together with the one at Happy Valley, provides the only legal betting outlet in Hong Kong. It's packed on race days (the season is from Sept to May); entry details are the same as for Happy Valley (see p.106). It even has its own KCR station, Racecourse (service on race days only). At other times, you can get into **Penfold Park** (closed Mon and race days) and its bird sanctuary, which are in the middle of the track, by taking the KCR to Fo Tan – the track and park are behind the Jubilee Garden estate.

The Ten Thousand Buddhas Monastery

A little way northwest of Sha Tin is the **Ten Thousand Buddhas Monastery**, known locally as Man Fat Sze. The monastery (daily 9am–5pm; free) is at the peak of Po Fook Hill. Its red-and-gold pagoda is visible from just outside the KCR station, just behind and above a larger white-and-green complex of Chinese buildings which house the Po (or Bo) Fook Ancestral Worship Halls (9am–5pm; free). It's a stiff climb up about 400 steps to the monastery, at the top of which you emerge onto a terrace, close to the main temple. Externally it's an undistinguished building, but the interior houses around thirteen thousand small black-and-gold statues of the Buddha, each around a foot high and sculpted in a different posture, which line the walls to a height of thirty feet or more. The building also contains the embalmed and gilded body of a monk, the founder of the monastery. Outside on the terrace there's a large pagoda that you can climb, and there are other shrines, statues of Chinese deities and a gigantic dog and elephant. Vegetarian lunches are available, and there are a couple of stalls selling snacks and drinks.

The **Po Fook Ancestral Worship Halls** are also worth a look. They include landscaped gardens, a temple complex and dozens of small shrines, each containing the memorial plaques and ashes of different families. You may see a funeral here, complete with the paper offerings which are burnt so as to join the deceased in the afterlife. The vans in the lower car park decorated with plastic flowers are the hearses.

To reach the hill and the temple, exit Sha Tin KCR following the sign for "Buses/Grand Central Plaza". Go down the ramp to the left of the bus terminal and walk past the old houses on the left towards the modern, glass Central Plaza building. Turn left there, and after about 20m you reach the entrance to the Po Fook Ancestral Worship Halls. A path to the monastery leads off to the right, between the entrance way and a public car park. Keep going left, passing some shacks after a couple of hundred metres, and you'll find the steps.

Tao Fung Shan

On the next ridge, the **Tao Fung Shan** Christian Centre is a complex of buildings built in the 1930s in a Chinese style, though this time the pagoda at the top holds a small Christian chapel. To get there, take the ramp by the bus terminal, but instead of walking straight on for the Ten Thousand Buddhas Monastery, turn back sharp left, parallel to the rail tracks, through Pai Tau village. You'll see a wooden post in front of a large tree, with a green arrow and logo. The path on the right leads up above the village, and, after about ten minutes' climb, brings you out on the main Tao Fung Shan Road, where it joins Pak Lok Path. Keep on up the road for another fifteen minutes or so and you can't miss the centre.

At the top, a marked path leads through pretty grounds to a large, white stone cross which faces directly out over the river. Away to the left are the blocks of Sha Tin and Fo Tan, while just visible through the apartment buildings at the foot of the hills opposite is Tsang Tai Uk village, a low, grey splash among the towers.

The views aren't the only reason to make the climb. In the grounds is a **porcelain workshop** (Mon–Fri 8.30am–12.30pm & 2–5pm, Sat

8.30am–12.30pm), where you can see good-quality porcelain being hand-painted. The decorated plates run to hundreds of dollars, but you can pick up a souvenir here – a cup and saucer, jug or decorated tile – for around $50.

Steps from the centre lead down to the **cemetery**, below the stone factory, just outside the main entrance, where there's the grave of Tao Fung Shan's founder, the Norwegian evangelist Karl Ludwig Reichelt (1877–1952), whose idea it was to convert Buddhist monks to Christianity. In part, this explains the centre's orthodox Buddhist look: Reichelt hoped that the buildings would dupe wandering Buddhist monks seeking sanctuary, and it certainly worked – until World War II, Tao Fung Shan was a prosperous Christian centre, although it's struggled to attract devotees in more recent times.

For lunch or a drink, drop in at the Yucca de Lac *restaurant, above the Tolo Highway; see p.248 for details.*

University, Ma Liu Shui and Tolo Harbour

Beyond Sha Tin, the train runs upriver before turning to hug the edge of Tolo Harbour. Just before the turn, there's a stop called **UNIVERSITY** (the Chinese characters translate as "Big School"), which serves Hong Kong's **Chinese University**, the campus spread back from the harbour up the hillside.

A shuttle bus from outside the station runs every 15–30 minutes up the steep hill to the central campus. If you get off at the second stop, at the top by the Sir Run Run Shaw Hall, the university's **Art Museum** (Mon–Sat 10am–4.45pm, Sun 12.30–5.30pm; free) is over to the left, in the middle of a block of buildings surrounding a square. The well-lit, spacious split-level galleries usually display items from the museum's own wide collection of Chinese paintings, calligraphy and ceramics dating from the Ming Dynasty onwards. Local and mainland Chinese museums often send touring exhibitions of art and archeological pieces here too.

Ma Liu Shui

The other reason to come here is for services from the ferry pier at **MA LIU SHUI**. From University KCR, follow the sign to Tung Ping Chau and Tap Mun out of the station, turn left, cross the highway by the flyover and descend to the waterfront – a fifteen-minute walk. Ferries go from here through **Tolo Harbour** and the Tolo Channel – either stay on board for the scenic round trip or jump off at Tap Mun Chau or another of the minor stops along the way; see pp.180–181 for details.

Tung Ping Chau

Ferries also run from Ma Liu Shui to the island of **Tung Ping Chau**, about as far away from central Hong Kong as you can get – which explains why hardly anyone goes there. Way to the northeast, beyond Tap Mun Chau and close to the Chinese coast, it's long been abandoned by its inhabitants, who must have been glad to be off the isolated speck. It's a flat place, its highest point precisely 37m high, but there are some good beaches and the odd overgrown trail along its banana-shaped, four-kilometre length. You could swim here in the clean water of Mirs Bay; indeed in recent times illegal immigrants from the Chinese mainland have been known to swim *to* the island.

The **ferry** runs only at weekends, leaving Ma Liu Shui at 9am (Sat & Sun) and 3.30pm (Sat only), returning at about 5.30pm; the journey takes ninety minutes. You can buy tickets up to a week in advance from Ma Liu Shui ferry pier; an ordinary return is $50, deluxe (top deck with air-conditioning) $70. This should give you quite long enough on the island, though some people come equipped with **camping gear** and everything else necessary for a pleasant night's stay – like an enormous bottle of something alcoholic. The campsite is at Kang Lau Shek, at the eastern end of the island; there's no fresh water.

Tai Po

Beyond University, the rail line runs alongside the sea. At **TAI PO**, on the western point of Tolo Harbour, you're roughly halfway up the KCR line. A market town since the seventeenth century, the manageable town centre is gradually being overwhelmed by new industrial and housing developments. Nonetheless, there's enough to warrant a short stroll, and regular buses from the station – called Tai Po Market – allow you to escape into the unspoiled hiking and picnic areas around Plover Cove.

CHINA

THE NEW TERRITORIES

The Town

The town's **market** – called Tai Po Temporary Market, although its position is virtually permanent – is the principal thing to see. It's at the end of the main road, Heung Sze Wui Street, a large covered run of stalls which extends into the surrounding streets, and is at its lively best in the morning. On the far side a gate leads up into the **Hong Kong Railway Museum** (Mon & Wed–Sun 9am–5pm; free), which occupies the site and buildings of the old Tai Po Market Railway Station, built in 1913. A small exhibition includes photographs of the opening ceremony of the Kowloon–Canton Railway, and outside on the preserved tracks you can clamber through coaches dating back to 1911. The other nearby diversion is the **Man Mo Temple**, on Fu Shin Street, built about a hundred years ago to mark the founding of the market and dedicated to the Taoist Gods of War and Literature. There are plenty of interesting old shops around here, too, selling dried seafood, religious paraphernalia and other Chinese wares.

Tai Po's other points of interest are across the river, which separates the old town from the new industrial developments. Over the bridge, Ting Kok Road leads up to the town's **Tin Hau Temple**, a few hundred metres up on the left. It's a particularly old relic, built around three hundred years ago and reflecting Tai Po's

TAI PO MARKET

traditional importance as a fishing centre. It's also one of the main centres for celebration and devotion during the annual Tin Hau festival (late April/May), when the whole place is decorated with streamers, banners and little windmills: come then and you're likely to catch a Cantonese opera performance on a temporary stage over the road.

Tai Wo

Rather than crossing the river again, you could pick up the train at the next KCR stop to the north, Tai Wo Station, which can be reached from the south end of Ting Kok Road. Follow the signs through the new housing estate to your right. This forms part of **TAI WO**, a brand new "town" with its own station, shops and arcades which is due to hold forty thousand people when completed. The first phase was built in just four years, giving an idea of the almost indecent haste with which the New Territories are being developed.

Plover Cove

The best thing about Tai Po is its proximity to the nearby country-side, notably **Plover Cove Country Park**, a few kilometres northeast. Bus #75K (roughly every 12–25min) from outside Tai Po Market KCR Station runs there in around thirty minutes, up Ting Kok Road and around the northern shore of Tolo Harbour.

THE NEW TERRITORIES

Tai Mei Tuk

The bus terminates at the few houses of **TAI MEI TUK** at the edge of the Plover Cove Reservoir. The bay here was once part of the harbour and has since been dammed to provide a huge fresh water supply for Hong Kong. Under the water is a sunken village – the population was moved to Sai Kung. Close to the terminus there's a clutch of restaurants, *dai pai dongs* and drinks stalls, and a line of **bicycle and tricycle rental** places. It'll cost $30–65 a day to rent a bike, $120 for the tricycles – not a bad idea if you intend heading straight for Bride's Pool (see below), but cumbersome if you want to tackle some of the excellent walks in the neighbourhood. Over the road, the little peninsula by the main dam shelters a barbecue site, and there's a watersports centre where you can rent rowing boats. If you're going no further into Plover Cover Country Park you could try the signposted nature trail here – about an hour's walk.

Bradbury Lodge Youth Hostel *is at Tai Mei Tuk. You'll need to book ahead as it's very popular; see p.215 for details.*

Local walks

The only road, Bride's Pool Road, heads north, alongside the reservoir and past endless barbecue sites to **Bride's Pool** – around an hour's stroll along a road that gets a fair bit of traffic at the weekend. A series of waterfalls, it's home to more barbecue sites and lots of picnickers, though you can escape the worst of the crowds by taking the trail thirty minutes back downriver to Chung Mei – an abandoned old village of scallop gatherers and vegetable farmers who moved to Tai Po when the reservoir construction destroyed their livelihood.

There are plenty of other local **walks**, none of them particularly exacting as long as you carry water. Marked paths lead off the Bride's Pool nature trail then on to the road to Wu Kau Tang. From there, a trail leads to Ha Miu Tin, which leads past some old, depopulated villages. Some way beyond this, there's a very small and basic **campsite** at Sam A Chung, and a circular route, difficult to follow, back to Wu Kau Tang. Better, if you're just around for the day, to follow the **Pat Sin Leng Nature Trail**, which runs for around 5km between Bride's Pool and Tai Mei Tuk, scrambling above the road for good views of the reservoir. At the Tai Mei Tuk end of the trail, just back from the main road, there's a **visitor's centre** (daily except Tues 9.30–11.30am & 1.30–4.30pm) with useful information boards on local flora, fauna and geology, as well as hiking advice and other details.

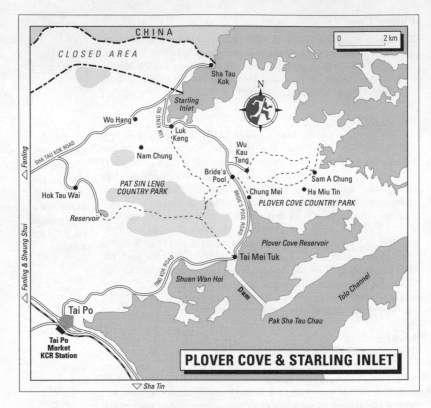

PLOVER COVE & STARLING INLET

For walks from Luk Keng on Starling Inlet, see p.158.

You can also walk on past Bride's Pool to **Starling Inlet** and **Luk Keng**. Keep on Bride's Pool Road, past the waterfall, and it's around another 4–5km to Luk Keng – two hours all told from Tai Mei Tuk. At Luk Keng you'll have to walk or take a taxi north to the main Sha Tau Kok–Sheung Shui road, where you can pick up the #78K (every 10–20min) to Sheung Shui. If you want to cut out the first part of the walk from Tai Mei Tuk, there's a **bus to Bride's Pool** (the #275R from Tai Po Market KCR, every 10–20min), though it only runs on Sundays and public holidays; at other times, you'll have to walk.

Fanling

By the time you reach **FANLING**, more than 20km from Tsim Sha Tsui, you're deep in the New Territories and – despite the inevitable new construction work – it becomes easier to appreciate the essentially rural aspect of the countryside. The people, too, begin to look different. Around Fanling, and especially in Sheung Shui to the north, many families are of **Hakka** descent – traditionally farmers and much in evidence around the area's vibrant markets. Most noticeable are the women, dressed in simple, baggy black suits and large fringed hats. Besides selling their produce in the markets, they take an active role in what would usually be seen as "male" jobs in the West – hauling barrows on building sites and doing the heavy work in local gardens and fields.

The KCR Route: Kowloon to Lo Wu

Although this is where Hong Kong's chief executive (and the governor before him) has his official country house, the town of Fanling itself is eminently missable. Much of it is being rebuilt and merged with neighbouring Sheung Shui to form another massive new housing development. A couple of destinations might tempt you, however. There's a large Taoist temple opposite the KCR station, the **Fung Ying Seen Koon**, serving vegetarian lunches, while expats come to play golf at the swanky Hong Kong Golf Club, founded in 1889 (and open to visitors; see p.302) or to ride at the Jockey Club's luxurious stable complex at Bea's River.

For most visitors, however, the main tourist attraction is the nearby **Luen Wo market** (Luen Wo Hui). The market has only been here since 1948 – though Fanling has been a trading centre for the local Hakka people for much longer – and is certainly worth a visit, without being nearly as good as the one further up the road in Sheung Shui. It's a ten-minute ride on one of the frequent buses (#78K) or minibuses (#53K) from outside Fanling KCR. Get there by 10am to see it at its best; if you do, you'll be able to **breakfast** very cheaply. The Chinese eat *congee* and a doughnut stick from one of the little noodle stalls around the covered market; for a few dollars more, other places will sell you a plate of duck or pork and rice.

You can reach Luen Wo market direct from Kowloon on the #70 bus from Jordan Ferry Bus Terminal, an hour's ride.

Sha Tau Kok, Starling Inlet and Luk Keng

East of Fanling, the new development peters out into the rural, border area with China. Bus #78K continues past Luen Wo Market to SHA TAU KOK, a twenty-minute ride past quiet farming and fishing villages dotted along the valley. Just before you get to Sha Tau Kok the road passes two villages (Wo Hang and Man Uk Pin) which are known for their Mid-Autumn Festival (see p.285) celebrations, when unmanned hot-air balloons built out of bamboo and rice paper, ten or fifteen feet high, are launched at night. In still conditions the balloons have been known to fly thousands of feet up and well into the Chinese mainland. The Sha Tau Kok area is not one you can easily explore, since the village itself lies in a restricted area, but it's a pleasant ride. At Starling Inlet there's a checkpoint on the road, where you'll be politely turfed off the bus. You'll have to wait for the return bus; the Sha Tau Kok locals have passes which enable them to cross in and out freely.

You can see more of this pretty area by taking a regular maxicab instead from Fanling KCR station – the #56K – which turns off the Sha Tau Kok road at **Starling Inlet** and runs around the cove and its mangrove swamps to LUK KENG. This is a very peaceful village,

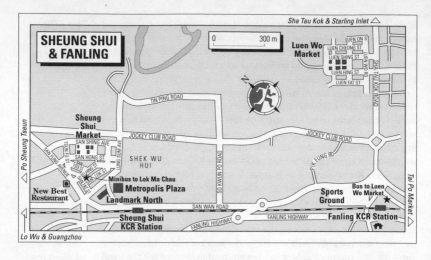

with a couple of noodle stalls on the road by the bus stop and two more old Hakka villages in the valley plain behind. The area is a popular wintering place for birds, white herons in particular. If you walk down the main Luk Keng Road, it soon becomes Bride's Pool Road (see "Plover Cove" on p.155); about five minutes from Luk Keng bus stop there's a noticeboard showing the path to Bride's Pool. It also indicates a circular half-hour "Family Walk" which takes you out along the inlet and then cuts back high above the villages and water to regain the main road. There are magnificent views as you go, across to the high-rises of the border town of Sha Tau Kok and China beyond, and down to the fish farms and junks of Starling Inlet itself.

A much longer hike is accessible by taking the #52K maxicab from Fanling KCR. This drops you at **Hok Tau Wai** (where there's a campsite), around 4km from Fanling, from where a trail runs past a small reservoir over the top of the Pat Sin Leng Country Park and down to Tai Mei Tuk at Plover Cove – a lengthy walk but easily done in a day.

Sheung Shui

A few minutes beyond Fanling, **SHEUNG SHUI** is as far as you can go on the KCR without continuing into China. Only 3km from the border, it's one of the most enjoyable of the New Territories' towns, well worth a visit, with a centre that's small enough to appreciate and a character not yet swamped by new development – though this will surely come since great apartment buildings are already encroaching upon the old centre. For the moment, though, Sheung Shui retains something of its traditional Hakka life.

The town divides into two areas. The main part, just five minutes on foot from the KCR station using the overhead walkways, is known as

Shek Wu Hui, an interconnected block of streets that can't be bettered as an example of a down-to-earth New Territories' market town. There are cheap clothes stalls, *dai pai dongs*, herbalists' shops and Hakka women on their way to market laden down with goods and bags. It's also one of the few places left in Hong Kong where you still see letter-writers at small roadside tables; for a fee, they'll write a dictated letter for those who can't manage it themselves. The **food market**, in the alleys behind San Hong Street (off the main San Fung Avenue), is one of the best in the territory, certainly the one that comes closest in appearance to those over the border. The covered stalls are stuffed with fruit and veg, preserved eggs and beancurd, while in a separate section live fish are picked from the slabs and clubbed on demand. It's no place for the squeamish, particularly when you notice the more peripheral trades going on in between the stalls: vendors selling from buckets of tied crabs and jumping prawns; the frog-seller who dispatches the beasts with a hatchet across the back, keeping the legs and throwing the twitching bodies away; the woman who spends all day wringing the necks of tiny birds, taken from a squeaking cage, and placing the pathetic plucked carcasses on a slab.

The other part of Sheung Shui is **Po Sheung Tsuen** – or Sheung Shui Wai (Sheung Shui Village) – the original village over to the west of the town. Down the main San Fung Avenue from the KCR station, take the first left (at the traffic lights) and walk past the Jockey Club playground up to the main Po Shek Wu Road, where you'll see the China Light and Power building over the way. Cross at the lights and go down the steps straight ahead of you, just to your right. Walk along by the side of the small drainage channel and through the car park, and behind the new apartment buildings is the old village. It's an almost medieval raggle-taggle of buildings with dank alleys between the houses, just wide enough for one person to walk down and with open gutters alive with rustling rats. The houses are a strange mixture, some brand new with bright tiling, others just corrugated iron and cheap plaster. It's actually much less alarming than it appears and, though you might be stared at, there's not much to fear. Every house pays protection money to the local "security" group, so opportunistic crime is rare. The only thing to see is the large local **ancestral hall**, Liu Man Shek Tong (Wed & Thur, Sat & Sun, 9am–1pm & 2–5pm) built in the eighteenth century. Giving directions to this is pointless, since the name and numbering system for the alleys is hopelessly confusing, but you'll stumble across it sooner or later and be glad that you did: unlike many such places in more touristy parts of Hong Kong, this one is firmly in use by the locals and still stands in its original crumbly surroundings, carved and decorated in traditional fashion.

Practicalities

Buses use the bays outside the KCR station. Many **minibuses** – including the #17 to Lok Ma Chau – leave from San Fat Street.

There are lots of **restaurants** in the small centre of Shek Wu Hui, including the rambling *New Best Restaurant*, on San Fung Avenue, good for *dim sum*: head up the escalators and try to attract the attention of the head waiter. The food is great, and very cheap – and you'll be the only tourist in the place. For just a plate of meat and rice, or bowl of noodles, the *Ming Yuen* on the corner of San Fat Street and Fu Hing Street, opposite Watson's, is worth a try. Also on San Fat Street, there's the *Malaysian Restaurant* (no. 26), which serves decent Malaysian food, as well as European lunches and dinners; the *Thai Food Restaurant*, next door, has more good-value Asian cooking. Even cheaper meals are available at the **dai pai dongs** in the town's market – they're all at the eastern end of San Shing Avenue.

CHINA

THE NEW TERRITORIES

The Border: Lo Wu, Lok Ma Chau and San Tin

The **border with China** remains a customs and immigration barrier under the "one country, two systems" policy which governs Hong Kong's relationship with the mainland. It follows the course of the Sham Chun river across the narrow neck of the New Territories' peninsula. There aren't any compelling reasons to go and look – it is only a fence and a river when all's said and done – but if you're in the area anyway, at Sheung Shui particularly, you may want to make the trip just to say you've been.

Lo Wu and the border

The crossing into China used by foreign travellers is the train link through the station of **LO WU**, one stop after Sheung Shui and the last stop on the Hong Kong side of the border. You're only allowed here if you're equipped with valid travel documents to go on into China; otherwise it's a closed area to visitors.

Local people make the crossing at a couple of other points – Sha Tau Kok and Man Kam To, just northeast of Sheung Shui. It's possible to cross the border here with the right documentation, but there's no real point without your own transport since onward connections are nonexistent.

Lok Ma Chau

For years, **LOK MA CHAU**, 4km west of Sheung Shui, was the place to come and peer over the border at Red China from a special viewing platform built above the river. It's a bit anachronistic these days, but still makes for a pleasant hour or two's diversion as Lok Ma Chau lies in some isolated, green surroundings. Even here, though, the jackhammers are falling as the fields are dug up to accommodate new developments.

The best way here is by **bus**: either the #76K from Sheung Shui KCR station or minibus #17 from San Fat Street (see p.159). Both take about fifteen minutes to reach the general area: ask the bus driver – you need to get off at the junction of Lok Ma Chau Road and Castle

Peak Road, and follow the signposts up the main road to the lookout point, which will take another fifteen to twenty minutes. A steep road leads up between souvenir stalls to a car park. Then a path takes you to a terrace overlooking Shenzhen, the Chinese border town. The river marks the boundary, the fishponds are on the Chinese side and the wire fence delineates a sort of no-man's land. There's a small Chinese-style pavilion, benches, and just below it a small shrine. The glazed pots contain human bones, a local burial custom. Back down the road there's a restaurant, and frequent minibuses heading back to the main road if you can't be bothered to walk.

From the main road, you don't need to head back to Sheung Shui for the return trip. If you set out early enough to get up to this part of the New Territories, flagging down the next #76K bus that runs past takes you into Yuen Long, a New Town around twenty minutes south (see p.171). From here, it's easy to circle right around the western New Territories before returning to Kowloon or Central, a couple of hours' travelling all told if you don't linger.

San Tin

If rural peace and quiet appeals, head for the traditional Chinese dwellings at the nearby village of **SAN TIN**. On foot from Lok Ma Chau, return to the main Castle Peak Road (20min) and turn right, heading along the busy main road towards Yuen Long; it's another ten minutes to San Tin. By bus, take the #76K or #17 minibus from Sheung Shui and get off in San Tin by the Esso service station.

Walk up the street beside the post office, just off the main road, and within five minutes you'll be at **Tai Fu Tai** (daily except Tues 9am–5pm; free), a fine example of a nineteenth-century home built for a wealthy Chinese family of the Man clan, who originally settled this area in the fifteenth century. There are some excellent murals inside, carved wood panels, and glazed friezes in high relief. Built in 1865, this is considered one of the most beautiful buildings of its kind remaining in Hong Kong – and you'll have the place to yourself. From here, continue through the maze of quiet streets and you'll find three ancestral halls. The best of these, the **Man Lun Fung Ancestral Hall**, was built in the mid-seventeenth century and restored in 1987. It's still in regular use as a place for worship and meeting by local people; the forest of wooden tablets commemorates men of the clan.

The West: Tsuen Wan, Tuen Mun and Yuen Long

Access to the **western New Territories** is a simple matter, and connecting transport means you can construct a day-trip which runs through all the major towns and villages. There are two routes, both of which start at **Tsuen Wan**, a New Town at the end of the MTR line,

**The West:
Tsuen Wan,
Tuen Mun
and Yuen
Long**

or reached by hoverferry from Central. Attractions here include the excellent **Sam Tung Uk Museum**, a restored Hakka village, and some good walks in the neighbouring **country parks**. From Tsuen Wan, the most popular route is the bus run up Route Twisk, past the famous walled villages of the **Kam Tin** area to **Yuen Long** town. Yuen Long is close to the oyster beds at **Lau Fau Shan**, where you might want to break for lunch. Alternatively, buses run from Tsuen Wan along the shore to **Tuen Mun**, passing several excellent **beaches** along the way. Yuen Long and Tuen Mun are connected by bus and train (the LRT), so completing the circle is easy. Alternatively, buses run east from Yuen Long to connect up with stations on the KCR rail line, from where it's an easy trip back to Kowloon.

Tsuen Wan

Approached by bus from the north or west TSUEN WAN ("shallow bay") appears as a stack of white high-rises nestling between the hills, overlooking Tsing Yi Island and the greater harbour beyond. Arriving by hoverferry from Central is similarly exhilarating, a short skim across the water providing a good view of the western side of Kowloon. The only approach that doesn't merit attention is the one that most people are likely to make: taking the tunnel-bound Tsuen Wan MTR line west to its terminal station, depositing you right in the centre of town in the midst of some major development. In 1898 there were only three thousand inhabitants, mostly farmers. Now, around a million people live or work in the area, and the town has the futuristic, concrete-bound look favoured by planners all over Hong Kong: flyovers and walkways spin off in all directions, and signposts point into interlinking malls and gardens. There's the usual complement of shops and stores, and if it's your first New Town it merits a brief look around. Apart from the **market**, three blocks south of the MTR, the only thing worth seeing in the centre is the first-rate Sam Tung Uk Museum, though there are several attractive **walks** on the outskirts if you've got time to spare.

The Sam Tung Uk Museum

The Tsuen Wan area was completely depopulated following the orders of the seventeenth-century Manchu government to abandon the coastal villages in response to constant pirate attacks. It wasn't populated again until the end of the century and permanent settlements only developed later, typified by the eighteenth-century Hakka walled village that survives today as the **Sam Tung Uk Museum** (daily except Tues 9am–5pm; free). The museum is on Kwu Uk Lane; exit left from the MTR and follow the signs to the museum along the pedestrian walkway.

Founded by a clan originally from China's Fujian province, who moved into Guangdong, the name of what was a farming village means "three-beamed dwelling" – a reference to the three-roofed halls

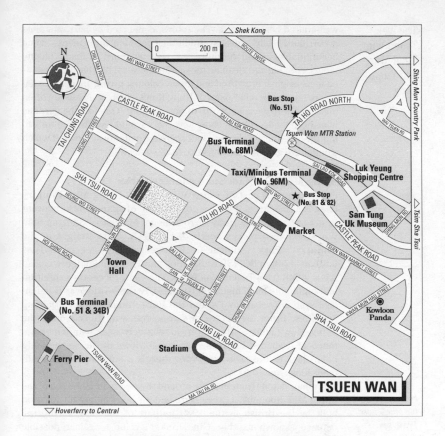

that form the central axis of the village, with new housing added on both sides as the village grew. At the entrance there's an **orientation room** which tells the fascinating story of the village's restoration. There's a particularly revealing photograph that shows Sam Tung Uk surrounded by similar adjacent villages when Tsuen Wan was just a gleam in a planner's eye, taken as recently as 1977, which indicates the speed of development here. As the New Town went up around it, the villagers moved out, and in 1981 Sam Tung Uk was declared a monument – cleaned, stripped and renovated to its original condition, with the furniture and most of the exhibits actually collected from two contemporary Hakka villages over the border in Guangdong.

It's a remarkable achievement, although critics might argue that the **buildings** are too pristine to be authentic. The basic layout is of three connected halls: a common room for villagers, with carts and sedan chairs; a central hall for banquets and gatherings; and the ancestral hall, which faced the main entrance. Everywhere, the walls are whitewashed and cool, the buildings sporting low lintels and well-crafted beamed roofs. The rooms, connected by narrow streets – corridors really – display traditional farming implements, some beautiful blackwood furniture, as well as more ordinary chairs, tables, cooking and cleaning tools. The ancestral hall has been painted in its original bright red and green colours, giving an idea of what you're missing in other parts of Hong Kong, where the halls are often ingrained with decades' worth of dust and dirt. Outside, the **gardens** have been landscaped to show how there would have been a threshing ground and a fishpond, and there's a gatehouse beyond which would have guarded the entrance to the village.

Shing Mun and Kam Shan country parks

Fifteen minutes east of Tsuen Wan by bus, **Shing Mun Country Park** is a fine target if you've got a couple of spare hours and want to get out into more rural surroundings. Maxicab #82 from Shiu Wo Street, two blocks south of the MTR, runs straight to the **Country Park Visitor's Centre** (daily except Tues 9.30am–4.30pm ☎2489 8598/1362) and on Sunday there is also a bus #94S from Tsuen Wan ferry. The visitor's centre exhibition hall highlights local history – particularly the World War II defensive system (see below) – and the flora, fauna and local mining activities. From the centre, a signposted walk runs around the Shing Mun (Jubilee) Reservoir, a relatively easy two-hour hike, much of it shaded by trees, with great views of the surrounding hills. Back at the visitor's centre there's a summertime refreshment kiosk and toilets.

For more on the MacLehose Trail, see p.178.

A minor detour from the hike around the reservoir takes you to the **Shing Mun Redoubt**, a twelve-acre underground hilltop fortification built by the British in the 1939 as part of the New Territories' defence (known as the "Gin Drinker's Line") against possible Japanese invasion. Based on a series of tunnels – each named after a London street or area – the system was taken by the Japanese after a short but bloody battle in 1941. Large parts of the system still remain intact, covered by undergrowth: if you're intent upon exploring, take a flashlight and be careful, since the tunnels aren't maintained. To get there from the visitor's centre, walk around the reservoir in an anti-clockwise direction; when you see a big overhead sign marked "MacLehose Trail (Stage Six)", leave the road and join the trail – the tunnels start about ten minutes after the sign, mostly on the left hand side of the track.

This section of the **MacLehose Trail** itself heads south towards Smuggler's Ridge, a ninety-minute climb that takes you into the neighbouring **Kam Shan Country Park**, known for its wild macaque monkeys. This section of the trail ends at the Kowloon Reservoirs and the park entrance, from where you can pick up buses back to either Jordan MTR (#81) or Sham Shui Po MTR (#72) stations in Kowloon.

Yuen Yuen Institute

To complete the tour of Tsuen Wan's outskirts, take maxicab #81 from Shiu Wo Street (two blocks south of Tsuen Wan MTR) to the Yuen Yuen Institute, a ten-minute ride into the green hills overlooking the city; the bus may be marked Lo Wai Village. It's a working temple dedicated to Taoism, Buddhism and Confucianism – which makes for an interesting mix of styles. The main building is a replica of Beijing's Temple of Heaven, and there are also bonsai trees, a collection of rocks (contemplated by scholars as an aid to meditation) and a dining room with very good vegetarian food. Lunch is around $60.

Practicalities

The **hoverferry** from Central docks down at Tsuen Wan Ferry Pier, a five-minute walk from the Town Hall; see p.51 for details. Bus #51 goes to **Kam Tin** via Route Twisk (see p.168) from the terminal next to the pier (it also makes a stop on the flyover above the MTR station). Also from the Ferry Pier, bus #34B runs along the coastal Castle Peak Road, passing the **beaches** covered in the section below.

The main **bus terminal** in Tsuen Wan is opposite the MTR station, underneath the shopping centre. From here, bus #68M goes to **Tuen Mun/Yuen Long**, which follows the new highway and not the parallel coastal road; this is the bus to take if you're heading for either the Ching Chung Koon Temple or the Mui Fat Monastery. The main **taxi/maxicab terminal** is along the main road (underneath the multistorey car park, opposite the Luk Yeung Shopping Centre). Maxicab #96, which skirts the coast for the beaches and the goose restaurants at Sham Tseng, departs from Hoi Pa Street, four blocks south of the MTR station. **Shiu Wo Street**, a couple of blocks south of the MTR, near the market, has the minibus and maxicab stops for the country parks and the Yuen Yuen Institute.

Tsuen Wan has one of the New Territories' few **hotels**, the *Kowloon Panda* (see p.229 for details); inside is the *Yuet Loy Heen* **restaurant**, on the second floor, which serves highly rated *dim sum* from 7am to 3pm; the seafood choices are especially good.

The coastal route: Castle Peak Road

Two parallel roads run along the **coast** of the western New Territories beyond Tsuen Wan: the new, fast highway, Tuen Mun Road, and the quieter and original **Castle Peak Road**. Finished in 1919, this road is the one to follow if you want to see any of the shoreline, as it winds around the **beaches** and small headlands between Tsuen Wan and Tuen Mun, before cutting up through the inland region to Yuen Long and continuing to Lok Ma Chau. The coastal part of the route is best done on maxicab #96 or bus #34B from Tsuen Wan: see "Practicalities" above for details.

THE NEW TERRITORIES

Tsing Yi Island which dominates the entire first half of the coastline, across Rambler Channel from Tsuen Wan, is home to container

terminals, oil depots and other industrial concerns. The various nox-
ious emissions haven't helped the water quality, which is already hit
by the junk flowing out of Tsuen Wan's harbour. Consequently, the
water hereabouts is off limits for swimming.

The beaches and Sham Tseng

The **beaches** nearest to Tsuen Wan are all pretty much affected by
the polluted water, but the sands are generally fine. You'll pass
Approach beach and **Ting Kau**, while further on are **Ho Mei Wan**
and **Gemini** beaches; beyond Sham Tseng come **Angler's** and
Dragon.

If none of these appeal, consider stopping at **SHAM TSENG** itself,
a little roadside village about fifteen minutes out of Tseun Wan. Get
off at the stop after the massive San Miguel brewery, directly opposite which there's a line of nine or ten **restaurants**, all specializing in
roast goose and duck. The *Chan Kee*, right opposite the factory, has
an English menu and tables under a marquee where you can spend a
very pleasant lunchtime eating goose, swigging the local San Miguel
beer, and avoiding the heavier Chui Chow-influenced items on the
menu – the rather alarming "pig's ding", as well as intestines and
goose blood.

*For more on
the LRT sys-
tem, see p.49.*

Tuen Mun and around

For the rest of the ride to Tuen Mun you can sit back and appreciate
the views over the water and the increasingly built-up coast. There
are a few beaches on the eastern side of town, but again the water
quality is very dodgy. **TUEN MUN** itself, a large and straggling town
of nearly half a million, doesn't do much to tempt you off the bus – a
couple of nearby Chinese temples are the only interest. The name of
the town means "Channel Gate", a reminder that this was once an
important defensive post, guarding the eastern approaches to the
Pearl River Estuary. These days it's a standard New Town sporting
the obligatory shopping and commercial development – **Tuen Mun
Town Plaza** – which at least makes an attempt at variation: there's a
fake Georgian square around a fountain, planted inside the plaza.

If you came from Tsuen Wan on the #68M bus, stick with it as it
runs right through the town, passing both temples. Otherwise, get off
in the centre and make your way to one of the stations of the **Light
Rail Transit** system (LRT), which links Tuen Mun with Yuen Long to
the north; there are terminals right in the centre, or down at the
Ferry Pier, where the **hoverferries** from Central arrive and depart.
To head back to Kowloon, bus #68X runs to Jordan Road Ferry Pier.

Ching Chung Koon Temple

There's a large Taoist temple complex, the **Ching Chung Koon
Temple** (daily 7am–7pm), just out of Tuen Mun, off Tsing Chung
Koon Road. It's a little complicated to find, but worth the effort. Alight

New Towns

The dominant feature of the New Territories' countryside are the seemingly ubiquitous **New Towns**, each a forest of residential and commercial towers, shopping centres and flyovers. Borrowing from similar British experiments of the 1950s and 1960s, the first plans were laid in 1972, with the proposed towns designed to provide homes for almost two million people. This resulted in the construction of Tsuen Wan, Tuen Mun and Sha Tin, still the three largest developments; Tsuen Wan alone will eventually house around 700,000 people. A second wave of projects saw the rapid rise of Yuen Long, Tai Po and Sheung Shui/Fanling, all of which are now substantially complete. The final wave this century will be the development of sites at Tung Chung (next to the new airport on Lantau), Tin Shui Wai (northwest of Yuen Long) and Tsueng Kwan O (Junk Bay, east of Kowloon City). When finished, the nine new towns will have a total capacity of over 3.5 million inhabitants; in 1898, when the New Territories were first leased to Britain, fewer than ten thousand farmers and fishermen lived in the region.

Each New Town is designed to be self-sufficient, in that they feature local employment opportunities, a full range of cultural, civic and leisure services, shops and markets, and co-ordinated transport facilities. For the majority, they offer a better environment to live in than the crowded tenement slums of Mongkok or Kowloon City. Residential living space is limited, but much thought was given to enhancing the quality of life outside the home: markets, shops, laundries and sports facilities are provided, sometimes within apartment buildings; pedestrian and vehicular traffic is segregated as far as possible; cinemas and theatres are on the doorstep.

But while they are supposed to be much more than mere "dormitory" towns for central Hong Kong, there is an awareness that to thrive in future the New Towns have to attract inhabitants who work elsewhere in the territory. Consequently, as part of the development programme currently underway in Hong Kong, many New Towns are looking at improved **transport links** both with each other and with the rest of the territory. Tung Chung already forms an integral part of the airport scheme (see pp.204–205) and is just half an hour from Central by rail; Tsueng Kwan O is scheduled to have its own MTR link by the year 2000; while the proposed 52-kilometre Western Corridor Railway will link Tuen Mun, Yuen Long and Tsuen Wan and connect them with interlinking stations on the MTR and KCR.

It's certainly worth taking the time to look round a New Town, if only to see the environment in which most local people live, and what can be achieved in just a few years given a coherent planning programme. Sha Tin (p.149) is perhaps the most attractive since it's splendidly sited and has had time to acquire a certain character. The town centre of Tuen Mun (see opposite) was only completed in 1990; while Sheung Shui/Fanling (p.158), close to the Chinese border, is set to change greatly in the next few years due to their proximity to the free-market antics of the adjacent Shenzhen Special Economic Zone. The most dramatic development, though, will be at Tung Chung (p.206). Just opposite the new airport, it's planned to serve as the future gateway into Hong Kong and to become a major residential and business centre in its own right.

at the #68M bus stop on Castle Peak Road, just a few minutes out of
the centre (ask the driver), then walk to the left over the small hill,
cross the river and you'll come to Affluence LRT station (line #507
from Tuen Mun Ferry Pier or #612 from the town centre); bear left
through the housing estate to the main road, and the temple is visible
to your right.

There's an altar to the Earth God at the entrance. Just inside is a
plan of the complex of temples, gardens and shrines, built in 1949
and dedicated to Lu Sun Young, an eighth-century "immortal" blessed
with magical and curative powers. The main temple is flanked by
small pavilions housing bells and drums, used to signal prayer times.
Vegetarian lunches (a set meal served for a minimum of two people)
can be booked in the room to the left, while next down is the
Ancestral Hall, unusually large and crammed full of photos and
records of the dead. People pray here for their ancestors' souls, and
occasionally you might catch a commemoration service, with chant-
ing monks accompanied by drums, cymbals and flutes. The best time
to see this is at either of the annual festivals which commemorate the
dead: Ching Ming or Yue Lan (see pp.283–284). At the end of the
buildings, there's an ornamental **garden**, carefully built in traditional
style, with imported Chinese rocks, a rock pool and pagodas, setting
off perfectly the air of formal prayer and devotion in the complex.

Mui Fat Monastery

The other local temple, this time strictly Buddhist in character, is
the **Mui Fat Monastery**, about 4km north of Tuen Mun on Castle
Peak Road, halfway to Yuen Long. You can get there on the #68M
bus, which stops virtually outside, or on the #68X direct from
Jordan Road Ferry Terminal; or ride the LRT from either Tuen Mun
or Yuen Long – get off at Lam Tei station, and the temple is just back
up the road.

The only part of the monastery you can get into is the tall, square
temple building set back from the main road, a garish building whose
entrance is guarded by two golden dragons, their bodies writhing up
the building, the usual pair of lions, and two six-tusked elephants.
There are three floors inside, the top one overwhelming in its opu-
lence, with three large golden Buddhas, massive crystal chandeliers,
marble tablets and little Buddha images lining the walls, and a bell
and a skin drum hanging at either side.

On the middle floor is a decorated dining room which, like Ching
Chung Koon, serves **vegetarian lunches** (noon–3.30pm): buy a ticket at the desk on the way in and you'll be brought platefuls of food
from the kitchens.

Route Twisk: Tai Mo Shan and Shek Kong

The other bus route through the western New Territories runs anti-
clockwise, inland north of Tsuen Wan and around to Yuen Long, on

the so-called **Route Twisk**, a high road pass which is sometimes blocked in part by landslides during the typhoon season. Twisk, incidentally, stands for "Tsuen Wan Into Shek Kong". Take the #51 bus (every 6–20min), which you can pick up at Tsuen Wan Ferry Pier.

The West: Tsuen Wan, Tuen Mun and Yuen Long

Tai Mo Shan and the MacLehose Trail

It's a splendid climb in the bus up the hillside above Tsuen Wan, with great views back to the sea. The road twists past bamboo groves and banana trees, while the occasional clearing off to the side harbours a picnic site perched on the edge of a hill. After 4–5km, just above the village of Chuen Lung, the bus stops at an entrance to the **Tai Mo Shan Country Park**, which contains Hong Kong's highest peak, **Tai Mo Shan**, 957m above sea level. The climb is straightforward enough, and can be combined with a night in the nearby **Sze Lok Yuen Youth Hostel**, which you reach by getting off the #51 at the junction with the smaller Tai Mo Shan Road – the hostel is signposted, around 45 minutes' walk up the road; turn right onto a small concrete track after passing the car park. You'll need to bring your own food. There's a visitor's centre near the bus stop with details of all the other local trails, including the walk to the magnificent series of waterfalls at **Ng Tung Chai**, in the north of the park.

At either the hostel or the peak, you're just off the **MacLehose Trail** (Stage 8), 22km from its western end at Tuen Mun. If you fancy a short day's hike, join the trail here and walk west to Tin Fu Tsai (6km), from where you can drop down the 3–4km to the coast at Tsing Lung Tau for buses east or west along the coast. There's also a **campsite** in the Tai Mo Shan Country Park, by the management centre, over on the western side of Route Twisk.

See p.178 for more details on the MacLehose Trail.

Shek Kong and the Kadoorie Experimental Farm

The #51 bus climbs up over the pass and rattles down the winding road into the **Shek Kong** (pronounced "Sek" Kong) area, through richly forested slopes, offering sweeping views of the plain below and of the runway formerly used by the Shek Kong military garrison.

To the east of Shek Kong is the **Kadoorie Farm and Botanical Gardens** (Mon–Sat 9.30am–4pm, free). Founded by the Kadoorie family in the 1950s, the farm's original purpose was as an experimental breeding station. It now also serves as a sanctuary for abandoned and injured animals – endangered species such as owls, birds of prey and snakes saved by the police on their way to the cooking pot often end up here – so it's popular with children. To get there take #64K from Tai Po KCR and get off on Lam Kam Rd. They like you to call one or two days in advance on ☎ 2488 1317.

Kam Tin

The #51 bus ends its ride in **KAM TIN**, an area famous for its surviving **walled villages**. One of them at least is firmly on the tourist map, but there are a couple of others in the area displaying the same characteristic buildings and solid defensive walls.

Kat Hing Wai is the most obvious walled village, 200m down the main road from the bus stop, opposite a small Wellcome supermarket. The square walls enclose a self-contained village, encircled by a moat, which has been inhabited for nearly four hundred years by members of the Tang clan, who once farmed the surrounding area. Their ancestors moved here from central and southern China almost eight hundred years ago, fortifying villages like these against pirate attacks and organizing their lives with little recourse to the measures and edicts of far-off Imperial China. As late as 1898, this village was one of those prepared to see action against the new British landlords, when local militias were raised to resist the handing over of the New Territories to Britain. As punishment the British confiscated the iron gates of the village – they were returned in 1925 after having been found in Ireland.

Today, the buildings are as defensively impressive as ever, with guardhouses on each corner, but otherwise Kat Hing Wai is rather a sad sight, with lots of bad modern buildings and TV aerials. Most of it is now geared to tourists: the main street is lined with tacky souvenir stalls and Hakka women posing for photos in their "costume" (still normal dress in many parts of the New Territories). They'll want money if you try and take a photo, and it'll cost you a dollar to set foot through the gate in the first place.

More rewarding is **Shui Tau Tsuen**, a few hundred metres back down the main road (towards Tsuen Wan) on the right; at the Mung Yeung Public School, follow the lane down and over the bridge. The village is much bigger, though not as immediately promising. New building on the outskirts has destroyed the sense of a walled settlement, and many of the old buildings are locked or falling down. But the elegant carved roofs are still apparent, and a walk around the tight alleys reveals the local temple and an ancestral hall, and gives at least some impression of normal village life. The other village in the area is **Wing Lung Wai**, up the main road in the opposite direction, beyond Kat Hing Wai, though this is mostly fenced off and inaccessible to visitors. You can, however, get into the market here for the usual mix of noise and activity.

Practicalities

The #51 **bus** stops on the main, traffic-choked Kam Tin Road, opposite the post office and Hongkong Bank. The road is virtually a bazaar, lined with hardware stores, grocers, restaurants, bars and even discos – slightly surprising in the middle of nowhere until you realize that this used to be the site of a big British military base. There are **cafés** all the way down Kam Tin Road serving noodles and the like. Scarcely any more formal, but providing a change, the *Gurkha Restaurant*, opposite the bus stop and next to the post office, has reasonably priced Nepali and Indian food.

There are various **onward routes**: #77K runs down the main road on its way from Yuen Long to Sheung Shui; minibus #18 runs along the same route; and #51 runs back to Tsuen Wan. You can also catch bus #54 to Yuen Long West, while #64K passes the walled villages on its run between Tai Po KCR and Yuen Long.

Yuen Long

There's a good chance you'll pass through the town of **YUEN LONG**, a major transport hub in the western New Territories. It's not a place to hang around in, however. A built-up New Town with more than 120,000 residents and an LRT train line running right down the middle of the main street, it's much the same as all the other New Towns and unrecognizable as the coastal fishing village it once was. There are still visible relics of an older life in the surrounding countryside, however – small temples and ancestral homes scattered across the fragmented coastline. Unfortunately, they're almost all difficult to reach and mostly run-down, though the government has preserved a series of buildings in nearby Ping Shan which you can visit. The closest Yuen Long itself gets to tradition are the big annual celebrations of the **Tin Hau Festival**, a throwback to the town's fishing days. The town is also renowned for the quality of its **moon cakes**, the small lotus-seed cakes with a preserved egg yolk that are eaten during the Mid-Autumn Festival – some of the best in the territory are the Wing Wah moon cakes made by the *Tai Wing Wah Restaurant*, 11 Tai Lee Street.

THE NEW TERRITORIES

On buses to the town, the destination indicator often reads "Un Long" and not "Yuen Long"; it's the same place.

Practicalities

The **bus terminal** is in On Tat Square, just off the main Castle Peak Road down Kik Yeung Road, from where you can catch buses #76K and #77K to Fanling; bus #276 or #276P to Sheung Shui; #68M to Tuen Mun (for Mui Fat Monastery and Ching Chung Koon Temple); #68X to Jordan Road Ferry Pier; or the #64K to Tai Po Market KCR station. There's a separate **minibus terminal** nearby on Tai Fung Street: to get to it, turn into Kuk Ting Street at 77 Castle Peak Rd (Bank of East Asia), follow Sai Tai Street, and Tai Fung Street is over on the right. This is where to come to catch the direct #33 maxicab to Lau Fau Shan.

Mai Po Marshes

North of Yuen Long, the **Mai Po Marshes** have been designated a site of international importance for migratory waterfowl such as Dalmatian pelicans and black-faced spoonbills, and are also home to other wildlife, including otters. The Mai Po Nature Reserve, at the centre of the marshes, has floating hides for bird-watching. Details of how to get there and organized tours are available on ☎2368 7111.

Lau Fau Shan

The main reason to visit Yuen Long is to take the bus out to nearby LAU FAU SHAN, an oyster-gathering and fishing village a few kilometres northwest. It's the most unusual of the places in Hong Kong in which to eat seafood: a ramshackle settlement built – literally – on old oyster shells. It's also the least visited of the seafood villages, so prices are realistic and a basic meal can be had without much fear of being ripped off. To get there, take #33 maxicab from the terminal on Tai Fung Street (see p.171) or the light railway feeder bus #655 from the main Castle Peak Road.

The West: Tsuen Wan, Tuen Mun and Yuen Long

The ride takes around twenty minutes, through some fairly drastic constructions necessary to protect the local villages from floodwater. The bus stop in Lau Fau Shan is right by the only street, Ching Tai Street, which leads down to the water past a succession of small restaurants, fishmongers' stalls and dried seafood provisions stores, many staffed by ladies in traditional Hakka dress. The oysters are turned into excellent oyster sauce, which is on sale everywhere. The main fish market is at the very end of the street. The dried foods – oysters, scallops, mussels and fish used to make soups – are interesting, but are something of a delicacy; a packet of dried scallops costs up to $500. Walk through the fish market to the main jetty, on either side of which, stretching away into the distance, are enormous dunes made out of piles of millions of old, opened oyster shells, among which are scattered fishing pots, wooden skiffs and wading birds looking for food. The village here looks out over Deep Bay and across to the skyscrapers of the Chinese mainland – a fine prospect.

There are plenty of **restaurants** in the village, all pretty reliable. Choose a fish and they'll bring it wriggling to your table for inspection before whisking it away to be cooked; the deep-fried oysters are also thoroughly recommended, a massive crispy plateful, easily enough for three, will cost about $100.

The East: Clearwater Bay and the Sai Kung peninsula

To visit the eastern limb of the New Territories you'll need to set aside another couple of days: one for the popular beaches and magnificent Tin Hau Temple at Clearwater Bay; another to visit the beautiful **Sai Kung peninsula**, with its fishing town, sands and nearby islands. The whole Sai Kung area is about the closest Hong Kong gets to real isolation, though on weekends and holidays even the large country parks here aren't big enough to absorb all the visitors. Happily, most people stick to two or three spots – those prepared to do some walking will be able to find a bit of space.

Access to both areas is by bus from **Choi Hung** MTR station, on the Kwun Tong line (take the Clearwater Bay North exit). All the buses leave from the bus ranks just outside the station.

To Clearwater Bay

Bus #91 (and #91R on Sun) or regular minibuses from outside Choi Hung MTR station run east and then south along **Clearwater Bay Road**, a pleasant half-hour's ride through striking countryside, dotted with expensive villas with precarious views over the bays below. About halfway, you'll pass the **Shaw Brothers'** and **Clearwater Bay film studios**, where countless Cantonese movies are churned out every year, before dropping down to **Tai Au Mun**, which overlooks **Clearwater Bay** itself.

There's a bus stop here, where you can get off for the first, smaller **beach** (known as #1 beach), though the bus does continue down the hill to stop at the terminus next to the much bigger #2 beach. You can count on this being packed on a sunny weekend, despite its size, and you should take your own food if you've come for the day as there's only a snack kiosk here. A path connects the two beaches if you want to check on space at either one.

Joss House Bay and back

Beyond the beaches the road climbs up and across the peninsula giving marvellous views over the sea, passing the tiny fishing and seafood village of **Po Toi o** over the other side of a small bay, which is guarded by two temples, one on each headland. At the end of the road, half an hour's walk away, is the **Clearwater Bay Country Club**, to which the HKTA sells day-passes if you're after a bit of civilized swimming and lounging about (see p.301).

By the side of the club entrance (the wider of two marked paths) leads down to **Joss House Bay**, or Tai Mui Wan, where one of Hong Kong's finest temples is situated. The short path runs past a rock bearing an inscription dating from 1274 (Southern Sung Dynasty) recording a visit made by an officer in charge of salt administration – the oldest known dated inscription in Hong Kong. Further on is the **Tin Hau Temple** itself – elaborately carved and beautifully sited, with a large terrace overlooking the bay. Built originally in 1266 (though reworked several times since, particularly in 1962 after Typhoon Wanda almost destroyed it), this is *the* major site of the annual Tin Hau celebrations in Hong Kong, and there's a long pier below the terrace where thousands of passengers disgorge from the special chartered junks and ferries to come to pay homage to the Goddess of the Sea. The temple entrance is guarded by two small stone lions with round stones in their mouths: turn the stones three times for luck. Inside are incense spirals, a drum and stalls selling religious items.

Back at the entrance to the Country Club, a second trail leads, circuitously, back to Clearwater Bay beach, near the village of

CHINA

THE NEW TERRITORIES

The East: Clearwater Bay and the Sai Kung peninsula

The East: Clearwater Bay and the Sai Kung peninsula

Sheung Lau Wan. Bypassing the village, the path heads over the ridge, where you can detour to climb to the nearby summit of **Tin Ha Shan** or simply drop straight down to the main road, just five minutes from the bus terminal. The whole walk – past Po Toi O, Joss House Bay, the temple and then around the headland – should take two to three hours depending on the heat and humidity. Take water, and be warned that the path is sketchily marked at times – you may spend periods scampering up and down the hill looking for the route. Paths also continue further north to Silverstrand Beach.

Tung Lung Chau

Lying just to the south of the peninsula, the small island of **TUNG LUNG CHAU** maintains a restored eighteenth-century Chinese fort on its northern shore. Overlooking the Fat Tong Mun (or Fat Tong) passage, the **Tung Lung Fort** kept a strategic eye on ships sailing to Hong Kong, but was finally abandoned to the elements at the beginning of the nineteenth century. It remained overgrown until 1979, when its rectangular walls and interior were restored and opened to the public. There's also an **information centre** here (daily except Tues 9am–4pm). Tung Lung's other historic attraction is Hong Kong's largest **rock carving**, a representation of a dragon some two metres tall – take the path from the fort and head back past the ferry pier; around 1500 metres in all.

Despite the island's proximity to the Clearwater Bay peninsula, it can only be reached by **ferry from Sai Wan Ho** (see p.116) on Hong Kong Island (Sat & Sun; $10). Ferries currently leave at 8.30am and 3.30pm and return at 9.30am and 5pm; they dock roughly halfway between the fort and the rock carving. The journey takes about 30 minutes. Check times with the HKTA or call the Coral Sea Ferry Company (☎2513 1835) for timetable information.

Sai Kung Town and its beaches

THE NEW TERRITORIES

North of Clearwater Bay, beaches and coves spread over a large area, incorporating a series of island retreats, good walking trails and even a folk museum. The whole area is known as **Sai Kung**, and is divided into two main **country parks**, with several approaches and little centres. The main centre is the rapidly developing resort of **SAI KUNG TOWN**. Bus #92 from Diamond Hill MTR or maxicab #1 from Choi Hung MTR take around half an hour, following Clearwater Bay Road before heading north along Hiram's Highway, passing Hebe Haven on the way. Alternatively, take bus #299 from New Town Plaza in Sha Tin.

The Town

New building is rather dwarfing the little fishing village that Sai Kung once was, but for the moment it remains a pleasant enough seaside

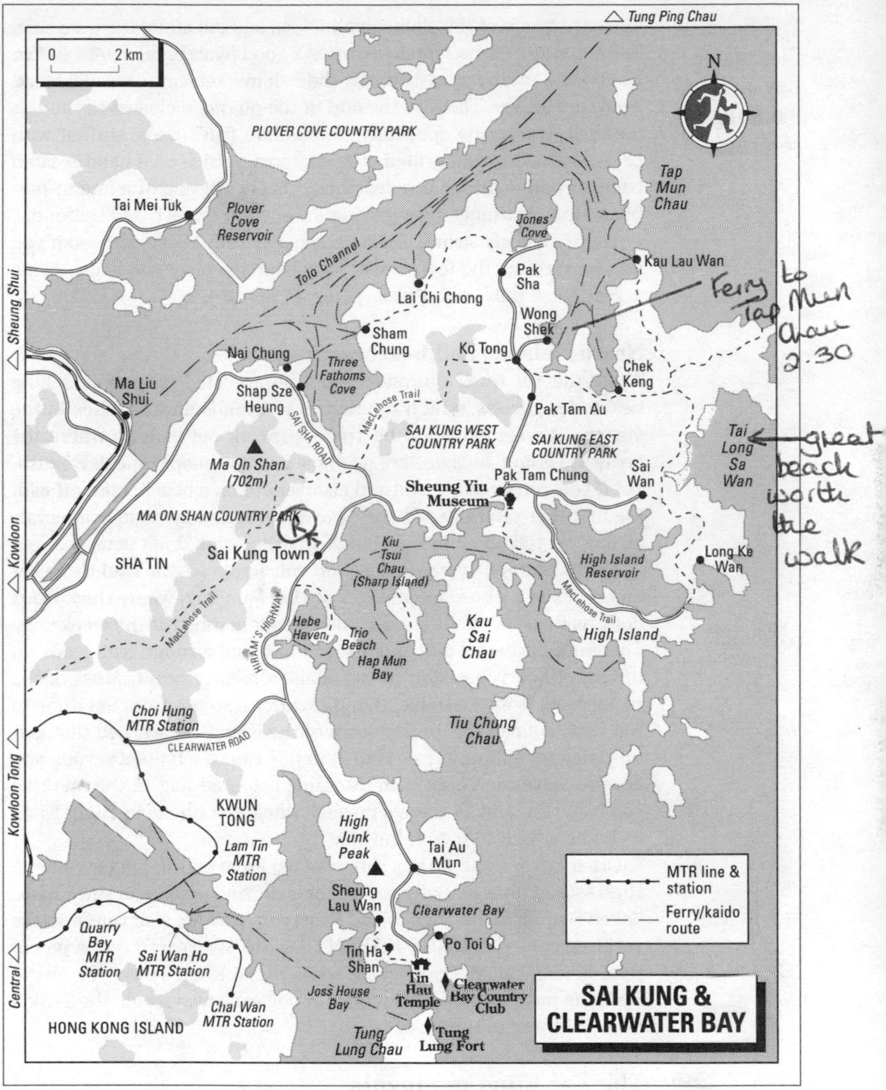
Tung Ping Chau
0 2 km
N
PLOVER COVE COUNTRY PARK
Tai Mei Tuk
Plover Cove Reservoir
Tap Mun Chau
Jones' Cove
Kau Lau Wan
Tolo Channel
Pak Sha
Lai Chi Chong
Wong Shek
Sheung Shui
Sham Chung
Ko Tong
Nai Chung
Three Fathoms Cove
Chek Keng
Ma Liu Shui
Shap Sze Heung
MacLehose Trail
Pak Tam Au
SAI SHA ROAD
SAI KUNG WEST COUNTRY PARK
SAI KUNG EAST COUNTRY PARK
Tai Long Sa Wan
Ma On Shan (702m)
Pak Tam Chung
Sai Wan
Sheung Yiu Museum
MA ON SHAN COUNTRY PARK
Kowloon
Kiu Tsui Chau (Sharp Island)
Long Ke Wan
Sai Kung Town
SHA TIN
High Island Reservoir
MacLehose Trail
HIRAM'S HIGHWAY
MacLehose Trail
Hebe Haven
Trio Beach
Kau Sai Chau
High Island
Hap Mun Bay
Choi Hung MTR Station
CLEARWATER ROAD
Tiu Chung Chau
Kowloon Tong
KWUN TONG
High Junk Peak
Lam Tin MTR Station
Tai Au Mun
MTR line & station
Ferry/kaido route
Sheung Lau Wan
Clearwater Bay
Quarry Bay MTR Station
Po Toi O
Tin Ha Shan
Sai Wan Ho MTR Station
Tin Hau Temple
Clearwater Bay Country Club
Central
Joss House Bay
Chai Wan MTR Station
HONG KONG ISLAND
Tung Lung Chau
Tung Lung Fort
SAI KUNG & CLEARWATER BAY
Ferry to Tap Mun Chau 2.30
great beach worth the walk

port. The bus terminal is just back from the sea, with the whole seafront promenade devoted to fish and seafood **restaurants**, most of which have outside seating overlooking the bay. A walk down the seafront takes you to the **fish market** in the older part of town, overlooking the junks tied up in the harbour. Stroll back, and you can pick up a fishing net, line and bait at one of the stalls, or choose your lunch from one of the slabs and buckets laid out along the quayside. The *Seaside Seafood Restaurant* is a good place to take your fish to be cooked, on the quay towards the fish market; or, for a real treat, head for the *San Shui*, at the end of the quayside closest to the bus terminal, where the speciality is "bamboo fish": carp, stuffed with preserved turnip and grilled over charcoal outside on a hand-rotated bamboo pole – pricey but delicious. This is just one of a line of harbourside restaurants here serving excellent fresh fish and seafood.

There's a fairly strong expat presence in town these days, so if you wander through the few streets back from the quay you'll also come across some pubs and a pizza place, *Pepperoni's*.

Nearby islands and beaches

Along the Sai Kung quayside you'll be accosted by people selling tickets for *kaidos*, which run across to **islands and beaches** in the vicinity. It's sometimes a bit tricky to work out exactly where the boats are going, as there are no signs and few people speak English, but if you don't really mind and just want to hit a beach, take off with the first that offers itself. They leave and return at regular intervals all day, so you shouldn't get stuck anywhere you don't want to.

The most popular trip is the short run across to **Kiu Tsui Chau** (or Sharp Island), whose main beach at Hap Mun Bay, where the *kaidos* dock, is fine, though it's small and can get mobbed at the weekends. There are barbecue pits and a snack bar, and a rough trail leads up through thick vegetation to the island's highest point. Most of the rocky coast is inaccessible, though *kaidos* also run from Sai Kung to Kiu Tsui, a small bay to the north of the island. Be warned that getting back to Sai Kung from Hap Mun Bay can be a bit of a scrum: you have to leave on a boat with the same coloured flag as the one that you came on, and as there's no such thing as a queue in Hong Kong it can be a fight to get on the boat.

Other *kaidos* and ferries run from Sai Kung on the longer route to **High Island**, now actually part of the mainland peninsula since dams linked it to form the High Island Reservoir. *Kaidos* also run from the yachting centre of **HEBE HAVEN** (Pak Sha Wan) across to a peninsular beach, called **Trio Beach**, south of Sai Kung Town: the bus to Sai Kung passes Hebe Haven first, or you can always walk the 2–3km from Sai Kung to the beach.

The Sai Kung peninsula

It takes a little more effort to get the best out of the rest of the **Sai Kung peninsula**, which stretches all the way north to the Tolo Channel and encompasses some supremely isolated headlands and coves. The whole region is one giant, 7500-hectare **country park**, split into two sections, **Sai Kung East** and **Sai Kung West**, along with neighbouring **Ma On Shan Country Park**, which reaches down to Sha Tin. There have been settlements here since the fourteenth century, mostly fishing villages, though the area was never widely populated: even thirty years ago most places in Sai Kung could be reached only on foot. Things changed with the opening of the High Island Reservoir and its associated road access in 1979, but Sai Kung has still not been spoiled – though it has become mightily popular with weekend-trippers who want a breath of country air. Following the marked paths through the grasslands and planted forests is very relaxing after a spell in the city: there's plenty of birdlife, some spectacular coastal geological formations due to the peninsula's volcanic history, and lots of quiet places just to plonk yourself down and tear into a picnic.

The best place to start is Sai Kung Town, from where regular buses run to many of the places covered in this section. The **MacLehose Trail** runs right across the peninsula, while you can see most of the more isolated northern coast from the **ferry** which departs twice daily from Ma Liu Shui to Tap Mun Chau (see p.180).

The Countryside Series Sheet 4 (Sai Kung and Clearwater Bay) and the Pak Tam Chung Nature Trail maps, both available from the Government Publications Centre (p.45) are useful. Bookshops also sell maps of the peninsula, worth buying if you're spending more than a day in the area.

Pak Tam Chung

From Sai Kung Town, bus #94 (hourly) and #96R (Sun only; starts in Choi Hung; every 20min) make the fifteen-minute run around the coast to **PAK TAM CHUNG** in Sai Kung Country Park (taxis can enter, but private cars without permits have to stop outside). Pak Tam Chung marks the start of the MacLehose Trail, although there's nothing much here apart from a bus terminal, a **visitor's centre** where you can pick up local hiking and transport information (daily except Tues 9.30am–4.30pm; ☎2792 7365) and the nearby **Sheung Yiu Folk Museum** (daily except Tues 9am–4pm; free). The museum is a thirty-minute walk from the bus terminal along the seashore down the **Pak Tam Chung Nature Trail**, a pleasantly shady and signposted route that includes a *feng shui* woodland, labelled with explanations of the *feng shui* principles involved in the layout of its trees and water. It's based around an abandoned village, Sheung Yiu, founded 150 years ago by a Hakka family who made their living from the produce of a local lime kiln. The kiln itself is on the outskirts of the village, on the path as you approach; the lime from it was used for local agriculture and building purposes. Further on, the village is a line of whitewashed houses built on a high terrace overlooking the water and defended by a thick wall and gate tower, which kept off the pirates who roamed the area in the nineteenth century. The tile-roofed houses, including an equipped kitchen house, have been restored and filled with farming implements, typical Hakka clothes and diagrams showing how the kiln worked.

The MacLehose Trailhead: High Island and Tai Long Wan

Keep on down the Pak Tam Road from Pak Tam Chung, past the turn-off for the museum, and the **trailhead** for the western end of the cross-New Territories **MacLehose Trail** is just a few minutes'

The MacLehose Trail

The **MacLehose Trail** (named after a former Governor) is a 100-kilometre-long hiking route which stretches from Pak Tam Chung on the Sai Kung peninsula to the new town of Tuen Mun. There's a sketch map of the trail below. It links seven different country parks and is divided into ten different signposted stages, each of which connects with public transport and some of which are provided with campsites, so that you can make a day's hike or complete the whole trail, as you wish. There's one official IYHF youth hostel right on the trail at Tai Mo Shan, as well as a couple close to the trail at Wong Shek. You could do the whole trail in four or five days, but most people take it slower, particularly if they're attempting it in the summer, when the going is hot; the easternmost sections are the most attractive. An annual charity race sets teams a 48-hour target for the course; the winners usually manage it in well under 24, while the record (set by Gurkha troops) is just 13.

Information on the trail, including 1:10,000 route maps, is available from the **Country Parks Division**, Agriculture and Fisheries Department, 12th Floor, 393 Canton Rd, Tsim Sha Tsui ☎2733 2235 (Mon–Fri 9am–5pm, Sat 9am–noon).

turn-off for the museum, and the **trailhead** for the western end of the cross-New Territories **MacLehose Trail** is just a few minutes' walk ahead. The first two stages of this hundred-kilometre route run off to the south from here, through the Sai Kung East Country Park, a twenty-kilometre hike around **High Island Reservoir** and then north to Pak Tam Road, from where you can continue the trail or cut back to Pak Tam Chung. This part of the trail takes the best part of a day to complete, but there are no less than seven **campsites** along the way, one of which, at Long Ke Wan on the southeastern edge of the reservoir, has a fine beach. Less committed hikers could short-

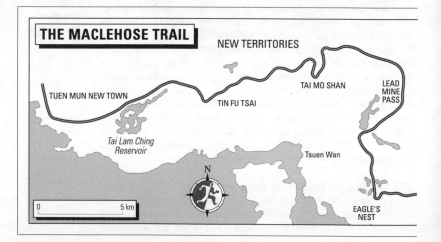

THE MACLEHOSE TRAIL

NEW TERRITORIES

TUEN MUN NEW TOWN

TIN FU TSAI

TAI MO SHAN

LEAD MINE PASS

Tai Lam Ching Reservoir

Tsuen Wan

N

0   5 km

EAGLE'S NEST

three-quarters of the way round (at Sai Wan), heading directly back to Pak Tam Chung.

If you're looking for a beach at the end of a walk, then a path just beyond Sai Wan leads north to the bay of **Tai Long Sa Wan** – a much better target from Pak Tam Chung if you're not interested in completing any part of the MacLehose Trail for its own sake. It'll still take three to four hours for the round trip (around 12km by concrete path), but the beach of unspoiled white sand, one of the finest in the territory, is very definitely worth it. The small village of Ham Tin, next to Tai Wan beach, has a couple of outdoor restaurants serving basic food and drinks, though they're usually only open at the weekend. Note that the last bus back from Pak Tam Road to Sai Kung is at around 7.30pm; don't miss it.

great beach & almost deserted (don't go @ weekends)

Wong Shek, Chek Keng and Jones' Cove
Bus #94 (also #95R on Sun from Diamond Hill MTR) continues on across the neck of Sai Kung East Country Park to **WONG SHEK** – little more than a pier and a few barbecue pits really, and only worth coming out to if you're going to be staying at one of the nearby youth hostels or catching the *kaido* to the island of **Tap Mun Chau** to the north (see p.181).

Two of Hong Kong's more remote **youth hostels**, both with over a hundred beds, are in the Wong Shek area. The most popular, *Bradbury Hall* (not to be confused with Bradbury Lodge) is near **CHEK KENG**, the next village and bay to the east. You can either reach it directly on the ferry from Ma Liu Shui (see p.180); or by getting off the bus at the top of the pass, at Pak Tam Au, before you reach Wong Shek, and following the signposted path down to Chek Keng – a 45-minute walk. The hostel is right next to the sea (which,

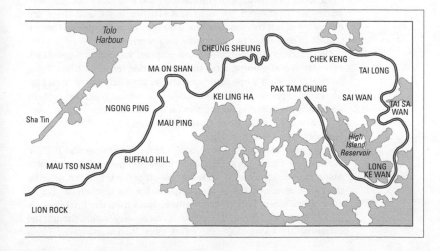

The East:
Clearwater
Bay and the
Sai Kung
peninsula

*For booking
details for both
hostels, see
"Accommo-
dation",
pp.214–215.*

for once, is clean enough to swim in), and there's space for **camping**, too; you can get cold drinks and basic **meals** in the village.

The other hostel, *Pak Sha O*, is at **JONES' COVE**, to the north – **Hoi Ha Wan** on some maps. Again, you could come by ferry from Ma Liu Shui, getting off at either Lai Chi Chong or Wong Shek and following the signs; around an hour's walk. But it's easier to take the #94 bus, getting off just before Wong Shek at Ko Tong. Take Hoi Ha Road, on the left, and it's around a thirty-minute walk to the hostel – though taxis are available if you hang around, and on Sundays and public holidays there's a maxicab service. Hoi Ha **beach** is around another fifteen minutes' walk from the hostel, and again, you can get simple food and cold drinks in the village.

The Northern Coast and the Tolo Channel

The most remote section of the Sai Kung peninsula is its **northern coast**, though you can easily see it by taking the **ferry from Ma Liu Shui** to Tap Mun Chau island (see opposite). The pier is a signposted fifteen-minute walk from the University KCR station (see p.152); current departures are at 8.30am and 3.15pm. There is a return service from Tap Mun Chau daily at 5.20pm, with additional departures at 10.40am (Mon–Sat) and 1.45pm (Sun).

Ma Liu Shui lies at one end of the **Tolo Channel**, which divides the New Territories' two most rural areas: Plover Cove and Sai Kung. The 75-minute **ferry** ride makes for a fine half-day trip if all you're going to do is stay on board and soak up the views: the early morning departure runs up the channel for Tap Mun Chau calling on the way at isolated bays along Sai Kung's northern coast. In the order reached from Ma Liu Shui, these are: Shap Sze Heung, Sham Chung, Lai Chi Chong (for *Pak Sha O* hostel), Tai Tan (for Wong Shek), Chek Keng (for *Bradbury Hall* hostel) and Kau Lau Wan. All these places are connected by paths and rougher trails, and there are campsites along the way, but you'll need to be well equipped with a tent, food and water to explore the area properly.

One place on the northern coast you can visit without too much difficulty is **Nai Chung**, a ten-minute bus ride from Sai Kung Town (#299; hourly). It's one of a dozen similar sites in the area, with barbecue sites, picnic areas, drinks stalls and rowing boats for rent. At weekends it's possible to continue on to Sha Tin following the coast north around **Ma On Shan Country Park** using bus #289R (Sat & Sun only; every 20–30min).

The climb up **Ma On Shan** itself – Hong Kong's second highest mountain at 702m – is accessible by bus #299 from Sai Kung Town. About five minutes out of Sai Kung, get off at the top of the ridge by the picnic area and follow the signposts for the MacLehose Trail – most of the steep, five-kilometre route, apart from the final peak, is part of Stage 4 of the trail. The climb can be very tough, though the extraordinary views make the effort more than worthwhile. You'll need decent footwear, plenty of water, and don't even think of attempting the walk in bad weather.

Tap Mun Chau

Right up in the northeast of the territory at the mouth of the Tolo Channel, **TAP MUN CHAU** island, although awkward to reach, is becoming an increasingly popular destination. There's not much to see: the relative isolation is the main draw.

The quickest way to get there is by *kaido* from Wong Shek – a twenty-minute crossing. There are currently services daily at 10.05am and at 5.00pm, but call to check (☎2771 1630). The alternative approach is by ferry from Ma Liu Shui ferry pier (see p.152). Perhaps the best option is to cross from Wong Shek by *kaido* and pick up the return ferry to Ma Liu Shui (current departures at 5.20pm daily).

Both ferry and *kaido* dock in a sheltered inlet on the island's west side which contains the only **village** – a single line of crumbling houses and small shops overlooking the fish farms that constitute the only industry. It's a run-down, ramshackle kind of place, nice and quiet, with the houses on the only street open to the pavement. There's a Tin Hau temple along here too (to the left of the pier), the venue for a large annual festival, while to the right of the pier, a fishermen's quarter straddles the low hill – nets and tackle stacked and stored in the huts and houses, many built on stilts over the water.

A couple of paths spread across the island, which is surprisingly green, leading to its English name of "Grass Island". After you've ambled around, the only thing to do is to head back to the main street and its one good **restaurant**, the *New Hon Kee*; left from the ferry pier and it's on the first corner. There's no English sign, but there is an English menu which offers reasonable seafood, fried rice and beer in a room overlooking the water.

Don't miss the last ferry whatever you do – be at the pier in plenty of time. There's no accommodation on Tap Mun Chau, and even the restaurant owners don't live on the island but back in the New Territories.

Chapter 5

The Outlying Islands

H ong Kong Island is only one of 260-odd other islands scattered in the South China Sea that, together with the Kowloon peninsula and New Territories, make up the territory of Hong Kong proper. The vast majority of these **outlying islands** are tiny, barren and uninhabited; others are restricted areas, used as detention centres or for rehabilitating drug addicts. The few you are able to visit form some of the territory's less cluttered reaches, and the southwestern trio of **Lamma**, **Cheung Chau** and **Lantau** are popular with locals and tourists alike: Lantau is actually much bigger than Hong Kong Island, and staying there overnight is an attractive possibility.

None of the islands is exactly uncharted territory. The easily accessible ones have suffered from the attentions of the developers over the years, and an increasing number of Hong Kongers – *gweilos* especially – choose to live on islands like Lantau and Cheung Chau. Some of the islands were inhabited way before Hong Kong Island itself, but their fishing communities have been abandoned and the buildings left to rot after their people moved to new cities and jobs on the mainland. Parts of the islands can still feel relatively deserted – especially if you're lucky enough to be invited onto a private (or chartered) boat, when you can reach some supremely isolated spots.

Many people visit for the **beaches** – not a bad idea given the crowded state of the sands on Hong Kong Island, although even those on Lantau are packed if you go at the weekend or on a public holiday. Pollution often puts many other island beaches out of bounds, at least as far as swimming goes (the local papers print water-quality ratings for the main venues every week) but there are other reasons to visit.

OUTLYING ISLANDS: TOP FIVE ATTRACTIONS

Cheung Chau Village (p.189)
Cheung Sha beach, Lantau (p.201)
Po Lin Monastery, Lantau (p.203)
Tai O Village, Lantau (p.202)
Yung Shue Wan, Lamma (p.184)

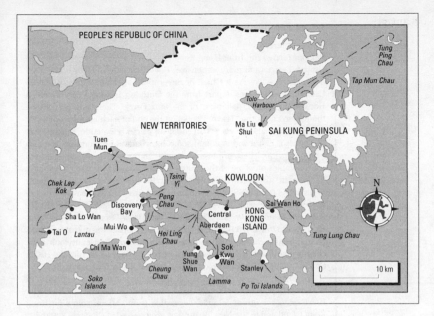

Lantau is a popular spot for **hiking**, and its cross-island trail, old villages and monasteries make it easily the most interesting island to head for. Lamma and, to a lesser degree, Cheung Chau are noted for their **seafood restaurants** and food stalls; while the quieter and less visited islands – including Peng Chau – still offer a slice of the traditional Chinese life that was once lived all over the territory. You may want to stay over at one or two of the places: there are **hotels** on Lantau, Lamma and Cheung Chau, and a couple of **hostels** on Lantau – see "Accommodation" (p.215 and p.230) for details.

There's a good **map** of the southwestern islands – Lantau, Cheung Chau, Peng Chau and Lamma – in the *Countryside Series* (available from the Government Publications Centre, Queensway Government Offices, 66 Queensway, Admiralty). The HKTA dishes out printed **ferry and hoverferry timetables** for all the major routes, which are well worth picking up, since the prices and times given below are all subject to change.

Lamma

The closest island to Hong Kong – Aberdeen is only around 3km from its northern point – **LAMMA** is perhaps the best to visit if your time is limited. Its elongated fourteen square kilometres are still largely unspoiled and you can round off a trip with a meal in one of its seafood restaurants. There's no motorized traffic on the island,

Lamma

THE OUTLYING ISLANDS

I go to last restaurant Wau Kok

Lamma

Island Practicalities

Getting there

Regular **ferries** run from Hong Kong Island to Lamma, Cheung Chau and Lantau. Faster (and more expensive) **hoverferries** also serve a few main destinations – like Peng Chau, or Silvermine Bay and Discovery Bay on Lantau. Most services depart from the **Outlying Islands Ferry Piers** on Hong Kong Island, just west of the Star Ferry. There are exceptions, though, so check the "Travel Details" at the end of each island account for specific information. Access to a couple of places is by **kaido**, a small ferry or licensed, motorized sampan; some **inter-island connections** are also made by *kaido*. These are less frequent than the ferries and though there are timetables on some of the routes, you'll often just have to ask around.

There are also weekend **excursion ferries** to some of the most popular destinations from the Star Ferry Pier in Tsim Sha Tsui: you have to reserve ahead for these with the HYFCO Travel Agency, Shop 3, Star House, Salisbury Road, Tsim Sha Tsui (Mon–Sat 10am–7pm, Sun 11am–6pm; ☎2736 1387 or 2516 9581). If you don't mind splashing out, arranging a **charter boat** is easy enough: enquire at ferry piers on the islands, look in the classified sections of the newspapers or *HK Magazine*, or ring the HKTA (☎2508 1234). For organized **tours** of the islands by boat, see p.59.

The islands covered in this chapter are the main ones in the southwest of the territory, to which there are regular ferries from Central and Kowloon. However, other **minor islands**, accessible from various points on Hong Kong Island and in the New Territories, are covered in Chapters 2 and 4:

Using the ferries

You can't reserve seats on the ferries: it's first come, first served, so get there early at busy times. **Tickets** to all main destinations cost around $15

---

something which attracts many expats in search of a rural existence within commuting distance of Hong Kong. By and large they've found it: development is relatively low-key and some of the more outrageous recent planning proposals have been defeated by conservationists, including the plan to construct an oil refinery here in the early 1970s. Nothing, however, could prevent the building of the power station at Po Lo Tsui, on the northwestern coast. This is the island's major eyesore, though it's gradually being rivalled by the quarrying operations on the other side of the island, overlooking Sok Kwu Wan. Still, once you're on the hilltops following the well-marked paths and trails, Lamma regains its peace and quiet.

Yung Shue Wan

Ferries run to the two villages on the island, Yung Shue Wan in the northwest and Sok Kwu Wan at the island's squeezed middle. As it's an easy walk between the two, and the best seafood is at Sok Kwu one-way for "ordinary class" and around $30 for "de luxe class" (upstairs, on the air-conditioned top deck). These fares virtually **double after noon on Saturday** for the duration of the weekend; children under 12 pay half-price at all times. All return tickets are double the price of a single. **Hoverferry** tickets cost around $24–32 one-way: children pay about half. If you can, especially at the weekend, buy a return ticket on all services so you won't have to queue on the way back.

None of the journeys is very long – around an hour maximum on all the main routes – and if you can't get a seat, you can always lounge on deck; coming back into Hong Kong, especially, the views are fabulous. Most ferries also have a small **bar** selling coffee, sandwiches, hot noodles, cold drinks and beer.

On a *kaido*, you generally pay the fare to the person operating the boat. It will usually only be around $5–10, though foreigners can expect to pay more than the locals on some routes, and you may have to bargain. Sometimes, when there's no regular service, you'll need to charter the whole boat – the text tells you when it's necessary and roughly how much it will cost; again, you may have to haggle.

When to go

Services to all the main islands are more frequent on **Sunday** for a good reason: the entire territory swaps its packed vertical apartment blocks for packed horizontal beaches. There are enormous queues at the piers, and, after noon on Saturday and all day Sunday, the fares shoot up, too. If you are planning to stay **overnight** on any of the islands, be prepared to pay double or more at the weekend, and book well in advance.

Midweek is much quieter, and some places can seem positively secluded. Note that major disruption to the timetables can occur during the **typhoon season** (June–Oct), when ferry services can be abandoned at very short notice. Listen to the bulletins and check with the harbour office if you want to avoid being stranded.

Wan, you're best off aiming first for **YUNG SHUE WAN** ("Banyan Bay"), which has connections to Central and Kennedy Town, and to Aberdeen via Pak Kok Tsuen on the island's north coast. The seafront street is **Yung Shue Wan Main Street**, at the end of which a typically gloomy, century-old **Tin Hau temple** overlooks the water. The expat presence in the village is manifest in the new bars, restaurants and shops, and the island has acquired a rather bohemian reputation. Unfortunately the number of second-rate apartment buildings is spreading rapidly up behind the village, but the place remains small-scale enough to be pleasant. Really the only things that spoil the village atmosphere are the three huge chimney stacks of the power station that glare down from behind the hill.

If you've come intending to walk across the island, there's nothing much to stop you heading straight off, though the narrow seafront street has a scattering of **restaurants**, a couple with terrace tables outside. Good places include *B & B's*, 22 Main Street, a pub-style

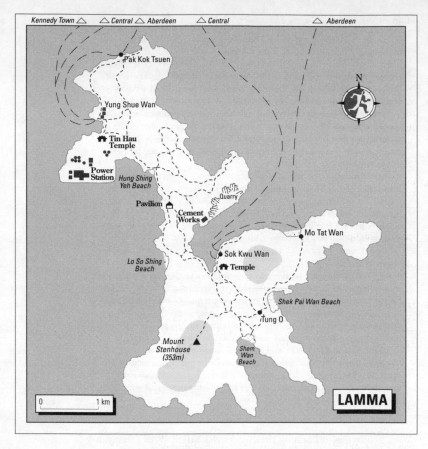

Pak Kok Tsuen

Yung Shue Wan

Tin Hau
Temple

Power
Station

Hung Shing
Yeh Beach

Pavilion

Quarry

Cement
Works

Mo Tat Wan

Sok Kwu Wan

Temple

Lo So Shing
Beach

Shek Pai Wan Beach

Tung O

Mount
Stenhouse
(353m)

Sham
Wan
Beach

N

0   1 km

LAMMA

place overlooking the water; the *Lamcombe Seafood Restaurant*, at no. 47, with no-nonsense fish specialities and decent prices; and the *Man Fung Seafood Restaurant*, at no. 5, one of the better of Yung Shue Wan's terrace restaurants, with *dim sum* in the morning, fresh fish and a long list of budget rice or noodle combination dishes, which will set you up for an afternoon's walk.

There is **accommodation** in the village too, including the *Lamma Vacation House*, at 29 Main Street on the left-hand side, the *Kathmandu Guest House*, and the *Man Lai Wah Hotel*, just by the ferry pier.

Lamma's accommodation is detailed on p.230.

The walk to Sok Kwu Wan

It's about an hour on foot to Sok Kwu Wan, across the hill from the northern half of the island and down through the narrow waist of land at Lo So Shing. In Yung Shue Wan, take the turning between 64

Main Street and the *Light House Pub* into Yung Shue Wan Back Street, and follow the signs to "Hung Shing Yeh" .

It's a twenty-minute walk along a good concrete path to **Hung Shing Yeh**, where there's a tiny sand beach with first-hand views of the power station. It's nice enough when it's empty and there are barbecue pits, a couple of places to get a drink and holiday apartments stretching back up the hillside from the sand. There's another hotel, too, the *Concerto Inn*, where you can also eat pigeon or seafood at the terrace tables.

From Hung Shing Yeh a clear footpath continues around the beach and up the hill on the other side, now signposted to "Sok Kwu Wan". It's quite a climb on a hot day, but it's not long until the path levels out to reach a viewing point marked by a **Chinese pavilion**, roughly halfway between the two villages. Carry on down the hill and views of Sok Kwu Wan gradually unfold – as do those of the vast cement works and quarry away to your left. At the bottom, amid the houses, there's a signposted diversion to **Lo So Shing**, to the right, a bigger and sandier beach than at Hung Shing Yeh, with changing rooms, showers, a snack kiosk and more barbecue pits. It's usually okay for swimming, too, though check the information board first. Back on the main path, it's only another fifteen minutes to Sok Kwu Wan. Just before you cross the bridge at the end of the inlet a sign points into the undergrowth to the **Kamikaze Caves**, constructed by the Japanese in 1944–45 to house a flotilla of suicide motor boats, but never used. Unfortunately, there's not much to see now.

Sok Kwu Wan

The bay at **SOK KWU WAN** is devoted to fish farming. Floating wooden frames cover the water, interspersed with rowing boats, junks and the canvas shelters of the fishermen and women. A concrete path runs the length of the village, from the obligatory Tin Hau temple to the main pier, along which Sok Kwu Wan's **seafood restaurants** form a line. They're the only real reason to come, though what was once a low-key array of simple eating houses has turned into a range of more polished restaurants, with outdoor tables overlooking the bay and large fish tanks set back on the street. Some restaurants have special set menus in English posted on the walls, but *always* ask the price first, certainly if you're choosing your fish straight from the tank. If you're having trouble choosing a restaurant, look for where the locals are eating.

The only drawback to eating on the terraces is the view over the bay: the whole hillside opposite has been quarried, scarred and despoiled by storage containers, corrugated-iron huts and a large conveyor belt; and the bay itself – sometimes known by its alternative name, Picnic Bay – is rapidly becoming polluted by the refuse generated by the intensive fish farming in the area. It's illegal for the fishermen to live on the floating rafts, but many do: they use the polystyrene floats at the pier to row themselves across to the fish frames, where they erect canvas shelters, from which they dump sewage and rubbish into the bay.

Mo Tat Wan and Mount Stenhouse

If you arrive early enough, there are a couple of other targets around Sok Kwu Wan to occupy the time before dinner. It's a 25-minute walk (left as you step off the ferry pier) to **MO TAT WAN**, another small beach village, usually quieter than the others on the island. It's one of the oldest settlements in Hong Kong, here in some shape or form for over three hundred years. There's not much to show for it now, although the *Coral* restaurant's reasonably priced seafood provides one reason to hang around. The **kaido** service to Aberdeen from Sok Kwu Wan calls in regularly every day; there's a timetable posted at Sok Kwu Wan pier.

A path from Mo Tat Wan leads the kilometre or so to the bigger beach of **Shek Pai Wan** on the southeastern coast, from where you can continue – past Tung O – to the smaller **Sham Wan** beach, perhaps the remotest on the island, and worth heading to if only for that reason.

Cast around a bit, either in Sok Kwu Wan or at Shek Pai Wan and Sham Wan, and it's not difficult to find one of the paths that lead eventually to the summit of **Mount Stenhouse** (also known as Shan Tei Tong), 353m up in the middle of the island's southwestern bulge. It's quite a climb, particularly since the paths aren't wonderful, but you'll be rewarded with some fine views. It should take around two hours from Sok Kwu Wan to climb up and down again; take plenty of water.

Lamma Travel Details

Outlying Islands Ferry Piers to Yung Shue Wan (16 daily; first at 6.45am, Sun at 8.15am, last at around 12.30am); to Sok Kwu Wan (10 daily; first at 7.20am, last at 11.40pm).

Kennedy Town to Yung Shue Wan (*kaido* service Mon–Sat 7–9 daily, Sun 16 daily, last at 6.40pm).

Aberdeen to Mo Tat Wan/Sok Kwu Wan (Mon–Sat 8 daily, Sun every 45min; first at 6.45am, Sun at 8am, last at 10.40pm); to Pak Kok Tsuen/Yung Shue Wan (9–11 daily, first at 6.30am Mon–Sat, 7.30am Sun, last at 7pm Mon–Sat, 7.30pm Sun).

Yung Shue Wan to Outlying Islands Ferry Piers (16 daily, first at 6.20am, Sun at 6.50am, last at 11.30pm); to Kennedy Town (9 daily, last at 6.05pm); to Pak Kok Tsuen/Aberdeen (9–11 daily, first at 6am Mon–Sat, 8am Sun, last at 7.30pm Mon–Sat, 8pm Sun).

Sok Kwu Wan to Outlying Islands Ferry Piers (10 daily; first at 6.30am, last at 10.50pm); to Mo Tat Wan/Aberdeen (8 daily, first at 6.05am Mon–Sat, 6.15am Sun, last at 6.45pm Mon–Sat, 6.45pm Sun, special late service at 10.40pm).

For ticket prices and other ferry details, see pp.184–185. For up-to-date ferry information, call the Hong Kong Ferry Co. (☎2542 3081) or, for Sok Kwu Wan–Aberdeen services, Chuen Kee Ferry Ltd (☎2982 8225 or their 24-hour information hotline on ☎2525 1108).

Cheung Chau

THE OUTLYING ISLANDS

An hour southwest of the city, **CHEUNG CHAU** is the most densely populated of the outlying islands, the central waist of its dumb-bell shape crammed with buildings; its harbour and typhoon shelter busy day and night. However, unlike some of the other islands, it's not an artificial development caused by invading outsiders seeking peace and quiet – though certainly these exist on Cheung Chau. Rather, the island is one of the oldest settled parts of Hong Kong, with a prosperity based on fishing, supplemented in the past with smuggling and piracy. There's a life here that's independent of the fortunes of Hong Kong, manifest in a surviving junk shipyard, several working temples and one of Hong Kong's best annual festivals.

Concrete **paths** cover the entire island and, despite the name, which means "long island" in Cantonese, you can whip around the place fairly quickly. Like Lamma, no cars are allowed here, though you'll have to listen out for the buzz of the motorized scooter-like work vehicles as you walk along – the paths aren't really wide enough for you both. Much of the relatively undeveloped parts of the island are taken up by youth camps, and the two or three fine beaches are regularly crowded. But for all that, the paths repay a dawdle: traditional life thrives in the main village, with its fishing boats and stalls; there are some excellent views as you go; and – as ever – sampling Cheung Chau's seafood is a good reason to visit.

Cheung Chau Village

The ferry from Central picks its way through the breakwaters and junks to dock at **CHEUNG CHAU VILLAGE**, where the island's population and activity is concentrated. The waterfront road, or **Praya** (the full name is Pak She Praya Road), is where the fishermen lay out their catch in water-filled trays and buckets; early morning and mid-afternoon this develops into a small market, with the fishermen joined by fruit-and-veg and clothes sellers. From opposite the ferry pier, Tung Wan Road leads across the island's waist to Tung Wan Beach (see p.191), a short walk through a couple of twists and turns lined with stalls and shops – the place to snap up bamboo hats and other essential beach gear.

One block in from the water the main thoroughfare, **San Hing Street**, leads up about 500m to the **Pak Tai Temple**, built in 1788 and set in its own little square. Not surprisingly, on an island once totally dependent on fishing, the inhabitants deemed it prudent to dedicate a temple to Pak Tai, the protector of fishermen and "supreme emperor of the dark heaven". Inside, there are relics appropriate to Pak Tai's status: an 800-year-old iron sword, fished out of the sea; a golden crown; a gilded nineteenth-century sedan chair, made to carry the god's image during festivals; and a plaque recording the 1966 visit of Princess Margaret.

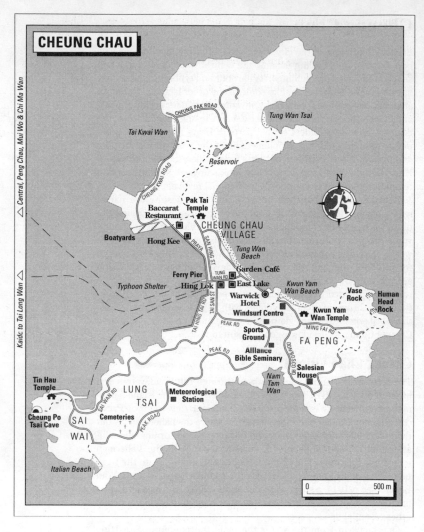

CHEUNG CHAU

Central, Peng Chau, Mui Wo & Chi Ma Wan

Kaido to Tai Long Wan

Cheung Pak Road

Tung Wan Tsai

Tai Kwai Wan

Reservoir

Cheung Kwai Road

Pak Tai Temple

Baccarat Restaurant

CHEUNG CHAU VILLAGE

Boatyards

Hong Kee

San Hing St

Praya

Tung Wan Beach

Garden Café

Ferry Pier

Tung Wan Rd

Tai San St

East Lake

Typhoon Shelter

Hing Lok

Warwick Hotel

Kwun Yam Wan Beach

Vase Rock

Human Head Rock

Tai Hing Tai Rd

Windsurf Centre

Kwun Yam Wan Temple

Peak Rd

Sports Ground

Ming Fai Rd

FA PENG

Peak Rd

Alliance Bible Seminary

Don Bosco Rd

Salesian House

Tin Hau Temple

San Wan Rd

LUNG TSAI

Meteorological Station

Nam Tam Wan

Cheung Po Tsai Cave

SAI WAI

Cemeteries

Peak Road

Italian Beach

N

0   500 m

The temple is also the venue for the annual four-day **Cheung Chau Bun Festival**, or "Tai Chiu", in late April/early May, held since the ravages of a series of eighteenth- and nineteenth-century plagues that supposedly appeased the vengeful spirits of those wrongly killed by Cheung Chau's pirates. Outside the temple, several sets of bamboo scaffolding are erected, each around twenty metres high and topped with pink and white buns. Up until 1978, at midnight on a designated day, people were encouraged to clamber up the frames to grab the buns, which would bring good luck –

the higher the bun, the better the luck. This particular activity was stopped after what the tourist authorities refer to darkly as "an unfortunate accident"*, and these days the buns are just handed out from the bottom of the frames. The festival's other great draw is the teams of costumed children riding on floats through the streets, some of their peers strapped onto stilts on which they glide over the crowds. The village is packed for the four days of the festival – extra ferries are laid on from Hong Kong – and it's a fascinating time to come: as well as the displays, there is a host of religious services, Chinese opera performances, unicorn and lion dances, and all the bluster and bustle that the Cantonese bring to any celebration.

North of the village

Just down from the temple, at the water, are the **boatyards**, where junk-builders still work largely by hand, working without plans and using skills that haven't changed much in five hundred years – though electric drills and saws have been introduced. You may also catch sight of blocks of ice being shipped out of the adjacent ice-making factory and loaded onto boats for removal to Hong Kong.

Beyond here, the **northern** stretch of the island only has views to offer, but they're worth the effort. On the seafront, just after the fire station, some steep steps on the right lead up to a housing estate, from where you can look down over the village and harbour. Or continue around the headland, following the waterfront Cheung Kwai Road: there's a path off to the left after a few hundred metres (marked "Family Trail") which leads up to a hilltop **reservoir**, from where there are splendid views over the whole island. You can descend straight back down to the village from here, past a small cemetery – you'll come out close to the Pak Tai Temple.

The East Coast: Tung Wan and Kwun Yam Wan

Across the waist of land from the ferry pier, a few minutes' walk up Tung Wan Road, is the island's main beach, **Tung Wan Beach**: 700–800m of fine sand and as popular as anywhere in the territory at the weekend. There are a couple of restaurants, as well as Cheung Chau's bid for the weekend set, the *Warwick* hotel, at the southern end. Just past here, around the little headland, there's another sweep of sand, **Kwun Yam Wan Beach** (or "Afternoon Beach"), probably the best on the island. The **windsurf centre** here rents out all the relevant bits and pieces, and offers tuition – it's run by the family of Lee Lai Shan, better known as San San, Hong Kong's windsurfing heroine who won a gold medal in the 1996 Olympics. The café here has a nice terrace and is a good place for a beer or snack.

---

*In fact, a couple of the towers collapsed and 24 people were injured.

A walk around the island

If you've got a couple of hours, the **southern** part of the island offers a good, circular walk along tree-shaded paths. From the waterfront in the village, close to the ferry pier, jump on a *kaido* to **Sai Wan**, across the harbour at the southwestern tip of the island: you'll hear the name of the village being called by the *kaido* operators, or just ask someone on the quayside. It's a five-minute crossing and on the way the *kaido* sometimes calls at one or two of the junks in the harbour, depositing people laden with shopping at their floating homes.

From Sai Wan's pier, a path leads up to one of the island's several **Tin Hau** temples, where there's a pavilion overlooking the harbour. A path runs over the brow of the hill to a rocky bluff, part of which has been landscaped. Follow everyone else scrambling over the rocks and you'll come to the so-called **Cheung Po Tsai Cave**, touted as the HQ of a notorious Cheung Chau pirate. Whether it was or wasn't, the adventurous and agile can climb through the underground passage here: unless you follow someone else, you'll need a flashlight, which you can buy or hire from a woman sitting at the entrance – it'll cost around $30, though make it clear if you only want to hire it and you'll get $20 or so back when you return it. The climb is fairly hard going, though faint hearts will be shamed by the queue of elderly women risking the drop into the abyss with their grandchildren.

Back at Sai Wan pier, follow Peak Road for several hundred metres and detour right down to Pak Tso Wan, known as **Italian Beach** – small and sandy, though a little grubby. The road climbs up through a series of **cemeteries**, with occasional pavilions providing views over the sea, into Lung Tsai Tsuen, once a separate village but now a southern outpost of the main village. Just after the Alliance Bible Seminary building, take Fa Peng Road to the right and then follow Don Bosco Road, which leads down to Salesian House, a religious retreat, before doubling back to **Fa Peng Knoll**, the island's eastern bulge. Turn left here and the path runs down past **Kwun Yam Temple** to Kwun Yam Wan beach, only a short walk from the centre of the village. Alternatively, a path from Fa Peng leads around the eastern headland, climbing down the cliffside to view a series of weirdly shaped **rocks** that have supposedly self-explanatory names – Vase Rock, Human Head Rock and Loaf Rock; they could equally be called Big Splodge Rock, Amorphous Rock and Vague Shape Rock.

Practicalities

There are **bike rental** shops on the road between the Pak Tai Temple and the Praya, as well as at the northern end of the Praya itself. There's no shortage of **holiday apartments** to let, either, from the stalls opposite the ferry pier; most come with bathroom and kitchen and many overlook the beach. During midweek, they're reasonably cheap, especially if you can get three or four people together. Prices start at around $280 per night, at the weekend you could be charged double that. The only time to avoid, or book months in advance, is the period of the Bun Festival. Of the **hotels**, the obvious – if most expensive – place to stay is the *Warwick*, overlooking Tung Wan Beach.

For **eating**, most of the village's waterfront Praya is lined with small restaurants. At night, the whole street is decked out with tables and chairs as the *dai pai dongs* arrive to dish out cheap and excellent seafood; take your pick and point to what you want. Quite a few places offer menus in English, including the *East Lake Restaurant*, up Tung Wan Road on the way to the main beach. In the evening, the *Garden Café* – also known as Betty's – is popular with locals, or try the strip of restaurants at the northern end of the Praya near the Pak Tai Temple, especially the *Baccarat*, the *Hing Lok* or the *Hong Kee*, which serve tasty things like garlic fried prawns, scallops and Yang Chow fried rice. You should get away with $150-200 a head. For **bottled water** and cold **beer**, there's a Wellcome supermarket opposite the ferry pier.

Note that if you're on Cheung Chau during the Bun Festival, the island goes **vegetarian** for a few days – no great hardship since the food on offer remains excellent.

For details of hotels on Cheung Chau, see p.230.

Cheung Chau Travel Details

Ferries
Outlying Islands Ferry Piers to Cheung Chau (daily: at least hourly; first at 6.25am, last at 12.30am).

Tsim Sha Tsui to Cheung Chau (Sat at 4pm, Sun at 8am &10am).

Cheung Chau to Outlying Islands Ferry Piers (daily: at least hourly; first at 5.35am, last at 11.30pm); Tsim Sha Tsui (Sun at 12.45pm).

Fast Ferries: Mon–Sat
Outlying Islands Ferry Piers to Cheung Chau (at 8.50am, 10.15am, 12.15pm, 2.15pm, 4.05pm & 5.25pm).
Cheung Chau to Outlying Islands Ferry Piers (at 7.00am, 8.10am, 9.40am, 10.50am, 12.50pm, 2.50pm & 4.50pm).

Sundays
Outlying Islands Ferry Piers to Cheung Chau (at 10.15am, 12.15pm, 2.15pm, 4.05pm & 5.25pm).

Cheung Chau to Outlying Islands Ferry Piers (at 10.50am, 12.50pm, 2.50pm & 4.50pm).

Inter-Island Ferry Service: daily
Cheung Chau to Chi Ma Wan and Mui Wo (both on Lantau) and on to Peng Chau (roughly every 2hr; first at 5.35am, last at 10.10pm; not every departure calls at every stop, so check the timetable at the pier).

For ticket prices and other ferry details, see pp.184–185. For up-to-date ferry information, call the Hong Kong Ferry Co. (☎2542 3081).

THE OUTLYING ISLANDS

Peng Chau

Some ferries to Lantau (see opposite) call at **PENG CHAU**, a tiny horseshoe-shaped blob of land fifty minutes from Hong Kong and just twenty minutes from its larger neighbour. Few tourists bother to get off the boat, and although there are no obvious attractions, the quiet streets are a pleasant alternative to the busy antics of Lantau's Mui Wo. You could see the whole of Peng Chau in the couple of hours before the next connection, and there are ferries between Peng Chau and Mui Wo throughout the day.

Wing On Street, just back from the pier, is a typical island street: part market, part residential, with an eighteenth-century Tin Hau temple, noodle shops, Chinese herbalists and no traffic. Some shops sell hand-painted porcelain, a local cottage industry. Signs point you in the direction of **Tung Wan**, the island's only real beach. It's five minutes' walk away and is pretty enough, with a barbecue site and a few fishing boats. Really, though, you won't want to hang around, unless you've been tempted into one of the **seafood restaurants**, where the food is as good and as cheap as on any of the islands.

Hei Ling Chau

A fairly frequent service runs from the quayside to **Hei Ling Chau**, an island south of Peng Chau and around twice its size, though don't get on the ferry by mistake, since part of the island is used as a drug rehabilitation centre – the chattering trippers are actually visiting relatives.

Peng Chau Travel Details

Ferries
Outlying Islands Ferry Piers to Peng Chau (approximately hourly; first at 7am, last at 12.20am).

Peng Chau to Outlying Islands Ferry Piers (approximately hourly; first at 6.30am, last at 11.30pm).

Hoverferries: Mon–Fri only
Outlying Islands Ferry Piers to Peng Chau (at 9.35am, 11.20am, 2.25pm & 4.25pm).

Peng Chau to Outlying Islands Ferry Piers (at 7.50am, 10.25am, 12.20pm, 3.20pm & 5.20pm).

Inter-Island Ferry Service: daily
Peng Chau to Mui Wo/Chi Ma Wan/Cheung Chau (roughly every 2hr; first at 5.40am, last at midnight; check the timetable at the pier).

Kaido
Peng Chau to Tai Shui Hang (Trappist Monastery, Lantau; roughly hourly; 7.45am–4.20pm).

For ticket prices and other ferry details, see pp.184–185. For up-to-date ferry information, call the Hong Kong Ferry Co. (☎2542 3081).

Lantau

By far the biggest island in the territory, **LANTAU** and its charms could occupy several days. Twice the size of Hong Kong Island, it's wild and rugged enough in parts to make hiking an attractive option; some of the beaches are among the best in Hong Kong; and there's a full set of cultural diversions, including several monasteries and the world's largest seated outdoor bronze Buddha statue.

Most people's first sight of Hong Kong is now of Lantau. The new **airport** brings you in to Chek Lap Kok island, just off Lantau's north coast, and the airport highway and rail line run along the island's north shore, until recently one of the more isolated stretches of Hong Kong coastline. The next few years will probably see this area change beyond recognition as urban expansion follows the new transport links.

There is still room to get away from it all, even so: more than half the island is designated country park, and the circular **Lantau Trail** loops for 70km around the southern half of the island, passing campsites and the island's two youth hostels along the way. For detailed information on the trail's 12 stages, pick up the free *Lantau Trail* leaflet, published by the Country Parks Authority (CPA), which lists the route stages and picks out the relevant camping and transport details. There's a CPA booth at the ferry pier in Mui Wo, although don't rely on too much help in English. You don't have to tackle the whole thing: there are a couple of easy stages and other half-day walks accessible from Mui Wo, the village where the ferries dock. Don't underestimate the trails, though: parts are steep and unshaded, which can take its toll in the tropical heat and humidity. Take a hat, sunscreen and water.

Lantau has a small **bus** network (see p.208) which connects nearly all of the places covered below, and there are **taxis**, too.

Mui Wo (Silvermine Bay)

The large ferries from Hong Kong all dock at **MUI WO** ("Five Petal Flower"), generally known by its English name of Silvermine Bay, after the silver mine which once brought prosperity to the village. The mine has long since been boarded up, but the walk there is pleasant enough – about a kilometre inland from the village and close to a waterfall. The village itself is actually about the least interesting place on the island and most people head from the ferry straight to the **bus terminal** outside, where queues build up quickly for buses to the most popular destinations on the island. **Taxis** leave from the same square.

To the north of the bus terminal is the **Cooked Food Market** (6am–midnight) – a dozen or so covered stalls with outside tables overlooking the bay. They're all fairly cheap, serving bowls of noodles, seafood and the like. A little more salubrious, and not much

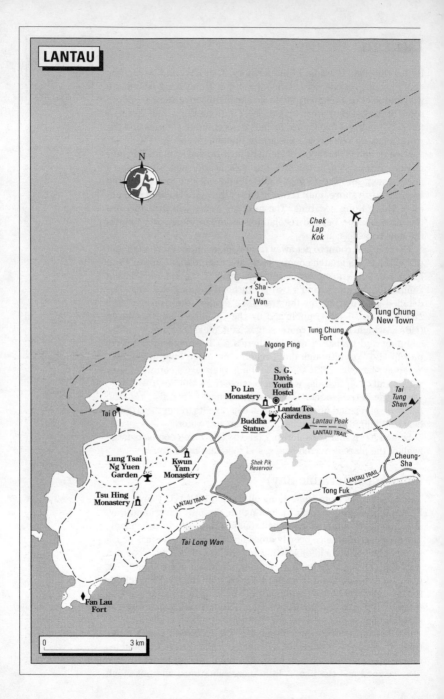

LANTAU

Chek
Lap
Kok

Sha
Lo
Wan

Tung Chung
New Town

Tung Chung
Fort

Ngong Ping

S. G.
Davis
Youth
Hostel

Po Lin
Monastery

Tai
Tung
Shan

Lantau Tea
Gardens

Buddha
Statue

Lantau Peak

Tai 0

LANTAU TRAIL

Lung Tsai
Ng Yuen
Garden

Kwun
Yam
Monastery

Shek Pik
Reservoir

Cheung
Sha

LANTAU TRAIL

Tsu Hing
Monastery

LANTAU TRAIL

Tong Fuk

Tai Long Wan

Fan Lau
Fort

0   3 km

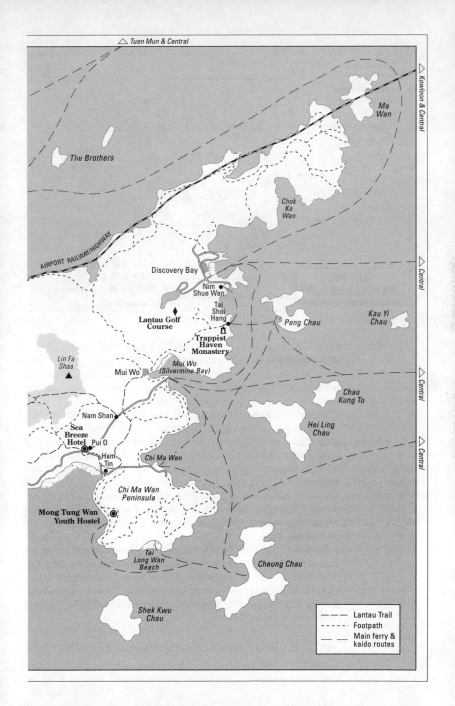

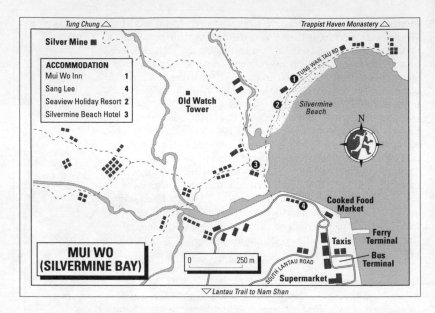

Silver Mine ■

ACCOMMODATION

Mui Wo Inn	**1**
Sang Lee	**4**
Seaview Holiday Resort	**2**
Silvermine Beach Hotel	**3**

TUNG WAN TAU RD

■ **Old Watch Tower**

Silvermine Beach

N

Cooked Food Market

Ferry Terminal

Taxis

Bus Terminal

MUI WO (SILVERMINE BAY)

0   250 m

SOUTH LANTAU ROAD

Supermarket

▽ Lantau Trail to Nam Shan

more expensive, is the welcoming *Sang Lee*, a simple **restaurant** with a terrace overlooking the bay – it's a little way beyond the market on the way to the beach. Other nearby options are a Wellcome **supermarket** and a Park 'N' Shop around the main square, and the Rome cake shop, across the square from the ferry pier.

Beyond the Cooked Food Market, a path leads around to the long, curving, sandy **beach**, backed by restaurants, barbecue pits, showers and toilets. The water here is too polluted for swimming, though that doesn't seem to stop the locals fishing in it, or dredging the sands for shellfish. Still, it looks attractive from a distance, and there are three **hotels** which capitalize on the views across the bay: the large *Silvermine Beach Hotel* (which has a reservations booth at the ferry pier and a terrace café with bay views), the rather characterless *Seaview Holiday Resort* and the smaller, more pleasant *Mui Wo Inn*, further along.

For details about Lantau's hotels, see p.230.

It's possible to **rent bicycles** along the beach at Mui Wo (around $30 an hour), though given the island's steep hills and excellent bus service, there's no compelling reason to do so (although mountain biking is becoming an increasingly popular, if technically illegal, activity on Lantau's trails). Mui Wo is also the starting and finishing point of the **Lantau Trail**.

North: to the Trappist Monastery and Discovery Bay

One of the best short hikes from Mui Wo is over the hills to the Our Lady of Joy Monastery, better known simply as the **Trappist**

Monastery, in the next bay north. It takes around an hour and a half. Head along the seafront Tung Wan Tau Road (past the hotels) to the end, cross the bridge over the river and follow the path as it loops round to the right. It's steep and very overgrown to start with, then a signpost to the left directs you up on top of the bare hills. There are some excellent views as you go, over Peng Chau and to Hong Kong in the distance, and a detour to the peak on your left offers a view over the golf course above Discovery Bay. Otherwise, stick to the path to the right of the peak, which brings you out at the Trappist Monastery. Founded by refugees from mainland China, the institution used to run a dairy farm that sold milk throughout Hong Kong. They sold the dairy a few years ago – the Trappist insignia on milk cartons is now just a brand name. You can wander round parts of the compound, but most is closed to the public. There's a **kaido** service across to Peng Chau (from where you can return directly to Central) from the small pier at the end of the road beyond the monastery. There are only a few daily crossings, the last one at 4.30pm; if you miss it, you'll have to walk back to Mui Wo.

Discovery Bay and the North
A couple of kilometres beyond the monastery is **Nim Shue Wan**, reached either by a downhill path from the monastery (marked by large crucifixes signifying the Stations of the Cross) or by *kaido* from the monastery's pier, at the bottom of the hill. There's a small beach here, at which you should be able to swim. Back up the hill, the road to the left leads down into **DISCOVERY BAY** ("Disco Bay" to the *gweilo* locals), a fast-growing New Town popular with young families, with its own beach, restaurants, shops, markets, banks and watersports facilities. The atmosphere is slightly Orwellian: like an almost too-perfect copy of idealized middle-American suburbia, with happy blonde families zipping about in golf carts, despite the fact that there are no roads out of town. The main attraction is the 24-hour **hoverferry service** back to Hong Kong (every 20min during peak hours), which delivers you to the pier next to the Star Ferry in Central in half an hour. There are also direct fast-ferry services to the airport, with connections on from there to Tuen Mun in the New Territories.

North of Discovery Bay a network of **hiking trails** heads into the rough countryside, though there's nowhere particularly exciting to head for and nowhere to stay. Moreover, what destinations there are – principally the inlets of Chek Ko Wan (Penny's Bay) and Yam O Wan – will soon be overwhelmed forever by construction work associated with the airport highway and rail line.

Chi Ma Wan Peninsula
The other short walk from Mui Wo is to the **CHI MA WAN PENINSULA**, a foot of land around 4km south of the ferry pier. The most direct route is to follow the first section of the Lantau Trail as far as Nam

Shan (where there's a campsite) and then switch to the last section of the trail, following it south to the peninsula: you'll come out on Chi Ma Wan Road, which runs east–west across the neck of the peninsula.

East along the road it's only a short walk to **Chi Ma Wan** itself. From the pier, there's a handy **ferry** service, either back to Mui Wo or on to Cheung Chau to the south. With a good map you could make your way around the peninsula clockwise from Chi Ma Wan (there's another campsite at the peninsula's easternmost point), but it's more rewarding to take in the **western side**. There's a youth hostel to aim for, and you can cut out the walk from Mui Wo by taking the bus (#1 or #7) from the Mui Wo ferry pier to **Pui O**, or from the airport (#3 or #13). There's an excellent beach at Pui O, one of the most popular on the island, with barbecue pits, a campsite at its eastern end and, back on the main road, a few simple restaurants, like the Thai *Nam On*. You might find an apartment for rent if you ask around, or try the reasonable *Sea Breeze Hotel* on the main road.

For reservation details for Mong Tung Wan Hostel, see p.215. You can reach the hostel by kaido *from the waterfront at Cheung Chau. Ask for Mong Tung Wan; it should cost around $100 for the boat.*

From the bus stop on the main road at Pui O, follow the signpost to **Ham Tin**. A concrete footpath leads you across the fields and alongside the river to a small temple, from where another signpost points up towards **Mong Tung Wan** – just under an hour's walk, with lovely views over Pui O beach. The quiet bay has a **youth hostel**, the *Jockey Club Mong Tung Wan Hostel*, made up of white bungalows set back from the harbour – a nice, clean place, though packed to the gills on Saturday nights from June to August. Camping is allowed here, and there are barbecue pits outside. The path from the hostel leads down to a tiny harbour, where you could swim, though it's rocky and a little murky. The hostel warden can arrange for a **kaido** to pick you up and take you to Cheung Chau: it'll cost around $100 and you'll need to order it the night before.

Yi Long and Tai Long Wan

A footpath runs on from Mong Tung Wan around the peninsula, climbing steeply above the coast, and you can clamber down to good beaches at a couple of places. At **Yi Long** there's a swanky and rather deserted private development, *Sea Ranch*, and the next bay along, **Tai Long Wan**, has some long and usually empty sands. It's hard going, though, especially to reach Tai Long Wan; it's easier to take a *kaido* from Cheung Chau's waterfront ($80–100, depending on numbers).

The real attraction at Tai Long Wan is the **Frog & Toad** (☎2989 2300), a splendid bar/restaurant at the back of the tiny village behind the beach. A three-storey village house with a roof terrace, at the weekend it's crowded with expats drinking enormous amounts of beer and tucking into the pub food. The downstairs bar turns into a sweaty disco after about the fifteenth tequila slammer and the whole thing shuts when the last person leaves. Other than walking, the only realistic way out is by junk or *kaido*, either arrange for the one that brought you from Cheung Chau to return at a certain time, or get someone at the bar to ring for one when you're ready to go.

The south coast: Pui O to Fan Lau

Lantau's best beaches are all on the **south coast**, and most are easily accessible by **bus** from Mui Wo; bus #1 (to Tai O), #2 (to Po Lin Monastery), #4 (to Tong Fuk) and #5 (to Shek Pik) run along the coast, so you can get off wherever you like.

Pui O beach (see opposite) is the closest to Mui Wo, around a fifteen-minute bus ride away. The next one along, at **Cheung Sha**, is considered by many to be the best in the territory. There are a couple of cafés here, serving simple Chinese food and cold drinks; a campsite; and the possibility of renting a **room** at the *Cheung Sha Resort House*.

Cheung Sha beach stretches all the way down to **Tong Fuk** (more cheap Chinese cafés as well as *The Gallery*, an English-style pub only open on Sundays), where the road strikes inland to reach the **Shek Pik Reservoir**, an impressive construction whose surroundings have been planted and landscaped to provide picnic areas and walking trails. There's a beach below the reservoir at Tai Long Wan, a short walk away. The road up to Tai O/Po Lin (see p.202) skirts the reservoir; crane your head up to the opposing hilltop for a first view of the seated Buddha – his back to you at this point.

A longer walk from Shek Pik follows a section of the Lantau Trail, past a couple of fairly isolated campsites to **FAN LAU**, 5km away on the southwestern tip of the island. It takes around two hours to walk from Shek Pik, via Kau Ling Chung. There are two excellent beaches here, a large east-facing one and a smaller west-facing one a few minutes' walk away, as well as the remains of a 1300-year-old rectangular **fort**, from which there are fine views across the water. Built to garrison troops, the fort overlooked a strategic sea route into the Pearl River Estuary, but was abandoned at the turn of this century. The Lantau Trail swings north from Fan Lau, with Tai O village around two to three hours' walk further on.

The Pink Dolphins

The waters around the western end of Lantau are where Hong Kong's few remaining **pink dolphins** are most likely to be found. These rose-coloured creatures are beautiful but rare: only a few hundred are now left, the remainder having been killed by a combination of polluted waters, disturbance by fishermen and, arguably, the development of the new airport. This didn't stop the Hong Kong authorities – without any apparent sense of irony – choosing the pink dolphin as one of the symbols of the handover celebrations. You can visit the dolphins on trips organized by Hong Kong Dolphinwatch (☎2984 1414; Web site *www.zianet.com/dolphins*), who also raise money to help protect these threatened creatures.

Tai O and around

The largest village on Lantau, **TAI O**, on the northwestern coast, was once the centre of a thriving salt export trade to China, as well as being one of Hong Kong's oldest fishing settlements. The saltpans are still visible, though the local fishermen have converted them into fish-breeding ponds – an enterprise which hasn't stopped the village population from falling rapidly as people move to the city to look for jobs. There are still around two thousand people left though, and it's a favourite tourist destination, with plenty of interest in the village's old streets, shrines and temples. The government has plans to revitalize the village and develop it as a major tourist destination.

The village is in two halves: a land side, where the **bus** stops (#1 from Mui Wo; 45min), and an island settlement, across a narrow creek lined with fishermens' houses built on stilts. To get there from the bus stop, walk down to the main street, follow it round to the right, and then turn left by the vendors selling live seafood. There are lots of restaurants and shops as you go, dried fish being a particular speciality.

On the island side are more small shops, a market, shacks alive with the clack of *mahjong* tiles and a few local **temples**. One – originally founded in the Ming dynasty – is dedicated to Kuan Ti, the God of War and Righteousness, to whom people pray for protection. Another, the renovated Hau Wong temple (spelt on local signs "Hou Wang"), is a five-minute walk away along the main street, Kat Hing Back Street, at the end of the village on a small headland facing the sea. Built a little later, in 1699, it contains the local dragon-racing boat, some sharks' bones, a whale's head found by Tai O's fishermen, and a lovely carved roof frieze displaying two roaring dragons. If you're taking the ferry out of Tai O, you'll pass a third temple, the Hung Shing Temple, on the way down Shek Tsai Po Street towards the pier, about 15 minutes on foot from the village centre.

The number of tourists that descend upon Tai O also means that you'll have no trouble getting something **to eat**. Try the *Wing On* or *Good View Seafood* restaurants on the land side, or cross to the island where, at the end of the street, the *Fook Moon Lam* (open 11am–9.30pm) next to the market has a short English-language menu featuring good fresh scallops and prawns.

Kwun Yum, Ng Yuen and Tsu Hing Monastery

On the way to or from Tai O, not far from the village, the #1 and #21 buses make a stop at the **Kwun Yum Monastery**, where you can get a simple vegetarian meal. A half-hour's walk up from here is the **Lung Tsai Ng Yuen** ornamental garden, at its best in February and March, and a further kilometre beyond this is the **Tsu Hing Monastery** – situated in one of the most isolated spots on the island and guarded by a six-metre-long stone dragon. The monks and nuns here aren't really geared up to receiving visitors, though no one will object if you turn up and have a vague interest in Buddhism: Sunday is the recommended visiting day. There is accommodation available too, but only for those seriously interested in a meditational retreat. The return walk via Lung Tsai Ng Yuen, then directly to Tai O, takes about an hour.

The Po Lin Monastery and Lantau Peak

The one place that everyone makes for in Lantau is the Po Lin Monastery in the central **Ngong Ping** region, north of the Shek Pik Reservoir. There's always a massive queue for the bus from Mui Wo after the ferry comes in, especially at the weekend, but it's worth the wait – partly for the fifty-minute ride past the reservoir and slowly up the valley, with swirling views below to the coast.

Po Lin Monastery and Tian Tan Buddha

The **Po Lin Monastery** was established in 1927 on the Ngong Ping plateau surrounded by mountains, including Lantau Peak itself. The temple complex is on a much grander scale than is usual in Hong Kong, reminiscent more of a Peking opera set than a place of worship; an impression of grandeur enhanced by other features of the site such as the huge bronze urn, a gift from the mainland Chinese government to mark the 1997 handover. The hundred monks and nuns here led a relatively peaceful existence until the 1970s, when the main temple and its pavilions were opened to the public, since when they've been besieged by swarms of people posing for photos on the temple steps and in the gardens. The main temple houses a noted group of three statues of the Buddha – fairly restrained under the circumstances, at only around three metres high each. There's nothing at all restrained about the temple itself, though, which is painted and sculpted in an almost gaudy fashion, its surfaces awash with vibrant gold, red, pink, orange and yellow.

All this pales into insignificance besides the gigantic but serene **Tian Tan Buddha** statue, at the top of a flight of 268 steps up the hillside in front of the monastery. The bronze figure seated in a ring of outsized lotus petals is 34m high and weighs 250 tonnes – roughly the same as a jumbo jet. It was built at a reputed cost of $68 million and, following its consecration in 1993, is now Lantau's top tourist attraction. It will probably get even more crowded if the government goes ahead with plans to build a cable car linking the monastery to Tung Chung and the airport – a key element in its strategy to boost the tourist industry. Climb the steps for supreme views over the surrounding hills and down to the temple complex – there's no charge. Inside the base are four paintings depicting the Buddha's spiritual journeys, while if you've bought a meal ticket (see overleaf), you'll also be allowed into the (rather dull) exhibition galleries underneath the statue.

Book ahead if you want to stay at the S. G. Davis Youth Hostel at Ngong Ping. Take bus #S51 ($3.50) from the airport to Tung Chung bus terminal, then #23 ($16 Mon–Fri, $25 Sat–Sun) to the end of the line; see p.215.

Access to the Buddha statue is from 10am to 6pm only, so make sure you set out early enough if you want to climb to the top: it's an hour's ferry ride from Central, plus 50min on the bus.

Everything else in the complex is firmly aimed at the weekend tourist invasion, too. Inside the temple courtyard there's a huge and chattering **dining hall**, where you can get a filling meal of inventive vegetarian food ($60, or the "deluxe" meal, served in air-conditioned surroundings, for $100, or a "snack" for $25; sittings every 30 minutes from 11.30am to 5pm). Buy a coupon from the ticket office at the bottom of the steps leading to the Buddha and sit at the table numbered on your ticket. On the other side of the temple courtyard from the dining hall a traditional pagoda shelters a collection of vending machines.

Just to the left of the steps for the statue, a path leads the few hundred metres up to the **Lantau Tea Gardens**, once Hong Kong's only

---

Chek Lap Kok and the new airport

During the 1980s, with the old airport at Kai Tak at saturation point and the danger of the flight approach amongst the buildings of Kowloon a major concern, Hong Kong's need for a **new airport** was generally acknowledged. Despite this, plans for a new airport, announced in 1989, were highly controversial and led to a long-running spat between the British authorities in Hong Kong and the Chinese government, who saw it as a plot to spend Hong Kong's reserves – and give work to British construction companies – before the handover.

What was surprising was the choice of site – isolated **Chek Lap Kok island**, off the north coast of Lantau – and the sheer scale of the proposals, which were to make the airport and its associated developments the world's largest civil engineering project. Before the redevelopment Chek Lap Kok had supported a dwindling population of around two hundred. Now the island was completely levelled, forty thousand tonnes of explosive were used to blast out 75 million cubic metres of rock, and reclamation more than doubled its size. The airport platform is 6km long, while the dimensions of the airport buildings on the reclaimed island are no less staggering: the terminal building alone is twice the size of London Heathrow and New York's JFK put together. It is currently designed to handle 35 million passengers a year, a figure that will rise to more than 80 million by 2040.

The construction of the airport has been only the start of an entire new phase of development in Hong Kong: the **Airport Core Programme** (ACP), comprising ten major projects. Some of these were needed to provide transport links – the siting of Chek Lap Kok in one of the more inaccessible corners of Hong Kong meant the territory's communications and transport infrastructure had to be redrawn almost from scratch – whilst entire new towns and industrial areas are planned to grow up along the new transport routes in areas such as Tsing Yi, Tai Kok Tsui and West Kowloon. Tung Chung New Town, opposite the airport on Lantau, is due to house sixty thousand people and serve as a gateway into Hong Kong. From here the six-lane North Lantau Expressway, the 32-kilometre Airport Express Railway and the Tung Chung MTR line follow the northeast coast of Lantau, crossing the islands of Ma Wan and Tsing Yi on suspension bridges before hitting the mainland and turning south into Kowloon.

Naturally, there were objections to a scheme of such magnitude. The residents of Tung Chung have seen their village and way of life transformed,

---

tea-producing estate, though its future has become uncertain since it was sold in 1993. It contains the little *Tea Gardens Restaurant*, where you can sit outside, eat fried rice and drink a beer – the tea is good too. Despite its proximity to the monastery, it's usually fairly peaceful. Signs just beyond the restaurant indicate the paths to the *S. G. Davis Youth Hostel*, Lantau Peak and the Po Lam Zen Monastery.

Lantau Peak

A very steep path leads up from the Tea Gardens to the 934-metre-high peak of Fung Wong Shan, as **Lantau Peak** is properly known,

some say ruined; fishermen on nearby Cheung Chau claim that the dumping of mud from the project has killed the fish; while environmental groups have pointed to the detrimental effect on species like the pink dolphin which once inhabited the waters around Chek Lap Kok. More vociferous objections came from the Chinese government, worried – perhaps with some justification – that the airport was a last, grand gesture from a departing British government which wouldn't have to foot the bill after 1997 if things went wrong. The cost (although a matter of some debate) is astronomical: estimates put the entire ACP budget at around $155 billion, of which the airport site accounted for around $70 billion. For a while there was real concern that arguments over the cost would derail the entire project, though a final financing package between Britain and China was eventually agreed in June 1995.

The first planned opening date was mid-1997 (so that the last governor could leave – symbolically – from the new airport when China took over). That was put back to July 1998 when – entirely coincidentally, according to the SAR government – it was ready just in time to be opened by President Jiang Zemin of China during celebrations marking the first anniversary of the handover. The transfer of services from Kai Tak to Chek Lap Kok was achieved in an extraordinary overnight operation using hundreds of lorries, barges and planes. The old airport closed at 1.15am, the equipment was dismantled, transported and reassembled, and the new one opened for its first landing at 6.30am.

Unfortunately things went wrong from there. On the first day – and for some days afterwards – the luggage carousels malfunctioned, the automatic gates didn't work properly, the signage was unreadable and the computer system crashed. Passengers got locked in lifts and buildings, and tons of perishable freight rotted in warehouses, attracting a plague of rats. Thousands of people waited hours to check in or retrieve their luggage, only to then find the transport links malfunctioning. It amounted to a massive loss of face for a city which prided itself on its efficiency, and whose officials hadn't hesitated to boast of their superiority. The result was a certain amount of soul-searching and the setting up of a number of public enquiries, all of which attempted to pin the blame on someone else – preferably someone who wasn't still in power. The airport itself was working properly within a few weeks, and most of the associated projects are due to be completed by 2001. The wheel should turn full circle in the first decades of the new century with the redevelopment of the old Kai Tak site in Kowloon City, which is scheduled to become another new town with a quarter of a million inhabitants.

the second highest in Hong Kong, and renowned as an excellent venue for sunrise watching. This will mean a crack-of-dawn start, but the views – as far as Macau on a clear day – are justly famous.

The peak is on the Lantau Trail and depending on how energetic you feel the path then heads east, reaching the slightly lower **Tai Tung Shan**, or "Sunset Peak", after about 5km. A fairly sharpish two-hour descent from there puts you on the road at Nam Shan, within shouting distance of Mui Wo.

Tung Chung

The other main village on the island, **TUNG CHUNG**, on the northern shore below Chek Lap Kok island, was once a trading and fishing port with close links with Tai O. It slipped gradually into twentieth-century obscurity and for decades Tung Chung and its fourteen associated settlements lived an unassuming, though self-sufficient life, dependent on a bit of fish- and pig-farming, some local shallot growing and occasional visits by tourists. Then came the decision to site Hong Kong's new airport on Chek Lap Kok, just 400m to the north, and Tung Chung suddenly found itself at the heart of one of the world's most extensive development programmes. The fish vanished from Chek Lap Kok – indeed, Chek Lap Kok itself vanished; two of the local settlements were torn down to make way for access roads; the bridge from the airport was completed; and Tung Chung New Town began to take shape.

It's still worth the ride out here to see the relics of the old Tung Chung, and the bus ride (#3 or #13 from Mui Wo) alone is sufficient reason to head out here, climbing slowly over the hills before rattling down the valley to the village. The one road out of Tung Chung leads north past the nineteenth-century **Battery**, while a kilometre or so back inland, the road winds to **Tung Chung Fort**, six cannons lining its northern wall, though these days the fortifications protect a school. There was a fortress here as long ago as the seventeenth century, though this building dates back only to 1817, built on the orders of the Viceroy of Guangdong (Canton province) to defend Lantau's northern coast. Over the road from the fort are two paths, the unmarked one on the right leading back over the fields to Ma Wan Chung, the part of the village where the bus drops you.

There are some good **walks** in the vicinity, most obviously the one down to Tung Chung from **Po Lin Monastery**, a pleasant two- to three-hour hike passing several smaller temples scattered along the Tung Chung valley. Longer hikes are those from Mui Wo and the coastal walk from Tai O, both of which take around five hours; don't forget to take water, suncream, strong shoes and a hat. There's also a **bus** (#23) to and from the Po Lin Monastery, with frequent services, especially on Sundays; it's a 50-minute ride.

Lantau Travel Details

For up-to-date ferry information, call the Hong Kong Ferry Co. (☎2542 3081) between 8am and 6pm.
For Discovery Bay hoverferry service call Discovery Bay Transportation Services Ltd (☎2987 7351).
For Chek Lap Kok services call Airport Ferry Services Ltd at Tuen Mun (☎2459 9799), at Chek Lap Kok (☎2949 0022), at Discovery Bay (☎2987 7351).
For bus information call New Lantao Bus Co. (☎2984 9848).

Ferries

Outlying Islands Ferry Piers to Mui Wo (hourly; first at 7am, last at 12.20am; to Tuen Mun/Sha Lo Wan/Tai O (Sat at 9.15am & 2.15pm, Sun at 8.15am).

Star Ferry Pier, Tsim Sha Tsui to Mui Wo (Sat at 1pm, 2pm, 3pm, 5pm & 7pm; Sun 9am, 11am then hourly 1pm–6pm).

Mui Wo to Outlying Islands Ferry Piers (approximately every hour; first at 6.10am, last at 11.10pm); to Tsim Sha Tsui (Sat at 2pm, 3pm, 4pm & 6pm; Sun at 10am, noon & hourly 2pm–7pm).

Tai O to Tuen Mun/Sha Lo Wan/Central (Sat at 11.50am & 5pm, these services terminating at Tuen Mun; Sun at 3pm terminating at Tuen Mun, & 5.30pm terminating at Central).

Tai Shui Hang (Trappist Monastery) to Peng Chau (Mon–Sat at 8.10am, 9.30am, 11.30am, 12.30pm, 2.45pm & 4.30pm; Sun at 8.10am, 10.15am, 12.30pm, 3pm & 4.45pm).

Inter-Island Ferry

Mui Wo to Peng Chau (7–8 daily; first at 6.10am, last at 10.50pm); Chi Ma Wan/Cheung Chau (8 daily; first at 6.05am, last at 9.35pm, Sun, first at 6.25am, last at 9.40pm).

Hoverferries

Outlying Islands Ferry Piers to Mui Wo (via Peng Chau) (Mon–Sat at 9.35am, 11.20am, 2.25pm & 4.25pm; Sun at 9.35am, 11.25am, 2.25pm & 4.25pm).

Chek Lap Kok to Discovery Bay (Mon–Fri at 6.45am, 8.10am, 9.10am, 5.30pm, 6.10pm, 7.50pm & 8.40pm; Sat additional service at 4.15pm; Sun additional services at 9.50am & 4.45pm); to Tuen Mun (every 20–30 mins between 6am and 10pm).

Discovery Bay to Star Ferry Pier, Central (24hr service; every 20–30min at peak times); to Chek Lap Kok (Mon–Fri at 5.50am, 7.10am, 8.10am, 4.30pm, 6.50pm & 7.40pm; Sat additional service at 3.15pm; Sun additional services at 8.50am & 3.45pm).

Star Ferry Pier, Central to Discovery Bay (24hr service; every 20–30min at peak times).

Mui Wo to Peng Chau/Outlying Islands Ferry Piers (Mon–Sat at 7.40am, 10.15am, 12.10pm, 3.10pm & 5.10pm).

Tuen Mun to Chek Lap Kok (every 20–30 mins between 6am and 10pm).

Kaidos

Kaido services operate on the following routes with varying degrees of regularity; specific details are given in the text where appropriate.
Tai Shui Hang–Nim Shue Wan.
Tai Long Wan–Cheung Chau.
Mong Tung Wan–Cheung Chau.

continued overleaf

Lantau

Buses

On regular services, fares are between $3.60 and $9.50 one-way; air-conditioned services cost about a third more. You pay on board; fares are just under double on Sundays and holidays. The special air-con bus from Mui Wo direct to Po Lin Monastery costs $16.

#1 Mui Wo–Tai O (via Pui O and Kwun Yam Temple); approximately every 30 mins until 1.30am.

#2 Mui Wo–Ngong Ping (Po Lin Monastery); Mon–Sat hourly from 8.20am until 6.35pm, Sun every 30min. The direct air-con service runs every 5–15min, last departure back to the ferry pier at 7.30pm.

#3 Mui Wo–Tung Chung; approximately every hour; first at 6.15am, last at 7.35pm.

#4 Mui Wo–Tong Fuk (via Nam Shan and Cheung Sha beach); Mon–Sat hourly until 10.30pm, Sun every 30min until 10pm.

#5 Mui Wo–Shek Pik; Mon–Sat hourly until 9.30pm, Sun every 30min until 7.30pm.

#7 Mui Wo–Pui O (via Nam Shan); Mon–Sat hourly until 10.30pm, Sun every 30min until 7.30pm.

#11 Tung Chung–Tai O; approximately every 30 mins, first at 6.20am, last at 00.50am.

#21 Tai O–Ngong Ping; 7 daily; first at 7.45am, last at 3pm.

#23 Tung Chung–Ngong Ping; first bus at 8.10am, last at 6.10pm.

Hong Kong Listings

Chapter 6

Accommodation

Accommodation in Hong Kong doesn't have to be a major expense. There are plenty of rock-bottom choices, starting at around $70 a night for a bed in a dormitory (even cheaper if you stay in an IYHF hostel), which are bearable if all you're doing is passing through. However, for extended stays – even just three or four nights – they cease to be an attractive proposition: they're often crowded, dirty and hot. If you can afford a little more, then a room in a guest house with fan or air-conditioning starts at around $200–250 double, slightly more with an attached bathroom. Above that, some of the three- and four-star hotels, hit hard by the downturn in tourism which followed the handover, now offer deep discounts when their occupancy rate is looking low. If money is no object, Hong Kong also has some of the world's finest hotels, offering an unparalleled degree of comfort and service.

There isn't really a high or a low season so far as hotel bookings are concerned because of the constant inflow of business travellers. But given the sheer number of options, **booking in advance** isn't strictly necessary – especially at the cheaper end of the market – if you don't mind a bit of legwork, although if you want a bargain rate at one of the mid-price hotels it's a good idea to find out what packages and deals are available before you arrive The only time you will be chasing too few hotel beds is during Chinese New Year, which falls in January or February, but even then you should find something. Still, for peace of mind (and certainly if you want to guarantee space in one of the plusher hotels) it's as well to have at least your first night's accommodation sorted out before you arrive.

Airport arrivals can reserve rooms through the offices of the Hong Kong Hotel Association in the A and B Halls of Chek Lap Kok airport (daily 6am–1am). There's no booking fee, but they'll only contact hotels which are members of their association, which rules out the bulk of the budget hostels and hotels; the cheapest rooms you'll get through them start at around $500 double. The HKTA also issues a Hotel Guide which includes maps, contact numbers and prices.

Beware of the **touts** at the airport and elsewhere, who will accost you and offer you a cheap room. The place you're taken to might, in fact, be all right, but if you decide you don't want to take the room having seen it they'll probably try to pin a charge on you for taking you there in the first place. If this happens, don't pay, but don't expect them to be happy about it. On the other hand, don't be too paranoid: the people handing out guest-house business cards are harmless enough – you can always take the card and go and look on your own later.

> **Hong Kong Hotel Association:**
> ☎ 2383 8380
> fax 2362 2383
> email *hkhahrc@att.net.hk.*

Accommodation

The bulk of the very cheapest places – dormitories and guest houses – are Kowloon-side, in and around Tsim Sha Tsui, but with money to burn you can take your pick of the hotels on Hong Kong Island or in Tsim Sha Tsui East. There is also a string of YMCAs and equivalent places on the island and in Kowloon, offering more downmarket (but thoroughly decent) hotel-style accommodation; and there's a small network of youth hostels (and a few cheap hotels) in the New Territories and on the outlying islands – both under-used options for the most part.

> The various **Airbuses** from the airport can take most people right to their hotel; see p.214 for more details.

Dormitory accommodation

The cheapest beds in Hong Kong are those found in **dormitory-style accommodation**, either in offical IYHF youth hostels or in non-IYHF hostels and guest houses.

IYHF youth hostels

There are seven official International Youth Hostel Federation (IYHF) **youth hostels** in Hong Kong, of which three are regularly used by foreign travellers: Ma

Wui Hall on Hong Kong Island, and Mong Tung Wang and S.G. Davis, both of which are close to Chek Lap Kok airport. The others are in fairly remote parts of the New Territories and on Lantau Island, but if you want to escape the cloying atmosphere of central Hong Kong, it's worth making an effort to stay at them. They are all very cheap – $35–65 per person, $200-260 per family – and have cooking and washing facilities. You'll need an IYHF membership card to use them, available from the national organizations in your home country (see the box below), or you can buy a "Welcome Stamp" ($30 per night) at your first Hong Kong hostel – buying six is the equivalent of having international membership. The **head office** of the Hong Kong Youth Hostels Association (open Mon, Wed, Fri 9.30am–5.30pm, Tues, Thurs 9.30am-7pm, Sat 9.30am-1pm) is at Room 225, Block 19, Shek Kip Mei Estate, Sham Shui Po, Kowloon (☎2788 1638, fax 2788 3105, email *hkyha@datainternet.com*).

It's best to book beds at the hostels **in advance**, either by writing to or telephoning head office, or by telephoning the hostels themselves, although you can also walk in and try your luck. The HKTA office in the Buffer Hall at the airport has a leaflet on how to reach the

---

Youth Hostel Organizations

Australia Australian Youth Hostels Association, 422 Kent St, Sydney ☎02/9261 1111.

Canada Hostelling International/Canadian Hostelling Association, Room 400, 205 Catherine St, Ottawa, ON K2P 1C3 ☎613/237-7884 or ☎1-800/663-5777.

England and Wales Youth Hostel Association (YHA), Trevelyan House, 8 St Stephen's Hill, St Alban's, Herts AL1 2DY ☎01727/855215. London shop and information office: 14 Southampton St, London WC2 7HY ☎0171/836 1036.

Ireland An Oige, 61 Mountjoy Square, Dublin 7 ☎01/830 4555.

New Zealand Youth Hostels Association of New Zealand, PO Box 436, Christchurch 1 ☎03/379 9970.

Northern Ireland Youth Hostel Association of Northern Ireland, 56 Bradbury Place, Belfast BT7 ☎01232/324733.

Scotland Scottish Youth Hostel Association, 7 Glebe Crescent, Stirling FK8 2JA ☎01786/451181.

USA Hostelling International–American Youth Hostels (HI-AYH), 733 15th St NW, Suite 840, PO Box 37613, Washington DC 20005 ☎202/783-6161.

Ma Wui Hall, S.G. Davis and Bradbury Lodge hostels; use the free phones to check on space with the warden or the head office. The hostels are **closed** between 10am and 4pm on weekdays, between 1 and 2pm at weekends (some also close one day midweek), and there are separate dormitories for men and women – couples must take two-person family rooms. On Friday and Saturday nights throughout the year the New Territories hostels are nearly always packed with groups of young Chinese: go in midweek and you'll often be on your own. You'll also need a sheet sleeping bag, which you can rent at the hostel for a few dollars.

MOUNT DAVIS

Ma Wui Hall, Mount Davis, Hong Kong Island ☎ 2817 5715. The most popular – and central – hostel in Hong Kong, above Kennedy Town on top of Mount Davis, with superb views. It's open 7am–midnight, there are cooking facilities, lockers, air conditioning and 112 beds, including two- and three-person family rooms. However, it fills up quickly. To get there take bus #47A from Admiralty, or minibus #54 from the Outlying Islands Ferry Terminal in Central, alight near the junction of Victoria Road and Mount Davis Path. Walk back 100m from the bus stop and take Mount Davis Path to the hostel – a tough, two-kilometre, 45-minute climb with luggage. There is also a hostel shuttle bus ($10) from the bus terminal next to the Shun Tak Centre at the Macau Ferry Terminal, near Sheung Wan MTR station. The shuttle leaves the Shun Tak Centre at 9.30am, 7pm, 9pm, 10.30pm; the return service leaves Ma Wui Hall at 7.30am, 9am, 10.30am, 8.30pm. Alternatively, take a taxi from the Macau Ferry Terminal (around $70) or Kennedy Town (around $50).

NEW TERRITORIES

Bradbury Hall, Chek Keng, Sai Kung Peninsula ☎ 2328 2458. 100 beds, including two- and four-person family rooms; see p.179

Bradbury Lodge, Tai Mei Tuk, Tai Po ☎ 2662 5123. 94 beds and five family rooms, camping facilities; see p.155.

Pak Sha O, Hoi Ha (Jones' Cove), Sai Kung Peninsula ☎ 2328 2327. 112 beds, camping facilities; see p.180.

Sze Lok Yuen, Tai Mo Shan, Tsuen Wan ☎ 2488 8188. 92 beds, camping facilities; see p.169.

LANTAU

Mong Tung Wan, Chi Ma Wan peninsula ☎ 2984 1389. 88 beds; closed 1–2 days a week, advance booking essential, camping facilities available; see p.200.

S.G. Davis, Ngong Ping ☎ 2985 5610. 48 beds, camping facilities available ($16 members, $25 non-members); see p.203.

Other hostels

Mostly located in Tsim Sha Tsui, dormitories in non-IYHF hostels are rather thinner on the ground than they used to be, due to more toughly enforced health and safety restrictions, but some places still maintain a few bunk beds here and there. Typically, you'll pay around $70–80 for a space in a multi-bedded dorm, sharing with other backpackers. There will normally be separate shower and laundry facilities, and sometimes a TV room and cooking facilities. The dorms are generally friendly places, good for meeting people, but can be cramped, and some are less than secure. The *Oriental Pearl Hostel* (p.225), *STB Hostel* (p.229), *Travellers' Hostel* (p.223) and *Victoria Hostel* (p.226) are among the places with dorm space – see the listings below for more information.

Guest houses, YMCAs and hotels

Most budget travellers end up in one of Tsim Sha Tsui's **guest houses**. Given the high rents in Hong Kong, most of the rooms are shoe-box sized, with paper-thin walls and a turnover that's fast and furious (qualities shared by many of the owners). Often the decor looks as if someone has tried to swing a cat – and

Accommodation

Accommodation

failed. However, if you're prepared to spend a little more than you'd perhaps planned, you should be able to find somewhere reasonable.

Most guest houses are contained inside large mansion blocks on and around **Nathan Road** in Tsim Sha Tsui, most notoriously **Chungking Mansions** (36–44 Nathan Rd), where there are dozens of relatively cheap places, although many are not that inviting. Instead, you might want to try one of the other slightly more appealing blocks, like the nearby **Mirador Mansions** (56–58 Nathan Rd) or the **Lyton Building** (42–48 Mody Rd). After years of procrastination, and repeated warnings of massive fire risks, Chungking Mansions and similar buildings have finally undergone improvement programmes, though you may find this hard to believe on a first viewing – Chungking especially is still an endlessly confusing warren of dingy corridors, and safety and hygiene standards are still not what they should be. On the other hand, Chungking Mansions has developed a reputation among travellers as a place to meet people and swap information.

When **renting your room**, *always* ask to see it first, and don't be afraid to try and bargain the price down. If you're staying a few days, you'll often be able to get a reduction, but be wary about paying out the whole lot at once: if the guest house turns out to be roach-infested or noisy, or both, you'll have a hard job getting your money back if you want to leave early. The best advice is to take the room for a night and see what it's like before parting with your cash.

Check that the **air-conditioning** unit actually works and isn't too noisy – some places make an extra charge ($20–30 per night) for its use; other rooms simply come equipped with a ceiling fan. **Bathrooms** are rarely that: rather, a tiny, very musty additional room with toilet and hand-held shower, although even this is usually better than sharing what can be fairly grim communal facilities. Most rooms also come with TV, though the reception in places like

Chungking Mansions can leave a lot to be desired. Guest houses nearly all charge for the room, which usually sleeps two (sometimes three) people, so **single travellers** will find themselves paying over the odds – the best you can do is ask for the smallest available room, but it will often be terribly claustrophobic.

There are several **YMCAs** and **religious organizations** offering accommodation somewhere in between the most expensive of the guest houses and the cheapest of the regular hotels. The rooms are all well appointed (with air-conditioning and TV) and comparatively spacious. Most importantly, at these prices, you can start to pick and choose the area you want to stay in; some of the places below are in excellent locations. Rooms at all of them can be booked at the airport's accommodation office.

At the top end of the scale, Hong Kong has some of the world's finest and most expensive **hotels**, competing for the massive business custom that passes through the colony. The *Peninsula* is the longest-established, and arguably the most famous, an elegant colonial hotel just behind the Tsim Sha Tsui waterfront. Of the others, the *Mandarin Oriental* and the *Conrad* are often mentioned in surveys of the world's best hotels. There are many cheaper, mid-range hotels around too, though beware those at the lower end of this range which are little more than guest houses using the official designation, "hotel" – the YMCAs might prove better value. With most hotels, the only choice to be made is location since most are fitted with everything that you could possibly want – business centres, gyms and restaurants, hair stylists and gift shops.

Lots of hotels don't distinguish between singles and doubles; you're just charged for the room; breakfast is not usually included, but is worth negotiating over. It pays to shop around, since most places offer discounts and deals at odd times of the year and you might save a couple of hundred dollars here and there. It's worth remembering, too, that many hotels work out better value if booked as

Price Categories

Accommodation in this guide is classified in eight price categories. Dormitory beds (①) are classified according to the cost per person per night; the guest house and hotel categories refer to the cost of a double room, *excluding taxes*. Guest houses tend to have a range of rooms on offer – singles, doubles, with and without air-conditioning or bathroom – and some reviews have multiple price categories to reflect this. In hotels (roughly speaking category ④ and upwards), you can count on rooms coming with a bathroom, air-conditioning and TV. Again, most have a range of available rooms and the price categories sometimes reflect this (eg. ⑥–⑦).

Accommodation

① Under $80 per person	⑤ $500–800 per room
② Under $200 per room	⑥ $800–1200 per room
③ $200–300 per room	⑦ $1200–2000 per room
④ $300–500 per room	⑧ Over $2000 per room

part of an **inclusive package or tour**. Count on adding a ten percent **service charge** and a three percent government **tax** to the quoted room price. If you want a **harbour view**, you'll always pay much more than the standard room rate.

Central and Admiralty

On the whole, this is the most expensive area in Hong Kong to look for a room. There are no guest houses and the few hotels are of international quality and price – the locations, though, are superb. Sadly the *Hilton* – a local favourite – has been demolished and replaced by another office block. The #A11 Airbus from the airport passes most of the Central hotels; otherwise, take the MTR to either Central or Admiralty (for Pacific Place).

Bishop Lei International House, 4 Robinson Rd ☎ 2868 0828, fax 2868 1551, email *resvtion@bishopleihtl.com.hk*. Above Central, and convenient for the mid-levels escalator, the hotel is associated with the local Catholic church. Some of the 205 rooms have great views but the place has a rather basic feel, which makes its rates seem rather high, particularly compared to discount or package rates available from smarter establishments. ⑦.

Conrad International, Pacific Place, 88 Queensway ☎ 2521 3838, fax 2521 3888, email *reservation@conradintl.com.hk*.

Spiffy modern hotel which takes full advantage of its position in the upper floors of one of the Pacific Place towers. Great views and superb restaurants, though its luxury is slightly characterless. ⑧.

Furama Hotel, 1 Connaught Rd ☎ 2525 5111, fax 2845 9339, email *reservation@furama.com.hk.*. Slightly dated décor compared to the others, so slightly cheaper prices, despite an excellent location. It has harbour or Peak view rooms (provided you're above the 16th floor), a revolving restaurant and a faithful business clientele. ⑦–⑧.

Garden View International House, 1 Macdonnell Rd ☎ 2877 3737, fax 2845 6263. A rare budget option in Central, this YWCA-run hotel has an excellent location near the botanical gardens and is handy for the Peak Tram terminal. Book well in advance. Take the Airbus to Central Bus Terminal and bus #12A from there to Macdonnell Rd. ⑤.

Island Shangri-La, Pacific Place, 88 Queensway ☎ 2877 3838, fax 2521 8742. Classy hotel at Pacific Place and, if anything, with the best Peak or harbour views of the lot, particularly from the top-floor *Cyrano's* bar. ⑧.

Mandarin Oriental, 5 Connaught Rd ☎ 2522 0111, fax 2810 6190, email *reserve-moht@moht.com.hk*. The *Mandarin* is considered by many to be the best hotel in the world: there's no faulting the service (the staff run into

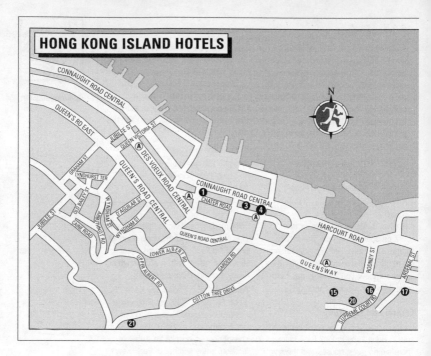

hundreds), facilities (the rooms have
antiques and balconies, the corridors
eighteenth-century Chinese textiles) or
location (close to the Star Ferry). You
don't need to stay here to appreciate its
atmosphere – people-watching in the
lobby is a great way to see Hong Kong's
finest at work and play. The café is a
favourite *tai tai* lunch spot, the *Chinnery
Bar* is where bankers come to unwind,
and the *Mandarin Grill* is where government officials and *Taipans* also have
their power lunches. If you really want to
put the staff through their paces, they
claim that the restaurants will prepare
any dish that has ever appeared on the
menu over the last thirty years. ⑧.

JW Marriott, Pacific Place, 88 Queensway
☎2810 8366, fax 2845 0737, email
guest@marriott.com.hk. Flash Pacific
Place complex, exuding Hong Kong luxury and hi-tech – the spectacular lobby
even has a waterfall. Rooms with harbour views cost an extra $200. ⑦.

Ritz-Carlton, 3 Connaught Rd ☎2877
6666, fax 2877 6778, email
ritzrchk@hk.super.net. In a prime city
centre location, it's probably the best
alternative in Central to staying at the
Mandarin Oriental. Rooms (just over 200
of them) are eminently comfortable and
there's a high staff-guest ratio. ⑧.

Wan Chai

Again, there are no real bargains here –
at least at the full rate – except for the
Wesley and the *Harbour View
International House*, which are popular
enough to warrant booking well in
advance. Mostly, the hotels here are
patronized by business people and the
better package tours: you certainly don't
need to stay in Wan Chai to get the best
out of its nightlife and the Arts Centre.
Access is by buses #1, #18, or Airbus
#N11; Wan Chai MTR puts you close to
most, too, while from Wan Chai Ferry
Pier it's an easy stroll to the *Grand Hyatt*,

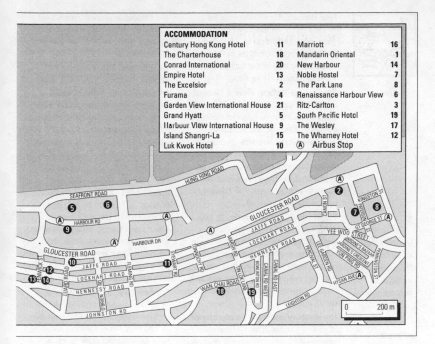

Renaissance World Harbour View and *International House*.

Century Hong Kong Hotel, 238 Jaffe Rd ☎2598 8888, fax 2598 8866. Modern, not completely outrageously priced hotel, handy for access to the Convention and Exhibition Centre and Wan Chai's nightlife. It's at the bottom of this price range. ⑦.

Empire Hotel, 33 Hennessy Rd ☎2866 9111, fax 2861 3121, email *info@empire-hotel.com.hk*. Convenient for Wan Chai's nightlife and featuring a small lounge which looks onto Lockhart Road. Two levels of basement food outlets. ⑦.

Grand Hyatt, 1 Harbour Rd ☎2588 1234, fax 2802 0677, email *www.grandhyatt.com.hk*. Part of the Convention and Exhibition Centre complex (along with the neighbouring *Renaissance Harbour View*), and bulging with fine harbour views, this is a prime example of the territory's bid for the busi-

ness trade – massively expensive, luxurious rather than tasteful, and bristling with bars, restaurants, pools, gardens, tennis courts and a health club. ⑧.

Harbour View International House, 4 Harbour Rd ☎2802 0111, fax 2802 9063, email *hvihymca@netvigator.com*. One of the best-value Hong Kong Island locations, and good views to boot, right next door to the Arts Centre and handy for the Wan Chai ferry pier. It's operated by the YMCA, and the doubles, complete with all facilities, come at the bottom of this category. Rooms with a harbour view are $400 extra. ⑥.

Luk Kwok Hotel, 72 Gloucester Rd ☎2866 2166, fax 2866 2622, email *lukkwok@lukkwokhotel.com*. This is one of the city's landmark hotels – famous as the hotel name and location used in the film *The World of Suzie Wong* (see p.96). Not that you'd recognize it anymore, with its brown-marble-and-glass exterior and standard, mid-range interior. ⑦.

Accommodation

*① Under $80
per person
② Under $200
per room
③ $200–300
per room
④ $300–500
per room
⑤ $500–800
per room
⑥ $800–1200
per room
⑦ $1200–2000
per room
⑧ Over $2000
per room*

New Harbour, 41–49 Hennessy Rd
☎2861 1166, fax 2866 7615. Pretty
good value for its location, though the
rooms and public areas are quite small
– and it's on one of the busiest (read
noisiest) routes in Hong Kong. ⑦.

Renaissance Harbour View, 1 Harbour
Rd ☎2802 8888, fax 2802 8833, email
nwhv@com.hk. More splendid views, as
the name suggests, and the same
expense-account business clientele as
the *Grand Hyatt*, though the rooms are a
shade cheaper (and smaller) – you get
to use the *Grand Hyatt's* facilities, too. A
favourite with air crews. The breakfast is
particularly good here. ⑧.

The Wesley, 22 Hennessy Rd ☎2866
6688, fax 2866 6633, email
wesley@hanglung.com.hk. Knock-down
room rates in a quiet and comfortable
modern hotel with coffee shop close to
the Arts Centre. The restaurant isn't all it
could be though – eat elsewhere.
⑥–⑦.

The Wharney Hotel, 57–73 Lockhart Rd
☎2861 1000, fax 2865 6023, email
wharney@wlink.net. Nice guest quarters
and facilities – gym, whirlpool, subterranean bar (from where you look up
through plate-glass windows to Lockhart
Rd) and daily papers delivered to your
room. An extra $100 gets you the buffet
breakfast. ⑦.

Causeway Bay

Hong Kong's premier shopping district
isn't well endowed with decent hotels.
Of those listed below, the *Excelsior* and
Park Lane often feature as part of package tours, and are worth asking about if
that's how you're travelling to the territory, since room rates will then be eminently affordable. Causeway Bay does
have several cheap guest houses in its
back streets, though most are the sort of
places you rent by the hour – worth
avoiding on the whole. Access is by
Airbus #N11, tram or Causeway Bay
MTR.

The Charterhouse, 209–219 Wan Chai
Rd ☎2833 5566, fax 2833 5888, email
info@charterhouse.com.hk. Good services

and catering, and some rooms have a
good view of the Happy Valley racecourse. Coming by MTR, take the Times
Square exit. ⑦.

The Excelsior, 281 Gloucester Rd
☎2894 8888, fax 2895 6459, email
info@exhkg.com.hk. Best sited of
Causeway Bay's major hotels – with
many rooms overlooking the water –
though it's getting on in years and does-
n't feature the same up-to-the-minute
facilities as other similar places. Rooms
are better value than at most large
hotels though. ⑦.

Noble Hostel, 7th Floor, C1, Paterson
Building, 37 Paterson St ☎2576 6148,
fax 2577 0847. This is the contact
address and number for a series of budget-rated air-con rooms in Causeway Bay
run by the same owner. Well worth trying
first for good, central accommodation,
with and without private bathroom. ④.

The Park Lane, 310 Gloucester Rd
☎2890 3355, fax 2576 7853, email
info@parklane.com.hk. With views over
Victoria Park, this is the most convenient
hotel for the department stores, with a
wide variety of rooms on offer. ⑦.

South Pacific Hotel, 23 Morrison Hill Rd
☎2572 3838, fax 2893 7773, email
info@southpacifichotel.com.hk.
Architecturally, one of the most striking
hotels in Hong Kong. The style continues
inside the green cylinder: rooms are well
sized and quiet and the tram runs right
past the door. Coming by MTR, take the
Times Square exit. ⑦.

Tsim Sha Tsui

Most visitors – and nearly all those travelling on a budget – stay in Tsim Sha
Tsui, which breaks down into several
specific areas, though wherever you end
up, you're supremely well sited for all
the shops, bars, restaurants and nightlife.
The main road, Nathan Road, runs the
gamut from high-class hotels like the
Sheraton and *Miramar* to the myriad
cheap guest houses in Chungking
Mansions and other buildings. In the
streets east and west of Nathan Road,
there's a similar mix: it's just to the west

of the road that you'll find possibly the two best-sited hotels in the territory, the colonial *Peninsula* and the affordable *Salisbury YMCA*. The #A21 and #N22 Airbuses run through the area. Tsim Sha Tsui MTR also puts you within walking distance of all the places listed below.

ALONG NATHAN ROAD

Golden Crown Guest House, 5th Floor, Golden Crown Court, 66–70 Nathan Rd ☎ 2369 1782. Golden Crown Court is about the least awful of the blocks along Nathan Road, and this is a very friendly place, though there's not much space in

Accommodation

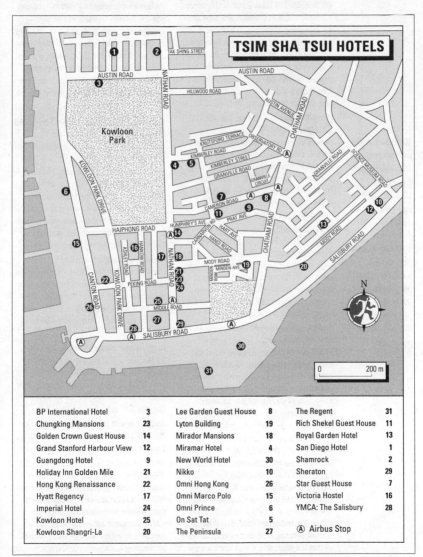

BP International Hotel	3	Lee Garden Guest House	8	The Regent	31
Chungking Mansions	23	Lyton Building	19	Rich Shekel Guest House	11
Golden Crown Guest House	14	Mirador Mansions	18	Royal Garden Hotel	13
Grand Stanford Harbour View	12	Miramar Hotel	4	San Diego Hotel	1
Guangdong Hotel	9	New World Hotel	30	Shamrock	2
Holiday Inn Golden Mile	21	Nikko	10	Sheraton	29
Hong Kong Renaissance	22	Omni Hong Kong	26	Star Guest House	7
Hyatt Regency	17	Omni Marco Polo	15	Victoria Hostel	16
Imperial Hotel	24	Omni Prince	6	YMCA: The Salisbury	28
Kowloon Hotel	25	On Sat Tat	5		
Kowloon Shangri-La	20	The Peninsula	27	Ⓐ Airbus Stop	

Accommodation

① Under $80
per person
② Under $200
per room
③ $200–300
per room
④ $300–500
per room
⑤ $500–800
per room
⑥ $800–1200
per room
⑦ $1200–2000
per room
⑧ Over $2000
per room

the dorms and the other rooms smell musty; a couple have showers, otherwise communal bathroom. Clean, though, and with laundry facilities, China visas available and soft drinks for sale. Dorms ①, rooms ③.

Holiday Inn Golden Mile, 46–52 Nathan Rd ☎2369 3111, fax 2369 8016, email *reserv@goldmile.com.hk*. Right next door to Chungking Mansions, which must annoy the owners, the rooms here are typically good value from the *Holiday Inn* chain, recently renovated, relatively spacious and with plenty of single rooms, too. There's also a pool, a popular bar and several restaurants. ⑧.

Hyatt Regency, 67 Nathan Rd ☎2311 1234, fax 2739 8701, email *general@hyattregency.com.hk*. Fully refurbished, with a spectacular lobby and ground-floor shopping arcade. Perfectly positioned for shopaholics: seventeen floors and over 700 rooms, all very decently equipped with marble bathrooms and hair dryers. ⑧.

Imperial Hotel, 30–34 Nathan Rd ☎2366 2201, fax 2311 2360, email *imperial@imperialhotel.com.hk*. A surprising bargain if you're looking for a proper hotel on Nathan Road itself, though you'll need to book ahead – and don't expect too many frills. Prices tend to fluctuate throughout the year. ⑥–⑦.

Kowloon Hotel, 19–21 Nathan Rd ☎2369 8698, fax 2739 9811, email *khh@peninsula.com*. Regular hotel comfort (mostly to business travellers) in a large (700-room) sleek building whose jagged glass facade soars off Nathan Road. You're paying for the location, however, since the rooms are among the smallest on offer in any hotel of this standard, though some have fine Wan Chai and harbour views. ⑧.

Miramar Hotel, 130 Nathan Rd ☎2368 1111, fax 2369 1788, email *miramar@netvigator.com*. Right opposite Kowloon Park, this is a fairly garish hotel, dating from the 1950s and bursting with shops. It's enormous (the rooms are larger than average too), and pricey, but for all that it's often full. If you want a view

over the park, you'll need to be in a more expensive room at the top. ⑦.

Sheraton, 20 Nathan Rd ☎2369 1111, fax 2739 8707, email *res_hongkong@ittsheraton.com*. Lording it over the bottom of Nathan Road, the *Sheraton* is swanky and expensive, though for the price of a cocktail you can ride the exterior elevator to the *Sky Lounge* for superb harbour views; yuppies congregate in the basement *Someplace Else* bar. Rooms and public areas are nicely turned out; the lobby, incidentally, is one of the easiest places in Tsim Sha Tsui from which to make a phone call. ⑧.

Chungking Mansions, 36–44 Nathan Rd
Chungking House, Block A, 4th Floor ☎2366 5362. The only real hotel in the Mansions, its "de luxe" single and double rooms come with air-con, bath and TV, though the decor is rather institutional. There's also a dining room serving a $25 breakfast and the rooms are actually reasonably spacious though, frankly, with this much money to spend, you can do better than Chungking Mansions. ④.

Fortunate Guest House, Block A, 11th Floor ☎2366 5900. Clean, modern guest house that would do well for a group of friends or family: two of the rooms have four beds. Otherwise the doubles come with air-con and TV but shared bathroom. ②–③.

Happy Guest House, Block B, 10th Floor, B3 ☎2368 1021. Popular and friendly, you'll have to go to "reception" on the 9th floor (B3) first. Singles available, as well as doubles with fan and TV, some with bath. You pay $20 extra for air-con. ②–③.

Harbour Guest House, Block B, 4th Floor ☎2368 1428. Only four floors up, which saves a lot of elevator trouble. Relatively pricey double rooms with own toilet and air-con. ③.

Hawaii Guest House, Block A, 14th Floor ☎2366 6127. One of the bargains in the Mansion, with en-suite air-con rooms the same price however many people occupy it – though three would be pushing it. ②.

Himalaya Guest House, Block A, 14th Floor ☎2368 6520. Clean and slightly larger-than-usual rooms with air-con and their own bathroom. TV and fans in the dining room, and helpful staff. ②.

Jinn's Ti Guest House, Block B & C, 7th Floor ☎2366 6742. Long-standing cheapie with a range of rooms spread across two blocks. Shared bathrooms. Not great at the less expensive end; worth splashing out on air-con. ③.

Kamal Guest House, Block B, 6th Floor ☎2739 3301. Rooms in two apartments on this floor, all have baths, no extra charge for air-con. ②.

London Guest House, Block A, 6th Floor, A1 ☎2366 5975. Slightly down-at-heel, but with friendly, conscientious staff. Basic doubles, some with shower and TV, and one room with a bathtub. ②

New Carlton Guest House, Block B, 15th Floor, ☎2721 0720. Basic place where all the rooms have private bathroom. It's friendly and good value. ②–③.

New Harbour Guest House, Block C, 9th Floor ☎2367 2777. Reasonable doubles with air-con; shared bathroom. ②.

New International, Block A, 15th Floor, A7 ☎2366 7972. Fairly standard doubles and singles with bath, though each room has a fridge and TV. The staff are very helpful and speak good English; laundry service available. Air-con costs $20 extra. ②.

New Washington Guest House, Block B, 13th Floor ☎2366 5798. Not terribly well maintained rooms, without air-con and private bathrooms (or, let's face it, windows). ③.

Park Guest House, Block A, 15th Floor, A1 ☎2368 1689, fax 2366 7936. A guest house you can rely on, this has been renting out rooms for years. Clean, very tidy box-like singles and doubles, some with fridges and shower, some claiming a mythical "sea view". ②.

Payless Guest House, Block A, 7th Floor A2 ☎2723 0148. You only do if you opt for a longer stay, in which case there'll be $20 knocked off the price per night. Clean and comparatively spacious single rooms only. ②.

Peking Guest House, Block A, 12th Floor, A2 ☎2723 8320. Bargain-priced but small doubles with air-con ($20 extra) and TV, some with shower. The best rooms face Nathan Road, which can be a bit noisy for some. Welcoming manager. ②–③.

Ranjeet Guest House, Block C, 4th & 6th Floors ☎2368 9943. Cramped rooms done out in lurid pink, though undeniably cheap; Indian movies shown every night. ②.

Rhine Guest House, Block A, 11th & 13th Floors ☎2367 1991 or 2721 6863. Very friendly, family-run place offering two singles and basic doubles with and without bath. ②.

Royal Inn/Royal Inn Plaza, Block D, 5th Floor ☎2366 2121. Slightly more upmarket place under the same management as the Rhine Guest House. They'll usually have a room, though they're not greatly attractive. ③.

Taj Super Deluxe, Block C, 3rd Floor ☎2366 4466. Slightly faded, but with doubles (with bath and air-con) that could sleep three, and helpful staff. Not bad value (at the top of this price range). ②.

Tokyo Guest House, Block A, 14th Floor, A5 ☎2367 5407. Nice big doubles ($50–100 more for one with a bath) and a welcoming owner; the single rooms are less impressive though. ②.

Tom's Guest House, Block A, 8th Floor, A5 ☎2722 4956; Block B & C, 16th Floor, C1 ☎2367 9258 or 2722 6035, fax 2366 6706. Pleasant sets of rooms with a friendly owner flitting between them, though the cool doubles with air-con and TV fill quickly. Not surprisingly: it feels safe, you get the use of a fridge, there's chilled water on demand, and the bathrooms are clean and decent. The Block A rooms are more expensive, but come with en-suite shower. ②–③.

Travellers' Hostel, Block A, 16th Floor ☎2368 7710. Best known of the backpackers' hostels, with mixed dorm beds and a few singles, as well as regular doubles. All have shared baths. There is also a kitchen, TV, lockers and a good noticeboard. Air-con is $20 extra. However, the

Accommodation

Accommodation

A Chungking Checklist

If you're going to stay in **Chungking Mansions** (36–44 Nathan Rd), it's as well to know what you're letting yourself in for. Despite new licensing restrictions and renovations, which dealt with the most extreme of the mansions' health and safety shortcomings (and closed dozens of guest houses), it still remains a fairly alarming place: seventeen storeys high, a gloomy collection of apartments housing dimly lit accommodation, gift shops, basic restaurants and loitering locals. Not a good option if you are claustrophobic, keen on hygiene or worried about fire.

Located next to the *Holiday Inn*, the ground and first floors are shopping arcades; the guest houses are on the floors above. Wander around and you'll find five sets of **elevators**, labelled A to E, two for each block – one for the even floors, one for the odd floors. Noticeboards tell you which guest houses are on each floor: the numbers, A3, B4, etc, are the address on that floor for each guest house. Confusingly, once you're up in the mansions, some of the **blocks** connect with each other by corridors: one wrong turn through a swing door and you could be coming down Block C having gone up Block B.

Searching for a room, it's best to leave one person downstairs with the luggage as the elevators are very small. When they get overloaded, an alarm sounds and the last one in has to get out. If you're really going to shop around, go straight to the top floor of a block and work your way down: the lists below have been drawn up on that principle. Big queues form for the elevators (especially Blocks A and B), and if you're staying on the 16th floor, walking up the stairs instead isn't always an option.

Most of the **guest houses** themselves are all right and some are really good. A few owners run more than one place, so don't worry if you're packed off to another block or another floor when you try to check in: just make sure to see the room first and establish the price. The **lists** below let you check out the possibilities block by block, and floor by floor; cross-check with the reviews for more detailed information.

Block A

16th Floor: *Travellers' Hostel.*
15th Floor: *Park Guest House, New International.*
14th Floor: *Hawaii Guest House, Tokyo Guest House, Himalaya Guest House.*
12th Floor: *Peking Guest House.*
11th Floor: *Fortunate Guest House, Rhine Guest House.*
8th Floor: *Tom's Guest House.*
7th Floor: *Payless Guest House, Welcome Guest House.*
6th Floor: *London Guest House.*
4th Floor: *Chungking House.*

Block B

16th Floor: *Tom's Guest House.*
15th Floor: *New Carlton Guest House.*
13th Floor: *New Washington Guest House.*

12th Floor: *Hong Kong Guest House.*
10th Floor: *Happy Guest House.*
7th Floor: *Jinn's Ti Guest House.*
6th Floor: *Kamal Guest House.*
4th Floor: *Harbour Guest House.*

Block C

16th Floor: *Tom's Guest House.*
9th Floor: *New Harbour Guest House.*
7th Floor: *Jinn's Ti Guest House.*
4th Floor: *Ranjeet Guest House.*
3rd Floor: *Taj Super Deluxe.*

Block D

5th Floor: *Royal Inn, Royal Inn Plaza.*

Block E

8th Floor: *Yan Yan Guest House.*

weirdos the hostel sometimes attracts make it one to avoid for a long-term stay. China visas sorted out at the travel agency next door. Dorms ①, rooms ②.

Welcome Guest House, Block A, 7th Floor, A5 ☎ 2721 7793. A recommended first choice; air-con doubles with and without shower. Nice clean rooms, luggage storage, laundry service and China visas available. ③.

Yan Yan Guest House, Block E, 8th Floor ☎ 2366 8930. Helpful staff renting out doubles with all facilities; you could sleep three in some at a squeeze, making them pretty good value. ②–③.

Mirador Mansions, 56–58 Nathan Rd

City Guest House, 3rd Floor, F2 ☎ 2724 2612. The reasonably friendly *City* has cheaper-than-usual dorm beds (though the room's very dark) as well as regular air-con rooms with TV. Discounts offered for longer stays; laundry service available. Dorms ①, rooms ③.

Dzin Hun Guest House, 9th Floor, E3 ☎ 2301 3018. English-speaking staff offering clean double rooms with air-con and shower (at the bottom of this price category) – not much space in them, however. ③.

Kowloon Hotel, 13th Floor, F1 and 10th Floor, E10; reception at 13th Floor, F4 ☎ 2311 2523. A guest house, despite the name, the smart, well-kept rooms are looked after by a friendly set. The F1 rooms all have shower, TV and air-con – and there are fridges and an iced-water dispenser, too. The 10th-floor rooms are slightly cheaper, but not as nice. You should get a 10% discount for staying two nights or more. Recommended. ④.

Man Hing Lung Guest House, 14th Floor, F2 ☎ 2722 0678 or 2311 8807. The rooms here are very small and clean (there's barely room to dirty anything), but all come with shower, TV and air-con – the very cheapest don't have a window. The owner speaks good English and has several other rooms scattered around the block, so it's not a bad first choice. ③.

Mei Lam Guest House, 5th Floor, D1 ☎ 2721 5278. The nice, very helpful, English-speaking owner here has very presentable singles and doubles, all spick-and-span and with full facilities. Worth the higher-than-usual prices. ③

Oriental Pearl Hostel, 6th Floor, A3 & A4 ☎ 2723 3439 or 2723 1344. The dorm looks like an overstuffed furniture warehouse, or there are air-con doubles too. If you want the luxury of a window, you'll pay another $80. Dorms ①, rooms ③.

EAST OF NATHAN ROAD

Guangdong Hotel, 18 Prat Ave ☎ 2739 3311, fax 2721 1137, email *gdhotel@guanghotel.com.hk*. CTS-owned hotel that's no real bargain, but within staggering distance of some of the better bars and restaurants. Rooms with street views are pricier the higher up the building you go. ⑤.

Lee Garden Guest House, 8th Floor, 34–36 Cameron Rd ☎ 2367 2284 or 2367 5872. Renovations have taken this place slightly upmarket and the decent singles, doubles and triples have bath, air-con and TV; prices are in the middle of this category. ④.

Lyton House Inn, Lyton Building, 42–48 Mody Rd, 4th & 6th Floor ☎ 2367 3791. The Lyton Building (on the south side of Mody Road, beyond Blenheim Ave) has a few guest house options. This is one of the longest-standing, with rooms on two floors, whose big doubles with shower are modern and clean. ④.

On Sun Tat, 7th Floor, Flat F, Champagne Court, 16 Kimberley Rd ☎ 2723 9143, fax 2311 2680. The pleasant people here have well-kept rooms with shower, air-conditioning and TV (ask in the travel agency). A good first call, since the rooms are cool and quiet, if not enormous; most of them have a window. ③.

Rich Shekel Guest House, 5th Floor, James Lee Mansion, 33–35 Carnarvon Rd ☎ 2369 6535 or 2739 6434. No English bar the price is spoken here – negotiate your way in, and you'll get a reasonable double room with air-con and shower

Accommodation

① *Under $80 per person*
② *Under $200 per room*
③ *$200–300 per room*
④ *$300–500 per room*
⑤ *$500–800 per room*
⑥ *$800–1200 per room*
⑦ *$1200–2000 per room*
⑧ *Over $2000 per room*

Accommodation

for the money. The friendly manager also offers discounts for longer stays. ④.

Star Guest House, 6th Floor, 21 Cameron Rd ☎2723 8951. Small, reasonably well-equipped rooms that can accommodate one or two people; under the same management as the *Lee Garden*. ④.

Tourist House, Lyton Building, 42–48 Mody Rd, 6th Floor; use lift no.3 ☎2721 8309. Chinese-run place with doubles with shower and TV, though the small rooms are nothing special. It might also be "full" to Westerners. ③.

WEST OF NATHAN ROAD

Hong Kong Renaissance, 8 Peking Rd ☎2375 1133, fax 2375 6611, email *resv@gehotel.com*. Serious prices for rooms for jaded business travellers – there are even fax machines provided, as well as TVs and all the usual comforts, including a pool. It's at the Canton Road end of the street and you'll pay more for a harbour view. ⑧.

Omni, Harbour City, Canton Rd; *The Hongkong* ☎2113 0088, fax 2311 0011, email *mphkkh97@asiaonline.net*; *The Marco Polo* ☎2113 0888, fax 2113 0022, email *mphkgdc@wlink.net*; *Prince* ☎2113 1888, fax 2113 0066, email *mpphh@asiaonline.net*. The massive Harbour City development houses three different hotels under the same Omni umbrella. They're all fairly fancy, at least in the public areas – the rooms aren't overwhelming – and you can use each hotel's facilities at will; the rest of the time, you'll spend lost in the endless shopping mall corridors. Only the *Hongkong* (the largest) has harbour views; those at the *Prince* overlook the park. ⑧.

The Peninsula, Salisbury Rd ☎2366 6251, fax 2722 4170, email *pen@penin-sula.com.hk*. Possibly the grandest hotel in Hong Kong, the *Peninsula* has been putting visitors up in unrivalled style since the late 1920s. Its elegant colonial wings have been overshadowed by the new central tower, which provides harbour views to match the style and quality of the hotel – the top-floor bar-restaurant, *Felix*, is the work of hotshot designer

Philippe Starck. Service is impeccable, as you might expect. The hotel's restaurants include some of the best food in the whole of Hong Kong. At least drop in for afternoon tea, which lets you gawp at the splendid lobby, or a drink at *Felix* (some locals like to combine a drink here with dinner in one of Chungking Mansions' Indian restaurants). See p.128 for more on the hotel's history. ⑧.

Victoria Hostel, 1st Floor, 33A Hankow Rd ☎2376 1182. Small, mixed dorms (cheaper without air-con), cooking facilities, lockers and a little sitting-out area. The paintwork's peeling, though, and the pushy management isn't to everyone's taste. Double rooms, too, are not the bargain they might be. Dorms ②, rooms ③.

YMCA: The Salisbury, 41 Salisbury Rd ☎2369 2211, fax 2739 9315, email *room@ymcahk.org.hk*. Spruced up and expanded, this is the best semi-cheap hotel location in this part of town, next to the *Peninsula* and in the middle of Tsim Sha Tsui. It may be a Y, but the facilities are excellent, including two indoor pools, fitness centre, squash court and a good café. The air-con doubles with TV and shower are booked up weeks in advance – try making a reservation two months ahead. Harbour-view rooms are an extra $270 and nearly push into the next price category. There are also 56 budget beds available in four-bedded rooms ($190 per person), though you can't stay more than seven days in these. ⑥.

Tsim Sha Tsui East and Hung Hom

Thirty years ago, Tsim Sha Tsui East didn't exist, but extensive land reclamation allowed the developers to run riot with a spate of high-class hotels sporting harbour views. A couple are as posh as anything in Hong Kong. Otherwise, you're a little far from the action in Tsim Sha Tsui itself to make most worth the bother, though inclusive tour holidays often put up in this part of town. The #A21 Airbus runs close, but it's easiest to take a taxi or walk along the seafront to the Star Ferry.

Grand Stanford Harbour View, 70 Mody Rd ☎2721 5161, fax 2732 2233. Fair-sized rooms with good views over the harbour to Hong Kong Island. There's also a reasonable roof-top health club and pool, but a safety wall hides the view. ⑨.

Holy Carpenter Guest House, 1 Dyer Ave ☎2362 0301, fax 2362 2193. Easily the best value in this district, this small church-run guest house only has four-teen rooms; it's close to Whampoa Garden and Hung Hom ferry pier. All rooms have modern furnishings, TV and attached bathroom. You'll need to book a good two weeks in advance. ⑤.

Kowloon Shangri-La, 64 Mody Rd ☎2721 2111, fax 2723 8686, Website and email www.shangri-la.com. The hov-erferry from Central stops right outside, though the mainly business clientele doesn't get much use out of it, holed up in the entire floor given over to "execu-tive" use. Elsewhere inside, the design makes the usual extravagant use of mar-ble, crystal and splashing fountains. ⑦.

New World Hotel, 22 Salisbury Rd ☎2369 4111, fax 2369 9387, email nwhhkres@netvigator.com. One of Tsim Sha Tsui East's earliest fixtures, the sprawling red-brick New World has already been completely renovated and it's not even twenty years old. ⑧.

Nikko, 72 Mody Rd ☎2739 1111, fax 2311 3122, email nikkl@hotelnikko.com.hk. Plush Japanese-owned business hotel, popular with Japanese package tours. It has all the contemporary luxury you'd expect, and is only a step away from the KCR station – which makes it quite a hike from Tsim Sha Tsui's restaurants, though naturally it has its own excellent Japanese restaurant. ⑧.

The Regent, 18 Salisbury Rd ☎2721 1211, fax 2739 4546, email reservation.rhk@fourseason.com. The only real rival to the Peninsula on this side of the water (and the preferred hotel of many international business tycoons), the Regent has an extraordi-nary glassed-in lobby (in which mere mortals can take a drink) and a twisting

marble staircase that pops up in fashion shoots. As well as its waterfront site it has its own pool, a top-rated Cantonese restaurant (the Lai Ching Heen) and is connected to the New World Centre, a huge shopping mall. With a fistful of credit cards, you need never leave. ⑧.

Royal Garden Hotel, 69 Mody Rd ☎2721 5215, fax 2369 9976, email htlinfo@theroyal.com.hk. Hong Kong is notoriously short of green space, so the Royal Garden incorporates its own – an interior garden-atrium, overlooked by room terraces and serviced by wall-hugging ele-vators. It's an extraordinary conceit, even by Hong Kong standards. ⑧.

Jordan

Staying up around Jordan Road, just north of Kowloon Park, is no great hard-ship. You're still within walking distance of the shops and restaurants of Tsim Sha Tsui (and the streetlife of lower Yau Ma Tei), and although there's no let up in noise you usually get a little more for your money. Jordan MTR is the most convenient station.

BP International, 8 Austin Rd ☎2376 1111, fax 2376 1333, email reserva-tions@megahotels.com.hk. Just north of Kowloon Park, with basic, clean, charac-terless rooms popular with long-stay visi-tors and business people from Asia and the Indian subcontinent. ⑥–⑦.

City Guest House, 6th Floor, Cumberland House, 227 Nathan Rd ☎2730 0212, fax 2730 0336. A large variety of rooms, all at reasonable prices, overseen by a friendly and helpful manager. ④.

Eaton Hotel, 380 Nathan Rd ☎2782 1818, fax 2782 5563, email ehhk04@asiaonline.net. On the fringes of Yau Ma Tei, this large, modern hotel fea-tures all the facilities you'd expect at the price, including a good coffee shop (with dinner buffet). It's also very close to the Jade Market and some interesting street life. ⑦.

Evergreen Hotel, 42–52 Woo Sung St ☎2780 4222, fax 2385 8584, email evergrhtl@netvigator.net. Cramped chain-style hotel catering largely to overseas

Accommodation

Accommodation

① *Under $80*
per person
② *Under $200*
per room
③ *$200–300*
per room
④ *$300–500*
per room
⑤ *$500–800*
per room
⑥ *$800–1200*
per room
⑦ *$1200–2000*
per room
⑧ *Over $2000*
per room

Chinese tour groups, so spoken English is limited. ⑤.

International House, 5th Floor, Cumberland House, 227 Nathan Rd ☎2730 9276. As long as you don't expect a sumptuous room like those in the pictures outside, you'll be happy with your clean, nicely furnished room with bath. ④.

Majestic Hotel, 348 Nathan Rd ☎2781 1333, fax 2781 1773. One of the better hotels in this area, recently renovated throughout, with a shopping complex and two-screen cinema beneath. ⑥.

Nathan Hotel, 378 Nathan Rd ☎2388 5141, fax 2770 4262, email *nathan@nathan.hkstar.com*. Sitting between the *Eaton* and *Majestic*, this doesn't have the character of either, which explains why there's room to spare. However, it's comfortable enough, slightly cheaper, and has a high proportion of single rooms. Discounts for stays of two days or more. ⑤.

Prudential Hotel, 222 Nathan Rd ☎2311 8222, fax 2311 1304. Great city views and a swimming pool on the roof do a lot to attract custom, and the MTR exit couldn't be closer. Staff are very helpful, too. ⑦.

San Diego Hotel, 169–189 Woo Sung St ☎2735 3855, fax 2736 0297. Modern and slightly garish hotel block tucked into the street parallel to Temple Street. Perfect for early-morning and late-night market bustle; less charming for a quiet break. ⑥.

Shamrock, 223 Nathan Rd ☎2735 2271, fax 2736 7354, email *shamrock@iohk.com*. Old-style hotel with a bit of character, typical of the first wave of building along Nathan Road in the 1950s. Renovations over the years have made the rooms personable, if not exactly stylish; there's an inexpensive restaurant, with a lunch buffet, and a clientele that's mostly Asian. ⑥.

Siu Hing Hostel, 4th Floor, Siu Hing Building, 230 Temple St ☎2770 9798, fax 2388 6901. Good-value rooms with air-con and shower, though you may feel you should get a window for this price. ④.

Yau Ma Tei

Comparative hotel prices start to drop once you get up around Waterloo Road and you can pick up some bargains this far north up Nathan Road, especially at the hotels operated by religious organizations. Regular buses run up and down Nathan Road, or you can get to all those listed below via Yau Ma Tei MTR. Each one is marked on the map on p.135.

Booth Lodge, 7th Floor, 11 Wing Sing Lane ☎2771 9266, fax 2385 1140. A smart, modern (built in the mid-1980s) Salvation Army hotel just off Nathan Road, close to the Jade Market and Temple Street Night Market. Not exactly brimming with comforts, it's at the bottom of this category; adding an extra bed to a double room costs around $120. ⑤.

Caritas Bianchi Lodge, 4 Cliff Rd ☎2388 1111, fax 2770 6669. Almost next door to *Booth Lodge*, and around twice as big, the air-conditioned rooms in this Roman Catholic-run hotel have bath and TV. Continental breakfast is included and there's a restaurant serving cheap lunches and dinners. There's also a second branch, further north on Boundary St (see "Mongkok" opposite). ⑤.

Chinese YMCA, 23 Waterloo Rd ☎2771 9111, fax 2388 5926, email *ymcares1@netvigator.com*. Smart and well-equipped YMCA guest house with some budget single rooms for men: you can't book these in advance, just turn up early. Otherwise, standard singles and doubles come with air-con, bath and TV; laundry service too. The restaurant serves a good buffet breakfast. ⑥.

King's Hotel, 473–475a Nathan Rd ☎2780 1281, fax 2782 1833. A budget hotel with passable rooms (at the bottom of this category) and a splendid Thai restaurant. Ask for a room at the back; the rooms above Nathan Road can be very noisy. ④.

Pearl Seaview Hotel, 262 Shanghai St ☎2782 0882, fax 2388 1919, email *pearlsea@netvigator.com*. Excellent location, next to Temple Street Night Market, and with all the comforts of a proper hotel at relatively reasonable prices.

Worth venturing beyond the confines of Tsim Sha Tsui for. ⑥–⑦.

STB Hostel, 2nd Floor, Great Eastern Mansion, 255–261 Reclamation St (junction with Dundas St) ☎2710 9199, fax 2385 0153. Terrific bustling environment outside; inside, segregated dorm beds (slightly pricier than in Tsim Sha Tsui), and very small twin-bedded rooms and triples. Newish, clean and pleasant, with a common room. Book in advance if you can. Dorms ②, rooms ④.

Mongkok

Not many tourists choose to stay this far north in Kowloon, with many of the hotels solely the preserve of Chinese businessmen and tour groups. But certain places have a tempting proximity to attractions like the Bird Market or Ladies' Market and you won't have to look far for something decent to eat. Each hotel is marked on the map on p.135.

Caritas Bianchi, 134 Boundary St, Mongkok, Prince Edward MTR ☎2339 3777, fax 2338 2864. Second branch of the religious-run lodge, though this one is too far out to be of any use other than as a standby if everywhere else is full. Rooms are pleasant enough, though. ④.

Concourse, 22 Lai Chi Kok Rd, Prince Edward MTR ☎2397 6683, fax 2381 3768, email concours@hkstar.com. Large (over 400 rooms), fairly new CTS-owned hotel, with good prices. You're a fair way from any downtown action, but there are two restaurants, a bar and coffee shop on the premises. ⑦.

Grand Tower, 6th floor, 627–641 Nathan Rd, Mongkok MTR ☎2789 0011, fax 2789 0945, email gthotel@hanglung.com.hk. Not exactly a stand-out hotel, but well sited, right by the MTR station and with a free shuttle bus to Tsim Sha Tsui. Rooms (many at the bottom of this range) are comfortable, if on the small side, and triples are good value. There's a very good dim sum restaurant on the 5th floor. ⑥.

Lucky Hostel, 13th Floor, Chun Yee Building, 731 Nathan Rd, Mongkok MTR

☎2308 1264, fax 2787 6948. Good rooms in a Chinese-spoken-only hostel. ③.

YWCA Guest House, 5 Man Fuk Rd, Waterloo Hill Rd, Mongkok MTR/KCR ☎2713 9211, fax 2761 1269, email annblack@ywca.org.hk. Basic singles and doubles with shower at pretty good rates; men can stay here too now. It's a little bit off the beaten track, though only a short walk from Mongkok KCR station which puts you in easy reach of New Territories' day trips. ④.

The New Territories

Most people tend to see the New Territories on a day trip, but if you want a night away from the manic centre, stay either at one of the youth hostels (see p.214) – which are all fairly remote – or one of the three major hotels below,

Kowloon Panda, 3 Tsuen Wan St, Tsuen Wan, Tsuen Wan MTR ☎2409 1111, fax 2409 1818, email reservation@megahotels.com.hk. Easily accessed on the MTR (though admittedly at the end of the line), the enormous, 1000-roomed Panda has plenty of space, some rooms with water views, masses of facilities (including a pool and two good restaurants) and offers the chance to see a bit of New Town life at first hand. ⑥.

Regal Riverside, Tai Chung Kiu Rd, Sha Tin ☎2649 7878, fax 2637 4748, email regalrrh@netvigator.com. The New Territories' best hotel – though there's not a lot of competition – close to Sha Tin and all its New Town amenities. This comfortable hotel often appears on holiday packages; there's a fine Asian lunch buffet served here too. ⑦.

Royal Park Hotel, 8 Pak Hok Ting St, Sha Tin ☎2601 2111, fax 2601 3666. Email resvn@royalpark.com.hk. In the same complex as the town hall and shopping malls. Very near the Regal Riverside although without as many facilities, something that is reflected in the cheaper rates. ⑦.

The Outlying Islands

If you want to get away from the city and stay on any of the outlying islands, you'll

Accommodation

Accommodation

need to book rooms in advance – especially if you're planning to go at the weekend, when half of Hong Kong heads out of the urban areas. As well as the places listed below, there are two youth hostels on Lantau, for details of which, see p.215.

LAMMA

Concerto Inn, 28 Hung Sing Yeh Beach, Yung Shue Wan ☎2982 1668, fax 2982 0022. Lamma's best hotel, offering rooms with balconies overlooking the beach, satellite TV and a video and fridge in every room – some have kitchens too. The restaurant is sited on a nice garden terrace. Expect around 40% discount on weekdays. ⑤–⑦.

Lamma Vacation House, 29 Main St, Yung Shue Wan. ☎2982 0427. Down the street from the ferry pier, on the left-hand side. Pleasant rooms (which sleep two) with a separate bathroom and kitchen. You should be able to get a discount midweek. ②.

Man Lai Wah Hotel, Yung Shue Wan ☎2982 0220 or 2982 0600, fax 2982 0347. Right by the ferry pier, overlooking the harbour, this hotel has nine rooms, with discounts during the week. ④.

CHEUNG CHAU

Warwick, East Bay ☎2981 0081, fax 2981 9174. Overlooking Tung Wan Beach, this is the obvious – if most expensive – place to stay: a concrete box whose rooms have balconies, private baths, cable TV. There's also a terrace café and a swimming pool. Sea-view rooms are pricier than others, though there's a forty percent discount from Monday to Friday and during winter. ⑥.

LANTAU

Cheung Sha Resort House, Cheung Sha ☎2980 2872. Self-contained apartments big enough to sleep six (the price doubles at the weekend). ⑤–⑥.

Mui Wo Inn, Mui Wo ☎2984 8597. Further along from the *Silvermine Beach*, this small hotel has attractive rooms with balcony and cheaper rooms at the back. During the week rooms are almost half price with breakfast thrown in too. ④.

Sea Breeze Hotel, Pui O ☎2984 2383. On the main road and popular with weekenders who pack out the nearby beach. Expect a discount of around forty percent during the week. ④.

Silvermine Beach Hotel, Mui Wo ☎2984 8295, fax 2984 1907. Overlooking the beach at Silvermine Bay, this is comfortable, almost luxurious, and great value for money compared to the hotels back in the centre. Rooms are discounted from Sunday to Thursday. ⑥.

Camping

There are around forty official **campsites** throughout the territory, most in the various country parks. There are large concentrations on Lantau Island and on the Sai Kung Peninsula in the New Territories; several of the most usefully sited are detailed in the text. All of them cost just a few dollars but you can't reserve a space, so getting there early at the weekend or on a public holiday is a good idea. All the sites have basic facilities: toilets, barbecue pits and a water supply. But generally you'll need to take your own food and equipment, and be prepared to walk to most of them as they're often well away from shops and villages. There's a free combined information sheet/map of the sites called *Campsites of Hong Kong Country Parks*, available from the HKTA.

You can sometimes **camp at the youth hostels** on Lantau and out in the New Territories; see the list on p.215 and call first to check before setting out. Camping this way, you'll be able to use the hostel facilities too.

Chapter 7

Eating

Don't underestimate the importance of **food** in Chinese culture. Meals are a shared, family affair, full of opportunities to show respect for others – by the way the food and drink is served, accepted and eaten. Although they're generally informal in tone, there's a structured form to each meal that reflects the importance of the food being eaten. As a visitor, especially as a foreigner, the nuances might pass you by, but it will soon become apparent that the Hong Kong Chinese live to eat – every café and restaurant is noisy and packed, the shrill interiors more reminiscent of school cafeterias than fancy eateries. On the street, too, stalls and stands do a brisk trade in snacks and cheap meals.

Almost everyone eats out regularly and the vast Chinese restaurants organize their opening hours around the long working days of most of the population. You can also pick and choose from one of the world's widest selections of cuisines. Quite apart from the **regional Chinese** variations on offer – of which the local **Cantonese** cooking is the most familiar to foreigners – there isn't any kind of **Asian** food you can't sample, from Burmese to Vietnamese. Probably the biggest surprise is the number of excellent **Indian** and **Pakistani**

Eating

Children are welcomed in most Chinese restaurants; see "Children's Hong Kong" p.307 for more details.

restaurants in the territory. **American** and **European** food is well represented too, though it's cooked with varying degrees of skill: generally speaking, the high-class hotel, French and Italian restaurants are good, but other food can often leave a lot to be desired. There's also a catch-all category of **international** restaurants and bars, where you can eat anything from burgers and steaks to *nouvelle cuisine*. There are also pubs which put on **British**-style food of the pie-and-chips variety, as do a growing number of **Irish** theme pubs. At the other end of the scale there are the **dai pai dongs** – street stalls or snack bars shovelling calories and fuel into office workers.

Food needn't be expensive, certainly if you stick to Chinese and Asian restaurants. The important thing is to retain your spirit of adventure at all times: some of the best dining experiences in Hong Kong are in the most unlikely-looking places, and some of the best food is eaten almost in passing, on the street or taken quickly in a *dim sum* restaurant or café.

The **listings and reviews** below should help you decide where and what to eat in Hong Kong. We've started with cafés, coffee shops, delis and street food, followed by *dim sum* restaurants and Chinese food in its various guises, succeeded by all the other cuisines available in the territory, listed in alphabetical order. At the end of the chapter are details about buying your own food in markets and supermarkets.

You'll find **descriptions** of Cantonese food, including *dim sum*, as well as other regional Chinese food and Asian cuisines in the introductions to the various sections. **Vegetarian** restaurants, and those that serve vegetarian meals, are included throughout, though bear in mind that the only solely vegetarian places are either Cantonese or Indian/Pakistani – there's a round-up on p.259. To go straight to the listings for the kind of food you want to eat, check the **food index**.

The **opening hours** given throughout are daily, unless otherwise stated.

Chinese restaurants tend to close early, and the kitchen is usually winding down by 9pm or so. Don't count on being able to use **credit cards** everywhere. Many restaurants – especially the smaller ones – will only take cash, so always check first if you're unsure. In addition to our list, pick up the HKTA's *Official Dining Directory*, and check out the restaurant reviews in *HK Magazine* or its more glossy sister publication, *Where Hong Kong*. Restaurants in Hong Kong open and close even more quickly than in other cities and these publications will help you stay up to date.

Two factors you might want to consider when choosing your restaurant are hygiene and MSG. While the ingredients used in most restaurants – particularly Chinese – are extremely fresh, the conditions in which they are handled can leave a lot to be desired. Things to look out for are the general cleanliness of the staff, the condition of the kitchen and utensils, the water in which live fish and seafood are kept and whether cooked and fresh food are handled separately. MSG, or monosodium glutamate, is also a common additive in many Chinese restaurants (and is also sold in supermarkets for domestic use). It acts not on the food but by stimulating your sense of taste – in other words part of your nervous system. Large amounts can produce an allergic reaction in some people, and if you feel slightly 'buzzy' after a meal, that's why. Some restaurants have a policy of no MSG, and you can get others (or at least try) to leave it out.

Cafés, coffee shops, delis and fast food

Whether it's breakfast, coffee and cake, sandwich, burger or ice cream you want, Hong Kong isn't going to present you with any difficulty. **Cafés** and **hotel/department store coffee shops** are ubiquitous, while all the familiar Western **burger and pizza joints** are represented in Hong Kong – McDonald's has more than 200 outlets, almost as many as in the rest of China

Tea, coffee and soft drinks

You can sometimes get **non-Chinese tea** in cafés and snack bars (but not in Chinese restaurants): it's generally *Lipton's* and comes hot or cold on request. It's common to drink it with lemon; tea with milk is rarer – and be careful when you ask for milk that you don't get the condensed variety. For the real thing, venture into one of the big hotels for afternoon tea, something which is well worth doing at least once for the atmosphere alone. **Coffee** is the more usual hot drink, but in Chinese cafés is invariably instant and weak and, again, is served with condensed milk and sugar unless you specify otherwise. However, there's a fast-growing band of European and American coffee shops and stands, where you can get espresso, cappuccino, mocha, latte and all the other caffeine drinks that civilization demands. Some of these double as cyber cafés offering Internet access. You'll also get a decent cup of coffee in most of the larger hotels and many European restaurants, although this comes at a high price: $20 or so for an espresso.

Coke and all the usual international fizzy **soft drinks** are available from stalls and shops everywhere, as are a variety of fruit juices – though the small boxed ones are packed with sugar and additives. Fresh fruit juice is always expensive. Try the local soft drinks: Vitamilk is a plain or flavoured soya milk drink – a few dollars a carton – while lemon tea, chocolate milk, iced teas and lots of other infusions all come cold and in cartons. Regular milk isn't drunk very much by the Cantonese (most of whom have a lactose intolerance), but you can buy it in supermarkets.

Eating

combined. Burgers here are the same as anywhere else in the world, and prices are kept low in order to establish American fast-food in a culture that has been producing its own more appetizing equivalent for thousands of years. Burger bars are now terribly popular with Chinese kids; they are also, incidentally, the cheapest places to get a reasonable cup of coffee, a cold drink or a welcome blast of air-conditioning. Other Western delights include a growing number of **sandwich bars** and **delis**, a few specialist **ice-cream shops**, and some fine independent **coffee bars**.

A couple of Chinese chains sell Asian-influenced snacks (radish cake, chicken wings and the like) and there are lots of Chinese **cake shops** too – although the products may be too sweet and sickly for the Western palate. **Chinese cafés**, often just hole-in-the-wall affairs, dish out polystyrene and foil boxes of more substantial food – rice and meat, noodles and so on – which you can generally eat perching on a stool or take away, for around $20–40 a go.

Territory-wide

Café de Coral. Branches on every corner serving Chinese takeaway snacks from bright, plastic interiors. Chicken wings, radish cakes, salads and sandwiches at low prices.

Délifrance. Pseudo-French deli-cafés selling croissants, French-bread sandwiches, okay cakes and coffee. Rapidly expanding, and consequently the service and cleanliness can be patchy.

Haagen-Dazs. The best ice cream in Hong Kong – the chain also does cakes and drinks. Branches (among others) at 1 Lan Kwai Fong, Central; Shop C1, Ground Floor, World-Wide House, Central; Shop B209, Times Square, 1 Matheson Rd, Causeway Bay.

KFC. Branches at 6 D'Aguilar St, Central; 40 Yee Woo St, Causeway Bay; 28 Beach Rd, Repulse Bay; 2 Cameron Rd, Tsim Sha Tsui; 241 Nathan Rd, Yau Ma Tei.

Maxim's. BBQ chicken legs, hamburgers, salads, roast-meat dishes, drinks and sandwiches. Garish and synthetic-tasting cakes, too. At MTR and KCR stations, and at the Star Ferry terminals.

Eating

McDonald's. Two 24-hour restaurants at 21 Granville Rd and 12 Peking Rd (both in Tsim Sha Tsui), plus many other branches.

Oliver's Super Sandwiches. Reliable but crowded deli and sandwich shop chain (most open Mon–Sat 8am–6pm), also serving breakfast, afternoon tea and baked potatoes. Branches (among others) at: Shop 104, Exchange Square II, 8 Connaught Place, Central; Shop 201–205, Prince's Building, 10 Chater Rd, Central; Repulse Bay Hotel, 109 Repulse Bay Rd, Repulse Bay; Ocean Centre, Canton Rd, Tsim Sha Tsui; Tower One, Lippo Centre, Queensway, Admiralty; Shop A, Fleet House, 38 Gloucester Rd, Wan Chai.

Pizza Hut. The many branches include: B1, Edinburgh Tower, The Landmark, Des Voeux Rd, Central; Pacific Place, 88 Queensway, Admiralty; Shop 22, Basement, Silvercord Shopping Centre, 30 Canton Rd, Tsim Sha Tsui; Shop 008, Ocean Terminal, Harbour City, Canton Rd, Tsim Sha Tsui.

Central and Admiralty

Café Chater, *Furama Kempinski*, 1 Connaught Rd. Hotel coffee shop which prepares pretty much anything, at a price: fresh fruit and eggs, Japanese breakfasts, the full American and British works, or just coffee and pastries – from around $80–150. Breakfast served 6–11am.

Cafe Piatti: at Exchange Square, Connaught Rd; 108 Prince's Building, 10 Chater Rd; Far East Finance Centre, Harcourt Rd; Lippo Centre, Queensway; and Seibu Food Court, The Mall, Pacific Place, 88 Queensway. Five coffee stands dotted around Central and the business districts, with a range of high-quality real coffees. Experts recommend the chocolate chip cookies. Open 8am–6pm.

Cappucci, Government Offices Lower Block, 66 Queensway. Popular Italian coffee bar/sandwich kiosk, run by people with disabilities. Open 8am–5.30pm.

La Cité, Basement, Pacific Place, 88 Queensway. Smart bistro-cum-café that pushes all the right buttons – soup, snacks, set lunches, or just teas and coffees while you take the weight off your shopping feet. Open 11am–11pm.

Dan Ryan's Chicago Bar and Grill, 114 The Mall, Pacific Place, 88 Queensway. American restaurant (see p.251) serving classic breakfasts at weekends – eggs, pancakes and all the fixings. Very good with children. Served Sat & Sun 7.30–11am.

Joyce Café, One Exchange Square, Connaught Rd; The Galleria, 9 Queen's Rd. In a league of its own for stylish café surroundings, making it one of the most popular haunts for local *tai tais*. Expensive, although there are set breakfast menus (7.30am–noon) and the Exchange Square branch has a cheaper snackbar/takeaway facility. The menu is mostly soups, sandwiches, pastas and salads, with East-West fusion and

---

Breakfast

The traditional Chinese breakfast is *congee*, a gruel made from rice boiled for a long time in lots of water, served with chopped spring onions or morsels of meat or fish. It's available from some early opening restaurants or street stalls (*dai pai dongs*), and often comes with long sticks of fried dough – a bit like doughnuts. *Congee* is an acquired taste, but it's something that Chinese kids get used to from a very early age, since it's virtually force-fed to babies and sick children. It's more appealing to breakfast on *dim sum*, served from many restaurants, many of which erect stalls outside to sell takeaway *dim sum* to passers-by – though the stalls have usually disappeared by 9am or so. Western breakfasts – cooked and continental – are available in most of the bigger hotels, and in an increasing number of cafés, coffee shops and some pubs. Check the reviews under "Cafés, Coffee Shops, Delis and Fast Food" and "Dim Sum" for full details of where serves what.

Cyber Cafés

Not surprisingly in a city obsessed with technology, there are many cafés where you can log on for free whilst enjoying a decent cup of coffee or a snack at the same time. Juices, sandwiches, newspapers and magazines are also available.

Bookworm Café, Yung Shue Wan Main St, Lamma.

Cyber X, Empress Plaza, 17–19 Chatham Rd, Tsim Sha Tsui ☎2366 0702; *www.cyber-x.com.hk*.

Pacific Coffee Company, Ground Floor, Bank of America Tower, Garden Rd, Central; Star Ferry Pier, Central; Basement, Citibank Plaza, Ice House St, Central; Shop 1022, International

Finance Centre, Harbour View St, Central; Shop C3–4 Queensway Plaza, Queensway, Admiralty; Seibu Food Hall, Pacific Place, 88 Queensway, Admiralty; Shop 101, Great Eagle Centre, Harbour Rd, Wan Chai. Star Ferry Pier, Tsim Sha Tsui.

Xyberia, A4, 3rd Floor, Mui Wo Center, 3 Ngan Wan Rd, Silvermine Bay, Lantau ☎2984 9983; *www.xyberia.com*.

health-food overtones. Open Mon–Sat 10am–7.30pm, Sun noon–6.30pm.

Mandarin Oriental Hotel, 5 Connaught Rd. *The* serious hotel power breakfast (served 7–11am in the Grill Room) where around $250 gets you unlimited stabs at an enormous buffet, from fresh fruit juice and cereals, eggs and all the works, through to strudels and cheese. Sunday brunch (11am–3pm) is similarly stylish, though costs around $350. For coffee, all-day snacks and light meals *The Cafe* (7am–1am) is the favoured see-and-be-seen haunt, although its breakfast gets mixed reviews.

Marriott Café, *Marriott Hotel*, Pacific Place, 88 Queensway. Good Western/Asian snacks and meals in an elegant hotel coffee shop whose long hours are a boon in this district. Open 7am–1am.

Movenpick Marché, Levels 6 & 7, The Peak Tower, The Peak. Good and inexpensive fresh food from this Swiss chain. Salads, sandwiches, soups and daily hot dishes, plus Swiss ice cream. The 6th floor café has an outside terrace. Open 11am–11pm.

Pacific Coffee Company, Ground Floor, Bank of America Tower, Garden Rd (Mon–Sat 7.30am–6pm); Basement, Pacific Place, 88 Queensway, Admiralty (Mon–Sat 7.30am–1pm, Sun 8am–9pm); Star Ferry Pier, Central (Mon–Fri

8am–8pm, Sat & Sun 8am–10pm). Stylish little coffee shop chain with great coffee, good fruit juices, cookies and sandwiches, plus newspapers and friendly staff.

Tiffany Delicatessen, 13–14 Connaught Rd (Ground Floor of Euro Trade Centre). Takeaway sandwiches; freshly baked European-style bread, cooked meats, smoked fish, cakes and wines. Open 8am–5pm.

Uncle Russ, California Tower, 30 D'Aguilar St. Stand-up booth serving excellent coffee and cookies. Open 7.30am–11pm. Branches with similar hours at Shop B216, Times Square, 1 Matheson Rd, Causeway Bay; and Ground Floor, 2 Canton Rd, Tsim Sha Tsui.

Wyndham Street Deli, 36 Wyndham St. European-style deli offering moderately priced sandwiches, pastas, grills, salads plus wonderful cakes and desserts. Good, reasonably priced (for Hong Kong) wine list. Open Mon–Sat 7am–11pm, Sun 9am–6pm.

Wan Chai

The Big Apple, Harbour Centre, Harbour Rd. Friendly sandwich bar with huge variety of breads and fillings. They also do breakfasts and other hot dishes throughout the day. There's a small sitting area and they also have a deli round the corner.

Eating

Food Courts

Hong Kong has several Food Courts – areas in shopping malls devoted to inexpensive takeaway shops serving different types of food. Pick and mix your cuisine and sit at one of the central tables. They include:

The Majestic Centre, 348 Nathan Rd, Tsim Sha Tsui.

Seibu, The Mall, Pacific Place, 88 Queensway, Admiralty.

Festival Walk, Kowloon Tong

Grand Café, *Grand Hyatt*, 1 Harbour Rd. Hotel coffee shop with some of the finest window seats in the territory and stylish, elegant surroundings. The food matches these step for step – always pricey, but top quality. Open 6.30am–1am.

Renaissance Harbour View Hotel, 1 Harbour Rd. In the same block as the Grand Hyatt, the *Lobby Lounge* offers equally spectacular views, with slightly cheaper prices.

Causeway Bay

New York Deli, 17 Lan Fong Rd. You'll know what to expect from the name, and servings are up to scratch – just don't expect the food to be terribly authentic. Eat in and takeaway services. Open noon–11pm.

Phoenix Congee and Noodle, 13–15 Cleveland St. *Congee* and all the trimmings for a real Cantonese breakfast; noodles too. Open 7.30am–11.30pm.

Kowloon

Cherikoff, Allied Plaza, Nullah Rd, Mongkok. Good, budget Western breakfasts, and coffee and cakes served all day. Open 8am–6pm.

Chungking Mansions, 36–44 Nathan Rd, Tsim Sha Tsui. Cheap curried breakfast, for those with cast-iron constitutions, at *Kashmir Fast Food* (Ground Floor, no. 17) and *Lahore Fast Food Centre* (Ground Floor, no. 19); served from around 8am.

Delicatessen Corner, 1st Basement, *Holiday Inn Golden Mile*, 46–52 Nathan Rd, Tsim Sha Tsui. Lunch-boxes, soups, salads and sandwiches. Open 7.30am–11.30pm.

Mall Café, Ground Floor, *YMCA*, 41 Salisbury Rd, Tsim Sha Tsui. Favourite Tsim Sha Tsui spot for a leisurely breakfast – Continental, English or Chinese for $30–40 – set lunch or sandwich. The Hong Kong daily papers are available. Open 7am–midnight.

New Territories

Coffee Shop, University of Science and Technology, Clearwater Bay Rd, Tseung Kwan O, Kowloon. Snacks, sandwiches, salads, hot dishes and specialist coffees. There is a large outdoor terrace. A hot dish or large sandwich is around $20–30. Get there by bus #91M from Choi Hung MTR or #298 from Lam Tin MTR.

Street food: dai pai dongs

A short walk through some of the densely populated parts of the territory offers you a vast choice of **street food**; dozens of different snacks, all at incredibly cheap prices. If you're worried about **hygiene**, most of the snacks are fairly innocuous anyway, made out of fresh or preserved ingredients, while more elaborate food – noodles and the like – is freshly cooked in front of you.

The street stalls you'll see all over the territory are called **dai pai dongs** (a term which is also used for small restaurants). Most are mobile mini-kitchens and you just point to what you want and pay – most things are usually just a few dollars. Common snacks are fish, beef and pork balls (threaded onto bamboo sticks and dipped in chilli sauce), fresh and dried squid, spring rolls, steamed buns, *won ton* (stuffed dumplings), simple noodle soups, pancakes, *congee* (rice gruel served with a greasy, doughnut-type stick), cooked intestines, tofu pudding and various sweets. In some places – open-air and indoor markets and on a couple of the outlying islands – *dai pai dongs* are more formal affairs, grouped together with simple tables and chairs, and with more elaborate food: seafood, mixed rice and noodle dishes, stews and soups, and bottled beer. There'll rarely be a menu, but everything will still be dirt cheap, and you should be able to put together a decent meal for around $50-60.

The following central Hong Kong and Kowloon locations are the most accessible places to sample *dai pai dong* food. Every New Territories town has its own particular area for *dai pai dongs*, as do various of the outlying islands; see the text for more details.

Graham St market, at the bottom of Stanley St, Central.

Haiphong Rd, bottom of Kowloon Park, Tsim Sha Tsui.

Hau Fook St, Off Carnarvon Rd, between Cameron Rd and Granville St, Tsim Sha Tsui. The street tables here serve basic Cantonese and Shanghai food, especially seafood.

Kung Wo Tau Pan Chong, 118 Shanghai St, Sham Shui Po. A traditional *dai pai dong* in an ordinary market, except this one still uses a stone mill to grind its soybeans, not an electric mill. Its popularity with local people reflects the good food. Open 7.15am-8pm.

Luard Rd, opposite Southorn Playground, Wan Chai.

Sheung Wan Market, Urban Council Complex, 345 Queen's Rd, Central. The Cooked Food Market on the second floor is one of the more authentic culinary experiences in town: no frills, no foreigners. Open 6am-2am.

Sutherland St and Hing Lung St, off Des Voeux Rd, Sheung Wan.

Temple St, Yau Ma Tei. Reliable seafood-based street food at the Temple Street Night Market, from 7pm; see p.136.

Dim sum

Some of the most exciting of all Cantonese food is **dim sum**, which, literally translated, means "to touch the heart". Basically it's steamed or braised stuffed dumplings, small cakes and other appetizers served in little bamboo baskets. This might not sound like much, but there are scores of different varieties. A list of the most common dishes is given overleaf, but everyday items include pork, prawn, crab, beef or shark's fin dumplings, as well as spring rolls, prawn toast, rice and cooked meats in lotus leaves, curried squid, chicken feet, turnip cake, stuffed peppers, pork and chicken buns, custard tarts and steamed sweet buns.

Restaurants that specialize in *dim sum* **open early** in the morning, from around 7am, and serve right through lunch up until around 5pm; nearly all regular Cantonese restaurants also serve *dim sum*, usually from 10-11am until 3pm. If you can't make breakfast, the best time is before the lunch rush – say around noon; after lunch there won't be much left. The opening hours given in the reviews below (daily, unless otherwise stated) are the *dim sum* hours for that particular restaurant: most of the places convert into regular restaurants for the evening session.

Eating

Eating

For more details about restaurants – etiquette, the bill and service charges – see "Restaurants", p.240.

Central

City Hall Chinese Restaurant, 2nd Floor, City Hall Low Block ☎2521 1303. Harbour views and a good range of *dim sum* served by friendly types throughout the day. You'll have to wait for a lunchtime table; take a ticket at the door. Open Mon–Sat 10am–3pm, Sun 8am–3pm.

Jade Garden, Shop 5, Lower Ground Floor, Jardine House, 1 Connaught Place ☎2524 5098. One of a chain (with two more in Causeway Bay); dependable *dim sum* meals served by staff who are used to novice *gweilo* visitors. Open Mon–Sat 11am–11pm, Sun 10am–5pm.

Luk Yu Teahouse, 24–26 Stanley St ☎2523 5464. Excellent, if rather pricey, *dim sum* from this traditional wood-panelled and screened Chinese tea-house, with service by white-coated waiters. You order from a Chinese order-paper, but a waiter will choose a selection for you if you ask – though don't expect the service to be particularly welcoming or polite. You really need to book, or be prepared to wait if you're not a regular. Open 7am–6pm.

Summer Palace Restaurant, *Island Shangri-La Hotel*, Pacific Place, Admiralty ☎2877 3838. Superb *dim sum* in relaxed, stylish and reasonably quiet surroundings. Expensive though. Daily 11.30am–3pm.

Tai Woo, 15–19 Wellington St ☎2524 5618. All-day *dim sum* ordered from a short English menu – a lunchtime favourite with local office workers and shoppers. Open 10am–2pm.

Tsui Hang Village Restaurant, 2nd Floor, New World Tower, 16–18 Queen's Rd ☎2524 2012. Weekends only. Get there early for the good *dim sum* in splendid, traditional surroundings. Open Sat 11am–5.30pm, Sun 10am–5.30pm.

Yung Kee Restaurant, 32–40 Wellington St ☎2522 1624. Classic Cantonese restaurant which gets mobbed for its fine *dim sum*. Open Mon–Sat 2pm–5pm, Sun 10am–5.30pm.

Zen, LG1, The Mall, Pacific Place, 88 Queensway, Admiralty ☎2845 4555. Sharp designer-style and expertly cooked *dim sum*, which means considerably higher prices than usual. Expect to pay $150 a head. Unfortunately, they have a rather casual attitude to reservations when they're busy. Open Mon–Fri 11.30am–3pm, Sat 11.30am–4.30pm, Sun 10.30am–4.30pm.

Sheung Wan

Diamond Restaurant, 267–275 Des Voeux Rd ☎2544 4708. A swarming Cantonese diner on several floors, you may have to wait (or share a table), but it's loud, authentic and cheap. Trolley women shout out their wares and you'll have to speak up if you want to eat anything – learn the names of a few dishes before you go. It's near Western Market. Open 6.30am–4pm.

Treasure Island Seafood Restaurant, 2nd Floor, Western Market, 323 Des Voeux Rd ☎2850 7780. Galleried restaurant trying hard for that traditional look. Order from the cards left at the table: the food isn't bad, though the restaurant is slightly pricier than normal and not overwhelmingly friendly. Open 11am–3pm.

Wan Chai

Canton Room, 1st Floor, *Luk Kwok Hotel*, 72 Gloucester Rd ☎2866 2166. Weekend only *dim sum* hours in this rather splendid hotel dining room with wood panelling and Deco touches. Open Sat & Sun 10.30am–3pm.

Dynasty Restaurant, *Renaissance Harbour View*, 1 Harbour Rd ☎2802 8888. Harbour views from one of Hong Kong's best hotels. Excellent, creative but pricey *dim sum*. Open Mon–Sat noon–3pm, Sun 11.30am–3pm.

Round Dragon Chinese Restaurant, 60th Floor, Hopewell Centre, 183 Queen's Rd East ☎2861 1668. *Dim sum* sixty floors up, with views to match, which on the whole is what you're paying for, since the food is unremarkable. There's an English menu to help you out. Open 11.30am–3pm.

Causeway Bay

Maxim's Chinese Restaurant, 1st & 2nd
Floors, 1 Yee Wo St (entrance on Great
George St) ☎2894 9933. Not many
tourists find themselves in this refreshing-
ly down-to-earth *dim sum* palace, where
the relatively cheery trolley-pushers
muster up the odd word of English. Open
7.30am–5pm.

Happy Valley

Dim Sum, 63 Sing Woo Rd ☎2834
8893. Old-style wooden booths make
this a nice, cosy place to experiment
with *dim sum* – the food is top quality
too. Open 11am–11pm.

Aberdeen

Jumbo Floating Restaurant, Shum Wan,
Wong Chuk Hang ☎2553 9111. This
famous floating restaurant (see
"Cantonese" on p.246) serves *dim sum*
from breakfast onwards, as does its
neighbouring sister ship, the *Jumbo
Palace*. It's the cheapest way to have a
meal here, but both restaurants are now
horribly touristy and the quality of food
reflects that – few locals eat here. Open
7am–5pm.

Tsim Sha Tsui

Beijing Restaurant, 34–36 Granville Rd
☎2721 1808. A Beijing restaurant that
trots out northern-style *dim sum* at
lunchtime – stodgy dumplings a speciality. There's not a huge choice and it's
very meat-orientated: the noodle soups
and mixed cold cuts of meat are the
local choice. Open 11am–5pm.

The Chinese Restaurant, 2nd Floor,
Hyatt Regency, 67 Nathan Rd ☎2311
1234. Extremely elegant traditional tea
house surroundings, complete with
booth seating and deferential waiters,
make for one of the finer *dim sum* experiences. Pricey, but worth every cent.
Open 11.30am–3pm.

East Ocean Seafood Restaurant, 3rd
Floor, East Ocean Centre, 98 Granville Rd
☎2723 8128 or 2367 1133. Noisy
basement dining with excellent *dim sum*,
as well as other dishes. Considered one

of the best in town. Open Mon–Sat
11am–midnight, Sun 10am–midnight.
Moderate–Expensive.

Fontana Restaurant, 2nd Floor,
Multifield Plaza, 3-7A Prat Ave ☎2369
9898. *Dim sum* palace, where waitress-
es with two-way radios find you a table
in the bowels of the restaurant. There's
a wider range of dishes than usual,
served from trolleys, but get there early
as it attracts a bustling local clientele.
Open Mon–Sat 11am–3pm, Sun
10am–3pm.

Jade Garden, 4th Floor, Star House, 3
Salisbury Rd, by the Star Ferry terminal
☎2730 6888. Part of the *Maxim* chain,
serving *dim sum* with harbour views.
Open Mon–Sat 10am–3pm, Sun
8am–3pm. There's another branch, also
with reasonable *dim sum*, at 25–31
Carnarvon Rd ☎369 8311. Open
7.30am–5pm.

Tao Yuan, 1st Floor, China Hong Kong City,
33 Canton Rd ☎2736 1688. Authentic
Cantonese *dim sum* for a clientele that
couldn't be more critical: Chinese travellers
from the adjacent departure level for China
ferries. It's usually packed. Open Mon–Sat
11am–5pm, Sun 10am–5pm.

Vegetarian dim sum

The majority of *dim sum* restaurants
have enough options on their menu to
keep most vegetarians happy.
Healthy Mess, Ground Floor, 51–53
Hennessy Rd, Wan Chai ☎2527 3918.
Stylish little place with veggie *dim sum*
and snacks served all day – take a look
in the window first to see what you
fancy. Open 11am–11pm.

Kung Tak Lam, Lok Sing Centre, 31 Yee
Wo St, Causeway Bay ☎2890 3127.
Shanghainese vegetarian cuisine with
more than 120 choices. No meat, no
MSG and organic vegetables. Open
11am–11pm. Inexpensive.

Pak Bo Vegetarian Kitchen, Ground
Floor, 106 Austin Rd, Tsim Sha Tsui
☎2380 2681. Point to what you want
from the window and eat inside; it's all
cheap and very tasty.

Eating

Eating

Dim Sum Restaurants

Most *dim sum* restaurants are enormous and noisy, often with tables on several floors; in the smarter places, staff with two-way radios check on space before letting you through. In many the decoration is completely over-the-top: they're used for wedding receptions and parties and are covered in dragons, swirls, painted screens and ornate backgrounds that can easily cost millions of Hong Kong dollars.

Going in, you'll either be confronted by a *maître d'*, who'll put your name on a list and tell you when there's space, or often you can just walk through and fight for a table yourself. It's busiest at lunchtime and on Sunday when families come out to eat, when you'll have to queue. This is not an orderly concept: just attach yourself to a likely looking table where people appear to be finishing up, and hover over the seats until they leave. Any hesitation and you'll lose your table, so keep an eye out.

It's best to go in a group if you can, in order to share dishes. As all the tables seat about ten or more, you'll be surrounded by others anyway, which is fun if the experience is new to you.

How to order, how to pay

Sit down and you'll be brought tea – apt since if you're Chinese you don't go just to eat *dim sum*, but to *yum cha* ("drink tea"). You don't pay for this, though in some places there'll be a small cover charge. Foreigners will generally be given jasmine tea (*heung ping*), which is light and fragrant, but the Chinese mostly drink *bo lay*, a strong black or fermented tea which is particularly suited to cutting through the oil and stodge. If you want this (and hot water too, to dilute it), ask for *bo lay gwan soy*. When you want a refill, just leave the top off the teapot and it'll be replaced for free.

At this stage, if you're Chinese you'll have already started to wash your chopsticks and rinse your bowls in the hot tea or water: everything should be clean anyway, but it's almost an obsession with some people.

In most places you'll see trolleys being wheeled through the restaurant. These contain the bamboo baskets which, typically, contain three or four little dumplings or similar-sized bites to eat. Somewhere, too, there'll be people frying stuffed vegetables at mobile stands, others with trays of spring rolls and cakes, and different trolleys dispensing noodle soups, *congee* and other food. Just flag down the trolleys as they pass and see what you fancy by lifting the lids. Each time you pick something, the basket or plate will be dumped on the table, and a mark made on a card left at your table when the tea was brought. In some of the more upmarket *dim sum* restaurants, you'll have to order your dishes from the kitchen, in which case there'll invariably be a short menu in English on the table.

When you've finished, cross your chopsticks over the pile of rubble left on your table and flag down a waiter, who will take your card. He or she counts the number of empty baskets/plates on the table, checks it off against the ticks on your card and goes away to prepare the bill. Most things cost the same, just $30–40 a basket. Even if you absolutely stuff yourself on *dim sum*, you'll find it hard to spend more than $90–120 a head, perhaps rising to $150 if you eat in one of the fancier or more famous *dim sum* places. On top of this, you'll nearly always pay a ten percent service charge.

Vegi-Food Kitchen, 8 Cleveland St, Causeway Bay ☎ 2890 6663. One of Hong Kong's best-known and most inventive vegetarian restaurants (p.243) serves *dim sum* too. Open 11am–5pm.

Restaurants

If you've mastered the *dim sum* palaces, no Chinese or Asian **restaurant** in Hong Kong need hold any fears. Most places have **menus** in English and the only real

Savouries

Steamed prawn dumplings	*har gau*	蝦餃
Steamed beef ball	*au yuk*	牛肉丸
Steamed spare ribs in spicy sauce	*pai gwat*	排骨
Steamed pork and prawn dumpling	*siu mai*	燒麥
Steamed bun stuffed with barbecued pork	*cha siu bau*	叉燒包
Gelatinous rice-flour roll stuffed with shrimp/meat	*cheung fun*	長粉
Steamed glutinous rice filled with assorted meat, wrapped in a lotus leaf	*nor mai gai*	糯米雞
Deep-fried stuffed dumpling served with sweet and sour sauce	*won ton*	餛飩
Half-moon shaped steamed dumpling with meat/shrimp	*fun gwor*	粉角
Congee (thick rice gruel, flavoured with shredded meat and spring onion)	*djuk*	粥
Spring roll	*chun kuen*	春卷
Turnip cake	*law bak go*	羅蔔糕
Chicken feet	*fung jao*	鳳爪
Stuffed beancurd	*yeung do fu*	釀豆腐
Taro/yam croquette	*woo kok*	蕃薯糊角
Crabmeat dumplings	*hie yuk gau*	蟹肉角
Shark's fin dumplings	*yu chi gau*	魚鰭餃
Curried squid	*gar li yau yu*	咖喱魷魚
Steamed, sliced chicken wrapped in beancurd	*gai see fun kuen*	雞絲粉卷
Fried, stuffed green pepper	*yeung chen jiu*	釀青椒
Deep-fried beancurd roll with pork/shrimp	*seen chuk guen*	鮮春卷
Steamed dumpling with pork and chicken	*guon tong gau*	豬肉雞水餃
Steamed chicken bun	*gai bau tsei*	雞包仔
Barbecued pork puff	*cha siu so*	叉燒酥
Mixed meat croquette	*ham shui kok*	咸水角

Sweets

Water chestnut cake	*ma tai go*	馬蹄糕
Sweet beancurd with almond soup	*do fu fa*	豆腐花
Sweet coconut balls	*nor mai chi*	糯米池
Steamed sponge cake	*ma lai go*	馬來糕
Mango pudding	*mango bo din*	芒果布丁
Sweet lotus seed paste bun	*lin yung bau*	蓮蓉糕
Egg-custard tart	*daan tat*	蛋撻

Eating

problem is that often the translations leave a lot to be desired. Also, the English-language menu is generally much less extensive and exciting than the Chinese one: you may have to point at what other Chinese diners are eating if you want seasonal, traditional food rather than the more bland tourist menu.

Most Cantonese restaurants open early in the morning and, in certain parts

Eating

The restaurants reviewed in this book have been given price categories as follows: Inexpensive under $150 Moderate $150–300 Expensive $300–500 Very Expensive $500–800+

of the city like Tsim Sha Tsui and Wan Chai, can stay open until midnight or beyond. The ones that serve *dim sum* start serving their regular menu from mid- to late afternoon onwards. In the evenings most local people like to eat early, which means that kitchens start closing at around 9.30pm. Other regional Chinese and Asian restaurants keep pretty much the same hours, though they perhaps won't open until 11am or so. Western restaurants generally have shorter hours, but you'll never have a problem finding somewhere to eat up until around midnight.

For the intricacies of **eating and ordering** in a Chinese restaurant, see the box below. To ask for **the bill** you say *mai dan*, which – with the wrong intonation – can also mean to "buy eggs". Sign language works just as well. Nearly all restaurants will add a ten percent **service charge** to your bill, and if there are nuts and pickles on your table you'll often pay a small cover charge too. In places where there's no service charge, leaving ten percent or a few dollars from your change is fine. Even if you've paid service, the waiter may wave your change airily above your head in the leather wallet that the bill came in; if you want the change, make a move for it or that will be deemed a tip, too.

Chinese

Lots of Chinese restaurants offer a set tourist menu, which can be good value but is unlikely to be very adventurous.

Also, if you're going on into China, you'd do best to sample all the foods first in Hong Kong: on the whole the quality and choice here are infinitely better than in most cities on the mainland.

CANTONESE

Central and Admiralty

Fat Heung Lam, 94 Wellington St ☎2593 0404. It's hard to fault this small, cheap and cheerful vegetarian restaurant. Inexpensive.

Jade Garden, Shop 5, Lower Ground Floor, Jardine House, 1 Connaught Place ☎2524 5098. Reliable member of the *Maxim* restaurant chain with a decent – if unsurprising – menu. There'll be plenty that's recognizable, all well cooked, and served by English-speaking staff. Mon–Sat 11am–3pm, 5–11.30pm, Sun 10am–11.30pm. Moderate.

Man Wah, *Mandarin Oriental Hotel*, 5 Connaught Rd ☎2522 0111. If you've got the cash for one extravagantly priced Cantonese meal, blow it here on some beautiful food (which follows a seasonal menu) and spectacular views. If they don't take your breath away, the bill will. Reservations are essential. Open noon–3pm & 6.30–11pm. Very Expensive.

Treasure Inn Seafood, 2nd Floor, Western Market ☎2850 7780. Serves a wide range of seafood, although the quality is adversely influenced by the number of tourists who eat here. Moderate–Expensive.

Tsui Hang Village Restaurant, 2nd Floor, New World Tower, 16–18 Queen's Rd ☎ 2524 2012. Named after the home town of Sun Yat-sen, the restaurant is well thought of – the food and decor are traditional and prices not too bad for this part of the city. Open Mon–Fri 11.30am–3pm, 5.30–11.30pm, Sat 11am–11.30pm, Sun 10am–11.30pm. Moderate.

Yung Kee Restaurant, 32–40 Wellington St ☎ 2522 1624. Impressive four-storey eating-house into whose nether regions you're led by walkie-talkie-wielding staff. Diners are presented with "hundred-year-old eggs" and preserved ginger as they sit down – traditional Cantonese appetizers – and the house speciality is roast goose (there's a roaring trade in takeaway roast goose lunch boxes during the week). Don't be surprised when the goose arrives cold, that's the local custom. You can also try hot-pot dishes and various forms of frog. Open 11am–11.30pm. Moderate.

Zen, Lower Ground Floor 1, The Mall, Pacific Place, 88 Queensway, Admiralty ☎ 2845 4555. Designer-led, new Cantonese cuisine – which means hi-tech surroundings, imaginative Cantonese food which borrows influences extensively from the rest of Asia and competent, English-speaking staff. Open Mon–Fri 11.30am–3.00pm & 6–11pm, Sat 11.30am–4.30pm & 6–11pm, Sun 10.30am–4pm & 6–11pm. Expensive.

Wan Chai

Fook Lam Moon, 35–45 Johnston Rd ☎ 2866 0663. Among Hong Kong's finest and most famous Cantonese restaurants, this is no place to come if you're skimping on costs. Classic cooking, pricey ingredients (shark's fin, bird's nest) and consistently reliable quality. Open 11.30am–11.30pm. Expensive–Very Expensive.

Healthy Mess, Ground Floor, 51–53 Hennessy Rd ☎ 2527 3918. Bright and busy mock-traditional Cantonese vegetarian restaurant specializing in tofu (beancurd) dishes. It's next to the New

Harbour Hotel. Open 11am–11pm. Inexpensive.

Honey Honey Desert House. Ground Floor, Wah Fat Mansion, 404–419 Lockhart Rd ☎ 2836 6970. Delicious noodles and chicken rice, but primarily famous for its desserts. Don't miss the signature dish sago, which comes with 13 seasonal fruits – a great way to cool down in summer. Open daily noon–4am. Inexpensive.

One Harbour Road, *Grand Hyatt*, 1 Harbour Rd ☎ 2588 1234. The high-ranking Chinese businessmen's favourite, and they know a thing or two about quality food. Superb meals and spot-on service. Reservations advised. Open noon–2.30pm & 6.30–10.30pm. Very Expensive.

Yat Tung Heen Chinese Restaurant, 2nd Floor, Great Eagle Centre, 23 Harbour Rd ☎ 2878 1212. Large, busy, noisy restaurant, popular with local office workers. Good food – particularly the noodles. Inexpensive.

Causeway Bay

Ah Yee Leng Tong, Basement, Hang Lung Centre, 2–20 Paterson St ☎ 2576 8385; 1st Floor East, South Building, 475–481 Hennessy Rd ☎ 2834 2278. Old-style Cantonese cafés serving warming soups and casseroles, and simple family-style meat dishes, all guaranteed MSG-free. Open 11.30am–11.30pm. Moderate.

Heng Fa Garden, 1st Floor, 57 Lee Garden Rd ☎ 2915 7797. The main reason for coming here is the desserts, although there's also a full menu of noodle and *congee* dishes. The dumplings and steamed egg are recommended. Open 11.30am–midnight. Inexpensive.

Lee Yuen Restaurant, 539 Lockhart Rd ☎ 2834 4978. Unpretentious place using very fresh ingredients, although the portions are quite small. Excellent beef noodles. Open 11.30am–2am. Inexpensive.

Vegi-Food Kitchen, 8 Cleveland St ☎ 2890 6663. A sign at the entrance warns "Please do not bring meat of any kind into this restaurant", which gives

Eating

Eating

Eating Chinese Food

Don't be unnecessarily intimidated by the prospect of eating in a Chinese restaurant in Hong Kong. The following tips will help smooth the way.

Chopsticks and other utensils

You eat, naturally enough, with chopsticks, which – with a bit of practice and patience – are easy enough to master.

The idea is to use them as pincers between thumb and forefinger, moving the bottom one to grip the food, but really any method that gets your meal into your mouth is acceptable. If you can't manage, use the china spoon provided, or shrink with shame and ask for a fork and spoon – many restaurants will have them. You eat out of the little bowl in front of you (the smaller cup is for your tea), putting your rice in and plonking bits of food on top. Then, raise the bowl to your lips and shovel it in with the chopsticks (much easier than eating with chopsticks from a plate), chucking bones and other grungy bits onto the small plate as you go (you can ask for clean ones as you go along) . They'll change the cloth when you leave, so it's no problem if your table looks like culinary Armageddon.

Don't stick your chopsticks upright in your bowl when you're not eating (it's a Taoist death sign); place them across the top of the bowl, or on the chopstick rests.

There may well be one or two tiny dishes laid at your place too: at some stage someone will come round and fill one of them with soy sauce, the other with chilli sauce, and you dip your food into either.

Ordering food and drink

For ordering Chinese food, you're best off in a group; as a rough guide, order one more dish than there are people. The idea is that you put together a balanced meal, including the "five tastes" – acid, hot, bitter, sweet and salty – best achieved by balancing separate servings of meat, fish and vegetable, plus rice and soup. Soup – normally meat, fish or vegetable stock in a tureen – is drunk throughout the meal (or, in very old-fashioned restaurants, at the end) rather than as a starter, though if you want your individual bowl of chicken and sweetcorn soup you'll usually be able to get that too. Rice with food is white and steamed; fried rice comes as a fancier dish as part of a large meal. It's bad manners to leave rice, so don't order too much. The food will either come with various sauces (like plum sauce or chilli sauce), which are poured into the little dishes provided, or you can use the soy sauce and sesame oil on the table to flavour your food. Bear in mind that you use the sauces as dips: sloshing soy sauce over your rice and food will pick you out as an uncouth foreigner straight away. Dessert isn't always available, though you'll often get a sliced orange with which to cleanse the palate.

The classic drink with your meal is tea (see "Dim Sum" box on p.240), which will be brought as a matter of course. Beer also goes well with most Chinese food. Wine is generally expensive, and the stronger taste and higher alcohol content makes it a less suitable accompaniment, although that hasn't stopped it becoming increasingly popular among Chinese diners (at the expense of the traditional drink of brandy or whisky), who increasingly regard wine (red, particularly) as healthy. Having a couple of bottles from an expensive, well-known French chateau on your table is also a way of indicating status when entertaining or celebrating (even if it is then diluted with Coke or Sprite to make it sweeter!). Westerners usually prefer a dry white so as not to kill the taste of the food.

The cuisines

Cantonese cuisine is the most common cooking style in Hong Kong, but most types of Chinese food can be eaten, if not in specialist regional restaurants, then as individual dishes in places that are otherwise firmly Cantonese – the waiter should always be able to point you towards the house speciality. One thing common to most of the regional cuisines is the inclusion of things that Westerners often baulk at eating at all. Chinese cooking over the centuries has been essentially starvation food: nothing is ever wasted, and intestines, bone marrow, fish heads, chicken feet and blood are all recycled in various forms. Some are not as disgusting as they sound; others – like braised chicken blood – can challenge even the most robust palates.

Eating

Cantonese

Cantonese cuisine, from China's southeastern Guangdong province, is that which has been exported in bastardized forms to virtually every country in the world by Cantonese immigrants, and it is at its supreme best in Hong Kong. Throw away all your ideas of "Chinese" food when you sit down at a good Cantonese restaurant: apart from the cooking methods – mainly stir-frying and steaming – there's little similarity, and no self-respecting Chinese person would eat what they dismiss as the "foreign food" served up in restaurants and takeaway shops at home.

Ingredients are based around fish and seafood, pork, beef and vegetables, either stir-fried at high temperatures with a little oil, or either steamed or braised and flavoured with fresh ginger, spring onion, soy and oyster sauce. Everything is bitingly fresh and full of flavour, as a walk around any market proves – too fresh for some sensibilities, who can't bring themselves to choose their dinner from a restaurant fish tank. Fish and seafood are readily available and often excellent (although the pollution of Hong Kong's waters is creating a widespread preference for imported fish): garoupa, mullet and bream (which are often steamed whole), prawns, scallops, crayfish, mussels, clams, crabs, oysters, abalone, squid, octopus and lobster. In particular, prawns and crabs, served in spicy black-bean sauce, are classic dishes.

Chicken is the most widely eaten meat, and duck is popular too: commonly, it'll either come sliced and stir-fried with vegetables or marinaded and braised with things like lemon and soy or black-bean sauce. Other specialities are *dim sum* (see p.240) and roast or barbecued meats, especially pork and duck, as well as pigeon, all of which you'll see hanging up in restaurant windows, served with plain rice. Frog's legs are eaten, too; snake is one of the territory's more notorious delicacies, along with various intestinal dishes, and (more appealing) preserved eggs (p.101).

Chiu Chow

Another southeastern cuisine (from the Swatow district of Guangdong), Chiu Chow food is strong on seafood, including thick shark's fin soup and eel, and also encompasses the famous (and very expensive) bird's nest soup – made from the dried saliva which binds the nests of the sea swallow; cold roast goose is another favourite. The food uses much the same ingredients but is oilier than Cantonese, and you assist the digestion with a drink of bitter tea, known as "Iron Maiden" or "Iron Buddha".

continued overleaf

Eating

Eating Chinese Food (continued)

Beijing (Peking)

Beijing food is a heavier, northern style of cooking which relies more on meat, and supplements rice with bread and dumplings. One speciality is the Mongolian-influenced hot pot of sliced meat, vegetables and dumplings cooked and mixed together in a stock that's boiled at your table in a special stove; you dip the raw ingredients in, eat them once cooked and then drink the resulting soup at the end of the meal. The most famous Beijing food of all is Peking duck – a recipe that's existed in China for centuries – slices of skin and meat from a barbecued duck, wrapped in a pancake with spring onion and radish and smeared with plum sauce. The local ducks are usually rather fattier than that you may be used to at home. If you order this, be sure to ask for the duck carcass to be taken away after carving and turned into soup with vegetables and mushrooms, which is then served later.

Hakka

The Hakka people originated in northern China, but migrated south over the years and have been farming in what are now the New Territories for centuries. Their food is often taken to be Cantonese, and although there are few Hakka restaurants in Hong Kong, most Cantonese restaurants serve some Hakka dishes. These use beancurd a lot, and salted and preserved food, deriving from the days when the Hakka carried their food with them as they moved: salted, baked chicken, pork and preserved cabbage, intestines and innards cooked in various ways are staple dishes. One real speciality is boned duck, stuffed with rice, meat and lotus seeds.

Shanghai

Shanghainese is also a heavier cuisine than Cantonese, using more oil and spices, as well as preserved vegetables, pickles and steamed dumplings. It's warming, starchy food, particularly suited to the winter. Meals often start with cold, smoked fish, and include "drunken chicken", cooked in rice wine. Seafood is widely used, particularly fried or braised eels, while the great speciality is the expensive hairy crab – sent from Shanghai in the autumn, it is steamed and accompanied by ginger tea; the roe is considered a delicacy.

Szechuan (Sichuan)

Szechuan food is spicy and hot, using garlic, fennel, coriander, chillies and pepper to flavour dishes, which are served with hot dips and bread and noodles. Salted bean paste is a common cooking agent. Marinades are widely used and specialities include smoked duck (marinaded in wine, highly seasoned and cooked over camphor wood and tea leaves). Other dishes you'll see are braised aubergine, beancurd with chilli sauce, prawns with garlic, chilli and ginger, and braised beans. You'll get through a lot of beer with a Szechuan meal.

you an inkling of what to expect – inventive Cantonese vegetarian food at very fair prices. Open 11am–midnight. Moderate.

Aberdeen

Floating restaurants, Shum Wan, Wong Chuk Hang. Docked in Aberdeen Harbour, Hong Kong's famous floating restaurants are, in truth, a disappointment. You can eat better, cheaper seafood at various other venues around the territory, and you won't be surrounded by package-tour groups either. However if you still hanker after a meal in surroundings that look like a set from Bertolucci's *The Last Emperor*, you have a choice of three: the *Jumbo* ☎ 2553 9111; the *Jumbo Palace*

2554 0122; and the *Tai Pak* **2554 1026**. Each has its own private boat that will run you there across the harbour. The two *Jumbos* are open 7.30am–11.30pm, the *Tai Pak* 11.30am–11.30pm. Moderate–Expensive.

Tse Kee, 80 & 82 Old Main St, Aberdeen. Well-known noodle and fish-ball restaurant. There are two separate entrances, which can be confusing. Open 10.30am–6pm. Inexpensive.

Repulse Bay

Hei Fung Terrace, 1st Floor, The Arcade, The Repulse Bay, 109 Repulse Bay Rd **2812 2622**. Delicious food in elegant surroundings including speciality *dim sum* at lunchtimes. Open Mon–Sat 11.30am–3pm & 6–11pm. Moderate–Expensive.

Kowloon

East Ocean Seafood Restaurant, 3rd Floor, East Ocean Centre, 98 Granville Rd, Tsim Sha Tsui **2723 8128** or 2367 1133. Noisy basement dining with excellent seasonal cooking and approachable waiters. Open Mon–Sat 11am–midnight, Sun 10am–midnight. Moderate–Expensive.

Good Hope Restaurant. Ground Floor, 146 Sai Yeung Choi St, Mongkok **2393 9036**. Friendly restaurant specializing in noodles – the beef and fish ball varieties are particularly recommended; the vegetables are very fresh too. Open noon–midnight. Inexpensive.

Good Taste Restaurant, Ground Floor, 148–50 Sai Yeung Choi St, Mongkok **2394 8414**. Another noodle specialist. Here they come with vegetables, beef balls, fish balls, Taiwanese-style pork balls and more. Open 24 hours. Inexpensive.

Lai Ching Heen, *Regent Hotel*, 18 Salisbury Rd, Tsim Sha Tsui **2721 1211**. Reckoned one of Hong Kong's best for cutting-edge Cantonese cooking – and for the excellent service and amazing harbour views. Count on $800 a head for the works, though a $600 set menu relieves the pain a little.

Reservations essential. Open noon–2.30pm & 6–11pm. Very Expensive.

Nathan Restaurant, 11 Saigon St, Yau Ma Tei **2771 4285**. Many different combinations of *congee* available for $20–30. Open 7.30am–midnight. Inexpensive.

Tai Leung Pak Kee Sweet Shop, 266 Shanghai St, Yau Ma Tei **2384 7271**. All sorts of traditional Chinese desserts, including red bean, green bean, sesame flower, almond and walnut. Open noon–11.30pm. Inexpensive.

Ying Do Restaurant, 20 Sheung Fung St, Fung Wong Estate **2329 7275**. Typical old-style restaurant near Wong Tai Sing MTR, not too difficult to find and with friendly service. Recommended dishes include roast duck cooked to a house recipe and chicken with soya sauce. Open 7am–9pm. Inexpensive.

Shang Palace, Basement 1, *Kowloon Shangri-La Hotel*, 64 Mody Rd, Tsim Sha Tsui East **2733 8754**. Marvellous restaurant which seems to cook everything well, including pigeon, complete with over-the-top Imperial decor. It's busy at lunchtime – go early. Open Mon–Sat noon–3pm & 6.30–11pm, Sun 10.30am–3pm & 6.30–11pm. Expensive–Very Expensive.

Sun Tung Lok, Shop 63–64, Ocean Galleries, Harbour City, 17–19 Canton Rd, Tsim Sha Tsui **2730 0288**. Famous shark's fin restaurant, serving the (wildly expensive) delicacy in several different ways, alongside other excellent food. For a cheaper meal try the eel in black bean sauce and one of the chicken or pigeon dishes – all authentically Cantonese. (There's a second branch at Sunning Plaza, 1–5 Sunning Rd, Causeway Bay **2882 2899**). Open 11am–11pm. Expensive.

New Territories

Lung Wah Hotel and Restaurant, 22 Ha Wo Che, Sha Tin **2691 1594**. The best place in Hong Kong to eat hot, greasy pigeon – a Cantonese speciality. It's tricky to find, but worth the effort. The

Eating

The restaurants reviewed in this book have been given price categories as follows:
Inexpensive under $150
Moderate $150–300
Expensive $300–500
Very Expensive $500–800+

Eating

restaurant's traditional, with a garden full of *mahjong* players and outdoor tables, and gets packed at the weekend. You can eat inside in the air conditioning or in the garden. Good beancurd and almond desserts too. Get there by taxi or minibus #60X from Sha Tin KCR, or bus #48 – from Tsuen Wan ferry to Wo Che – to Sha Tin Police Quarters, then take the footbridge over the motorway at the end of Wo Che St. Open 11am–11pm. Moderate.

Yucca de Lac, Ma La Shui, Sha Tin ☎ 2691 1630. Long-established open-air restaurant in the hills overlooking the Chinese University and Tolo Harbour. There's an extensive menu – the pigeon is recommended, as are the beancurd dishes. It's on the old Tai Po Road, above Tolo Highway – take a taxi from Sha Tin and walk back down on foot to University KCR; or take bus #70, from Jordan Rd Ferry Terminal to Sheung Shui, which passes the restaurant. Open 11am–11pm. Moderate.

HAKKA

Chuen Cheung Kui, 91–95 Fa Yuen St, Mongkok ☎ 2396 0672. Large portions of family-style cooking make this a pop-

ular place with locals – weekends are always packed. Not much English spoken; you may have to point. Open 11am–11pm. Moderate.

New Home Hakka & Seafood Restaurant, 19–20 Hanoi Rd, Tsim Sha Tsui ☎ 2366 9243. Fairly austere tile-and-mirror decor, but attentive service and authentic Hakka food. The tangy salt-baked chicken is excellent (and half a bird is big enough for two), as are the beancurd dishes and soups. Open 11am–11pm. Moderate.

CHIU CHOW

Chiu Chow Garden, Basement, Jardine House, 1 Connaught Place, Central ☎ 2525 8246; 3rd Floor, Vicwood Plaza, 199 Des Voeux Rd, Central ☎ 2545 7778; 6th Floor, Windsor House, 311 Gloucester Rd, Causeway Bay ☎ 2882 2232. Chiu Chow food from the *Maxim* people. Always reliable and not expensive; goose a speciality. All open 10am–3pm & 5.30pm–midnight. Moderate.

City Chiu Chow Restaurant, 1st Floor, East Ocean Centre, 98 Granville Rd, Tsim Sha Tsui East ☎ 2723 6226. One of a chain (look for the words "City Chiu

---

Shark's Fin

If there's one dish that epitomizes both the Chinese propensity for eating unlikely animal body parts and their willingness to pay through the nose for the privilege, it's shark's fin. Many Cantonese restaurants offer it up as thick, fibrous shark's fin soup, not so much an acquired taste but an outrageously expensive one: suffice to say that if there's a cheap bowl of shark's fin on the menu, it isn't the real thing.

Quite how and why it came to be eaten in the first place is unclear, though – as with most obscure animal parts – the Chinese claim medicinal properties for the fin. Modern medical thought is sceptical, to say the least, though the wider concern is that eating shark's fin soup is putting the various fish species at risk. Economic growth in Southeast Asia and the Pacific Rim has fuelled demand for shark's fin and, consequently, shark fishing is now very big business. Numbers are declining rapidly and since the shark is an important part of the food chain, the destruction of large numbers of them has disturbing implications for the marine environment.

For this reason alone, there's a growing move to boycott the eating of shark's fin products. If you need any more convincing, it's worth noting that shark flesh is not usually eaten in the Far East, so the fish are killed just for their fins. These are cut off while the shark is still alive and then the fish is thrown back into the sea, where – without its fins to give it mobility – it drowns.

Chow" in the name) selling reasonably priced food, even if the cooking doesn't always inspire. Open 11am–midnight. Moderate.

BEIJING (PEKING)

American Restaurant, 20 Lockhart Rd, Wan Chai ☎ 2527 7277. Misleadingly named, averagely priced Beijing restaurant with a large menu and some good spicy dishes. A favourite with tourists, although the food can be indifferent. Open 11.30am–11.30pm. Inexpensive–Moderate.

Beijing Restaurant, 1st–3rd Floor, 34–36 Granville Rd, Tsim Sha Tsui ☎ 2721 1808. Peking duck and other warming northern specialities. Open 11am–11pm. Moderate.

Peking Garden, branches at Basement, Alexandra House, 6 Ice House St, Central ☎ 2526 6456; Shop 003, The Mall, Pacific Place, 88 Queensway, Central ☎ 2845 8452; 1st Floor, Hennessy Centre, 500 Hennessy Rd, Causeway Bay ☎ 2577 7231. High culinary standards in all three restaurants, with particularly renowned Peking duck and interesting desserts. Tourist side shows include nightly noodle-making displays and the occasional impromptu cookery demonstration. Open 11am–10.30pm & 5.30pm–midnight. Moderate–Expensive.

Peking Restaurant, 227 Nathan Rd, Jordan ☎ 2730 1316. Don't be put off by the fairly glum decor: this place serves some of the best Beijing food in Hong Kong, with the duck especially recommended. Open 11am–10.30pm. Moderate.

Spring Deer, 1st Floor, 42 Mody Rd, Tsim Sha Tsui ☎ 2366 4012. Long-established place noted for its barbecued Peking duck (which is carved at the table), among a barrage of authentic dishes, such as shark's fin and baked fish on a hot plate. Try the smoked chicken and the beancurd with minced pork. Open noon–11pm. Moderate.

SHANGHAINESE

Dai Pai Dong, Ground Floor, 128 Queen's Rd, Central. Typical street food,

but served in 1950s Shanghai-style restaurant. Open 7am–10.30pm. Inexpensive.

Great Shanghai, 26 Prat Ave, Tsim Sha Tsui ☎ 2366 8158. One of the most reliable of Hong Kong's Shanghai restaurants, with well-presented food (fine fish and seafood) served in small or large portions. A good choice for a first Shanghai meal. Open 11am–11pm. Moderate.

New 369 Restaurant, 73 Austin Rd, Jordan ☎ 2730 8113. Well known locally, their *xia-long bao* and *won ton* with chicken are particularly good. They're also famous for their traditional Chinese New Year cake made of chicken or pork. Open 11am–midnight. Inexpensive.

Peace Restaurant, Ground Floor, Pai Trade Centre, 40 Nga Tsin Wai Rd, Kowloon City ☎ 2382 2189. Own versions of many traditional Shanghai dishes – the noodles and dumplings are especially recommended. Friendly staff. Open 11am–2am. Moderate

Shanghai Garden, Hutchison House, 10 Harcourt Rd, Central ☎ 2524 8181. More upmarket than the Tsim Sha Tsui Shanghai eating places, the *Shanghai Garden* also mixes in dishes from other regions. But the scrumptious food is authentic and prices aren't too extreme for Central (though they are higher than all the other places listed in this section). Open 11.30am–3pm & 5.30pm–midnight. Moderate–Expensive.

Wu Kong Shanghai Restaurant, Basement, Alpha House, 27 Nathan Rd, Tsim Sha Tsui ☎ 2366 7244; *Food Forum*, 12th Floor, Times Square, 1 Matheson St, Causeway Bay ☎ 2506 1018. Popular restaurants with a wide menu, and – given their handy positions – not destined to break the bank either. There are some challenging specialities alongside more mainstream dishes like chicken with garlic and chilli or beancurd with sliced pork. Fish is pricier. In Tsim Sha Tsui, go early for dinner or expect to wait in line. Open 11.30am–midnight. Moderate.

Yin King Lau Restaurant, 113 Lockhart Rd, Wanchai ☎ 2520 0106. Traditional

Eating

Eating

The restaurants reviewed in this book have been given price categories as follows:
Inexpensive under $150
Moderate $150–300
Expensive $300–500
Very Expensive $500–800+

restaurant serving Peking and Szechuan food. Popular with both local Chinese and expats. Open 6pm–10.30pm. Moderate.

SZECHUAN (SICHUAN)

Kam Kong Restaurant, 60 Granville Rd, Tsim Sha Tsui ☎2367 5397. Good, no-nonsense food, highly spiced and with lashings of hot green and red chillies. Try the "green fish", the dumplings (*won ton*) and the smoked fish; the dishes come in three sizes so you don't need to over-order. Open noon–11pm. Inexpensive–Moderate.

The Red Pepper, 7 Lan Fong Rd, Causeway Bay ☎2577 3811. The name says it all – a good choice for devilishly hot food and a favourite with expats, which means higher-than-warranted prices and pushy staff. The smoked duck and beancurd are standard favourites here. You might want to book in advance, since it can get very busy. Open noon–11.45pm. Moderate.

Szechuan Lau, 466 Lockhart Rd, Causeway Bay ☎2891 9027. Classic Szechuan food, with all the best-known dishes served in relaxed, old-style surroundings. The chilli prawns are great, and there are more elaborate (and expensive) seafood dishes, too. The waiters keep the beer coming – go easy if you're trying to cut costs. Open noon–midnight. Moderate.

OTHER CHINESE REGIONS

Bistro Manchu, 33 Elgin St, Mid-Levels ☎2536 9218. Manchu cuisine seems to be a mix of northern Chinese with a bit of Mongolian and Korean thrown in. Stylish East-meets-West décor. The food, while generally tasty, can be a bit variable. Open noon–11pm. Moderate–Expensive.

Forever Green Taiwanese Restaurant, 93 Leighton Rd, Causeway Bay ☎2890 3448; BIC Centre, 18 Cheung Lok St, Yau Ma Tei ☎2332 7183. Despite the OTT decor and traditionally dressed staff, there's more than just curiosity value at these late-opening Taiwanese restau-

rants. Both have interesting and comparatively cheap menus. Open noon–3pm & 6pm–4.30am. Moderate.

Hunan Garden, 3rd Floor, The Forum, Exchange Square, 8 Connaught Place, Central ☎2868 2880. Hunan province features spicy dishes akin to those from Szechuan; the menu points out what's hot and what isn't. Excellent dishes from Chairman Mao's home province. Open 11.30am–3pm & 5.30pm–midnight. Expensive.

Islam Food, 1 Lung Kong Rd, Kowloon City ☎2382 2822. This restaurant focuses mainly on the traditional food of China's Muslim minority peoples, but also serves some Beijing and Szechuan dishes. Open 11am–10.30pm. Inexpensive.

Ning Po Residents Association, 4th Floor, Yip Fung Building, 10 D'Aguilar St, Lan Kwai Fong ☎2523 0648. Some of the best Ning Po and Shanghainese food in town. The steamed pork dumplings and the pork dipped in vinegar and ginger are recommended. Open noon–2.30pm & 6pm–9pm. Inexpensive.

Taiwanese Icy Fruit House, 240 Sai Yeung Choi St, Mongkok ☎2380 5109. Unappealing exterior, but the food is good – the sweet-and-spicy pork and the fruit served on a bed of ice are particularly fine. Open 10.30am–midnight. Inexpensive.

Yunnan Kitchen, 12th Floor, Times Square, 1 Matheson St, Causeway Bay ☎2506 3309. Yunnan province specialities make for a change after the Canto dishes on offer in most of Hong Kong's restaurants, but they don't come particularly cheap and you have to endure the usual Times Square thematic shenanigans and costumed staff. Open 11.30am–3.30pm & 5.30–11.30pm. Moderate–Expensive.

African

The Gallery Pub and Restaurant, Tong Fuk Village, South Lantau Rd, Lantau ☎2980 2582. South African food in relaxed surroundings. Not surprisingly, barbecued food figures prominently.

Open Wed-Fri 6–11pm, Sat & Sun noon–11pm. Moderate.

American

Al's Diner, 37 D'Aguilar St, Lan Kwai Fong, Central ☎2869 1869. Straightforward diner food – burgers, dogs, chilli and sandwiches – and late opening at weekends for ravenous clubbers. Open Mon–Thurs 11am–12.30am, Fri & Sat 11am–3.30am, Sun 6pm–12.30am. Inexpensive–Moderate.

American Pie, 4th Floor, California Entertainment Building, 34–36 D'Aguilar St, Lan Kwai Fong, Central ☎2877 9779. Forget the overpriced *à la carte* meals in this rather chic, if cramped, restaurant and come instead for the excellent Sunday brunch; if you book ahead, you can eat out on the terrace. Or simply call in for a coffee and hog out on the superb desserts and cakes (regularly voted Hong Kong's best in restaurant surveys). Open Mon–Thurs noon–2.30pm & 6–11pm, Fri–Sun noon–1am. Moderate–Expensive.

The Bayou, 9–13 Shelly St, Mid-Levels ☎2526 2118. Popular Cajun restaurant, which also runs a small takeaway next door. The Sunday brunch with jazz/Gospel accompaniment is usually packed out. Open 12.30pm–2.30pm & 6.30pm–midnight. Moderate.

California, California Tower, 24–26 Lan Kwai Fong, Central ☎2521 1345. Restaurant/café/bar that oozes Americana and serves a classic menu – burgers, potato skins, salads and barbecues. Pricey and flash. Mon–Thurs noon–1am, Fri & Sat noon–4am, Sun 5pm–1am. Expensive.

Dan Ryan's Chicago Bar and Grill, 114 The Mall, Pacific Place, 88 Queensway, Admiralty ☎2845 4600; Ocean Terminal, Harbour City, Canton Rd, Tsim Sha Tsui ☎2735 6111. Bumper American-size portions of ribs, burgers, steaks, salads and home-made desserts. You'll get enough food to sink a battleship, but it doesn't come cheap. Open 11am–midnight. Moderate–Expensive.

Hard Rock Café, Ground–3rd Floor, 100 Canton Rd, Tsim Sha Tsui ☎2377 8118.

A branch of the burger-and-rock chain, with menus short on surprises, though portions are decent enough. There are live bands and dancing every night after 10.30pm, and a daily 3–7pm Happy Hour. Open noon–midnight, later at weekends. Moderate.

LA Café, Ground Floor, Lippo Centre, Admiralty ☎2526 6863. Complete with Harley Davidson above the bar, Californian cuisine and international beer served by staff with attitude. Open 11am–2am. Moderate–Expensive.

Napa, 21st Floor, *Kowloon Shangri La Hotel*, Tsim Sha Tsui ☎2733 8752. Excellent Californian food in stunning art deco surroundings, with possibly the best view of the harbour available anywhere. Live jazz in the evenings. Open noon–3pm & 6.30pm–midnight. Expensive–Very Expensive.

Planet Hollywood, 3 Canton Rd, Tsim Sha Tsui ☎2377 7888. Sly, Bruce and Arnie's venture heads east: burgers, fries, Tex-Mex specials and ice cream, with some Asian additions, in regulation movie-heaven surroundings. Open 11.30am–2am. Moderate.

Australian

Brett's Seafood, 72 Lockhart Rd, Wan Chai ☎2866 6608. Seafood café/takeaway joint doing good business in fish and seafood platters (the raw ingredients flown in from Australia) served with rice or fries. Open Mon–Thurs & Sun 7.30am–2am, Fri & Sat 7.30am–4am. Inexpensive–Moderate.

Ned Kelly's Last Stand, 11a Ashley Rd, Tsim Sha Tsui ☎2376 0562. Laid-back Aussie bar with live jazz (see "Live Music") and a filling range of tucker – meat pies much in evidence. Open 11.45am–1.45am. Inexpensive.

UC Bistro, University Centre, University of Science and Technology, Clearwater Bay Rd, Tseung Kwan O, Kowloon ☎2335 1875. Western food with emphasis on modern Australian-type cooking. Great sea views over the Sai Kung peninsular. Set lunches $58-68, buffets $80. Inexpensive.

Eating

Eating

British

For no-nonsense portions of fish and chips, steak-and-kidney pie or an all-day English breakfast, most pubs can do the honours; see the next chapter for full pub and bar listings.

Bentley's Seafood Restaurant & Oyster Bar, B4 Basement, Prince's Building, 10 Chater Rd, Central ☎2868 0881. British fish-and-seafood/oyster restaurant serving classic grills alongside a smattering of Southeast Asian-inspired dishes. Open Mon–Sat 11.30am–3pm & 6–10.30pm. Expensive.

Harry Ramsden's, Wu Chung House, 213 Queen's Rd East, Wan Chai ☎2832 9626. The famous British fish-and-chip shop moves out east – and remains remarkably true to its origins. The best fish and chips for thousands of miles, served under imported Yorkshire chandeliers. Full takeaway service too. Open 11.30am–11pm. Moderate.

SoHo SoHo, 9 Old Bailey St, Central ☎2147 2618. Excellent modern British-style cooking offering traditional English ingredients with a twist. The menu changes regularly, according to what's fresh in the markets. Friendly staff and very reasonably priced set lunch. Open Mon–Sat noon–2.30pm, 7–10.30pm. Moderate–Expensive.

Buffets and set meals

Most of the larger hotels put on self-service **buffets** – for breakfast, lunch or afternoon tea, and sometimes for dinner too. Many also offer two- or three-course set meals. Check advertisements or the "Hotel Fare" section of the daily *South China Morning Post* for special deals. Buffet lunch (around $110) is usually noon–2.30pm, dinner ($160–250) 6.30–10pm, but ring for exact times; ten percent service is added in all cases and drinks are usually extra.

Burmese

Rangoon, Ground Floor, Hoi Kung Mansion, 265 Gloucester Rd, Causeway Bay ☎2893 0778. This quiet Burmese restaurant – the only one in Hong Kong – is a real treat, with a high-quality menu (with vegetarian dishes) that's not particularly expensive. Subtly spiced curries predominate. The food is beautifully presented and comes in hefty portions. Open 11.30am–11.30pm. Moderate.

Filipino

Cinta-J, 69–75 Jaffe Rd, Wan Chai ☎2529 6622. Just around the corner from the associated *Cinta*, this has good-value meals (and a long Happy Hour) – soups, casseroles and seafood. Open 11am–midnight. Inexpensive.

Cinta Restaurant, Shing Yip Building, 10 Fenwick St, Wan Chai ☎2527 1199. Selection of Filipino and Indonesian dishes. Reliable and does good business with tourists. Open 11am–2am. Moderate.

Mabuhay, 11 Minden Ave, Tsim Sha Tsui ☎2367 3762. Crispy fried pig's intestines are fairly typical of the authentic dishes offered here, but there are plenty of other choices – hearty soups, garlicky baked clams (actually green mussels) and grilled fish. Basic, bustling canteen dining accompanied by Western pop and cheap schooners of beer. Thoroughly recommended. Open 9am–11.30pm. Inexpensive.

French

Au Trou Normand, 6 Carnarvon Rd, Tsim Sha Tsui ☎2366 8754. This long-standing restaurant dishes up fine provincial French food in rustic surroundings, with calvados to wash it all down. Open noon–3pm & 7–11pm. Moderate.

Café Gypsy, 29 Shelley St, Mid-Levels ☎2521 0000. Mediterranean rather than strictly French cuisine, but inventive and good. The small terrace at the front allows you to sit and watch the world – or the escalator – go by. Open Mon–Fri noon–5pm, 7–11pm, Sat 10.30am–5pm, 7–11pm, Sun 10.30am–2pm.

Gaddi's, 1st Floor, *Peninsula Hotel*, Salisbury Rd, Tsim Sha Tsui ☎2366 6251. One of the most respected Western restaurants in Hong Kong.

Extraordinary food, extraordinary prices (at least $800 per person for a full meal); advance booking and smart dress essential. Open noon–2.30pm & 7–11pm. Very Expensive.

Papillon, 8–13 Wo On Lane, Central ☎ 2526 5965. Extensive and not overly expensive menu of French bistro classics in a pleasing little place, close to Lan Kwai Fong. Best value is the three-course set meal for $260 or so; the desserts are wantonly attractive. Open noon–2.30pm & 7–11pm. Moderate–Expensive.

2 Sardines, 43 Elgin St, Mid-Levels, ☎ 2973 6618. Small restaurant with a big reputation for reliable, reasonably priced French food. Open Mon–Sat noon–2.30pm, 6.30–10.30pm. Moderate.

Stanley's French Restaurant, 1st & 2nd Floors, 90B Stanley Main St, Stanley ☎ 2813 8873. Chic French restaurant in Stanley Village which is winning a lot of friends with its imaginative, regularly changing menu and bay views. Try to book in advance. Open noon–3pm & 7pm–midnight. Expensive.

W's Entrecote, 13th Floor, Times Square, 1 Matheson St, Causeway Bay ☎ 2506 0133. Not exactly a thoroughbred French restaurant, but it does serve the one thing that matters: steak (it's the only dish on the menu) which comes with a green salad and unlimited *frites*. Open noon–11pm. Moderate.

German, Austrian and Swiss

Chesa, 1st Floor, *Peninsula Hotel*, Salisbury Rd, Tsim Sha Tsui ☎ 2366 6251. The *Pen*'s top-price Swiss restaurant with great fondue and superb meat and fish dishes. Reservations essential. Open noon–2.30pm & 6.30–10.30pm. Very Expensive.

Mozart Stub'n, 8 Glenealy, Central ☎ 2522 1763. Meat dishes predominate in this small Austrian restaurant. If you're looking for filling central-European food, this is about the best value in the territory – book ahead for dinner. Open Mon–Sat noon–2pm & 7.30–11pm. Moderate–Expensive.

Greek, Turkish and Lebanese

Bacchus Taverna, Basement, Hop Hing Centre, 8–12 Hennessy Rd, Wan Chai ☎ 2529 9032. Extensive menu featuring Mediterranean and Greek dishes. Now that the *Bacchus* is more of a bar it makes for a fun evening out. Open noon–2.30pm & 6pm–midnight. Moderate–Expensive.

Beirut, Shop A, Winner Building, 39 D'Aguilar St, Central ☎ 2804 6611. A chic setting for Lebanese food, kebabs and mixed grills – though the bar gets just as much custom as the restaurant. Open Mon–Sat 11am–midnight, Sun 4pm–midnight. Moderate.

Midnight Express, 3 Lan Kwai Fong, Central ☎ 2525 5010. Pitta bread stuffed with all kinds of fillings at bargain prices. Just the place after a drinking bout in Lan Kwai Fong. Open Mon–Sat 11.30am–3am, Sun 6pm–12.30am. Inexpensive.

Indian, Pakistani and Nepalese
See also "Burmese" and "Sri Lankan".

CENTRAL
The Ashoka, 57–59 Wyndham St ☎ 2524 9623. A very popular, comfortable restaurant serving highly recommended Northern Indian food. There are very good-value set lunches and dinners, and several vegetarian choices. A second branch in Wan Chai (185 Wan Chai Rd ☎ 2891 8981) also gets rave reviews. Open noon–2.30pm & 6–10.30pm. Moderate.

Gunga Din's Club, Lower Ground Floor, 59 Wyndham St ☎ 2523 1276. Among the very best of Hong Kong's small, club-like Indian restaurants. Prices are extremely reasonable; booking recommended. Open 11.30am–2.30pm & 6–10.30pm. Moderate.

India Curry Club, 3rd Floor, 10 Wing Wah Lane, Winner Building (off D'Aguilar St) ☎ 2523 2203. A very limited menu, but fine food (always some vegetarian) and friendly service in basic, cramped surroundings. Open 11.30am–2.30pm & 6.30–10.30pm. Inexpensive.

Eating

The restaurants reviewed in this book have been given price categories as follows:
Inexpensive
under $150
Moderate
$150–300
Expensive
$300–500
Very
Expensive
$500–800+

Eating

The restaurants reviewed in this book have been given price categories as follows:
Inexpensive under $150
Moderate $150–300
Expensive $300–500
Very Expensive $500–800+

The Mughal Room, 1st Floor, Carfield Commercial Building, 75–77 Wyndham St ☎ 2524 0107. Upmarket north Indian restaurant, with costumed staff, historical notes on a decent-looking menu that's strong on tandoori dishes and also features some Afghan and Pakistani specialities. The food can be a bit hit-and-miss, but the surroundings are worth paying for. Open noon–3pm & 6–11.30pm. Moderate.

Sherpa Himalayan Coffee Shop, 11 Staunton St, Mid-Levels ☎ 2973 6886. Friendly restaurant with an interesting range of vegetarian dishes. If they send you over the road to another restaurant, don't worry, it's the same management and kitchen. Cheap set lunch. Open 10am–11pm. Moderate.

WAN CHAI

Jo Jo Mess Club, 1st Floor, 86–90 Johnston Rd, Wan Chai (entrance on Lee Tung St) ☎ 2527 3776. Hardly luxury surroundings, but a deservedly popular spot with tandoori specialities and views out onto the busy street. Open 11am–3pm & 6–11pm. Inexpensive.

Viceroy, 2nd Floor, Sun Hung Kai Centre, 30 Harbour Rd, Wan Chai ☎ 2827 7777. Food from all parts of India and terrace dining, too, with harbour views. The lunch buffet is particularly well regarded. Open noon–2.30pm & 6pm–midnight. Moderate.

STANLEY

The Curry Pot, 6th Floor, 90B Stanley Main St ☎ 2899 0811. Very friendly little restaurant with ocean views from its sixth-floor windows and delicately judged Indian food from all regions. The set lunch is remarkable value, but you can't go wrong choosing *à la carte* either. Open noon–3pm & 6–10.30pm. Inexpensive–Moderate.

TSIM SHA TSUI

Delhi Club , Block C, C3, 3rd Floor, Chungking Mansions, 36–44 Nathan Rd, ☎ 2368 1682. A curry house *par excellence*, once you ignore the spartan surroundings and slap-down service. The ludicrously cheap set meal would feed an army. Open noon–2.30pm & 6–11.30pm. Inexpensive.

Gaylord, 1st Floor Ashley Centre, 23–25 Ashley Rd ☎ 2376 1001. Smarter-than-average décor for an Indian restaurant and the fresh and reliable food doesn't disappoint either. Open noon–3pm, 6–11pm. Moderate.

Koh-i-Noor, 1st Floor, 3–4 Peninsula Apartments (on corner with Minden Row), 16c Mody Rd ☎ 2368 3065. The garish, upmarket decor hides reasonable food. There are also seasonal promotions, highlighting different aspects of north Indian cooking. Open 11.30am–3pm & 6–11.30pm. Moderate.

Woodlands, Mirror Tower, 61 Mody Rd ☎ 2369 3718. Part of an international chain, this is a mainly southern Indian restaurant serving pure vegetarian food, with a menu that describes each dish in detail. Snacks as well as full meals, including biryani and excellent thalis, the portions large enough to share. Always popular, with friendly service. Open noon–3.30pm & 6.30–11pm. Inexpensive.

YAU MA TEI

Ah Long, Ground Floor, Tak Lee Building, 95B Woo Sung St, Jordan ☎ 2782 1635. Chinese-run place cooking halal curries. Usually busy and worth a look if you're in the market for a cheap and cheerful meal. Open 11am–11pm. Inexpensive.

Indonesian

Bali Restaurant, 10 Nanking St, Yau Ma Tei ☎ 2780 2902. Affordable, but often fairly unimaginative, Indonesian food (though the fish in chilli sauce is very tasty) served in extremely kitsch surroundings – lanterns, bamboo and drapes as far as the eye can see. Open noon–11pm. Inexpensive–Moderate.

Cinta Restaurant, Shing Yip Building, 10 Fenwick St, Wan Chai ☎ 2527 1199. Filling *rijstafel* among other reliable meal choices; does good business with tourists. Also serves Filipino dishes. Open 11am–2am. Moderate.

Indonesia Padang Restaurant, 85 Percival St, Causeway Bay ☎2576 1828. An unassuming spot with better-than-usual food and highly recommended desserts, which are also sold as take-away snacks. Open 11am–11pm. Moderate.

Indonesian Restaurant, 28 Leighton Rd, Causeway Bay ☎2577 9981. Recommended place with canteen-style surroundings and staff who'll help you get the best out of the extensive menu – the curries or spicy eggplant are great. Open 11.30am–11.30pm. Inexpensive.

Java Rijstafel, 38 Hankow Rd, Tsim Sha Tsui ☎2367 1230. Bang in the middle of Tsim Sha Tsui and consequently popular; you might want to book ahead since it's a tiny place. The *rijstafel* ("rice table") – a buffet of ten or more little dishes – is certainly worth considering, though it's only served for a minimum of two people; the satay scores highly, too. Open noon–10.30pm. Moderate.

International

Cafe Deco Bar & Grill, Level 1 & 2, Peak Galleria, 118 Peak Rd, The Peak ☎2849 5111. Superbly located restaurant with unrivalled views and a stylish Art Deco interior that extends to the rest rooms. The menu ranges over gourmet pizzas, curries, Thai noodles, grilled meats and oysters; prices, surprisingly, are not too high. Or just call in for a drink, or cake and coffee; the bar stays open an hour or so after the kitchen closes (until 1am on Fri & Sat) and there's often live jazz. Kitchen open Mon–Thurs & Sun 10am–11pm, Fri & Sat 10am–11.30pm. Moderate–Expensive.

Felix, 28th Floor, *Peninsula Hotel*, Salisbury Rd, Tsim Sha Tsui ☎2366 6251. As chic as can be, with a Philippe Starck-designed bar, supreme aerial views, and a guest list that's pure Hollywood. Oh, and the Eurasian food's good, too, but it costs a packet. Reservations required. Or just come for a drink and enjoy the view. Open 6–11pm. Very Expensive.

Jimmy's Kitchen, Basement, South China Building, 1–3 Wyndham St, Central ☎2526 5293; 1st Floor, Kowloon Centre, 29 Ashley Rd, Tsim Sha Tsui ☎2376 0327. Old European restaurant, popular with expats and serving a menu of standards from French onion soup to steak pie. It's relatively cheap given its decent-sized portions, but the cooking isn't always greatly accomplished. Open noon–midnight. Moderate–Expensive.

M at the Fringe, 2 Lower Albert Rd, Central ☎2877 4000. Stylish restaurant much favoured by the glitterati for its boldly flavoured, health-conscious dishes – meat, fish and veggie – whose influences range the world. Reservations advised. Open Mon–Sat noon–2.30pm & 7–10.30pm. Expensive.

Peak Café, 121 Peak Rd, The Peak ☎2849 7868. Furbished in Californian designer style, the East–West food at the *Peak* is spot on, as are the views out to sea from one of Hong Kong's finest vantage points. Set meals are good value and there are weekend barbecues and vegetarian choices too. Open 10.30am–10.45pm. Expensive.

Post 97, 1st Floor, 9–11 Lan Kwai Fong, Central ☎2810 9333. Relaxed, brasserie surroundings for an eclectic menu of Mediterranean and American food, plus a daily vegetarian choice. There's also real coffee and herbal teas, while an imaginative list of brunch specials is served all day on Sunday. Open Mon–Fri 9am–2am, Sat–Sun 24hr. Moderate–Expensive.

Stanley's Oriental Restaurant, 90b Stanley Main St, Stanley ☎2813 9988. Excellent location, with a terrace overlooking Stanley's bay, and featuring an enterprising mix of Indian, Thai, Cajun and Chinese cooking. Daily specials are always worth trying, including a set vegetarian menu and a set lunch. Open 9am–midnight. Moderate–Expensive.

Tables 88, 88 Stanley Village Rd, Stanley ☎2813 6262. Bizarrely furnished, upmarket village restaurant in Stanley's old police station building. It serves

Eating

Eating

mainly Mediterranean-style food. Prices are quite high considering it's a long way from Central. Open 11.30am–3pm & 6.30–10.30pm.

Tiffany Restaurant, 148 Prince Edward Rd, Mongkok ☎ 2381 1516. Steak is the best thing here. The set dinner is $100–140 with nice atmosphere and music. Open 8am–11.30pm. Moderate.

Italian

Baci Restaurant and Pizza, 1 Lan Kwai Fong, Central ☎ 2801 5885. Quality Italian dishes, including crisp pizzas with good toppings. The pizza section is on the first floor, below the restaurant. Moderate.

Grappa's, Pacific Place, 88 Queensway, Admiralty ☎ 2868 0086. A good place to meet or eat, whether you want a glass of wine, a snack or a full meal. The restaurant is usually pretty full, but turnover is quick. There's also a branch in Tsim Sha Tsui, but the food isn't nearly so good. Open 11.30am–10.30pm. Moderate–Expensive.

Pepperonis, 18B Stanley Main St ☎ 2813 8605; 1592 Po Tung Rd, Sai Kung ☎ 2813 8605. Good, tasty and filling pizzas. They also have a takeaway service. The same management also runs two other Sai Kung restaurants – *Jaspa's* and *Al Fresco's* . Open 10am–10pm. Inexpensive.

The Pizzeria, 2nd Floor, *Kowloon Hotel,* 19–21 Nathan Rd, Tsim Sha Tsui ☎ 2369 8698. Smart and highly rated pizzeria (takeaway available too), with pricier pasta dishes and main courses. Open noon–3pm & 6–11pm. Moderate.

Rigoletto's, 14–16 Fenwick St, Wan Chai ☎ 2527 7144. Established Italian restaurant whose decent food draws lots of visitors. Open Mon–Sat noon–3pm & 6pm–midnight, Sun 6pm–midnight. Moderate.

Tivoli, 130 Austin Rd, Tsim Sha Tsui ☎ 2366 6424. A cosy, candlelit, checked-tablecloth joint, serving good pasta and authentic thin-crust pizzas. Open noon–midnight. Moderate.

Toscana, *Ritz-Carlton,* 3 Connaught Rd, Central ☎ 2532 2062. Fashionable Tuscan restaurant in one of the fanciest of the city's hotels. Stylish Italian food, some of it good value, in posh surroundings. But style comes at a price. There are set lunches and dinners, too, from around $320. Open noon–2.30pm & 7–10.30pm. Very Expensive.

Tutto Meglio, 33 D'Aguilar St, Central ☎ 2869 7833. Just about every Italian region gets a look-in around Lan Kwai Fong – the Florentine food served here is a little unusual, but pricey. You can usually just turn up and get a table, too, though maybe there'd be more of a queue if they turned the music down. Open Mon–Sat noon–3pm & 7–11pm (midnight Fri/Sat). Moderate.

Va Bene, 58–62 D'Aguilar St, Central ☎ 2845 5577. Regularly rated as either Hong Kong's best or Hong Kong's most over-rated Italian. Considered over-priced and over-crowded by some, nevertheless this astonishingly successful restaurant continues to pack them in, despite the fact that its authentic touch of Venice is also a painful financial experience. Open Mon–Fri noon–2.30pm & 7–10.30pm. Sat 7pm–2am. Very Expensive.

Japanese

Beppu Menkan Japanese Noodle Restaurant, Ground Floor, 3 Pak Sha Rd, Causeway Bay ☎ 2881 0831. Delicious Japanese-style noodles, particularly the spicy dishes. Open 11.30am–midnight. Inexpensive.

Department stores. For informal, cheap Japanese food, try the supermarkets in the Sogo (555 Hennessy Rd), and Seibu, Pacific Place, and department stores, which feature takeaway *sushi* and Japanese snack bars. Inexpensive.

Genroku. Some thirty branches around Hong Kong, including 376 Lockhart Rd, Wan Chai; 22 Stanley St, Central; 733 Nathan Rd, Tsim Sha Tsui. The S-shaped conveyor belt delivers your food – about the cheapest way to eat Japanese in Hong Kong. There are a dozen other

branches too. Open 11am–11pm.
Inexpensive.

Katiga Japanese Food, 37 Sung Kit St, Hung Hom ☎ 2764 6436. Beef rolled with noodles and grilled sardines are among the specialities. Nice atmosphere and surroundings. Open 11.30am–11.30pm. Moderate.

Kiku Express, Lower Ground Floor, Jardine House, Connaught Rd, Central ☎ 2845 9541. Popular Japanese café serving *sushi*, noodles and other dishes, as well as takeaway lunch boxes. Open Mon–Sat 7.30am–7pm. Inexpensive.

Ichizen, Lower Ground Floor 1, Seibu, The Mall, Pacific Place, 88 Queensway, Admiralty ☎ 2523 0185. Plenty of Japanese diners attest to the quality here, with *teppanyaki* and *sashimi* dishes in constant demand. Open Mon–Sat 11.30am–3pm & 6–11pm, Sun 12.30–9.30pm. Moderate–Expensive.

Momoyama, Shop 15, Lower Ground Floor, Jardine House, Connaught Rd, Central ☎ 2845 8773. Jardine House's other Japanese option, this time for the flash and speedy business-lunch brigade. Medium-to-pricey set meals. Open Mon–Sat 11am–3pm & 6.30–10pm. Moderate–Expensive.

Nadaman, Basement 2, *Kowloon Shangri-La*, 64 Mody Rd, Tsim Sha Tsui East ☎ 2721 2111. Traditional, minimalist Japanese dining room where most of the Japanese business clientele tucks in at the *sushi* bar or spends big on the other house specials – like the *kaiseki*, a set dinner of various small, beautifully presented dishes. Open noon–3pm & 6.30–11pm. Expensive.

Tokyo Joe, 16 Lan Kwai Fong, Central ☎ 2525 1889. The designer-refectory look hits Hong Kong: great food and set *sushi* meals served at large pine tables. Open noon–2.30pm & 6.30pm–midnight. Moderate–Expensive.

Unkai, 3rd Floor, *Sheraton Hotel*, 20 Nathan Rd, Tsim Sha Tsui ☎ 2369 1111. If you're going to blow your money on one expensive Japanese meal, it may as

well be somewhere fairly true to its origins. In this case, the chefs are from Osaka and the food is beautifully presented. Open noon–2pm & 6.30–10pm. Expensive.

Yorohachi, 5–6 Lan Kwai Fong, Central ☎ 2524 1251. Small restaurant in the trendy heart of Central serving good *sushi* and other delicately prepared dishes. Book in advance. Open 11am–3pm & 6–11pm. Moderate.

Korean

Nearly all Korean restaurants in Hong Kong feature a "barbecue" (*bulgogi*) as part of the menu – the table contains a grill, over which you cook marinaded slices of meat, fish or seafood; assorted pickles (including *kimchi*, spicy, pickled cabbage), rice and soup come with the meal. One odd feature of many restaurants is the ginseng-flavoured chewing gum handed out when you leave.

Arirang Korean Restaurant, 11th Floor, Food Forum, Times Square, 1 Matheson St, Causeway Bay ☎ 2506 3298; 2nd Floor, The Gateway, 25 Canton Rd, Tsim Sha Tsui ☎ 2956 3288. Dependable restaurant offering the usual Korean specialities.

Korean Restaurant, 4th Floor, 8 King Kwong St, Happy Valley ☎ 2573 6662. Spacious restaurant, well used to *gweilos* who fill the place up at weekends. Ginseng chicken is a speciality, though most stick with the budget-rated barbecues – there's chicken, beef, shrimp and squid, though frog's legs, deer and offal get a look in too. Open 11am–2.30pm & 6–11pm. Inexpensive–Moderate.

Koreana, 55 Paterson St, Causeway Bay ☎ 2577 5145. Decently priced barbecue restaurant with all the standard dishes as well as some interesting vegetable choices and good noodles. Open 11am–11pm. Moderate.

Malaysian and Singaporean

Banana Leaf Curry House, Lockhart House, 440 Jaffe Rd, Wan Chai ☎ 2573 8187; 3rd Floor, Golden Crown Court, 68 Nathan Rd, Tsim Sha Tsui ☎ 2721 4821;

Eating

The restaurants reviewed in this book have been given price categories as follows:
Inexpensive under $150
Moderate $150–300
Expensive $300–500
Very Expensive $500–800+

Eating

The restaurants reviewed in this book have been given price categories as follows:

Inexpensive
under $150
Moderate
$150–300
Expensive
$300–500
Very
Expensive
$500–800+

3rd Floor, 440 Prince Edward Rd (at Lung Kok St), Kowloon City ☎2382 8189. Malaysian and Singaporean standards, served on banana leaves, as is traditional. Curries are notable, too, particularly fish-head curry; pad out your meal with satay, samosas and breads. Note that no alcohol is served at any of the restaurants, but there's plenty of fresh fruit juices. Open 11am–3pm & 6pm–midnight. Inexpensive.

Satay Hut, 1st Floor, Houston Centre, Mody Rd, Tsim Sha Tsui East ☎2723 3628. Authentic satay dishes and other Singaporean staples in a friendly restaurant. Open 11.30am–10.30pm. Moderate.

Mexican

Casa Mexicana, Ground Floor, Victoria Centre, 15 Watson Rd, North Point ☎2566 5560. Ropey Mexican food but everyone comes to get blind on the *margaritas* and beer. Open 11.30am–midnight. Moderate.

La Placita, 13th Floor, Times Square, 1 Matheson St, Causeway Bay ☎2506 3308. With an arcaded interior modelled on a Mexican village square, staff in ponchos, and pastel paint thrown about like it was on special offer, you know you're in themeland. It's the best Mexican food in town (not much of a recommendation, admittedly) and the bar is a good place for a drink. Open noon–midnight. Moderate–Expensive.

Mongolian

Kublai's, 3rd Floor, One Capitol Place, 18 Luard Rd, Wan Chai ☎2529 9117; 53–59 Kimberley Rd, Tsim Sha Tsui ☎2722 0733. Mongolian "barbecue" restaurant: pick your own ingredients – noodles, spices, vegetables, sliced meat and fish, and sauces – and then take it to be cooked. Highly entertaining if there's a crowd, and you can keep going back for more – though the whole affair can be a little rushed at busy times. Open noon–3pm & 6.30–11pm. Moderate.

Spanish and Portuguese

La Bodega, 31 Wyndham St, Central ☎2877 3101. Stylish bar-restaurant that specializes in "Nueva Cocina Española", which means fancy cooking, fancy decor and fancy prices. Daily specials are always worth investigating, and there's a grand wine list, although this can push the cost of a meal skywards. Open noon–midnight. Expensive-Very Expensive.

Lucky Joy Restaurant. Mei Tung House, Mei Tung Estate, Kowloon City ☎2338 5688. Near the old Kai Tak airport site. Specialities of this comfortable and casual place include grilled cuttlefish and roast pig (yes, a whole one). You can eat outside on the roof. Open 11.30am–3pm & 5–11pm. Inexpensive.

Rico's, 44 Robinson Rd, Mid-Levels ☎2840 0937. It's always busy at this homely tapas bar, where you can put together a meal from a score of different bits and pieces – shrimp, croquettes, meatballs, fried squid, spicy potatoes and tortilla. Wash it down with the house wine, not bad and relatively cheap for once. Open noon–midnight. Moderate-Expensive.

Sri Lankan

Club Sri Lanka, Basement, 17 Hollywood Rd (at the Wyndham St end) ☎2526 6559. Sri Lankan restaurant with some fine vegetarian dishes and a different bread baked every day; the food is similar to southern Indian, although it can be highly spiced. There's a help-yourself buffet meal as well as a limited menu. Extra-friendly staff and nice surroundings make this one of Central's better choices. Open noon–2.30pm & 6–11pm. Inexpensive.

Thai

There are some classy Thai places about, especially in Central, but almost without exception the best places are the cheaper restaurants in Kowloon City, near the old Kai Tak airport site – take buses #11 (from Jordan Rd Ferry), #5, #5C and #9 (Star Ferry), or #5K and #5C (Kowloon Station) and get off at Carpenter Road, opposite the abandoned airport terminal.

The Chilli Club, 88 Lockhart Rd, Wan Chai ☎2527 2872. A shade too popular for its own good these days, full of in-the-know *gweilos*, the *Chilli Club* continues to knock out splendid meals on the spicy side. Booking – especially at night – is wise. Open noon–3pm & 6–10.30pm. Inexpensive–Moderate.

Phuket Thai Seafood Grill Club, 30–32 Robinson Rd (entry on Mosque St), Mid-Levels ☎2869 9672. Good-value, noisy, reliable Thai haunt with all the spicy

---

Vegetarian Food

The main problem with being **vegetarian** in Hong Kong is the language barrier in restaurants; often, even when waiters do speak English, they will insist that things like chicken or pork aren't really meat. In Chinese restaurants it's better to say "I eat vegetarian food" (*ngor sik tzai*), or Buddhist monk's food as it's thought of, which is an accepted concept. Even committed Chinese meat-eaters eat strictly vegetarian meals fairly regularly in order to clean out the system and balance their diet, while a fair number of the population are vegetarian for religious reasons, either permanently or on certain religious holidays.

It's fairly easy to stick to vegetarian Chinese food, either eating the mainstream veg-etable, mushroom and beancurd (tofu) dishes on the menu or ordering a regular noo-dle dish without the meat. Bear in mind, though, if you're a purist, that many Chinese dishes start off life with a meat stock. Some strictly vegetarian dishes to order are *lo hon tzai* ("monk's vegetables"; a mixture of mushrooms, vegetables and beancurd) and *bak choy* (Chinese cabbage), usually stir-fried and served with oyster sauce.

To avoid any problems, it's easiest to eat in one of the excellent **Cantonese vege-tarian restaurants**, where the food is based on tofu, which can be shaped into – and made to taste of – almost anything. Several places also specialize in **vegetarian dim sum** (p.239), where all the food looks exactly like its meaty counterpart (you even call it by the same names), but is all strictly vegetarian. In regular *dim sum* restaurants, you'll have a much harder time eating widely and well unless you eat prawns, though the various cakes and puddings are usually harmless enough.

Other than these places, you're best off in the territory's **Indian and Pakistani restaurants** (p.253), which have lots of non-meat choices, at a **pizza** (see "Italian" p.256) place, or a hotel buffet (p.252), which will always have a good salad bar and other vegetarian options. A meal at one of the **Buddhist monasteries** in Hong Kong will also consist of strictly vegetarian food; see especially Lantau (Chapter 5) and the various temples in the New Territories (Chapter 4).

Vegetarian restaurants
The places listed below are completely vegetarian, and are reviewed elsewhere in this chapter.

Bookworm Café, Yung Shue Wan Main St, Lamma; p.235.

Fat Heung Lam, 94 Wellington St, Central; p.242.

Woodlands, Mirror Tower, 61 Mody Rd, Tsim Sha Tsui; p.254.

Healthy Mess, Ground Floor, 51–53 Hennessy Rd, Wan Chai; p.243.

Kung Tak Lam, 31 Yee Wo St, Causeway Bay; p.239.

Vegi-Food Kitchen, 8 Cleveland St, Causeway Bay; p.243.

Eating

favourites. Good fresh fish which you can pick yourself. Open Mon–Fri noon–3pm, 6–11pm, Sat–Sun noon–11pm. Moderate.

Shek O Chinese Thai Seafood Restaurant, near the bus stop, main corner, Shek O ☎2809 4426. On Hong Kong Island's east coast (see p.117 for transport details), this open-air café gets crowded quickly, and deservedly so. Excellent food from an extensive menu, and a fine atmosphere. Open noon–10pm. Inexpensive.

Supatra's, Allied Capital Resources Building, Ice House St, Central ☎2522 5073. Flash setting and decor, as befits the trendy end of town. A good choice of good quality dishes. Open noon–11.30pm. Moderate.

Sweet Basil Thai, 73 Kai Tak Rd, Kowloon City ☎2718 8077. Good, spicy Thai food in friendly surroundings. Open 11.30am–11.30pm. Inexpensive–Moderate.

Thai Lemongrass, California Tower, 30–32 Lan Kwai Fong, Central ☎2905 1688. Chic surroundings and high quality, imaginative Thai food. One of the best in town. Open Mon–Thurs noon–2.30pm, 7–11pm, Fri noon–2.30pm, 7–11.30pm, Sat noon–2.30pm, 6.30pm–3am, Sun 6.30pm–midnight. Expensive–Very Expensive.

Thai Thai, 5th Floor, 90B Stanley Main St, Stanley ☎2813 7818. Friendly Thai restaurant, offering views out over Stanley Bay. They also do takeaways. Open Mon–Fri noon–3pm, 6–11pm, Sat–Sun noon–11pm. Moderate–Expensive.

Wong Chun Chun Thai Restaurant, 70–72 Nga Tsin Wai Rd, Kowloon City ☎2383 4680; 21–23 Prat Ave, Tsim Sha Tsui ☎2721 0099. Bright and clean Thai places serving reasonably priced meals. Open noon–2am. Inexpensive.

Wyndham Street Thai, 34 Wyndham St, Central ☎2869 6216. Probably the best Thai restaurant in town. Superb food in minimalist surroundings. Everything is very fresh. They also do a good-value set lunch. Expensive–Very Expensive.

Vietnamese

Golden Bull Restaurant, Level 1, 17, New World Centre, 18 Salisbury Rd, Tsim Sha Tsui ☎2369 4617. Impressive, top-of-the-range Vietnamese restaurant with approachable staff and a fair choice of dishes. The barbecued prawns are always good or try one of the specials – the "seven kinds of beef", the house platter or, best of all, the mixed meat satay, actually a hot pot in which you cook thinly sliced squid, shrimp, fish, beef, chicken and rice noodles. Open noon–11.30pm. Moderate–Expensive.

Indochine 1929, 2nd Floor, California Tower, Lan Kwai Fong, Central ☎2869 7399. The very elegant *Indochine* serves up some of the tastiest Vietnamese food in the territory. There's a whiff of French colonial style about the place – stuffed snails feature on the menu – and every dish is a winner. Reservations advised. Open Mon–Sat noon–2.30pm & 6–11pm, Sun 6–11pm. Moderate–Expensive.

Perfume River, 89 Percival St, Causeway Bay ☎2576 2240. Ignore the owner's tendency to cover everything in the interior in green paint and this is one of the better Vietnamese restaurants in town. Open 11am–11pm. Inexpensive.

Saigon Beach Restaurant, 66 Lockhart Rd, Wan Chai ☎2529 7823. Good little restaurant that's a draw with young travellers and locals because it sticks to the basics and cooks them well. Open noon–3pm & 6–10pm. Inexpensive.

Vong, *Mandarin Oriental Hotel,* 5 Connaught Rd, Central ☎2825 4028. The *Mandarin's* venture into Vietnamese-French cuisine has met with mixed reviews. Whether you like the style or not it is undoubtedly carried out to the highest standards (as usual in this hotel). Open noon–3pm, 6pm–midnight. Very expensive.

Yuet Hing Yuen, 17 Cannon St, Causeway Bay ☎2832 2863. Popular,

Eating

Special Diets

Some of the Pakistani restaurants in Chungking Mansions advertise themselves as serving **halal** food, as does the occasional Chinese Muslim restaurant.

For **kosher** food, enquire about the kosher kitchen and restaurant at the Ohel Leah synagogue, 76 Robinson Rd, Mid-Levels ☎ 2801 5442, or contact the Jewish Community Centre, 70 Robinson Rd, Mid-Levels ☎ 2801 5440. There's also the *Shalom Grill*, 2nd Floor, Fortune House, 61 Connaught Rd, Central ☎ 2851 6300, serving kosher Middle Eastern food and couscous.

Any other dietary requirements can probably be catered for by the biggest hotel restaurants; it's always worth a phone call. Or check the list of **supermarkets** given under "Markets, supermarkets, bakeries and barbecues" (below) if you want to play safe and buy your own provisions.

busy place, offering good-value, no-frills food. Open 11.30am–10.30pm. Inexpensive.

Markets, supermarkets, bakeries and barbecues

With hot food and snacks so cheap in Hong Kong, there isn't much incentive to buy **picnic food**. There are, however, **supermarkets** right across Hong Kong which may be useful if you're going to use any of the hundreds of **barbecue sites** throughout the territory, if you're on a special diet, or if you simply want to know exactly what it is you're eating. Be warned, though, that for anything recognizably Western, you'll pay a lot more than you would at home.

Markets

A walk around a Cantonese **market** is a sight in itself, and several are detailed in the text, including Hong Kong Island's Central Market (p.75), Sheung Wan market (p.82) and Luen Wo (p.157) and Sheung Shui markets (p.159) in the New Territories. A market is where the bulk of the population buys its fresh food, shopping at least once a day for meat, fish, fruit and vegetables. All the towns and residential buildings, especially in the developments in the New Territories, have a market hall.

They can look a bit intimidating at first, but no one minds you wandering around and checking out the produce. Most food is sold by the **catty**, which

equals 1.3lb or 600g. Prodding and handling **fruit and veg** is almost expected: just pick out the items you want and hand them over. They'll invariably be weighed on an ingenious set of hand-held scales, and, although the metric system is in official use, will almost certainly be priced according to traditional Chinese weights and measures. No one's out to cheat you, but it can help to know some Cantonese numbers and prices. Some stallholders will let you sample some of the more obscure fruit: one to watch for is the durian, a yellow, spiky fruit shaped like a rugby ball, that is fairly pricey and decidedly smelly – very much an acquired taste.

Buying **meat and fish** is also straightforward, though if you're going by sight alone make sure that the pretty fish you're pointing at isn't extremely rare and very expensive. It's perfectly all right to have several things weighed until you find the piece you want. For the best fish, either get to the market early in the morning, or come back in the mid-afternoon when the second catch is delivered. Every market will also have a **cooked meat** stall, selling roast pork, duck and chicken, which can perk up a picnic lunch no end.

Supermarkets

There are plenty of **supermarkets** around, but apart from a couple of notable exceptions they're pricey and concentrate on tinned and packet foods.

The restaurants reviewed in this book have been given price categories as follows:
Inexpensive under $150
Moderate $150–300
Expensive $300–500
Very Expensive $500–800+

Eating

Territory-wide **supermarket chains** include Wellcome and Park 'N' Shop (see below). They're generally open daily from around 8am to 8pm, though stores throughout the territory vary their hours.

TERRITORY-WIDE SUPERMARKETS

Park 'N' Shop: including branches at Basement, The Landmark, Des Voeux Rd, Central; Pedder St, Central; Admiralty Centre, Central.

Wellcome: including branches at The Forum, Exchange Square, Central; 78 Nathan Rd, Tsim Sha Tsui.

SPECIALIST STORES

Big Apple Deli, Shop 105-9, 1st Floor, Harbour Centre, Wan Chai. Small deli/supermarket with a good range of Western foodstuffs – cheese, milk, biscuits, fresh bread, pasta, tinned goods, chocolate. They also have a wine selection.

City'super, Times Square, 1 Matheson St, Causeway Bay. Large western supermarket and delicatessen.

Indian Provision Store, Ground Floor, 65–68, Chungking Mansions, 36–44 Nathan Rd, Tsim Sha Tsui. Indian spices, sweets and pickles as well as tins and dairy products.

Oliver's Delicatessen, 2nd Floor, Prince's Building, Central; Ocean Terminal, Canton Rd, Tsim Sha Tsui. A Mecca for Hong Kong's expat community, stocking bread, wine, cheese, biscuits, meat, and a huge range of other western products.

Sogo, East Point Centre, 555 Hennessy Rd, Causeway Bay. There's a Japanese supermarket inside the department store

– takeaway Japanese snacks and food as well.

Seibu, Basement, Pacific Place, 88 Queensway, Admiralty. Upmarket Japanese food hall, selling top quality fresh produce, alongside everything else you might need.

Bakeries

The bread sold in supermarkets tends to be white and horrible, and you're better off buying it from the **bakeries** you'll find in every market and on most street corners. It'll be substantially the same but will at least be fresher, and costs only a couple of dollars for a small sliced loaf. Brown and wholemeal are usually available only from shops patronized heavily by expats. **Cakes** from bakeries are cheap, too, only a dollar or two for very sweet, rather synthetic creations. More elaborate cream cakes and buns are sold from the *Maxim's* chain of shops, which you'll find in most MTR and KCR stations, as well as at the Star Ferry terminals. If you are interested in cakes that are closer to Western tastes, try the western-style supermarkets and delis.

Barbecues

Almost everywhere of scenic interest you go in Hong Kong (and at some youth hostels and campsites) there are special **barbecue pits** provided in picnic areas. They're inordinately popular and getting the ingredients together for a barbecue isn't difficult. Supermarkets sell fuel, barbecue forks, rubbish bags and all the food, as do kiosks at some of the more enterprising sites; either buy ready-made satay sticks or pick up cuts of meat and fish from the market.

Chapter 8

Nightlife: Bars, Pubs and Clubs

If you're not making eating your sole evening's entertainment, then Hong Kong has plenty to occupy you, lots of it carrying on until the small hours. There's no shortage of **bars, pubs and clubs** in which you can while away the night and although several of the pubs are, as you might expect, British in style – complete with homesick expats, horse brasses and dartboards – lots of other bars are either American or Australian, with food and drink to match. And because Hong Kong doesn't have so much of that desperately trendy edge that bedevils London and New York, most of them are good, down-to-earth fun. That doesn't mean they're scruffy. Some are, but plenty of others are expensively decorated and dripping with sophistication, so if you're planning to go out much, bring (or buy) clothes that won't wilt under a supercilious Hong Kong glare. Most of the newer, trendier bars and clubs are in Central, especially **Lan Kwai Fong** and **SoHo**, the chic new eating and drinking area around the Mid-Levels escalator between Lyndhurst Terrace and Robinson Rd, where new bars and restaurants open almost every week. There are other possibilities at **Tsim Sha Tsui**, whose well established pubs and discos are much favoured by travellers staying in the nearby guest houses. Traditionally, **Wan Chai** has played host to the less refined, late-opening, hard-drinking dens, although this started to

change in the mid-1990s when the withdrawal from the colony of the British Army – the area's traditional patrons – combined with rising rents in Central encouraged more sophisticated establishments to move into the area.

Most bars are **open** from around lunchtime until well after midnight; some, especially in Lan Kwai Fong and Wan Chai, stay open until breakfast, and a few keep serving drinks right around the clock, particularly at the weekend. If there's a DJ or it's a **club night**, you might have to pay to get in; from around $60 at the smaller places to $150–200 at the flash designer clubs. Some include a drink or two in the entry price, and lots only charge an entrance fee on the busy Friday and Saturday nights. Many bars also put on **live music**, usually pseudo-folk (singer-guitarists mangling "Yesterday") or jazz: these are picked out in the lists below, but for fuller details of live music, turn to the following chapter.

The **music** played is generally mainstream European and American pop and dance music, although there's a minuscule Indie scene, while plenty of places also play Canto-pop (see "Live Music", p.273), and others have Japanese-style karaoke lounges. **Rave culture** made a belated appearance in Hong Kong, but is going strong now with several bars and other venues hosting seasonal and one-off party nights – keep an eye out for flyers and check local **listings magazines**

Nightlife: Bars, Pubs and Clubs

Alcoholic Drinks

The most readily available alcoholic beverage is **beer** – lager style and served ice cold. For years, the main brews were San Miguel (brewed in the territory for fifty years) and (better) Tsingtao, the latter a sharp Chinese beer made originally from a German recipe; where these weren't available, there was locally brewed Carlsberg. However, changes to the duty charged on imported alcohol in 1994 opened the floodgates and bars and restaurants (and lots of supermarkets) now sell British bitter, Guinness and untold other foreign beers, designer or otherwise, draft or bottled, Belgian to Venezuelan. There's even a Hong Kong-based microbrewery, selling decent unadulterated, locally produced ale: look for Crooked Island Ale in bars. In a supermarket, beer costs from around $7–8 a small can. In most restaurants, it's around $20–25 for the same can; while in bars and pubs this can rise dramatically – anything from $35 upwards for a small bottle, $45–60 for a draft pint.

Drinking **wine** in a bar or restaurant is similarly expensive, starting at around $25–45 a glass, $200 a bottle for even the most average of wines – considerably more for anything halfway decent. Buy your own in a supermarket, and you'll pay at least $100 for basic French plonk – the alternatives are mostly Australasian, although South African and South American wines are increasingly well represented. You can get wine from the Chinese mainland (Dynasty is a common label) but it's not terribly drinkable. Most internationally known **spirits** are available in bars and restaurants, again at a price. Cheaper, though much nastier and guaranteeing a miserable morning after, are the various brands of Chinese rice wine, the cheaper examples of which are best left for cooking, or stripping paint.

(*BC* and *HK Magazine*) for an accurate rundown of what's happening where.

The main drawback is that pubbing and clubbing – or at least drinking – is comparatively **expensive** and you'll need a fairly substantial amount of money to party every night (see the box above). The main thing to watch out for in this respect is the prevalence of **happy hour**, where you'll get two-for-one drinks. They generally last a lot more than an hour: some time between 5pm and 8pm is usual (though some places sell cheap drinks all afternoon); many places also try to lure you back in with the same deal at around 11pm–1am. Blackboards and notices in pubs and bars have details, and check the reviews below. Finally, it's worth noting that in the newer, trendier bars you're expected to **tip the barstaff**; ten percent will cover it.

Lan Kwai Fong

Beirut, 39 D'Aguilar St ☎ 2804 6611. Lebanese restaurant with a downstairs bar that opens onto the street. There's enough elbow space and style to attract a more-than-usually-sophisticated LKF crowd. Open noon–midnight. There's also a branch at Shing Yip Building, 48–50 Lockhart Rd, Wan Chai ☎ 2865 7271.

Bit Point, 31 D'Aguilar St ☎ 2523 7436. German bar with decent beer and schnapps. It throws its doors open on summer evenings; otherwise, it can be a claustrophobically male hang-out. Open noon–2am.

California, Ground Floor, California Tower, 24–26 Lan Kwai Fong ☎ 2521 1345. Expensive American bar and restaurant with a tiny dance floor on which the local yuppies strut their stuff. It's been around for too long to be at the cutting edge of anything, but can still be fun on occasion. Open Mon, Tues & Thurs noon–11pm, Wed, Fri & Sat noon–4am.

Club 64, Ground Floor, 12–14 Wing Wah Lane ☎ 2523 2801. Down-at-heel, back-alley drinking den playing blues and rock to an enthusiastic, vaguely Indie crowd most nights, many of whom spill out onto the pavement later. Drinks are affordable and happy hour is a long 11am–8pm. Open 11am–2am.

Club 97, 9 Lan Kwai Fong ☎2810 9333. A popular ground-floor disco, with a small dance floor and good Western rock and pop. Mobbed at the weekend, when there's a cover charge, but free and emptier during the week. Mon–Thurs & Sun 9pm–3am, Fri & Sat 6pm–5am.

La Dolce Vita, 9 Lan Kwai Fong ☎2810 9333. Too-happening-for-words Italian bar open to the street, this is very much where the beautiful people, their hangers on and aspirants congregate, sipping coffee and grappa, and contemplating the bizarre red satin nippled backdrop. Late-night dancing is rather less chic, with 70s and 80s disco trash the usual ticket. Happy hour 4–8pm. Open Mon–Thurs & Sun 11am–2am, Fri & Sat 11am–4am.

F-Stop, 14 Lan Kwai Fong ☎2868 9607. Self-consciously cool place with regular live bands and beer promotions. Open 11.30am–2.30pm & 4.30pm–12.30am.

Le Jardin, 10 Wing Wah Lane ☎2526 2717. Cosy alfresco bar with hit-and-miss service, set back from the hustle of Lan Kwai Fong. Nearly always full despite being a little difficult to find – head for the staircase at the end of the lane, after the bend. Look out for the Elvis impersonator. Mon–Thurs 9am–2am, Fri & Sat 9am–4am.

The Jazz Club, 2nd Floor, 34–36 D'Aguilar St ☎2845 8477. The narrow bar is open to non-members, who can drink to the jazz sounds coming from the video CD provided for customers' use. Happy hour 6–9pm. Open Mon–Thurs 5pm–2am, Fri & Sat 5pm–3am, Sun 7pm–2am; also see "Live Music", p.275.

Landau's, 1 On Hing Building, On Hing Terrace, Central ☎2827 7901. Reasonably priced European-style bar and restaurant. Attracts local yuppies and tourists alike. Open 9am–2am.

Mad Dogs, Century Square, 1 D'Aguilar St ☎2810 1000. Unashamedly British pub, with pictures of Queen Victoria, British

Nightlife: Bars, Pubs and Clubs

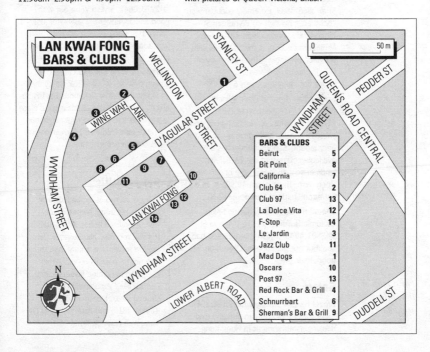

LAN KWAI FONG
BARS & CLUBS

BARS & CLUBS	
Beirut	5
Bit Point	8
California	7
Club 64	2
Club 97	13
La Dolce Vita	12
F-Stop	14
Le Jardin	3
Jazz Club	11
Mad Dogs	1
Oscars	10
Post 97	13
Red Rock Bar & Grill	4
Schnurrbart	6
Sherman's Bar & Grill	9

Nightlife: Bars, Pubs and Clubs

For a map of the SoHo area, see p.93.

beer on draught and comfy seating. It mostly attracts a business-district clientele, all of whom pack in for the 4–8pm and 10–11pm happy hours. Open Mon–Thurs 7am–2am, Fri & Sat 7am–3am, Sun 10am–2am.

Oscars, 2 Lan Kwai Fong ☎2804 6561. Crush-box bar-restaurant with propellor-blade fans and a few stools and seats for early arrivals. Everyone else piles outside for the Fong's good-natured street party, where it's standing room only and barely that at times. Open Mon–Sat 11.30am–2am, Sun 11.30am–midnight.

Post 97, Upper Ground Floor, 9 Lan Kwai Fong ☎2810 9333. The upstairs brasserie-bar in the *Nineteen 97* complex features sink-in-and-slouch chairs, arty surroundings, great coffee, all-day Sunday brunch and a decent list of beers and wines. Not a lot more to ask of life really. Happy hour is 5–7pm. Open Mon–Thurs & Sun 8.30am–1am, Fri 8.30am–4am, Sat 24hr.

Red Rock Bar & Grill, 57–59 Wyndham St ☎2868 3884. Extremely cool bar – so cool there's no sign on Wyndham St – behind the Ashoka Indian Restaurant. Minimalist decor and chic clientele, with a terrace overlooking the hurly-burly of LKF. The restaurant area becomes a dance floor later on. Open 6–11.30pm.

Schnurrbart, Ground Floor, Winner Building, 27 D'Aguilar St ☎2523 4700. German bar with bar stools, herring and sausage snacks, and some of the best beer around. Serious headaches are available courtesy of the 25 different kinds of schnapps – try the butterscotch. Open Mon–Thurs noon–12.30am, Fri & Sat noon–1.30am, Sun 6pm–12.30am.

Sherman's Bar & Grill, Ground Floor, California Building, 34–36 D'Aguilar St ☎2801 4946. Stylish open-fronted bar; cool but not pretentious. Open Mon–Sat noon–midnight.

SoHo

Brezel Haus, 23 Hollywood Rd ☎2541 5449. Proof that you can find any kind of drinking establishment in Hong Kong –

including a German *Bierkeller*. Serves German beer, snacks and food. Open noon–2am.

Club 1911, 27 Staunton St ☎2810 6681. Ignore the "members only" sign. This is one of SoHo's best established and most popular joints, offering comfortable seats and reasonable quiet if you want to talk. Not a bargain, but nowhere in this area is. Open Mon–Sat 5pm–midnight, Sun 5–11pm.

Dublin Jack, 37 Cochrane St ☎2543 0081. Irish pub, just under the escalator exit for Lyndhurst Terrace. Draft Guinness, Irish food, reasonable prices, occasional music, and room to stand outside. All this and well over a hundred different varieties of whiskey too. Happy hour noon–8pm. Open Mon–Fri 8am–2am, Sat–Sun 11am–2am.

The Globe, 39 Hollywood Rd ☎2543 1941. Cosy bar serving snacks. Popular with locals after work – can get rowdier later on.

Petticoat Lane, 1 Tung Wah Lane ☎2973 0642. Stylish wine bar with good snacks under the escalator just above Lyndhurst Terrace. Baroque hangings, topiary and candles lend atmosphere.

Staunton's Wine Bar and Café, 10–12 Staunton St ☎2973 6611. Right by the escalator, this rather cavernous bar fills up quickly in the evening and is a good place to gather before checking out neighbouring restaurants. Mon–Fri 11am–midnight, Sat & Sun 9am–midnight.

Gay Nightlife

The gay scene has expanded since the laws regarding homosexuality were liberalized in line with Britain's. It's still very discreet, however: there are few recognized venues, and these may not necessarily be exclusively gay. Current opinion favours bars in Central like *Propaganda* (Lower Ground Floor, 1 Hollywood Rd ☎2868 1316) and *Petticoat Lane* (1 Tung Wah Lane ☎2973 0642).

Central

Bank Bar at Portico, Basement, Citibank Plaza, 3 Garden Rd ☎ 2523 8893. High-priced drinking hole for city types drowning their sorrows. Best in the early evening. Open noon–11pm.

Bentley's Oyster Bar & Restaurant, Basement B4, Prince's Building, 10 Chater Rd ☎ 2868 0881. By day an oyster bar where you can have half a dozen of the finest shucked oysters with a glass of champagne for $350, in the evening an atmospheric bar popular with young bankers from nearby HSBC and Standard Chartered. Open 11.30am–3pm (oyster bar), 11.30am–10.30pm (restaurant and bar).

Captain's Bar, *Mandarin Oriental Hotel*, 5 Connaught Rd ☎ 2521 0111. Some say this is the only bar worth drinking in in Hong Kong. Certainly it's full of real movers and shakers. Knowledgeable bar staff can provide you with every cocktail known to man and the atmosphere is lively. Excellent Filipino band play nightly 9pm–2am. Not cheap. Open 11am–2.30am.

Cossacks, Basement, *Ritz Carlton*, 3 Connaught Rd ☎ 2869 0328. Full marks for a hotel bar actually worth drinking in. Russian theme bar with vodka, naturally enough, playing a significant part in most people's downfall. Good one-nighter club events, too. Mon–Fri 12.30pm–1am, Sat 6pm–1am.

The Gallery & Pier One, Shop 12, Basement, Jardine House, 1 Connaught Rd ☎ 2526 3061. Dark, nautical surroundings – oak barrels, ropes and maritime bric-a-brac – for this basement British pub with a city clientele and Filipino musicians struggling with "Smoke on the Water". Open Mon–Sat 8am–midnight.

Judgement AD, Bank of America Tower, 12 Harcourt Rd ☎ 2521 0309. Cavernous late-opening club playing techno to a free-spending city crowd; Tuesday nights can be wild. Open 5pm–4am.

LA Café, Ground Floor, Lippo Centre, Queensway ☎ 2526 6863. American designer bar: Harley Davidson in the bar, TVs in the toilets, trendies lurking in the corners. Friday and Saturday are club nights – usually some mix of retro, grunge, Indie and alternative sounds. Open daily 10.30am–1.30am, Fri & Sat 9.30am–3.30am.

Pomeroy's, Level 3, 349 Pacific Place, 88 Queensway, Admiralty ☎ 2523 4772. Not a bad stab at a London wine bar (though it lacks the genteel shabbiness of the *Rumpole of the Bailey* original). There's a decent, if predictably expensive, wine list, and British food and salad

Nightlife: Bars, Pubs and Clubs

For a map of Central, see p.68.

Bars with Views

The places below all offer views while you drink – mostly of the harbour, though the *Flying Machine* gives you a view over the old airport runway and the eastern harbour. Those on the Peak can be covered in mist in bad weather. Some have already been covered in the listings, but where they haven't (especially if they're hotel bars), you can expect to pay more than usual for your drink.

Cafe Deco, Level 1 & 2, Peak Galleria, 118 Peak Rd, The Peak ☎ 2849 5111. The terrace is particularly pleasant in hot weather.

Felix 28th Floor, *Peninsula Hotel*, Sailsbury Rd, Tsim Sha Tsui ☎ 2920 2888.

Flying Machine, 14th Floor, *Regal Airport Hotel*, 38 Sa Po Rd, Kowloon City ☎ 2718 0333.

Oasis Lounge, 8th Floor, *Renaissance Harbour View Hotel*, 70 Mody Rd, Tsim Sha Tsui East ☎ 2721 5161.

Peak Café, 121 Peak Rd, Victoria Peak ☎ 2899 7868.

Sky, 42nd Floor, The Centre, 99 Queen's Rd, Central ☎ 2186 6868.

Sky Lounge, 18th Floor, *Sheraton*, 20 Nathan Rd, Tsim Sha Tsui ☎ 2369 1111.

Nightlife: Bars, Pubs and Clubs

bar on offer all day. Open 9am–midnight.

Trattoria Restaurant & Bar, Ground Floor, The Landmark, Des Voeux Rd, Central ☎ 2524 0111. Modern, comfortable Italian-style restaurant and bar patronized by local yuppies wanting a quiet conversation. Offers a reasonable selection of wine by the glass and free happy hour nibbles.

Wyndham Street Deli, Ground Floor, 36 Wyndham St ☎ 2522 3499. Primarily a restaurant/deli but if you want to share a bottle of wine and perhaps some nibbles this is a civilized place. Good wine selection at – for Hong Kong – reasonable prices.

Wan Chai

Wall Street, 114–120 Lockhart Rd ☎ 2529 7702. Part of the Wan Chai new wave, *Wall Street* wouldn't look out of place in Lan Kwai Fong: open-fronted, mirror-and-marble bar packed with city types and cool dudes, microbrew beers on tap, decent Cal-Ital food, and dance and jazz after hours upstairs. Happy hour 4–9pm. Open 9.30am–3am.

Beer Castle, 15–19 Luard Rd ☎ 2527 7211. A barn of a drinking den with friendly staff but an unpredictably rambunctious clientele whose main interest is the maintenance of high alcohol levels. Open Mon–Sat 11am–6am, Sun 6pm–4am.

Big Apple, 20 Luard Rd ☎ 2529 3461. The hippest place in town at 4am on Sunday morning, when spaced-out socialites, chemically fuelled stockbrokers and Eurotrash mix it on the crowded dance floor – most of them are still there at 6am. During daylight, and up until midnight, it's a rather tame bar. Open Mon–Fri noon–5am, Sat & Sun 2pm–6am.

Carnegie's, 53–55 Lockhart Rd ☎ 2866 6289. Noise level means conversation here is only possible by flash cards, and once it's packed hordes of punters keen

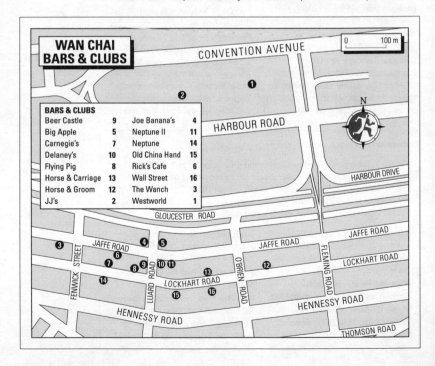

WAN CHAI BARS & CLUBS

BARS & CLUBS			
Beer Castle	9	Joe Banana's	4
Big Apple	5	Neptune II	11
Carnegie's	7	Neptune	14
Delaney's	10	Old China Hand	15
Flying Pig	8	Rick's Cafe	6
Horse & Carriage	13	Wall Street	16
Horse & Groom	12	The Wanch	3
JJ's	2	Westworld	1

to revel the night away fight for dancing space on the bar. Home of the much talked about topless barman on a Wednesday night; occasional riotous club nights, too, and regular live music. Open 11am–3am, often later.

Delaney's, 2nd Floor, One Capital Place, 18 Luard Rd ☎2804 2880. Take the elevator up to the second floor to reach this extremely popular re-creation of a Dublin pub, complete with live traditional music every night, *Guinness* flowing like water and loud, red-faced expats. Drinks are expensive. There's another branch in the Basement, Mary Building, 71–77 Peking Rd in Tsim Sha Tsui. Open Mon–Thurs & Sun noon–2am, Fri & Sat noon–3am.

Flying Pig, 2nd Floor, 81–85 Lockhart Rd ☎2865 3730. Extremely boisterous and young Wan Chai weekend party venue. A must if you've ever wondered what dancing in an overcrowded aeroplane to disco trash would be like. Weekdays are much quieter and, dare it be said, much nicer. Open Mon–Thurs 11.30am–3am, Fri & Sat 11.30am–4am, Sun 3.30pm–2am.

Horse & Carriage, 117 Lockhart Rd ☎2529 6914. Old-style Wan Chai hangout with very cheap food and budget drinks during the 11am–8pm happy hour. Open Mon–Sat 11am–6am, Sun 7.30pm–6am.

Horse and Groom, 161 Lockhart Rd ☎2519 7001. Recently smartened-up pub worth visiting for its inexpensive food. Open Mon–Sat 10.30am–4.30am, Sun 7pm–4am.

JJ's, *Grand Hyatt*, 1 Harbour Rd ☎2588 1234. Classy mainstream disco with a smart dress code, two bars, snooker and darts. There's live music every night from the (usually not bad) house band except Sunday, and a stiff cover charge. Open Mon–Thurs 5.30pm–2am, Fri until 3am, Sat 4am.

Joe Banana's, 23 Luard Rd ☎2529 1811. Lively, unsophisticated American bar with a late disco, occasional live music and marathon weekend opening hours; happy hour 11am–9pm. You need to be (or look) 21 and there's a

strict door policy – men need a shirt with a collar; non-drinkers will require tolerance and understanding. Open Mon–Thurs 11.30am–5am, Fri & Sat 11.30am–6am, Sun 5pm–5am.

Neptune, Basement, 54–62 Lockhart Rd ☎2527 5276; **Neptune II**, 98–108 Jaffe Rd ☎2865 3808. Dingy but good-natured club, the backdrop for mostly Western pop, interspersed with bouts of the Filipino house band playing cover versions. The clientele is mainly Filipina, too – which means significant numbers of sad Western men on the prowl. Open 6pm–7am.

Old China Hand, 104 Lockhart Rd ☎2527 9174. Pub for hard-core drinkers, hung-over clubbers (who come for breakfast) and those with a taste for formica surfaces. Open Mon–Thurs 7am–2am, Fri & Sat 24hr, Sun 9am–1am.

Rick's Café, 78–82 Jaffe Rd ☎2528 1812. Rowdy bar with a reputation – primarily, it seems, for being a cattle market and playing naff music. Open 11am–2am, Fri & Sat until 5am.

The Wanch, 54 Jaffe Rd ☎2861 1621. Another venue for all those party animals who know the words to various 1960s song classics and want to sing along – loudly. Open daily 11am–1am, Fri & Sat until 4am.

Westworld, 4th Floor, *Renaissance Harbour View Hotel*, 1 Harbour Rd ☎2824 0380. Glitzy dance club that's visually and financially extravagant – a decidedly non-Canto-pop experience. Open 9.30pm–3am, Thurs–Sat until 4am.

Causeway Bay

Dicken's Bar, Lower Ground Floor, *Excelsior Hotel*, 281 Gloucester Rd ☎2894 8888. One of the few decent hotel bars, this also features regular jazz sessions. Mon–Thurs & Sun 11am–2am, Fri & Sat 11am–3am.

The Jump, 7th Floor, Plaza Two, 463 Lockhart Rd ☎2832 9007. Entertainment is split between the small dance floor and the performance art of the bar ten-

**Nightlife:
Bars, Pubs
and Clubs**

**Nightlife:
Bars, Pubs
and Clubs**

ders. Its dentist's chair has been the scene of notorious episodes in the past – notably involving the England football squad; lie back and have drink poured straight down your throat. An office-party favourite. Open Mon–Wed noon–2am, Thurs–Sat noon–5am.

New China Max, 11th Floor, Times Square, 1 Matheson St ☎ 2506 2282. This has been through so many name changes recently the staff are getting dizzy, but the theme remains the same: in-your-face, funky Asian interior where Thai elephants and Vietnamese statues rub shoulders, great central bar, good restaurant and dance floor. Live bands and wired DJs complete the set-up. Open noon–2am.

La Placita, 13th Floor, Times Square, 1 Matheson St ☎ 2506 3308. The domed, horseshoe-shaped bar in this Mexican restaurant (see p.258) is a decent Times Square venue. Prices are spot on at happy hour (5–7.30pm) for splashing out on Mexican beers or *margaritas* – tortilla chips with salsa and the dulcet tones of the Filipino *mariachi* band are included free. Open noon–midnight.

Shooters 52, 13th Floor, Times Square, 1 Matheson St ☎ 2506 2626. Ersatz American bar and grill, mightily popular

with young execs. There's NFL on TV, but no good reason to drink here except during happy hour (Mon–Sat 4.30–8pm): no self-respecting barman would wear the "humourous" buttons sported by all the staff. Open Mon–Thurs & Sun 11am–midnight, Fri & Sat 11am–2am.

TOTT (Talk Of The Town), 34th Floor, *Excelsior Hotel*, 281 Gloucester Rd ☎ 2894 8888. Indifferent food but excellent bar with live band nightly and happy hour 5–8pm.

Tsim Sha Tsui

Bahama Mama's, 4–5 Knutsford Terrace ☎ 2368 2121. Beach-bar theme and outdoor terrace that prompts party crowd antics. It's all right as a mere bar, but for the best crack, stump up the cover charge and come along on club nights where a mixed music policy offers everything from Garage to World. Open Mon–Thurs 6pm–3am, Fri & Sat 6pm–5am, Sun 6pm–2am.

The Catwalk, *New World Hotel*, 22 Salisbury Rd ☎ 2369 4111. Mirrors and chrome and bland Western pop, or salsa and funk, depending on the night – which doesn't seem to have prevented it from acquiring a reputation as a Triad hang-out. Free midweek; steep cover

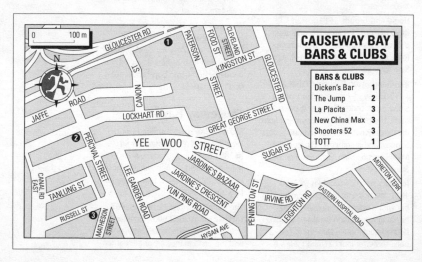

**CAUSEWAY BAY
BARS & CLUBS**

BARS & CLUBS	
Dicken's Bar	1
The Jump	2
La Placita	3
New China Max	3
Shooters 52	3
TOTT	1

Hostess Clubs

Hong Kong is notorious for its plethora of hostess clubs, or "girlie bars", which the HKTA tries hard to push as a tourist experience. Frankly, they're pathetic places for pathetic patrons, exploitative in every way, whose sleazy offers of "one drink $50" are distinctly worth resisting. Still, whatever your feelings about them, some have almost entered into Hong Kong legend. *Bottoms Up* (14 Hankow Rd, Tsim Sha Tsui) is a case in point, famous simply because a long time ago parts of the James Bond film *The Man With the Golden Gun* were shot there. *Red Lips* (1a Lock Rd, Tsim Sha Tsui) is notorious for the advanced age of its hostesses, most of whom are over sixty. And *Club BBoss* (New Mandarin Plaza, 14 Science Museum Rd, Tsim Sha Tsui East) is reputedly the largest hostess club in the world, an enormous, super-plush haunt, where a full-sized Rolls Royce-shaped model car drives you to your table. It was forced to change its name – from *Club Volvo* – after losing a court action brought by Volvo cars about the use of the name. The club argued, unsuccessfully, that the name was merely a transliteration of its Chinese name, Dai Fu Ho, or "big wealthy tycoon".

Nightlife: Bars, Pubs and Clubs

charge Thurs, Fri & Sat. Open 9pm–3am.

Dan Ryan's Chicago Grill, Shop 200, Ocean Terminal, Canton Rd ☎2735 6111. American-style restaurant and a good, friendly place to come for a quick beer, close to the Star Ferry.

Falcon, Basement, *Royal Garden Hotel*, 69 Mody Rd ☎2721 5215. Posh surroundings and mainstream Canto-pop for the well-heeled clientele. Open Mon–Thurs 9.30pm–2am & Fri–Sun 9pm–3am.

Gripps, *Hong Kong Hotel*, Canton Rd ☎2113 3114. Restaurant and bar featuring quality rock n' roll bands.

Hard Rock Café, 100 Canton Rd ☎2377 8118. Live bands playing cover versions and mainstream rock and pop keep the dance floor busy. The music starts at 10.30pm and there's a cover charge. Open 10.30am–2am.

Jousters II, 19–23 Hart Ave ☎2723 0022. Ludicrous drinking venue – mock medieval interior, suits of armour, coats of arms and other baronial trappings, washed down with loud rock music and very cheap drinks right up until 9pm. Open Mon–Thurs 3pm–2am, Fri & Sat 3pm–3am, Sun 6pm–2am.

Kangaroo Pub, 1st Floor, 35 Haiphong Rd ☎2376 0083. An old favourite, popular with travellers – split-level Australian pub, with windows overlooking the bottom of Kowloon Park. Australian beer, sports on the video, a fine jukebox and snacks or a full menu in the restaurant. Happy hour 4–7pm. Open 11am–3am.

Mad Dogs Kowloon, 32 Nathan Rd ☎2301 2222. More entertaining than the Central branch, this basement pub elevates serious drinking to an art form. Live musicians kick off the evening proceedings, which degenerate later on as guest DJs whip up the beer monsters. Great fun. Happy hour 4–7pm, plus two-for-one deals most nights on selected drinks. Mon–Thurs 8am–2am, Fri–Sun 8am–4am.

Ned Kelly's Last Stand, 11a Ashley Rd ☎2376 0562. Dark Australian bar with great live trad jazz after 9pm; good beer and meaty Aussie food served at the tables. It's a real favourite with travellers and good fun – after 9pm you'll be lucky to get a seat. Open 11.45am–1.45am.

Sky Lounge, 18th Floor, *Sheraton Hotel*, 20 Nathan Rd ☎2369 1111. Marvellous city and harbour views in stylish surroundings; dress up for the impeccable service, and free nibbles, accompanied by nightly crooners and instrumentalists. It's cheaper before 8pm, after which there's a steep minimum charge per person. Open Mon–Thurs & Sun 4pm–1am, Fri & Sat 11am–2am.

Nightlife: Bars, Pubs and Clubs

Someplace Else, Basement, *Sheraton Hotel*, 20 Nathan Rd ☎2369 1111. The *Sheraton*'s other bar (entered at the junction with Middle Rd) is much more accessible – an upmarket singles' bar, whose large, rowdy two-floor bar-restaurant has live music, free popcorn nibbles, Tex-Mex and Asian snacks and a good cocktail list. Happy hour 5–7pm. Open 11am–2am.

Elsewhere

Beaches, 92b Stanley Main St, Stanley Village ☎2813 7313. Expat bar-restaurant-disco haunt which pounds out 60s and 70s sounds nightly. Open until 2am.

Cafe Deco, Level 1 & 2, Peak Galleria, 118 Peak Rd, The Peak ☎2849 5111. Stupendous views from the picture windows and great Deco surroundings make this one of the island's highlights. Come for a meal, or just a drink; stop and listen to the jazz band. Open Mon–Thurs & Sun 10am–midnight, Fri & Sat 10am–1am.

Visage Too, 411–413 Shek O Village ☎2809 2129. The coolest bar on the island's south side, with staff as laid-back as the customers, snacky food and flexible opening hours. Live music, too, on occasions. Mon–Fri 8pm–1am, Sat 3pm–1am, Sun noon–1am.

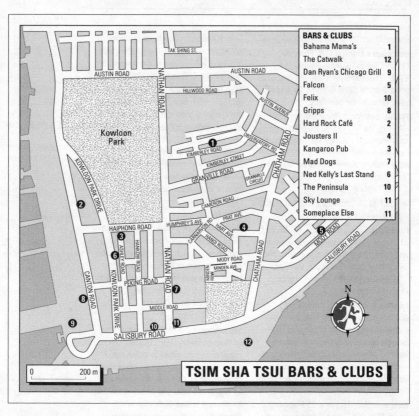

BARS & CLUBS

Bahama Mama's	1
The Catwalk	12
Dan Ryan's Chicago Grill	9
Falcon	5
Felix	10
Gripps	8
Hard Rock Café	2
Jousters II	4
Kangaroo Pub	3
Mad Dogs	7
Ned Kelly's Last Stand	6
The Peninsula	10
Sky Lounge	11
Someplace Else	11

TSIM SHA TSUI BARS & CLUBS

Chapter 9

Live Music

Hong Kong is never the first place that touring Western bands think of, but even so the **live music** scene has picked up considerably over the last couple of years. Venues, however, remain few: apart from the Hong Kong Coliseum, Hong Kong Stadium and the Queen Elizabeth Stadium, where the megastars play, there's no real middle-ranking concert hall for rock and pop music. If you're in Hong Kong during a quiet period for Western bands, check to see if any of the big names in the home-grown pop music scene are playing:

Canto-pop, a Chinese-language version of Western pop ballads and disco music, is easily the most popular music in Hong Kong. Its origins lie in the Cantonese movie musicals of the 1950s and 1960s, whose soundtracks became enormously popular in postwar Hong Kong. Until the 1970s, however, most true pop music in Hong Kong was either imported from the West or from Taiwan, whose Mandarin pop singers were among the first to receive star treatment. Sam Hui, in the mid-1970s, was the first Hong Kong-based artist to mix Cantonese lyrics with Western pop music – a style that quickly became known as Canto-pop. To Western ears, it's often fairly bland stuff – ballads are easily the most popular song form – but to the practitioners it's anything but straightforward. The nine tones in the Cantonese language cause major problems, since they limit the expressiveness that

singers can put into the songs; singing in Mandarin is actually much easier.

There's also a thriving local **jazz** scene, based around regular gigs in pubs and clubs, while many bars offer evening punters what is euphemistically referred to as **folk** music. You'll never see anyone very exciting, but if all you want to do is drink to the strains of Eagles cover versions, there's plenty of opportunity. Finally, most of the large **hotels** feature resident bands and visiting "international artists" in their bars – usually from the Philippines. It's invariably mood music and crooning as an accompaniment to expensive cocktail-sipping.

The choice of **Western classical** music is rather more limited – certainly when it comes to local musicians and orchestras. Hong Kong is, however, well established on the international touring circuit, and because of the limited interest in Western classical music you can often get last-minute tickets to see world-class artists when they're in town.

Hong Kong also offers plenty of opportunities to listen to **Chinese classical** music, not only Chinese opera but also concerts featuring traditional Chinese instruments, which most Westerners find rather easier on the ears than the opera.

To find out **what's on**, look in the free listings magazines *BC* and *HK Magazine*, available at many of the venues listed below and at bars and restaurants, particularly in and around

Live Music

Tickets for concerts at major venues such as the Hong Kong Coliseum and Queen Elizabeth Stadium can be booked through URBTIX on ☎2734 9009. For full details, see p.277.

Lan Kwai Fong, and SoHo. The *South China Morning Post* also has a daily "What's On" page (which lists the hotel-bar music in detail) and a weekly "Gig Guide", published every Friday.

Rock and pop

Outside the big venues, less well-known bands tend to appear in bars and pubs, or are served up as PAs ("personal appearances" singing or miming to backing tapes) in one or two of the clubs. You'll find details of forthcoming events in the local press, or contact the places listed below direct. Ticket prices vary, but you'll usually pay $50–100 for local bands and second-rank visiting groups and artists, more like $400–700 for someone famous.

BB's, Ground Floor, 114–120 Lockhart Rd, Wan Chai ☎2529 7702. Well-known bar, popular with locals. Live rock music 11pm–3am on Thursdays and Saturdays.

Bruce Lee Café, 22 Robinson Rd, Mid-Levels ☎2525 3977. Small cafe dedicated to the deceased Kung Fu star. Different bands every night.

Carnegies, Ground Floor, 53–55 Lockhart Rd, Wan Chai ☎2866 6289. Regular gigs by local acts; usually no cover charge.

The Dublin Jack, 37 Cochrane St, Central ☎2543 0081. Irish pub with live rock and pop.

Fringe Club, Ice House St, Central ☎2521 7251. Rock and pop gigs by local bands and visiting artistes; Saturday night is open-mike night when anyone can have a go, using the club's equipment – this is not always as entertaining as it sounds.

F-Stop, Ground Floor, 14 Lan Kwai Fong, Central ☎2525 5445. Regular rock n' roll acts. Ring for details.

Hard Rock Café, 100 Canton Rd, Tsim Sha Tsui ☎2302 0375. A live band every night from 10.30pm, with an occasional name act to thrill the crowds.

Hong Kong Coliseum, 9 Cheong Wan Rd, Hung Hom, Kowloon ☎2355 7233. Fairly regular performances by major international rock and pop bands, and lengthy concert series by Canto-pop superstars.

Hong Kong Stadium, 55 Eastern Hospital Rd, Causeway Bay ☎2895 7895. Very occasional gigs by megastars, although the organisers seem increasingly uninterested. Elton John cancelled when they insisted the audience wear gloves to keep the noise of clapping down – this in one of the world's noisiest cities.

New China Max, 11th Floor, Times Square, 1 Matheson Rd, Causeway Bay ☎2506 2282/4471. Mixed music, but generally enough R & B and rock 'n roll (with bands every night) to keep things moving; no cover charge either.

Queen Elizabeth Stadium, 18 Oi Kwan Rd, Wan Chai ☎2591 1347. Major rock and pop bands.

The Viceroy, 2nd Floor Sun Hung Kai Centre, 30 Harbour Rd, Wanchai ☎2827 7777. Popular venue hosting everything from salsa to disco. Call for details.

Folk

Entrance to all these bars and pubs is free, but you must expect to buy a drink or two.

Cinta 2, 69 Jaffe Rd, Wan Chai ☎2529 4183. Filipino singers after 9pm.

Cinta Restaurant and Lounge, *Hotel New Harbour*, 8–10 Fenwick St, Wan Chai ☎2527 1199. Popular with Filipina *amahs*.

Delaney's, 2nd Floor, One Capital Place, 18 Luard Rd, Wan Chai ☎2804 2880; Basement, Mary Building, 71–77 Peking Rd, Tsim Sha Tsui ☎2301 3980. Genuine traditional Irish folk, every night at both venues. Sunday afternoon in Wan Chai sees a jam session.

Hardy's Folk Club, Winner Building, 35 D'Aguilar St, Central ☎2526 7184. Inoffensive folk singers (and enthusiastic, drunk amateurs) every night doing cover versions. Starts at 9.30pm.

Mad Dogs, Century Square, 1 D'Aguilar St, Central ☎2810 1000; Asian House, 1 Hennessy Rd, Wan Chai ☎2861 3191. Early-evening singer-guitarists most nights at both pubs, and occasional bands too.

The Wanch, 54 Jaffe Rd, Wan Chai
☎2861 1621. Solid folk and pub rock venue, with live music seven nights a week from 9pm to 2am.

Jazz

Mostly, entrance to pub and bar jazz gigs is free (except where stated below), and the standard of playing is high. Visiting name acts play at The Jazz Club, while the Arts Festival in January also attracts some names; details from the HKTA.

BB's, Ground Floor, 114–120 Lockhart Rd, Wan Chai ☎2529 7702. Jazz 8pm–midnight on Sunday evenings.

Cafe Deco, Levels 1 & 2, Peak Galleria, 118 Peak Rd, The Peak ☎2849 5111. Regular jazz and cool sounds in the Peak's Art Deco extravaganza (with occasional cover charge for special events).

Dickens Bar, Lower Ground Floor, *Excelsior Hotel*, 281 Gloucester Rd, Causeway Bay ☎2894 8888. Jazz sessions every Sun 3–6pm.

Fringe Club, Ice House St, Central ☎2521 7251. Occasional jazz gigs; cover charge for non-members.

The Jazz Club, 2nd Floor, 34–36 D'Aguilar St, Central ☎2845 8477. A unique venue in Hong Kong. Live jazz nightly from about 9.30pm. Admission varies from free to around $100, with more expensive tickets for big-name

bands and soloists throughout the year.

Ned Kelly's Last Stand, 11a Ashley Rd, Tsim Sha Tsui ☎2376 0562. Trad and Dixieland jazz every night after 9pm from the stomping resident band, the "Kowloon Honkers". Recommended.

Western and Chinese classical

The main local exponent of **Western classical music** is the Hong Kong Philharmonic Orchestra, formed in 1975, whose season runs from September through to June, and which regularly employs excellent guest conductors and soloists. Performances are at a variety of venues, primarily the Cultural Centre; information on ☎2832 7121. The Hong Kong Sinfonietta is another professional orchestra, although their performances can be rather ragged.

For **Chinese orchestral music**, watch for performances by the Hong Kong Chinese Orchestra, founded in 1977 and the territory's only professional Chinese music group. The orchestra plays one weekend every month at City Hall and the Cultural Centre, performing reworkings of Western classical music on traditional Chinese instruments – a combination not to everyone's taste, but certainly worth hearing. For other Chinese classical music, look out for student concerts at the university or Academy of Performing Arts, or ask the HKTA.

Live Music

For details of Chinese opera performances, see p.277

Chapter 10

The Arts and Media

For years Hong Kong has had a poor cultural reputation among visitors, though it's not for want of trying: the **Cultural Centre** in Tsim Sha Tsui and the **Hong Kong Arts Centre** and the adjacent **Academy for Performing Arts**, in Wan Chai, both put on high-quality work. Nevertheless, Western arts receive only limited exposure in Hong Kong. The only art form that commands a mass audience is **film**, with the cinemas packed for every new Hollywood release or Chinese film. Local **Chinese culture** is less formally presented in the territory though, as you might expect, there's much more of it around. The main venues host traditional dance, opera and music performances, but you're just as likely to see something exciting in the night markets, or during religious holidays at temples and on the street.

Cantonese might be the language of the overwhelming majority in Hong Kong, but for tourists it's the English-language **media** that make the territory such an easy place to come to terms with. Television, radio and newspapers are immediately accessible to English-speaking visitors.

Information, listings and tickets

Information about cultural events and performances can be picked up at any of the venues listed below. Several free magazines give detailed **listings** of forthcoming events: the Urban Council's dual-language monthly *City News* (available in City Hall and other government buildings); the Hong Kong Arts Centre's monthly *Artslink* magazine, HKTA publications such as *Essential – The Official Hong Kong Guide* and *Hong Kong Now!*, and the weekly *HK Magazine* (available at bookshops, bars, clubs and restaurants throughout the centre). Take a look, too, at the English-language daily newspapers, the *Hong Kong Standard* and the *South China Morning Post*, whose Friday and weekend editions have reviews and listings.

Tickets for most events can be bought at any of the main venues, and from offices called **URBTIX** outlets; there's a list opposite of venues and outlets. URBTIX also has a good telephone-booking service (see opposite). Cultural events are very good value in Hong Kong. Many are subsidized by the government and, as a result, you won't pay anything like the prices you would at home. Seats for most local productions cost around $50–120, rising to $250–800 for anything international.

Main venues

Academy for Performing Arts, 1 Gloucester Rd, Wan Chai ☎ 2584 8514. Six separate stages for local and international drama, modern and classical dance. Box office 10am–6pm.
Alliance Française, 123 Hennessy Rd, Wan Chai ☎ 2527 7825; Ho Kwan Bldg, 52 Jordan Rd, Kowloon ☎ 2730 3257.

Films and culture at the French Cultural
Institute. Box office 8.30am–9.30pm.

City Hall, 1 Edinburgh Place, Central
☎2921 2840. Drama, concerts, recitals,
exhibitions and lectures. Box office
10am–9.30pm.

Fringe Club, 2 Lower Albert Rd, Central
☎2521 7251. Offbeat venue for cabaret,
alternative theatre, jazz, concerts and
poetry, as well as exhibitions, classes
and workshops. Pick up the schedule
from the venue; temporary membership
available. Box office Mon–Sat
noon–10pm.

Goethe Institute, 14th Floor, Hong Kong
Arts Centre, 2 Harbour Rd, Wan Chai
☎2802 0088. Films and events at the
German Cultural Institute.

Hong Kong Arts Centre, 2 Harbour Rd,
Wan Chai ☎2582 0232. Local art,
drama, concerts, film screenings, galleries
and exhibitions. Box office 10am–6pm.

Hong Kong Coliseum, 9 Cheong Wan
Rd, Hung Hom ☎2355 7233. Hong
Kong's largest venue (12,000 seats) for
concerts, dance and sports events. Box
office 10am–6.30pm.

**Hong Kong Convention and Exhibition
Centre**, 1 Harbour Rd, Wan Chai ☎2582
8888. Major conventions, exhibitions,
concerts and performances. Box office
varies according to the promoter; check
press for details.

Hong Kong Cultural Centre, 10 Salisbury
Rd, Tsim Sha Tsui ☎2734 2010. Dance,
drama and concerts in Hong Kong's
newest and most controversial building,
drawing on local and international per-

formers. See p.126 for more details. Box
office 10am–9.30pm.

Ko Shan Theatre, 77 Ko Shan Rd (off
Chatham Rd North), Hung Hom ☎2330
4742. Hong Kong's first open-air theatre,
located in a disused quarry. Film, theatre,
Chinese opera and concerts. Box office
10am–6.30pm.

Ngau Chi Wan Civic Centre, 2nd Floor,
Ngau Chi Wan Complex, 11 Clearwater
Bay Rd, New Territories ☎2325 1970.
Drama, dance and film. Box office
10am–6.30pm.

Queen Elizabeth Stadium, 18 Oi Kwan
Rd, Wan Chai ☎2591 1347. Stadium
with 3500 capacity for large concerts
and sports events. Box office
10am–6.30pm.

Sha Tin Town Hall, 1 Yuen Wo Rd, New
Town Plaza, Sha Tin, New Territories
☎2694 2536. Drama, dance and concerts. Box office 10am–9.30pm.

Sheung Wan Civic Centre, 345 Queen's
Rd, Sheung Wan ☎2853 2678. Drama,
concerts, lectures and exhibitions. Box
office 10am–6.30pm.

Tsuen Wan Town Hall, 72 Tai Ho Rd,
Tsuen Wan, New Territories ☎2414
0144. Large venue for concerts, dance
and drama. Box office 10am–9.30pm.

Tuen Mun Town Hall, 3 Tuen Hi Rd,
Tuen Mun, New Territories ☎2450 1105.
Local venue for concerts, dance and
drama. Box office 10am–9.30pm.

**The Arts
and Media**

Chinese cultural performances

Chinese cultural performances are widespread in Hong Kong – every town and
village has a hall, theatre or outdoor
space where traditional opera and dance
are put on. All performances are highly
theatrical; coming across one by accident can be a real highlight of your stay.

The best known is **Chinese opera**,
which you'll see performed locally at festivals, on religious holidays, and in some of
the larger venues by visiting and local
troupes. In Hong Kong, the style is mostly
Cantonese (though visiting mainland
Chinese groups perform Peking Opera on

*For more
details of
Chinese classi-
cal music per-
formances, see
p.175.*

The Arts
and Media

Arts Festivals

There are several main arts festivals in Hong Kong each year. More information about all of them can be obtained from the HKTA, but it's worth knowing that tickets for the best performances can be hard to come by; book well in advance, or be prepared to settle for what performances you can get into.

Hong Kong Arts Festival (Jan/Feb). Wide-ranging international arts festival bringing together leading artists from China and the West. Usually includes opera, theatre, ballet and concerts.

Hong Kong International Film Festival (April). A month of international films at various venues – very popular and imaginative. The City Hall has specific information if you want to try booking in advance.

Festival of Asian Arts (Oct/Nov). Held every two years, featuring artists from all over Asia in folk singing and dancing, and classics of Asian drama.

Fringe Festival (Jan/Feb). Runs in conjunction with the official HK Arts Festival, supplementing (and clashing with) its offerings. Information from the Fringe Club (see p.277).

occasion too) – a highly stylized affair, a musical drama with mime, set songs and responses based on well-known legends and stories. The costumes and garish make-up are magnificent, and although the strident singing and percussion are decidedly awkward to untuned Western ears, it becomes compelling after a while – particularly as the story is interspersed with bouts of elaborate swordfighting and acrobatics. Performances often go on for three hours or more, but the ones held in or near temples at festivals are usually informal, with people walking about, chatting and eating right the way through.

Other cultural shows you might catch include traditional Chinese **music**, **puppet theatre**, **folk dancing**, **acrobatics** and **tumbling**, **magic** and **martial arts** – all things that are soon evident if you're in Hong Kong for any length of time. Street markets and festivals are good places to look; or check in the local press for specific performances at some of the main venues listed above.

Obviously, it's most rewarding to stumble on performances as you travel around the territory: **religious festival events** (see pp.282–285) and cultural shows out in the New Territories (often listed in the press) are put on for the locals and have few pretensions. But if you want to ensure you see at least

something of the traditional culture during your stay, the HKTA organizes frequent free shows at various locations such as the New World Centre (Tsim Sha Tsui) and Cityplaza (Taikoo Shing), where there'll usually be a bit of everything on display from opera extracts to glove puppetry. For more information, contact any of the HKTA offices (see p.45).

There are also Chinese craft and culture displays at **Middle Kingdom**, Ocean Park (p.110). And make an effort to visit the **Temple Street Night Market** (p.136), where you can often see enthusiastic amateurs performing Cantonese opera.

Film

There are at least thirty **cinemas** in Hong Kong, with the current trend firmly towards multi-screen complexes showing a mixture of new Hollywood and Cantonese releases. Going to the movies is inexpensive and it's worth taking in one of the **Chinese-language films** if you can: most are lightweight pot-boilers, slapstick comedies, gangster movies or martial arts thrillers, though interesting films from the mainland are increasingly on view as well. Look for a showing with English subtitles. Reviews of current films in both English-language daily newspapers will help you choose what to see. All the major **English-**

language films make it to Hong Kong soon after release, and are usually shown in their original language, with Chinese subtitles – but check the performance you want isn't a dubbed version.

All the major venues offer computerised booking systems, so you can either telephone in advance and let the system select the best available seats, or go in person and pick your seat from those available, shown on the video monitor by the box office. Entrance is around $55 a ticket (the *loge*, incidentally, is equivalent to the dress circle).

As all Hollywood films are subtitled it's not uncommon for Chinese members of the audience to talk right through them – sometimes on their mobile phones. It can be hard to concentrate as the couple in front of you argue heatedly and chicken feet snacks are strewn around your feet, but it's undeniably different.

The **major cinemas**, and a few interesting minor ones, are listed below, but for a full rundown of what's on where, consult the local press. If you're just wandering and fancy a movie, the biggest concentration of cinemas is in Wan Chai and Causeway Bay. There are also regular film shows (often free) sponsored by the Alliance Française and Goethe Institute; see "Main Venues" on pp.276-277 for addresses. Real film buffs will want to try to coincide with the annual **film festival** (see the "Arts Festivals" box opposite), which always has an excellent and entertaining international programme, though it can be hard to get seats.

Astor Classics, 380 Nathan Rd, Jordan ☎ 2781 1833. Sister cinema of London Classics, 219 Nathan Rd, Kowloon ☎ 2736 8282; both offer a similar programme of new releases.

Broadway Cinematheque, Prosperous Gardens, Public Square St, Yau Ma Tei ☎ 2332 9000. Modern complex with four screens, restaurants and shops. Successfully mixes art-house and mainstream films.

Cine-Art House, Sun Hung Kai Centre, Harbour Rd, Wan Chai ☎ 2827 4820. Arty foreign films in two mini-cinemas.

Hong Kong Arts Centre, 2 Harbour Rd, Wan Chai ☎ 2582 0232. Seasons of alternative and foreign films and Chinese cinema.

Majestic Cinema, 348 Nathan Rd, Jordan ☎ 2782 0272. Long runs for new releases.

New York Cinema, 463-483 Lockhart Rd, Plaza II, Causeway Bay ☎ 2838 7380. Plush cinema for new Western and Chinese releases.

Silvercord Cinema, Silvercord Plaza, 30 Canton Rd, Tsim Sha Tsui ☎ 2317 1083. A triple-screen cinema offering mostly Hollywood blockbusters.

United Artists, One Pacific Place, 88 Queensway, Admiralty; Times Square, Causeway Bay; Level 2, Whampoa Plaza, Hung Hom; New Town Plaza, Sha Tin, New Territories; 128 Carpenter Rd, Kowloon City Plaza, Kowloon City; Bonds, Yue Man Square, Kwung Tong; 13-23 Nam Ning St, Aberdeen Centre, Aberdeen. Modern multi-screen venues for all new releases. All bookable on Cityline ☎ 2317 6666.

Windsor, Windsor House, 311 Gloucester Rd, Causeway Bay ☎ 2882 2621. Well-located three-screen cinema with smoochy double-seats at the back.

The Arts and Media

Television and radio

Every hotel and most guest houses lay TV and radio on for their guests, and you'll be hard pushed to escape them in bars and restaurants – although what you'll get is likely to be quantity rather than quality.

There are four main domestic channels, two English-language and two Cantonese, operated by two companies. Television Broadcasts (TVB) runs Jade (Cantonese) and **TVB Pearl** (English); Asia Television (ATV) runs Home (Cantonese) and **ATV World** (English). In addition, domestic and hotel TVs can often receive cable and satellite channels, including ESPN, CNN and BBC World. Hong Kong's broadcasting companies, unlike their mainland counterparts, are privately run and uncensored, although it's generally felt that self-censorship is practised instead.

The Arts and Media

For details of Hong Kong's daily newspapers, see p.315.

Much of the domestic **English-language programming** is imported – documentaries, soaps and sitcoms – mostly from the USA. The quality is average, or sometimes below, but unfortunately most of the home-grown products are even worse. It's an indication of the way that English-language broadcasting (in both TV and radio) is increasingly regarded as a minority interest – perhaps not surprisingly in a place where the vast majority of the six million-plus inhabitants speak Cantonese as a first language. Nevertheless, the lack of commitment to English-language TV and radio is an indication that the image of Hong Kong as an international business city is not always matched by the reality. Future priorities have already been signalled by TVB, which now carries Mandarin news, weather and financial reports on its English-language Pearl channel. In the meantime, however, the saving grace of the English-language channels is that both regularly feature **films** in the evening, some made for TV but plenty of recent Hollywood productions too. Also, they're fairly good on **sporting events**, particularly horse racing, and you can count on getting live coverage of important soccer matches, as well as tennis, rugby and other sports, although these are often shown in the early hours because of the time difference. Be warned, though, that the constant commercials are no respecter of film plot or goalmouth action.

If you speak Cantonese, try the **Chinese channels** which put on a lot more locally produced stuff – including some good Cantonese and mainland Chinese drama series and feature films – but on the whole it's a diet of soaps and variety shows.

On the **radio**, there's plenty in English to tune in to. Stations include those operated by the main broadcasting outfit, Radio Television Hong Kong (RTHK); there are commercial stations too, as well as the BBC World Service.

Full **programme details** for TV and radio are contained in the daily newspapers.

Theatre and the performing arts

Hong Kong has recently become the home of excellent local **drama and performance art**, alongside the usual international touring companies and artists who enliven the cultural year. Big musical productions have also become popular – recent visitors have included *Phantom of the Opera, Les Misérables,* and *Joseph and the Amazing Technicolor Dreamcoat.* There's a wealth of **venues** (details on pp.276-277) – the Cultural Centre in particular – most of which host drama and performance art throughout the year, but check whether **productions** are in English or Cantonese.

Other than straight drama, some of the most exciting local performances are of **dance**, which doesn't have the disadvantage of a language barrier and often mixes Western and Chinese forms very successfully. **Fringe events** are common, too: the Fringe Club (see p.277), especially, hosts its fair share of mime, magic, cabaret and comedy.

Some interesting **local companies** to watch out for, who perform at venues all over the territory, include:
City Contemporary Dance Company.

Very good, full-time professional company; they usually perform at the Arts Centre.

Conrad Hotel Dinner Theatre. Light comedy from visiting British West End stars.

Hong Kong Ballet Company. Classical and contemporary ballet performances at various venues.

Hong Kong Dance Company. Modern and classical Chinese dance.

Hong Kong Singers. Musical comedy of the Gilbert and Sullivan variety.

Zuni Icosahedron. Very avant-garde theatre-dance company, performing in Cantonese and English.

Visual arts

Some of the main venues listed above have **gallery and exhibition space** that's worth checking for current displays. Otherwise, keep an eye on the territory's **museums**, which host occasional lectures and exhibitions. The Urban Council's district **libraries** also put on year-round lectures (sometimes in English) and exhibitions that might be of interest; full details in each month's *City News* magazine (available from City Hall).

There are many **private art galleries** in Hong Kong. The *South China Morning Post* highlights a good selection of current exhibitions in its daily *What's On* section, as does the weekly *HK Magazine*. The places listed below are usually worth dropping in on:

Agfa Gallery at the Fringe, Fringe Club, 2 Lower Albert Rd, Central. ☎ 2521 7251. Works mostly by local artists. Quality varies but often interesting.

Alisan Fine Arts, 315 Prince's Building, 10 Chater Rd, Central ☎ 2526 1091. Mainly Chinese contemporary work of a not-too-challenging variety.

Altfield Gallery, 248–9 Prince's Building, 10 Chater Rd, Central ☎ 2525 2738. China Trade paintings, maps, prints, Chinese furniture and rugs, for the home rather than the museum.

Artland Gallery, 3rd Floor, Lockhart Centre, 301–307 Lockhart Rd, Wan Chai ☎ 2511 4845. Watercolours.

Galerie La Vong, 13th Floor, One Lan Kwai Fong, Central ☎ 2869 6863. Leading modern Vietnamese painters.

Hanart TZ Gallery, 2nd Floor, Henley Building, 5 Queen's Rd, Central ☎ 2526 9019. Leading dealer of modern Chinese painters.

The Museum Annex, One Exchange Square ☎ 2530 9609. Changing commercial exhibitions of painting, furniture, jewellery and more.

Plum Blossoms Gallery, 17th Floor, Coda Plaza, Garden Rd, Mid-Levels ☎ 2521 2189. Contemporary Chinese painters and antique Tibetan furniture and rugs.

Pottery Workshop, The Fringe Club, 2 Lower Albert Rd, Central ☎ 2525 7634. Interesting work by local potters.

Wattis Fine Art, 2nd Floor, 20 Hollywood Rd, Central ☎ 2524 5302. Antique maps and watercolours.

Zee Stone Gallery, Yu Yuet Lai Building, 43–55 Wyndham St, Central ☎ 2845 4476. Modern Chinese paintings and antique furniture, including Tibetan.

The Arts
and Media

Chapter 11

Festivals

Timing your trip to coincide with one of Hong Kong's traditional **Chinese festivals** can add greatly to its interest. Below is a round-up of the year's events, with details of what to expect and where to see the associated celebrations. We've given the likely months and dates for the festivals (as well as the lunar dates), but for the exact dates look in the HKTA's free publications, *The Official Hong Kong Guide* and *Where Hong Kong*. The festivals below are dealt with **chronologically**, starting with the Chinese New Year.

Chinese New Year

Most famous and most important of the Chinese festivals, **Chinese New Year** falls some time between the end of January and the end of February. Decorations go up everywhere, there's a huge **flower market** in Victoria Park on Hong Kong Island (and in Fa Hui Park and Cheung Sha Wan playground in Kowloon), where locals buy lucky flowers – peach and plum blossom – oranges, lanterns and sweets. You might also catch an impromptu **lion dance**. These are mostly held in residential areas, but ask the tourist office which large hotels are likely to put on a dance display. The most obvious manifestations of New Year are the red scrolls and posters pasted to walls and houses all over the territory: the Chinese characters wish long life, prosperity and happiness.

Not all the Chinese festivals are also public holidays. For a full rundown of public holidays in Hong Kong, see p.26.

Most years there is a firework display over the harbour and a parade in Kowloon, but other than that there's not actually a great deal to see at Chinese New Year. Most offices, banks, official buildings and some shops are closed for three days or even longer (traditional New Year celebrations last fifteen days). It's a family festival, when people clean their houses, settle debts, visit friends and relations, buy new clothes and generally ensure a fresh start for the year. Married couples hand out money (new notes only) in red envelopes (*lai see*) to their families, and tip their doormen, cleaners and other staff in the same way; people on salaries get a bonus; and shop assistants and waiters are feasted by their employers. Some services like hairdressing can cost double in the run-up to the festival. But many places, particularly restaurants, stay open since families also go out to celebrate. To wish someone a "Happy New Year", you say "*kung hay fat choi*".

Arriving in Hong Kong and trying to find a **room** during Chinese New Year is something you should avoid. And don't even think about travelling to China during the festival: everything is jam-packed solid as literally millions of Hong Kong Chinese stream across the border to visit relatives.

Yuen Siu (Lantern) Festival

The **Yuen Siu Festival** marks the last official day of the Chinese New Year celebrations (the fifteenth day of the first moon), and so falls about two weeks after the public holidays. Traditionally designed and brightly coloured lanterns symbolizing the moon are hung in restaurants, shops, temples and houses. Yuen Siu is also known as "Lovers' Day", a kind of Chinese Valentine's Day. There's a second lantern festival in September; see "Mid-Autumn Festival" on p.285.

Ching Ming Festival

Generally falling in April, **Ching Ming** is when families visit their ancestral graves to perform traditional rites. The day – the beginning of the third moon, a public holiday – signals the beginning of spring and a new farming year, but it's more noted for the sweeping of graves at the territory's cemeteries. Whole families take along joss sticks, incense and food offerings (roast pork and fruit), which are left for the dead at the graves while prayers are said for the departed souls and blessings sought for the latest generations of the family. Extra public transport is laid on for trips to the cemeteries, on Hong Kong Island and out in the New Territories, as well as extra ferries to carry people to the outlying islands: it's one enormous scrum.

Tin Hau Festival

A traditional fishing festival, this is one of the most spectacular of the year's events. Falling in late April or May (on the 23rd day of the third lunar month), it is in honour of **Tin Hau**, a legendary fisherman's daughter of a thousand years ago, who could forecast the weather, calm the waves and generally help the fishermen to a decent catch; not surprisingly, she is regarded as the goddess of the sea and of fishermen, and as the protector of sailors. Fishing boats are colourfully decorated with flags, streamers and pennants as fishermen and others who follow the goddess gather at the various Tin Hau temples throughout the territory to ask for luck in the coming year and to offer food, fruit and pink dumplings as a mark of respect. The main temple is the one at

Joss House Bay in Sai Kung (p.173), where massive crowds congregate every year, and there is always a good celebration in **Yuen Long** in the New Territories, another large centre of Tin Hau worship. Special ferry services run out to some of the brightly decorated temples, many of which put on Chinese opera displays, dances and parades.

Birthday of the Lord Buddha

A low-key celebration in May when the Buddha's statue is taken out of the various Buddhist monasteries in the territory and "bathed" in scented water. The monasteries on Lantau are an obvious place to head for to see the rites being performed, but there are important monasteries in the New Territories too, at Sha Tin and Lam Tei (see Chapter 4).

Tam Kung Festival

The second patron saint of the fishing people is **Tam Kung**, whose festival is celebrated in May (eighth day of the fourth lunar month) at the temple in Shau Kei Wan on Hong Kong Island (p.116).

Tai Chiu (Cheung Chau Bun) Festival

A week-long extravaganza in May (starting on the same day as the Tam Kung Festival, above) on Cheung Chau Island, the **Tai Chiu Festival** is one of the highlights of the festival year. The buns that give the festival its English name are distributed for luck at the end of the celebrations, which consist of dances, operas, parades – and the famous "floating children" and bun towers. See (p.190) for more details; and expect the island and all the transport there and back to be in a state of siege during this time.

Tuen Ng (Dragon Boat) Festival

The **Tuen Ng Festival** is one of the oldest of Cantonese festivals, held to commemorate the Chinese hero Ch'u Yuen,

Festivals

Festivals

an advisor to the king who committed suicide by jumping in a river in Hunan Province and drowning, in protest against a corrupt third-century-BC government. The local people tried to save him in their boats, while others threw rice dumplings into the water to feed the fish that would otherwise have eaten his body.

Today, the festival is celebrated in June (fifth day of the fifth moon) with noisy dragon boat races – narrow rowing boats with a dragon's head and tail – throughout the territory, while rice dumplings are eaten, too. The boats are crewed by anything up to eighty people (though most are smaller), the oar-strokes set by a drummer, and the races are accompanied by cymbals and watched from scores of junks and launches. You can see **races** in many places, particularly on the Sha Tin waterfront, where it's become a major spectacle. There are races, too, at Tai Po, Stanley, Aberdeen and Yau Ma Tei – watch the local press for details or ask the tourist office. Since 1976 there's been an annual International Dragon Boat Race, with teams from all over the world competing.

Birthday of Lu Pan

Held in July, this is a holiday for anyone connected with the building trades. **Lu Pan** was a Master Builder in around 600 BC, a skilled carpenter and possessor of miraculous powers. Banquets are held in

his honour on his festival day (the thirteenth day of the sixth moon) and there are ceremonies at the Lu Pan Temple in Kennedy Town (p.87).

Maiden's Festival

Also known as the Seven Sisters' Festival, the **Maidens' Festival** is held in mid-August, on the seventh day of the seventh moon. It is observed mostly by young girls and lovers, who burn incense and paper and leave offerings of fruit and flowers. The festival dates back more than 1500 years and, like many Chinese festivals, there are many different versions of the legend accompanying it. A common one is that it marks the story of the youngest of seven sisters who was separated from her lover and only allowed to see him once a year – on this date. Like most other Chinese festivals you will see offerings placed on rooftops, by the roadside, or burnt in the gutters of quiet streets – a more formal setting can be found at the Bowen Road Lover's Stone Garden above Wan Chai (p.95).

Yue Lan Festival

The **Yue Lan Festival** is held in late August (the fifteenth day of the seventh moon). It's known as the "Festival of the Hungry Ghosts", commemorating the lunar month when ghosts are released from the underworld to roam the earth. It's generally seen as an unlucky day, when accidents or sinister events can

---

The Maiden's Festival: the Legend

While you're considering the wonderful views from Lover's Stone Garden, over Wan Chai and the harbour beyond, you can muse on the **legend** commemorated by the festival. A cowhand stole the clothes of a weaving girl, a daughter of the Kitchen God (or, in a different version, the Emperor of Heaven), while she was bathing, and having seen her naked, had to marry her, after which they lived together happily. But the gods ordered her to return to heaven to continue her weaving, and said that the couple could meet only once a year. The cowhand died and became an immortal, but to prevent the couple meeting in heaven, the Queen of Heaven created the Milky Way, leaving the weaving girl on one side and the cowherd on the other. Although they can see each other, they only meet on the seventh day of the seventh moon, when magpies form a bridge so that they might cross to each other.

happen. To forestall them, people give offerings to the ghosts in the form of paper models of food, cars, houses, money, furniture, etc – which are then ceremoniously burnt so that the ghosts can take them back to the underworld with them. It's not a public holiday, but you may see fires on the pavements and at the roadside during this time where the elaborate models are burnt. See the account of the Pak Tai Temple in Wan Chai (p.100) for more details about the dying craft of making paper models.

Mid-Autumn Festival

Another major festival, the **Mid-Autumn Festival** is also called the **Moon Cake Festival** after the sweet cakes eaten at this time – mostly made from sesame and lotus paste and stuffed with an egg. The festival takes place in September, on the fifteenth day of the eighth moon, roughly equivalent to the Western Harvest Festival. It purportedly commemorates a fourteenth-century revolt against the Mongols, when the call to arms was written on pieces of paper, stuffed inside the cakes and distributed to the population. Nowadays, the various kinds of moon cake (*yuek beng*) are stacked up in bakeries for the occasion – they're all wonderfully sickly and cost around $100 for a box of four, though the better, more elaborate double-yolk cakes are pricier. The festival is also accompanied by lantern displays on hillsides throughout the territory. You'll see the charming paper, cellophane or silk lanterns for sale in many shops; many shaped like animals, flowers, ships or cars. The Peak

and various spots in the New Territories are favourite places to go and light your lantern while watching the moon rise – at which point you scoff the cakes. There's a lantern display, too, in Victoria Park on Hong Kong Island, but expect transport to anywhere near a hill (like the Peak Tram) to be packed. Some more traditional villages in the New Territories celebrate by building large sausage-shaped hot air balloons out of paper and bamboo, and launching them at night; fuelled and illuminated by burning wadding they can travel hundreds of feet up if the air is still. Tradition links this practice to ancient military signalling, but its true origins are obscure. The day after the festival is a public holiday.

Birthday of Confucius

The **Birthday of Confucius** in September, is marked by low-key religious ceremonies at the Confucius Temple in Causeway Bay.

Cheung Yeung Festival

A public holiday in October (on the ninth day of the ninth lunar month), the **Cheung Yeung Festival** relates to a tale from Han Dynasty times, when a soothsayer advised an old man to take his family to the mountains for 24 hours to avoid disaster. On his return, everything else in the village had died. The same trip to high places is made today in remembrance, with the result again that all transport to hilly areas is packed. Lots of people also take this as another opportunity to visit family graves.

Festivals

Chapter 12

Shopping

A lot of people still come to Hong Kong mainly to **shop**, although the stories you've heard about give-away prices for clothes, electrical goods and other items aren't really true any more. That's partly because the stability of the Hong Kong dollar has kept prices up compared to other parts of Asia, and partly because other cities have sharpened up their act. However, you can still get some very good deals on items like clothing, computer gear, jewellery, silk and other Chinese arts and crafts, old and new. There are also some specialist niches, like porcelain and antiques, worth investigating. In addition, since Hong Kong is a largely **tax-free zone**, the only imported goods to attract duty are alcohol, tobacco, perfumes, cosmetics and cars, and the prices you pay should reflect that (worth remembering when a sales clerk tries to persuade you that a discount of less than your home sales tax rate represents a big concession).

The key is to approach your shopping as you would at home: with scepticism. For big-ticket items – particularly electronics – there is no substitute for research. There are too many horror stories of visitors, in Kowloon especially, being charged three or four times the real price. If you don't have the information you need, a phone call home, or the ads in a foreign newspaper could save you a lot of money and grief. At the very least, compare prices with the local fixed-price retailers or department

stores. Remember that almost every purchase you make will be non-refundable (and being overcharged won't negate that), so keep an eye out for the small print and the warranty, check whether an electronic item will work in your home country, and make sure you know exactly what is and is not included. A fully itemized receipt will help.

You shouldn't have any difficulty finding designer gear or hi-fi and electrical equipment in Hong Kong. All the big names are sold absolutely everywhere and specific addresses, if you need them, are given in the HKTA's *Official Dining, Entertainment & Shopping* guide and a dozen other publications and leaflets. We've listed more mainstream places – markets, bookshops and department stores – that should be useful for anyone staying in Hong Kong, as well as a selection of more unusual shops, any of which can occupy a spare half-hour or so, or provide an offbeat souvenir or interesting purchase.

Shop opening hours vary according to which part of Hong Kong you shop in; most areas have late-night shopping once a week too. Shops generally open seven days a week, though some smaller shops close on Sunday and Japanese department stores open on Sunday but close for one day mid-week instead. Otherwise, the only time shops close is for two to three days around Chinese New Year, and even then by no means all do so. Opening hours for street **markets** (apart from fresh-food markets) are even longer: daily until 11pm or midnight usually, though with a couple of exceptions which are dealt with in the text.

Antiques and art galleries

Hong Kong offers good opportunities to buy Chinese antiques and arts, although bargains are rarer than you might think. There is also an increasing number of items from other Asian countries, particularly Thailand and Burma, although prices are higher than they would be in Bangkok (but lower than in Europe). For antiques, the best place to start (at least to get your eye in) is Hollywood Road. The majority of the customers here are still foreigners – few locals have much of a taste for antiques yet – and include many dealers. Most of the items come from China, usually by "unofficial" routes. There are no problems in exporting antiques once they are in Hong Kong, but if you're worried, pieces which have left China legitimately will have a small red seal on them.

The type of stock available changes from year to year. What never changes though is the premium on really good pieces. However, if you are happy with something that is attractive rather than valuable you'll have much more choice and leeway for bargaining (which, incidentally, is a must). It's quite possible to get some very nice pieces of embroidery or small Han or Tang figures for a couple of hundred dollars. When dealing with larger items like furniture or burial ceramics don't be swayed by vendors showing you a similar item in an international auction catalogue – if the two were really

the same they would both have gone to Sotheby's. They may also be composite pieces – made from remnants of a number of different items. Many of the Hollywood Road shops maintain larger warehouses elsewhere (including over the border), so if you're really interested ask about visiting. Art and antiques more than one hundred years old are usually allowed into most countries duty-free, though check first with your consulate (there's a list on p.312). The shop should provide the necessary certificate of authenticity.

If you're interested in more **modern art**, Hong Kong is also a good place to view the work of some of the best Chinese contemporary painters. Once again, the best isn't cheap, not least because there is a local market for modern Chinese art.

A good source of information is *A guide to buying Antiques, Arts & Crafts* by Valery M. Garrett (Times Books International), available in local bookstores. There are also two locally published glossy magazines, *Orientations* and *Arts of Asia*, which cover antiques and the arts throughout the region.

Antique shops

Buying antiques is always a case of "buyer beware", so buy it because you like it, not as an investment. The shops below are all well established. Some are closed on Sunday.

The Antique Express, Unit 1114, Horizon Plaza, 2 Lee Wing St, Ap Lei Chau, Aberdeen ☎ 2856 9720. Competitive prices and helpful staff selling furniture and decorative objects.

Art Treasures Gallery, 42 Hollywood Rd, Central ☎ 2543 0430. Helpful small gallery. Core specializations are furniture and burial items, but they are branching out into other things. They have a warehouse in Zuhai. Bargain hard on the furniture.

Altfield Gallery, 2nd Floor, Prince's Building, 10 Chater Rd, Central ☎ 2537 6370. Furniture, carpets, paisley shawls and textiles, Buddha figures from Burma,

Shopping

A list of art galleries with regular exhibitions and sales is given on p.281.

Shopping

Shopping: A Survival Guide

Although it may sometimes seem like it, not everyone's out to rip you off, but there are some rules to follow and dodges to be aware of before you part with any cash. The key ground-rule is to shop around to get an idea of what things cost. Pirate and fake goods (CD-ROMs and clothes particularly) are common, so if you see something that's spectacularly cheap, always check it out elsewhere. **Parallel imports** (imports which come via a third party, rather than directly from the manufacturer, and so are not covered by warranties) of electronic goods are also on the increase. In itself this may not be a problem: these imports are usually aimed at local consumers whose demand for the latest models often outstrips supply. But buying parallel imports can cause problems if you are not aware of what they are; guarantees are often invalid and the manufacturer may be unwilling to service them. Take your time; find out *exactly* what's included, ask for demonstrations and – on principle – don't buy the first one you see. If you're being unduly pressurized to buy, you're probably in the wrong shop.

Choosing a shop

For expensive items, it's often recommended that you use shops that are members of the Hong Kong Tourist Association (HKTA); they pay an annual membership fee and identify themselves by a sign in the window of a red junk within a red circle. Obviously, only a fraction of the territory's shops and stores are in the HKTA and the ones that don't belong aren't necessarily all villains – far from it. But it's a starting point if you're worried.

All the registered shops are listed in the HKTA's *Official Dining, Entertainment & Shopping* guide (available free from HKTA offices), which has plenty of information on shopping for various items and goods. Look, too, at the newspaper *Hongkong Now!* and the monthly guide, *Essential Hong Kong*, both available from HKTA offices, for their articles on shopping and factory outlets. Advertisements in the *South China Morning Post* and the free *HK Magazine* are also good sources of information.

Fiona Campbell's *The Guide to Shopping in Hong Kong* (FDC Services) is a reliable and regularly updated guide to local retail outlets, written as much for locals as for visitors, whilst Carolyn Radin's *The Complete Guide to Hong Kong Factory Bargains* (Delta Dragon) is a useful pocket-sized guide to the fast-changing world of factory outlets.

For questions about shopping in Hong Kong, or complaints against HKTA members, ring ☎ 2508 1234 (Mon–Fri 9am–5pm, Sat–Sun 9am–1pm).

Agents and importers

Many of the products sold in Hong Kong are handled by a sole agent or importer, who can give you reliable information about the particular model you're interested in if the shop is vague or unhelpful. The agents' and importers' names and telephone numbers are given in the HKTA *Shopping* guide.

Guarantees

Always check the guarantee you're given for photographic, electronic or electrical goods. Some are international guarantees, in which case they should carry the name of the sole agent in Hong Kong for that product; but most are purely local guarantees, which are only valid in Hong Kong, usually for a period of twelve months. All guarantees should carry a description of the product, including a model number and serial number, as well as the date of purchase, the name and address of the shop you bought it from and the shop's official stamp. In either case, don't put too much reliance on the protection of a piece of paper. Parallel imports may not carry any kind of guarantee.

Shopping

Deposits and refunds

You don't need to put down a deposit on anything unless it's being made for you. For tailored clothes, expect to put down fifty percent of the price, or a little more. On other items, if the shop tries to insist (to "secure" the item, or to order a new one because they're "out of stock") go somewhere else – there are always plenty of alternatives. Generally, goods are not returnable or refundable, though if something is faulty or missing the better shops may replace your goods. It will help if you have your receipt itemized and go straight back to the shop if there's something wrong.

Compatibility

It's important to check that electrical goods are compatible with your domestic mains voltage, and that television sets and VCRs are compatible with each other, and with your domestic broadcasting system. Beware of the "bait and switch" scam, when having paid for a certain product, you are then told it can't be used in your home country. The shop refuses to refund the transaction, forcing you to pay more for a "better, compatible" model.

Customs, shipping and insurance

Before making large purchases, check with the relevant consulate (see p.312) or the HKTA about customs regulations for the country you want to import the goods to. The shop may be able to arrange to have your purchase packed and sent overseas, but make sure you have it insured to cover damage in transit as well as loss (and of course that you keep the receipt). To send items home yourself, you need to go to a main post office (see p.315), where you can also arrange insurance (though check first to see if you're covered by your own travel insurance). Parcels usually take about a month by surface mail and a week by airmail to reach Europe or North America.

Avoiding rip-offs

Having checked all the main points, you still need to be armed against the out-and-out bad guys – or simply against the shopkeepers who see their chance to make some extra profit from an unsuspecting visitor.

• Always ask the price, and what that price includes. Ask the latter question more than once to ensure a consistent answer.

• Bargaining: for most large items in the bigger shops and department stores, the price will be fixed and you won't be able to bargain, though you might be able to wangle extra accessories and the like before completing the sale. However, you can bargain in markets and smaller shops, though bear in mind that the seller always wins.

• Switching goods: if you've paid for goods, don't let them out of your sight as it's not unknown for bits and pieces to have mysteriously vanished by the time you get home, or for cheaper gear to have been substituted. Either pack your purchases yourself, or check everything before you leave the shop. If things like camera cases or electrical leads are part of the package, make sure they're there and itemized on the receipt: otherwise if you return later to complain you may be told that they're "extras" which you now have to pay for.

continued overleaf

Shopping

Shopping: A Survival Guide (continued)

• Fake and pirate gear: sometimes you know that goods are fakes or copies and it doesn't matter. Pirated CD-ROMs, computer programmes and video discs for instance, are available in many places. Fake Rolex watches are fun. Copies (in gold and precious stones) by local jewellers of the signature designs of leading international jewellery brands are also good value. Fake designer-label gear from markets may also have a certain cachet. But if you want the real McCoy, don't buy anything from anyone on the street; also, don't be tempted by stupid "bargains" – pay the going rate and get receipts and guarantees. In any case the traffic in pirated items like watches and CDs is being increasingly heavily stamped on by the customs authorities, who are under heavy international pressure to clean up.

Boycotting products

There's almost nothing you can't buy in Hong Kong, which means that there is trade in several products you may not feel entirely happy about, including furs, leather and skin goods made from rare and exotic or endangered species and, most importantly, **ivory**. There are huge stocks of ivory in Hong Kong, one of the world's largest markets in the product, and the territory is still home to a big ivory processing industry – you'll see the results in shop windows. However, both the Chinese government and the Hong Kong authorities are a party to CITES (the Convention on International Trade in Endangered Species) and, since 1990, the Hong Kong authorities have abided more stringently by the rules of the worldwide ban.

There is also a growing trade in **Shatoosh**, a fibre even finer than cashmere. It comes from Tibetan antelopes which are shot by poachers (the fur isn't gathered after being rubbed off on thorns, as vendors would have you believe). The shawls produced can go for US$10,000 or more.

The trade in endangered species also rears its head in traditional **Chinese medicine**, which often uses the body parts of animals like tigers and rhinos. Many of the medicines (surprisingly) carry bilingual ingredient lists – if you're going to buy anything, check first.

---

and a good selection of oriental prints, paintings and maps. Expensive but good quality. Very helpful, unpushy staff.

Dragon Culture, 231, 184 & 77A Hollywood Rd, Central ☎ 2545 9098. Vast selection of burial ceramics and other items (including fossilized dinosaur eggs) in all price ranges.

Gorgeous Arts and Crafts, Al Aqmar House, 26 Hollywood Rd, Central ☎ 2973 0034. Entrance is by the escalator at the bottom of Shelley St. Fascinating selection of small bits of embroidery, dress accessories and other bits and pieces. A good place for reasonably priced decorative souvenirs.

Honeychurch Antiques, 29 Hollywood Rd, Central ☎ 2543 2433. One of the longest established galleries, offering a wide selection of small items from throughout Asia, including Japan. Silver, porcelain, books, prints and many other things. Expensive but interesting.

Karin Weber Antiques, 32A Staunton St, Mid-Levels. Large selection of mid-price items. Also organizes trips to warehouses in mainland China.

Low Price Shop, 47 Hollywood Rd, Central. A Hong Kong institution. More of a stall really, selling bric-a-brac, old photos and general junk. Bargain hard.

Schoeni, 27 Hollywood Rd, Central ☎ 2542 3143. Long-established furniture dealer, which also deals in Tibetan furniture and Burmese Buddhas. One of their warehouses of unrestored furniture is just round the corner and is open every Saturday.

Teresa Coleman, 36 Wyndham St, Central ☎2526 2450. One of Hong Kong's best-known dealers, with an international reputation for dealing in Chinese textiles and a good selection of pictures and prints. They also run The Tibetan Gallery, at 55 Wyndham St.

Books and magazines

All the **bookshops** below sell English-language books, and many sell overseas newspapers and magazines too. There are, of course, hundreds of other bookshops selling Chinese-language books only.

Bookazine, 102–103 Alexandra House, Chater Rd, Central; 3rd Floor, Prince's Building, 10 Chater Rd, Central; Room 117, Shui On Centre, Harbour Rd, Wan Chai; Shop 8 & 9, 3rd Floor, Hopewell Centre, Queen's Rd East, Wan Chai; Shop 208, Caroline Centre, 2 Yun Ping Rd, Causeway Bay; Peak Tower, the Peak. Excellent selection of foreign magazines and books.

Cosmos Books, 1st Floor, 30 Johnston Rd, Wan Chai. Good for travel, novels and history.

Data Bank, The Goldmark, 502 Hennessy Rd, Causeway Bay; Shop 206 & 313A, Mongkok Computer Centre, 8 Nelson St, Mongkok. Specialist shops for computer books, magazines and accessories.

Fleet Arcade, Lung King St, Wan Chai. Good book and magazine store selling mostly American publications at reasonable prices. The arcade was originally built for visiting American servicemen, but they don't seem to mind the public shopping there.

Government Publications Centre, Queensway Government Offices, Low Block, Ground Floor, 66 Queensway, Admiralty. Official government publications, Hong Kong maps, exhibition catalogues, and books on local flora, fauna, politics, environment, industry and anything else you can think of.

Hong Kong Book Centre, Basement, On Lok Yuen Building, 25 Des Voeux Rd, Central. Cramped, library-like interior, but well stocked with novels and travel books, and good on Chinese history and politics. Foreign newspapers, too.

Joint Publishing, Chung Sheung Building, 9 Queen Victoria St, Central. Sole agent/distributor for mainland Chinese publications, with a good stock of Marxist-Leninist works, foreign-language books and magazines, and books published in Hong Kong and Taiwan.

Kelly and Walsh, Shop 348, The Mall, Pacific Place, 88 Queensway, Admiralty. Big, central, general bookshop, good on travel and art.

New Age Shop, 7 Old Bailey St, Mid-Levels. Stocks a wide range of "alternative" books from east and west, as well as the usual paraphernalia for alternative health and healing.

Page One, Times Square, 1 Matheson St, Causeway Bay; Festival Walk, Kowloon Tong. One of the territory's best bookshops, with a big selection.

South China Morning Post Family Bookshop, 2nd Floor, Times Square, 1 Matheson St, Causeway Bay; Star Ferry Concourse, Central; 313 Ocean Centre, Harbour City, Canton Rd, Tsim Sha Tsui; Basement One, New World Centre, 18–24 Salisbury Rd, Tsim Sha Tsui East. Fine selection of English-language novels, travel guides, dictionaries, maps and books on Hong Kong and China, and foreign newspapers.

Swindon Book Co. Ltd, Star Ferry Concourse, Tsim Sha Tsui; 13–15 Lock Rd, Tsim Sha Tsui; 249 Ocean Terminal, Harbour City, Canton Rd, Tsim Sha Tsui; 310 Ocean Centre, Harbour City, Canton Rd, Tsim Sha Tsui. A general bookshop with a fairly large travel section; the Star Ferry branch is particularly good for publications on Hong Kong and glossy art books.

Tai Yip Chinese Art Book Gallery, 54 Hollywood Rd, Central. Large selection of books and magazines on Chinese arts and crafts – new and secondhand. Also books and gifts relating to Hong Kong.

Shopping

Shopping

China and porcelain

Porcelain has been a traditional export of Hong Kong for hundreds of years, and is still a good buy. The available quality varies enormously – from the cheapest household blue and white (still very pretty) to museum-quality replicas of old patterns.

Chinese Arts and Crafts, China Resources Building, 26 Harbour Rd, Wan Chai; 230 The Mall, Pacific Place, 88 Queensway, Admiralty; Star House, 3 Salisbury Rd, Tsim Sha Tsui; *Nathan Hotel*, 378 Nathan Rd, Kowloon. A good selection of all types and qualities of china in traditional styles. Also a few antique pieces.

Henry's Lampshades. Large selection of porcelain lamps in traditional designs and shapes. They will make to order.

Wah Tung China Ltd, 59 Hollywood Rd, Central. Very high-quality selection, representing all the major decorative trends in Chinese porcelain. They pack and dispatch worldwide.

Lee Fung Chinaware, 18 Shelley St, Mid-Levels. You'll pass this as you ride the Mid-Levels escalator up. Good-quality selection, well displayed. Prices higher than Supercase up the road.

Supercase Ltd, 49c Elgin St, Mid-Levels. Dusty barn-like shop with a huge range of stock at good prices. Right next to the Mid-Levels escalator.

L&E, Nam Wa Po, Tai Po, New Territories. A warehouse full of decorative porcelain. They have another a few hundred metres up the road full of old furniture and china. Packing and shipping can be arranged.

Chinese and oriental products stores

These stores specialize in products made in mainland China, including silk clothes and underwear, cashmere, fabrics, furniture, porcelain, antiques, herbal medicines, electrical goods, household linen, jewellery, and decorative items.

Chinese Arts and Crafts, China Resources Building, 26 Harbour Rd, Wan Chai; 230 The Mall, Pacific Place, 88 Queensway, Admiralty; Star House, 3 Salisbury Rd, Tsim Sha Tsui; *Nathan Hotel*, 378 Nathan Rd, Kowloon. The largest and best branches are those in Star House and Wan Chai. Some items are very good value and it's always worth a look around, although some of the silks and linens can be had cheaper in Stanley Market.

CAC Home Furnishing Plaza, Site 3, Whampoa Garden, Hung Hom.

CRC Department Store, Chiao Shang Building, 92 Queen's Rd, Central; Lok Sing Centre, 31 Yee Wo St, Causeway Bay. Cheap department-store products plus Chinese specialities such as medicines, foodstuffs, porcelain and handicrafts.

Chun Sang Trading, 3–4 Glenealy, Central. Chinese-made cotton and linen products – embroidered sheets, cushion covers, tablecloths, etc. Cheap.

Shanghai Tang, Pedder Building, 12 Pedder St, Central. As well as fashion this store stocks a small selection of household goods, watches, glassware, china and gifts, all in exclusive designs.

Yue Hwa Chinese Products Emporium, 301–309 Nathan Rd, Yau Ma Tei; 1 Kowloon Park Drive, Tsim Sha Tsui; 54–64 Nathan Rd, Tsim Sha Tsui; Park Lane Shoppers' Boulevard, 143–161 Nathan Rd, Tsim Sha Tsui; 24-32 Paterson St, Causeway Bay. Long-standing department store; particularly good for Chinese medicines.

Clothes

For the addresses of the big-name **designers** – from Armani to Valentino, as well as local Hong Kong whiz-kids – look no further than the HKTA *Shopping* guide, which lists them all in exhaustive detail. Otherwise, simply check out stores as you wend your way around the city. Be aware though that Western designer clothes are often significantly more expensive here than they are back home because of the extra cachet attached to foreign labels. For cheaper clothes shopping, check out the main **local fashion chain stores** – Giordano, U2, 2000 and Bossini – for decent-quality, value-for-money casual wear, including shirts, chinos, jackets, skirts and socks. There are countless branches in all areas of the city. Or track down the **factory and warehouse outlets** (see p.294), whose bargain prices for designer shirts and jackets really start to save you money. For other ideas, visit the various **markets** (p.298) that specialize in clothes, and keep an eye out for barrow sellers in the underpasses and by the Star Ferry. The Chinese products stores are also worth checking for fabrics, silk clothing, cashmere and padded winter jackets. Make sure you try everything on – particularly women's clothes – the sizes on the labels don't mean that much. There are also some **local designers** whose work you might want to check out – see below.

Blanc De Chine, 2nd Floor, Pedder Building, 12 Pedder St, Central. Designs loosely based on traditional Chinese clothes, in silk and cashmere using muted colours.

Joyce Boutique, 14 Queen's Rd, Central; Shop 344, Pacific Place, 88 Queensway, Admiralty. Hong Kong's most fashionable boutique offers its own range of clothing, as well as many top overseas designer brands.

Shanghai Tang, Pedder Building, 12 Pedder St, Central. A must to visit, if not to buy. The store has been beautifully done up in 1930s Shanghai style. It specializes in new takes on traditional Chinese designs – often in vibrant colours – and they can also make to order (see p.294). They also do some household items and gifts. Watch out for the regular, competitive sales.

Vivienne Tam, The Galleria, Queen's Rd, Central. Funky shirts and dresses in David Hockney-meets-Vivienne Westwood style, often featuring Chairman Mao and other icons of the East.

Walter Ma, 16 Wellington St, Central. Party clothes for Hong Kong's smart set.

Shopping

Clothing and Shoe Sizes						
Dresses						
USA	8	10	12	14	16	18	20
UK	10	12	14	16	18	20	22
Continental	40	42	44	46	48	50	52
Women's shoes						
USA	4.5	5.5	6.5	7.5	8.5	9.5
UK	3	4	5	6	7	8
Continental	35.5	36.5	37.5	38.5	39.5	40.5
Men's suits/coats						
USA	36	38	40	42	44	46
UK	36	38	40	42	44	46
Continental	46	48	50	52	54	56
Men's shirts						
USA	14	15	16	17		
UK	14	15	16	17		
Continental	36	38	41	43		
Men's shoes						
USA	6	7	8	9	10	11
UK	6	7	8	9	10	11
Continental	39	41	42	43	44	46

Shopping

Factory and warehouse outlets

One unusual aspect of shopping in Hong Kong is the chance to buy from a wide variety of **factory and warehouse outlets**. These are in commercial buildings, not shops, and sell clothes, fabrics and jewellery direct to the public. Prices are competitive, either because there's a low mark-up or because you're buying samples, ends-of-lines or high-quality seconds. The HKTA puts out a brochure, *Factory Outlets*. If you're really serious, locally published guides like *The Smart Shopper in Hong Kong* or *The Complete Guide to Hong Kong Factory Bargains*, available in most bookshops, list a wide range of outlets by area and type of goods, with maps, transport details and average prices. Also keep an eye out for ads in the local press, particularly the *Shopping Guide* in the *South China Morning Post*.

Many outlets can be difficult to find if you don't have the exact address. If you just want to browse, **Granville Road** in Tsim Sha Tsui (off Nathan Rd), is a good place to look. In Central, look for signs in doorways in **Wyndham St** and **D'Aguilar St**, and don't forget the **Pedder Building**, (12 Pedder Street), which is full of discount outlets. If you find yourself in Aberdeen check out the **Joyce Warehouse** in the **Hing Wai Centre**. It's where Hong Kong's most fashionable shop puts all last season's stuff that didn't sell – with discounts up to eighty percent. The nearby **Horizon Plaza** on Ap Lei Chau is also worth a look for other discount outlets.

Tailors

Hong Kong has long been known for the speed and value of its **tailors**, but whatever you've heard don't ask for a suit in 24 hours. If you're foolish enough to do so it either won't fit, will fall apart, or both. You'll need at least two or three fittings for a decent tailor to make a suit or jacket (one fitting for a shirt or skirt) spread over several days. The result may not be spectacularly cheap, but it will be considerably better value than the same suit made at home (the rule-of-thumb is that a handmade men's suit in Hong Kong costs the same as an off-the-peg version in the West). Bargaining is usually not appropriate. When it comes to style, the easiest way is to bring the tailor something to copy, perhaps with some alterations. If that's not possible, a picture is useful – most shops have piles of magazines to help you choose. The best way to find a good tailor is personal recommendation - if you don't know anyone try asking in your hotel. Alternatively, look for a tailor who relies on regular clients, not passing tourists; the big hotels, shopping malls or areas around Mid-Levels, Happy Valley and Causeway Bay are promising locations. Ask to look at some of the garments they have underway. Women may want to choose a tailor with an established Western clientele, as they will be used to dealing with the rather different body shape. Some suggestions include:

Italian Tailor, 1st Floor, Prince's Building, 10 Chater Rd, Central. Upmarket men's tailor which makes suits for many of the local businessmen. Quality fabric selection.

Johnson & Co., 44 Hankow Rd, Tsim Sha Tsui. Does a lot of work for military and naval customers. Mostly male clientele.

Linva Tailor, 38 Cochrane St, Central. Well-established ladies tailor, whose core business is making party clothes (*cheongsam*) for local ladies. Also does embroidery.

Sam's Tailors, 94 Nathan Rd, Tsim Sha Tsui. A Hong Kong institution, as much for Sam's talent for self-publicity as for the quality of his clothes. A long list of distinguished clients.

Shanghai Tang, 12 Pedder St, Central. This boutique's tailoring service specializes in modern adaptations of traditional Chinese styles for men and women. A fabulous selection of fabrics. They are very geared up to helping visitors and can arrange quick fittings and the posting of finished garments.

Fabrics

All tailors keep a selection of fabrics or samples, but if you want to choose your own, or don't have time to wait for theirs to arrive in stock, there are a number of fabric shops around town, particularly at the junction of Queen's Rd and Wellington St, and in D'Aguilar St. You could also try the following:

Western Market, Sheung Wan (p.82). There are lots of cloth shops there, with a wide variety of silk, cotton, linen and wool fabrics. Yau Shing Piece Goods at Shop 105 has an interesting selection, including some designer fabrics.

China Products, China products, Tsim Sha Tsui (p.130). Both shops keep a good range of Chinese fabrics, such as silk and brocade.

Shanghai Tang, 12 Pedder St. You don't have to have your fabric made up here, you can just buy by the metre.

Computers and electronics

Hong Kong is an excellent place to stock up on hardware and software. There's no tax on computers, and the locals want nothing but the latest model – creating big discounts on older versions. For other types of electronics, such as cameras and video players, the picture is more complicated. Some shops will try and charge you two or three times the true price – whilst swearing blind that they're offering huge discounts. The Nathan Road area seems to be the worst for this. Department stores – Chinese and Western – make a good reference point, as do the fixed-price electronic retail chains such as Fortress, which has branches all over Hong Kong. The electronics shops in the Prince's Building (10 Chater Rd, Central), or in hotels like the *Furama* are also pretty straight and may not be as expensive as you think. Stanley Street in Central has a good range of **camera shops**. See also **Secondhand** (p.298).

For the latest offers on computers and accessories look at the ads in the *South China Morning Post*'s technology supplement every Tuesday. The main places to head for include:

Star House, Salisbury Rd, Tsim Sha Tsui. Near the Star Ferry. Reliable computer mall, including a specialist computer bookshop.

Golden Shopping Arcade, 156 Fuk Wah St, Sham Shui Po, Kowloon. Famous for its supply of cheap computer goods, but notorious as a centre for pirate software.

Windsor House, 311 Gloucester Rd, Causeway Bay. Useful Hong Kong-side arcade, which also stocks secondhand computers.

Computer Zone, 298 Hennessy Rd, Wan Chai. Warren-like place, full of shops selling new, secondhand, official and pirated computer gear.

Crafts

In addition to what's available in the Chinese products stores, these shops offer various types of modern arts-and-crafts products from throughout Asia.

Amazing Grace Elephant Company, 349 Ocean Centre, Harbour City, Canton Rd, Tsim Sha Tsui. Assorted Asian handicrafts, collectables and knick-knacks.

Banyan Tree, 214–218 Prince's Building, 10 Chater Rd, Central; 257 Ocean Terminal, Canton Rd, Tsim Sha Tsui. Antiques, reproduction furniture and pricey Asian handicrafts.

G.O.D. Horizon Plaza, Ap Lei Chau, Aberdeen; Festival Walk, Kowloon Tong; Discovery Park, Tsuen Wan. Simple modern household products and furniture for Chinese yuppies. Some very good designs and colours, in natural materials and at reasonable prices.

Kinari, 27 Staunton St, Mid-Levels. Selection of Asian crafts and antiques.

King and Country, 3rd Floor, Pacific Place, 88 Queensway, Admiralty. An amazing shop which sells beautiful hand-painted lead soldiers and models. Many have military themes, but there are also wonderful sets showing Chinese life, the Qing dynasty court, and a traditional wedding.

Mountain Folkcraft, 12 Wo On Lane (off D'Aguilar St), Central. Beautiful handmade folk arts and crafts from Southeast Asia and elsewhere.

Museum Shop, Hong Kong Arts Centre, Cultural Centre, Salisbury Rd, Tsim Sha Tsui. Art books and supplies, calligraphy

Shopping

Shopping

materials, prints, postcards, gifts and stationery.

The Pottery Workshop, 2 Lower Albert Rd (entrance on Wyndham St), Central. Small gallery for locally produced pottery and ceramic art. Affordable and interesting.

Tequila Kola, 115 Prince's Building, 10 Chater Rd, Central. A similar selection to the Banyan Tree – furniture, rugs, lamps, brassware, etc.

The Welfare Handicrafts Shops, Shop 7, Lower Ground Floor, Jardine House, 1 Connaught Place, Central; Salisbury Rd, Tsim Sha Tsui. Locally made arts and crafts sold on behalf of charities.

Department stores

There is a vast selection of mammoth, air-conditioned **department stores**, owned by parent companies from different countries; pick your culture and dive in. Most have cafés and coffee shops inside, too.

Local stores

Lane Crawford, 70 Queen's Rd, Central; Levels 1–3, The Mall, Pacific Place, 88 Queensway, Admiralty. Hong Kong's oldest Western-style department store – the first branch listed is the main one.

Sincere, 173 Des Voeux Rd, Central; 83 Argyle St, Mongkok. A more downmarket store; the Argyle St branch is good for shoes.

Wing On, 26 Des Voeux Rd, Central; 211 Des Voeux Rd, Central; 183 Queen's Rd East, Wan Chai; Cityplaza I, 1111 King's Rd, Tai Koo Shing; 361 Nathan Rd, Yau Ma Tei; Wing On Plaza, 62 Mody Rd, Tsim Sha Tsui East; Site 11, Whampoa Garden, 6 Tak Hong St, Hung Hom. Standard department store with branches all over the territory, good for everyday items.

Japanese stores

Mitsukoshi, Hennessy Centre, 500 Hennessy Rd, Causeway Bay; Sun Plaza, 28 Canton Rd, Tsim Sha Tsui. Flashiest of all the Causeway Bay stores.

Seibu, Pacific Place, 88 Queensway, Admiralty. Includes a great food hall.

Sogo, East Point Centre, 555 Hennessy Rd, Causeway Bay. Ten floors' worth of consumerism, including a good Japanese supermarket.

Other stores

Marks & Spencer, Shop 120 & 229, The Mall, Pacific Place, 88 Queensway, Admiralty; Shop 313–316 & 418–421, Times Square, 1 Matheson St, Causeway Bay; Shop 102 & 254, Ocean Centre, Harbour City, Canton Rd, Tsim Sha Tsui. Classic British department store selling sensible underwear and biscuits.

Food and drink

For a list of **bakeries, delicatessens, take-aways** and **supermarkets**, consult the relevant sections of Chapter 7. You'll find accounts of **markets** where you can buy food throughout the book. The main ones are Central and Sheung Wan markets (Chapter 2); Temple Street Night Market (Chapter 3); and Luen Wo Market and Sheung Shui Market (both Chapter 4). For **wines and spirits** and other drinks, most of the supermarkets have adequate selections. Wine is expensive because of high tax rates. There is also an increasing number of wine shops, mostly in Central and Mid-Levels (where some restaurants don't have licenses). If you want a bigger selection, try Olivers in Prince's Building (10 Chater Rd, Central) and Ocean Centre, Tsim Sha Tsui; Citysuper, Times Square, 1 Matheson St, Causeway Bay; The Big Apple Deli, 105–109 Harbour Centre, 25 Harbour Rd, Wan Chai; Seibu's Food Hall, Pacific Place, 88 Queensway, Admiralty; Watson's Wine, D'Aguilar St, Central; or a branch of Marks & Spencer (see above). Most of these sell a range of Western foods (cheese, bread, chocolates) too.

When buying food in markets, you need to know that **Chinese weights and measures** are different from Western ones. Most things (vegetables, beansprouts, rice, dried foods) are sold by the **catty**, which is the equivalent of 1.3 lb or 600g; the smaller unit is the **tael**, equivalent to 1.3 oz or 38g. That said, unless you can speak and read Chinese, you'll probably find that simply picking up the amount you want and handing it to the stallholder is the best way to go about things. Fruit is sold by the piece or the pound, meat and fish by the ounce.

Jewellery

Jewellery prices are low in Hong Kong (since precious stones can be imported without paying duty) and there are literally thousands of jewellers, reflecting the local population's love for glitter and sparkle. Most of their designs tend towards the flashy – this is a town where you wear your wealth on your sleeve, or your finger – although many also do pieces which are extremely close to the signature designs of some of the most famous international jewellers, so if you've always coveted that Cartier necklace, this could be your opportunity. Alternatively, given time they can make or copy to your requirements. Again if you're buying, shop around, take what you hear with a pinch of salt, and check the fixed-price shops before venturing to Nathan Road.

If you're going to buy, first get hold of the HKTA's free *Shopping Guide to Jewellery*, which explains the different quality and grade of various precious stones sold in Hong Kong. This is particularly important if you're buying **jade**, which is very popular here: there's a special Jade Market in Kansu Street, Yau Ma Tei (see p.134).

If you need help or information on buying **diamonds**, contact the Diamond Importers' Association Ltd, Room 1707, Parker House, 70 Queen's Rd, Central ☎ 2523 5497.

For **opals**, a fun place to visit is The Opal Mine (Burlington House, Ground Floor, 92 Nathan Rd, Tsim Sha Tsui), which also has an informative exhibition on the mining of opal in Australia, where ninety percent of the world's supply comes from.

Elissa Cohen Jewellery, 209 Hankow Centre, 5–15 Hankow Rd, Tsim Sha Tsui. Individual designs, lots of pearls.

Gallery One, 31–33 Hollywood Rd. A huge selection of semi-precious beads and necklaces – amber, amethyst, tiger's eye, crystal and much more. They will string any arrangement you want.

Johnson & Co., 44 Hankow Rd, Kowloon. Straight, middle-of-the-road jeweller, not too pushy.

Just Gold, Ground Floor, Pacific Place, 88 Queensway, Admiralty; 453 Hennessy Rd, Wan Chai; The Landmark, Des Voeux Rd, Central. Local chain specializing in fun, fashionable, cheapish designs for young women. They have the licence for Mickey Mouse gold jewellery – very popular locally.

Kai-Yin Lo, 3rd Floor, Pacific Place, 88 Queensway, Admiralty; Shop M6, *Mandarin Hotel*; Shop BE11a, *Peninsula Hotel*. Hong Kong's best-known jewellery designer, who also sells in New York. Makes interesting use of old jade, carvings and semi-precious stones. Expensive, but nice to look.

New Universal Jewelry Company, 23rd floor, Diamond Exchange Building, 8–10 Duddle St, Central. Reliable, quality jewellers with wide range of styles. Competitive prices.

Regal Jewelry, Empire Centre, 68 Mody Rd, Tsim Sha Tsui East. Good, large selection of gold, including some very well-known designs. Unfortunately the sales force are very shark-like. You need to be an experienced and persistent bargainer.

Leather goods

There are lots of outlets selling inexpensive leather **shoes and bags**, often of good quality and design. You'll find stalls in many of the markets (see p.298), Stanley Market particularly, while the area around Nathan Rd also has lots of outlets. On the Island try the Pedder Building (12 Pedder St, Central) or – strangely – the Landmark (Des Voeux Rd, Central) and the Prince's Building (10 Chater Rd, Central). If you just want to browse go to Wong Nai Chung Road in Happy Valley where there are lots of leather shops, who will also make to

Shopping

Learn to say "gay dor chin?" ("how much is it?"), the numbers (see p.403), the word for dollar (mahn), catty (gan) and ounce (onsi), and you might just be able to buy something in a Hong Kong market.

Shopping

order if you have time.

Nancy & Prima, 173 Wong Nai Chung Rd, Happy Valley; 606B Pedder Building, 12 Pedder St, Central. Well established shop that will make to order.

Perfect Borne Ltd, Star Ferry Pier, Tsim Sha Tsui. Wide selection at the cheap-and-cheerful end of the range.

Markets: clothes, fabrics and bric-a-brac

The cheapest clothes and fabrics can be found in markets, but shop around and haggle. You won't be able to try anything on and you'll never be able to take anything back, but be sensible and you shouldn't go too far wrong.

Jade Market, Kansu St, Yau Ma Tei. Jade jewellery, artefacts and statues; p.134.

Jardine's Bazaar, Causeway Bay. Clothes and household goods; p.104.

Li Yuen Street East and West, Central. Women's and children's clothes; p.75.

Man Wa Lane, Sheung Wan. Traditional Chinese seals; p.81.

Marble Street, North Point. Shirts and shorts; p.116.

Stanley Market, Stanley Village. Clothes, silk, cashmere; some fake designer labels a speciality; p.114.

Temple Street, Yau Ma Tei. The territory's best night market: clothes, tapes, watches, jewellery, digital bits and pieces, everything; p.136.

Tung Choi Street, Mongkok. Women's and children's clothes and accessories; p.136.

Upper Lascar Row (Cat Street), Central. Flea market; p.84.

Western Market, Sheung Wan. Fabrics, arts and crafts; p.82.

Music: CDs and tapes

Most mainstream CDs and tapes (laser discs too) can be found in Hong Kong: prices are generally around twenty to thirty percent lower than in the UK (and slightly higher than in the US). Check out the locally produced Canto-pop releases,

as well as recordings of mainland Chinese artists. Note that artists are almost always filed under first names. If you come across market barrows selling CDs, they're almost certainly pirate copies.

Chungking Mansions, 36–44 Nathan Rd, Tsim Sha Tsui. Cheap tapes and CDs at various stalls inside Nathan Road's most labyrinthine shopping centre.

DoReMi Records, D16, Queensway Plaza, 93 Queensway, Admiralty. A bit limited in range, but with the odd bargain.

Good Times Music Store, Shatin Plaza, Sha Tin. You can listen to your selection before buying here.

Hong Kong Records, Shop 252, The Mall, Pacific Place, 88 Queensway, Admiralty. Good mixture of styles and prices; no vinyl in sight, despite the name.

HMV, Ground Floor, Windsor House, Great George St, Causeway Bay; Sands Building, Peking Rd, Tsim Sha Tsui. Megastores with listening stations and a mammoth choice, as good for World and Canto-pop as for Western releases.

Satellite Record Co., B9–10, United Centre, Queensway Plaza, 93 Queensway, Admiralty. Good for classical music.

Tower Records, 7th Floor, Times Square, 1 Matheson St, Causeway Bay. Huge selection of music (often a few dollars less than HMV), with in-store appearances to pull in the punters.

Secondhand

Bizarrely, Hong Kong is rather a good place to buy secondhand stuff, or – as it's coyly known locally – "pre-owned". The local population is so fashion- and brand-conscious that there is a lot of turnover, and apartments are so small people don't have room to keep last season's stuff.

Books: *Collectables*, 1st Floor, Winning House, 26 Hollywood Rd, Central; *Ann Chan Books & So Forth*, 66 Lockhart Rd, Wan Chai; *Flow*, 40 Lyndhurst Terrace, Central (also stocks CDs).

Computers: *Computer Exchange Sq*, 298 Hennessy Rd, Wan Chai; *Carion Computer Solution*, 1248 Windsor House, 311 Gloucester Rd, Causeway Bay.

Cameras: try the shops in Stanley St, Central or: *David Chan Co*, 15 Champagne Ct, 16 Kimberley Rd, Tsim Sha Tsui; *Tin Cheung Camera Co.*, 26 Tung Yung Building, 100 Nathan Rd, Tsim Sha Tsui; *Hing Lee Camera Co.*, 25 Lyndhurst Terrace, Central.

Clothes: The Pedder Building, 12 Pedder St, Central, has some outlets such as *La Place* which deal in upmarket second-hand. Other outlets include *Mak Yau Saw*, 12A Haven Commercial Building, Tsing Fung St, North Point; *Re-Fashion*, 221 Hankow Centre, 14 Hankow Rd, Tsim Sha Tsui.

Watches: *Berne Horology*, Kam On Building, 176A Queen's Rd, Central. Huge selection of secondhand and antique watches, including the top brands.

Shopping malls

Even if you hate shopping, it's impossible to avoid walking through a **shopping mall** sooner or later, since half the pedestrian overpasses and walkways in Central and Tsim Sha Tsui East pass straight through one or more of them. You may as well accept that you're going to see the inside of more shopping malls than you thought existed; you may even enjoy them when the weather is hot or wet since they're air-conditioned. The main concentrations are in Central, Admiralty and Tsim Sha Tsui, with a few in Causeway Bay and a couple of other major malls in the New Territories. Many are sights in themselves: gleaming, climate-controlled consumer paradises, serviced by state-of-the-art elevators, enlivened by galleries, lights and fountains, and sustained by bars, cafés and restaurants. All the important ones are covered in the text, but a quick checklist of the best includes:

Cityplaza, 111 King's Rd, Taikoo Shing. Popular mid-range mall, catering mainly for local shoppers.

Festival Walk, Kowloon Tong. Linked by underpass to Kowloon Tong MTR. The newest and shiniest of the Hong Kong malls, designed by the super-trendy Miami architectural practice, Arquitechtonica. The design incorporates feng shui principles, so there are no pointed edges and lots of references to nature – water with the fountains, a glacier with the ice rink, a cave for the food court. There are also more than 200 shops.

The Landmark, Des Voeux Rd, Central. Central MTR. Five minute's walk from the Star Ferry, you're almost certain to pass through this mall as it's an intersection for Central's raised walkways. Check out the basement for local brands and a good bookshop. The designer boutiques on the upper floors are interesting in the sales.

New Town Plaza, Sha Tin, New Territories. Formerly one of the most important in the New Territories, but now easily outshone by Festival Walk.

Ocean Terminal, Tsim Sha Tsui. Near the Kowloon Star Ferry terminal. A warren-like building which incorporates Harbour City and Ocean Centre. Includes a couple of posh antique shops, a good bookshop, Toys 'R Us, and a number of local jewellers, as well as dozens of the usual boutiques.

Pacific Place, 88 Queensway, Admiralty. Linked by underpass directly to Admiralty MTR. One of the swankiest malls around, but in addition to the designer outlets on the upper floors it also has a good range of ordinary shops and local boutiques on the lower ones.

Prince's Building, 10 Chater Rd, Central. Next to Chater Square and two minutes from the Star Ferry. Not really a mall, but it has become a second home for many of Hong Kong's expats because of the deli on the third floor which stocks loads of foreign foods and wines. Some interesting fashion accessory shops, jewellers and tailors, a good bookshop and stationers, and an expensive but totally straight antique shop.

Shun Tak Centre, 200 Connaught Rd, Sheung Wan. Mid-range shopping centre

Shopping

Shopping

with a local clientele – nothing fancy, but handy if you're in the area.

Times Square, 1 Matheson St, Causeway Bay. Linked by walkway to Causeway Bay MTR; the tram also runs nearby. The main mall in Causeway Bay, with the usual selection of local and international retailers, plus lots of restaurants, a cinema complex, and a forum area often used for special exhibitions.

Tea shops

Chinese tea in decorative tins and boxes makes a nice, portable souvenir, and can be bought from any of Hong Kong's numerous specialist tea shops, or in prepacked selections from Chinese products shops (see p.292). In traditional tea shops the tea is treated like wine, with different vintages and producers. There are dozens of different varieties, and some shops will let you taste before you make your choice. You buy in small amounts, since tea loses its flavour after a while.

Most shops also stock **teapots** – often fanciful creations, shaped as animals, plants or fruits. Some are collector's items, made by well-known potters and priced accordingly.

Best Tea House, 3 Lock Rd, Tsim Sha Tsui; Unit 201, Causeway Bay Plaza II, 463–483 Lockhart Rd, Causeway Bay.

Fook Ming Tong Tea Shop, Ground Floor, Shop 5C, Prince's Building, 10 Chater Rd, Central; The Landmark, Des Voeux Rd, Central; Lower Ground 3, Mitsukoshi, Hennessy Centre, 500 Hennessy Rd, Causeway Bay; Shop 200A, Ocean Terminal, Harbour City, Canton Rd, Tsim Sha Tsui; East Point Centre, Yee Wo St, Causeway Bay. Lovely selection of teapots. Expensive.

Kee Heung Chun Tea Co., 30A Sands St, Kennedy Town.

Ying Kee, Siu Ying Building, 151 Queen's Rd, Central; 33 Staunton St, Mid-Levels; Silver Commercial Building, Nathan Rd, Mongkok.

Chapter 13

Sports and Recreation

The only drawback to Hong Kong's varied range of **sporting and recreation opportunities** is the inevitable lack of space for such things. **To play** some sports – particularly racket sports – you'll generally have to book well in advance, which is why so many residential buildings have private sports facilities. Still, as a tourist, you should be able to find something energetic to do – the possibilities are detailed below in alphabetical order.

Spectator sports are more limited, primarily because the territory's available space restricts the number of stadiums and sports grounds, not to mention teams. That said, there are events throughout the year – some of them of international standard – again, you'll find details below.

The territory's main sporting venue is the **Queen Elizabeth Stadium**, 18 Oi Kwan Rd, Wan Chai ☎ 2591 1346. The major municipal stadiums and sports grounds are run by the Urban Council, whose free monthly magazine *City News* (from City Hall) carries a "Sports Diary" listing current events and competitions. Also, check out the listings in the free *HK Magazine* and *Where Hong Kong*, both distributed via bars, restaurants and cafes. The HKTA's publications also give full details of forthcoming events, or alternatively contact the **Sports Promotion Office**, 9th Floor, Fa Yuen Street Complex Building, 1238 Fa Yuen St, Mongkok ☎ 2309 1000.

One privately run sports centre is the **Hong Kong Sports Institute** in Sha Tin

(☎ 2681 6888), which has excellent facilities and is open to non-members during off-peak hours (Mon–Fri 8am–6pm) – see the badminton, squash, swimming and tennis listings below for fuller details. A second centre offering visitor's passes for $30 is the **South China Athletic Association** (Caroline Hill, Causeway Bay ☎ 2577 6932; membership enquiries ☎ 2577 4427), which has facilities for all kinds of sports and keep-fit activities.

Finally, you can let someone else do the organizing by signing on for the HKTA's **sports and recreation tour** (information from any HKTA office). Around $400 gets you a day-return trip to the Clearwater Bay Golf and Country Club on the Sai Kung peninsula, the Kau Sai Chau Public Golf Course on an island near Sai Kung, or the Hong Kong Golf Club at Fanling. The fee includes admission and transport. At Clearwater Bay there are other facilities too – you'll pay $55 for swimming, sauna and jacuzzi; $75 per session for squash, badminton and tennis; and a much heftier charge if you want to play golf. There's a bar and restaurants, too. Book a day in advance (departures are at around 7.30am).

Badminton

You can rent **badminton** courts for $60–80 an hour at the two places listed below, or play at the Clearwater Bay Golf and Country Club (see introduction, above). More general information is

Sports and Recreation

available from the Hong Kong Badminton Association on ☎2504 8318.

Hong Kong Sports Institute, Sha Tin ☎2681 6888. Off-peak hours only for visitors; Mon–Fri 8am–10pm.

Queen Elizabeth Stadium, 18 Oi Kwan Rd, Wan Chai ☎2591 1346.

Bowling

For **ten-pin bowling**, try one of the bowling alleys below. At either, you'll pay around $50 an hour; avoiding weekends is a good idea, as alleys are extremely popular. For **lawn bowls**, which also costs from around $50 an hour, try the green at Victoria Park, Causeway Bay (☎2570 6186).

South China Bowling Centre, 88 Caroline Hill Rd, Causeway Bay ☎2890 8528. Open 10am–midnight.

Top Bowl Ltd, Whampoa Garden, Hung Hom ☎2764 0811. Open 9am–1am.

Fishing

The **fishing** season in Hong Kong's reservoirs lasts from September to March; if you're over thirteen, you can get a licence from the Water Supplies Department, 7 Gloucester Rd, Wan Chai ☎2824 5000. They'll also give you information about what you can and can't catch.

Golf

Golf is a pricey sport in Hong Kong, and you'll have to be keen to play at any of the territory's clubs. Most, if they are open to non-members at all, take them only during the week. The **Hong Kong Open Golf Championship** is held at the Hong Kong Golf Club in Fanling every February. Less serious golf is catered for by the

> You can't play **golf** on a whim in Hong Kong. Clothes specifically banned from the greens include tracksuits, T-shirts, collarless shirts, shorts more than four inches above the knee, jeans, vests and bathing gear. If you're going to play, pack or buy accordingly.

minigolf course at Shek O, right by the beach, and a similar set-up, with a driving range, at Sha Tin's New Town Plaza.

Clearwater Bay Golf and Country Club ☎2335 1271. The HKTA runs an inclusive day trip to this club. Green fees on the Executive Nine course are around $400, golf cart and clubs extra; playing the 18-hole championship course starts at $1200.

Discovery Bay, Lantau ☎2987 7273. Among the newest of Hong Kong's golf clubs, with a course spectacularly laid out on top of the island's hills. Fees here are around $900 from Monday to Friday, around $1600 at weekends, plus extras.

Hong Kong Golf Club, Fanling, New Territories ☎2670 1211. The territory's major club, and home of the HK Open, there are three 18-hole courses at which visitors can play on weekdays for around $1400 per person (Hong Kong residents $1200), plus caddies and clubs. The HKGC also operate a course at **Deep Water Bay** on Hong Kong Island (☎2812 7070); visitors pay around $450 plus extras, again on weekdays only (9.30am–1.30pm). You should book well in advance for all these courses.

Shek O Golf and Country Club ☎2809 4458. The swishest golf course on the south side of Hong Kong Island, open to members only – with membership restricted to only three hundred people.

Hiking

One of the most pleasant and unexpected discoveries to be made in Hong Kong is the countryside. Despite the density of its urban areas, nearly three-quarters of the territory's land is still undeveloped, and – even more surprising – forty percent of the territory is officially classified as country park. There are 22 different parks in the New Territories and on Lantau and Hong Kong Island, and it's worth making the effort to get out into at least one for the totally different perspective it will give you on the territory.

The countryside varies from subtropical vegetation to pine forests and barren hillsides. There are also wonderful views, interesting flora and fauna, and some rare peace and quiet. All the parks are easily accessible by public transport and are well supplied with trails varying in difficulty from afternoon strolls to challenging hikes.

Don't be deceived, however, into thinking that because of their closeness to the city the country parks are easy or tame countryside. They are not. Every year a couple of walkers simply disappear or are found dead, having fallen down slopes or met with accidents. Much of the terrain is mountainous and unshaded and can be dangerous in the tropical sun and humidity if not treated with respect. Wear good shoes and sun protection, take water and – if possible – a mobile phone.

All the territory's **long-distance hikes** are covered in the text. The three main routes are the Lantau Trail (p.195), the 100-kilometre MacLehose Trail (p.178) and the Hong Kong Island Trail (p.63). You can get trail maps from the Government Publications Centre, 66 Queensway, Admiralty ☎ 2537 1910. The HKTA also have information.

Horses: racing and riding

The only sport in Hong Kong to command true mass appeal, **horse racing** is a spectating must if you're here during the season, which runs from September to May. There are two courses, both run by the **Hong Kong Jockey Club**: the original one at Happy Valley (meetings every Wednesday evening during the season) and a much newer, state-of-the-art affair at Sha Tin in the New Territories, which stages races most weekend during the season. For information, call the HKJC hotline on ☎ 2966 8397; alternatively the HKTA can organize tours and tickets for the enclosures. If you want to go on your own you can just turn up and pay $10 to get into the public stands. Alternatively, take your passport to the racecourse (over-18s only) and the HKJC will sell you a guest badge for $50, which gives you access to a more pleasant stand near the finish. See p.106 and p.150 for full details of each course.

If you want to get on the back of one of the beasts, then there are a couple of places where you can go **horse-riding**, though it's necessarily a limited, and expensive, option given the lack of flat space. Most establishments are owned by the Jockey Club, and the best of them are for members only. The public can, however, ride at **Tuen Mun Riding**, Lot 45, Lung Mun Rd, Tuen Mun ☎ 2461 3338 (lessons from $275 per hour) or the **Pokfulam Public Riding School**, 75 Reservoir Rd, Pokfulam, Hong Kong Island ☎ 2550 1359 (lessons around $340/hour; closed Mon and for 2–3 weeks in July/Aug). Most of the horses are thoroughbreds retired from the racetrack. Pokfulam also has riding facilities designed for disabled people, and long waiting lists, especially for children and beginners. You need to book well in advance.

Indoor sports: snooker, billiards, pool and darts

There are dozens of private clubs at which you can play table games like **billiards**, **snooker** and **pool**. You usually have to join, though sometimes you only need to pay a nominal fee, and then

Sports and Recreation

Betting on the Horses

Minimum bet at the racecourses is $10 and you can only bet in multiples of this sum. Aside from simply betting on a win or place, try betting a **quinella** (predicting first and second horse, in any order); a **tierce** (first, second and third in correct order); **double or triple trio** (first three horses, in any order, in two or three designated races); or a **treble** (winners of three designated races). Betting **tax** is 11.5 percent, rising to 17.5 percent on a more complicated bet.

Sports and Recreation

pay for your games. Look in the Yellow Pages (under "Billiards") for a club near you and ring for opening hours and membership details before setting out. You can also usually get a game at Top Bowl, Whampoa Garden, Hung Hom ☎ 2764 0811. Alternatively, a growing number of bars now have games tables.

Another recreational possibility is a game of darts in one of the pubs. Several have boards (including the *Kangaroo Pub* in Tsim Sha Tsui); check the pub listings in Chapter 8 for more possibilities.

A good place for all these games is *The Stadium Bar & Grill* at the Hong Kong Stadium, 55 Eastern Hospital Rd, So Kon Po, Happy Valley ☎ 2915 7114. As well as pool and darts, there's table soccer and table hockey, and big-screen action of all the major sports events.

Martial arts

As in China, **martial arts** are phenomenally popular in Hong Kong, where every second film released features combat of some sort or other. Though born in the United States, **Bruce Lee** (1940–73) spent the later part of his childhood in Hong Kong, and every kid still wants to be him, or one of the dozens of other movie practitioners who have emerged since. Bruce's actor son, Brandon Lee, died tragically young like his father in an accident on a film set in 1993; his daughter is now starting her film career. Meanwhile Hong Kong-born Jackie Chan remains one of the most prolific of the current stars, although he's getting a bit old for flying kicks – you'll see his name everywhere in magazines and on film posters.

The martial art you see most of in Hong Kong outside the cinema, however, is **tai chi**, also known as shadow boxing – a series of slow, balletic exercises designed to stimulate both the mind and the body. Early morning in most of the parks and gardens is the best time to watch or participate in this extraordinarily uplifting exercise. Popular venues include Kowloon Park, Victoria Park, Chater Gardens, around Central Plaza, and the Botanical and Zoological Gardens.

Hong Kong Chinese Martial Arts Association, 687 Nathan Rd, Jordan ☎ 2394 4803.

Hong Kong Tai Chi Association, 60 Argyle St, Mongkok ☎ 2395 4884.

Rugby

Rugby (Union, not League) is generally of a good standard and each Easter a couple of days are devoted to a series of Rugby Sevens matches with international teams – the boisterous crowd is as entertaining as the matches themselves. The event is organized by the **Hong Kong Rugby Football Union** (Room 2003/4, Sports House, 1 Stadium Path, So Kon Po, Happy Valley; ☎ 2504 8300), who can provide more information and tell you how to go about joining a team in Hong Kong.

Running

You'll see people **jogging** at dozens of places throughout the territory, some of which have marked routes and exercise stops along the way. A few of the most popular spots are along Bowen Road in Mid-Levels; around the roads at the top of Victoria Peak; along the Tsim Sha Tsui East waterfront; around Victoria Park; and in Kowloon Park, off Nathan Road. If you do run or jog, remember that the summer heat and humidity are crippling; run in the early morning or evening and take some water along.

An increasingly wide variety of **races** now take place for walkers and runners – traditional marathons, endurance events, and adventure racing. Notable events include the **Hong Kong Marathon**, held in January, the **MacLehose Trailwalker** in November, and the **Action Asia Challenge** in December. You can get information, and entry forms for the Hong Kong Marathon, from the Hong Kong Amateur Athletic Association (☎ 2504 8215; the HKTA can help with the others). All such events start early, because of the climate. In the past the Hong Kong Marathon has attracted a large contingent of disabled athletes in wheelchairs.

More offbeat running is provided by the **Orienteering Association of Hong Kong** (Room 1014, Sports House, 1 Stadium Path, So Kon Po, Happy Valley ☎ 2504 8111), who maintain an orienteering course in Pokfulam Country Park on Hong Kong Island. Write or ring for a map of the course.

Skating

There are a number of **ice-skating** rinks in Hong Kong and one fairly central **roller-skating** rink, too. On the streets, try Victoria Park, the Tsim Sha Tsui East waterfront promenade, or Bowen Road in Mid-Levels (good views, clean air, but not such a good surface) which are all popular with skateboarders and rollerbladers.

Ice-skating

Cityplaza Ice Palace, Cityplaza, Taikoo Shing ☎ 2885 4697 (Taikoo Shing MTR). Open Mon–Fri 8am–10pm, Sat & Sun 12.30–10pm; $50 all day during the week, $60 at the weekend, including skates.

The Glacier, Festival Walk, Kowloon Tong ☎ 2265 8888. Open 8.30am–10pm; $40–60 per session, skates extra.

Whampoa Super Ice, Whampoa Garden, Hung Hom ☎ 2774 4899. Open 10am–11pm; two-hour sessions $40 weekday, $50 weekend, including skates.

Roller-skating

Sportsworld Association, Telford Gardens, Kowloon Bay ☎ 2757 2211. Open 9am–11pm; $40 a session.

Soccer

Soccer is played widely throughout the territory. Hong Kong's First Division is littered with has-been or never-were players from other countries (mostly Britain) – teams are allowed five overseas players. Good local talent is fairly thin on the ground, but games can be entertaining, not least because the foreign players tend to be bought as strikers and consequently face local defences comprising people much shorter than themselves.

If you're sufficiently interested, teams to watch are Happy Valley, South China and Eastern. The "national team", such as it is, usually has a torrid time in the World Cup qualifying matches, making heavy weather against such footballing giants as Bahrain and Lebanon. The best advice for soccer fans is to find a TV on Saturday evenings during the English soccer season, when you get an hour's worth of the previous week's top English matches; most major cup and international matches are televised live, too.

Sports and Recreation

Squash

Squash is about the most popular indoor racket sport. Book well in advance and expect to pay around $50 an hour at the public courts listed below – or you can play at the Clearwater Bay Golf and Country Club (see introduction on p.301). For beginners, the Urban Council (☎ 2529 7960) organizes courses, and the **Hong Kong Squash Association** (☎ 2869 0611) has private lessons for intermediate players.

Hong Kong Sports Institute, Sha Tin ☎ 2681 6888; off-peak hours only: Mon–Fri 8am–5.45pm, Sat 8am–1pm.

Hong Kong Squash Centre, Cotton Tree Drive, Central ☎ 2521 5072; book up to ten days in advance in person (no bookings taken by phone).

Lai Chi Kok Sports Hall, Lai Chi Kok, Kowloon ☎ 2745 2796.

Queen Elizabeth Stadium, 18 Oi Kwan Rd, Wan Chai ☎ 2591 1346.

Victoria Park, Causeway Bay ☎ 2570 6186.

Swimming

If you don't want to risk the water at any of the territory's **beaches** – the best of which are covered in the text – then you'll have to take your dip in one of the few, and crowded, **swimming pools** operated by the Urban Council: call the Sports Promotion Office (☎ 2309 1000) or the Urban Services Department for

Sports and Recreation

information (Hong Kong Island ☎2801 5225; Kowloon East ☎2320 6542; Kowloon West ☎2309 1058). Most of the bigger hotels have pools, though these are usually open to residents only.

Aberdeen, 2 Shum Wah Rd, Aberdeen ☎2553 3617. Daily 7am–10pm; adults $19, children $7. Good facilities for the disabled.

Hong Kong Sports Institute, Sha Tin ☎2681 6888. You can use the pool during off-peak hours: Mon–Sat 7–8.30am & noon–2pm, Sun 7–9am; $40 per person. Call first to check times.

Kowloon Park, Nathan Rd, Tsim Sha Tsui ☎2724 3577. Open 6.30am–9pm; adults $19, children $8.

Morrison Hill, Oi Kwan Rd, Wan Chai ☎2575 3028. Daily 6.30am–9pm; adults $19, children $8.

Victoria Park, Hing Fat St, Causeway Bay ☎2570 4682. Daily 6.30am–10pm; adults $19, children $8.

Tennis

Public **tennis** courts are often solidly booked, but if you can get a court you'll pay around $40 an hour. Try at one of the following places, or play at the Clearwater Bay Golf and Country Club (see introduction on p.301). The Queen Elizabeth Stadium also has the facilities for **table tennis**, which costs about half as much per hour.

Hong Kong Sports Institute, Sha Tin ☎2681 6888. Off-peak hours only for visitors; Mon–Fri 9.30am–5.45pm.

Tennis Centre, Wong Nai Chung Gap Rd, Happy Valley, and King's Park, Kowloon. ☎2574 9122.

Victoria Park, Causeway Bay ☎2570 6186.

Watersports

As you might expect, there's plenty of choice for watersports in a territory of 230 islands. **Sailing** enthusiasts who are members of an overseas club can contact the prestigious Hong Kong Yacht Club on Kellet Island, Causeway Bay (☎2832 2817), which has reciprocal arrangements with many foreign clubs. The Hong Kong Yachting Association (☎2504 8158) operates intensive instruction courses at Clearwater Bay. For plain **boating and pleasure cruising**, contact any of the tour companies listed under "Organized Tours", p.59, or ask the HKTA for recommendations.

You can rent **windsurfing** equipment at quite a few of the territory's beaches: there are government-funded centres at Tai Po and Sai Kung where you can learn the basics fairly cheaply, or try the Windsurf Centre (☎2981 8316, open 10am–7pm) on Kwun Yam Wan Beach on Cheung Chau (p.191), which also offers courses and rental. The Windsurfing Association of Hong Kong (1 Stadium Path, or PO Box 1083, Central ☎2504 8255) can help with other enquiries.

Some beachside operations also offer **water-skiing** and **canoeing** (particularly at the Cheung Chau Windsurf Centre); you can get more information from the Hong Kong Water-Skiing Association (☎2504 8168).

Chapter 14

Children's Hong Kong

It's some kind of achievement in itself to have got children unscathed through a long-haul flight, so once in Hong Kong it's nice to know that there's lots for them to do. Not that there's an enormous amount in the way of specialized activities and events, but the territory itself can be a playground. Most of the things that you'll want to do anyway – from visiting island beaches to trawling through space-age shopping malls – are of sufficient general interest to keep everyone amused. The transport, particularly the trams and ferries, is exciting; most of the views and walks more so; and there are several venues with a real

family slant – Ocean Park is only the best known. The sections below should give you some ideas for day-to-day **activities**. You'll need to follow the page references for the full accounts of each sight, activity or sport. There's also a round-up of **dangers** to be aware of if you're travelling with small children.

Outings

Base a day trip around the places and activities below, all of which can occupy several hours with kids in tow. Some also offer a way to get out of the crowds – lunchtimes in Central and

---

Babysitting
Most large hotels can organize babysitting for you; the HKTA has a full list of those that will oblige, if you want to check before you leave.

Playgroups and information
Playgroups and parent-toddler groups are run by a variety of organizations, although most are aimed at residents rather than short-term visitors. Information from – among others – the Pre-School Playgroups Association ☎2523 2599 (Mon–Fri 9am–12.45pm, term-time only); St Andrew's Church, 138 Nathan Rd, Tsim Sha Tsui ☎2367 1478 (playgroups every Tues & Fri); St John's Cathedral, Garden Rd, Central ☎2523 4157 (parent and childrens' group every Tuesday). There's also a bi-monthly *Mother and Baby* magazine published in Hong Kong, available in many kids' clothes stores and toddler shops.

Clothes and supplies
Hong Kong has two branches of the specialist store Mothercare (Shop 338–340, Prince's Building, Chater Rd, Central; Shop 137, Ocean Terminal, Harbour City, Canton Rd, Tsim Sha Tsui) and there are children's clothes and toy shops in most of the large shopping malls – check the listings in HKTA's shopping guide (available free at HKTA offices).

Children's Hong Kong

Causeway Bay can be frightening for small children.

Botanical Gardens, Central (p.76). A pleasant green area, housing tropical birds and some small mammals. The best known inhabitants are two over-weight jaguars, but don't miss the lemurs and orangutans.

Festival Walk, Kowloon Tong MTR, Exit C (p.299). Massive shopping mall with an ice rink, a Rainforest Café, and endless shops.

Hong Kong Park, Central (p.78). Across the road from the Botanical Gardens. Enormous aviary, greenhouses, gardens, picnic areas, restaurant and the best playground in Hong Kong. Also close to the pedestrian walkways that snake off into the hi-tech buildings of Central.

Kadoorie Farm, near Kam Tin, New Territories (p.169). Farm with experimental breeding programme, lots of animals, abandoned and injured wildlife, walks, views and plants.

KCR train to Sheung Shui and back, New Territories (p.146). A train ride, with stops at traditional markets, brand-new towns and shopping centres, and a railway museum. Start from Festival Walk at Kowloon Tong.

Ocean Park and Water World, Deep Water Bay, Hong Kong Island (p.110). Multi-ride amusement and theme park, with moving dinosaurs, marine animals, shows, gardens, and, in summer, an adjacent slide-and-splash park. Plus Hong Kong's giant pandas An-An and Jia-Jia in their purpose-built home. Next door, Middle Kingdom recreates life in ancient China, with acrobats, lion dancing, and the chance to try skills like calligraphy.

Outlying islands (Chapter 5). Ferry rides to all the main islands, where there are beaches, walks, temples, watersports and – on Cheung Chau particularly – cycling trails.

Sea cruises (see "Organized tours", p.59). Cruises lasting anything from an hour to a whole day through the harbour and around the outlying islands; many

include lunch. The Dolphinwatch trip to see the endangered pink dolphins is particularly good.

Stanley Village, Hong Kong Island (p.112). Beaches, watersports, a covered market, some child-friendly restaurants, and a good bus ride there and back.

Victoria Peak (p.88). A trip up on the Peak Tram; easy flat walks around the Peak with great views; the shops of the Peak Galleria; Ripley's *Believe It Or Not!* Odditorium; and panoramic views and picnic areas.

Whampoa Garden, Hung Hom (p.132). Huge concrete ship-shaped shopping mall, with musical fountain, coffee shop, ice-skating rink, cinema and children's play area.

Museums and temples

The following places will interest an inquisitive child. The museums are ones where participation is encouraged – operating robots, clambering on old train carriages, exploring a renovated village – and while nearly all the temples in Hong Kong are unusual enough for most visitors, the ones listed below are particularly large and colourful.

Ching Chung Koon Temple, Tuen Mun, New Territories (p.166).

Po Lin Monastery, Lantau (p.203).

Railway Museum, Tai Po Market, New Territories (p.153).

Sam Tung Uk Folk Museum, Tsuen Wa, New Territories (p.162).

Science Museum, Science Museum Rd, Tsim Sha Tsui East (p.131).

Space Museum, Salisbury Rd, Tsim Sha Tsui (p.127).

Wong Tai Sin Temple, Kowloon (p.140).

Sport

See Chapter 13, "Sports and Recreation", for details of all **sporting activities** in Hong Kong. You should be able to persuade even the most slothful child that there's something they'd enjoy, whether it's bowling, skating or swimming. If you want your sport self-contained, think about the HKTA trips to the Clearwater Bay Golf and Country Club, where there's a variety of activities on offer in one well-equipped complex.

Entertainment

Obvious ideas include **cinemas**, which show the latest films in English; the HKTA-organized **cultural shows**, with song, dance and mime in various venues; and a (brief) visit to a **Chinese opera** for the singing and costumes. Some places, like the Arts Centre and local libraries, organize **special events** for children throughout the school summer holiday: the HKTA will have current information, or call into City Hall and look at the noticeboards, and pick up the *City News* magazine. There's more information on all these activities and events in Chapter 10. Coinciding with one of Hong Kong's **festivals** (see p.282) is another way to expose kids to a bit of cultural entertainment. If they're happy with crowds and loud noise they'll particularly enjoy the Cheung Chau Bun Festival. Dragon boat racing and any of the colourful Tin Hau celebrations are also popular. Suitable **arts events** (see p.276) include the Arts Festival in January and February, and the Christmas pantomimes.

Shopping

Shopping can keep children amused, too, especially when it's raining, since if you pick one of the huge shopping malls you don't have to set foot outside for hours on end, even to eat.

There's a list of the main malls on p.299; while specific **shops** that you might want to take in include the enormous *Toys R Us*, Shop 003, Basement, Ocean Terminal, Harbour City, Canton Rd, Tsim Sha Tsui; *The In Square*, Windsor House, 311 Gloucester Rd, Causeway Bay and Shop A197–199, Level I, New Town Plaza, Sha Tin, New Territories; *Hobby Horse*, Prince's Building, 10 Chater Rd, Central; *Wise Kids*, Pacific Place, 88 Queensway, Admiralty. Mitsukoshi and Sogo, the Japanese department stores in Causeway Bay (see p.296), are good, with games, toys, comics and cafés, as is the entire Festival Walk complex in Kowloon Tong (see p.299).

Eating

It's good to know that **restaurants** in Hong Kong (certainly Chinese restaurants) generally welcome kids with open arms; nearly all have high chairs available. Eating is a family affair, as a trip to any *dim sum* restaurant shows. Chapter 7

Children's
Hong Kong

Dangers

• Hong Kong can be extremely **hot and humid**. Small children should wear a hat and suncream when outside, and make sure they're drinking plenty of liquids.

• **Pollution** is a growing problem. Air contamination in urban areas – especially Causeway Bay – makes them worth avoiding at peak times, particularly if your child is asthmatic. The seawater in many popular swimming spots may not be healthy for small children with no immunity to local bugs. Don't even *think* of touching the water in Victoria Harbour.

• **Restaurant hygiene** may also be an issue, particularly for children who are not used to Chinese food. Use your eyes and common sense when choosing where to eat.

• Keep a close eye on children when riding **public transport**. Tram rides on Hong Kong Island, the Peak Tram and the MTR are all exciting, but they're nearly always packed. Keep kids away from tram windows, and from the edges of the cross-harbour ferries. It's easy to get separated in crowds, although it's very unlikely that anyone will try to abduct them.

• Don't encourage or allow children to play with **animals** found on the street. Rabies is still a problem here, and if your child gets bitten or scratched by a stray kitten, you're in for lengthy hospital visits.

Children's Hong Kong

details all the eating possibilities. You can get fish and chips in Hong Kong (Yorkshire's famous *Harry Ramsden's* has a branch here), as well as pizzas, hamburgers and all manner of calorific junk, so no one needs to starve. Other restaurants regarded as particularly child-friendly are the *Hard Rock Café, Planet Hollywood, Dan Ryan's, Tony Roma's*

Pizza Hut, Ruby Tuesday, Rainforest Café, Haagen-Dazs, the Peak Café, Stanley's Italian, and *Spaghetti Kitchen.* For more of an occasion, visit one of the specialist **fish restaurants** in Lau Fau Shan (p.172) or Lei Yue Mun (p.141) or on one of the outlying islands (Chapter 5), where youngsters can pick dinner out of the fish tanks.

Chapter 15

Directory

AIRLINES All the airlines in Hong Kong are listed in the Yellow Pages under "Air Line Companies". The main ones include:
Aeroflot ☎2845 4232
Air India ☎2522 1176
Air New Zealand ☎2524 9041
British Airways ☎2868 0303
Cathay Pacific ☎2747 1888
China Airlines ☎2868 2299
Dragon Air ☎2590 1188
Emirates ☎2526 7171
Japan Airlines ☎2523 0081
Korean Air ☎2368 6221
Lufthansa ☎2868 2313
Philippine Airlines ☎2369 4521
Qantas ☎2842 1438
SAS ☎2865 1370
Singapore Airlines ☎2520 2233
Swissair ☎2529 3670
Thai International ☎2876 6888
United Airlines ☎2810 4888

AIRPORT ENQUIRIES Hong Kong International (Chek Lap Kok) Airport ☎2181 0000. For Airbus routes and times call ☎2873 0818.

AMBULANCE Call ☎999, or the St John's Ambulance Brigade, which runs a free ambulance service, on ☎2576 6555 (Hong Kong Island), ☎2713 5555 (Kowloon) or ☎2639 2555 (New Territories).

AMERICAN EXPRESS Ground Floor, New World Tower, 16–18 Queen's Rd, Central ☎2801 7300 (Mon–Fri 9am–5.30pm, Sat 9am–noon); stolen cheques ☎2885 9331; stolen cards ☎2811 6122.

AMNESTY INTERNATIONAL 3rd Floor, Besto Best Building, Unit C, 32–36 Ferry St, Kowloon ☎2300 1250/1.

BANKS AND EXCHANGE There are banks of every nationality and description throughout Hong Kong, seemingly on every street corner. Opening hours are Mon–Fri 9am–4.30pm, Sat 9am–12.30pm, with small fluctuations – half an hour each side – from branch to branch. Most charge commission for exchanging travellers' cheques (around $50 per transaction), though generally, the Hang Seng Bank, Wing Lung Bank, Wing On Bank and the Union Bank of Hong Kong don't. There's no commission either if you change American Express or Thomas Cook cheques at their respective offices (see above and p.316). You can also change money and cheques at a licensed money changer – there are several in Tsim Sha Tsui which are open late (and on Sun). They won't rip you off, but they do charge a big commission (around nine percent of the sum changed). The signs on the windows of the moneychangers which say "No Commission" only apply if you're *selling* Hong Kong dollars. Otherwise, you can change travellers' cheques and cash at the big hotels and in some stores, but the rates will be lower than at the bank.

BIKE RENTAL Not an option in central Hong Kong, though possible on the islands and in the New Territories. Check with the HKTA, or contact the Hong Kong Cycling Association, at the Queen

Directory

Elizabeth Stadium, 18 Oi Kwan Rd, Wan Chai ☎2573 3861, fax 2834 3715.

BRITISH COUNCIL 1 Supreme Court Road, Wan Chai ☎2913 5500. There's a lending library on the first floor (Mon–Fri noon–8.00pm, Sat 10.30am–5.30pm, Sun 1.30–5.30pm) which costs $500 a year (or $300 for six months) to join. Members can borrow books, talking books and videos. There's also a reference section, open to anyone, with British newspapers and magazines. For French and German equivalents, see "Cultural Groups" below.

CAR PARKS The biggest firm is Wilson, which has car parks at Kowloon (Hung Hom) Station, City Hall (Central), 310 Gloucester Rd and 475 Lockhart Rd, among other places; other central car parks are at Exchange Square and Central Plaza. Charges are roughly $13–22/hour.

CAR RENTAL You'll pay from around $850 a day, $3,900 a week, for the smallest available car. You need to be over 18 (21 or 25 with some firms), have been driving for at least a year, and have a valid overseas driving licence (with which you can drive in Hong Kong for a year) or an international driving licence. Remember that you drive on the left. Agencies include: Avis, Ground Floor, Bonaventure House, 85 Leighton Rd, Causeway Bay ☎2890 6988; Hertz, Miramar Tower, 1–23 Kimberley Rd, Tsim Sha Tsui ☎2525 2838 or toll free ☎8009 62321; and Intercontinental Hire Cars Ltd, *Mandarin Hotel*, Central ☎2336 6111. Hiring a car and driver by the day or hour may be cheaper. Try Fung Hing Hire ☎2572 0333.

CLOTHING REPAIRS AND ALTERATIONS The many small shops in World-Wide House, Des Voeux Rd in Central are cheap and reasonably quick.

CONSULATES AND EMBASSIES British citizens who need consular assistance, particularly with regard to passport issues, should contact the Hong Kong Immigration Department, 7 Gloucester Rd, Wan Chai ☎2824 6111. The other main consulates and embassies are:

Australia, Harbour Centre, 23rd Floor, 25 Harbour Rd, Wan Chai ☎2827 8881.

Canada, 14th Floor, One Exchange Square, Central ☎2810 4321.

China, 5th Floor, China Resources Building, 26 Harbour Rd, Wan Chai ☎2827 1881.

India, 504 Admiralty Centre, Tower One, 18 Harcourt Rd, Admiralty ☎2528 4028.

Indonesia, 127 Leighton Rd, Causeway Bay ☎2890 4421.

Ireland, 6th Floor, Chung Nam Building, 1 Lockhart Rd, Wanchai ☎2527 4897

Japan, 46th Floor, One Exchange Square, Central ☎2522 1184.

Korea, 5th Floor, Far East Financial Centre, 16 Harcourt Rd, Central ☎2529 4141.

Malaysia, 23rd Floor, Malaysia Building, 50 Gloucester Rd, Wan Chai ☎2527 0921.

New Zealand, Room 2705, Jardine House, Connaught Rd, Central ☎2877 4488.

Philippines, 6th Floor, United Centre, 95 Queensway, Admiralty ☎2823 8500.

Portugal, 905 Harbour Centre, 25 Harbour Rd, Wanchai ☎2802 2587.

Singapore, 9th Floor, Tower One, Admiralty Centre, 18 Harcourt Rd, Admiralty ☎2527 2212.

South Africa, 27th Floor, Sunning Plaza, 10 Hysan Ave, Causeway Bay ☎2577 3279.

Thailand, 8th Floor, Fairmont House, 8 Cotton Tree Drive, Central ☎2521 6481.

Taiwan Chung Hwa Travel Service, 4th Floor, East Tower, Lippo Centre, 89 Queensway, Admiralty ☎2525 8315.

UK 1 Supreme Court Road, Central ☎2901 3000.

USA, 26 Garden Rd, Central ☎2523 9011.

Vietnam, 15th Floor, Great Smart Tower, 230 Wanchai Rd, Wan Chai ☎2291 4510.

CONTRACEPTION Condoms are available in supermarkets, the Pill over the counter from chemists. For anything else, contact a family planning clinic: the HQ is at

Southorn Centre, 130 Hennessy Rd, Wan Chai ☎2575 4477.

COUNSELLING AND ADVICE Community Advice Bureau, St John's Cathedral, New Hall, 8 Garden Rd, Central ☎2815 5444 (Mon–Fri 9.30am–4pm), deals with day-to-day problems and advice for new-comers and tourists. The AIDS Concern counselling service is on ☎2898 4411 (Thurs & Sat 7–10pm); Alcoholics Anonymous on ☎2522 5665 (daily 6–7pm). The Samaritans have an English-speaking 24-hour service on ☎2896 0000.

COUNTRY PARKS The Country Parks Division, Agriculture and Fisheries Dept, 12th Floor, 393 Canton Rd, Kowloon ☎2733 2235 (Mon–Fri 9am–5pm, Sat 9am–noon) has information and trail maps for all Hong Kong's country parks. Maps are also on sale from the Government Publications Centre (see p.314).

COURIER FLIGHTS For international couri-er flights, contact Aeronet Express (for Singapore Airlines) ☎2751 6120, Bridges Worldwide ☎2305 1412/3, Jupiter Air ☎2735 1946, or look at the classified ads in the *South China Morning Post*.

CULTURAL GROUPS Alliance Française, 2nd Floor, 123 Hennessy Rd, Wan Chai ☎2527 7825 (Mon–Fri 10am–1pm & 2–6pm; bus #11 passes by) has a French-language library and films; there's a second branch at 52 Jordan Rd, Kowloon ☎2730 3257. The Goethe Institute, 14th Floor, Hong Kong Arts Centre, 2 Harbour Rd, Wan Chai ☎2802 0088 (Mon–Fri 9.30am–7.45pm) has a general-purpose German-language library (as well as some English-language books), and also newspapers and a video library.

DENTISTS Dentists are listed in the Yellow Pages under "Dental Practitioners"; or ring the Hong Kong Dental Association (☎2528 5327) for a list of qualified dentists. Treatment is expensive.

DEPARTURE TAX Airport departure tax is $50 for anyone over 12.

DISABLED TRAVELLERS For a full run-down of services, pick up a copy of the *Guide to Public Transport Services in Hong Kong for Disabled Persons*, issued by the Transport Department (41st Floor, Immigration Tower, Gloucester Rd, Wan Chai ☎2829 5258). In particular, a spe-cial twelve-seater bus service, Rehabus, operates a scheduled service on 34 routes in the territory, as well as a dial-a-ride service; phone the Hong Kong Society for Rehabilitation on ☎2817 6277 in advance to make a reservation. Other useful numbers include: Hong Kong Red Cross ☎2802 0021 (wheelchair loans and other services); Hong Kong Society for the Blind ☎2778 8332; Hong Kong Society for the Deaf ☎2527 8969.

DOCTORS Look in the Yellow Pages under "Physicians and Surgeons", or con-tact the reception desk in the larger hotels. Make sure you ask for a doctor who speaks good English. You'll have to pay for a consultation and any medi-cines they prescribe, which will start at around $350 for the consultation; if the medicine is not prescription-only it's often cheaper to write down the name and pick it up from an ordinary chemist, rather than buy it from the surgery. Ask for receipts for your insurance. It's cheap-er to visit the nearest local government clinic (often with the words "Jockey Club" in the title, since that's who partly funds them): they stay open late, and you'll only pay a few dollars if you need a basic prescription or treatment at the casualty desk – though you may have to queue. All the clinics are listed in the Hong Kong phone book (at the begin-ning, in the Government directory).

DRESS Dress as you would in any city where it's usually hot and humid, though bear in mind that a lot of the smarter hotels and restaurants insist on some kind of dress code. So no shorts, sandals or flip-flops if you're going for tea at the *Peninsula* and a jacket and tie if you're eating in an expense-account restaurant. For formal dinners, you'll need the pen-guin suit and tie rental services of Tuxe Top Co. Ltd, 1st Floor, 18 Hennessy Rd,

Directory

Directory

Wan Chai ☎2529 2179 and 3rd Floor, Wing Lok Hse, 16 Peking Rd, Tsim Sha Tsui ☎2366 6311 (both branches open daily 10am–7pm).

DRY CLEANING There are shops inside the MTR stations at Jordan, Admiralty, Causeway Bay, Central and Tsim Sha Tsui, although the service can take up to a week.

ELECTRICITY Current is 200 volts AC. Plugs are a mixture of square or round three-pin or two round pins, so a travel plug is useful.

EMBASSIES see "Consulates."

EMERGENCIES Call ☎999 for fire, police or ambulance; also see "Ambulance", "Counselling and Advice" and "Doctors" on pp.311-313, and "Hospitals" below.

ENVIRONMENTAL MATTERS Contact Friends of the Earth (2nd Floor, 53–55 Lockhart Rd, Wan Chai ☎2528 5588) for details of local issues and campaigns.

GAY LIFE Until very recently, homosexuality was completely illegal; the statutes carried a maximum penalty of life imprisonment for committing a homosexual act. The law was brought into line with Britain's in 1990, but there is still only a limited gay scene in the territory. Few people are prepared to speak about their homosexuality, and there's no open, obvious place for gay men and women to meet. There's an advisory service, Horizons (☎2815 9267) for gays and lesbians; other than that, you'll have to rely on one of a very few places where you might meet other gay people, listed in the box on p.266.

GOVERNMENT PUBLICATIONS CENTRE Queensway Government Offices, Low Block, Ground Floor, 66 Queensway, Admiralty (Mon–Fri 9am–5pm, Sat 9am–1pm ☎2537 1910). For maps of the islands, New Territories and other useful publications.

HOSPITALS Government hospitals are the cheapest; they're listed in the Hong Kong phone book. Hong Kong ID Card holders pay $60 per day if admitted to a public ward; some private beds are also available in public hospitals at a higher charge. Those who aren't local residents pay around $3000 a day, though casualty visits are free – the government hospitals below have 24-hour casualty departments. Private hospitals are more expensive, but the standard of care is higher.

Government Hospitals Princess Margaret Hospital, 2–10 Lai King Hill Rd, Lai Chi Kok, Kowloon ☎2990 1111; Queen Elizabeth Hospital, 30 Gascoigne Rd, Kowloon ☎2958 8888; Queen Mary Hospital, Pokfulam Rd, Hong Kong Island ☎2855 3111; Tang Shiu Kin Hospital, Queen's Rd East, Hong Kong Island ☎2831 6800.

Private Hospitals Hong Kong Baptist Hospital, 222 Waterloo Rd, Kowloon Tong ☎2339 8888; Canossa Hospital, 1 Old Peak Rd, Hong Kong Island ☎2522 2181; Hong Kong Adventist Hospital, 40 Stubbs Rd, Hong Kong Island ☎2574 6211; Matilda Hospital, 41 Mount Kellett Rd, The Peak ☎2849 0111.

ID CARDS Available to long-term residents from the Immigration Department, Wan Chai Tower, Gloucester Rd, Wan Chai ☎2598 0888.

INTERNET ACCESS Internet access is available at larger hotels and branches of the *Pacific Coffee Company* and other cyber cafés – see p.235 for full details.

LAUNDRY There's a same-day laundry service in most hotels (though it's usually fairly expensive); guest houses generally have a cheaper service. Otherwise, look in the Yellow Pages, which lists hundreds of laundries. Most charge by the weight of your washing.

LEFT LUGGAGE There's an office in the departure lounge at the airport (daily 6.30am–1am), and at the Central and Kowloon stations for the Airport Express. Alternatively you can usually leave luggage at your guest house or hotel – but don't leave anything valuable unless you're confident it's secure.

LIBRARIES The main English-language library is in the City Hall High Block in Edinburgh Place, Central (open Mon–Fri 10am–9pm, Sat 10am–5pm, Sun 10am–1pm) and contains lending, reference, record and junior libraries, plus a newspaper reading room. To join, you need a passport and $150 deposit (ID card holders free). There's also the British Council library (see p.312).

LOST PROPERTY Police ☎2860 2000; MTR, Admiralty Station (daily 11am–6pm); KCR, 8th Floor, KCR House, Sha Tin, New Territories ☎2606 9392 (Mon–Sat 9am–noon). To recover items left in taxis call ☎7385 8288, although you'll pay a steep fee up front – even then, they don't have a very good record for finding anything.

NEWSPAPERS There are five English-language newspapers published in Hong Kong. The *South China Morning Post* is the most reliable, a firmly cen-trist publication that's the best thing to read on the various problems that face Hong Kong. It carries a good, daily "what's on" listings section. The *Hong Kong Standard* is the *Post's* main rival, duller and notable only for its reason-able daily listings section. The other two papers are the *Asian Wall Street Journal* and the *International Herald Tribune* – the first business-led, the second culled mostly from American newspapers. Published in China, but widely available in Hong Kong, the *China Daily* makes interesting reading in an Alice-in-Wonderland kind of way – straight-down-the-line Beijing government pro-paganda. There are also over forty Chinese newspapers published daily in Hong Kong of various political hues. Beijing objects to the hard reporting of several of them, though there are a few pro-China papers as balance.

British, European and American newspa-pers are widely available too, normally a couple of days late. They're on sale at both Star Ferry concourses; or try inside the South China Morning Post Family Bookshop in Central's Star Ferry con-course. Many bookshops, including this one, also stock a wide range of local and foreign magazines. For local listings magazines and free sheets, see p.276.

PHARMACIES The largest Western-style pharmacy is Watson's (open daily

9am–7pm or later), which stocks toiletries, contact-lens fluid and first-aid items. A number of products are available over the counter which are prescription-only in many Western countries, notably contraceptive pills and melatonin. Watson's has branches all over Hong Kong (for your nearest, phone ☎2606 8833) including Entertainment Building, 30 Queen's Rd, Central; Shop 301–307, 3rd Floor, Prince's Building, 10 Chater Rd, Central; 241 Nathan Rd, Tsim Sha Tsui.

PHOTOCOPYING There's a photocopy service in the City Hall library (see "Libraries" opposite for address).

POLICE. For emergencies dial ☎999. The Police Headquarters is at Arsenal St, Wan Chai ☎2860 2000 and Kowloon Regional HQ, 190 Argyle St, Mongkok ☎2761 2228. For lost property and gen-eral enquiries call ☎2860 2000 and you'll be given the address and tele-phone number of the local police station that will deal with your loss. For Crime Hotline and Taxi Complaints, call ☎2527 7177; for Complaints Against the Police, call ☎2574 4220.

POST OFFICES The main General Post Office (GPO) building is at 2 Connaught Place, Central ☎2921 2222 (Mon–Fri 8am–6pm, Sat–Sun 8am–2pm). It's just behind the Star Ferry on Hong Kong Island, to the right as you get off. The ground floor is for collecting registered letters and parcels, and there are public payphones as well; the first floor is for stamps, sending registered letters and other counter services. Kowloon-side, the main post office is at 10 Middle Road, Tsim Sha Tsui ☎2366 4111. Letters sent poste restante will go to the Central GPO building, where you can collect them Mon–Sat 8am–6pm; take your passport.

TELEPHONES For local calls, you'll find phones at public transport terminals, in shops, hotels, restaurants and bars – local calls are free, except for a $1 charge in coin-operated phones, which will give you five minutes. For long-dis-tance calls, either use an IDD payphone – many accept phone cards or credit cards – or go to one of the following

Directory

Directory

Hong Kong Telecom Service Centres: Telecom House, 3 Gloucester Rd, Wan Chai (Mon–Fri 8am–9pm, Sat 8am–3pm); S26–7, 2nd Floor, Kornhill Plaza North, Kornhill Rd, Quarry Bay (Mon–Fri 9am–6pm, Sat 9am–4pm); Hermes House, 10 Middle Rd, Tsim Sha Tsui (open 24hr). See pp.26 for more information. You can rent mobile phones from the D'Aguilar Street and Hermes House offices.

Useful telephone numbers include:

AT&T Direct Service access code ☎80096 1111

Collect calls ☎10010

Directory Enquiries (English) ☎1081

Emergencies (ambulance, police or fire) ☎999

IDD and Cardphone enquiries ☎10013

International Operator ☎10013

International Operator assistance for foreign credit card calls ☎10011

Telefax operator ☎10014

Telephone problems/repair ☎109

Time and temperature ☎18501

Tourist information (multilingual) ☎2508 1234

Weather (English) ☎2187 8066

THOMAS COOK Changes travellers' cheques at 18th Floor, Vicwood Plaza, 199 Des Voeux Rd, Central ☎2544 4986 (Mon–Fri 9am–5.30pm, Sat 9am–1pm); Ground Floor, Mirador Mansions, 58a Nathan Rd, Tsim Sha Tsui ☎2366 9687 (daily 8am–10pm).

TIME Eight hours ahead of the UK (seven in summer), sixteen hours ahead of Los Angeles, thirteen hours ahead of New York, and two hours behind Sydney.

TIPPING Large hotels and most restaurants will add a ten percent service charge to your bill. In restaurants where there's no service charge, they'll expect to pick up the dollar coins change. In taxis, make the fare up to the nearest dollar. Porters at upmarket hotels and at the airport aren't carrying your bags for the love of the job – tip at your discretion.

TOILETS You'll find public toilets at all major beaches, sights and country parks – there's usually no paper, though there might be an attendant on hand to sell you a couple of sheets. Public toilets are scarcer in the centre, but that's no problem given the number of restaurants and hotels in Tsim Sha Tsui and Central. The swankier the place, the less likely you'll be challenged; indeed some of the very top hotels have rest rooms incorporated into their high-class ground-floor shopping arcades. The finest (and most intimidating) toilet experiences are those in the arcade of the *Peninsula* hotel (men should go up to the *Felix* restaurant) or the *Mandarin* on the Island. Amid brass and marble elegance attendants turn on the taps, hand over the soap and retrieve the towels; there's talc, eau de toilette, hairbrushes, and when you've finished you can sit on the chaise longue and make phone calls all afternoon. Needless to say, you're expected to tip.

TRANSPORT ENQUIRIES See "Getting Around", p.46, for public transport information.

TRAVEL AGENCIES As well as flights to the rest of Southeast Asia and beyond, most of the places below can help with travel to China, including organizing visas. If you're looking for budget flights or tours, you should also look in the classified sections of the *South China Morning Post* and *HK Magazine*.

China Travel Service (CTS): 4th Floor, CTS House, 78–83 Connaught Rd, Central ☎2851 1700; China Travel Building, 77 Queen's Rd, Central ☎2522 0450; Southorn Centre, Wanchai ☎2832 3888; HK–Macau Ferry Terminal, Shun Tak Centre, Central ☎2559 2991.

Efficient Travel Co., Rm 1505, Tak Shing House, 20 Des Voeux Rd, Central ☎2110 1088; Rm 604, Hollywood Plaza, 610 Nathan Rd, Mongkok ☎2771 0313. Hotel packages and flights.

Four Seasons Travel Service, Room 102–3, Commercial House, 35 Queen's Rd, Central ☎2523 9147. Packages throughout Asia, flights, China visas.

Hong Kong Student Travel Ltd, Hang Lung Centre, Yee Wo St, Causeway Bay ☎ 2833 9909. Very popular place for flights, package tours, boats and trains to China, visas, ISIC and YIEE cards.

Honour Tourist Company, Metropole Building, Hankow Rd, Tsim Sha Tsui ☎ 2311 4211. Worth trying for flights.

Phoenix Services, Room B, 6th Floor, Milton Mansions, 96 Nathan Rd, Tsim Sha Tsui ☎ 2722 7378. Chinese visas, train tickets, and flight- and hotel-booking services.

Shoestring Travel, 4th Floor, Alpha House, 27–33 Nathan Rd, Tsim Sha Tsui ☎ 2723 2306 (entrance on Peking Rd). Flights, visas and bus tickets to Guangzhou.

Time Travel, Block A, 16th Floor, Chungking Mansions, 36–44 Nathan Rd, Tsim Sha Tsui ☎ 2366 6222 and Hyatt Regency Hotel Arcade, 67 Nathan Rd, Tsim Sha Tsui ☎ 2722 6878. Helpful place with visas, tickets, passport photos and telex/fax service.

Wah Nam Travel, Ground Floor, Star House, Tsim Sha Tsui ☎ 2753 7979. Visas, boat and train tickets.

WESTERN UNION United Centre, Queensway, Central ☎ 2528 5631.

WOMEN'S HONG KONG Women's issues have yet to make much of an impact in Hong Kong. There are, however, a number of associations for women, including the Hong Kong Federation of Women (☎ 2833 6133). The International Association for Business and Professional Women (IABC), GPO Box 1526, Central, ☎ 2813 7827 hold monthly 'mixers' in a wine bar or club to which visitors are welcome. There is also a refuge – Harmony House (24-hour hotline on ☎ 2522 0434) – for battered women and their children. It's also worth knowing that there's a long-term residential hotel/club for women in Hong Kong, the *Helena May* (35 Garden Road, Mid-Levels ☎ 2522 6766), but check well in advance if you want to stay – you'll need to ensure they have room and will take a non-member.

Directory

Part 4

Macau

Chapter 16

Introducing Macau

T he territory (or enclave, as it's often called) of Macau is 60km west of Hong Kong and 145km south of Guangzhou. It's split into three small, distinct parts – a peninsula and two islands – and the whole enclave covers less than nineteen square kilometres (making it the fourth smallest country in the world), in which lives a population of roughly half a million.

The city of Macau itself is built on a **peninsula** of the Chinese mainland, about 4km by 2km at its widest points and easy to negotiate on foot. It's here that you'll find most of the real sights, the colonial buildings, lots of restaurants and the bulk of the casinos for which Macau is famous. Two bridges link the peninsula with **Taipa** island, from where a slightly shorter causeway runs across to the southernmost **Coloane** island. Both islands are small, easily reached by bus, and feature more good restaurants and the odd church and temple; Coloane also has the enclave's only beaches.

See the colour plates for a street map of central Macau.

Although the bulk of the population is Chinese, there are times when you could imagine yourself in the Mediterranean. The pace of life is slower than in Hong Kong, there's time to have a drink at an outdoor café and, as you climb up to old fortresses through hilly, cobbled streets, you pass small squares lined with pastel-coloured mansions and cracked, whitewashed Catholic churches.

But Macau is gradually losing its sleepy colonial image with the completion of a series of **construction projects** designed to allow it to compete with the other burgeoning Southeast Asian economies. The face of the peninsula itself has been changed markedly by the enclosing of the Praia Grande bay and by the construction of a huge trade-and-entertainment project on reclaimed land between Taipa and Coloane islands. Macau's new international airport and container port are designed to attract trade and investment, in an attempt to challenge Hong Kong's dominance as the business gateway to China. A planned highway from Macau and the neighbouring Chinese Special Economic Zone of Zhuhai will run up to Guangzhou, joining with the Hong Kong–Guangzhou highway – and linking the territory firmly with the rapidly expanding southeastern Chinese economy.

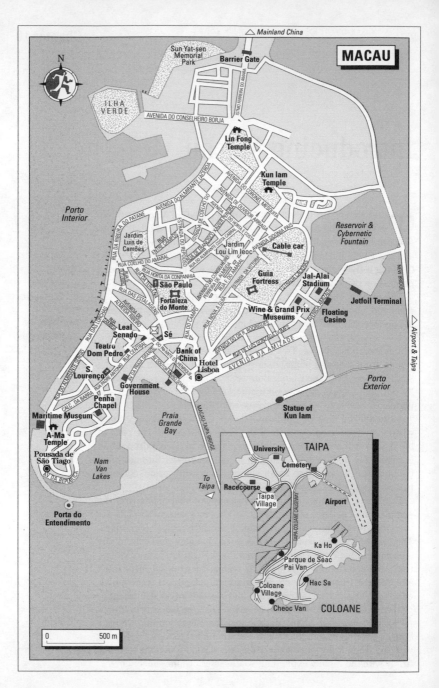

If you're pushed for time, a day trip from Hong Kong can take in most of the interesting things in the whole of Macau, but it really warrants a longer visit. Two or three days is enough time to get around everything comfortably and gives you the chance to sample a few of the excellent restaurants. It's also worth considering leaving for China from Macau – you don't need to return to Hong Kong to move on, since there are regular bus and ferry connections.

Getting to Macau

Getting to Macau

For Macau's visa regulations, customs and currency matters, see pp.15–24).

Although the airport has been operational since 1995, the majority of visitors still arrive **by sea from Hong Kong**, a journey of between an hour and an hour and forty minutes, depending on the vessel. Most departures are from the Macau Ferry Terminal in Central, on Hong Kong Island, though there are links with Kowloon, too. **From China**, there's a direct bus service from Guangzhou, and also boat services from cities in Guangdong province, though these are rarely used by foreigners. For all **arrival details**, see below.

If you're travelling on to Macau directly after arriving in Hong Kong, take the #A11 or #A12 airport buses (daily every 12–15min, 6am–midnight) which run from Chek Lap Kok to the Macau Ferry Terminal.

By air

Macau International Airport, which opened in late 1995, is located at the eastern end of Taipa island. Services are still somewhat limited, though there are currently flights from Beijing, Shanghai, Taiwan, Singapore and Bangkok among others, and provisional service agreements with some other countries: it's hoped that eventually there will be direct flights from elsewhere in Asia, Europe and North America.

There's also a **helicopter service** between Hong Kong and Macau, with 22 flights daily operated by East Asia Airlines (information in Hong Kong on ☎2559 9800) costing around $1210 one-way ($1310 at weekends) – the journey takes twenty minutes. Departures are from the helipad at Hong Kong's Macau Ferry Terminal (see above), where you can buy tickets from a window adjacent to the jetfoil ticket offices; see the "Directory" (p.376) for the telephone number of East Asia Airlines in Macau.

By sea

Most departures by sea **from Hong Kong** – whether by jetfoil, high-speed ferry or catamaran – leave from the **Macau Ferry Terminal** (☎2859 3333), Shun Tak Centre, 200 Connaught Road, Central, Hong Kong Island (Sheung Wan MTR). Other, less frequent catamaran services depart from the **China Ferry Terminal** at 33 Canton Road, Tsim Sha Tsui. Ticket details are covered in the box on pp.324–325. Jetfoils provide the quickest service; high-speed ferries the slowest but cheapest.

Hong Kong to Macau by Sea

The Hong Kong government charges a departure tax of $26 per person on sea journeys to Macau, which is included in the price of your ticket – there's a similar charge when you leave Macau. At the Macau Ferry Terminal, you can book same-day and advance tickets for all services, as well as tickets for the jetfoils up to 28 days in advance. Advance jetfoil and high-speed ferry tickets are also available from MTR Travel Services Centres, which you'll find in Hong Kong at the MTR station concourses of Tsim Sha Tsui, Mongkok, Tsuen Wan, Kwun Tong, Causeway Bay, Central and Admiralty.

Try to book in advance for all crossings, especially at the weekend and on public holidays, when all the transport is packed; buying a return ticket is also recommended since it saves time at the other end. Standby tickets are available, but you'll have to join the queue – though frequent departures from the Macau Ferry Terminal mean you shouldn't have too long a wait. All prices given below are for one-way fares; returns are double. All tickets are for a specific departure time; aim to be at the ferry terminal at least thirty minutes before departure as you'll have to fill in immigration forms before boarding; also allow extra time if you have to pick up pre-booked tickets. Carry-on luggage on the jetfoils is limited to hand luggage. You'll be allowed on with a suitcase or rucksack, but anything more and you'll have to check it in at the counter on the third floor of the Shun Tak Centre at least thirty minutes before departure – you'll pay an extra $20–40 depending on weight. Alternatively, take the high-speed ferry instead, which has baggage racks.

Jetfoils and foil-cats

Run by the Far East Jetfoil Company (☎2859 3333), jetfoils and foil-cats provide the quickest ride to Macau, taking 55 minutes. Services leave from

By land

Twice-daily **buses** run from Guangzhou direct to Macau, a six-hour trip. They exit China at Gongbei, the town immediately over the border in the Zhuhai Special Economic Zone, and run right through to the centre of Macau. There's nothing much to see in Gongbei, but if you decide to get off for a look around, walk over the border (open daily 7am–9pm) afterwards and jump on a #5 bus, which will take you to Avenida de Almeida Ribeiro and Avenida da Praia Grande.

Arriving in Macau

For details about the peculiarities of the Macanese currency, see p.24.

All jetfoils, catamarans, hoverferries and high-speed ferries dock at the **Macau Maritime Terminal** on Avenida da Amizada in the Outer Harbour (Porto Exterior), on the eastern side of the Macau peninsula; the helicopter service from Hong Kong lands on a helipad on the roof. The terminal is usually known as the **Jetfoil Terminal**, which is the name used on the buses that stop here. If you're only staying for the Macau Ferry Terminal in Hong Kong, running every fifteen minutes between 7am and 5pm, and every thirty to sixty minutes during the evening and overnight. Tickets are priced according to class and departure time (and there are some special return deals), but, in general, day services from 7am to 5pm cost around $130 for economy class (lower deck) and $145 first-class (upper deck); weekend prices are around $140 and $155 respectively. Night services, from 6pm to 7am, cost around $160 (economy) and $175 (first-class).

Telephone credit-card bookings in Hong Kong for Jetfoil services can be made on ☎2859 6596; Visa, Mastercard, American Express and Diners Club are all accepted.

Catamarans

China Travel Service (☎2921 6688) has crossings by turbo-cat, departing from the Macau Ferry Terminal every 30 minutes between 7.30am and 5.30pm; regularly but less frequently between 6pm and 10.30pm. The journey takes an hour, but is usually slightly more comfortable than in the jet-foils, since the craft are larger and more modern. The fare is $130 (economy) or $232 (first-class) on weekdays, $141/247 at weekends, and $161/260 at night (6pm–7.30am). There are also twelve catamarans daily from the China Ferry Terminal in Kowloon, operated by HYFCO Travel Agents Ltd (☎2730 8608). The journey takes 70 minutes, and there is only one class. Fares are $113 on weekdays, $134 at weekends, and $154 after 6pm. Both types of catamarans also have six-seater VIP cabins available for around $1200 each way.

Hong Kong Yaumatei Ferry Co. (☎2236 1387 or 2516 9581) operate a jet-cat service twelve times daily from the China Ferry Terminal between 8.30am and 8pm. It takes around seventy minutes and costs $90 on weekdays, $110 at weekends and $120 after 6pm.

the day, use the **left-luggage office** on the second floor of the terminal building (daily 6.30am–midnight) or the luggage lockers on the ground and first floors (24hr). There's also a money-exchange office here, though you can use Hong Kong dollars in Macau.

Pick up a map at the Visitor Information Centre inside the terminal (see p.326). It takes around twenty minutes to **walk into central Macau**; otherwise, **buses** from the stops directly outside the terminal run into the centre, past several of the main hotels and out to Taipa and Coloane: #3, #3A, #28A, #28B and #32 all go past the *Lisboa*; #28A goes on to Taipa Island. Other transport options from the terminal are taxis and pedicabs – for details see "Getting Around" below.

From the airport, the **airport bus #AP1** (3.50ptcs) runs across the new Macau–Taipa bridge and makes a stop outside the Jetfoil Terminal before heading on to the *Hotel Lisboa*. **Ferries** from Shekou and Kongman in Guangdong Province dock at the inner harbour pier, from where it's a short walk to the main avenue, Avenida de Almeida Ribeiro; buses run down here towards the *Lisboa*.

For all departure details from Macau, see "Directory", pp.376–377

Arriving in Macau

The **bus from Guangzhou** stops outside the CTS office on Rua de Nagasaki (mark on map), midway between the Jetfoil Terminal and the *Hotel Lisboa*.

Information

In Hong Kong, the office of the **Macau Government Tourist Office** (MGTO) at the Shun Tak Centre, Room 1303, 200 Connaught Road (Mon–Fri 9am–1pm & 2–6pm, Sat 9am–1pm; ☎25498884) has lots of useful leaflets and maps. Otherwise, **in Macau**, you can pick up the same information at various MTIB offices, including the Visitor Information Centre at the Jetfoil Terminal (daily 9am–6pm; ☎726416). The main office is in the middle of Macau at Largo do Senado 9 (daily 9am–6pm; ☎315566), and there are smaller information counters at a few of the city's fortresses.

Free **literature** to look out for includes separate leaflets on Taipa and Coloane; Macau's churches, temples, and walks; a bus timetable; hotel brochures; and the free monthly newspaper, *Macau Travel Talk*, which lists forthcoming cultural events and entertainment and carries useful reviews of hotels and restaurants.

Getting around

You'll be able to **walk** almost everywhere in Macau, though to reach Taipa and Coloane and a couple of the more far-flung sights, you'll need transport. **Buses and minibuses** are run by two companies – Transportes Colectivos de Macau (TCM) (☎850060) and TRANSMAC – and operate on circular routes from 7am daily until 11pm or midnight; a few stop running after 6–8pm, though the short distances mean you shouldn't get stuck. **Fares** are low: around 2.5ptcs for any single trip on city routes; slightly more for trips to Taipa or Coloane. The airport bus costs 3.50ptcs – pay the driver as you get on with the exact fare.

The main **terminals** and bus stops are outside the Jetfoil Terminal; in front of the *Hotel Lisboa;* at Barra district in the southwest of the peninsula (near the Maritime Museum and A-Ma temple); along Avenida de Almeida Ribeiro; and at Praça Ponte e Horta. The main routes from these places are listed in the box opposite; details of individual buses are given in the text where useful.

Taxis, pedicabs, car and bike rental

It's cheap enough to get around Macau by **taxi**, and you'll find ranks outside all the main hotels and at various points throughout the enclave. All rides are metered: minimum charge is 9ptcs (for the first 1500m), after which it's 1ptcs for every 220m, plus 3ptcs for each piece of luggage. Going by taxi to the islands of Taipa and Coloane,

Bus Terminals and Routes

Jetfoil Terminal: #AP1 to *Hotel Lisboa/Hyatt* hotel/airport; #3 and #3A to *Hotel Lisboa/*Av. de Almeida Ribeiro; #28A to *Hotel Lisboa/Hyatt* hotel/Taipa village; #28B to *Hotel Lisboa/*Av. da Praia Grande; #32 to Lisboa/Av. de Horta e Costa.

Hotel Lisboa: #AP1 to airport; #3 and #3A to Jetfoil Terminal; #11 to *Hyatt* hotel/Taipa village; #21 to Taipa village/Coloane village; #21A to Coloane village/Parque de Coloane/Hac Sa beach; #26A to Taipa/Coloane village; #28A to *Hyatt* hotel/Taipa village.

Avenida de Almeida Ribeiro: #3 to Jetfoil Terminal; #3A to Jetfoil Terminal (eastbound) or Floating Casino (westbound); #5 to Rua do Campo/Av. de Horta e Costa/Barrier Gate; #10 to *Hotel Lisboa* (eastbound) or Barra (southbound); #11 to Barra (southbound) or *Hotel Lisboa/*Taipa (eastbound); #21 to Barra (southbound) or *Hotel Lisboa/*Taipa/Coloane (eastbound).

Barra: #5 to Av. de Horta e Costa/Portas do Cerco; #9 to *Hotel Lisboa/*Av. de Ferreira Almeida/Av. de Horta e Costa/Portas do Cerco; #10 to *Hotel Lisboa*; #11 to Taipa; #21 to Taipa/Coloane; #18 to M. Russa; #21A to Hac Sa beach.

Praça Ponte e Horta (close to Floating Casino): #3A, #21A and #34 all pass through.

---

there's a 5ptcs surcharge, though there's no surcharge if you're coming back the other way. There's also a 5ptcs surcharge if you are picked up at the airport.

Outside the Jetfoil Terminal and the *Hotel Lisboa* you'll be accosted by the drivers of **pedicabs** – three-wheeled bicycle rickshaws. They're more suited for short tourist rides – say around the Praia Grande – than for serious getting around, since Macau's hills prevent any lengthy pedalling. You're supposed to bargain for rides, which cost around 40–50ptcs for a short turn along the harbour, around 100ptcs for an hour's sightseeing.

Renting a car doesn't make an awful lot of sense: it's easy to get around cheaply by public transport and on foot and also extremely difficult to find parking spaces in central Macau. You might, however, want to pay for the novelty of driving a **moke** – a low-slung jeep – particularly if you intend to see a bit of Taipa and Coloane, where transport is less common. See "Directory" (p.376) for details.

For organized tours of Macau, see "Directory", p.378.

Renting a **bicycle** is the best bet if you want a little more mobility, though be warned that the traffic in the centre is as manic as in Hong Kong, and that you're not allowed to ride over the Macau–Taipa bridge. Bike-riding is most enjoyable on the islands. On Taipa, you can rent bikes either from the *Hyatt Regency* hotel, the shop in the main square where the buses stop, or from Largo do Camões, next to the Pak Tai temple, or on Largo Governador Tamagnini Barbosa. In Coloane, the bike rental shop is at the bottom of Coloane village's main square, towards the water. They cost around 10-12ptcs an hour, depending on the bike, or 50ptcs a day. Note that if you want a bike for Coloane it's better to rent one there than ride over the causeway from Taipa.

Festivals and holidays

Macau's mostly Cantonese population celebrates the same Chinese religious and civil **holidays and festivals** as in Hong Kong: there's a round-up of the events and celebrations associated with the festivals on pp.282–285. The enclave also currently celebrates several holidays and festivals lent to Macau by Portugal, although this is expected to change after the handover to China – just as some holidays in Hong Kong were changed after 1997. Currently however, the major holidays:

Lent (first day): procession of Our Lord of Passos. An image of Christ is carried in procession from the church of Santo Agostinho to the Sé for an overnight vigil and then returned via the stations of the cross.

April 25: anniversary of the 1974 Portuguese revolution. Public holiday.

May 13: procession of Our Lady of Fatima, from São Domingos church to the Penha chapel to commemorate a miracle in Fatima, Portugal, in 1913. The biggest annual Portuguese religious celebration, though not a public holiday in Macau.

June 10: Camões Day (Portuguese Communities Day). A public holiday to commemorate Portugal's national poet.

June 24: procession in honour of St John the Baptist (the patron saint of Macau), with a special mass in the cathedral. Also in June is a procession in honour of St Anthony of Lisbon.

July 13: holiday on Taipa and Coloane celebrating the defeat of pirates in 1910.

October 5: Portuguese Republic Day; a public holiday to mark the establishment of the Portuguese Republic in 1910.

December 1: Portuguese Independence Day. Public holiday.

Language and addresses

Roughly 95 percent of the population of Macau is Chinese, three percent Portuguese and two percent of other ethnic origin. Nevertheless, as in Hong Kong, the colonial power has retained the primacy of its **language** and Macau's two official languages are Portuguese and Cantonese. In practice, for visitors, this means becoming familiar with Portuguese street and office signs, which are explained throughout the text if there's any confusion; a few useful Portuguese words are given below to help decipher signs and maps. Otherwise, you won't need Portuguese to get around, though you may find the menu reader on pp.365–366 useful. Although taught in schools, English is patchily spoken and understood – and a few words of Cantonese will always help smooth the way (for which see "Language", pp.403–405).

Addresses are written in the Portuguese style: street name followed by number. Abbreviations to be aware of are Av. or Avda. (Avenida), Est. (Estrada), Calç. (Calçada) and Pr. (Praça).

Some Useful Portuguese Words			
Alfandega	Customs	*Largo*	Square
Avenida	Avenue	*Lavabos*	Toilets
Baia	Bay	*Mercado*	Market
Beco	Alley	*Museu*	Museum
Bilheteira	Ticket office	*Pensão*	Guest house
Calçada	Alley	*Ponte*	Bridge
Correios	Post office	*Pousada*	Inn/Hotel
Edifício	Building	*Praça*	Square
Estrada	Road	*Praia*	Beach
Farmácia	Pharmacy	*Rua*	Street
Farol	Lighthouse	*Sé*	Cathedral
Fortaleza	Fortress	*Travessa*	Lane
Hospedaria	Guest house	*Vila*	Guest house
Jardim	Garden		

Chapter 17

Macau, Taipa and Coloane

O ver four hundred years of foreign trade and colonial rule have shaped **MACAU** into arguably the most intriguing of the southern Chinese settlements ceded to European powers over the centuries. When the Portuguese arrived off the southern Chinese coast at the turn of the sixteenth century, they were looking for trading opportunities to add to their string of successes in India and the Malay peninsula. In particular, they were hoping to break the Venetian monopoly of the Far Eastern spice trade, something that had seemed possible since the seizure of the Malay port of Malacca in 1510. Three years later, the first European to set foot in southern China, Portuguese explorer Jorges Álvares, opened up trade with the Chinese Empire. Later, with the Portuguese "discovery" of Japan in 1542 – accidentally, as it happens, by a ship blown off course – it became vital for the Portuguese to find a base from where they could direct trading operations between China and Japan, as well as between both countries and Europe. This base was Macau, first settled in 1557, and by the end of the sixteenth century nine hundred Portuguese settlers were living here. The area was already familiar to the local Chinese, who knew it as A-Ma-Gao ("Bay of A-Ma"), after the goddess of the sea A-Ma, who was reputed to have saved a ship from a storm off the Macau coast. From A-Ma-Gao is derived the modern name, Macau, linking it firmly with the territory's seafaring and trading history.

MACAU: TOP FIVE ATTRACTIONS

The casinos of the *Hotel Lisboa* (p.333)
The Leal Senado and around (p.338)
The Protestant Cemetery and Camões Museum (p.342)
The church of São Domingos (p.336)
The ruins of São Paulo (p.340)

Most of the interest is contained on the fist-shaped **peninsula** of land that reaches south from the Barrier Gate and the border with China. Most of the sights are within walking distance of one another, and though Macau's hills can make for tiring climbing in the heat of the day, there are excellent views from the churches and fortresses which crown their summits, most notably the ruined church of **São Paulo** and the adjacent **Fortaleza do Monte**. Other attractions include a couple of **temples** that are the equal of any of the better-known ones in Hong Kong; an excellent **Maritime Museum**, which illuminates the Macau's long association with fishing and trade; and a series of quiet **gardens** and squares reflecting the enclave's laid-back approach to life. Spare time, too, for trips out to the two islands: **Taipa**, best known for the fine restaurants in its one village, and **Coloane**, which sports a couple of good **beaches**, including the black sands at Hac Sa.

A little history

Following the initial Portuguese settlement, a city grew quickly on the peninsula, becoming an influential centre of Christian missionary activity. The **Jesuits** were pioneers, sending missionaries to China and Japan and using their vast trading funds to build great Baroque churches, São Paulo being the most notable. Given city status in 1586, Macau's civil and religious importance to the Portuguese was confirmed in a decree which named it as *Cidade do Nome de Deus de Macau*: "City of the Name of God, Macau".

Throughout the sixteenth and early seventeenth century Macau prospered, though from 1612 onwards the authorities were forced to build fortifications on the city's hills to ward off attacks from the **Dutch**, who coveted the valuable trade emanating from the city. The Dutch came close to taking Macau in 1622, but were beaten off, only to move in elsewhere in the Far East, encouraged by the failing Spanish Empire, which in 1580 had annexed Portugal. Before long, the Dutch had gained a foothold in Japan, turning the Japanese against the Jesuit missions there, and by 1639 Japan was closed to the Portuguese for trade, removing one of Macau's vital links. Another disappeared in 1641 with the Dutch capture of Malacca, and although Portugal regained its independence from Spain at around the same time, it was too late to restore the country's – and Macau's – trade with the Far East. From the end of the seventeenth century onwards Macau became impoverished by loss of trade and its proximity to a meddling Imperial Chinese authority. At its lowest political point, in the mid-eighteenth century, it was known rather contemptuously as the "City of Women", a reference to the number of child slaves and prostitutes abandoned in what was rapidly becoming a miserable backwater.

Ironically, it was the growing importance of other foreign traders in the South China Sea during the eighteenth century that saved

Macau. Forced to spend the summers away from the trading "factories" in Guangzhou by the Chinese, who wouldn't allow permanent foreign settlement on their soil, the British, Americans, Dutch, French and others moved to Macau instead. The city became a halfway house for foreign companies, whose merchants built fine mansions to live in – a time recalled in Timothy Mo's novel *An Insular Possession*. However, even this position was undermined after 1841 with the **founding of Hong Kong** as a British colony and free port, and the opening up of the other Chinese Treaty Ports in 1842 for direct trade.

The **nineteenth century** saw modern Macau begin to take shape. A new Governor, João Ferreira do Amaral, arrived in 1846 to stake a claim for Portuguese sovereignty over the peninsula; he annexed the neighbouring island of Taipa, expelled the Chinese customs officials from Macau and built new roads – although sovereignty wasn't ceded by China until 1887. Macau prospered again in a minor way, without being able to challenge Hong Kong, whose rapidly expanding infrastructure now attracted all the direct trade with China that Macau had once monopolized. The enclave became renowned for less salubrious methods of money-making, notably with the advent of **gambling** and prostitution rackets, which existed alongside the well-established opium trade that had run through Macau since the very earliest days.

Lurching on in its down-at-heel way, Macau's last upheavals came with the great **population movements** in Southeast Asia in the first part of the twentieth century. The population increased rapidly after the Sino-Japanese War in the 1930s; many Europeans arrived during World War II as the Japanese respected Portuguese neutrality; and after 1949 and the Communist victory in the civil war, Chinese refugees began to migrate to Macau in massive numbers. The fairly cordial relations between Portugal and China were strained in 1966 when the Chinese **Cultural Revolution** led to a series of riots in Macau, during which demonstrators were shot dead. Yet even this failed to encourage China to take back the land it had claimed for so long. In fact, since the late 1960s China has effectively had complete political control over Macau, finding Portugal's sovereignty a useful way of attracting Western business and investment. This position became clear in 1974 when, after the **revolution in Portugal**, the new left-wing government in Lisbon began to disentangle itself from its remaining colonial ties in Mozambique, Angola and elsewhere. Discussing the future of Macau, however, the Chinese made clear their preference for the enclave's remaining under nominal Portuguese sovereignty, whilst continuing to make money for the People's Republic – particularly through its developing tourist infrastructure and the vast amounts of money generated by the gambling industry.

Despite the Beijing government's equivocal attitude towards the enclave's sovereignty, with Britain and China reaching agreement in

1984 over the future of Hong Kong, it became clear that it was only a matter of time before Macau would also be **returned to China**. Following the **Joint Declaration** of 1987, this is now due to happen on 20 December 1999, when the last chapter in the long history of colonialism in the South China Sea will be closed. Officially, the agreed Basic Law (promulgated in 1993) means that Macau – like Hong Kong – will keep its capitalist structure intact for at least fifty years. In practice, though, Macau has always been far more under China's influence than Hong Kong. Local liberals and pro-democracy activists are in the minority and on the defensive, concerned that the enclave will rapidly lose its Portuguese heritage once it returns to China and pointing – with some justification – to the way the conservatives in government accede to China's every wish. The conservatives, for their part, talk of the need for "convergence" with China if Macau is to continue to be economically viable after 1999. Quite how Macau will develop as a "Special Administrative Region" (SAR) of China is anyone's guess, though the pace of infrastructure **development** (see box, pp.338–339) suggests that the die has already been cast in favour of close economic co-operation with China.

Around the Peninsula

In the early days of Portuguese settlement, a thriving town emerged on the bottom half of the **PENINSULA**. Grand buildings were erected around a network of streets which still forms the heart of the old town, and a fine central avenue was laid out across the peninsula. The central focus was the Praia Grande, a large, handsome bay from which all the streets radiated and along whose waterfront the locals would promenade in the evenings, much as they might have done back home in Portugal.

Along the Praia Grande

The **Praia Grande** now sits at the heart of a redevelopment programme (see pp.338–339) that is radically transforming the entire enclave. What was formerly a fine banyan-planted sweep today echoes with the sound of jackhammers as work continues on the plan to enclose the bay, forming two artificial lakes (the Nam Van Lakes) and reclaiming land for residential and commercial building – catapulting the Macau cityscape into the twenty-first century.

New buildings will eventually line the revised parameters of the bay, but for now the northern edge sports two prominent landmarks, both at odds with much of colonial Macau. The modern, snub-nosed **Bank of China** is the latest addition to an increasingly built-up waterfront, while just to the east sits the orange polka-dot bulk of the **Hotel Lisboa**, whose low flanks are fronted by a multi-storey circular drum done up like a wedding cake and lit to extravagant effect at night. No

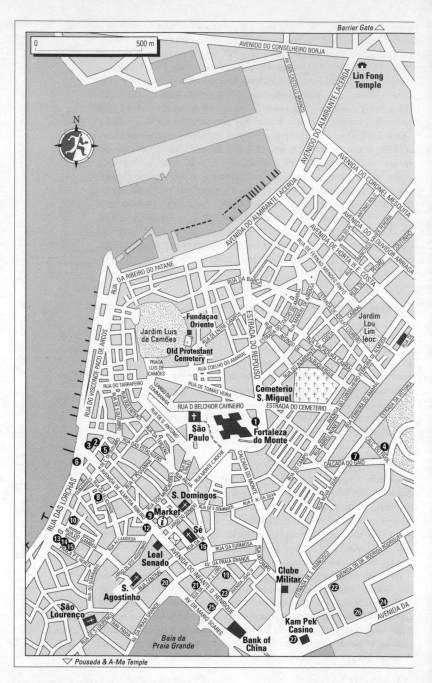

Barrier Gate △

AVENIDO DO CONSELHEIRO BORJA

0   500 m

N

♨ Lin Fong Temple

AVENIDO DO ALMIRANTE LACERDA

AV GEN CASTELLO BRANCO

AVENIDA DO CORONEL MESQUITA

AVENIDA DO OUVIDOR ARRIAGA

AVENIDA DE HORTA

AVENIDA DO ALMIRANTE LACERDA

RUA DE FERNAO MENDES PINTO

RUA DA BARCA

RUA DA RIBEIRO DO PATANE

ESTRADA DO REPOUSO

Jardim Lou Lim Ieoc

Fundaçao Oriente

Jardim Luis de Camões

RUA DE ENTRE CAMPOS

Old Protestant Cemetery

PRAÇA LUIS DE CAMÕES

RUA COELHO DO AMARAL

Cemeterio S. Miguel

RUA DO VISCONDE PAÇO DE ARCOS

RUA DE TOMAS VEIRA

RUA DO TARRAFEIRO

LARGO DA COMPANHIA

RUA D BELCHIOR CARNEIRO

ESTRADA DO CEMETERIO

São Paulo ✝

❌ ① Fortaleza do Monte

RUA DE S. ANTONIO

❷❸ ⑤

CALÇADA DO GAIO

⑦

④

⑥

CALÇADA DO MONTE

AVENIDA DE ALMEIDA RIBEIRO

RUA DAS ESTALAGENS

RUA DAS LORCHAS

⑧

S. Domingos ✝

⑨ Market ①

⑫

Sé ✝

RUA DE S. DOMINGOS

RUA P. N. DA SILVA

⑩

RUA DO GAMBOA

RUA DA FORMOSA

⑬⑭⑮

PRAÇA P. E. HORTE

⑯

Leal Senado

AVENIDA DO INFANTE D. HENRIQUE

⑲

Clube Militar

㉒

S. Agostinho ✝

⑳

㉑ ㉓

RUA CENTRAL

São Lourenço ✝

㉕

AVENIDA DA

㉔

㉖

Baia da Praia Grande

㉗ Kam Pek Casino

Bank of China

AV DR MARIO SOARES

▽ Pousada & A-Ma Temple

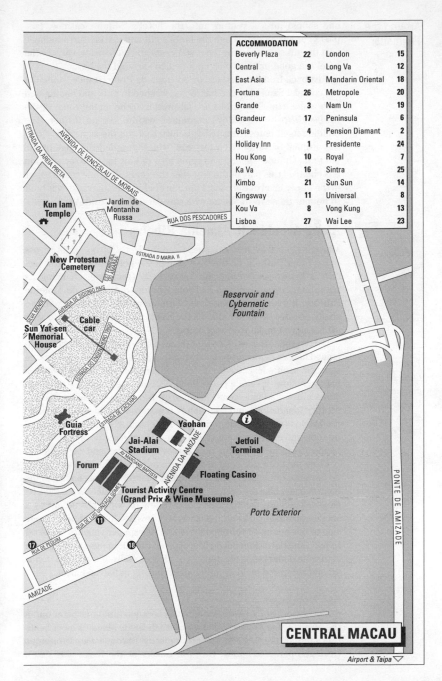

Estrada da Areia Preta

Avenida de Venceslau de Morais

Kun Iam Temple

Jardim de Montanha Russa

Rua dos Pescadores

New Protestant Cemetery

Estrada D Maria II

Rua Ferreira do Amaral

Silva Mendes

Avenida de Sidónio Pais

Reservoir and Cybernetic Fountain

Cable car

Estrada do Engenheiro Trigo

Sun Yat-sen Memorial House

Estrada de Cacilhas

Guia Fortress

Yaohan

Jai-Alai Stadium

Av Marciano Baptista

Forum

Avenida da Amizade

Jetfoil Terminal

Floating Casino

Tourist Activity Centre (Grand Prix & Wine Museums)

Rua de Luis Gonzaga Gomes

⑪

Porto Exterior

⑰

Rua de Pequim

⑱

Ponte de Amizade

Amizade

CENTRAL MACAU

Airport & Taipa ▽

one should miss a venture into the hotel's 24-hour casinos, (see p.372) or a wander through the hotel's gilt and marble surroundings, past the gift shops and the ten restaurants and bars inside. Outside the hotel is a good place to pick up a pedicab around the bay.

Just back from the *Lisboa*, on Avenida da Praia Grande, stand the old colonial São Francisco **barracks**, washed in pink and highlighted with white trim. The public are allowed into the dining room of the *Clube Militar* (see p.367) contained within, but no further. The building itself dates from 1864; before that, on the same site, stood the original São Francisco fortress, which guarded the edge of the old Praia Grande – giving you some idea of how far land reclamation has changed this part of the city over the years. The fine round tower in the upper level of the ornate gardens behind the barracks was built to honour those from Macau who saw service in World War I.

Along Avenida de Almeida Ribeiro

MACAU

Macau's central avenue stretches from the *Hotel Lisboa* right across to the Inner Harbour on the west side of the peninsula. The first section is known as **Avenida do Infante D. Henrique**, changing its name as it crosses Avenida da Praia Grande to **Avenida de Almeida Ribeiro**. It's a fine thoroughfare, with shops and banks tucked into shady arcades on either side of the road, and there's plenty to stop off for as you make your way along it.

To the local Chinese, the avenue is known as San Ma Lo ("new road").

On the right, the steps of Rua da Sé climb past some graceful balconied houses before dipping down into a large square which holds the squat **Sé** itself – Macau's Cathedral, hidden from the rest of town in a natural hollow. It's not a particularly distinguished church – rebuilt in stone in the mid-nineteenth century on top of its original sixteenth-century foundations and completely restored again in 1937 – though it's spacious enough inside, with some fine stained glass, and is flanked by some rather pretty colonial buildings. What must once have been a handsome cathedral square now serves as a market and car park.

From the Sé, a side road drops down into the rather grander **Largo do Senado**, or Senate Square, though it's better approached from the main avenue. Like the avenue, the pedestrianized square is arcaded, its elegant buildings painted pale pink, yellow or white and set off by a small fountained park with benches and flowers. In the arcade on one side of the square sit fortune tellers and newspaper vendors, while off to one side, down Rua Sul do Mercado de São Domingos and adjacent streets, is a **market**: a quadrangle of clothes stalls and *dai pai dongs* around a covered building which deals mostly in fish and meat.

São Domingos

At the bottom of Largo do Senado, the arcaded buildings peter out in the adjacent Largo São Domingos, which holds Macau's most beautiful church, the fine seventeenth-century Baroque **São Domingos** (usually open afternoons; ring the buzzer at the metal side gate).

Built for Macau's Dominicans, its restrained cream-and-stucco facade is echoed inside by the pastel colours on display on the pillars and walls, and on the statue of the Virgin and Child which sits on top of the altar. There's a museum of sacred art in the old belfry, which was opened in 1997 at the end of a major restoration of the entire building. On May 13 every year the church is the starting point for a major procession in honour of Our Lady of Fatima.

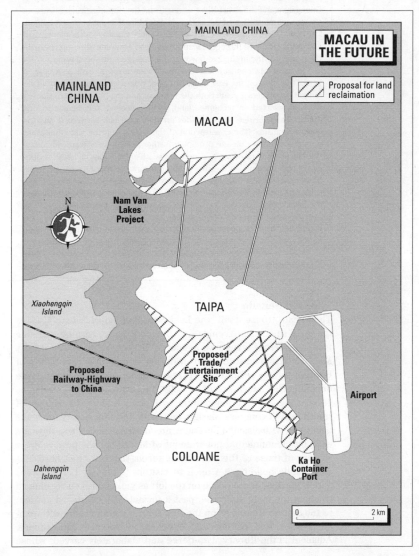

The Redevelopment of Macau

There's a startling amount of redevelopment taking place in Macau, much of it on the huge swathes of reclaimed land – the land area of the Macau peninsula alone is already two-and-a-half times bigger than it was 150 years ago – and a visitor returning to the enclave after a ten-year absence simply would not recognize the place. The impetus for change derives from Macau's close relation to the booming economies of Hong Kong, Guangzhou and the Pearl River estuary, and the new constructions are an obvious manifestation of the enclave's determination not to be left behind. The Joint Declaration with China of 1987 paved the way for the planning of new infrastructures linking Macau firmly with economic developments on the mainland, and in the last few years the progress has been rapid.

The most obvious new construction is the **airport**, built at a cost of US$975 million off the east coast of Taipa, with a potential capacity of six million passengers a year. Both the terminal and the 3.5-kilometre runway were constructed on reclaimed land, while a second, four-kilometre-long **Macau–Taipa bridge** now provides another road link between it and the Macau peninsula. The construction of the airport and the huge **container port** at Ka Ho on Coloane prompted further development plans, including the Macau Cultural Centre, a new Legislative Assembly building, a 300-metre-high communications tower and restaurant, a marine park on Taipa, a business city near the airport and the world's tallest statue of the goddess A-Ma on Coloane. Most extraordinary of all is a plan to fill in the sea between the islands of Taipa and Coloane (to the west of the current causeway) to provide space for a new business and trade centre called Cotai. With this completed, it will be possible to run a road and rail line into Zhuhai in mainland China, so that goods can be freighted directly from port and airport.

If this is ambitious, the ongoing work designed to close the **Praia Grande** is positively visionary. Prompted in part by the gradual silting

The Leal Senado

The Senate House itself, the **Leal Senado** ("Loyal Senate"), faces the main square on Avenida de Almeida Ribeiro, earning its name from a grateful Portuguese monarchy in recognition of the loyalty Macau had shown to the crown during the Spanish occupation of Portugal in the seventeenth century; alone of all the Portuguese dependencies, Macau refused to fly the Castilian flag. Founded as early as the 1580s, it's one of the truly great buildings in Macau, of traditional Portuguese design and with interior courtyard walls decorated with classic blue and white *azulejo* tiling. These days it's used by the municipal government of Macau, whose powers are a shadow of those of the democratic forum that once met here. But as a public building it's open to visitors (Mon–Sat 1–7pm; free) and, if you ask in the office on the left as you enter, you're allowed to climb the main staircase, past a formal little courtyard garden, to the **Senate Chamber** on the first floor – a grand room with panelled walls and ceiling and excellent views over the square. Adjacent is the **library**, two-tiered and elaborately carved, whose

up of the Pearl River estuary, it was decided to link the pockets of land
reclamation on the Macau peninsula by running four-lane roads on
causeways around them, thus forming two artificial lakes, the Nam Van
Lakes. The almost two million square metres of reclaimed land this
scheme has produced will be occupied by hotels, shops, office space,
leisure complexes and pedestrian precincts. The outline shape is
already visible, and the lake enclosures almost complete: buildings are
rising rapidly, too, though the most striking addition so far are the towers of the **Gate of Understanding** monument, towards the southern end
of the peninsula.

For tourists, the transformation of Macau is most obviously reflected in
the expanding range of facilities. Until the economic downturn of 1997
new hotels were opening every few months, many in the intensively developed strip of land between the Jetfoil Terminal and the Hotel Lisboa. The
pace will probably pick up again as the region's economy does. In the
same area, the new **Tourist Activity Centre**, next to the Forum, houses
Macau's Grand Prix and Wine museums. Other facilities include a new
Cultural Centre, and the new museum of sacred art and a shopping complex near the ruins of São Paulo.

It's an undeniably impressive achievement, with more to follow,
though the development comes at a price. Matching the economic expansion of its neighbours has not only changed the very geography of Macau,
but arguably affected its soul as well. It's already a noticeably busier and
noisier place, with traffic levels set to increase once all the new roads are
in place. The colonial peace of the once elegant Praia Grande has been
lost for ever, while new building is rapidly encroaching upon the remaining old-town pockets in the centre. Twenty-first-century Macau will
undoubtedly be an impressive Southeast Asian city, but along the way it
will have sacrificed much of its colonial charm.

wooden chambers house a large collection of books about China
dating from the sixteenth century.

The Inner Harbour and surrounding streets

The main avenue ends on the peninsula's western side, at the **Inner
Harbour** or Porto Interior – the main harbour of Macau for centuries
until the new terminals were built over on the Outer Harbour, or
Porto Exterior, on the eastern side.

The harbourside retains a turn-of-the-century atmosphere. Rua
das Lorchas leads down past **Praça Ponte e Horta**, an elongated
square that was obviously once grand, though its central expanse
now houses a produce market. It now sports only one surviving old
building: the green, four-storey, balconied house on the left. From
the square, **Rua do Almirante Sergio** is arcaded all the way down to
Barra and the tip of the peninsula, a fascinating twenty-minute walk.
The arcade pillars are painted with red Chinese characters advertising each shop, including chandlers and fishing-supply shops (selling
nets and great steel hawsers), greasy electrical and hardware stores,

MACAU

pawn shops, incense sellers, peddlers with jade ornaments, vegetable sellers and *dai pai dongs*. There's a small temple at no. 131, while the side streets around conceal a tumbledown world of dark, tatty shops and mildewed houses.

There are other similar streets closer to the Inner Harbour quayside. Some, like **Rua da Felicidade** – almost parallel with the main avenue – have been spruced up, and what was once a red-light district of sordid repute is now a fairly endearing run of small guest houses, shops selling luridly coloured strips of cured beef and pork (a local Cantonese speciality), seafood restaurants and cake shops. It was still considered suitably rough to double as old Shanghai when scenes from *Indiana Jones and the Temple of Doom* were filmed here in 1984.

More basic in every way are the streets over on the other side of the main avenue, which can have changed little since the last century. Turn down **Rua de Cinco de Outubro** for its traditional tea houses, one at no. 126–130, another at no. 159, and the splendid Farmacia Tai Neng Tong on the left at no. 146, which has a remarkable decorated facade and sculpted interior. Beyond, the street opens out into **Largo do Pagode do Bazar**, a small market square and site of the **Hong Kung temple**, past which things become more intense as the very old surrounding streets degenerate into a noisome wholesale market: wicker baskets full of vegetables and roots, chickens in coops waiting to be killed and plucked, and whole side alleys turned over to different trades – one full of ironmongers, another of street barbers. In a similar vein, **Rua das Estalagens**, **Rua da Tercena** and the parallel **Rua dos Ervanarios** are also worth investigating. Along these you'll find smiths beating metal, jade carvers, carpenters working wood and various stores selling joss sticks, wedding dresses, antiques, blackwood furniture, medicines, silk and shoes.

MACAU

São Paulo and the Fortaleza do Monte

Macau's most enduring monument – and its most famous image – is the imposing facade of the church of **São Paulo**, which stands high above the nest of streets to the north of the main avenue. Building began in 1602 on a Jesuit church here, attached to the Madre de Deus ("Mother of God") college, and its rich design reflected the precocious, cosmopolitan nature of early Macau. Designed by an Italian, it was built largely by Japanese craftsmen who produced a stunning Spanish-style facade that took twenty-five years to complete. The church and adjacent Jesuit college became a noted centre of learning, while the building evoked rapture in those who saw it: "I have not seen anything that can equal it, even in all the beautiful churches of Italy, except St Peter's" wrote one visitor in the 1630s. However, following the expulsion of the Jesuits from Macau, the college did duty as an army barracks and on a fateful day in 1835 a fire, which had started in the kitchens, swept through the entire complex leaving just the carved stone facade.

Approaching up the impressive wide swathe of steps (floodlit at night), you can just about convince yourself that the church still stands, but on reaching the terrace the **facade** is revealed, like a misplaced theatre backdrop, rising in four tiers and chipped and cracked with age and fire damage. The statues and reliefs carved on the facade over 350 years ago have lost none of their power and are worth a cricked neck to study more closely: a dove at the top (the Holy Spirit) is flanked by the sun and moon; below is Jesus, around whom reliefs show the implements of the crucifixion – a ladder, manacles, a thorn crown, a flail. Below are the Virgin Mary and Angels, flowers representing China (a peony) and Japan (chrysanthemum), a griffin and a rigged galleon, while the bottom tier holds four Jesuit saints, and the crowning words "Mater Dei" above the central door.

In what was the nave and crypt, behind the facade, there is now a **museum** (daily except Tues 9am–6pm; free) detailing the building and design of the church. The architects took great care to tailor the museum building to the extraordinarily elegant facade, which rather begs the question of why the square below the steps was not afforded the same protection. What was once a harmonious cobbled expanse is now disfigured by a shopping centre, of all things.

Fortaleza do Monte

To the right of the church, a path and steps lead up the few hundred metres to the solid **Fortaleza do Monte** (Tues–Sun 10am–6pm; 15ptcs), a fortress that was part of the Jesuit complex of São Paulo and dates from the same period. It saw action only once, when its cannon helped drive back the Dutch in 1622; like São Paulo, it fell into disuse after the Jesuits had gone. From the ramparts (made from a hardened mixture of earth, shells, straw and lime, packed in layers between strips of wood) you can appreciate its excellent defensive position, cannon still pointing out to the water and giving fine views around almost the whole peninsula – only the Guia fort and lighthouse to the east are higher. The well-kept grounds contain a meteorological station (in the pale yellow colonial building), and, most welcome after the climb, a small bar at the entrance; there's a tourist information counter here too.

The Camões Garden and Old Protestant Cemetery

From São Paulo, Rua de São Paulo and Rua do Santo António run northwest towards the Camões Garden, past the church of **Santo António**. This is rather plain in appearance, though given that it was wrecked by fire in 1809, 1874 and 1930 it's perhaps surprising that it survives at all. Each St Anthony's Day (June 13) the saint – a military figurehead – is presented with his wages by the President of the Senate, after which his image is paraded around the city to inspect the battlements.

Around the Peninsula

Beyond is **Praça Luís de Camões** (buses #17 & #18 run past), at the head of which the **Jardim Luís de Camões** is a garden of banyans, ferns and flowers commemorating the sixteenth-century Portuguese poet who is supposed to have visited Macau and written part of his epic *Os Lusíadas* (about Vasco de Gama's voyages) in the vicinity. There's a bust of Camões, encircled by rocks, and although there's no real evidence that he ever did come here, the Macanese have awarded themselves an annual holiday in his name, just in case. The garden was once part of the grounds of the adjacent building, a stylish late-eighteenth-century country villa, originally called the Casa Garden, and later the headquarters of the British East India Company in Macau. Now known as the **Fundação Oriente**, it contains the **Museu de Luís de Camões** (daily except Wed, 11am–5pm; 1ptc), whose wide-ranging collection of objects pertaining to Macau includes Chinese porcelain and some attractive old prints.

The Old Protestant Cemetery

For the full rundown of grave inscriptions, the MGTO sells a fascinating book called The Protestant Cemeteries of Macau *by Manuel Teixera, which covers both this cemetery and the New Protestant Cemetery over by the Kun Iam temple to the north of the city.*

Established in 1814 on land purchased by the East India Company, the **Old Protestant Cemetery** (to the side of the museum – you may need to knock to get in) houses many of the non-Portuguese traders and visitors who expired in the enclave. For decades Protestants had no set burial place in Macau: the Catholic Portuguese didn't want them cluttering up the city and the Chinese objected if they were interred on ancestral lands. Some of the graves were moved here from various resting places outside the city walls, as the pre-1814 headstones show.

The most famous resident is the artist **George Chinnery** (on the cemetery's upper tier), who spent his life painting much of the local Chinese coast; a plaque on his tomb recounts how he proclaimed the Christian message of Goodwill Towards All Men "by word and by brush". Some of the cemetery's most poignant graves are those belonging to ordinary **seamen** who died nearby. It was a dangerous, uncomfortable time to be a sailor: Samuel Smith "died by a fall from aloft"; the cabin boy of ship's master Athson similarly met his end "through the effects of a fall into the hold"; while poor Oliver Mitchell "died of dysentery". There's also the grave of the missionary Robert Morrison, who translated the Bible into Chinese, and his wife who died in childbirth. The small **Morrison Chapel** in the grounds, formerly the British Chapel, was consecrated in 1822.

East: across to the Outer Harbour

The largest cemetery on the peninsula is over to the east from here, the otherwise undistinguished **Cemeterio São Miguel** (daily 8am–6pm), from where Avenida do Conselheiro Ferreira de Almeida – with its fine colonial mansions set back from the road – takes you north to the quiet **Jardim Lou Lim Ieoc** (daily dawn–dusk; 1ptc). A formal Chinese garden enclosed by a high wall, with the usual grottoes, pavilions, carp ponds, shrubs and trees, it was built in the nineteenth century and modelled on the classical gardens of Suzhou, in China. It's known locally as Lou Kau, after the nineteenth-century Chinese merchant who funded its construction; Lou Lim Ieoc was his son.

Just to the east, on Avenida de Sidonio Pais (at the junction with Rua de Silva Mendes), the granite, Moorish-style **Sun Yat-sen Memorial House** (daily except Tues 10am–5pm; free) was built by the republican leader's family in the 1930s to house relics and photos. Sun Yat-sen lived in Macau for a few years in the 1890s, practising as a doctor, before developing his revolutionary beliefs, and while there's no massive interest here, you could spend half an hour quite happily in this odd building. There's a Chinese reading room on the ground floor, while upstairs Mrs Sun Yat-sen's former bedroom opens onto a balcony with green twisted pillars. Rooms off here are lined with photocopied manuscripts of less-than-thrilling content ("Dr Sun narrating the beginning of revolutionary activities") and some very poor copies of old photos of Dr Sun and various comrades and committees. Things pick up slightly on the top floor where there's a photographic record of the war against the Japanese, led by the "Great Man", Chiang Kai-Shek. Here scenes of Japanese atrocities (like the newspaper report of two soldiers engaged in a beheading competition) sit uneasily alongside pictures of Chiang hobnobbing with Roosevelt, Churchill, Gandhi and Mountbatten.

Guia Fortress

North of here, the steep hill leads up to the nearby **Guia Fortress**, completed in 1638, on the highest point in the enclave. It was originally designed to defend the border with China, though given its extraordinary perch above the whole peninsula it's seen most service as an observation post. It's either a long, hot walk up the quiet lane to the fort, or take the cable car which runs during daylight hours (10ptcs) from Flora Garden to the top of Guia Hill and then walk across to the lighthouse. From here you'll be rewarded by the pick of the views in Macau and a small seventeenth-century chapel within the walls dedicated to Our Lady of Guia, which contains an image of the Virgin that local legend says left the chapel and deflected Dutch bullets with her robe during the Dutch attack of 1622. You can only get into the chapel once a year, on August 5 (6–9am), the saint's day. The chapel's other function was to ring its bell to warn of storms, something now taken care of by the fortress's lighthouse, built in 1865 and crowning the hill. From the fortress walls, among other sweeping views are those over the **Outer Harbour**, the Porto Exterior, where you probably arrived. The bronze statue on a small artificial island in the harbour is that of Kun Iam, the Goddess of Mercy.

There's a small tourist information office within the ramparts (daily 9am–5.30pm) whose most useful function is to provide much-needed drinks in an adjacent bar.

The Jetfoil Terminal to the Hotel Lisboa

There's been a phenomenal amount of new development on the eastern side of the Guia hill, between the new **Jetfoil Terminal** and the

Hotel Lisboa, much of it on land reclaimed from the sea. For the most part, it's office and hotel buildings, though attractions around the terminal include the old **Jai-Alai Stadium** (now full of casino games) and a massive Yaohan department store.

Further down Rua Luis Gonzaga Gomes the so-called **Tourist Activity Centre** houses both the Grand Prix Museum and the Wine Museum. The **Grand Prix Museum** (Museu da Grande Prémio; daily 10am–6pm; 10ptcs) was established to commemorate the fortieth anniversary of the Macau Grand Prix in 1993 – a race now considered one of the highlights of the Formula 3 calendar. The subterranean hall displays vintage and modern racing cars with race videos and information boards – all frankly rather dull and rescued only by the opportunity of spending a few minutes strapped into a race simulator experiencing the twists and turns of the Formula 3 circuit. The **Wine Museum** (Museu do Vinho; daily 10am–6pm; 15ptcs) charts the history of viniculture from 10,000 BC and offers a chance to learn about – and sample – some Portuguese vintages.

Nearby is the so-called **Floating Casino** (properly called the Casino Macau Palace), a wooden vessel that was once a floating restaurant in Hong Kong and is now an incredibly popular gambling haunt, filled with all kinds of ways to lose money. It used to be moored in much sleazier surroundings in the Inner Harbour but was moved here, close to many of the other casinos, ostensibly for "security reasons", but probably also to attract a higher grade of clientele.

MACAU

North to the Barrier Gate

There are a couple of stops worth making on the way north to the Barrier Gate, though you're going to have to be very energetic to want to do it all on foot. Take bus #5, which runs from Avenida de Almeida Ribeiro in the city centre, and get off about halfway down Avenida Horta e Costa, from where it's only a short walk north to the Kun Iam Temple on Avenida do Coronel Mesquita.

Kun Iam Temple

Entered through a banyan-planted courtyard, the splendid **Kun Iam Temple** (daily 7am–6pm) is one of the most interesting in either Hong Kong or Macau. Dedicated to the Buddhist Goddess of Mercy (Kwun Yum or Kuan Yin in Hong Kong), the temple complex is around four hundred years old and was the venue for the signing of the first ever Sino-American treaty in 1844. There's an overpowering smell of incense inside, and from the formal gardens outside you can look up to the porcelain tableaux that decorate the eaves and roofs of the main buildings. A flight of stone steps approaches the three altars of the main temple, one behind the other; the third is dedicated to Kun Iam herself, dressed in Chinese bridal robes. She is surrounded by other statues of the eighteen wise men of China – the figure on the far left, nearest the fortune teller's desk, with the moustache, round eyes and pointy beard, is Marco Polo, said to have become a Buddhist during his time in China. If you want your fortune told, shake one of the cylinders on the fortune teller's desk in the main temple until a bamboo sliver falls out, when it's matched with the "correct" fortune hanging behind the desk – the Chinese characters are explained to you in return for a few *patacas*. Another traditional way of acquiring good luck used to be to touch the miniature tree shaped like the Chinese character for "long life" or to turn the stone balls in the mouths of the lions on the main steps three times to the left for luck. Unfortunately both are now fenced off.

Lin Fong Temple

Walk back northwest to Avenida do Almirante Lacerda and take the #5 bus as it runs on up past a second temple, the **Lin Fong Temple** or Lotus Temple (daily 7am–6pm) – smaller than the Kun Iam and Taoist rather than Buddhist. First established in 1592 in order to provide overnight accommodation for mandarins travelling between Macau and Guangzhou, it has a fine nineteenth-century facade, and altars dedicated to a variety of Chinese deities.

The Barrier Gate

Bus #5 from Lin Fong Miu runs through some less edifying parts of the Macau peninsula, primarily apartments and roadworks, before stopping outside the **Barrier Gate** which marks the border with China. Called the Portas do Cerco in Portuguese (or "Siege Gate"), a gate here has always marked the entrance to Portuguese territory, even when the old city walls were much further south. Once, all you could do was peer through the gate at the other side. These days the original stucco gate has been removed to a small park nearby and replaced with a far less romantic modern terminal building. You can walk across if you've the right documents and don't mind joining the queues of people and goods trucks that line up all day in both directions. The **Sun Yat-sen Memorial Park**, just to the west, sits against the canal that marks the border; there's a statue of the man outside; aviary, greenhouse and café inside.

South to Barra: the A-Ma Temple and the Maritime Museum

From the Leal Senado, it's around a half-hour walk south along Rua Central to the area known as Barra. Up a small side street, on the right, you pass the peppermint-coloured **Teatro Dom Pedro V**, built in 1873, across from which is the early nineteenth-century church of **Santo Agostinho**, whose pastel walls are decorated with delicate piped icing – the monthly accounts are pinned to the inside of the door, showing expenditure on flowers and "liturgical consumables". Further down Rua Central, the square-towered **São Lourenço** on

MACAU

SOUTHERN MACAU: PRAIA GRANDE TO BARRA

Lin Fong Temple & Barrier Gate △

△ São Paulo

N

S. Domingos

Sé

Leal Senado

S. Agostinho

Teatro Dom Pedro

São Lourenço

Palácio do Governo

Penha Chapel

Maritime Museum

A-Ma Temple

Portuguese Consul's Residence

Bank of China

Baia da Praia Grande

Nam Van Lakes

△ Jetfoil Terminal

△ Taipa

ACCOMMODATION

Lisboa	1
Pousada de S. Tiago	3
Ritz	2

RESTAURANTS

Afonço III	B
Clube Militar	D
Fat Siu Lau	A
Henri's Gallery	F
A Lorcha	E
Pele	G
Solmar	C

0   250 m

Rua de São Lourenço also dates from the early nineteenth century, though like Santo Agostinho it's built on much older foundations, both parishes having existed since the very early Portuguese days. Beyond the churches lies the **Barra district**, the road lined with cheap Chinese cafés, clothes-making workshops, car repairers and the work spaces of various craftsmen.

A-Ma Temple

By the water, turn left for the **A-Ma Temple** (A-Ma Miu in Cantonese), built underneath Barra Hill and probably the oldest temple in Macau, parts of it dating back six hundred years. A-Ma, the Goddess of the Sea and Queen of Heaven (known in Hong Kong as Tin Hau), is supposed to have saved a ship from a storm; where the ship landed, the goddess ascended to heaven and a temple was built on the spot. She subsequently gave her name to the whole territory

and is honoured here in a convoluted complex of temples and altars
dotted among the rocks. Red is the predominant colour, both in the
buildings and in the characters painted on the grey and green rocks.
Paths lead you above the carved roof joints, curved like prows and
topped by dragons; inside the cluttered pavilions are fortune tellers
and incense burners. The busiest time to come is during A-Ma's festival (late April/May; the 23rd day of the third moon), when alongside
the devotions there's also Cantonese opera in a temporary theatre.

The Maritime Museum
Over the road from the temple, in purpose-built premises designed to
look like wharf buildings, is Macau's superb **Maritime Museum**
(Museu Maritimo de Macau; daily except Tues 10am–5.30pm; 8ptcs,
children 5ptcs). Ranged across three storeys is an engaging and well-
presented collection relating to local fishing techniques and festivals,
Chinese and Portuguese maritime prowess and boat building. Poke
around and you'll find navigational equipment, a scale model of seventeenth-century Macau, traditional local clothing used by the fishermen, and even a small collection of boats moored at the pier,
including a traditional wooden *lorcha* – used for chasing pirate ships
– and a dragon-racing boat. The whole collection is made eminently
accessible with the help of explanatory English-language notes,
video displays and boat models. There's an outdoor café and half-
hour **junk rides** around the Inner Harbour – very definitely worth
doing for the different perspective of the enclave they offer, as you
chug past warehouses, floating homes, dredgers and tug boats
(departures daily at 10.30am, 11.30am, 3.30pm and 4.30pm; 10ptcs
for tickets which also include entry to the museum).

From the Fortaleza da Barra to the Palácio do Governo
Keep on past the museum and the road swings around the tip of the
peninsula past the swanky **Pousada de São Tiago**, built over the ruins
of arguably the most important of Macau's fortresses, the **Fortaleza
da Barra**. The fortress, finished in 1629, was designed to protect the
entrance to the Inner Harbour, a function it achieved by hiding two
dozen cannon within its ten-metre-high walls. Over the centuries, it
fell into disrepair along with all Macau's other forts, and was rescued
in 1976 when it was converted into a *pousada* or inn – no one will
mind if you have a look at the foundations and eighteenth-century
chapel inside. The *pousada*'s terrace bar is reasonably priced too,
and makes a good venue for a drink or a meal overlooking the water.

*For full details
of the* Pousada
de São Tiago,
*see "Accommo-
dation", p.362.*

At this point you're at the edge of the more southerly of the lakes
formed by the closing of the bay. A road runs from the tip of the
peninsula, skirting the outer edge of the lake to the unintentionally
bleak **Porta do Entendimento** ("Gate of Understanding") erected in
1993. Three interlocking black marble fingers, 40m high, reaching
up from a little circular platform, supposedly symbolize the "spirit of

Macau" – what's hardest to understand, however, is who'd want to eat whatever it is that the rows of fishermen on the flanks of the monument are intent upon catching from the filthy water.

Continue around the Praia Grande and the energetic can detour up to the left via **Penha Hill**, another steep climb, this time rewarded by the nineteenth-century Bishop's Palace and **Penha Chapel** (daily 9am–5.30pm), with more grand views over the city. The cream-coloured colonial building below, the former *Bela Vista* hotel, is now the home of Portugal's representative in Macau. Returning to the waterfront and heading back to the centre, you'll pass the pink **Palácio do Governo** (Government House), built in the mid-nineteenth century and as graceful as any of the colonial buildings already seen.

Taipa

Take the #11, #22, #28A or #33 if you're heading directly for Taipa village from Macau. All other buses to Taipa (#21, #21A, #26 and #26A) stop outside the Hyatt Regency, *at the roundabout outside Taipa village itself (a 15-minute walk) and at a stop close to the* Taipa House Museum, *before running on to Coloane.*

In the eighteenth century the island of **TAIPA** – just to the south of the peninsula – was actually two adjacent islands, whose sheltered harbour was an important anchorage for trading ships unloading their China-bound cargo at the mouth of the Pearl River. Silting of the channel between the two islands eventually caused them to merge, providing valuable farming land. With the emergence of Hong Kong and the development of the Macau peninsula, Taipa was left to get on as best it could, and for decades it was a quiet, laid-back sort of place, with little industry – just a couple of fireworks factories – and not much to it.

That all changed once it had been decided to build the new airport off the island's east coast, following which construction became almost frenzied. A second bridge now crosses to Taipa from the peninsula to cope with the increased traffic, and the modern business and residential area on the edge of old Taipa village is expanding daily. It's the original village that provides the only real attraction these days, with its fine restaurants and colonial waterfront houses, one of which has been turned into a museum.

Across the bridge: the north coast

Buses from the *Hotel Lisboa* cross the 2.5-kilometre **Macau–Taipa bridge**, and going either way there are terrific views from its highest section about halfway across. The **new bridge**, further to the east, is of a similar design, though even longer at around 4km; if you come into the city on the airport bus you'll cross on this one.

The first bus stop on the island is outside the **Hyatt Regency** hotel, a little way beyond the end of the bridge, from where some buses continue to Taipa village, five minutes beyond. Up from the hotel on the left, on the hill overlooking the water, is the **University of Macau**, just down from which – on a ledge east of the bridge – is a small **Kun Iam Temple**, with an image of the Goddess of Mercy in a

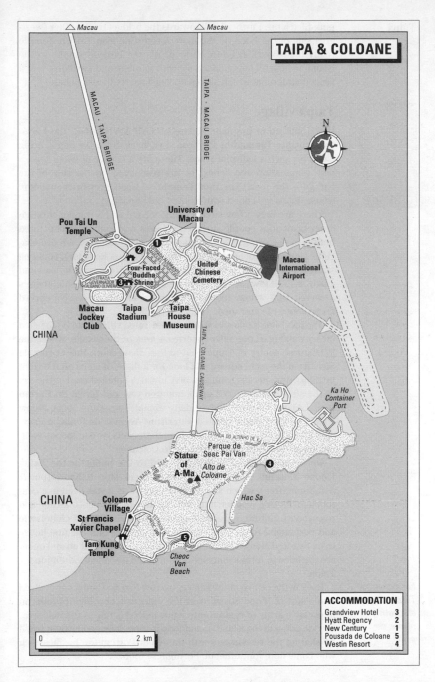

TAIPA & COLOANE

Macau △   △ Macau

MACAU - TAIPA BRIDGE

TAIPA - MACAU BRIDGE

N

University of
Macau

Pou Tai Un
Temple

ESTRADA NORDESTE DA TAIPA

ESTRADA ALMIRANTE

ESTRADA DA PONTA DA CABRITA

①

②

Four-Faced
Buddha
Shrine

United
Chinese
Cemetery

Macau
International
Airport

ESTRADA NOR DESTE DA TAIPA

ESTRADA
GOVERNADOR
ALBANO OLIVEIRA

③

Macau
Jockey
Club

Taipa
Stadium

Taipa
House
Museum

CHINA

TAIPA - COLOANE CAUSEWAY

Ka Ho
Container
Port

ESTRADA DO ALTINHO DE KA HO

ESTRADA DE SEAC PAI VAN

Parque de
Seac Pai Van

Statue
of
A-Ma

Alto de
Coloane

④

ESTRADA DE HAC SA

Hac Sa

CHINA

Coloane
Village

St Francis
Xavier Chapel

ESTRADA
COLOANE

Tam Kung
Temple

⑤

Cheoc
Van
Beach

ACCOMMODATION

Grandview Hotel   3
Hyatt Regency   2
New Century   1
Pousada de Coloane 5
Westin Resort   4

0   2 km

MACAU, TAIPA AND COLOANE

pink-tiled altar. Further back towards the bridge, on the other (western) side of the hotel, is the more interesting **Pou Tai Un Temple** (daily 9am–6pm). Brightly painted, it's the largest temple on the island and is still being added to, with gardens and pavilions, and a large dining room which serves up vegetarian Chinese meals.

MACAU

Taipa village

Buses pull up in the main square of **TAIPA VILLAGE**, the **Largo Governador Tamagnini Barbosa**, just back from the sea – a big name for such a half-pint place. There are a couple of cafés here, a bike rental shop and – next to the restaurant, to the side of the garage – the local **Tin Hau Temple**, a small grey-brick building whose doorway is lined with painted red paper.

There are only a few streets to the village and a wander through them takes in a couple of faded squares and some pastel-painted houses in narrow, traffic-free alleys. Largo do Camões, a more spacious square just behind Largo Barbosa (off Rua Regedor), could be straight out of rural Portugal, with its peeling, balconied houses and shady trees, if it wasn't for the large **Pak Tai Temple**. Inside, there's a carved altar whose figures are echoed in the impressive carved frieze above the entrance.

The half hour it takes to stroll around Taipa village can be finished off by walking to the older waterfront area of the village, where the Portuguese gentry of Taipa used to live. Head down Rua Correa da Silva from the main square and look for a flight of steps on the right by a bus stop, across from Rua do Cunha. A cobbled road at the top of the steps leads up to Taipa's hundred-year-old **Igreja do Carmo** (Our Lady of Carmel Church; daily except Tues 8am–5pm), below which, on the banyan-planted waterfront Avenida da Praia, are several late nineteenth- and early twentieth-century **mansions**, commanding fine views over the sound to Coloane.

One of the houses has been opened to the public as the **Taipa House Museum** (Casa Museu: daily except Mon 9.30am–1pm & 3–5.30pm; free), which shows off the house as it was lived in a century ago. Its airy, wooden interior is filled with period blackwood and rosewood furniture, an equipped kitchen, and assorted chinoiserie and Portuguese-influenced bits and bobs. This is only the first house to be restored along the Praia; the others, once spruced up and open, are intended to form a complete cultural and historical exhibition for Taipa.

For reviews of Taipa village's best eating places, see p.368.

Back in the centre of the village, narrow Rua do Cunha has evolved into a sort of "Food Street" over the years and now incorporates an impressive array of **restaurants** – this indeed is one of the main reasons to come to the island. Lunchtime is especially good, when you'll be sharing the restaurants with the expat Portuguese businessmen who come here for authentic Portuguese food.

The rest of the island

Rent a bike from one of the shops in the village square and you can cycle around the **eastern half** of Taipa in under an hour. Return to the main junction outside Taipa village and head straight over, following Estrada Coronel Nicolau de Mesquita, which leads uphill, past the university and above the island's north coast. At the top of the rise is the **United Chinese Cemetery**, with stepped rows of graves leading down to the water. The whole coast below is being reclaimed and the road passes what were once fairly nice beaches, now disfigured by water drainage pipes, dumper trucks and foundation works. Still, it's an exhilarating ride as the road swoops down the other side of the island, passing the causeway to Coloane and the Avenida da Praia before reaching the main road junction again.

Taipa

To the **west** of Taipa village, the only draw is the **racecourse**, operated by the Macau Jockey Club. It used to host horse-trotting races, no serious rival to the money-making horse racing in Hong Kong, until a new grass track was laid here at the end of 1989 and

Taipa

regular horse racing started up; the season runs from September to the end of June and a satellite dish beams the racing to other Asian countries, giving Hong Kong a run for its money at last. The **Four-Faced Buddha Shrine** outside the stadium is meant to bring luck to the punters. Incidentally, most of the buses come this way on their way back to Macau from Taipa village.

Coloane

To reach Coloane from the Macau peninsula, take buses #21, #21A, #26 or #26A, which run to Coloane village. Travelling from Taipa take the same buses from the stop near the Taipa House Museum.

COLOANE island is around twice the size of Taipa, and was until as late as the turn of the century a base for pirates who hid out in the cliffs and caves, seizing the cargoes of trading ships passing between Macau and Guangzhou. Like Taipa, there's little specifically to attract you other than some eminently peaceful surroundings and a village with a similar mix of temples and colonial leftovers. There's been massive land reclamation on the eastern side of the island at the Ka Ho container port, and ongoing reclamation to the west of the causeway. Despite this Coloane remains relatively enticing, especially as the island has a couple of good sand **beaches** and – with bike rental possible – the means to waste time gently in some fairly isolated bays and hills. Things are set to change beyond all recognition, however, if plans go ahead to build a huge US$300-million trade-and-entertainment **project** on reclaimed land between Taipa and Coloane islands, where the causeway currently stands (see box on p.338).

Parque de Seac Pai Van

On their way around the west coast of the island, buses pass the **Parque de Seac Pai Van** (Tues–Sun 9am–7pm; free), with gardens, ponds, pavilions, views out over the water, a display of the local flora and fauna, and a restaurant, the *Balichão*. Trails also provide good walking in the park, including one up to the heights of the **Alto de Coloane**. The 120-metre white marble statue of A-Ma here is the tallest of this goddess in the world but, other than giving a focal point to the hill, isn't of great interest.

Coloane village

Most buses end their run in **COLOANE VILLAGE** in a little central square surrounded by shops and cafés; a small covered market stands to one side. Signs point off to the few local attractions down roads that are all cobbles and cart-tracks. There's little traffic, chickens scratch around the pot-holes, and a ramshackle air hangs over the low, crumbling Chinese houses, shrines and temples.

Walk down to the bottom of the square and turn left along an alley of shops which winds around to the tiny, pale yellow chapel of **St Francis Xavier**, set back a few yards from the waterfront. The chapel dates from 1928 and honours the eponymous sixteenth-century missionary who passed through Macau on his way to China and Japan. If the friendly priest is around, you'll be let into the sacristy to see St Francis's elbow and a fine selection of other bones of the "Martyrs of Japan" – seventeenth-century Christians killed in Japan after the missionaries were expelled. The bones were rescued from the fire at São Paulo in Macau, kept in the Sé and then transferred here in 1976, since when an increasing number of Japanese visitors have come to pay their respects. The priest was born in Italy, but speaks excellent English and Cantonese. In front of the chapel, the **monument** with the embedded cannonballs commemorates the repelling of the last pirate attack in Coloane, which took place on July 12–13, 1910. The latter date is now an annual celebration on the island.

Further along the waterfront (to the left), past the library, a **Kun Iam Temple** is set back among the houses, though the **Tam Kung Temple** at the end of the road is more interesting, facing China across the narrow channel. The prize piece here is a whalebone shaped into a dragon boat with oarsmen – though the locally caught shark's snout runs it a close second. Like St Francis's chapel, if there's someone around to point out all the exciting religious exhibits you'll probably get stung for 10ptcs or so. Dig deep: there's not much else to spend your money on in Coloane.

Heading the other way along the harbour, past the junks moored offshore and people loafing around the rocks, it's not far to the village's last temple, the small **Sam Seng Temple**. Beyond here, shops are built out over the water, selling dried fish and seafood, while the road leads on to a tiny pier and police station. On the other side of the hill is Coloane's working **shipyard** – a fascinating place where junk building still takes place. Wooden planks fashioned from tree trunks lie around waiting to be seasoned, while work continues on the two or three half-finished boat hulls, pervaded by the intoxicating smell of sawdust and grease.

Back in the village, there are simple Chinese **cafés** around the church and the rather more attractive *Alem Mar* in the square.

Coloane's beaches

Coloane's good **beaches** are all easily reached by bike from the village, or by bus. The closest sandy beach to the village is at **Cheoc Van**, just a couple of kilometres east. It's fairly well developed, featuring cafés, the *Pousada de Coloane* (see "Accommodation", p.363) and generally murky seawater – though it's mud from the Pearl River rather than anything unsavoury. There's a swimming pool here too (daily 9am–1pm), which you'll have to pay a few *patacas* to use.

A few kilometres further east, **Hac Sa** is much the better choice. The grey-black sand beach (*hac sa* means "black sand") is very long and backed by a pine grove, with plenty of picnic places amid the trees. You can rent windsurfers here, and even go horse riding,

Coloane

Bus #21A from Taipa (every 20–40min) stops in Coloane village before moving on to Cheoc Van beach and Hac Sa; you can also get to Hac Sa on the #26 or #26A.

while if you don't fancy the sea or sands there's a **sports and recreation complex** behind the beach (daily 8am–9pm, Sat & Sun until midnight), where a dip in the olympic-size pool costs 15ptcs. On the sands there's a beach bar, as well as a couple of **restaurants** near the bus stop (including the excellent *Fernando's*; see p.368), while at the northeastern end of the beach the new, upmarket *Westin Resort* complex and golf course sprawls across the headland.

Ká Ho, at the far eastern end of the island, is really only for the curious, since the beach has disappeared under the massive new container port and local cement works. It's a nice ride there and back, though.

Macau Listings

Chapter 18

Accommodation

There is a huge number of places to stay in Macau, although weekends and public holidays are always busy with gamblers coming over from Hong Kong, so think about **booking in advance** if you're travelling to Macau at these times. You can do this through the MTIB office in Hong Kong in the Shun Tak Centre, 200 Connaught Rd, Sheung Wan (though not for the cheapest hotels), through the Hong Kong reservations offices of the larger hotels (see listings below), or directly with the hotels and guest houses themselves in Macau. To call Macau from Hong Kong dial 📞 001 853 followed by the subscriber number. Other busy times are Chinese New Year, Easter and during the Macau Grand Prix in late November. If you've arrived without a booking, there are **courtesy phones** in the Jetfoil Terminal from where you can make reservations at the larger hotels.

Guest houses and hotels are generally much better value than in Hong Kong – at the bottom end of the market you'll often be able to find a self-contained room for around the same price as a

sweatbox Kowloon dormitory bed. There are, however, no youth hostels or campsites in Macau.

Guest houses and hotels

As development takes hold, Macau is slowly losing many of its cheap hotels, and what new accommodation there is tends to be firmly mid- and upmarket; the strip of land between the Jetfoil Terminal and the *Hotel Lisboa*, in particular, has seen a frenzy of high-class hotel building in the last few years. For now, though, there's still no great shortage of budget accommodation, though many of the available rooms are small, dark and grubby. They're mostly used by weekend gamblers from Hong Kong who aren't too bothered about where they get their two hours' sleep a night before heading off to lose yet more money.

Most of Macau's **cheap hotels** – called either a *vila, hospedaria* or *pensão* – are located in two main areas: around the **Hotel Lisboa and Hotel Sintra** (the area bounded by Avenida da Praia Grande, Av. do Infante D. Henrique, Rua Dr. P. J. Lobo and Av. de Dom João IV) and near the **Inner Harbour** (bus #3A from the Jetfoil Terminal). However, few of the owners speak English, so telephoning in advance isn't always an option. The other problem is that many places are highly prejudiced against Westerners, particularly young ones with backpacks. Often, a place is "full", even when it patently isn't;

> All the hotels and guest houses below are **marked on the relevant maps**. For places from the Jetfoil Terminal to the *Lisboa* and across to the inner harbour, see the map of central Macau on pp.334–335; for southern Macau, see p.346; and for Taipa and Coloane see p.349.

Macau:
Accommodation

sometimes you won't even get your foot in the door. Basically you'll have to accept that there's no consistency – a hotel that we've said is all right, or you've found to be before, might just change its mind the next time you turn up. The places around the *Hotel Lisboa* are generally a better bet than the ones in the more traditional Chinese streets going towards the Inner Harbour, though there are notable exceptions in both areas. Bear in mind that you may have to grab the first available place you see at busy times, looking around later for something better.

You'll have no such problems with **mid-range** and **top-of-the-range** places, some of which offer very good value for money, especially during midweek when there may be **discounts** of up to fifty percent available. The biggest concentration of places is along the strip of land between the Jetfoil Terminal and the *Hotel Lisboa*, where most rooms come with good views. There are only a few choices on the islands of **Taipa** and **Coloane**, and they're all fairly expensive, although the idea of staying at a beach hotel on Coloane may appeal, if you don't mind the extra travel to and from the centre.

Between the Jetfoil Terminal and Hotel Lisboa

Holiday Inn Macau, Rua de Pequim 82–86 ☎783333, fax 782321.

Well-located four star, fairly typical of the chain and slightly anonymous. ⑤.

Hotel Fortuna, Rua de Cantão ☎786333, fax 786363; Hong Kong reservations ☎2517 3728. 368-room hotel, behind the *Lisboa*. Steel and glass outside, Chinese decor inside, and nicer-than-usual rooms, many with harbour views. ④–⑤.

Hotel Grandeur, Rua de Pequim 199 ☎781233, fax 781211; Hong Kong reservations ☎2857 2846. Top-notch business hotel with all the trimmings, including a revolving restaurant, sauna, pool, gym and coffee shop. ⑤.

Hotel Guia, Estrada do Eng. Trigo 1–5 ☎513888, fax 559822. Smart choice with views (if your room's high enough), on the southern fringes of the Guia hill, with an atrium and swish elevators. Decently priced for this sort of style, and with a shuttle bus to the *Lisboa* to save you the walk. ③–④.

Hotel Kingsway, Rua de Luis Gonzaga Gomes ☎702888, fax 702828. One of the newer and most glam of Macau's hotel creations, this bristles with facilities – 24-hour coffee shop, upmarket casino, sauna and health spa, and well-appointed rooms with views of the city or Taipa. There's a shuttle bus to and from the Jetfoil Terminal. ④–⑤.

Hotel Mandarin Oriental, Av. da Amizade ☎567888, fax 594589; Hong Kong reservations ☎2881 1988. Swanky comforts, including a pool, tennis courts, restaurants, gym and a casino, and considerably cheaper than its sister hotel in Hong Kong. The only drawback is that it's a little far out for an evening stroll. ⑥.

Hotel President, Av. da Amizade ☎553888, fax 552735; Hong Kong reservations ☎2857 1533. Just a block from the casinos of the *Lisboa*, this modern tower caters mostly to business clientele. It has some good restaurants (including a Korean one), decently priced rooms with harbour views, and a free shuttle bus from terminal to hotel. ④.

Hotel Royal, Estrada da Vitoria 2 ☎552222, fax 563008; Hong Kong reservations ☎2543 6426. A modern high-rise, close to the Guia fortress and some extremely good Thai restaurants. It's well-equipped, with standard and deluxe doubles, suites and a pool. ④–⑤.

Around the Hotel Lisboa and Hotel Sintra

Hotel Beverly Plaza, Av. do Dr Rodrigo Rodrigues 70 ☎782288, fax 780704. Conveniently located next to the CTS office and near the *Lisboa*, this 300-room hotel has all the facilities – restaurants, shops, entertainment, business centre. ⑤.

Vila Kimbo, 1st Floor, Av. do Infante D. Henrique 59 ☎710010. Small, clean rooms with TV, toilet and shower – worth a try even if they might not take you. ②.

Hotel Lisboa, Av. de Lisboa 2-4 ☎377666, fax 567193; Hong Kong reservations ☎2546 6944. A monstrous orange circular drum (with adjacent annexe) that has roughly 1000 rooms and a bundle of 24-hour casinos, shops, bars and restaurants, outdoor pool and sauna – some people never set foot outside the front door. Rooms in the rear block don't have the same atmosphere, but are cheaper than those at the front – all have nice bathrooms and decent furnishings. You can also pay considerably more than the price category shown for a superior double or suite. ⑤.

Hotel Metropole, Av. da Praia Grande 493-501 ☎388166, fax 330890; Hong Kong reservations ☎2833 9300. CTS-owned, this well-placed, central hotel is just back from the Praia Grande, and good value if you're looking for rooms with all the fixings. It also has a "fast food" centre, serving *dim sum*, roast meats and *congee* 8am–midnight ③–④.

Pensão Nam Un, Trav. da Praia Grande 3 ☎710008. Doubles with bath are good value and there are cheap singles with shared bathroom. ②.

Hotel Sintra, Av. de Dom João IV ☎710111, fax 567769; Hong Kong reservations ☎2546 6944. Close to the *Lisboa* and all the action, many of the smart rooms with bath and TV have views across the bay to Taipa – though building on the reclaimed land opposite may eventually change that. ④.

Wai Lee Guest House, 1st Floor, Av. de Dom João IV 38 ☎710199. The (rather indistinct) sign outside says "Vila Vai Lei" – nice, quiet and friendly and although the rooms are gloomy, they do have TV and shower. One of the better-value options in this price range. ②.

From Avenida Almeida de Ribeiro to São Paulo

Hotel Central, Av. de Almeida Ribeiro 26-28 ☎373888, fax 332275. One of Macau's oldest hotels, open since 1928. It's a good location, right on the central avenue, and many of the rooms have bathrooms. But ask to see the room first, since others don't even have windows. ③.

Holiday, Estrada do Repouso 36 ☎361696. Close to the Fortaleza de Monte and São Paulo. The compact rooms are just about worth the money. ②.

Pensão Ka Va, Calçada de São João 5 ☎574022. Just below the Sé, at the junction with Rua da Formosa, this smart *pensão* has affordable rooms with bath. ②.

Pensão Long Va, 8th floor, Av. de Almeida Ribeiro 21 ☎371867. Above the Wing Heng bank, there are lovely large rooms with bath, though you might well be told it's "full". ②.

Macau:
Accommodation

① *Under
150ptcs*
② *150–300ptcs*
③ *300–500ptcs*
④ *500–800ptcs*
⑤ *800–
1200ptcs*
⑥ *Over
1200ptcs*

Macau:
Accommodation

① *Under*
150ptcs
② *150–300ptcs*
③ *300–500ptcs*
④ *500–800ptcs*
⑤ *800–*
1200ptcs
⑥ *Over*
1200ptcs

Around the Inner Harbour

East Asia Hotel, Rua da Madeira 1 ☎922433; Hong Kong reservations ☎2540 6333. In the heart of old Macau, off Rua de C. de Outubro, the *East Asia* is a long-standing gamblers' haunt. Many of the rooms now have attached bath, and it has a good restaurant, too. ③.

Hotel Grande, Av. de Almeida Ribeiro 146 ☎921111, fax 922397. Splendid 1930s hotel with soaring Deco facade, featuring several restaurants and a nightclub. Rooms are reasonably good value and there are lots of them. ④.

Hou Kong Hotel, Travessa das Virtudes 1 ☎937555, fax 338884. On an alley off Rua da Felicidade and down Travessa do Auto Novo. More welcoming than most along here, a real hotel with clean, balconied rooms. ③.

Hotel Kou Va, 3rd Floor, Rua da Felicidade 71 ☎375599. A reasonably pleasant hotel on one of Macau's most interesting streets. It's seen better days, though most of the largish, refurbished rooms have bath and TV, making this one of the most attractive budget choices. ②–③.

Hotel London, Praça Ponte e Horta 4 ☎937761. Just about warrants the title "hotel", though things are never quite as impressive once you leave the lobby behind. Still, these are well-equipped rooms (singles, doubles and triples) in a decent location; prices tend to increase to the next category at weekends. ②.

Hotel Peninsula, Rua das Lorchas, Ponte Cais 14 ☎318899, fax 344933. Your money buys a modern, clean room in a building overlooking the water. Air-conditioning too, and some good-value suites. ③.

Pension Diamante Ltd, Rua Nova do Comercio 11 ☎923118. Behind the *Grande*, this used to be known as the Ruby Pension. It's slightly fancier than the guest houses further to the south. ②.

Hotel Sun Sun, Praça Ponte e Horta 14–16 ☎939393, fax 938822; Hong Kong reservations ☎2517 4273. Smart hotel with inner harbour views,

inoffensively furnished rooms with TV and bath, and plenty of marble and wood in the lobby. ③–④.

Vila Universal, Rua da Felicidade 73 ☎573247. Popular place, midway between guest house and hotel standard. There's a relatively friendly welcome here, some English spoken, and decent rooms for the price. ②.

Hospedaria Vong Kung, Rua das Lorchas 45 ☎574016. Opposite the Gulf service station, this is about as cheap as it gets in Macau, with rock-bottom singles and larger doubles; fairly spartan facilities, though. ①.

Southern Macau

Pousada de São Tiago, Av. da República ☎378111, fax 552170; Hong Kong reservations ☎2739 1216. A gloriously preserved seventeenth-century fortress now turned into an upmarket hotel with an unbeatable location at the foot of the peninsula. Rooms with views cost around 300ptcs extra; there's a swimming pool and terrace bar. Book well in advance if you want one of the 23 rooms at the weekend. ⑥.

Ritz, Rua da Boa Vista 2 ☎339955, fax 317826; Hong Kong reservations ☎2739 6993. Above the Portuguese consul's residence, this 163-room hotel has superb views from the terrace and some rooms, plus an indoor pool and billiards room, among other amenities. It's also the one luxury hotel in Macau likely to have a room at short notice. ⑥.

Taipa

Grandview, Estrada Governador Albano de Oliveira, ☎837788, fax 837736. Near the racecourse, a glitzy new addition to the hotels on Taipa. Pool, meeting rooms, games rooms, and a shuttle bus to the Jetfoil Terminal. ③–④.

Hyatt Regency, Estrada Almirante Marques Esparteiro ☎831234, fax 830195; Hong Kong reservations ☎2559 0168. Just over the bridge from Macau (all the Taipa buses run past it), it's what you'd expect from the *Hyatt* chain: smart rooms, casino, landscaped swimming pool and attentive staff. Rooms overlooking the water cost most; specify when booking if that's what you want. ⑤–⑥.

New Century, Av. Padre Tomás Pereira 889 ☎831111, fax 832222; Hong Kong reservations ☎2581 9863. Enormous five-star hotel across from the *Hyatt*, with similar high-class levels of comfort. Views are good, and the *Silver Court* restaurant here is also highly recommended. ⑥.

Coloane

Pousada de Coloane, Praia de Cheoc Van ☎882143, fax 882251. For years the only choice on Coloane, the *pousada* is surprisingly inexpensive given its location and facilities. It's a small place,

whose 22 rooms have balconies overlooking the beach; book in advance. ④.

Westin Resort, Estrada de Hac Sa ☎871111, fax 871122; Hong Kong reservations ☎2803 2015. The *Westin* lies at the far end of Hac Sa's fine beach – a white swathe of terraced rooms spread across the hillside. Good for a quiet day or two midweek, although at the weekend it fills up with Hong Kong families. The hotel offers excellent private sports facilities including an 18-hole golf course, two pools, and a jacuzzi. All rooms have terrace and beach or sea views. You're a little stranded once the sun goes down, though *Fernando's* (see p.368) is within walking distance and the hotel has three other restaurants. ⑥

Macau:
Accommodation

Chapter 19

Eating and Drinking

Although most of the **food** eaten in Macau is Cantonese, the enclave's unique combination of Portuguese and Asian cuisine – called **Macanese** – is well worth trying. A variety of cafés and restaurants serve straightforward and excellent **Portuguese** food – from *caldo verde* (a cabbage and potato soup), through different varieties of *bacalhau* (dried salted cod, Portugal's national dish), to *pudim flán* (crème caramel). Staples like steak, rabbit and sausages, grilled chicken, fried fish, sardines and other seafood dishes are also available, all served in huge quantities. From **Africa** and **India** (Goa particularly) the Portuguese took spices and chillies, and Macanese restaurants nearly always serve enormous spicy prawns and Macau's most famous dish, "African chicken" – chicken grilled with peppers and chillies. Food from Angola, including fine spicy meat and vegetable stews, is served in at least one of Macau's restaurants. From **Brazil**, there is *feijoada*, an elaborate meal traditionally made from meat, beans, sausage and vegetables.

Most restaurants mix and match these influences, also using local **Cantonese** ingredients and dishes, so that pigeon, quail and duck, as well as seafood (like crab and sole), are all available alongside the Macanese standbys. One result of this culinary cross-fertilization is that the Cantonese influence in some supposedly Macanese restaurants is very heavy-handed. Thus steaks are sometimes small, thick and grilled, rather than flat

and fried with garlic; Portuguese staples can be inexpertly cooked; and everything comes at once, as in a Cantonese meal. None of this matters very much, but can be annoying if you've taken the trouble to search out a "Portuguese" restaurant.

Eating in a **Portuguese/Macanese restaurant** in Macau is, however, a revelation if you've already spent time in Hong Kong's Cantonese diners. Freshly baked **bread** is common, as are custard tarts – *natas* – which have become a local speciality. Meals are washed down with cheap imported **Portuguese wine** – fine, heavy reds, chilled whites and slightly sparkling *vinho verde*, as well as any number of **ports** and brandies; and you can get decent **coffee** too. In most places, the **menu** is in Portuguese and English as well as Chinese; check the lists below for descriptions of food you don't recognize.

Vegetarians should do well for themselves. Every Portuguese restaurant serves excellent mixed salads; and most places will fry eggs and serve them up with some of the best French fries around. *Caldo verde* is always good (though you might have to fish out the piece of Portuguese sausage); *sopa álentejana* (garlic and bread soup) is harder to come by, but much tastier than it sounds.

People eat out earlier in Macau than in Hong Kong – you should aim to be at the restaurant by 8pm at the latest – and they rarely stay open later than 11–11.30pm. Meals are generally good

A Portuguese/Macanese Menu Reader

Basics and Snacks

Arroz	Rice
Batatas fritas	French fries
Legumes	Vegetables
Manteiga	Butter
Omeleta	Omelette
Ovos	Eggs
Pimenta	Pepper
Prego	Steak roll
Sal	Salt
Salada mista	Mixed salad
Sandes	Sandwiches

Meat

Almondegas	Meatballs
Bife	Steak
Chouriço	Spicy sausage
Coelho	Rabbit
Cordoniz	Quail
Costeleta	Chop, cutlet
Dobrada	Tripe
Figado	Liver
Galinha	Chicken
Pombo	Pigeon
Porco	Pork
Salsicha	Sausage

Fish and Seafood

Ameijoas	Clams
Bacalhau	Dried, salted cod
Camarões	Shrimp
Carangueijo	Crab
Gambas	Prawns
Linguado	Sole
Lulas	Squid
Meixilhões	Mussels
Pescada	Hake
Sardinhas	Sardines

Soups

Caldo verde	Green cabbage and potato soup, often served with spicy sausage
Sopa álentejana	Garlic and bread soup with a poached egg
Sopa de mariscos	Shellfish soup
Sopa de peixe	Fish soup

Cooking Terms

Assado	Roasted
Cozido	Boiled, stewed
Frito	Fried
Grelhado	Grilled
No forno	Baked

Specialities

African Chicken (Galinha á Africana)	Chicken baked or grilled with peppers and chillies; either "dry", with spices baked in, or with a thick, spicy sauce
Camarões	Huge grilled prawns with chillies and peppers
Cataplana	Pressure-cooked seafood with bacon, sausage and peppers (named after the dish in which it's cooked)
Cozido á Portuguesa	Boiled casserole of mixed meats (including things like pig's trotters), rice and vegetables
Galinha á Portuguesa	Chicken baked with eggs, potatoes, onion and saffron in a mild, creamy curry sauce
Feijoada	Rich Brazilian stew of beans, pork, sausage and vegetables
Pasteis de bacalhau	Cod fishcakes, deep-fried
Porco á álentejana	Pork and clams in a stew
Pudim flán	Crème caramel
Arroz doce	Portuguese rice pudding

Drinks

Água mineral	Mineral water
Café	Coffee
Chá	Tea
Cerveja	Beer
Sumo de laranja	Orange juice
Vinho	Wine (*tinto*, red; *branco*, white)
Vinho do Porto	Port (both red and white)

continued overleaf

Macau: Eating and Drinking

Vinho verde Green wine – ie a young wine, slightly sparkling and very refreshing. It can be white, red or rosé in Portugal but in Macau its usually white

Meals

Almoço Lunch
Comidas Meals
Jantar Dinner
Prato dia/ Dish/menu of the day
Menu do dia

value, certainly compared to Hong Kong. Soup or salad, a main course, half a bottle of wine and coffee comes to around 170ptcs almost everywhere; dessert and a glass of port adds another 40–50ptcs – though two courses in most restaurants will fill you to the brim since servings are so large. Eating Macanese specialities – such as curried crab and grilled prawns – pushes the price up a little. To all restaurant bills, add fifteen percent service charge and tax; it'll usually be included in the total. Be warned that many restaurants, bars and cafés don't take credit cards.

There isn't the **bar scene** that there is in Hong Kong, and most drinking is done with meals. There are a couple of late-night bars in the north of the city for a relaxed beer or glass of wine, while all the upmarket hotels have their own bars, or try one of the city's Portuguese cafés and restaurants.

Cafés

You'll find small **cafés** all over Macau, many serving a mixture of local Cantonese food and Portuguese-style snacks. Some are known as *Casa de Pasto*, a traditional Portuguese workers' dining room, though in Macau, as often as not, they're thoroughly Chinese in cuisine and atmosphere. Others specialize in the local custard tarts, *natas*. For late-night meals and snacks, many hotels have **24-hour coffee shops**, serving bleary-eyed gamblers: the handiest is the one in the *Lisboa*, but there are others in the *Kingsway* and *Holiday Inn*, to name just three.

Bolo de Arroz, Travessa de São Domingos 11. Near São Domingos church, this is a great place for

Portuguese pastries and some of the best coffee in town. Open 8am–7.30pm.

Café Girassol, *Mandarin Oriental*, Avenue de Amizade. High-quality café with a Mediterranean feel. Lots of choice on the menu, as well as a buffet on most days. Open 24 hours, except on Thursday, when it closes at midnight.

Café e Nata, 41 Rua Almirante Costa Cabral. On a main road northeast of the Fortaleza do Monte, this cafe has some of the best *natas* in Macau, amongst other snacks.

Caravela, Rua Comandante Mata e Oliveira 7. Excellent Portuguese *pastelaria*, with outdoor tables, great cakes and coffee and simple Macanese meals. Great for people-watching. It's a bit tricky to find: it's actually off the street, on an alley which runs between Av. Dom João IV and Rua P. J. Lobo, just northwest of the *Hotel Lisboa*. Open 9.30am–12.30am.

Fruitarian, Rua Pedro Nolasco da Silva. In a small lane off this street, south of the Fortaleza do Monte, serving amazing things with fruit – soups, ice creams, yoghurt. There are also Indonesian snacks. Clean and quiet, and the dishes are cheap and fresh. Open noon–midnight.

Garden Terrace, *Pousada de São Tiago*, Av. da República. Excellent breakfasts served on the *pousada* terrace: fresh fruit juices, eggs, home-baked pastries and bread and good coffee – a thoroughly civilized way to start the day. Breakfast served 7–11am; open for lunch, afternoon tea and cocktails too.

Lord Stow's Bakery, Coloane Town Square, Coloane. One of the best places to eat *natas*. The recipe is originally

Portuguese, but this bakery claims to use a secret, improved version.

Leitaria I Son, Largo do Leal Senado 7. A dairy-products café, with an endless variety of inexpensive milk puddings, ice cream and milkshakes, as well as fried-egg breakfasts and tea with real milk.

Noite e Dia, *Hotel Lisboa*, Av. de Lisboa 2-4. The *Lisboa*'s splendid 24-hour coffee shop, serving everything from *dim sum* and breakfast to good-value snacks and meals.

O'Barril 2, 14 Travessa de S. Domingos (near São Domingos church). Solid, satisfying well-cooked snacks, sandwiches and soups. Portions are large and prices cheap. Open Mon–Fri noon–11pm, Sat–Sun 10am–11pm.

Riquexo, Av. de Sidónio Pais 69. In an odd site, inside the Park n' Shop north of the Guia Fortress, but offering very good-value Macanese dishes. Open 9am–9pm.

Restaurants

The listings below concentrate on the enclave's excellent Portuguese and Macanese restaurants, but there are other options such as Italian, Indian and Chinese in the unlikely instance that you tire of this kind of food. Inexpensive wine can be bought in all Macau's restaurants, Portuguese or not.

Macanese and Portuguese

All the following restaurants, except the Montanha Russa, are marked on the map of southern Macau on p.346.

Afonso III, Rua Central 11A ☎586272. Split-level café-restaurant presided over by Afonso – former chef at the *Hyatt* – who will decipher the Portuguese menu for you. Provincial dishes feature, like a mammoth, oily serving of Álentejo pork with clams, drenched in fresh coriander. Other seafood dishes are pricier. Check the daily list of specials to see what the mainly Portuguese clientele is eating. Open noon–3pm & 7–11pm; closed first and third Thurs of every month.

Clube Militar, Av. da Praia Grande 795 ☎714009. This private club within the

São Francisco barracks has a dining room open to the public and, now that the *Bela Vista* is closed, it's probably the colonial dining experience in Macau – a grand setting with formal staff and sparkling silver service. That said, the food never quite matches the promise: competent Portuguese dishes, on the small side, though there's a very good-value daily three-course set meal. Otherwise, you'll spend 300ptcs for a full meal. Alternatively, go for afternoon tea or a drink – they have a large selection of ports. Open noon–3pm & 7–11pm.

Fat Siu Lau, Rua da Felicidade 64 ☎573585. One of Macau's oldest and most famous restaurants, with pigeon the speciality, best eaten with their excellent French fries. Nice, relaxed atmosphere, but – pigeon apart – not the best food in Macau, whatever the adverts say. Open 11am– midnight.

Henri's Gallery, Av. da República 4 ☎556251. Unexciting interior, but the spicy prawns are renowned as the best in Macau. Alternatively try the roast pigeon, quail or curried crab. The African chicken and *Galinha à Portuguesa* are also terrific. Go for an indoor window seat, the tables outside get a lot of traffic noise. Open noon–11pm.

A Lorcha, Rua do Almirante Sergio 289 ☎313193. Just around the corner from the Maritime Museum, this attractive wood-beamed restaurant is reputed to serve the best Portuguese food in Macau, and is consequently always busy – it's best to reserve in advance for lunch when the Portuguese business community are out in force. There's a large menu of Portuguese staples, superbly cooked, which the Governor of Macau is reputed to enjoy on his regular visits. Open 12.30–3.30pm & 7–11.30pm; closed Tues.

Montanha Russa, Jardim da Montanha Russa, Estrada Ferreira do Amaral ☎302731. Highly attractive set-up with outdoor dining under the trees in the little *jardim*. Steak, mullet, cod, pork and clams at reasonable prices, attracting a loyal Portuguese clientele, especially at lunchtime. Go for the daily specials – they

Macau: Eating and Drinking

Macau: Eating and Drinking

rarely miss. It's a bit far out in the north of the city, up near the Kun Iam Temple. Open noon–3pm, 7.30–10pm.

Pele, Rua de São Tiago da Barra 25 ☎969000. A dimly lit place with uninspiring decor, but the food is reasonably priced, the African chicken comes swimming in sauce and there are great spicy prawns to start. Close to the Pousada de São Tiago. Open noon–11.30pm.

Praia Grande, Praça Lobo d'Avila, Av. da Praia Grande. One of Macau's best restaurants, just south of the city centre. The dining rooms upstairs have a good harbour view. Pleasant staff and excellent food. Open noon–midnight.

Solmar Restaurante, Av. da Praia Grande 8–10 ☎574391. Old (since 1961), reliable Macanese restaurant with excellent seafood, as well as all the other classics. Prices slightly higher than average. Open 10am–11pm.

TAIPA

The restaurants below are marked on the map of Taipa village on p.351.

Galo, Rua do Cunha 45 ☎827423. Decorated in kitsch Portuguese country style with the cock (*galo*) – the national emblem of Portugal – much in evidence. The photographic menu is very Portuguese – plenty of boiled meats and pig's trotters – but mainstream dishes include steaks, great grilled squid and large mixed salads. You can eat cheaply and well, though the staff are grumpy. Open 10.30am–10.30pm.

Moçambique, Rua dos Clerigos 28a ☎827471. Small restaurant serving tasty Portuguese colonial food, with dishes from Goa and Africa – from samosas to African chicken. Standard prices and a popular place, so book ahead. Open 12.45–3pm & 7.30–10pm.

Panda, Rua Direita Carlos Eugénio 4–8 ☎827338. Reasonably priced and with good sardines but betrays its Chinese influence in the kitchen – unless you order your courses separately, everything comes at once, and not always delivered with good grace either. Open Mon–Fri

11am–2.30pm & 6–10.30pm, Sat & Sun 11am–10.30pm.

Pinocchio's, Rua do Sol 4 ☎827128. Good Macanese food in Taipa's best-known restaurant. Fish cakes, crab and prawns are well regarded, but the crispy roast duck is what it's known for. Open noon–midnight.

COLOANE

Balichão, Parque de Seac Pai Van ☎870098. Well-regarded Portuguese-Macanese food in an attractive restaurant in Coloane's park. This is a nice place for lunch since you can also sit outside (the buses to Coloane village all pass by the park entrance); at night, you'll probably want to come back in a taxi. Open 11am–11pm.

Caçarola, Rua das Gaivotas 8 ☎882226. Welcoming and deservedly popular restaurant with excellent daily specials and very affordable prices. It's off the main village square. Open Tues–Sun 12.30–3.30pm & 7.30–10.30pm.

Fernando's, Hac Sa Beach 9 ☎882531. The sign is hidden, but this is very close to the bus stop, at the end of the car park, under the Coca-Cola sign – the nearest to the sea in a small line of cafés. Walk past the café at the front to the back and there's a huge barn-like dining room, where Fernando explains the menu to novices – clams and crab are house specials, the grilled chicken is enormous and succulent. It's an institution with local expats, who fill it on Sundays with their large lunch parties. Slightly pricier than average. Open noon–10.30pm.

Pousada de Coloane, Praia de Cheoc Van ☎882143. Reserve a table if you want to eat here – deservedly popular for the *cataplana* dishes and other seafood specialities. Open noon–10.30pm.

Chinese

Dai pai dongs. Along Rua Escola Comercial, off Av. do Infante D. Henrique (to the side of the sports ground

between the hotels *Sintra* and *Lisboa).
Cheap and cheerful noodle and seafood
dishes, eaten outdoors.

Fook Lam Mun, Av. Dr Mario Soares 259
☎786622. Next to the *President* hotel,
this is the place to come for Cantonese
seafood specialities. High prices
(although more affordable in the morning
and at lunchtime for *dim sum*) but considered one of the best in town. Open
7.30am–11pm.

Long Kei, Largo de Senado 7B
☎573970. A huge menu takes in good
dim sum and Cantonese food. Open
11am–11pm.

Shanghai 456, New Wing, Mezzanine
Floor, *Hotel Lisboa*. Av. de Lisboa 2–4
☎388474. Long-established Shanghai
restaurant which does the rounds of
other regional cuisines, too, including
Szechuan and Beijing dishes. Open
11am–11pm.

Other Asian restaurants

Bangkok Pochana, Rua Ferreira do
Amaral 31 ☎561419. Near the gardens
across from the *Hotel Royal*. Prices are
reasonable as is the food. Open
5.30pm–6am.

Korean, Mezzanine Floor, *Hotel
Presidente*, Av. da Amizade ☎788213.
Top-quality Korean restaurant with bar-
becue grills. Open 11am–midnight.

Kruatheque, Rua de Henrique de
Macedo ☎330448. Authentic Thai food,
which might be too hot for some. It's
close to the *Hotel Royal*, one of several
Thai places in this district. Open
6.30pm–6am.

Maharaja, Av. Kwong Tong, Lojas do R/C,
Edifício Nam San, Block 5, Taipa
☎820499. Tandoori Indian cooking, or a
wide selection of curries. They do take-
aways too. Open noon–3pm &
6.30–11pm.

Thai, Rua Abreu Nunes 27E ☎552255
(east of the Fortaleza do Monte). Superb
Thai food with portions large enough to
defeat most people. Soups are marvellous (especially the mixed seafood) and
fish and shellfish are a strong point. Go

with a friend – on your own, two dishes
are plenty. Open 6pm–3.30am.

Italian

Mezzaluna, *Mandarin Oriental*, Av. da
Amizade ☎567888. Extremely elegant
contemporary Italian cooking in swish
surroundings; the wood-fired pizzas are
Macau's finest. Open Tues–Sun
12.30–3pm & 6.30–11pm.

Pizzeria Toscana, Av. da Amizade
☎963831. Don't be put off by the exterior. Genuine Italian food and not just
pizzas, though these are superb, as is
the coffee. Good for breakfast too if you
are catching an early ferry. It's out at the
Jetfoil Terminal, near the Grand Prix
stand. Open 8.30am–11.30pm, closed
first Tues of every month.

Buying your own food and wine

Apart from the market on Rua Sul do
Mercado de São Domingos, where you
can buy fruit and veg, there are branches
of the **supermarket** Park 'N' Shop at Av.
Sidonio Pais 69 and Praça Ponte e Horta
11. Days and Days, at Av. da Praia
Grande 57b, also sells cheap wine, spirits and a good selection of ports.

Bars

Café Nga Tim, Coloane Village Church
Sq., Coloane. A nice place to sit outside
on a warm evening and enjoy a drink.
Open until 1am.

The Embassy Bar, *Mandarin Oriental*, Av.
da Amizade. One of the better hotel
bars, with old Shanghai-type decor.
Weekdays 5–9pm and weekends
11am–9pm there's big-screen sporting
action. Happy hour 5–7pm.

Jazz Club, Rua das Albardas 9 (behind
São Lourenço church). This popular bar
only opens between 11pm and 4am on
Friday and Saturday nights, when there
is live music. Call ahead (☎596014) to
see what's on.

Portas do Sol Wine Bar, *Hotel Lisboa*. If
you don't mind the atmosphere in this
gambling palace, this bar, on the first floor,
offers a better than average selection of

**Macau:
Eating and
Drinking**

Macau: Eating and Drinking

Portuguese wines by the glass. Alternatively, it's not a bad refuge from the gambling as few serious punters come in here.

Pyretu's, Rua de Pedro Coutinho 106 (near Kun Iam Temple). Macau's liveliest drinking-and-dancing joint, with free-flowing sangria, African and Latin American sounds and a funky clientele. It's a good 25-minute hike north from the centre; take a taxi. Open 9pm–3am.

Talker Pub, Rua de Pedro Coutinho 104. Trendy bar with a decent beer list and juke-box, next door to *Pyretu's*; don't go before 11pm. Open 9pm–3am.

Chapter 20

Gambling and other Entertainment

Along with eating out, the main entertainment in Macau is **gambling** in various shapes and forms. Most people spend their evenings lurching from restaurant to casino – which is no bad thing in moderation, since a couple of nights is all you need to get around the more interesting venues in which to lose your money. In lots of cases, too, just being a spectator is entertainment enough, whether at the casinos or the horse- and dog-racing stadiums – which encourage betting (for which, see the next chapter, "Sports and Recreation").

Cultural activities of any kind are thin on the ground, though a couple of annual music and arts festivals do their best to bridge the gap.

Gambling

The main thing about **gambling** in Macau is that – with the exception of the casinos in the *Mandarin Oriental, Kingsway* and *Hyatt Regency* hotels – it's a downmarket, no-frills occupation, designed to rake in the largest amount of money in the shortest possible time. If you're expecting the gilt and glitter of Las Vegas (as well as the free drinks and cheap buffet dinners), you're in the wrong town.

The vast majority of the **punters** are Hong Kong Chinese who – since there's no legal betting except on horse racing in their own territory – flock to Macau to pursue games of chance (and some deprivation this is, bearing in mind that gambling is second only in importance to breathing in China, even though, technically, it's illegal under communism). It's not a subdued, high-class pastime, and the casinos are noisy, frenetic places, nearly always packed, especially at the weekend, with a constant stream of people who leg it off the jetfoil and into the gaming rooms.

Given that the sole object of the casinos is to take money off ordinary people, there aren't the **dress restrictions** you might expect. **Cameras**, however, aren't allowed in any of the casinos and if you've got a bag you'll have to check it in, noting down the serial numbers of any valuable items on a pad provided.

The casinos

The gambling franchise in Macau is held by the Sociedade de Turismo e Diversões de Macau (STDM), which operates ten **casinos**, nine of which are open to the general public (the exception being the *Landmark*, which is a private club). The controlling interest in STDM is owned by Stanley Ho, probably Macau's best-known citizen, and certainly its richest. Most of the casinos are located in a strip between the Jetfoil terminal and Avenida do Doutor Mario Soares. Each has its own character and variety of games. To get in, visitors officially need to be (or

Macau: Gambling and other entertainment

How to Win

Basically, you won't win unless you're very lucky, so don't look upon Macau as the way out of your money troubles. You can bet on a series of casino games, some of which are outlined below, or on one of several sporting events which take place regularly throughout the year. Wherever you go, and whatever you do, the same **warnings** apply. Gamble for fun only; never bet more than you can afford to lose. It's notoriously easy to get carried away, particularly if you're trying to make up for money that you've already lost. The best advice is to decide beforehand how much you're prepared to lose 'and then walk away when it's all gone. The same applies if you actually win, since the speed with which you can pour it all back is phenomenal. Remember, too, that the only system that works is the casino's. Recent figures show Macau's casinos pulling in around US$450 million a year.

The Casino Games

There's an astounding number of games on offer in any of Macau's casinos. Many are familiar: you'll need no coaching to work the **one-armed bandits** or slot machines (called "hungry tigers" locally), which either take Kong Kong dollars or *patacas* and pay out accordingly. Many of the card games are also the ones you would expect, like **baccarat** and **blackjack**.

However, local variations and peculiarly **Chinese games** can make a casino trip more interesting. To sort them all out, ask at the tourist information centres where you can buy the *A-O-A Macau Gambling Guide*, which details all the games, rules and odds. **Boule** is like roulette but with a larger ball and fewer numbers (25) to bet on. **Pai Kao** is Chinese dominoes and is utterly confusing for novices. **Fan tan** is easier to grasp, involving a cup being scooped through a pile of buttons which are then counted out in groups of four, bets being laid on how many are left at the end of the count – about as exciting as it sounds. In **dai-siu** ("big-small" in Cantonese) you bet on the value of three dice, either having a small (3–9) or big (10–18) value – this is probably the easiest to pick up if you're new to the games. In all the games, the **minimum bet** is usually $50 ($100 on blackjack).

---

look) 18; there's no entry fee. Except for the *Victoria*, all the casinos are open 24 hours a day.

Casino Jai-Alai, Outer Harbour, by the Jetfoil Terminal. All-night table action in a stadium that used to host *jai-alai* (Basque *pelota*) games. Also has an off-course betting centre for the dogs.

Casino Kam Pek, Av. de Amizade. This casino has recently moved to a modern building near the *Lisboa*. Known also as the Chinese Casino on account of the mainly Chinese card and dice games played here. Very popular and very intense. Also has an off-course betting centre for the dogs.

Casino Macau Palace, Outer Harbour, Av. de Amizade. Otherwise known as the Floating Casino, housed in a new two-

decked vessel and still delightfully downmarket.

Hotel Kingsway, Rua de Luis Gonzaga Gomes. Fairly flash and not terribly interesting unless you've come to risk your all – there are very high minimum stakes here.

Hotel Lisboa, Av. da Amizade. The biggest casino in Macau, a four-level extravaganza featuring every game possible. There are enough comings-and-goings here to entertain you without losing a cent. Bars, restaurants and shops are all within chip-flicking distance and there's also an off-course betting centre for the dog track.

Hotel New Century, Taipa. The second of Taipa's casinos, and one of the newest in town.

Hyatt Regency, Taipa. One of the smaller casinos. Very select and for high-rollers only.

Mandarin Oriental Macau, Av. da Amizade. Upmarket hotel casino. Still no Las Vegas, but you'll need decent clothes to play the small range of games.

Victoria, Macau Jockey Club. Over on Taipa, this is only in operation at week ends and on midweek race days.

The arts and culture

The free newspaper, *Macau Travel Talk*, lists the month's **concerts and exhibitions**. The usual **venues** for these include the new **Cultural Centre** in the Tourist Activity Centre (Rua de Luis Gonzaga Gomes, near the Jetfoil Terminal) for art displays and exhibitions; the gallery in the **Leal Senado**, which puts on temporary art displays; the **University of Macau** (☎831622) on Taipa, whose auditorium is used for concerts; and – more rarely – the **Jardim Lou Lim Ieoc**, by the Sun Yat-sen Memorial Home, which also hosts recitals and concerts. Other occasional concerts are given in a couple of the central churches (like São Lourenço) and the **Macau Forum** (Av. Marciano Baptista ☎702986), which puts on occasional rock gigs.

Cinema

The **Cineteatro Macau**, Rua de Santa Clara (☎572050), near the junction with Rua do Campo, has three screens; there should usually be something in English. Tickets are 35ptcs. There's also a **UA** cinema (☎712622) at the Jai-Alai Stadium, near the Jetfoil Terminal, which shows a few English-language films.

Annual arts festivals

Annual arts events worth catching include the **International Music Festival**, in October, when Chinese and Western orchestras and performers put on theatre, opera and classical music at all the above venues over a two- or three-week period. Tickets go for 100–300ptcs; check with the MTIB for details. There's also the **Macau Arts Festival**, usually held in February/March, which features a month's worth of events and performances by local cultural and artistic groups.

Every autumn Macau hosts an international **fireworks festival**, with teams competing to produce the biggest and brightest bangs over the Praia Grande. The festival usually lasts several weeks around November, with different competitors putting on displays each weekend, before a grand final between the best two. Check dates with the MTIB.

A **wine festival** exploring styles and developments in Portuguese wines is also held in December – there are seminars, tastings, music and dancing.

Macau: Gambling and other entertainment

For a roundup of Macau's religious and national festivals and holidays, see p.328.

Chapter 21

Sports and Recreation

Apart from horse and dog racing, Macau's biggest sporting draw is the annual **Macau Grand Prix**, which takes place on the enclave's streets, part of the circuit following the enlarged shoreline along Avenida da Amizade. Accommodation and transport is mobbed over this weekend, and you'll need to book well in advance if you want to see it.

There are various other recreational **sports** on offer too, from squash to horse riding, though most people will probably be content with a swim at one of the beaches on Coloane.

Spectator sports

Most **spectator sports** take place either at the **Forum** (Av. Marciano Baptista, near the Jetfoil Terminal ☎702986) – which hosts things like volleyball, table tennis and indoor athletics meetings – or the **Taipa Stadium**, a 20,000-seater next to the racecourse, for soccer, track and field events. Major events are listed in *Macau Travel Talk*, or look for posters around the city.

Macau Grand Prix

Held on the third weekend in November, the **Macau Grand Prix** is a Formula 3 event (plus a motorbike race). **Tickets** for the stand on race days run to around 350–600ptcs (100ptcs on qualifying days) and are available from the Macau Government Tourist Office or from overseas tourist representatives. Be sure to book well in advance.

Horse racing

Horse racing is as popular as in Hong Kong, with races held on the enlarged and converted racecourse on Taipa. The Macau Jockey Club hosts regular weekend **horse racing** from September to June; more information on ☎821188, or consult the MTIB. The minimum bet on a race is 10ptcs. The buses to Taipa (#11, #22, #28A or #33) from close to the *Hotel Lisboa* all return via the racecourse.

Greyhound racing

There's **greyhound racing** at the Canidrome (Canidromo; ☎221199) in Av. General Castelo Branco, very close to the Lin Fong Temple; buses #1, #2 and #5 go right past it. There are races on Tuesday, Thursday, Saturday and Sunday at 8pm, and also on Sunday afternoons; entrance is 2ptcs to the public stand, 5ptcs for the members' stand. Again, the minimum bet is 10ptcs. There's a bar and restaurant alongside the betting facilities.

Participatory sports

Participatory sports available include **squash**, which you can play at the *Hyatt Regency* (☎831234), the *Mandarin Oriental* (☎567888) or the *Westin Resort* (☎871111) for around 90ptcs a session. Otherwise, head for the *Hotel Lisboa* (☎377666), whose labyrinthine twists and turns conceal a **swimming pool** open to the public and a **snooker and billiards** room.

Hac Sa beach (p.353) on Coloane has a **recreation centre** (Mon–Fri 9am–9pm, Sat & Sun 9am–10pm; 5ptcs) with swimming pool (another 15ptcs), roller-skating, mini-golf, children's playground and tennis courts. You can rent **windsurfing** equipment on the beach here too.

Walking/jogging trails criss-cross the land around the Guia Fortress, the most popular a 1700-metre trail reached from the lower car park, just up the hill from the *Guia Hotel*. There are also signposted walking trails on Coloane: the Trilho de Coloane and Trilho Nordeste de Coloane – the latter, a six-kilometre walk that begins and ends near Ká Ho beach, is the more accessible.

At the end of November the **Macau Marathon** clogs up the enclave's streets, the course running from Taipa, across the peninsula and back again.

Macau: Sports and Recreation

Finally, the **Macau Horse Riding Centre** (Tues–Sun; around 400ptcs/hr; ☎828303), also at Hac Sa beach on Coloane, has horses for hire and arranges instruction.

Chapter 22

Directory

AIRLINES Airlines represented in Macau include: Air France (c/o Agencia de Viagens Turisticas Luis Chou, Av. do Dr. Mario Soares ☎712622); Air India (c/o Estoril Tours, *Lisboa Hotel* ☎710361); Air Macau (Av. da Praia Grande 639 ☎396 6888); East Asia Airlines (Hong Kong helicopter service; ☎727288). For other companies, contact the airport.

AIRPORT Macau International Airport (☎861111). Current destinations include Beijing, Bangkok, Manilla, Fuzhou, Haikou, Nanjing, Ningbo, Shanghai, Kaohsiung and Taipei (with Air Macau); Kuala Lumpur (Malaysia Airlines); Singapore (Singapore Airlines); Taipei and Kaohsiung (EVA Airways); Pyongyang (Air Koryo), Kunming (Yunnan Airlines) and Xi'an (China Northwestern).

BANKS AND EXCHANGE Banks are generally open Monday–Friday 9am–4pm, Saturday 9am–noon, though a bank in the arcade of the *Hotel Lisboa* keeps much longer hours than this. Most of the main banks will exchange travellers' cheques, including Banco Nacional Ultramarino (Av. de Almeida Ribeiro 2); Banco Comercial de Macau (Av. da Praia Grande 22; Av. Sidónio Pais 69A); Bank of China (Av. Dr. Mario Soares, and in *Hotel Lisboa*); Standard Chartered Bank (Av. do Infante D. Henrique 60–64); and Hongkong and Shanghai Bank (Av. da Praia Grande 639; Av. Horta e Costa 122–124), which gives cash advances on Visa. The large hotels will also change money, at a

price, and there are also licensed money-changers (*casas de cambio*), including one at the Jetfoil Terminal and a 24-hour service in the *Hotel Lisboa*. There are also banks on both Taipa and Coloane.

BOOKSHOPS It's hard to find bookshops in Macau that carry English-language books. However, books about Portugal and Macau are available from the Portuguese Bookshop and Cultural Centre, Rua de São Domingos 18–22 (near the Sé).

CAR RENTAL Contact Avis ☎336789 (or in Hong Kong ☎2541 2011) or Happy Mokes (Macau Ferry Terminal ☎727868). For moke rentals, expect to pay 500ptcs for 24 hours, with slightly cheaper midweek rates available; rates are inclusive of vehicle and third-party insurance. You need to be at least 21, to have held a driving licence for two years and have an international driving licence. Remember to drive on the left.

CHINA DEPARTURES There's no longer a ferry to Guangzhou, though there are still departures to Kongman (daily at 1.40pm, arrive 3.40pm; around 80ptcs, reserve 3 days in advance); and Shekou (daily at 2.30pm, arrive 4pm; around 100ptcs). Tickets can be bought from Yuet Tung Shipping Co., 14 Rua Lorchas Ponte (daily 8am–noon & 2–5.30pm; ☎564306). Buses to Guangzhou leave daily at 9am and 2pm from outside the main CTS office on Rua de Nagasaki (see "Tour Operators" on p.378). Tickets cost 55ptcs one-way, bought from any CTS office.

DEPARTURE TAX By sea, 26ptcs per person, included in the price of your jetfoil/ferry ticket. By air, 130ptcs if your stay exceeds 24 hours. There is no departure tax if you leave by land.

DOCTORS Go to the hospital casualty departments (see below) or look in the telephone directory Yellow Pages under "Médicos".

DRINKING WATER It comes straight from China and is perfectly safe to drink. It doesn't always taste wonderful, though, and you might be happier with bottled water, sold in shops everywhere.

ELECTRICITY Most of Macau's electricity is supplied at 220V, although some buildings in the older parts of the city still use power at 110V. Plugs use three round pins.

EMERGENCIES Call ☎999. For the police call ☎919. Other numbers include fire brigade ☎572222 and ambulance ☎577199.

HONG KONG DEPARTURES Jetfoil, catamaran and high-speed ferry tickets (and East Asia Airlines helicopter tickets) can be bought at the Jetfoil Terminal ticket offices (☎727288); the various companies' windows sell tickets for all immediate and advance sailings. For information call the following numbers: jetfoils (☎790 7039); turbo-cats (☎7903211); catamarans (☎726301). Departure frequencies are the same as from Hong Kong (see "Getting to Macau", p.323), as are the prices – though they're expressed in *patacas*.

HOSPITALS There are 24-hour casualty departments at Centro Hospitalar Conde São Januário, Calç. Visconde São Januário ☎313731 (English-speaking), and Hospital Kiang Wu, Est. Coelho do Amaral ☎371333 (mostly Chinese-speaking).

LAUNDRY Two central laundries (*lavanderia*) are the *Fok Sang*, Rua da Felicidade 55, opposite the *Fat Siu Lau* restaurant, and *Fai Kit* at 4A on the north side of the Mercado S. Domingos.

NEWSPAPERS You can buy Hong Kong's English-language daily newspapers in Macau, as well as imported copies of foreign newspapers, from the newspaper stands along the central *avenidas*. Macau's local newspapers are, of course, in Cantonese and Portuguese.

PHARMACIES Farmácia Popular, Largo do Leal Senado 16 ☎573739; Farmácia Tsan Heng, Av. de Almeida Ribeiro 215 ☎572888; Farmácia Lap Kei, Calç. do Gaio 3D ☎590042; Farmácia Chun Cheong, Rua de S. Domingos 8 ☎332252. Each takes it in turn to open for 24hr; details posted on the door.

POLICE The main police station is at Av. Dr Rodrigo Rodrigues ☎573333.

POST OFFICES The main post office is the large granite building on the central Largo do Leal Senado, just off Avenida de Almeida Ribeiro (Mon–Fri 9am–6pm, Sat 9am–1pm); this is where poste restante mail is sent. There's also a post office at the Jetfoil Terminal (Mon–Sat 10am–8pm). Otherwise, little booths all over Macau sell stamps, as do the larger hotels, and there's a post office on both Taipa and Coloane. *Correios* is Portuguese for post office; *selos* are stamps.

TAXIS To order a taxi, call ☎519519.

TELEPHONES Local phone calls from pay phones cost 1ptc, though, like Hong Kong, local calls are free from courtesy phones in hotels and restaurants. There are groups of payphones around the Largo do Leal Senado and at the Jetfoil Terminal. Some take telephone cards, available from the telephone office at the back of the main post office (open 24hr), from where you can make international calls. See p.28 for details of dialling abroad.

Useful telephone numbers include:

Directory enquiries ☎185 (Portuguese); ☎181 (Chinese and English);

Emergencies ☎999;

Time ☎140 (English);

Weather information ☎1311 (Portuguese).

Macau: Directory

Macau: Directory

TELEVISION You can pick up Hong Kong's television stations in Macau, as well as some from mainland China; there's also a local station, Teledifusão de Macau (TdM), whose programmes are mostly in Cantonese and Portuguese, though a few are in English. TdM's programme listings are carried in Hong Kong's daily newspapers.

TIME Macau is eight hours ahead of GMT, thirteen hours ahead of New York, sixteen hours ahead of Los Angeles, and two hours behind Sydney.

TOUR OPERATORS There's no shortage of companies who will show you the sights by bus and there are endless tour combinations available – half-day whisks around the peninsula and islands, from around 120ptcs a head, to pricey three- or four-day trips that take in Zhuhai and parts of Guangdong province. Most can be booked in Hong Kong as well, though it's generally cheaper to book in Macau.

For details, ask at any of the MTIB offices in Hong Kong or Macau or contact one of the tour operators, some of which are listed below – all offer the same tours at broadly similar prices.

China Travel Service, Rua de Nagasaki ☎700888.

Macau Tours, Av. Dr. Mario Soares 35 ☎710003.

New Sintra Tours Ltd, Jetfoil Terminal ☎728050.

VACCINATION CENTRE At Direcção dos Serviços de Saúde (Health Dept), Av. Conselheiro Ferreira de Almeida 89 ☎569011.

VISAS For China visas, visit the main office of the China Travel Service, on Rua de Nagasaki (see above), which issues visas and tickets (including tickets for the bus to Guangzhou) and organizes tours. Most other tour agencies can sort out a visa for you, too; see "Tour Operators", above, for addresses.

Contexts

Hong Kong: a history

To Western eyes, the history of Hong Kong starts with the colonial adventurers and merchants who began settling on the fringes of southeast China in the mid-sixteenth century. The Portuguese arrived in Macau in 1557; almost three hundred years later, the British seized Hong Kong Island. However, the whole region has a long, if not greatly distinguished, history of its own that is thoroughly Chinese – an identity that can only be strengthened with the handing back of both Hong Kong and Macau to China by the end of this century.

Early times

Archeological finds point to settlements around Hong Kong dating back six thousand years, and while there's little hard evidence, it's accepted that the archipelago off the southeastern coast of China was inhabited in these very early times by fishermen and farmers. There was no great living to be made: then, as now, it was a largely mountainous region, difficult to cultivate and with trying, tropical weather. Disease was common, and though the sea was rich in fish, the islands formed a base for bands of marauding pirates.

Later, though far from the Imperial throne in Peking, the land became a firm part of the great Chinese Empire, which was unified in 221 BC. Throughout the series of ruling dynasties that dominated the next 1500 years of Chinese history, the area around Hong Kong was governed – after a fashion – by a magistrate who report-

ed to a provincial viceroy in Guangdong (Canton province).

The local population was made up of several **races**, including the Cantonese, who were the most powerful and divided into clans; the Hakka people, a peripatetic grouping who had come down from the north; and the Tankas, who lived mostly on the water in boats. Villages were clan-based, self-contained and fortified with thick walls, and the inhabitants owned and worked their nearby ancestral lands. The elders maintained temples and ancestral halls within the villages, and daily life followed something of an ordained pattern, activities and ceremonies mapped out by a geomancer, who interpreted social and religious ideas through a series of laws known as **feng shui** or "wind and water".

Examples of these **walled villages** still survive in the New Territories, most notably at Kam Tin and Tsang Tai Uk (near Sha Tin), while geomancy is a flourishing art in modern Hong Kong, where the design of all new buildings takes into account the ancient principles of favourable location.

This village-based life continued uneventfully for centuries, the small population of the peninsula and islands mostly untroubled by events elsewhere in the empire. Recorded history made its mark only in the thirteenth century AD when a boy-emperor of the **Song Dynasty** was forced to flee to the peninsula of Kowloon in order to escape the Mongols who were driving south. They cornered him in 1279 and he was killed, the last of his dynasty. The Mongol victory caused a great movement of local tribes in southern China, and general lawlessness and unrest followed, characterized by continuing pirate activity based on Lantau Island.

Trade and the Chinese

The wider Chinese Empire, however, had begun to engineer links with the Western world that were to bring Hong Kong into the historical mainstream. Although the empire considered itself superior to other lands, supreme and self-sufficient, there had been **trade** between China and the rest of the known world for hundreds of years, often conducted under the guise of "tribute" from other countries and leaders, so as to preserve the idea of Chinese pre-eminence. Out from China went silk, tea and fine art; in came horses, cloth and other luxuries.

The concept of superiority was a resilient one, with foreigners seen as "barbarians" by the Chinese and kept at arm's length. Foreign merchants had to petition the authorities to be allowed to trade; they were not allowed to live within the borders of the empire; they were forbidden to learn the Chinese language, and were generally treated with disdain by Chinese officials.

The relationship changed slightly in the sixteenth century, when some of the first of the Western traders, the **Portuguese**, were given a toehold in the Chinese Empire by being granted permission to establish a trading colony at **Macau**, 60km west of Hong Kong. To the Chinese, it was a concession of limited importance: the Portuguese were confined to the very edge of the empire, far from any real power or influence, and when the same concessions were given to other Western nations in the eighteenth century, the Chinese saw things in the same light. As long as the barbarians kept to the fringes of the Celestial Empire, their presence was accepted – and mostly ignored.

For the West, and especially Britain, such trading territories were viewed altogether differently. Allowed to establish trading operations in **Canton** (Guangzhou) from 1714 onwards, many Western countries saw this as a first step to opening up China itself, and by the turn of the nineteenth century, the Dutch, American and French had joined the British in Canton hoping to profit from the undoubtedly massive resources at hand.

For the time being, however, foreign traders in Canton had to restrict themselves to the peculiar dictates of the Chinese rulers. Their **warehouses** (called "factories") were limited to space outside the city walls on the waterfront, and there they also had to live. All their operations were supervised, their trade conducted through a selected group of Chinese merchants, who formed a guild known as a **Cohong** (from which is derived the Hong Kong word *hong*, or company). In the summer, foreigners had to leave for Portuguese Macau, where most of them kept houses (and, often, their families). Under these circumstances foreign merchants somehow prospered and trade thrived. The British East India Company was only one of the firms involved, seeing their Chinese enterprises simply as an extension of

the worldwide trade network they had built up on the back of the British victory over Napoleon and their mastery of the seas.

The opium trade

The problem that soon became apparent was that trade took place on terms eminently favourable to the Chinese. Foreigners had to pay for Chinese tea and silk in silver, while the Chinese wanted little that the Westerners had. The breakthrough was the emergence of the trade in **opium**, in demand in China but illegal and consequently little grown. The Portuguese had been smuggling it into Macau from their Indian territories for years, and as it became clear that this was the one product that could reverse the trade imbalance, others followed suit. Most energetic were the British, who began to channel opium – "foreign mud" as the Chinese came to call it – from Bengal to Canton, selling it illegally to corrupt Chinese merchants and officials in return for various goods. Illegal or not, the trade mushroomed and opium became the linchpin of the relationship between the Chinese and the ever-richer foreign merchants.

Familiar Hong Kong names began to appear in Canton, most of whom were connected with the opium trade. **William Jardine** and **James Matheson** were two of the most successful and unscrupulous traders, both Scottish Calvinists who had no qualms about making fortunes from an increasing Chinese reliance on drugs. The trade was also encouraged by the British government, and by corruptible Chinese government officials who ignored what had become an overt smuggling operation. By 1837, around forty thousand chests of the drug were landed annually in China, unloaded at Lin Tin Island in the Pearl River estuary, transferred onto Chinese barges and floated upriver to Canton.

As silver began to flow out of China to pay for the increasing amounts of the drug being imported, the trade imbalance came to the attention of the Chinese Emperor in Peking (Beijing), who also began to show concern for the adverse effect that the opium was having on the health of his population. In 1839, the Emperor appointed an opponent of the trade, the Governor of Hunan province, **Lin Tse-Hsu**, to go to Canton to end the import of opium – something he'd achieved fairly spectacularly in his own province by brute force. Once in Canton, Lin Tse-Hsu ordered the surrender and destruction of all the foreigners' opium chests, twenty thousand in all, and much to the disgust of the enraged merchants, the British Chief Superintendent of Trade, **Captain Charles Elliot**, did just that. His was a difficult position, since he represented the traders, yet personally stood against the opium trade, and his actions did nothing to diffuse the affair. Governor Lin ordered a blockade against the merchants' factories and demanded they each sign a bond, promising not to import opium into China in future. Under Elliot's direction, the traders left Canton and retreated to Macau and their boats, anchored in Hong Kong harbour, fearing further trouble. The situation deteriorated when Lin reminded the Portuguese of their official neutrality, which they upheld by refusing Elliot a secure base on Macau and by forbidding the selling of supplies to the British merchant fleet, which still waited nervously off Hong Kong.

The First Opium War

If it was Governor Lin's intention to force the British back to Canton to trade on his terms, then he miscalculated disastrously. The mood in Britain, where Lord Palmerston was Foreign Secretary in the Whig government of Lord Melbourne, was one of aggressive expansionism. Merchants like Jardine and Matheson had long been urging the government to promote British free trade in China, demanding gunboats if necessary to open up the Chinese Empire. The first Superintendent of Trade in China, Lord Napier, had been given precisely those instructions, but had been humiliated by the Chinese when he had tried to press British claims in the region. Canton had been closed to him and his frigates forced to retreat, a disgrace in British eyes that Palmerston had not forgotten.

Captain Elliot had already begun the skirmishes that would degenerate into the so-called **First Opium War**, having replied to Lin's threats by firing on a Chinese fleet in September 1839 and sinking a number of ships. It was these threats, rather than the protection of the opium trade, that gave Britain the excuse it sought to expand its influence in China. There was opposition to the trade in Britain, particularly among the ranks of the Whigs, who had already made their mark with the abolition of the slave trade. But potential attacks on British personnel and overseas livelihoods couldn't be ignored.

Palmerston ordered an **expeditionary fleet** from India, comprising four thousand men, which arrived off Hong Kong in June 1840 with the express purpose of demanding compensation for the lost opium chests and an apology from the Chinese, and – most importantly – acquiring a base on the Chinese coast, which could be used like Portuguese Macau to open up the country for free trade. Several ports up and down the Chinese coast had been suggested by traders over the years, including Canton itself, and the expedition (led by Admiral George Elliot, a cousin of Charles) was authorized to grab what it could. The British fleet soon achieved its military objectives: it attacked the forts guarding Canton, while other ships sailed north, blockading and firing on ports and cities right the way up the Chinese coast. When part of the fleet reached the Yangtze river, approaching Beijing itself, the Chinese were forced to negotiate.

Governor Lin was dispensed with by the Emperor, who appointed a new official, Kishen, to deal with the British fleet, by now again under the command of Charles Elliot. The fighting stopped and the British withdrew to the Pearl River to negotiate, but after six weeks of stalling by the Chinese, the fleet once again sailed on Canton and knocked out its forts. Kishen capitulated and Elliot **seized Hong Kong Island**; the British flag was planted there on January 26, 1841.

Fighting began again soon after, when in August 1841 Elliot was replaced by Sir Henry Pottinger, who was determined to gain more than just Hong Kong Island. The fleet sailed north, taking ports as they went, which were later recognized as free-trade "Treaty Ports" by the 1842 **Treaty of Nanking**, which halted the fighting. In this way, Shanghai, Amoy (Xiamen), Fuzhou, Canton and others were opened up for trade; the Chinese were forced to pay an indemnity to the British; but most important of all, the treaty ceded Hong Kong Island to Britain in perpetuity.

The new colony

Not everyone was thrilled with Britain's new imperial acquisition. The small island was called Hong Kong by the British, after the Cantonese name (*Heung Gong*), most commonly translated as meaning "Fragrant Harbour". But aside from the excellent anchorage it afforded to the British fleet, Palmerston for one saw Elliot's action as a lost opportunity to gain further parts of China for

Britain. It was a move which cost Elliot his job, while at home Queen Victoria was amused by the apparent uselessness of her new out-of-the-way colony.

Nevertheless, the ownership of Hong Kong – which formally became a British Crown Colony in 1843 – gave a proper base for the opium trade, which became ever more profitable. By 1850 Britain was exporting 52,000 chests of opium a year to China through the colony.

Sir Henry Pottinger, who replaced Elliot, became the colony's first **governor**, a constitution was drawn up, and from 1844 onwards, a Legislative Council and a separate Executive Council were convened – though the governor retained a veto in all matters. In colonial fashion, pioneered elsewhere in the world by the British, government departments were created, the law administered and public works commissioned. At first, though, the colony remained something of a backwater, since the British were still ensconced at Canton and most of the China trade went through the other Treaty Ports. The population of around fifteen thousand was mostly made up of local Chinese, many of whom were attracted by the commercial opportunities they thought would follow; many of them sold land rights (that often they didn't own in the first place) to the newly arrived British, who began to build permanent houses and trading depots.

The first buildings to go up were around Possession Point, in today's Western district – offices, warehouses (called "godowns") and eventually European-style housing. This area was abandoned to the Chinese when the first colonists discovered it to be malarial and mistakenly moved to Happy Valley – which turned out to be even more badly affected. Gradually, though, sanitation was improved. Happy Valley was drained and turned into a racecourse; summer houses were built on The Peak; and a small but thriving town began to emerge – called **Victoria**, on the site of today's Central. The number of Europeans living there was still comparatively small – just a few hundred in the mid-1840s – but they at least now existed within a rigid colonial framework, segregated from the Chinese by early governors and buoyed by new colonial style and comforts. Streets and settlements were named after Queen Victoria and her ministers; St John's Cathedral was opened in 1849; Government House finished in 1855; the first path up The Peak cut in 1859; and the

Zoological and Botanical Gardens laid out in 1864. As Hong Kong began to come into its own as a trading port, the British merchants who lived there started to have more say in how the colony was run: in 1850, two merchants were appointed to the Legislative Council.

The Second Opium War and colonial growth

Relations between Britain and China remained strained throughout the early life of the colony, flaring up again in 1856 when the Chinese authorities, ostensibly looking for pirates, boarded and arrested a Hong Kong-registered schooner, the *Arrow*. With London always looking for an excuse for further intervention in China, this incident gave Britain the chance to despatch another fleet up the Pearl River to besiege Canton – instigating a series of events sometimes known as the **Second Opium War**. Joined by the French, the British continued the fighting for two years and in 1858 an Anglo-French fleet captured more northern possessions. The **Treaty of Tientsin** (Tianjin) gave foreigners the right to diplomatic representation in Peking, something Palmerston and the traders saw as crucial to the future success of their enterprise. But with the Chinese refusing to ratify the treaty, the Anglo-French forces moved on Peking, occupying the capital in order to force Chinese concessions.

This second, more protracted series of military engagements finally ended in 1860 with the signing of the so-called **Convention of Peking**, which ceded more important territory to the British. The southern part of Kowloon peninsula – as far north as Boundary Street – and the small Stonecutter's Island were handed over in perpetuity, increasing the British territory to over ninety square kilometres. This enabled the British to establish control over the fairly lawless village that had grown up on the peninsula at Tsim Sha Tsui, while the fine Victoria Harbour could now be more easily protected from both sides. Almost as a by-product of the agreement, the opium trade was legalized, too.

The period immediately after was one of **rapid growth**. With a more secure base, the colony's commercial trade increased and Hong Kong became a stop for ships en route to other Far Eastern ports. They could easily be repaired and refitted in the colony, which began to sustain an important shipping industry of its own. As a result of the increased business, the **Hongkong and Shanghai Bank** was set up in 1864 and allowed to issue banknotes, later building the first of its famous office buildings. The large foreign trading companies, the **hongs**, established themselves in the colony: Jardine, Matheson was already there, but it was followed in the 1860s by Swire, which had started life as a shipping firm in Shanghai. The town of Victoria spread east and west along the harbour, around its new City Hall, taking on all the trappings of a flourishing colonial town, a world away from the rather down-at-heel settlement of twenty years earlier. One of the major changes was in the size of the **population**: the Taiping rebellions in China greatly increased the number of refugees crossing the border, and by 1865 there were around 150,000 people in the colony. With Hong Kong soon handling roughly a third of China's foreign trade, the colony began to adopt the role it assumes today – as a broker in people and goods.

By **the 1880s**, Hong Kong's transformation was complete. Although the vast majority of the Chinese population were poor workers, the beginnings of today's meritocracy were apparent as small numbers of Chinese businessmen and traders flourished. One enlightened governor, **Sir John Pope Hennessy**, advocated a change in attitude towards the Chinese that didn't go down at all well: he appointed Chinese people to government jobs, there were Chinese lawyers, and even a Chinese member of the Legislative Council. It was an inevitable move, but one that was resisted by the bigoted colonialists, who banned the Chinese from living in the plusher areas of Victoria and on The Peak.

1898: the leasing of the New Territories

Following Japan's victory in the **Sino-Japanese War** (1894–95), China became subject to some final land concessions. Russia, France and Germany had all pressed claims on Chinese territory in return for limiting Japanese demands after the war, and Britain followed suit in an attempt to defend Hong Kong against possible future attack from any foreign source in China. One British gain was the lease of Weihaiwei in Shandong, in the north, to be held as long as the Russians kept Port Arthur (Lushun), on which they'd secured a 25-year lease in 1897.

More significant, though, was the British government's demand for a substantial lease on the land on the Kowloon peninsula, north of Boundary Street. Agreement was reached on an area stretching across from Mirs Bay in the east to Deep Bay in the west, including the water and islands in between, and this territory was **leased from China for 99 years**, from July 1, 1898. It came to be known as the **New Territories**, and it and the treaty under which it was granted became the legal focus for the return of the whole colony to China in 1997. Although the British undoubtedly thought they'd got a good deal in 1898 – a 99-year lease must have seemed as good as an outright concession – it was to become clear over the years that Hong Kong could never survive as a viable entity once the greater resources of the New Territories were handed back. Thus had the British authorities effectively provided a date for abolition of what subsequently became one of their most dynamic colonies.

The colony of Hong Kong was now made up of just under 1100 square kilometres of islands, peninsula and water, but there was an indigenous Chinese population of around 100,000 in the newly acquired territory which resisted the change. Many villagers feared that their ancestral grounds would be disturbed and their traditional life interfered with, and local meetings were called in order to form militias to resist the British. There were clashes at **Tai Po** in April 1899, though British troops soon took control of the main roads and strategic points. Resistance in the New Territories fizzled out and civil administration was established, but the villagers retained their distrust of the authorities. One further problem caused by the leasing agreement was the anomalous position of **Kowloon Walled City**, beyond the original Boundary Street – a mainly Chinese garrison that had evolved into a fairly unpleasant slum by 1898. For some reason, the leasing agreement didn't include the Walled City, and China continued to claim jurisdiction over it, hastening its degeneration over the years into an anarchic crime-ridden settlement and a flashpoint between the two sets of authorities.

The years to World War II

By the turn of the **twentieth century** the population of Hong Kong had increased to around a quarter of a million (and more came after the fall of the Manchu Dynasty in China in 1911), and the colony's trade showed an equally impressive performance, finally moving away from opium –

which had still accounted for nearly half of the Hong Kong government's finances in 1890. In 1907 an agreement was reached between Britain and China to end the opium trade, and imports were cut over a ten-year period – though all that happened was that the cultivation of poppies shifted from India to China, carried on under the protection of local Chinese warlords. Opium smoking wasn't made illegal in Hong Kong until 1946, and three years later in China.

Alongside the trade and manufacturing increase came other improvements and developments. The **Kowloon Railway**, through the New Territories to the border, was opened in 1910 (and completed, on to Canton, by the Chinese in 1912); the **University of Hong Kong** was founded in 1911; **land reclamation** in Victoria had begun; and the **Supreme Court** building was erected in the first decade of the new century (and still stands today, in Central, as the LEGCO building).

Despite this activity, movements outside the colony's control were soon to have their effect, and the years following World War I saw a distinct economic shift away from Hong Kong. Shanghai overtook it in the 1920s as *the* Chinese trading city, and Hong Kong lost its pre-eminence for the next thirty years or so. The polarization in Chinese politics began to have an effect, too. Sun Yat-sen was elected President of the Republic in Canton, and a militant movement on capitalistic Hong Kong's doorstep was bound to cause trouble. Most of Hong Kong's Chinese were desperately poor and there had been the occasional riot over the years, which erupted in 1926 (following Sun Yat-sen's death) into a total **economic boycott** of the colony, organized and led by the Chinese Nationalists (the Kuomintang), based in Canton. There was no trade, few services and – more importantly – no food imports from China, a state of affairs which lasted for several months and did untold damage to manufacturing and commercial activity. Expat volunteers had to keep things going as best they could, while the strike leaders in Hong Kong encouraged many Chinese people to leave the colony so as to press home their demands: a shorter working day, less discrimination against the local Chinese population and a reduction in rent.

The strike didn't last, but the colony's confidence had been badly dented. And although business picked up again, new worries emerged in the 1930s as the **Japanese occupied southern China**. Hundreds of thousands of people fled into the colony, almost doubling the population, and many saw the eventual occupation of Hong Kong itself as inevitable.

Japanese occupation 1941–45

The Japanese had been advancing across China from the north since 1933, seizing Manchuria and Beijing before establishing troops in Canton in 1939 – an advance which had temporarily halted the civil war then raging in China. What was clear was that any further move to take Hong Kong was bound to succeed: the colony had only a small defensive force of a few battalions and a couple of ships, and couldn't hope to resist the Japanese army.

Some thought that the Japanese wouldn't attack, and certainly, although Hong Kong had been prepared for war since 1939, there was a feeling that old, commercial links with the Japanese would save the colony. However, when the Japanese occupied Indo-China, the colony's defences were immediately strengthened. A line of pillboxes and guns was established across the New Territories, the so-called Gin Drinkers Line, which it was hoped would delay any advancing army long enough for Kowloon to be evacuated and Hong Kong Island to be turned into a fortress from which the resistance could be directed.

On December 8, 1941 the **Japanese army invaded**, overran the border from Canton, bombed the planes at Kai Tak airport and swept through the New Territories' defences. They took Kowloon within six days, the British forces retreating to Hong Kong Island where they were shelled and bombed from the other side of the harbour. The Japanese then moved across to the island, split the defence forces in hard fighting and finished them off. The **British surrender** came on Christmas Day, the first time a British Crown Colony had ever been surrendered to enemy forces. Casualties amounted to around six thousand military and civilian deaths, with nine thousand more men captured. The soldiers were held in prisoner-of-war camps in Kowloon – although some officers were held elsewhere, including in camps in Japan itself – while those British civilians who had not previously been evacuated to Australia were interned in Stanley Prison on the island.

It was a dark time for the people of Hong Kong, who faced a Japanese army out of control.

Although some Chinese civilians collaborated, many others helped the European and Allied prisoners by smuggling in food and medicines, and helping to organize escapes. It wasn't necessarily a show of support for the British, but an indication of the loyalty most Hong Kong Chinese felt towards China, which had suffered even worse under the Japanese. Atrocities faced the Allied prisoners, too: during the short campaign, the Japanese had murdered (sometimes after rape) hospital staff, patients and prisoners, and in prison beatings, executions for escape attempts and torture were commonplace. Life in Stanley meant disease and malnutrition, and being a civilian was no guarantee of safety: in 1943, seven people were beheaded on the beach for possessing a radio.

The Japanese meanwhile sent a military governor to Hong Kong to supervise the **occupation**, but found the colony to be much less use to them than they had imagined. It wasn't incorporated into the Japanese-run parts of China, and apart from changing the names of buildings and organizations – and adding a few Japanese architectural touches to Government House – nothing fruitful came of their time there. The New Territories became a battleground for bandits, various factions of the Chinese defenders and the Japanese invaders; towns and villages emptied as many of the local Chinese were forcibly repatriated to the mainland; food and supplies were run down; the cities on either side of the harbour were bombed out. As the Japanese gradually lost the battle elsewhere, Hong Kong became more and more of an irrelevance to them, and when the **Japanese surrendered to the Allies** in August 1945, colonial government picked itself up surprisingly quickly.

Postwar reconstruction: the 1950s and 1960s

The immediate task in Hong Kong was to rebuild both buildings and commerce, something the colony undertook with remarkable energy. In 1945, the population had been reduced to around 600,000 people, who were faced with an acute housing shortage. Within five years the population had risen to over two million, the harbour had been cleared and the trading companies were back in business. This was, however, achieved at a price, and Hong Kong lost out on the democratic reforms that were sweeping the rest of the world. There had been suggestions that the colony become a free-trading "international" state after the war, or that it be handed back to China, but quick thinking by the imprisoned British leaders on Japan's surrender – who declared themselves the acting government – ensured that Hong Kong remained a British colony. Liberal measures designed to introduce at least some democratic reforms into the running of the colony were treated with virtual disdain by the population, which was interested only in getting its business back on its feet.

The boost the economy needed came in 1949–50, when the **Communists came to power in China**, unleashing a wave of new refugee migration across the border. The civil war in China had been fought in earnest since the end of World War II, and with the fall of Nationalist China, traders and businessmen were desperate to escape. Thousands arrived, many from Shanghai, to set up new businesses and provide the manufacturing base from which the colony could expand. By 1951, the population had grown to around two-and-a-half million, and Hong Kong had moved from being a mere entrepôt to become an industrial centre. New, lucrative industries – directly attributable to the recent refugees – included textiles and construction. A further incentive for a change in emphasis in the colony came with the American embargo on Chinese goods sold through Hong Kong during the **Korean War**, so that the territory was forced into manufacturing goods as a means of economic survival.

The new immigrants unleashed new problems for the colony, not least the fact that there was nowhere for them to live. **Squatter settlements** spread like wildfire and faced with a private housing sector that couldn't build new homes fast enough, the government established approved squatters' areas throughout the territory. In addition, virtually all of the new immigrants were ardently anti-Communist, many supporting the Kuomintang, and they took every opportunity during the 1950s to unsettle the relationship between Hong Kong and China. This resulted in **riots** in the colony between Communists and Nationalists, pointing the way towards future conflict. In an attempt to solve the problem thousands of ex-Kuomintang soldiers and their families – who had been unable to join the bulk of their colleagues in Taiwan – were forcibly moved to the village of Rennies Mill, on Hong Kong Island, which until its redevelopment just before the handover remained a bastion of Nationalist support.

This uneasy link with China was exploited by both sides throughout the 1960s, each action emphasizing Hong Kong's odd position as both a British colony and a part of China, prey to the whims and fortunes of the Chinese leadership. In 1962, the point was made by the Chinese government in the so-called **trial run**, which allowed (and encouraged) upwards of sixty thousand people to leave China for Hong Kong. The border was flooded, and though the British authorities were determined to keep such an influx out, there was little they could do in the face of blatant provocation from the Chinese army, which was directing the flow of people.

Things finally got out of hand in 1966–67, as the worst excesses of the Chinese **Cultural Revolution** began to spill over into the colony. There had already been serious rioting in Hong Kong in April 1966, ostensibly against a price rise in the first-class Star Ferry fare. Against the background of increasing political turmoil in mainland China (where the Red Guards emerged in Beijing in August 1966), local strikes and unrest began to dominate the colony in spring of the following year. After deaths and rioting in neighbouring Macau, where the Portuguese authorities were overrun by Red Guard agitators, the situation in Hong Kong deteriorated, and May and June 1967 saw the worst violence yet: Government House was besieged by pro-China activists, there were cases of Europeans being attacked in the streets, and some policemen were killed on the Hong Kong–Chinese border. There were also riots and strikes, a curfew was imposed, and in July a bomb exploded on Hong Kong Island, injuring nine people. However, apart from supportive and vociferous press reports in the pro-China newspapers, and a virulent anti-Imperialist/British poster campaign taken directly from the mainland, the organizers of the riots and unrest took little comfort from the attitude of Beijing. Chairman Mao was intent upon pursuing the Cultural Revolution to its fullest extent in China and had little time for what was happening in Hong Kong. Mao was also keen to avoid destabilizing the colony, as it was an important source of revenue – a pragmatic attitude that determined the Chinese approach towards Hong Kong throughout this period. Although there were more

disturbances throughout the rest of 1967, the protests fizzled out as tourism and confidence in the local economy gradually picked up again.

The 1970s: social problems

The economic gains of the postwar period were accompanied by the growth of a number of social problems that still trouble the colony today. The **population** continued to grow, bolstered by the ever-increasing number of immigrants, legal and (mostly) illegal, from China. There had been a housing shortage since the end of World War II, which this growth exacerbated, and squatter settlements evolved throughout Hong Kong. A fire in 1953 in Shek Kip Mei, Kowloon, had already demonstrated the inherent danger of such settlements: over fifty thousand people were made homeless in just one night. An emergency housing programme – taking people out of wooden huts and into fairly basic resettlement estates – went some way to addressing the problem, though it wasn't until the development of the New Town programme in the early 1970s that the problem of adequately housing Hong Kong's burgeoning population was fully addressed. The first **New Town**, Tuen Mun, opened in 1973, was a prototype of the concrete block cities that have now spread right across the New Territories, housing more than 2.5 million people. Taken together the new developments have made the Hong Kong government the world's largest landlord. Roughly half the population lives in public housing, although one reason for this is the fact that the government owns all the land in Hong Kong and carefully controls how many new plot leases reach the market every year. This has enabled property developers to ensure incredibly high prices, something that has made buying even the smallest flat well beyond the means of many. For more on the development of the New Towns, see the feature on p.169.

The rise in population caused concern in Hong Kong for other reasons. Although there was no unemployment, there were water and power shortages over the years, limited welfare facilities and poor public services, all of which had to be shared by more and more people. Resentment against the new arrivals was nothing new but was to have an importance after 1975, when the first of the **Vietnamese boat people** – fleeing their country after the North Vietnamese victory – fetched up in the colony. Although no one was turned away (a credit to the Hong Kong authorities even now), the numbers involved soon soared to frightening proportions – 65,000 refugees in 1979, many of whom had no chance of subsequent resettlement in other parts of the world.

The other major problem during this period was that of **crime and corruption**, endemic in Hong Kong since the founding of the colony. In modern times, crime was fuelled in particular by the number of Chinese illegal immigrants. Some imported their criminal networks and rackets with them, others had little else to turn to once the Hong Kong authorities began to crack down, making it hard to get a job without official papers. These developments were accompanied by an increase in **official and police corruption** throughout the 1960s, something that touched most aspects of life, from accepting bribes from street traders through to police cover-ups of serious illegal activity – a state of affairs only partly redeemed by the setting up in 1974 of the **Independent Commission Against Corruption**.

The Triads

Behind much of the major crime and corruption in Hong Kong were the various secretive **Triad** organizations, akin to the Sicilian Mafia in scale and wealth, though probably unrivalled in terms of sheer viciousness. Triads (so called because their emblem was a triangle denoting harmony between Heaven, Earth and Man) were first established in the seventeenth century in China, in an attempt to restore the Ming Dynasty after its overthrow by the Manchus. They moved into Hong Kong early in the colony's history, where they were able to organize among the new immigrants, splitting up into separate societies with their own elaborate initiation rites and ceremonies. The Triad organizations relied on a hierarchical structure, with ranks denoted by numbers that begin with 4 – representing the four elements, compass points and seas.

After World War II, with the colony in tatters, refugees and immigrants from newly Communist China moved into Hong Kong, many to the Walled City in Kowloon, which became a notorious criminal haven, protected by the Chinese assertions of legal rule over this small enclave on Hong Kong territory. The Walled City became a no-go area for the Hong Kong police, while the number of groups operating throughout the colony rose to around fifty – with possibly 100,000 members in all, operating everything from street gangs upwards to organized crime.

Towards 1997: the political moves

As China began to open up to the wider world in the early 1970s, Hong Kong's relationship with its neighbour improved dramatically. Trade between the two increased, as did Hong Kong's role as economic mediator between China and the West. Chinese investment in Hong Kong became substantial – in Chinese-owned banks, hotels, businesses, shops – and Hong Kong was a ready market for Chinese food products, even water. This shift in relationship was recognized in the mid-1970s, when the word "colony" was expunged from all official British titles in Hong Kong: in came the concept of Hong Kong as a "territory", which sounded much better to sensitive Chinese ears.

Against this background came the realization that 1997 – and the handing back of the New Territories – was fast approaching. There was a general belief that it would be absurd to pretend that Hong Kong could survive without the New Territories, and that it was unlikely that China would want them without the money-making parts of Kowloon and Hong Kong Island.

It hasn't always been so clear cut to observers. Ian Fleming, author of the James Bond books, visiting in the 1950s, thought that "when the remaining forty years of our lease on the mainlands territory expire, I see no reason why a reduced population should not retreat to the islands and the original territory which Britain holds in perpetuity."

The first tentative moves towards finding a solution occurred in **1982**, when British Prime Minister Margaret Thatcher visited China and Hong Kong. Certain injudicious remarks by her on that tour, concerning British responsibility to Hong Kong's citizens and the validity of the original treaties ceding the territory to Britain, caused the Chinese to make an issue of the sovereignty question. As far as they were concerned, Hong Kong and its people were Chinese, so any responsibility was that of Beijing. To the Chinese government, historically the treaties had been "unequal" (that is, forced by a strong nineteenth-century Britain on a weak China) and therefore illegal. After Thatcher had gone home, and the dust had settled, talks continued, with both sides agreeing that their aim was the "prosperity and stability" of a future Hong Kong, while arguing about the question of sovereignty. It became clear during 1983 that Britain would eventually concede sovereignty to China, and that Britain would abandon all claims to Hong Kong, not just the New Territories.

After two years of debate and uncertainty, which had a negative influence on business and confidence in the colony, the **Sino-British Joint Declaration** was signed in September 1984, with Britain agreeing to hand back sovereignty of the entire territory to China in 1997. In return, Hong Kong would continue with the same legal and capitalistic system for at least the next fifty years, becoming a "Special Administrative Region" (SAR) of China, in which it would have virtual autonomy – a concept the then Chinese leader Deng Xiaoping described as "one country, two systems". Almost immediately, the declaration began to haunt the British government. No changes to the document were allowed after it was signed and, as people began to point out in the colony, with virtually no democratic institutions in place in Hong Kong, the Chinese would effectively be able to do what they liked after 1997. Only the economic necessity to retain Hong Kong's wealth-producing status would limit their actions, and even that wouldn't be enough in the face of any radical change in leadership in Beijing.

The Joint Declaration was followed by the publication in Beijing in 1988 of the **Basic Law**, a sort of constitutional framework for explaining how the SAR of Hong Kong would work in practice. Again, in theory, the Basic Law guaranteed the preservation of the existing capitalist system in Hong Kong, along with various freedoms – of travel, speech, the right to strike – that were deemed necessary to sustain confidence. But, in spite of this, concern grew steadily in Hong Kong. Only a third of the Legislative Council seats were to be directly elected by 1997 (with half elected by 2003); vague references to the outlawing of "subversion" were disturbing to anyone who was even remotely critical of Beijing's actions; and China refused a referendum in Hong Kong on the provisions of the Basic Law. Despite a consultation exercise in Hong Kong, where the Hong Kong government invited direct comment from the public on the Basic Law, confidence wasn't restored. Liberals in Hong Kong, in the Legislative Council and elsewhere, accused the British government of a sell-out, and of failing to implement democratic reforms that would at least provide some guarantee of stability after 1997. The **brain drain** of educated, professional people leaving Hong Kong for new countries, which had been picking up ever since 1984, began to increase more rapidly.

1989: shattered confidence

1989 was a grim year for Hong Kong. On June 4, following student-dominated pro-democracy demonstrations in China, Deng Xiaoping sent the tanks into **Tiananmen Square** in Beijing to crush the protest – an act which killed hundreds, possibly thousands, of people, with many more arrested, jailed and executed in the following weeks. This put China on show as never before, and confirmed the worst fears of almost the entire Hong Kong population that the British government had indeed sold them out to a dangerous and murderous regime. No one now doubted that with the People's Liberation Army due to be stationed on Hong Kong territory after 1997, any future dissent in the colony against Chinese authoritarian rule could be stamped upon as easily as in Beijing, whatever the Basic Law said. And to indicate the seriousness of this view, the Hang Seng Index, the performance indicator of the Hong Kong Stock Exchange, dropped 22 percent on the Monday following the massacre.

Tiananmen Square was a particularly galling experience for Hong Kong's own **pro-democracy movement**, which had staged extraordinary rallies in support of the Beijing students – and which spirited several dissident Chinese students out of China to safety in the following months. Successive protest rallies in Hong Kong had brought up to a million people out on to the streets – around twenty percent of the population – to demand democracy in China, and more significantly, more democracy in Hong Kong itself. A copy of the Goddess of Democracy statue, which had been created by the Tiananmen students, was erected in Hong Kong after the massacre; Cantonese pop stars recorded a song, *For Freedom*, in support of the Chinese students; while in typical Hong Kong fashion, manufacturers cashed in on the protests with stores selling democracy armbands, headbands and T-shirts. Everywhere, the point was being made loudly and angrily that without democratic institutions in place well before 1997, the territory and its people would be entirely at the mercy of the whims of the leaders in Beijing.

If there had been a brain drain from Hong Kong before June 4, it was now a flood. Embassies and consulates were swamped by people desperate for an escape route should things go wrong in the future. Singapore's announcement that it would be taking up to 25,000 Hong Kong Chinese over the next five to eight years led to fighting for application forms. Surveys and opinion polls showed that sixty percent of the population wished (and expected) to qualify for a foreign passport, and that one in six people would leave anyway before 1997.

On top of all this, the territory was enduring the worst problems yet caused by the continuing influx of the **Vietnamese boat people**. The summer sailing season saw the numbers top fifty thousand, the highest for a decade – and with fewer countries prepared to accept new immigrants, most Vietnamese arrivals were doomed to a protracted and unpleasant stay in Hong Kong's closed camps. As the camps filled and then burst, isolated and uninhabited outlying islands were used to hold the boat people. Shelter was in makeshift tents, conditions were unsanitary, food was poor, and, not surprisingly, trouble followed. There were disturbances in some of the camps – fighting between rival groups of Vietnamese, break-outs into the local villages, a few attempted suicides and the occasional murder – all of which the Hong Kong authorities could see no end to, given the numbers still arriving daily from across the South China Sea.

Into the 1990s

The turn of the decade brought no respite for Hong Kong. The two main problems were still the question of what would happen in 1997 and what to do with the Vietnamese. They were complicated and, in many ways, related questions, attracting emotional debate both in the territory and in Britain. Both matters affected the quality of life in Hong Kong, with many feeling that there was no assured future. Yet certain features of life in Hong Kong, like the **economy**, were still to be envied. The territory now ranks eighth in the world league of trading nations; it's the busiest container port in the world, has the third largest foreign exchange reserves, and is the fourth largest source of foreign direct investment in the world. Its economic growth has averaged eight percent a year for more than a decade; its citizens enjoyed virtually full employment and a GDP per capita of more than US $25,000 – higher than the United Kingdom and not far below that of the United States. In addition, more than half of all China's exports pass through Hong Kong, while the territory accounts for well over fifty percent of foreign investment in China – a formidable record for a place that was devastated only fifty years ago, and founded just a century earlier.

Domestic troubles

However, to pretend that during the early 1990s everything else was rosy in this capitalistic garden would be naive. **Crime** was on the increase – although the Triads seemed happy to move at least some of their activities out of Hong Kong before 1997, following the Cantonese exodus to places like London, Australia and Canada. **Drug addiction** was a major worry, with estimates of around forty thousand active drug users, 96 percent of them heroin addicts. And though the Far Eastern **sex trade** had largely moved away during the 1980s – to Thailand and across the border into China – the combination of prostitution and needle-sharing contributed to marked increases in the AIDS figures.

Most disturbing of all, however, was that despite Hong Kong's long association with Britain, and British protestations that she had a duty to the territory's citizens, Hong Kong's population had few of the **rights and privileges** that people in Britain enjoyed and expected. There was no democracy worth the name; citizens could be stopped and searched by the police at any time, and had to carry an ID card; and public welfare provision was limited. In addition, over the years the citizens of Hong Kong had been stripped of the right of abode in Britain by successive Immigration Acts. Told to consider themselves British for a century and a half for the purposes of government and administration, the vast majority of the Hong Kong Chinese found that having given up Chinese nationality when they fled that country in favour of a British administration, they were effectively stateless.

The passport question

The problem of the duty of the British government to the territory's population was crystallized into the **passport question**. Since the events in Tiananmen Square, increasing numbers in Hong Kong had sought a second passport so that if China went back on the promises enshrined in the Joint Declaration they would have an "insurance policy" – the right to leave the territory and live elsewhere.

The issue was not strictly whether or not people were able to get hold of such passports. Many countries, from Paraguay to The Gambia, were willing virtually to sell passports (and thus citizenship) to the large numbers of Hong Kong Chinese wishing to leave. All it took was the money. However, this was obviously an option open only to the relatively wealthy or well connected. The moral question faced by the British government was whether or not to grant the **right of abode** to all the citizens of Hong Kong, so that people would have a choice of where to live after 1997.

The arrangement was that after 1997, anyone without a foreign passport would automatically become a citizen of the PRC and so eligible for a Special Administrative Region (SAR) passport. The view in Hong Kong was that Britain had a duty to the territory's people, which involved overturning the various Immigration Acts passed in Britain and restoring their right of abode in Britain by giving them full British passports. It was argued that most people wanted to stay in Hong Kong anyway, and that, given the choice, most certainly wouldn't want to come to Britain – by far the most popular destinations for Hong Kong Chinese leaving the territory are Canada and Australia, where there are large Chinese populations. But the right to a passport, it was held, would give the residents of Hong Kong more security, and thus lend the territory more stability.

The view of the **British government** was confused from the start. Having effectively made many Hong Kong people stateless through the provisions of the 1981 British Nationality Act (Hong Kong people hold a British "dependent territories" or "overseas national" passport, without right of abode in the UK), the government argued that insurance policies exist to be used. It claimed all those with passports would in fact come to Britain, which would be disastrous for housing and social security measures, and for race relations in the UK. The figures were uncertain (it depends whether you count the whole Hong Kong population or just those with dependent territory passports), but the spectre of between three and a half million and five million people flooding into Britain was raised. Instead, the government – by way of the British Nationality (Hong Kong) Act – offered full passports and space in Britain for fifty thousand "key personnel", in effect, high-ranking civil servants and police officers, technical and professional people, business people and the wealthy, plus their families – a figure of around 225,000 in all. This was designed to ensure that these people stayed in Hong Kong, unless things became intolerable; placements were determined by a points system and the governor had the final judgement on the matter.

This was clearly a token offer, and although it's arguable whether anything like three and a half million people would have come in any case, there was fierce opposition in the UK to the plan. In fact, with lowering of barriers within Europe, as part of the European Union, those who did come would have had the right to settle anywhere in the European Community, not just Britain (which most Hong Kong Chinese people find cold and economically backward). Ironically, this is the right that the Chinese from Macau will enjoy. The Portuguese government is offering them passports which will theoretically allow them to live and work in Britain.

The situation was further confused by the **attitude of the British people**, who in repeated opinion polls said that they opposed letting any substantial number of Hong Kong Chinese settle in Britain. The opposition Labour Party particularly was torn between its moral heart and its political head: it knew that to call for a large influx of non-white immigrants into Britain would cost it dear in terms of support from the very people it needed to put it back into power.

The Chinese government, too, started to criticize Britain for supposedly reneging on the terms of the Joint Declaration. The Beijing line was that whatever happened, it wouldn't honour the full British passports issued, as the people in Hong Kong would be Chinese citizens after 1997 – and thus not entitled to leave or enter the territory on so-called "foreign" passports. This of course conveniently ignored those Hong Kongers not of ethnic Chinese origin – such as Indians or Filipinos.

The Vietnamese

There was an ironic twist to the nationality debate for the people of Hong Kong regarding the fate of the **Vietnamese boat people**, who had been landing in the territory since 1975. These were part of a mass exodus from Vietnam of over 800,000 people, fleeing in the wake of the Communist takeover. While seeking overseas passports themselves, the people of Hong Kong were increasingly adamant that the unfortunate refugees from Vietnam should not be allowed to stay in the territory. From having initially offered sanctuary to the boat people – the only Southeast Asian state to do so – Hong Kong now felt inclined to tow the Vietnamese back out to sea. Partly it was frustration with the lack of any progress in finding an international solution to the problem – successive Geneva conferences failed to come up with sufficient quotas from countries prepared to take the boat people. But it was a little rich coming from a people which one day hoped to seek sanctuary itself.

The situation became even more ironic once the British government decided upon its course of action towards the boat people in Hong Kong. Those deemed "economic migrants" were to be repatriated to Vietnam – forcibly if necessary – while long screening procedures would sort out the genuine refugees, thought to be ten percent of the total, who would be guaranteed resettlement in a third country. The first **forced repatriation** took place in December 1989, and a pathetic sight it was, as 51 men, women and children were herded into trucks by armed police and forced on to an aeroplane back to Vietnam. It drew worldwide condemnation, but was supported in Hong Kong at most levels – though quite what the distinction was between Vietnamese economic migrants and those Chinese who fled China in the 1950s to set up in Hong Kong, or those who now seek to flee Hong Kong for whichever third country will have them, was never satisfactorily explained.

Britain's tougher stance led to a marked decrease in the numbers sailing to Hong Kong, though there is considerable evidence that the Vietnamese simply headed to other nearby countries instead, like Thailand and Malaysia – shifting rather than alleviating the problem. There was also an upturn in the Vietnamese economy at the turn of the decade, which perhaps persuaded many would-be migrants to stay. Whatever the truth, the last boat recorded as entering Hong Kong was in late 1991.

Meanwhile, in Hong Kong, conditions deteriorated in the nine **camps** in which the Vietnamese were held. At its peak, the camps' population was just over 64,000 people – conditions were basic and exacerbated by violent clashes between the different Vietnamese factions contained within. In the worst incident, 21 people died at Shek Kong camp in a fire set alight during a fight between north and south Vietnamese groups.

By mid-1993, the camps' population had diminished to around 42,000 as the number of **voluntary returnees** steadily increased, following agreement between Britain and Vietnam on the method of return. Overseen by the United Nations High Commission for Refugees (UNHCR), those who volunteered to return to Vietnam received a US$50 bonus and US$30 a month during their first year back; forced returnees were supervised by the Orderly Return Programme and received only the $30 a month, not the bonus. By the end of 1996 – just six months before the handover – the number of Vietnamese people still detained in Hong Kong was down to around six thousand migrants awaiting repatriation to Vietnam, and thirteen hundred bona fide refugees waiting for offers of new homes in third countries. Many of these were difficult cases – convicted criminals, drug addicts, or those who the Vietnamese government claimed were not nationals. In the run-up to the handover China had demanded Britain take note of its "unshirkable responsibility" for any Vietnamese – migrants or refugees – remaining in the colony, which was Beijing-speak for saying that Britain should take the Vietnamese away when they left in June 1997. Britain, not surprisingly, made no such commitment, and the issue still rumbles on, although the small number of Vietnamese now remaining in Hong Kong has taken the sting out of the dispute.

The new politics

The **Basic Law** – the projected "constitution" for Hong Kong as a Special Administrative Region of China after 1997 – was finally approved by China's National People's Congress in April 1990, and immediately provided a focus around which people in Hong Kong began to question the lack of democratic progress in the territory.

Leaders in Hong Kong were particularly outraged by the attitude of the British government, which – in their eyes – during the consultations on the Basic Law had capitulated every step of the way to the Chinese. China, for obvious reasons, was keen to have as little democracy as possible in place in Hong Kong by 1997, and the final draft of the Basic Law as passed had

For more on the colonial system of government, see p.72.

worrying implications for the future – a promise of eventual universal suffrage was deleted, Beijing maintained the power to declare martial law in Hong Kong, and an anti-subversion clause was added.

Out of the protests against the Basic Law grew a new **political awareness**, which expressed itself in a number of emerging pressure groups and fledgling political parties. The **Hong Kong Alliance in Support of the Patriotic and Democratic Movement** organized a 10,000-strong rally in April 1990, defying warnings from China to stop this kind of "provocation". One of the leading liberal activists in Hong Kong, the barrister Martin Lee, became head of a new pro-democracy party, the United Democrats of Hong Kong, now known as the **Democratic Party**; the other main grouping was the conservative, business-led (and confusingly named) **Liberal Democratic Federation**.

In **elections in September 1991** – the territory's first direct elections – United Democrat candidates swept the board, winning sixteen of the eighteen seats on the sixty-seat Legislative Council (LEGCO) that were up for grabs. It was a limited exercise in democracy – 21 other candidates were selected by so-called "functional constituencies", consisting of trade and professional groups, while the rest were appointed by the governor – but it sent a powerful message to Beijing that Hong Kong people were dissatisfied with the provisions of the Basic Law. Even more alarming for Beijing was the fact that pro-China candidates failed to win a single seat.

Despite the advance of the United Democrats, the governor, David (later Sir David) Wilson refused to appoint liberals to his Executive Council (EXCO) – a move welcomed in Beijing, though denigrated in Hong Kong. Indeed, Wilson's role in Hong Kong's government became increasingly suspect in the eyes of many, who accused him of giving in too readily to the Chinese. His fate was sealed when new British prime minister John Major was forced to travel to Beijing to sign the agreement for Hong Kong's new airport. Major's presence at the signing ceremony was virtually a condition of the agreement, and it was seen as an embarrassment for the British that Wilson, with his diplomatic skills, should have avoided.

Fortuitously, as it turned out for the prime minister, his close ally **Chris Patten** – Conservative Party chairman – lost his parliamentary seat in Britain's April 1992 elections, even as his party was returned to power. Major offered him the governorship, which he eventually accepted, ushering in a new political era in Hong Kong.

The last governor

Chris Patten was the 28th – and last – governor to be appointed, but the first career politician to take the post. His arrival caused consternation all round: among the local population, who complained about having Britain's cast-off politicians imposed upon them, and among the Chinese leadership who – rightly as it turned out – feared Patten's motives for taking the job.

Any thoughts that Chris Patten was there to make up the numbers until 1997 soon disappeared. He quickly jettisoned much of the colonial paraphernalia associated with his position, while in talks with Beijing it became clear that he – and Britain – sought an extension in the franchise for Hong Kong before the handover to China, that arguably went beyond the provisions made in the Basic Law. New LEGCO elections were due in 1995, which – under the provisions of the Basic Law – would see the number of elected members rise from eighteen to twenty (and to thirty by 2003). This had already been dismissed by Hong Kong liberals as too slow a move towards democracy: the Democratic Party wanted fifty percent of LEGCO directly elected in 1995, rising to a hundred percent by 2003. Patten's proposal was to stick to the number of directly elected members agreed with China, but to **widen the franchise**, by lowering the voting age from 21 to 18; by increasing the number of indirectly elected council members; and by creating extra "functional constituencies" which would effectively enfranchise 2.7 million Hong Kong people – as opposed to the roughly 200,000 voters allowed by the previous system.

The Chinese government began a loud campaign against the new governor and his proposals, and **relations between Britain and China** worsened considerably. Patten was personally branded a "serpent", a "prostitute", a "sinner for all millennia" and – most intriguingly – a "tango dancer" by the mainland Chinese press, reflecting the (correctly held) view of the Chinese government that his attempts to meddle with the franchise were a

Western attempt to import democracy into China by the back door. As talks dragged on, and relations soured, new threats were made to Hong Kong's stability. China vowed to renege on all contracts and commercial agreements signed by the Hong Kong government without its consent as soon as the colony was returned to its control in 1997 – something that threatened the future of several major infrastructure projects, including the new Chek Lap Kok airport. The Hang Seng Index reflected a general lack of confidence in the territory's future by recording massive falls; and rumours of destabilization by the Chinese government caused huge runs on two of Hong Kong's largest banks, Citibank and the Standard Chartered. China also reiterated that it would not recognize the UK passports which were to be offered to the fifty thousand key Hong Kong personnel and their families – even though in theory the names of recipients would be kept secret. In the meantime, Britain announced a new British National Overseas (BNO) passport to replace the British Dependent Territories passport after 1997 – the BNO passport would grant British consular protection outside China, and visa-free entry to, but not the right of abode in, the UK.

The situation reached something of a stalemate, with both sides playing a nerve-wracking poker game with the territory's future. Meetings throughout 1993 consistently failed to provide any breakthrough with China hostile to Governor Patten's very presence in any negotiations and Britain adamant that its limited democratic proposals should prevail.

In the end, the governor prevailed, simply by ignoring the threats and gambling that the Chinese government wouldn't abandon its commercial agreements, thus cutting off its nose to spite its face. **Elections in September 1995** marked the first time that each of LEGCO's sixty seats was contested and brought gains for the Democratic Party, which could, for the first time, count on the support of almost half of LEGCO's members. The main pro-Beijing grouping, the Democratic Alliance for the Betterment of Hong Kong, came a distant second, despite vociferous Chinese backing. Beijing responded to the result by announcing that it would not recognize the sitting LEGCO.

The governor's firm line continued to command respectable support in Hong Kong, although pro-democracy LEGCO members changed their stance from supporting his electoral reforms to

complaining that the reforms did not go near far enough. Conservative business groups, for their part, pressed for an accommodation with China, arguing that the territory's future prosperity rested on co-operation and not confrontation. Yet the various conservative and pro-Beijing factions failed to command majority support.

The democracy activists were bound to lose out by the breakdown in relations between the governor and China. They had hoped for a so-called "through train" which would allow legislators elected in 1995 to see out their terms through the handover. Clearly, the Chinese government had no intention of allowing itself to be confronted by a robust democratic legislature that would turn the recovery of its prize into a political nightmare played out on worldwide television.

In the end the Chinese resorted to classic Communist Party tactics to change the political landscape and to bestow legitimacy on a legislative council of its own choice. Simply ignoring the eloquent denunciations of Patten and the democrats, the Chinese convened a series of hand-picked committees across the border in the boomtown of Shenzhen. Out of this labyrinthine and carefully scripted process there emerged a "provisional legislature" made up of compliant politicians and a **Chief Executive** who would assume the governor's role in the new Special Administrative Region.

The lucky man was **Tung Chee-hwa**, a shipping magnate in his sixties. Originally from a wealthy Shanghai family, Tung fled to Hong Kong after the communist revolution and took over his father's shipping business in the 1980s. An urbane, patriarchal figure, Tung came from the cloistered and deferential world of the traditional Chinese family boardroom. He was unused to the rough-and-tumble of political debate and unhappy in front of Hong Kong's unfettered media. Patten, by contrast, played a losing hand with consummate skill with his mastery of modern techniques of public relations. He was to end his term as the most highly esteemed British figure among the population of Hong Kong in 156 years of colonial history.

The countdown to 1 July 1997 ticked away in a poisonous atmosphere of mistrust and resentful rhetoric. Democrats feared the worst, dissidents departed for other countries and the British packed their bags. In truth, most of the business community would stay, but the military and colonial administrators were all to go – as would thousands of young Britons who had found Hong Kong an easy visa-free place to find work while on their travels in Asia.

The handover and beyond

The **handover** turned out to be one of history's great non-events. The bands played, the British flags came down, Patten shed a tear and Her Majesty's armed forces paraded perfectly under a drenching tropical downpour in a farewell display of the imperial stiff upper lip. China's president, Jiang Zemin, led his country's most senior politicians to the ceremony, where the British side was led by the Prince of Wales, representing the Queen. The actual event, at midnight on 30 June, was marked by rigid protocol and no warmth between the two sides, wearied by long and bitter disputes.

As the royal yacht sailed away, Hong Kong's embittered democrats were demonstrating at the LEGCO building. The morning after, they were thrown out and Beijing's chosen few filed in.

It seemed as if the same old arguments over politics would dominate the new Hong Kong. But just 48 hours after the handover, the devaluation of the Thai baht set off the **Asian Financial Crisis** which was to wreak havoc throughout the region. As one country after another saw its currency and stockmarket collapse, Hong Kong found itself in the eye of the storm.

The new administration waged a fierce battle against currency speculators to preserve the Hong Kong dollar's value and hold the link of $7.80 to the US dollar. But the price of preserving a stable currency was paid with dramatic falls in the local stock and property markets, reducing people's wealth and raising popular discontent. A collapse in tourism after the handover made matters worse. International business confidence in the government's adherence to its free-market doctrine was also shaken. In fighting off the speculators the government entered the stockmarket heavily, buying key stocks and propping up share prices to the tune of billions of dollars – becoming in the process one of the largest shareholders in many of Hong Kong's most important companies.

Tung seemed unable to rise to the occasion. A poor communicator, he vanished from sight as one public relations disaster after another beset an administration once renowned for its competence. An outbreak of lethal bird flu forced a mass slaughter of poultry – millions of birds were gassed – but this proved to be only one of a series of health scares and hospital blunders that did nothing to revive the flagging tourist trade or boost local confidence. In addition, Hong Kong's dreadful environmental neglect finally brought retribution: a disgusting red algae ruined popular swimming beaches, while record pollution levels sent thousands to hospital.

Ordinary people had other problems to face. In 1998 Hong Kong officially entered recession. Unemployment rose to record levels – albeit only a little over five percent, but a serious problem in a place with very limited social protection, and the retail and property sectors were badly hit, causing more job losses. One of the most interesting consequences of this was an end to the reticence many ordinary people had felt about commenting on government policy when times were good, and everyone was getting richer. Criticism of officialdom, its policies and relationship with business was voiced in a way and at a level that it never had been before.

Amid such doom and gloom one reassuring thing for Hong Kong people was the way that China kept its promise not to interfere in their affairs. In 1998 there were **new elections** to LEGCO and although the system was rigged against them, the democratic parties profited from the record turnout and easily won most of the votes. The new voting system, which had dramatically cut the number of people eligible to vote in functional constituencies, restricted them to a few seats, which voters found frustrating, but many of Beijing's most loyal friends were sent packing by the electorate. Democracy in Hong Kong was cramped, curbed and, for the moment, hedged about with deliberate barriers. But there could be no doubt that the will of the Hong Kong people and the dramatic changes in Asia were on its side.

Books

There's no shortage of books written about Hong Kong and Macau, and you'll find that you can get most of them in Hong Kong, too; for a list of main bookshop addresses in Hong Kong, see p.291. What there is a lack of – certainly in translation – is books about both territories written by Chinese authors. In the reviews below, the UK publisher is listed first, followed by the publisher in the US – unless the title is available in one country only, in which case we've specified the country; o/p signifies out of print.

Hong Kong

History and politics

Nigel Cameron, *Power* (OUP East Asia, o/p). Immensely detailed history of the China Light & Power Co, one of Hong Kong's biggest economic successes. More interesting, though, for the insight it offers into one of the territory's main power-broking families, the Kadoories.

Austin Coates, *Myself a Mandarin* (OUP East Asia, UK). Light-hearted account of the author's time as a magistrate in the colonial administration during the 1950s. For more from the prolific Coates, see "Macau" on p.398.

Maurice Collis, *Foreign Mud* (Faber, o/p). Useful coverage of the opening up of China to trade and of the opium wars.

Jonathon Dimbleby, *The Last Governor* (Little Brown, UK & US). An insider's account of the battle for democracy between the last British governor and the Chinese government, with a dash of Whitehall treachery thrown in. Colourful portraits of many of Hong Kong's leading figures.

E. J. Eitel, *Europe in China* (OUP East Asia, UK). First published in 1895, this is an out-and-out colonial history of early Hong Kong – lively, biased and interesting.

Jean Gittins, *Stanley: Behind Barbed Wire* (HK University Press, HK/State Mutual, US). Well-written and moving eyewitness account of time spent behind bars at Stanley Prison during the internment of civilians by the Japanese in World War II.

Christopher Patten, *East and West* (Random House, UK & US). An elegant account from the last British governor of his controversial term in office up to the 1997 handover, and a thoughtful assessment of where the Asian "miracle" went wrong.

Stephen Vines, *Hong Kong: China's New Colony* (Arum Press, UK). Lively anecdotal account of the new Hong Kong after the resumption of Chinese rule, containing astringent assessments of the city's business elite and a hard-headed view of its future prospects.

Frank Welsh, *A History of Hong Kong* (Harper Collins, UK). Much applauded and sweeping general historical survey of the "barren rock" from early times to the balmy days of colonial rule, and Hong Kong's modern transformation into a prosperous Chinese City. A standard text.

Peter Wesley-Smith, *Unequal Treaty 1898–1997* (OUP, o/p). Sound and detailed review of the leasing of the New Territories to Britain in 1898, recording the reaction of both the British and Chinese authorities along the way. Some parts are now dated, since it was written before the Joint Declaration was made.

Travel, architecture, reference and contemporary life

Frederick Dannen and Barry Long, *Hong Kong Babylon* (Faber & Faber, UK & US). Subtitled "An Insider's Guide to the Hollywood of the East", this pacy reference book gets to grips with every facet of the Hong Kong movie scene, from plot summaries to interviews with stuntmen.

Emily Hahn, *China to Me* (Virago, o/p/Da Capo). A breathless account of pre- and post-war hi-jinks in (mainly) Shanghai and Hong Kong, including time when the American author and her child lived under Japanese rule in the territory while her friends were interned.

Susanna Hoe, *The Private Life of Old Hong Kong* (OUP East Asia, UK & US). A history of the lives of Western women in Hong Kong from 1841 to 1941, re-created from contemporary letters and diaries. A fine book, and telling of the hitherto neglected contribution of a whole range of people who had a hand in shaping modern Hong Kong.

Ken Hom, *Fragrant Harbour Taste: The New Chinese Cooking of Hong Kong* (Bantam Press, UK). Details modern Hong Kong cooking as dished up in some of the swankier designer restaurants, which culls its influences from all over Asia, as well as the West.

Hong Kong (Hong Kong Government Press, HK). The Hong Kong government's official yearbook, published annually, and a detailed – if uncritical – mass of photos, statistics, essays and information. Available in most HK bookshops.

The Other Hong Kong Report (Chinese University Press, HK). An alternative to the rosy picture presented in the government's official yearbook, collating the observations of experts on such fraught subjects as corruption, political freedom, the rule of law, the housing crisis, and the appalling environmental degradation of this prosperous but filthy city.

Vittorio Magnago Lampugnani (ed), *Hong Kong Architecture: The Aesthetics of Destiny* (Prestel, UK). Beautifully produced, large-format account of Hong Kong's most important and innovative architectural projects, with fine colour pictures and sketches and an informative background history.

John and Kirsten Miller (ed), *Hong Kong* (Chronicle Books, UK). A nice little compendium of extracts from novels and travelogues based in Hong Kong, encompassing all the usual suspects: Somerset Maugham, Jan Morris et al.

Jan Morris, *Hong Kong: Epilogue to an Empire* (Penguin/Vintage). Hong Kong – historical, contemporary and future – dealt with in typical Morris fashion: which means an engaging mix of anecdote, solid research, acute observation and lively opinion. One of the best introductions there is to the territory.

Madelaine H. Tang et al., *Historical Walks: Hong Kong Island* (The Guidebook Company). An invaluable little book detailing five walks through parts of Hong Kong Island, with clear maps and directions. Available in most Hong Kong bookshops.

Fiction

John Burdett, *The Last Six Million Seconds* (Coronet UK). Fast paced cops-and-commissars thriller involving stolen nuclear fuel, triad gangsters and headless corpses. Written with reeking authenticity from the girlie bars of Mongkok to the bloody roast beef at the Hong Kong Club.

James Clavell, *Tai-Pan* (Coronet/Dell), *Noble House* (Coronet/Dell). Big, thick bodice-rippers set respectively at the founding of the territory and in the 1960s, and dealing with the same one-dimensional pirates and businessmen. Unwittingly verging on parody in places. A much better read, incidentally, is his *King Rat*, set in Changi prisoner-of-war camp in Singapore where Clavell was a POW.

John Le Carré, *The Honourable Schoolboy* (Coronet/Bantam). Taut George Smiley novel, with spooks and moles chasing each other across Hong Kong and the Far East. Accurate and enthusiastic reflections on the territory and the usual sharp eye trained on the intelligence world.

Elizabeth Darrell, *Concerto* (Michael Joseph/St Martin's Press). Blockbuster novel set against the background of the Japanese invasion of Hong Kong in 1941.

Somerset Maugham, *The Painted Veil* (Mandarin/Viking Penguin). First published in 1925, this colonial story of love, betrayal and revenge unfolds in Hong Kong before moving on to cholera-ravaged mainland China.

Timothy Mo, *An Insular Possession* (Pan/Random House o/p). A splendid novel, re-creating the nineteenth-century foundation of Hong Kong, taking in the trading ports of Macau and Canton along the way. Mo's ear and eye for detail can also be glimpsed in The Monkey King (Vintage/Double day, o/p), his entertaining first novel about the conflicts and manoeuvrings of family life in post-war Hong Kong, and his filmed novel Sour Sweet (Vintage/Random House, o/p) – an endearing tale of an immigrant Hong Kong family setting up business in 1960s London.

Macau

C. R. Boxer, *Seventeenth Century Macau* (Heinemann US, o/p). Interesting survey of documents, engravings, inscriptions and maps of Macau culled from the years either side of the restoration of the Portuguese monarchy in 1640. An academic study, but accessible enough for some informative titbits about the enclave.

Daniel Carney, *Macau* (Corgi/Kensington). Improbable characterization in a Clavell-like thriller set in the enclave.

Austin Coates, *Macao and the British* (OUP East Asia, UK), *A Macao Narrative* (OUP East Asia, UK), *City of Broken Promises* (OUP East Asia, UK). Coates has written widely about the Far East, where he was Assistant Colonial Secretary in Hong Kong in the 1950s. *Macao and the British* follows the early years of Anglo-Chinese relations and underlines the importance of the Portuguese enclave as a staging post for other traders. *A Macao Narrative* is a short but more specific account of Macau's history up to the mid-1970s; *City of Broken Promises* is an entertaining historical novel set in Macau in the late eighteenth century.

Cesar Guillen-Nunez, *Macau* (OUP, UK & US). Decent, slim hardback history of Macau, worth a look for the insights it offers into the churches, buildings and gardens of the city.

Books about China

David Bonavia, *The Chinese* (Penguin, o/p/Viking Penguin). Excellent introduction to the Chinese – their lives, aspirations, politics and problems. Intended as a discussion of the Chinese of the People's Republic, it remains useful and instructive for all travellers to Asia.

Michael Fathers and **Andrew Higgins**, *Tiananmen: the Rape of Peking* (Doubleday UK & US, o/p). Eyewitness account of the events leading up to the massacre in and around Tiananmen Square in 1989.

Christopher Hibbert, *The Dragon Wakes: China and the West 1793–1911* (Penguin/Viking Penguin). Superbly entertaining account of the opening up of China to Western trade and influence. Hibbert leaves you in no doubt about the cultural misunderstandings that bedevilled early missions to China – or about the morally dubious acquisition of Hong Kong and the other Treaty Ports by Western powers.

Alain Peyrefitte, *The Collision of Two Civilisations: the British expedition to China in 1792–4* (Harvill Press, UK) Excellent account by a scholar and former French diplomat of the Macartney embassy to the Chinese court and the misunderstandings it produced, placed in the context of contemporary European events.

Jonathan Spence, *The Search for Modern China* (WW Norton, US). From the pen of the distinguished Yale University historian and scholar of Chinese culture, this comprehensive, impartial and wise book is the definitive single volume account of the violent sweep of Chinese history from the decline of the emperors to the twilight years of Deng Xiaoping.

Zhisui Li, *The Private Life of Chairman Mao* (Arrow/Random House). The most intimate portrait of any modern dictator, an unsparing account from Mao's own doctor who watched what the book's introduction calls "a shadow world, where great visions became father to great crimes."

Frances Wood, *No Dogs and Not Many Chinese* (John Murray, UK). Historical snapshot of the treaty ports and the life lived within them – entertaining and instructive.

Astrology: the Chinese Calendar and Horoscopes

Most people are interested to find out what sign they are in the **Chinese zodiac system**, particularly since – like the Western system – each person is supposed to have characteristics similar to those of the sign which relates to their birthdate. True Chinese astrologers, however, eschew the use of the animal symbols in isolation to analyse a person's life, seeing the zodiac signs as mere entertainment. There are twelve signs in the Chinese zodiac, corresponding with one of twelve animals, whose characteristics you'll find listed below. These **animal signs** have existed in Chinese folk tradition since the sixth century BC, though it wasn't until the third century BC that they were incorporated into a formal study of astrology and astronomy, based around the device of the lunar calendar. Quite why animals emerged as the vehicle for Chinese horoscopy is unclear. one story has it that the animals used are the twelve which appeared before the command of Buddha, who named the years in the order in which the animals arrived. Another says that the Jade Emperor held a race to determine the fastest animals. The first twelve to cross a chosen river would be picked to represent the twelve earthly branches which make up the cyclical order of years in the lunar calendar.

Each **lunar year** (which starts in late January/early February) is represented by one of the twelve animal symbols. Your sign depends on the year you were born – check the calendar chart below – rather than the month as in the Western system, but beyond that the idea is the same: born under the sign of a particular animal, you will have certain characteristics, ideal partners, lucky and unlucky days. The details below will tell you the basic facts about your character and personality, though it's only a rough guide: to go into your real Chinese astrological self, you need to be equipped with your precise date and time of birth and one of the books listed below, which can explain all the horoscopical bits and pieces. The animals always appear in the same order so that if you know the current year you can always work out which one is to influence the following Chinese New Year.

The Rat

Characteristics: usually generous, intelligent and hard-working, but can be petty and idle; has lots of friends, but few close ones; may be successful, likes challenges and is good at business, but is insecure; generally diplomatic; tends to get into emotional entanglements.

Partners: best suited to Dragon, Monkey and Ox; doesn't get on with Horse and Goat.

Famous Rats: Wolfgang Amadeus Mozart, William Shakespeare, Marlon Brando, Yves St Laurent, Leo Tolstoy, Jimmy Carter and Prince Charles.

The Ox

Characteristics: healthy; obstinate; independent; usually calm and cool, but can get stroppy at times; shy and conservative; likes the outdoors and old-fashioned things, always finishes a task.

Partners: best suited to Snake, Rat or Rooster; doesn't get on with Tiger, Goat or Monkey.

Famous Oxen: Walt Disney, Adolf Hitler, Napoleon Bonaparte, Richard Nixon, Vincent Van Gogh, Peter Sellers, Dustin Hoffman, Margaret Thatcher, Jane Fonda, Pieter Paul Rubens.

The Tiger

Characteristics: adventurous; creative and idealistic; confident and enthusiastic; can be diplomatic and practical; fearless and forward, aiming at impossible goals, though a realist with a forceful personality.

Partners: best suited to Horse for marriage; gets on with Dragon, Pig and Dog; avoid Snake, Monkey and Ox.

Famous Tigers: Karl Marx, Queen Elizabeth II, Alec Guinness, Stevie Wonder, Ludwig van Beethoven, Marilyn Monroe, Princess Anne, Charles de Gaulle, Rudolf Nureyev, Ho Chi Minh.

The Rabbit

Characteristics: peace-loving; sociable but quiet; devoted to family and friends; timid but can be good at business; needs reassurance and affection to avoid being upset; can be vain; long-lived.

Calendar Chart

Date Of Birth	Animal		
29.1.1903 – 15.2.1904	Rabbit	27.1.1952 – 13.2.1953	Dragon
16.2.1904 – 3.2.1905	Dragon	14.2.1953 – 2.2.1954	Snake
4.2.1905 – 24.1.1906	Snake	3.2.1954 – 23.1.1955	Horse
25.1.1906 – 12.2.1907	Horse	24.1.1955 – 11.2.1956	Goat
13.2.1907 – 1.2.1908	Goat	12.2.1956 – 30.1.1957	Monkey
2.2.1908 – 21.1.1909	Monkey	31.1.1957 – 17.2.1958	Rooster
22.1.1909 – 9.2.1910	Rooster	18.2.1958 – 7.2.1959	Dog
10.2.1910 – 29.1.1911	Dog	8.2.1959 – 27.1.1960	Pig
30.1.1911 – 17.2.1912	Pig	28.1.1960 – 14.2.1961	Rat
18.2.1912 – 5.2.1913	Rat	15.2.1961 – 4.2.1962	Ox
6.2.1913 – 25.1.1914	Ox	5.2.1962 – 24.1.1963	Tiger
26.1.1914 – 13.2.1915	Tiger	25.1.1963 – 12.2.1964	Rabbit
14.2.1915 – 3.2.1916	Rabbit	13.2.1964 – 1.2.1965	Dragon
4.2.1916 – 22.1.1917	Dragon	2.2.1965 – 20.1.1966	Snake
23.1.1917 – 10.2.1918	Snake	21.1.1966 – 8.2.1967	Horse
11.2.1918 – 31.1.1919	Horse	9.2.1967 – 29.1.1968	Goat
1.2.1919 – 19.2.1920	Goat	30.1.1968 – 16.2.1969	Monkey
20.2.1920 – 7.2.1921	Monkey	17.2.1969 – 5.2.1970	Rooster
8.2.1921 – 27.1.1922	Rooster	6.2.1970 – 26.1.1971	Dog
28.1.1922 – 15.2.1923	Dog	27.1.1971 – 14.2.1972	Pig
16.2.1923 – 4.2.1924	Pig	15.2.1972 – 2.2.1973	Rat
5.2.1924 – 23.1.1925	Rat	3.2.1973 – 22.1.1974	Ox
24.1.1925 – 12.2.1926	Ox	23.1.1974 – 10.2.1975	Tiger
13.2.1926 – 1.2.1927	Tiger	11.2.1975 – 30.1.1976	Rabbit
2.2.1927 – 22.1.1928	Rabbit	31.1.1976 – 17.2.1977	Dragon
23.1.1928 – 9.2.1929	Dragon	18.2.1977 – 6.2.1978	Snake
10.2.1929 – 29.1.1930	Snake	7.2.1978 – 27.1.1979	Horse
30.1.1930 – 16.2.1931	Horse	28.1.1979 – 15.2.1980	Goat
17.2.1931 – 5.2.1932	Goat	16.2.1980 – 4.2.1981	Monkey
6.2.1932 – 25.1.1933	Monkey	5.2.1981 – 24.1.1982	Rooster
26.1.1933 – 13.2.1934	Rooster	25.1.1982 – 12.2.1983	Dog
14.2.1934 – 3.2.1935	Dog	13.2.1983 – 1.2.1984	Pig
4.2.1935 – 23.1.1936	Pig	2.2.1984 – 19.2.1985	Rat
24.1.1936 – 10.2.1937	Rat	20.2.1985 – 8.2.1986	Ox
11.2.1937 – 30.1.1938	Ox	9.2.1986 – 28.1.1987	Tiger
31.1.1938 – 18.2.1939	Tiger	29.1.1987 – 16.2.1988	Rabbit
19.2.1939 – 7.2.1940	Rabbit	17.2.1988 – 5.2.1989	Dragon
8.2.1940 – 26.1.1941	Dragon	6.2.1989 – 26.1.1990	Snake
27.1.1941 – 14.2.1942	Snake	27.1.1990 – 14.2.1991	Horse
15.2.1942 – 4.2.1943	Horse	15.2.1991 – 3.2.1992	Goat
5.2.1943 – 24.1.1944	Goat	4.2.1992 – 22.1.1993	Monkey
25.1.1944 – 12.2.1945	Monkey	23.1.1993 – 9.2.1994	Rooster
13.2.1945 – 1.2.1946	Rooster	10.2.1994 – 30.1.1995	Dog
2.2.1946 – 21.1.1947	Dog	31.1.1995 – 18.2.1996	Pig
22.1.1947 – 9.2.1948	Pig	19.2.1996 – 6.2.1997	Rat
10.2.1948 – 28.1.1949	Rat	7.2.1997 – 27.1.1998	Ox
29.1.1949 – 16.2.1950	Ox	28.1.1998 – 15.2.1999	Tiger
17.2.1950 – 5.2.1951	Tiger	16.2.1999 – 4.2.2000	Rabbit
6.2.1951 – 26.1.1952	Rabbit	5.2.2000 – 23.1.2001	Dragon
		24.1.2001 – 11.2.2002	Snake

Partners: best suited to Pig, Dog and Goat; not friendly with Tiger and Rooster.

Famous Rabbits: Fidel Castro, Bob Hope, David Frost, Martin Luther King, Josef Stalin, Queen Victoria and Albert Einstein.

The Dragon

Characteristics: strong, commanding, a leader; popular, athletic; bright, chivalrous and idealistic, though not always consistent; likely to be a believer in equality.

Partners: best suited to Snake, Rat, Monkey, Tiger and Rooster; avoid Dog.

Famous Dragons: Joan of Arc, Ringo Starr, Mae West, John Lennon, Frank Sinatra, Salvador Dali, Jimmy Connors, Che Guevara and Yehudi Menuhin. and Bruce Lee.

The Snake

Characteristics: charming, but possessive and selfish; private and secretive; strange sense of humour; mysterious and inquisitive; ruthless; likes the nice things in life; a thoughtful person, but superstitious.

Partners: best suited for marriage to Dragon, Rooster and Ox; avoid Snake, Pig and Tiger.

Famous Snakes: J. F. Kennedy, Abraham Lincoln, Edgar Allan Poe, Mao Zedong, Pablo Picasso, Johannes Brahms, Franz Schubert and Ferdinand Marcos.

The Horse

Characteristics: nice appearance and deft; ambitious and quick-witted; favours bold colours; popular, with a sense of humour, gracious and gentle; can be good at business; fickle and emotional.

Partners: best suited to Tiger, Dog and Goat; doesn't get on with Rabbit and Rat.

Famous Horses: Neil Armstrong, Barbara Streisand, Paul McCartney, Theodore Roosevelt, Rembrandt and Igor Stravinsky.

The Goat

Characteristics: a charmer and a lucky person who likes money; unpunctual and hesitant; too fond of complaining; interested in the supernatural.

Partners: best suited to Horse, Pig and Rabbit; avoid Ox and Dog.

Famous Goats: Andy Warhol, Billie Jean King, Liberace, Mohammed Ali, Michelangelo, Laurence Olivier, James Michener and Diana Dors.

The Monkey

Characteristics: very intelligent and sharp, an opportunist; daring and confident, but unstable and egoistic; entertaining and very attractive to others; inventive; a sense of humour but with little respect for reputations.

Partners: best suited to Dragon and Rat; doesn't get on with Tiger and Ox.

Famous Monkeys: Leonardo da Vinci, Mick Jagger, Bette Davis, Charles Dickens, Julius Caesar, Paul Gauguin and René Descartes.

The Rooster

Characteristics: frank and reckless, and can be tactless; free with advice; punctual and a hard worker; imaginative to the point of dreaming; likes to be noticed; emotional.

Partners: best suited to Snake, Dragon and Ox; doesn't get on with Pig, Rabbit and Rooster.

Famous Roosters: Prince Philip, Charles Darwin, Peter Ustinov, Elton John, Katharine Hepburn, Yves Montand and Michael Caine.

The Dog

Characteristics: alert, watchful and defensive; can be generous and is patient; very responsible and has good organizational skills; spiritual, home-loving and non-materialistic.

Partners: best suited to Rabbit, Pig, Tiger and Horse; avoid Dragon and Goat.

Famous Dogs: David Niven, Henry Moore, Brigitte Bardot, Liza Minnelli, Zsa Zsa Gabor, Winston Churchill, Elvis Presley, Sophia Loren and Voltaire.

The Pig

Characteristics: honest; vulnerable and not good at business, but still materialistic and ambitious; outgoing and outspoken, but naive; kind and helpful to the point of being taken advantage of; calm and genial.

Partners: best suited to Dog, Goat, Tiger and Rabbit; avoid Snake and Rooster.

Famous Pigs: Alfred Hitchcock, Ronald Reagan, Maria Callas, Henry Kissinger, Woody Allen, Julie Andrews, Humphrey Bogart, Al Capone and Ernest Hemingway.

Language: a Cantonese Survival Guide

The language spoken by the overwhelming majority of Hong Kong and Macau's population is **Cantonese**, a southern Chinese dialect used in the province of Guangdong – and the one primarily spoken by the millions of Chinese emigrants throughout the world. Unfortunately, Cantonese is one of the world's most difficult languages for Westerners to learn: it's tonal, and the same word can have several different meanings depending on the pitch of the voice; there are up to nine different tones. To learn to speak it fluently would take years, and even mastering the basics can be fraught with misunderstanding. Things are further complicated by the fact that

Cantonese Words and Phrases

Basics	
Good morning	jo san
Hello/how are you?	nei ho ma
Thank you	m goy
Goodnight	jo toe
Goodbye	joy gin
What is your name?	nei gwei sing ah?
My name is...	or sing...
What time is it?	cheung mun, gay dim le?
How much is it?	cheung mun, gay dor chin?
Where is the train	cheung mun, for che
station/	tjam hay been doe ah/
bus stop/	ba-si tjam hay been doe ah/
ferry pier?	ma-tou hay been doe ah?
Hong Kong	heung gong
China	chung kwok
Britain	ying kwok

Transport and Essentials	
Train	for che
Bus	ba-si
Ferry	do shun
Taxi	dik-si
Airport	gei-cheun
Hotel	lui dim
Restaurant	fan dim

Campsite	yer ying way ji
Toilets	chi sor
Police	ging-tchak

Numbers	
1	yat
2	yih
3	saam
4	sei
5	ngh (um)
6	luk
7	tchat
8	baat
9	gau
10	sahp
11	sahp yat
12	sahp yih
20	yih sahp
30	saam sahp
100	yat baak
1000	yat tin

Note that the number two changes when asking for two of something – long wei (a table for two) – or stating something other than counting – long mung (two dollars).

written Chinese is a different matter altogether – meaningful phrases and sentences are formed by a series of characters, or pictographs, which individually represent actions and objects.

Most visitors get by without knowing a word of Cantonese. Hong Kong is officially **bilingual**, although this doesn't necessarily mean much. All signs, public transport and utility notices and street names are supposed to be written in English as well as Chinese characters; most are, although you may have problems making out the tiny English script written on the front of the buses. Many of the people you'll have dealings with in Central, Tsim Sha Tsui and most other tourist destinations should speak at least some English, although it may be hard going, particularly in taxis, restaurants

SOME SIGNS

Entrance	入口	No smoking	請勿吸菸
Exit	出口	Danger	危險
Toilets	廁所	Customs	關稅
Gentlemen	男廁	Bus	公共汽車
Ladies	女廁	Ferry	渡船
Open	營業中	Train	火車
Closed	休業	Airport	飛機場
Arrivals	到達	Police	警察
Departures	出發	Restaurant	飯店
Closed for holidays	休假	Hotel	賓館
Out of order	出故障	Campsite	野營位置
Drinking/mineral water	礦泉水	Beach	海灘
		No swimming	禁止游永

PLACE NAMES

Hong Kong	香港	Jordan	佐敦
Hong Kong Island	香港島	Central	中環
Tsim Sha Tsui	尖沙咀	Wan Chai	灣仔
Kowloon	九龍	Causeway Bay	銅鑼灣
New Territories	新界	Aberdeen	香港仔
Happy Valley	跑馬地	Stanley	赤柱
Sha Tin	沙田	Lantau	大嶼山
Tsuen Wan	荃灣	Cheung Chau	長州
Mongkok	旺角	Lamma	南丫島
Yau Ma Tei	油痲地		

and on the telephone. In Macau, the dominant colonial language is **Portuguese** (for more on which, see pp.328–329). English is increasingly spoken, at least in hotels and larger restaurants.

To help out, we've provided a small, basic guide to everyday Cantonese on p.403. The problem with it is that the accepted way the Cantonese words are written in English often bears little relation to how they're actually pronounced by a Chinese person. The many different tones in Cantonese can mean a simple two letter word can have up to nine different, completely unrelated meanings, so the romanized word is at best an approximation of the Chinese sound, and in any case no one will understand you without the correct intonation. You'll only get it right by listening and practising. As far as the characters go, we've provided some examples of the most important signs and place names, but that's all – it's incredibly difficult for the untrained eye to read them, and anyway, they don't help with pronunciation.

Glossary of Hong Kong Words and Terms

Lots of strange words have entered the vocabulary of Hong Kong people, Chinese and Westerners alike, and you'll come across most of them during your time here. Some are derivations of Cantonese words, adapted by successive generations of European settlers; others come from the different foreign and colonial languages represented in Hong Kong – from Chinese dialects to Anglo-Indian words. For words and terms specifically to do with Chinese food, see the chapter on "Eating", p.241.

Amah Female housekeeper/servant.

Ancestral Hall Main room or hall in a temple complex where the ancestral records are kept, and where devotions take place.

Cheongsam Chinese dress with a high collar and long slits up the sides.

Chop A personal seal or stamp of authority; also used by the illiterate instead of signatures.

Dai pai dong Street stall or modest café selling snacks and food.

Expat Expatriate; a foreign worker living in Hong Kong.

Feng shui Literally "wind and water", the Chinese art of geomancy.

Godown Warehouse.

Gweilo Literally "ghost man"; used by the Cantonese for all Westerners (*gweipor*, "ghost woman"); originally derogatory, but now in accepted use.

Hong Major company.

Kaido A small ferry, or a boat used as a ferry, a sampan (also *kaito*).

Junk Large flat-bottomed boat with a high deck and an overhanging stern.

Mahjong A Chinese game played with tiles, like souped-up dominoes.

Miu The Cantonese word for temple.

Nullah Gully, ravine, or narrow waterway.

Praya The Portuguese word for waterfront promenade (in occasional use).

Sampan Small flat-bottomed boat.

Shroff Cashier.

Tai chi Martial arts exercise.

Taipan Boss of a major company.

Tai tai Literally means "wife", but often used to describe rich ladies who lunch and shop.

Acronyms

CE Chief Executive.

EXCO Executive Council.

HKTA Hong Kong Tourist Association.

KCR Kowloon–Canton Railway.

LEGCO Legislative Council.

LRT Light Rail Transit.

MTR Mass Transit Railway.

SAR Special Administrative Region.

Index

Stay in touch with us!

ROUGH*NEWS* **is Rough Guides' free newsletter. In three issues a year we give you news, travel issues, music reviews, readers' letters and the latest dispatches from authors on the road.**

I would like to receive ROUGH*NEWS*: please put me on your free mailing list.

NAME . . . .

ADDRESS . . . .

Please clip or photocopy and send to: Rough Guides, 62–70 Shorts Gardens, London WC2H 9AB, England or Rough Guides, 375 Hudson Street, New York, NY 10014, USA.

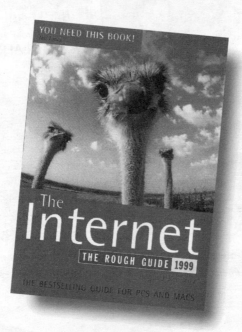

ROUGH GUIDES: Travel

Amsterdam
Andalucia
Australia

Austria
Bali & Lombok
Barcelona
Belgium &
  Luxembourg
Belize
Berlin
Brazil
Britain
Brittany &
  Normandy
Bulgaria
California
Canada
Central America
Chile
China
Corfu & the
  Ionian Islands
Corsica
Costa Rica
Crete
Cuba
Cyprus
Czech & Slovak
  Republics

Dodecanese
Dominican
  Republic
Egypt
England
Europe
Florida
France
French Hotels &
  Restaurants 1999
Germany
Goa
Greece
Greek Islands
Guatemala
Hawaii
Holland
Hong Kong
  & Macau
Hungary
India
Indonesia
Ireland
Israel & the
  Palestinian
  Territories
Italy
Jamaica
Japan
Jordan

Kenya
Laos
London
London
  Restaurants
Los Angeles
Malaysia,
  Singapore &
  Brunei
Mallorca &
  Menorca
Maya World
Mexico
Morocco
Moscow
Nepal
New England
New York
New Zealand
Norway
Pacific Northwest
Paris
Peru
Poland
Portugal
Prague
Provence & the
  Côte d'Azur
The Pyrenees
Romania

St Petersburg
San Francisco
Sardinia
Scandinavia
Scotland
Scottish Highlands
  & Islands
Sicily
Singapore

South Africa
Southern India
Southwest USA
Spain
Sweden
Syria
Thailand
Trinidad & Tobago
Tunisia
Turkey
Tuscany & Umbria
USA
Venice
Vienna
Vietnam
Wales
Washington DC
West Africa
Zimbabwe &
  Botswana

AVAILABLE AT ALL GOOD BOOKSHOPS

ROUGH GUIDES: Mini Guides, Travel Specials and Phrasebooks

MINI GUIDES

Antigua
Bangkok
Barbados
Big Island of
  Hawaii
Boston
Brussels
Budapest

Seattle
Sydney
Tokyo
Toronto

Spanish
A ROUGH GUIDE DICTIONARY PHRASEBOOK

TRAVEL SPECIALS

First-Time Asia
First-Time Europe
More Women Travel

Women Travel
A ROUGH GUIDE SPECIAL

Dublin
Edinburgh
Florence
Honolulu
Jerusalem
Lisbon
London
  Restaurants
Madrid
Maui
Melbourne
New Orleans
St Lucia

London Restaurants
THE ROUGH GUIDE 1999

CHARLES CAMPION

Egyptian Arabic
European
French
German
Greek
Hindi & Urdu
Hungarian
Indonesian
Italian
Japanese

Mandarin
  Chinese
Mexican Spanish
Polish
Portuguese
Russian
Spanish
Swahili

PHRASEBOOKS

Czech
Dutch

Thai
Turkish
Vietnamese

Bangkok
MINI ROUGH GUIDE

AVAILABLE AT ALL GOOD BOOKSHOPS

ROUGH GUIDES:
Reference and Music CDs

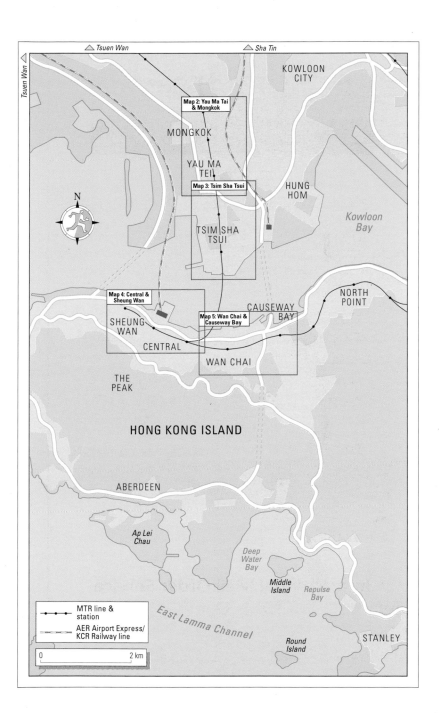

Tsuen Wan △ △ Sha Tin

KOWLOON
CITY

**Map 2: Yau Ma Tai
& Mongkok**

MONGKOK

YAU MA
TEI

HUNG
HOM

Map 3: Tsim Sha Tsui

Kowloon
Bay

TSIM SHA
TSUI

N

NORTH
POINT

**Map 4: Central &
Sheung Wan**

CAUSEWAY
BAY

SHEUNG
WAN

**Map 5: Wan Chai &
Causeway Bay**

CENTRAL

WAN CHAI

THE
PEAK

HONG KONG ISLAND

ABERDEEN

Ap Lei
Chau

Deep
Water
Bay

Middle
Island

Repulse
Bay

East Lamma Channel

Round
Island

STANLEY

●—●—● MTR line &
station

AER Airport Express/
KCR Railway line

0   2 km

Tsuen Wan

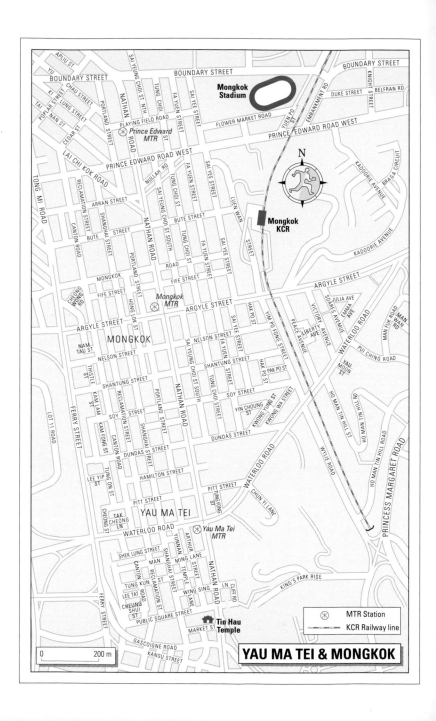

YAU MA TEI & MONGKOK

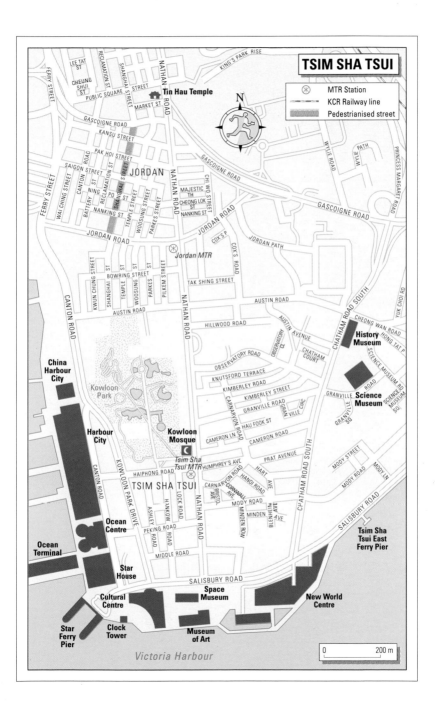

TSIM SHA TSUI

- ⊛ MTR Station
- ∙∙∙∙∙ KCR Railway line
- ▓▓▓ Pedestrianised street

Tin Hau Temple

JORDAN

Jordan MTR

China Harbour City

Kowloon Park

Harbour City

Kowloon Mosque

Tsim Sha Tsui MTR

TSIM SHA TSUI

Ocean Terminal

Ocean Centre

Star House

Star Ferry Pier

Cultural Centre

Clock Tower

Museum of Art

Space Museum

Salisbury Road

New World Centre

Tsim Sha Tsui East Ferry Pier

History Museum

Science Museum

Victoria Harbour

0   200 m

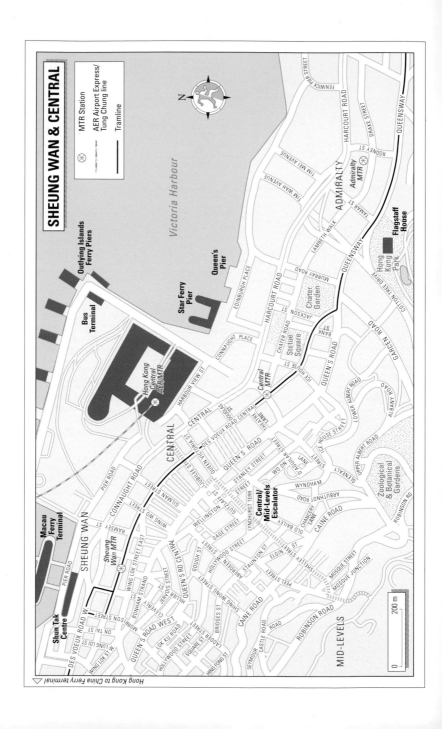

SHEUNG WAN & CENTRAL

MTR Station

AER Airport Express/
Tung Chung line

Tramline

N

Victoria Harbour

Outlying Islands
Ferry Piers

Bus
Terminal

Star Ferry
Pier

Queen's
Pier

Hong Kong
Central
AER/MTR

EDINBURGH PLACE

CONNAUGHT PLACE

HARBOUR VIEW ST

HARCOURT ROAD

TIM MEI AVENUE

TIM WAH AVENUE

LAMBETH WALK

MURRAY ROAD

ADMIRALTY

Admiralty
MTR

TAMAR ST

RODNEY ST

DRAKE STREET

HARCOURT ROAD

FENWICK PIER STREET

QUEENSWAY

Chater
Garden

Hong
Kong Park

Flagstaff
House

COTTON TREE DRIVE

GARDEN ROAD

CENTRAL

DES VOEUX ROAD CENTRAL

CONNAUGHT ROAD

PIER ROAD

Central
MTR

Statue
Square

JACKSON RD

CHATER ROAD

BANK ST

ICE HOUSE ST

QUEEN'S ROAD

GARDEN ROAD

LOWER ALBERT ROAD

ALBANY
ROAD

QUEEN'S ROAD

THEATRE LANE

ICE HOUSE STREET

D'AGUILAR STREET

WO ON LANE

WELLINGTON STREET

STANLEY STREET

WYNDHAM

ARBUTHNOT ROAD

GLENEALY

UPPER ALBERT ROAD

Zoological
& Botanical
Gardens

ROBINSON RD

CAINE ROAD

CHANCERY
LANE

OLD BAILEY
ST

GAGE STREET

GUTZLAFF ST

LYNDHURST TERR

ABERDEEN STREET

STAUNTON ST

ELGIN STREET

SHELLEY STREET

PEEL STREET

Central/
Mid-Levels
Escalator

Macau
Ferry
Terminal

Shun Tak
Centre

PIER ROAD

SHEUNG WAN

RAMSEY
ST

WING WO STREET

GILMAN STREET

JUBILEE ST

DES VOEUX ROAD W

WING LOK ST

BONHAM STRAND

MORRISON STREET

CLEVERLY ST

MILLAR ST

N TAI ST

LUNG LOI ST

Sheung
Wan MTR

WING LOK STREET EAST

QUEEN'S RD CENTRAL

GOUGH ST

HILLIER ST

SHING WONG STREET

JERVOIS STREET

QUEEN'S ROAD WEST

MOSQUE JUNCTION

MOSQUE STREET

ROBINSON ROAD

MID-LEVELS

CAINE ROAD

BRIDGES ST

LADDER STREET

SQUARE ST

HOLLYWOOD STREET

KAU YU KOK

SEYMOUR

CASTLE ROAD

ROBINSON ROAD

CAINE ROAD

HING KONG FONG ST

0   200 m

Hong Kong to China Ferry terminal

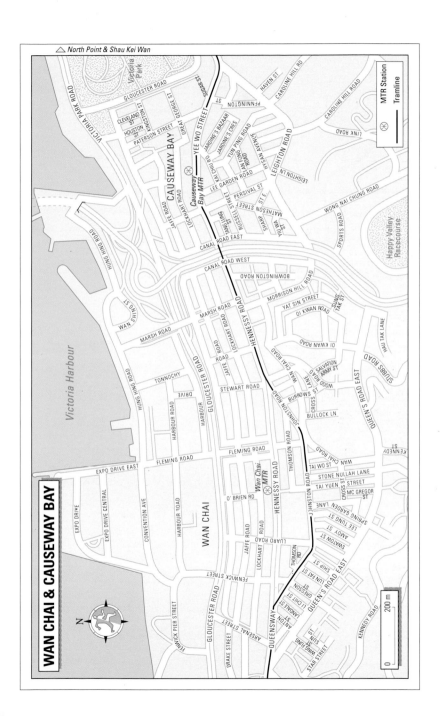

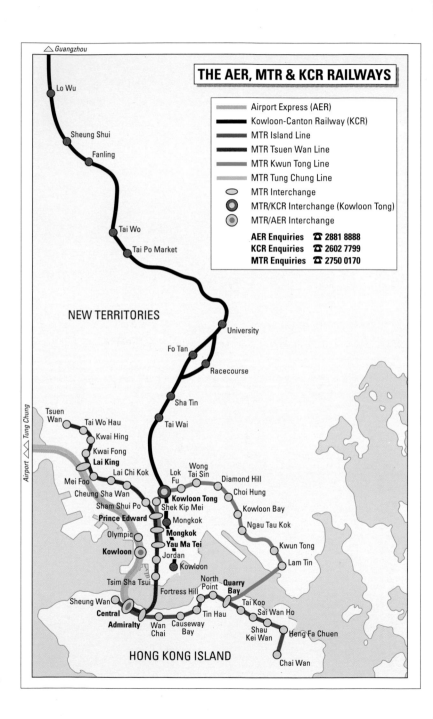

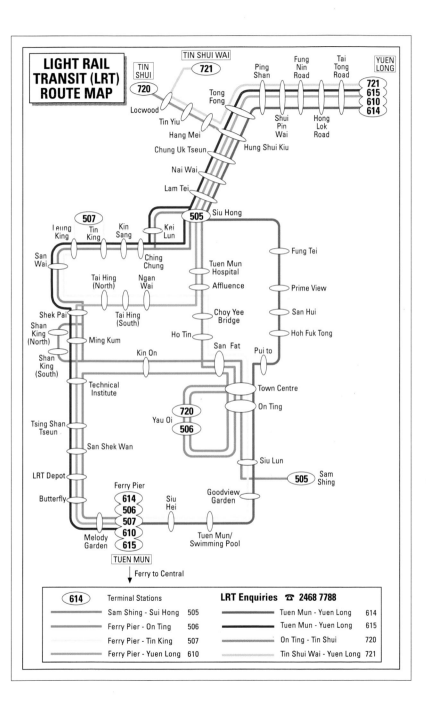

LIGHT RAIL TRANSIT (LRT) ROUTE MAP

TIN SHUI WAI
721
720
Locwood
Tin Yiu
Hang Mei
Chung Uk Tseun
Tong Fong
Nai Wai
Lam Tei
Siu Hong
Hung Shui Kiu

TIN SHUI

Ping Shan
Shui Pin Wai
Fung Nin Road
Hong Lok Road
Tai Tong Road

YUEN LONG
721
615
610
614

507
Leung King
Tin King
Kin Sang
Kei Lun
505
San Wai
Ching Chung
Tai Hing (North)
Ngan Wai
Tai Hing (South)
Ho Tin
Tuen Mun Hospital
Affluence
Choy Yee Bridge
Fung Tei
Prime View
San Hui
Hoh Fuk Tong

Shek Pai
Shan King (North)
Ming Kum
Shan King (South)
Kin On
San Fat
Pui to
Technical Institute
Tsing Shan Tseun
San Shek Wan
LRT Depot
Butterfly
Ferry Pier
614
506
507
610
615
Siu Hei
Yau Oi
720
506
Town Centre
On Ting
Siu Lun
505
Sam Shing
Goodview Garden
Tuen Mun/ Swimming Pool

Melody Garden

TUEN MUN
↓ Ferry to Central

614	Terminal Stations		**LRT Enquiries** ☎ **2468 7788**	
	Sam Shing - Sui Hong	505	Tuen Mun - Yuen Long	614
	Ferry Pier - On Ting	506	Tuen Mun - Yuen Long	615
	Ferry Pier - Tin King	507	On Ting - Tin Shui	720
	Ferry Pier - Yuen Long	610	Tin Shui Wai - Yuen Long	721

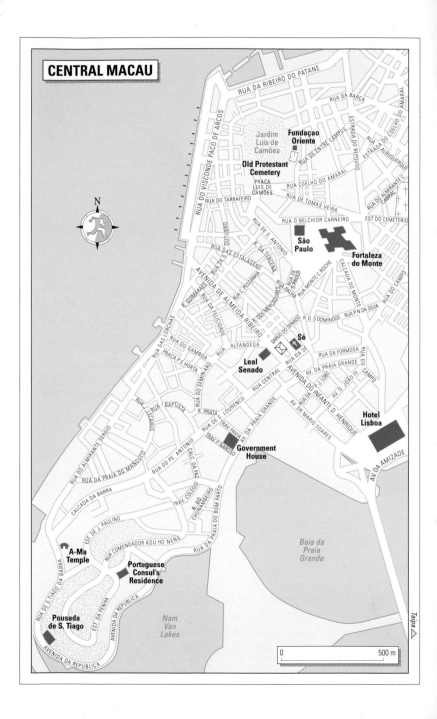

CENTRAL MACAU

N

RUA DA RIBEIRO DO PATANE

RUA DA BARCA

Jardim Luis de Camões

Fundaçao Oriente

ESTRADA DO COELHO DO AMARAL

RUA DO COELHO DO AMARAL

ESTRADA DO REPOUSO

ESTRADA ALBUQUERQUE

RUA DE ENTRE CAMPOS

Old Protestant Cemetery

PRAÇA LUIS DE CAMÕES

RUA COELHO DO AMARAL

RUA DE TOMAS VEIRA

RUA DO ALMIRANTE C. CABRAL

RUA DO VISCONDE PAÇO DE ARCOS

RUA DO TARRAFEIRO

RUA D BELCHIOR CARNEIRO

EST DO CEMETERIO

RUA DE S. ANTONIO

São Paulo

Fortaleza do Monte

RUA DAS ESTALAGENS

RUA DE 5 DE OUTUBRO

RUA DA TERCENA

RUA C. PESSANHA

CALÇADA DO MONTE

RUA DO CAMPO

AVENIDA DE ALMEIDA RIBEIRO

R. GUIMARAES

RUA DA FELICIDADE

R. DOS MERCADORES

RUA DE P PAULO

RUA DA PALHA

RUA MONTE C. ROCHE

R. D. S DOMINGOS

RUA P N DA SILVA

RUA DAS LORCHAS

RUA DO GAMBOA

ALFANDEGA

LARGO DO SENADO

Sé

PRAÇA P E HORTA

RUA DA SÉ

RUA DA FORMOSA

RUA DO SEMINARIO

Leal Senado

RUA CENTRAL

AVENIDA DO INFANTE D. HENRIQUE

AV. DA PRAIA GRANDE

AV. D. JOAO IV

RUA J ICARUS

RUA I BAPTISTA

R. PRATA

RUA DE S. TRAV PAVIA

AV DA PRAIA GRANDE

AV. DO P J LOBO

Hotel Lisboa

RUA DE S. LOURENCO

TRAV P. NARCISO

Government House

AV. DR MARIO SOARES

AV DA AMIZADE

RUA DO AMIRANTE SERGIO

RUA DO PE ANTONIO

CALC. DA PAZ

TRAV. COLEGIO

RUA DO CHUNAMBEIRO

RUA DA PRAIA DO MANDUCO

CALÇADA DA BARRA

EST DE J. PAULINO

RUA DA PRAIA DO BOM PARTO

RUA COMENDADOR KOU HO NENG

RUA DA PRAIA DO BOM PARTO

Baia da Praia Grande

A-Ma Temple

Portuguese Consul's Residence

RUA DE S. TIAGO DA BARRA

EST DA PENHA

AVENIDA DA REPUBLICA

Pousada de S. Tiago

Nam Van Lakes

AVENIDA DA REPUBLICA

Taipa ▷

0   500 m